MW00611012

MVS Systems Programming

Recent Titles in the IBM McGraw-Hill Series

Open Systems and IBM
Integration and Convergence
Pamela Gray

Risk Management for Software Projects
Alex Down
Michael Coleman
Peter Absolon

The New Organization
Growing the Culture of Organizational
Networking
Colin Hastings

Investing in Information Technology
Managing the Decision-making Process
Geoff Hogbin
David Thomas

Commonsense Computer Security 2nd Edition
Your Practical Guide to Information Protection
Martin Smith

The Advanced Programmer's Guide to AIX 3.x
Phil Colledge

The CICS Programmer's Guide to FEPI
Robert Harris

Business Objects
Delivering Cooperative Objects for Client-Server
Oliver Sims

Reshaping I.T. for Business Flexibility
The I.T. Architecture as a Common Language
for Dealing with Change
Mark Behrsin
Geoff Mason
Trevor Sharpe

Practical Queueing Analysis
Mike Tanner

MVS Capacity Planning for a Balanced System
Brian MacFarlane

Supercharging the AS/400
A Guide to Performance Management
Ron Fielder
Carolyn Machell

Details of these titles in the series are available from:

The Product Manager, Professional Books
McGraw-Hill Book Company Europe
Shoppenhangers Road, Maidenhead, Berkshire SL6 2QL
Telephone: 01628 23432 Fax: 01628 770224

David Elder-Vass

MVS Systems Programming

McGRAW-HILL BOOK COMPANY

London · New York · St Louis · San Francisco · Auckland
Bogotá · Caracas · Lisbon · Madrid · Mexico
Milan · Montreal · New Delhi · Panama · Paris · San Juan
São Paulo · Singapore · Sydney · Tokyo · Toronto

Published by
McGRAW-HILL Book Company Europe
Shoppenhangers Road, Maidenhead, Berkshire SL6 2QL, England
Tel 01628 23432 Fax 01628 770224

British Library Cataloguing in Publication Data

Elder-Vass, David
     Introduction to MVS Systems Programming.
     (IBM McGraw-Hill Series)
     I. Title II. Series
     005.4
     ISBN 0-07-707767-9

Library of Congress Cataloging-in-Publication Data

Elder-Vass, David
     An introduction to MVS systems programming / David Elder-Vass.
         p.   cm. -- (The IBM McGraw-Hill series)
     Includes bibliographical references and index.
     ISBN 0-07-707767-9
     1. Systems programming (Computer science) 2. IBM MVS. I. Title.
     II. Series.
     QA76.66.E43 1993
     005.4'429--dc20   92-31695
                                                                        CIP

Copyright © 1993 David Elder-Vass. All rights reserved. No part of this publication
may be reproduced, stored in a retrieval system, or transmitted, in any form or by any
means, electronic, mechanical, photocopying, recording, or otherwise, without the prior
permission of David Elder-Vass and of McGraw-Hill International (UK) Limited, with
the exception of material entered and executed on a computer system for the reader's
own use.

2345CUP 965

Typeset by Alden Multimedia
and printed and bound in Great Britain at the University Press, Cambridge

Printed on permanent paper in compliance with ISO Standard 9706

To
Alisa

Contents

IBM Series Foreword   xi

Preface   xiii

Part One   Background   1
1   The systems programmer's job   3
    1.1   You and your employer   3
    1.2   Your responsibilities   4
    1.3   Be a professional   8

2   System/370 and System/390 hardware   15
    2.1   Introduction   15
    2.2   Central processor complexes   16
    2.3   Channels   20
    2.4   DASD and DASD controllers   23
    2.5   Tape devices   29
    2.6   Communications devices   31
    2.7   Other devices   33
    2.8   Hardware environments   35

3   MVS internals   37
    3.1   Introduction   37
    3.2   Storage management   38
    3.3   Task management   47
    3.4   I/O management   50
    3.5   Job management   53
    3.6   Serialization   56
    3.7   Program management   62
    3.8   Catalogs   68
    3.9   Inter-address space communication   73

Part Two   Tools of the trade   81
4   Basic tools   83
    4.1   Introduction   83
    4.2   Using TSO   83
    4.3   MVS utility programs   90
    4.4   Console commands   94

5   **SMP/E**   **105**
    5.1   SMP/E fundamentals   105
    5.2   Standard SMP processes   117
    5.3   Problem resolution   127
    5.4   Special SMP processing   131
    5.5   SMP implementation and customization   134

6   **Assembler programming for systems programmers**   **136**
    6.1   Introduction   136
    6.2   Accessing MVS control blocks   136
    6.3   Using system macros   141
    6.4   31-bit addressing   142
    6.5   Re-entrant coding   146
    6.6   Authorized functions   152
    6.7   Dynamic allocation   154
    6.8   More advanced techniques   157
    6.9   Assembler installation and customization   158

Part Three   Creating a working system   **161**
7   **MVS initialization and implementation**   **163**
    7.1   Introduction   163
    7.2   MVS initialization   163
    7.3   The SYSRES pack   173
    7.4   Creating an I/O configuration   179
    7.5   SYS1.PARMLIB   192
    7.6   The catalog structure   209
    7.7   Major system datasets   212
    7.8   MVS installation processes   219

8   **JES2 implementation**   **232**
    8.1   Introduction   232
    8.2   JES2 datasets   237
    8.3   Defining JES2 facilities   247
    8.4   Defining JES exits   260
    8.5   JES2 communications facilities   261

9   **Basic network configuration**   **270**
    9.1   Introduction   270
    9.2   Basic VTAM implementation   274
    9.3   Basic NCP implementation   284

10 **TSO, ISPF, and ISPF/PDF implementation**   **293**
    10.1   Introduction   293
    10.2   TSO implementation   294
    10.3   ISPF and PDF implementation   302
    10.4   Extending ISPF   315

Part Four   Maintaining and enhancing MVS   **323**
11 **Maintaining your MVS system**   **325**
    11.1   Introduction   325

11.2   When and how to put on maintenance and upgrades   325
11.3   Cloning and the MVS maintenance process   331

12   Enhancing your MVS system   343
12.1   Making system modifications   343
12.2   Commonly used MVS exits   346
12.3   JES2 exits   346
12.4   Common data management exits   353
12.5   Common TSO exits   353

13   Multi-image environments   357
13.1   Introduction   357
13.2   Multiple processor complexes   358
13.3   Physical partitioning   360
13.4   Logical partitioning   361
13.5   Implementing PR/SM   363
13.6   Software partitioning   365
13.7   Implementing VM   367
13.8   Which option should you choose?   370
13.9   Sysplex   370

14   Sharing I/O devices   374
14.1   Introduction   374
14.2   Switchable devices   374
14.3   Sharing communications controllers   376
14.4   Shared DASD integrity   378
14.5   RESERVE/RELEASE   378
14.6   Multisystem GRS   380
14.7   GRS resource name lists   382
14.8   Multi-Image Integrity   386
14.9   Sharing system datasets   388

Part Five   Housekeeping and security   391
15   MVS security   393
15.1   Elements of MVS security   393
15.2   Preventing MVS security loopholes   403

16   DASD management   408
16.1   Systems programmers and DASD management   408
16.2   DASD initialization   409
16.3   DASD pooling   415
16.4   DASD housekeeping   420
16.5   Catalog management   425
16.6   DASD problems   430

17   System data housekeeping   436
17.1   Housekeeping overview   436
17.2   SMF data   438
17.3   SYS1.LOGREC data   441
17.4   The SYSLOG   446
17.5   System DUMP datasets   448

Part Six   Dealing with problems   **451**
18   Problem diagnosis and resolution   **453**
     18.1   How to approach problems   453
     18.2   Controlling and using dumps   463
     18.3   Other diagnostic information and tools   482
     18.4   Getting help from IBM   486

19   Emergency recovery facilities   **492**
     19.1   Why you need emergency recovery   492
     19.2   Level 1 recovery – Alternative startup options   493
     19.3   Level 2 recovery – Alternative MVS systems   498
     19.4   Level 3 recovery – Non-MVS facilities   507
     19.5   Level 4 recovery – Standby sites   509

     Glossary of acronyms   **511**

     Index   **516**

Foreword

The IBM McGraw-Hill Series

IBM UK and McGraw-Hill Europe have worked together to publish this series of books about information technology and its use in business, industry and the public sector.

The series provides an up-to-date and authoritative insight into the wide range of products and services available, and offers strategic business advice. Some of the books have a technical bias, others are written from a broader business perspective. What they have in common is that their authors — some from IBM, some independent consultants — are experts in their field.

Apart from assisting where possible with the accuracy of the writing, IBM UK has not sought to inhibit the editorial freedom of the series, and therefore the views expressed in the books are those of the authors, and not necessarily those of IBM.

Where IBM has lent its expertise is in assisting McGraw-Hill to identify potential titles whose publication would help advance knowledge and increase awareness of computing topics. Hopefully these titles will also serve to widen the debate about the important information technology issues of today and of the future — such as open systems, networking, and the use of technology to give companies a competitive edge in their market.

IBM UK is pleased to be associated with McGraw-Hill in this series.

Sir Anthony Cleaver
Chairman
IBM United Kingdom Limited

Preface

Objectives of this book

When I first became an MVS systems programmer, I searched for a book which would give me an overview of the knowledge and the skills I needed to do my new job well. I found plenty of IBM manuals which assumed you already had a general overview, and plenty of books on assembler coding and MVS JCL. But I searched in vain for the book I really needed — an introduction to MVS systems programming. Instead I had to acquire that overview for myself by painstakingly piecing together the details from dozens of courses, hundreds of manuals, and a certain number of highly educational mistakes! Some years later, I realized that I was ideally placed to provide the book I had searched for at the beginning of my own systems programming career — and that there was still no such book on the market. So I decided to write a book which would:

- Explain how, when, and why to perform the major tasks of the systems programmer's job.
- Provide the background knowledge required to understand those tasks and do them well.
- Pass on hints, tips, and rules of good practice which I have learnt by experience, by word of mouth, and from the available literature.
- Point the reader to sources of further information, particularly in the IBM manuals — which can sometimes be confusing until you have found your way round them.

These are the objectives of the book you are holding now.

Scope

The book aims to provide its reader with the knowledge required to install, start, and maintain a basic MVS system and the essential IBM systems software, including JES2, VTAM, TSO, and ISPF. It includes background information on how MVS works, the hardware it runs on, and the tools of the systems programmer's trade, and it looks briefly at problem determination and how to run multiple copies of MVS.

It does not, however, cover the myriad of other systems software products available from both IBM and other vendors, which it would not be practical to discuss in detail. Nor does it cover related responsibilities which often fall into the ambit of the systems programmer, such as performance management, capacity planning, or security administration.

Of course, the contents are limited by my own knowledge and experience at the time of writing. One notable omission is coverage of JES3. Perhaps more importantly, the highest level of MVS I have worked on so far is 3.1.3, so although I have a theoretical knowledge of MVS version 4, which I have included, there are no practical hints on new facilities available in version 4. As time goes by, MVS will continue to evolve rapidly, and more new facilities will appear. No doubt these will make some of my comments on how to use the old facilities redundant. However, I am confident that the main body of MVS, and of the systems programmer's job, will remain relatively stable, as it has for many years, and therefore that the main body of this book will continue to be relevant and useful.

Intended audience

Although the primary audience for the book is new (and not-so-new!) MVS systems programmers, there are many others who will find it of value. Each MVS system is supported by a wide range of technical professionals with an interest in understanding how to manage MVS. In addition to MVS systems programmers themselves, there are CICS, network, and database systems programmers, technical managers, operations analysts, capacity planners, storage, security and database administrators, and staff aspiring to all of these roles. I believe many of these people will find this book helps them to understand their job and its relationship with MVS systems better, and to do that job better as a result.

I should point out, however, that it will be difficult or impossible for anyone to benefit from this book unless they have already acquired the basic prerequisite skills for systems programming. Most staff who have spent a couple of years in other technical roles on MVS sites will have these skills (e.g. operators, operations analysts, and application programmers). In particular, readers will need to be familiar with:

- Basic computing concepts
- MVS JCL
- How to use TSO (including the ISPF/PDF editor)

It will also be helpful, though not essential, to know a little about System/390 assembler language and VSAM.

Approach

Each chapter aims to give the reader an understanding of its subject at the overview level, and practical information on how to perform the main duties of the systems programmer in the area it covers. Where detail is required to make this comprehensible, it is provided; where it is not, the book points the reader to the relevant place in the IBM manuals. I have tried to use diagrams and examples to clarify complex and difficult points whenever I felt they would help. Given the variations between MVS systems, though, I cannot guarantee that any examples will work unchanged on your system, so please check them out before using them.

Each chapter also includes a bibliography which provides a brief guide to the relevant IBM manuals (including their order numbers) and other published material. Unfortunately, IBM's constant efforts to improve and update their manuals lead to numerous changes in their titles, contents, and order numbers. My references are generally correct as at MVS/ESA 3.1.3, and where major changes were made between MVS/XA and MVS/ESA I have also tried to list the appropriate XA manuals. If you are using a different version of MVS from those I have listed manuals for, and you cannot identify the manual corresponding to one I have listed, you may need to ask your IBM representative for assistance.

MVS versions and releases

The terminology used to describe different levels of MVS can be confusing. Some IBM documentation refers to *all* current releases of MVS as '3.8' — this is actually the version number of the level of MVS's predecessor, OS/VS2, which became the base version of MVS. There are currently four different 'versions' of MVS in use, numbered one to four, and IBM regards each version as a separate product, at least for billing purposes. Within each version, major upgrades are labelled 'releases', and minor upgrades are considered 'modification levels'. The numbers used to identify levels of MVS consist of the version number, followed by the release, followed by the modification level; thus MVS 4.2.2 is version 4, release 2, modification 2. At any one time, there will only be one or two different levels of each version available, and the older versions have now been stabilized, meaning that no further upgrades will be made to them.

Version 1 of MVS is often referred to as MVS/SP or MVS/370, to differentiate it from the versions which followed, but neither of these terms really applies uniquely to version 1, so do not be surprised to find references to MVS/SP version 3, for example. Version 2 which introduced 31-bit addressing and therefore required processors to run in a different 'extended architecture' mode, is universally referred to as MVS/XA. Version 3, which once again requires the processor to run in a new mode, this time to support the use of access registers, is referred to as MVS/ESA. Version 4, however, does not require any mode change, and is still referred to as MVS/ESA. If you are interested in a more detailed discussion of the history and development of MVS, I would recommend the first chapter of Stephen Samson's book *MVS Performance Management* (McGraw-Hill, 1990).

One implication of all this is that processors which cannot support the new operating modes, cannot support the new versions of MVS either. So, because some organizations are still running these older processors, there are still people running MVS systems at many different version and release levels. In addition, some non-standard applications written for one version of MVS could not be moved over to higher versions without considerable modifications, and some older MVS systems are still running to support these. This book therefore aims to provide information which is relevant to staff working on MVS systems at various levels. In general, it relates to MVS version 3, which, at the time of writing, accounts for the majority of MVS systems, but it also refers to versions 2 and 4 where I am aware of major differences. Version 1 is now virtually extinct, so I have not made any specific references to it.

Another group of products which has gone through a confusing series of metamorphoses is the Data Facility family. DFP has sometimes been DFP, sometimes MVS/DFP, and has now become DFSMSdfp — part of the DFSMS/MVS product which provides the data management functionality for MVS 4.3. DFHSM started off as plain HSM, became DFHSM, and has now extended its name to DFSMShsm. And DFDSS has gone through an equivalent series of changes, ending up as DFSMSdss. No doubt these products will come to be known as dfp, hsm, and dss, but in this book I follow current usage and refer to them as DFP, DFHSM, and DFDSS.

Sources of further information

Although there are no other books I am aware of on the subject of MVS systems programming, there are related volumes on MVS facilities, assembler programming, and MVS performance management in McGraw-Hill's IBM series, which are well worth a look.

Technical journals also provide a useful source of educational material. Table 0.1 shows some of the most useful.

Another useful source is, of course, your fellow professionals, and systems programmers meet to exchange experiences under a variety of banners. These include the IBM user groups GUIDE and SHARE, the systems programmers' organization NASPA and CMG, an independent organization which was originally oriented mainly to capacity planning and performance, but now covers a wide variety of technical and computer management issues. In the UK, the two-monthly meetings of the GUIDE Large Systems Group are probably the most relevant gatherings for MVS systems programmers, although the UKCMG conferences are also useful. GUIDE and SHARE contacts for your country can be obtained from IBM; NASPA is at the address given in Table 0.1; and your local CMG will probably find you themselves once you are on the mailing lists of any of the software vendors who help to publicize their events.

Most of these organizations hold annual conferences where a wide variety of subjects are discussed, and even if you do not attend them, the proceedings are

Table 0.1. Technical journals relevant to MVS systems programmers

Journal	Coverage	How to get it
Candle Computer Report	In-depth technical articles on subjects like MVS internals, CICS, IMS, VTAM, and SNA.	Just ask Candle to put you on the mailing list! They are at: 1999 Bundy Drive, Los Angeles, California 90025, USA and other addresses around the world.
Enterprise Systems Journal	A mixture of technical articles on systems software and more management-oriented material.	Subscribe by writing to: ESJ, 10935 Estate Lane, Suite 375, Dallas, TX, 75238, USA Subs are free in North America, but not elsewhere.
MVS Update	Some educational articles and lots of examples of useful assembler and REXX code submitted by practising systems programmers.	Published by Xephon. Subscriptions from: Xephon plc, 27–35 London Road, Newbury, Berks RG13 1JL, England.
Technical Support	MVS, VM, and VSE-related articles from a systems programmer's point of view; also useful extracts from discussions held by systems programmers on the NASPA bulletin board.	Join NASPA — the National Association of Systems Programmers. Their address is: Suite 210, 4811 South 76th Street, Milwaukee, Wisconsin 53220, USA

usually published afterwards. These provide another useful source of educational material, particularly on user experiences of implementing relatively recent technical developments.

But the ultimate and definitive source of technical information on MVS and related subjects is, of course, IBM itself. IBM's manuals used to have a reputation for being both incomprehensible and incomprehensibly organized, but over the years they have steadily improved, and it is always worth finding your way round the relevant manuals when you turn to a new area. Finding your way round the manuals should also now become much easier as a result of the online search facilities provided by the various flavours of IBM's Bookmanager software.

Finally, IBM also provides other sources of information, such as printed marketing material and the online information services known as DIAL-IBM in the UK and IBMLink in the USA. These can be very useful for information on new products and for relatively obscure technical queries respectively.

Trademarks

Throughout the book I refer to numerous IBM products, many of whose names are trademarks or registered trademarks of IBM. Some of which I am aware are: MVS/SP, MVS/XA, MVS/ESA, ESA/370, MVS/DFP, DFSMS, Hiperspace, 3090, PR/SM, ES/9000.

In addition, I have made a few references to trademarked products from other suppliers. These include: Multi-Image Manager and its components, and MICS (Legent); CA-1, Top Secret and ACF2 (Computer Associates); SAS (SAS Institute); Omegamon (Candle); The Monitor (Landmark Systems); Stand-Alone Edit (New Era Software).

The commercial and intellectual property rights of all trademark holders whose products are listed in this book are hereby acknowledged.

Acknowledgements

This book would not have been possible without the assistance of many people, and I would like to thank all those who have helped me. In particular, I would like to thank:

- My colleagues at Dixons Data Centre in Stevenage, England, who have helped me in numerous ways, particularly Ron Armstrong for reviewing the chapter on networking, and Duncan Painter, upon whose work several of my examples are based, most notably Ex. 16.5.
- My managers at Dixons for their understanding and support.
- All those systems programmers from whom I have learned my craft over the years (and I am still learning, so please do not hesitate to let me know if you think this book could be improved).
- Everyone at McGraw-Hill for being so positive, efficient, and helpful.
- Microsoft for creating Word for Windows and Windows Paintbrush, which made creating this book an enjoyable experience.
- NASPA and *Technical Support* for publishing Sec. 11.3 of this book under the title 'MVS cloning strategies' in their April 1992 issue.
- And above all, Alisa, my wife and best friend, for her constant support and for believing in me.

But the responsibility for all that is contained in this volume, right or wrong, is, of course, ultimately mine!

Dave Elder-Vass

Part One
Background

1
The systems programmer's job

1.1　You and your employer

There is a traditional view of systems programmers as remote, unapproachable supertechnicians, working on obscure mysteries that even their managers do not understand, arbitrarily determining what changes should be made to 'their' system and laying down rules for other users of 'their' machine. Some systems programmers actually seem to aspire to such an image. They may sometimes seem to get away with it because of the scarcity of their skills on the open market, but the cost of the image is high. Many MIS managers see them as unreliable and unbusiness-like prima donnas, and approach them with open scepticism and distrust.

If you are going to surmount these obstacles and get the most out of your working life, you need to find out what your employers really do want from a systems programmer, and show them you can provide it.

So what do they want from you? Given that they are probably paying you a higher salary than many middle managers, they will generally expect you to be a highly skilled professional, with a professional attitude to match. If their expectations have not been worn down by generations of 'traditional' systems programmers, they will also expect a professional's understanding of both the business you are supposed to be working for and how you fit into it.

How do you fit into it? On the one hand, the systems programmer, like the whole operations department, plays essentially a service role — it is your job above all to make sure the system works when it is needed, performs adequately, and provides the function required by the applications the business wishes to use. On the other hand, you need to be a businessperson — you need to understand the impact of what you do on the organization you work for, you need to think about how you can contribute to its goals and policies, and you need to be prepared to stand up for getting things done in whatever way is best for the organization; whether that means implementing a rule that will protect the integrity or performance of the system or making do with a less-than-perfect piece of hardware because the benefits of replacing it would not justify the cost. You may still end up in contentious situations, but you will end up receiving the respect and rewards accorded to a businessperson — someone who thinks about what is best for the organization, not for the systems programmer or even for the 'machine'.

And just as important as understanding where you fit in and what is expected of you, is to ensure that those around you understand you! That means explaining to them what you are doing and why, consulting them when appropriate, and letting them see that you are a professional, with a professional attitude and professional methods.

I shall return to the subject of being a professional in Sec. 1.3, but first, of course, you have to know just what it is that is part of your job.

1.2   Your responsibilities

The term 'systems programmer' is very misleading — 'programming' is only one small aspect of the modern systems programmer's job. The heart of the job is to install, maintain, and enhance the system software that provides the environment in which the applications required by the organization can run (SHARE estimates that systems programmers spend 65 per cent of their time installing, upgrading, and maintaining software). The systems programmer's other responsibilities however, vary considerably from organization to organization, depending not only on its size and type, but also on the personalities and politics that have gone before you.

The following sections outline some aspects of your role in a little more detail.

1.2.1   System installation

The MVS systems programmer is responsible for creating all the datasets, load modules, catalogs and catalog entries, parameters, and procedures required to get the MVS system up and running. This awesome task (described in rather more detail in Chapters 7 to 10) is immensely simplified by the Custom-Built Installation Process Offering (CBIPO) process—IBM's method of packaging new releases of the operating system. The CBIPO is a set of tapes that includes not only all the modules you need to install your system but also the job control language (JCL) you need to do it, a tailoring process to correct the JCL for your site requirements, and a set of documentation including step-by-step instructions on how to generate your MVS system (and a wide range of IBM program products at the same time). You need to have an operating system installed already, of course, to run the CBIPO jobs, so for 'green field' sites IBM also supplies very basic pregenerated and preconfigured versions of MVS, which give you enough function to build a proper system from your CBIPO tapes.

Once you have created a system from your CBIPO, you must test it, apply any site-specific modifications required to make it consistent with your current version of MVS, and apply any fixes required (either to correct errors discovered in testing, or because IBM recommends them to prevent the occurrence of known high-impact problems (HIPERS)). Finally, you will have to bring up your new system in place of the old one, migrate your real users onto it, then sit back and wait for the problems!

1.2.2   Problem diagnosis and resolution

When those problems happen (or any others for that matter), the MVS systems programmer will generally be the 'expert of last resort' for the entire installation. Any problem that does not have an obvious and simple explanation (and many others that have) will be brought to you — and more often than not blamed on you! Your first task will be to separate the wheat from the chaff, passing back simple problems with a judicious mixture of scorn and succour, and tracking down exactly which piece of software is responsible for the others (Chapter 18 is dedicated to helping you with this task). If the problem is caused by a bug in a piece of IBM or third-party software, you will have to contact the supplier, obtain a 'fix', install it on your testing system, check that it does not introduce more problems than it solves (many fixes do), and migrate it onto your production system. You may also be required to install 'preventative' maintenance on a regular basis (though the wisdom of this is questionable to say the least).

1.2.3   System modifications

From time to time the systems programmer will either be asked to, or feel some need to, 'enhance' the operating system or other system software. While the thought of messing around with assembler code usually brings a shine to the eyes of any weary sysprog, it is one that should generally be firmly resisted — to dull that shine, just ask them to maintain the last mod that somebody else made! In fact, every system modification that does not use the standard IBM interfaces (generally documented exit points) poses the potential nightmare of having to be rewritten to fit every new release of the product that has been modified. Even well-behaved exits make the system more complex to maintain and harder to understand, so you should think twice before coding these, too. Nevertheless, there will be times when they are of value, and some techniques and examples are discussed in Chapter 12 (Chapter 6, which covers assembler programming for systems programmers, should also help here).

1.2.4   Hardware configuration

You will have to decide how devices such as disks, printers, and tape drives should be attached to the mainframe — on which channels, control units, and addresses for example. You will also generate the control blocks which both the processor hardware and the operating system use to identify which devices are attached to which channels and what protocols to use to drive them. The tools you will use to generate these are known as the IOCP and the MVSCP respectively (or HCD on MVS version 4 systems). You may also become involved in configuring ports on local communications cluster controllers, and other more 'hardware'-oriented work, depending on the lines of demarcation between the systems programming and other operations support groups.

1.2.5   Housekeeping

MVS generates large amounts of diagnostic and informational data, such as system logs, dumps, hardware error records, accounting and event-monitoring records, and it is the systems programmer's job to set up and maintain processes to collect, report on, and archive this information as required. Furthermore, MVS is not very good at tidying up after its users: it is also your job to set up the processes required to remedy this deficiency, e.g. to delete uncataloged datasets from DASD, defragment DASD packs, and reorganize catalogs with CI-splits and CA-splits. All these areas are discussed in Chapters 16 and 17.

1.2.6   Looking after other software

The range of 'other' software systems programmers have to look after (i.e. install, upgrade, maintain, and sometimes even administer) varies enormously from site to site. For example, you may have to look after:

- IBM program products (many of which may come on your CBIPO tape), including compilers, utilities, communications software, and system management products.
- Third-party system software such as storage management packages, security packages, tape management systems, scheduling packages, and many others.
- Major subsystems such as CICS, IMS, or DB2 (or third-party equivalents) — though in all but the smallest sites these will generally be looked after by specialists in the systems programming team.
- Possibly even application software packages bought in from external suppliers, particularly when the sort of expertise required to install these is lacking in the applications development areas of the MIS department.

1.2.7   Evaluating software packages

When someone needs a system software package to do a job and there are several alternative packages to choose between, you may be asked to perform an evaluation. Generally, you need to take the following sorts of action to do this:

- Decide on (and prioritize) criteria for choosing between them.
- Select the most appropriate packages to evaluate (from suppliers' fliers, industry surveys, asking around your contacts at other sites, etc.).

- Conduct trials of the candidates.
- Negotiate prices with the suppliers.
- Score the candidates against the criteria.
- Produce a report justifying your recommendation.

At the same time, you may have to put together the justification for spending the necessary amount of money on providing this function at all.

1.2.8 Dealing with software suppliers

Apart from raising problems with suppliers' technical staff and negotiating with their salespeople for deals on new products, you will probably have to deal with suppliers on many other occasions. Commonest and most irksome is having to deal with salespeople trying to sell you things you have never heard of and probably have no use for. Try to be polite, at the very least — they may actually come up with exactly what you need one day! Salespeople from companies you already deal with deserve more consideration again, as they may often be able to give you useful information about new releases with new functions, addon products, market trends, and competitors' products. You may also be able to squeeze them for useful 'goodies' such as free training or manuals!

1.2.9 Performance monitoring and tuning

In many organizations there is a separate team dealing with performance but in others you may have the opportunity to work in these areas as well as the others discussed above. In fact, the knowledge you will gain as an MVS systems programmer is an essential prerequisite for the task of tuning a system — you cannot tune a system well unless you know how it works in the first place. However, performance monitoring and tuning is a very large subject in itself, and I have not attempted to cover it in this book. If you want to learn more about MVS performance management, I can recommend [1].

1.2.10 Advice and assistance

As a systems programmer you should come to be regarded as something of a technical guru, and as such you may often be invited to give advice and assistance to those working in a wide range of other areas — particularly where those areas potentially overlap with your own. Many of these areas also deserve a book to themselves, so here I shall simply list a few of them to whet your appetite:

- Disaster recovery
- Capacity planning
- Applications development
- Automated operations

- Hardware strategy and purchasing decisions
- Security policy

Your assistance will be all the more sought after, and all the more positively received, if your colleagues perceive you as a true professional — which is what the next section is all about.

1.3   Be a professional

1.3.1   A professional attitude

The professional's attitude to work can be summed up in two simple words — taking responsibility. Those simple words mean a thousand different things in a thousand different situations, but here are a few examples:

- 'Owning the problem' — when someone brings a problem to you, you make sure that it is solved and the person with the problem knows when it is solved, even if you need to ask someone else to solve it.
- Admitting mistakes, putting them right as far as you can, and implementing measures to stop them happening again.
- Ensuring that anyone who might be adversely affected by what you are doing is consulted or at least informed — what they are doing might be a lot more important to the organization than what you are doing!
- Ensuring that you use methods which maximize the quality of your work and minimize any adverse consequences for your users.

The rest of this section is devoted to a discussion of some of these 'professional methods'.

Before going on to these, however, there is one more point which is well worth bearing in mind: professionals blow their own trumpet! Make it your objective to build a professional image — through the quality of your work and through your presentation of it. The benefits are enormous: colleagues and bosses will listen when you speak; you will get the resources you need to do your job; and your career will progress by leaps and bounds. Not least, you will have laid a firm foundation for feeling good about yourself and your work!

1.3.2   Project management

Some systems programmers seem to think that project management is only for applications projects. They are wrong — and they are depriving themselves of a vital technique for ensuring that they deliver high-quality work and deliver it on time. There are many PC-based tools available to help with project management, and if one is available to you, you will probably find it helpful, but whether or not you use one of these, there are certain basic rules that will help you with any major piece of work:

- Go for a slow start — many studies have shown that if you spend more time planning a project at the beginning, the total time taken to complete it (including the planning time) is reduced.
- List all the activities required to complete the project, decide who is going to do them, and schedule when they will do them, bearing in mind the availability of the people concerned, their other commitments, and the interdependencies between the activities themselves, allowing some slack for contingencies.
- Check the proposed schedule with everyone involved, including managers with potentially contending responsibilities, e.g. those who might be asking your project staff to do something else at the same time as your work, or those with projects which might require implementation on the same day.
- Once your schedule has been agreed, use it! Use it to remind yourself to do things, to ask other people to do things, and to check whether tasks have been completed on schedule.
- When a task is completed, check it — ask the person who did it to show you the results.
- Chase people who are behind schedule and get them to commit to complete by a specific date.
- If you realize you are going to miss a deadline, start talking to the people who will be affected straight away, and negotiate a new one, or increased resources. Changing the plan is not a failure — but missing the deadline is!

1.3.3   *Change management*

Change management is probably the number one bugbear of traditional systems programmers — there is nothing they hate more than having to fit their changes in with the rest of the business. But it is obvious that if the operations department is going to try to guarantee a service to its users, it has to control changes to the production environment. It needs to ensure that when something goes wrong, the people fixing it know what changes have been made recently, and are able to isolate the effects of one change from another. And it needs to ensure that any changes made to the production environment are well thought-out, adequately tested, and justified with good business reasons. Professional systems programmers recognize those needs and try to work within them. They realize it actually helps them to have to explain to other people what they are doing, why, and how they are going to test it — it is far too easy to make invalid assumptions when the only person you have to explain things to is yourself!

Generally change control systems will require you to:

- Record what it is you want to do, when, and what effect it will have on the production environment and online users.
- Explain what testing will be done and what provision will be made to back out the change if it goes wrong. (This is a vital one for systems programmers — when your changes go wrong you are often in danger of having corrupted the very

systems you need to use to put them right — and you should welcome any process that makes it harder for you to put yourself into that situation!)

- Obtain the approval of certain managers for the change and its timing.
- Inform any users who may be affected by the change — this gives you an opportunity to point out how the changes will benefit them and so improve your image too!

Of course, there are times when you need to make a change immediately to correct or prevent a system crash or other disaster. A good change control system should recognize that you will need to do this sometimes, and allow you to do it on your own authority then tell the relevant managers afterwards.

1.3.4   Change techniques

Every change that goes wrong is a blot on your reputation, and you will probably need five to ten changes to go right to cancel out the effect of the one that went wrong! So minimize the danger:

- Schedule major changes in 'maintenance slots' — regular times when you are given exclusive use of the production machine to make your changes. If you do not have these, fight for them. If you have, protect them by using them wisely — do not sneak changes in that nobody knows about, do not overrun your allotted time, and follow the rest of the guidelines below. Otherwise, you will be inviting the boss to remove your maintenance slots — often one of your most precious resources.
- Back up anything you might conceivably corrupt before you start changing it, and plan how to recover from every possible disaster (within reason) *before* you start making changes — this is the secret of turning disasters into minor delays.
- Have someone check your commands or JCL before you submit them if you are in any danger of causing a disaster should you have mistyped — and always check them against the manual if you are less than 100 per cent confident of what you are doing.
- Ensure users cannot access test systems or live systems you are in the process of changing.

1.3.5   Testing

Test all changes before implementing them on a production system! Ideally, you should have access to a full test system (possibly a VM virtual machine or a PR/SM partition reserved for systems programmer use — these options are discussed in Chapter 13) on which to test your changes before they are implemented. Alternatively, your change may be testable on the live system, or perhaps you will only be able to test it in your maintenance slot itself. Whatever the environment in which you run your test, though, the same rules apply:

- draw up a comprehensive test plan: consider what options need to be tested, and the possible things that could go wrong, consult users and specialists in the area you are dealing with, and prepare testing JCL or commands before your test session.
- Run through your test plan on the live system to see what the results ought to be before testing in earnest.
- Create whatever testing environment is required to enable you to test the new software without disrupting the users of the current version.
- Test from the plan!
- Check the results carefully.
- Rerun the whole test if you have to make changes to correct errors revealed by your testing.

1.3.6 Documentation

Fortunately, there is one area in which systems programmers are not alone in the industry in being notoriously unprofessional — and documentation is it! Unfortunately, that gives us just as bad a problem as the application programmers when we have to try and find out how our system is supposed to work. The objective of good documentation should be to make it easy for any reasonably skilled person to discover how the system works, down to whatever level of detail is required — remember that one day that person will be you. This does not mean, however, that you should keep reams of paper describing every detail of your system — with documentation like this you can guarantee that the piece of paper you need will always have been lost or allowed to go out of date by the time you need it! Simple guidelines for an effective documentation system are:

- document your work internally as you go, so every piece of JCL, assembler code, clist, etc., contains comments explaining what it is for, when it is used, and any peculiarities relating to it — unusual techniques, for example, or important things to check before you use it.
- Keep all your work in places where it will be easy to find — usually libraries with library names that follow a sensible standard and member names that are self-explanatory. If your work is part of a permanent system, it should be kept in permanent datasets that are regarded as part of that system, not in your personal datasets that may be deleted when you move on to pastures new.
- Create and keep up to date a high-level system manual. This should include summary documentation of key features of your system, including in-house modifications, with pointers to datasets where more detailed documentation can be found, and explanations of the naming standards which will allow someone new to find your detailed work easily. This document should be easily accessible to all systems programmers (e.g. in your technical library), there should only be one copy of it (except perhaps a spare at your disaster recovery site), it should be kept and updated in machine-readable form, and whenever

it is changed the entire document should be reprinted, the old hard copy thrown away, and the new one inserted in its place.

1.3.7   Problem resolution

You may have access to problem management software (e.g. using IBM's INFOMAN product), but there is more to problem management than this! In addition to recording each problem that is reported, ensuring it is dealt with, and recording the solution — which can be done using INFOMAN, an equivalent piece of software, or a plain old-fashioned notebook — a good systems programming team will ensure that problems are dealt with competently and with the minimum impact on your project work (and private life!) by:

- Training all members of the team to deal with the commoner types of problem in all areas for which the team is responsible.
- Maintaining an 'on call' rota so that each systems programmer carries a pager out of working hours and is responsible for dealing with any problems during those hours — but only for their week on the rota.
- Maintaining a 'problem duty' rota to handle problems during working hours in exactly the same way — junior staff can go onto this one earlier than the on call rota to help them learn the ropes, but with more experienced staff available to provide a safety net. This sort of rota is vastly preferable to the alternatives of: (a) directing all problems to the person in whose area they lie — this means everyone's project work is constantly disrupted, and the opportunity to spread basic problem resolution skills around the team is lost; or (b) having one or more members of staff dedicated full-time to problem resolution — the sort of mind-numbing job that drives away high-quality staff.

1.3.8   Standards

Your job will be easier to do and easier to learn if your site enforces proper standards. Good standards make the system run smoothly, with the minimum of administrative overhead, and make the system easy to understand and maintain. In the systems programming area, they consist mainly of naming standards for resources, and rules of good practice to be followed by staff. Examples will be found scattered throughout this book, but here are a few to serve as illustrations:

- Dataset names should include a high-level qualifier (HLQ) related to the application or user that owns them, so that rules for allowing access to them and for accounting for the space they use can be extremely simple, depending in 90 per cent of cases only on the HLQ.
- System dataset names should also follow simple rules, e.g. one HLQ could be allocated for installation JCL datasets, another for IBM program products, another for CICS datasets, another for third-party system software.

- When amending members of system libraries, follow a simple rule for naming backup copies — e.g. always make a backup copy with a name the same as the original, except replacing the suffix with your initials—and ensure that all members of the team follow the same convention.
- Never code tables of variable information into system programs (such as valid account codes, public holidays, etc.) — put them in an easily maintained file instead or you will constantly have to modify and reassemble the program itself.
- Make a rule about the use of SMP/E — i.e. always use it when possible—and about what products go in which CSIs — e.g do not put third-party products in your MVS CSI or you will not be able to throw it away when you install a new CBIPO.

If your site or section does not have effective standards, push for them! And remember the golden rule — a standard is only a standard if it is enforced. One of the best and commonest reasons for writing system exits to enforce standards.

1.3.9 *Manuals*

Manuals are the number one tools of your trade — *use them*! It never ceases to shock and amaze me how many people will attempt difficult and unfamiliar pieces of work without consulting the relevant manual first. True, IBM manuals used to have a poor reputation, but their quality is improving steadily, and even at their worst, there is a vast amount of useful information in them.

The best attitude is to regard every new piece of work as an opportunity to dig into the relevant manual. Never read 'just enough' to get the job done, but instead try to become an expert on whichever small area is involved by reading whatever is relevant in the manual. You may find a better way of doing your immediate task, and even if you do not, you will certainly be better prepared to deal with related issues in future.

One word of warning, though — manuals can be wrong. If anything does not seem to fit, or if things do not work quite as the manual says they should, contact the supplier (or check INFO/MVS for IBM manuals) and query it.

Manuals, however, are useless if you can never find the one you need when you need it. So you should ensure that the manuals you need are kept in a well organized and properly indexed technical library. Setting up an indexing system (and perhaps a booking-out system if your library is heavily used) is a useful way of familiarizing yourself with ISPF dialogs, CICS application writing, or any other online application technology.

Making and enforcing rules to keep the manuals in the library or on the desk of the current borrower is a little more difficult, but just as important, or you still will not be able to find that vital manual when the system is about to come tumbling down about your ears!

Finding IBM manuals and the relevant information in them has, thankfully, become much easier with the introduction of IBM's Bookmanager software and machine-readable manuals. If you do not have the MVS version of Bookmanager/ READ and a way of loading manuals onto mainframe storage you should try to get them as soon as possible — the cost is very easy to justify.

1.3.10 Time management

Professionals in all areas of life are coming to recognize that their own time is their most precious resource. Planning and managing that time effectively are probably the most important skills you can acquire if you want to perform to the best of your ability, not only at work but also in all other areas of your life. With these skills you can learn how to make realistic commitments, deliver on them, and get what you want from your time.

I will not go into the techniques you need here — they would require a book to themselves to do them justice. All I can do is recommend some other places to turn to. [2] is a great place to start. For a practical tool that helps you put serious time-management techniques into practice, I can highly recommend the purchase of a 'Time Manager System' from Time Manager International.

References

1. Samson, S.L.: *MVS Performance Management*, McGraw-Hill, New York, 1990.
2. Lakein, A.: *How to Get Control of Your Time and Your Life*, Gower, Aldershot, 1984.

2
System/370 and System/390 hardware

2.1   Introduction

MVS runs on machines that conform to the System/370 and System/390 architectures. IBM defines an architecture as 'the functions the computer system provides', including, most significantly, 'the set of machine instructions that the computer can recognize and execute' (these instructions are documented in [1]). The System/390 architecture was announced in 1990 and is currently only implemented by the ES/9000 series of processors. It is very much an evolutionary step forward from System/370, rather than a revolutionary one, and the differences between the two architectures are currently quite small, though no doubt additional functionality will progressively be added to the newer System/390.

System/370 has been around for a long time and all earlier processors running MVS conform to this architecture. In fact, there are several variations on the basic System/370 architecture, each representing an addition of more function, and almost all MVS users of System/370 machines are now using one of these more advanced versions — either System/370-XA (extended architecture), or System/370-ESA (Enterprise Systems Architecture, according to IBM's marketing department, but it is a fair bet that ES originally stood for 'expanded storage').

There are several families of IBM processors which implement these architectures, and several others produced and marketed by 'plug-compatible manufacturers' (PCMs), plus various types of peripheral devices which can be connected to them.

In this chapter I discuss those aspects of the hardware which are of most relevance to systems programmers. On one hand, you will need to understand some aspects of how the hardware works in order to understand how MVS makes use of it; and on the other, you will need to know more practical things like how different pieces of hardware can be configured so you can design and implement I/O configurations. We will return to both of these areas in later chapters; here we cover the basics. Each section deals with one type of hardware, beginning with the processors themselves.

2.2   Central processor complexes

Commonly referred to as the 'machine', 'mainframe', or 'CPU', the central processor complex (CPC) is the heart of your computer system — or more accurately, the brain. All the other devices we will discuss are dedicated to the task of delivering data to the processor complex; it is in the processor complex itself where both your users' programs and your systems software will execute.

2.2.1   Processor types

The most advanced family of MVS-capable IBM processor complexes currently available is the ES/9000 series. This consists of three subfamilies:

1   The 'rack-mounted' 9221 series, which are the smallest machines and are usually found running VSE rather than MVS.
2   The 'frame-mounted air-cooled' 9121 series, which replaced the old 4381 series but already matches the processing power of a 3090-300J at the top end. These are very viable as MVS machines for smaller and medium-sized sites.
3   The 'water-cooled' 9021 series, which are the biggest machines, replacing the old 3090 series and already providing much more power at the top end than the top-of-the-range 3090-600J.

A high proportion of MVS sites, however, are still running a 3090 of some description. The 3090 has gone through four major generations (the base, E, S, and J/JH series) and there is a range of different size models available in each series. The E and subsequent series support ESA, and there are upgrades available from any 3090 box to almost any later/bigger version.

Some sites are also still running MVS on various older/smaller machines. The 4381, for example, although mainly a VSE machine, is still running MVS on some smaller sites, and there is even a version of the 4381 that runs ESA, so they are likely to be with us for a few years more. Other machines of similar vintage, such as the 308x series (3081, 3084, etc.), which was the predecessor of the 3090, are no longer sold by IBM but there are still a few of them around. None of the 308x machines support ESA, so their future is now looking very limited.

There are two major manufacturers of plug-compatible processors, Fujitsu (whose boxes are sold by Amdahl in the West), and Hitachi. Amdahl is better established — its 580 series corresponds roughly to IBM's 308x series, and its 5990 to IBM's 3090 — but Hitachi is also producing high-quality boxes. Their main disadvantage is that because they are in the business of being compatible, they are constantly having to catch up with IBM's latest announcements, but there is no doubt that they provide realistic alternatives to buying from IBM, even for the largest corporations.

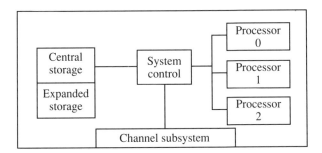

Figure 2.1. Logical structure of 3090-300x processor complex.

2.2.2   *Logical structure*

For the purpose of illustrating the logical and physical structure of a typical MVS-capable CPC, though, I will stick with an IBM example. Figure 2.1 shows the logical structure of a 3090-300x. Larger 3090s have two 'sides', one of them the same as this, and the other a mirror image, connected by links between the two system controllers.

Perhaps the first thing that leaps out of this diagram is the fact that there is more than one processor (this is a good reason for calling the box as a whole a 'processor complex' — if you call the whole box a 'processor' there is too much scope for confusion!). IBM supply 3090s with up to six processors, all of which can simultaneously be active, each executing a different stream of instructions, and all sharing the same main storage. One of the roles of the system controller is to prevent any integrity problems as a result of this, by serializing access to areas of main storage. The design of MVS must also take account of multiprocessing, which is handled in such a way that application programs need not be aware of it — each behaves more or less as if it had a dedicated machine.

The other obvious point is that the system controller is not directly attached to the peripheral devices, as it would be in a PC, for example. Instead there is a separate channel subsystem, which is a processor in its own right, with the specialized task of managing I/O to peripheral devices. This offloads some of the work involved in I/O operations from the main processors, allowing increased throughput on the complex as a whole.

Each of the main processors has a number of components, including the various registers you may use from an assembler program, and a high-speed buffer, which is used to speed up the fetching of the next instruction to be executed. On the assumption that most programs execute sequentially through their instructions, and frequently loop back to recently executed instructions, the buffer is preloaded with the next instructions in sequence and the previous instructions executed are kept in there for a period of time. When the next instruction to be executed is found in the high-speed buffer, it can be loaded much more quickly than if it had to be retrieved from main storage synchronously.

2.2.3   Key features for MVS

The processor hardware also provides a number of features that are fundamental to the way MVS operates, notably those that process interrupts and address translation.

Interrupts are a vital component of the multitasking process used by MVS. There is a long list of events that can occur which will prompt one or another of the components of the processor complex to generate an interrupt. The most common is the completion of an I/O request, which causes the channel subsystem to generate an interrupt, but others can be generated by the time-of-day clock, by the operator hitting an attention key on the system console, or by one of the processors themselves.

When an interrupt occurs, the hardware goes through the following process:

1 One of the processors is scheduled to process the interrupt.
2 On completion of the current instruction, the selected processor saves the current program status word (PSW) in a standard area (known as the OPSW — old PSW) in the prefixed save area (PSA) for the processor concerned, loads a new PSW (from an address in the PSA which depends on the type of interrupt), and resumes execution.

All this is done by instruction sequences which are hardwired into the processor. MVS, however, must provide the interrupt handlers themselves, at the addresses specified in the relevant new PSW. These are known as 'first-level interrupt handler' routines, and they must: (a) save the environment in use by the program that was executing when the interrupt occurred (including the registers); then (b) process the event that caused the interrupt to occur. During the execution of these routines, the processor is disabled for further interrupts.

Interrupts therefore provide a mechanism for preventing a single task from monopolizing a processor when there are urgent events to be processed, and they are vital to the working of the MVS dispatcher and to MVS processing of I/O requests, both of which we shall return to in the next chapter.

The dynamic address translation (DAT) feature is equally vital to MVS. It provides the mechanism which enables MVS to map virtual storage onto real storage and still to process work efficiently. However, we will defer a detailed discussion of DAT until the next chapter, as it is rather artificial to attempt to separate the workings of DAT from the MVS implementation of virtual storage.

2.2.4   Physical structure

Physically, a modern processor complex consists of a number of boxes; these however, do not correspond to the logical components discussed above. For a 3090, for example, all these logical components are contained in one cluster of boxes known as the 3090 processor unit, but you also require a number of other boxes to make your 3090 work:

- A 3092 processor controller, which provides IPL, power on/off, configuration, monitoring, error recovery, and diagnostic facilities, including remote diagnostic capabilities.
- Two or three system/service consoles, attached to the 3092, allowing the operator to control the functions of the 3092 — note that this is completely different from the MVS operator console. We will refer to these as 'hardware consoles' to distinguish them from MVS consoles.
- A pair of 3370 disk drives, holding data used by the 3092, notably the I/O configuration dataset (IOCDS), which the systems programmer must provide, and the microcode, i.e. software which is independent of the operating system and implements functions which appear to the operating system as if they were being provided by the hardware.
- A modem and telephone link for use by the 3092's remote diagnostic facility.
- A 3097 power and coolant distribution unit.
- A 3089 power unit (or a third-party equivalent).

Within the 3090 processor unit itself, there are numerous chips mounted on printed circuit boards or 'cards' which implement the logical components we have discussed. The processors themselves are held within 'thermal conduction modules' (TCMs). Each TCM contains around 100 chips mounted on ceramic cards in a helium-filled module, surrounded by a 'cold plate' through which chilled water circulates. This special design is required to dissipate the heat created as a by-product of the vast amounts of high-speed processing required from these chips. The TCMs can be slid in and out, making both maintenance and upgrades to them fairly straightforward — the TCMs are never altered at customer sites, they are simply replaced.

Such maintenance will be performed by your IBM hardware customer engineer (CE) if you have a maintenance contract with IBM, or by the equivalent personnel from the company concerned if you have a third-party maintenance contract. The engineers are also able to make the engineering changes (ECs) that IBM releases from time to time, which are the hardware equivalents of PTFs — in other words, fixes and minor enhancements. These are usually implemented through upgrades to the microcode on your machine, and may be brought in by the engineer on a diskette or sent down your remote support link.

Usually your site will need to perform a 'power-on-reset' to bring such changes into effect, and this may also be required for other reasons, e.g. to implement a new IOCDS, to switch between XA and ESA modes, or to recover from some types of hardware failure. This is more radical than an initial program load (IPL) of the operating system, as it also involves reloading the microcode, IOCDS, etc. In effect this duplicates the power-up sequence of events, though most sites will only physically power their machines up and down at installation time, in emergencies, and for major disruptions such as machine moves and changes to the power supplies.

You should familiarize yourself with the use of the hardware console to initiate and control actions such as IPLs, power-on-reset, and IOCDS changes.

2.3   Channels

Channels are the interface cards within the channel subsystem into which channel cables are plugged. One or more I/O devices can be attached to each channel cable, and the channel and channel cables carry the control information which the processor uses to control the attached devices, as well as the data which is flowing between the processor complex and the attached devices.

Until 1990, all channels on System/370 machines used a parallel protocol to send data down bulky copper cables known as 'bus and tag' cables. In 1990, however, IBM announced ESCON channels, which use a new serial protocol to send data down thin fibre optic cables at potentially far higher speeds. These two types of channel have quite different characteristics and configuration requirements, as we will see below. Some of the main ones are:

- Parallel channel cables cannot be more than 400 feet long, while ordinary ESCON channels can be up to 3 kilometres long, and special Extended Distance Facility (XDF) ESCON channels can be up to 20 kilometres long. Furthermore, up to three ESCON cables can be used in series with ESCON directors (see below) connecting them, so a control unit could in theory be 60 km from the processor to which it is connected — no doubt these distances will increase as the technology develops further. However, not all devices support these distances, since the timing of the I/O operation can be disrupted by the increase in the time taken for a signal to reach the device.
- Parallel channel cables support a maximum data transfer rate of 4.5 Mb per second, while ESCON channels support up to 18 Mb per second at the time of writing and will inevitably become even faster as time goes by.
- ESCON channels are far less bulky and far more easily manageable — most computer rooms feature a rat's nest of copper cables under the floor which are too heavy and mixed up to move, even though many of them are no longer connected to anything!
- The new ESCON channel architecture allows far greater flexibility in making channel connections, and allows many more connections to be made with a small number of channels. With the new ESCON Multiple Image Facility (EMIF), introduced at the end of 1992, it will even be possible to share an ESCON channel between multiple PR/SM partitions.
- ESCON channels, being optical rather than electrical, can be plugged in or pulled out without causing an electrical spark, and so can potentially be installed and removed without disrupting your system.

At the time of writing only a relatively small proportion of the I/O devices installed on customer sites have the capability to connect to ESCON channels, so parallel channels are likely to be common for some time, but it is clear that in the long term ESCON channels will tend to replace them.

Processor complexes are supplied with channels in blocks of 8 or 16, so you are likely to find you have 16, 24, 32, 48, or 64 on your box. Once upon a time most parallel channels were configured as 'byte multiplexor' channels, and these are still required for driving certain types of unit record device (e.g. card readers and punches), or if you are running PEP on a front-end communications processor (see Sec. 2.6). Usually only certain channels are capable of being configured this way (usually numbers 00, 01, 10, 11, 20, 21, etc.). All modern devices, however, run faster on the 'block multiplexor' type of parallel channel, and if you have none of the older devices, you will be able to configure all of your channels as block channels.

There are also two alternative protocols which may be used for I/O requests on a parallel channel, known as interlock (DCI) and data streaming (DS); data streaming is more efficient, and is used by most high-speed devices. You must specify channel types and protocols when you are defining your I/O configuration (using the IOCP and MVSCP programs or the HCD facility — see Chapter 7).

Parallel channel cables are thick (around 1 inch) round clusters of copper cables, usually in grey or blue sheathing. Each channel connection consists of a pair of cables, known as 'bus' and 'tag' lines. The 'bus' lines are parallel lines carrying the data itself, including channel command words, while the tag lines are used for hardware control signals.

Because of the technical difficulties of preventing signal skew over long parallel copper cables, parallel channel cables cannot be more than 400 feet long. It is, however, possible to buy channel extenders, which were the first step towards ESCON channels. These convert the channel signals from the OEMI protocol used on channel connections into a serial signal which is then sent down an optical fibre or a high-speed comms line to another extender. Here the signal is converted back to the OEMI protocol and fed down another channel cable to the I/O device. However, certain sorts of device, notably DASD devices, cannot sit on the end of channel extenders because they cannot handle the potential signal delays.

The other important constraint imposed by channels is that only one data transfer can occur up or down a given channel at any one time. However, there can be many devices attached to a single channel — not only can one control unit attached to a channel control multiple I/O devices, but there can also be multiple control units 'daisy-chained' on one channel (i.e. connected one behind the other — see Fig. 2.2). This means that there can be contention between different devices for the use of the channel, which can slow down I/O operations using those devices and contribute to degradation of the performance experienced by users of the system.

Figure 2.2 shows how devices are physically attached to parallel channel cables. A pair of bus and tag cables is connected from the channel itself to the 'in' side of the first device (or control unit), then another pair from the 'out' side of this device

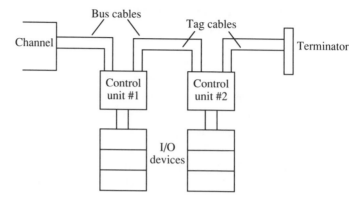

Figure 2.2. 'Daisy-chaining' control units.

to the 'in' side of the next one, and so on, until the last device on the channel. On this device, a terminator is attached to the 'out' side, which returns signals back down to the channel which have not been picked up by any device on the channel.

The ESCON channel architecture, however, allows connection of devices in quite new ways. The most interesting innovation of the ESCON architecture is a switching device known as an ESCON director, which dynamically switches paths to I/O devices between different MVS systems. Figure 2.3 illustrates a configuration using an ESCON director to share various I/O devices between two MVS systems. Note that:

- The ESCON director enables any of the host channels shown to connect to any of the I/O devices, or indeed to any of the other host channels.
- 3990 DASD control units, 3390 DASD, and 3490 cartridge drives are all discussed later in this chapter; the 9343/9345 DASD and integrated control

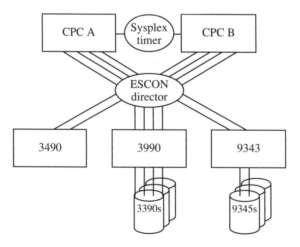

Figure 2.3. ESCON director configuration.

unit are uncached DASD which are supported by MVS but more commonly used on smaller systems.
- The sysplex timer enables the two CPCs to be configured as a sysplex — also known as 'closely coupled' systems.

We will return to sysplexes and the sharing of I/O devices between MVS systems in Chapter 14.

2.4   DASD and DASD controllers

Of all the devices attached to your processor complex, direct access storage devices (DASD) are likely to take the lion's share of your attention. The vast majority of the installed devices at the time of writing are IBM 3380s, 3390s, or plug-compatible equivalents. 3380 devices have been available for a long time and have now gone through a number of generations which can be intermixed with each other and with 3390s in your configuration.

2.4.1   3380 DASD and 3880 control units

The oldest 3380s are known as 'standards', which covers models A04, AA4, and B04. Each of these provides two spindles or head-disk assemblies (HDAs) per box, each of which carries two actuators — one actuator corresponds to one DASD volume, so each of these boxes contains four volumes. Up to four boxes can be bolted together to form a 'string', which can therefore contain a maximum of 16 actuators/volumes. The first box in the string must be an A box, as these contain the 'head of string' function, while the rest must be B boxes. The head of string is then connected to at least one control unit (typically an IBM 3880), which is in turn connected to a channel from the processor complex, so the basic configuration looks something like that shown in Fig. 2.4.

Later generations of 3380s provided enhanced function, performance, and data capacities, but were still attached in the same basic way. D devices (i.e. AD4 and BD4 boxes) and E devices (AE4 and BE4) were the next to come along; both offer improved function and performance, and the Es have double the data capacity of Ds and standards, which is achieved by doubling the number of cylinders of data,

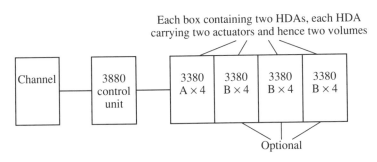

Figure 2.4. Basic 3880/3380 DASD configuration.

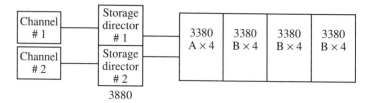

Figure 2.5. Multiple paths to 3380 string.

while keeping the track size and number of tracks per cylinder the same (these are often known as 'double density' drives). J and K devices completed the range, offering further perfomance improvements and, in the case of Ks, triple the data capacity of Ds and standards, again achieved by increasing the number of cylinders (these are known as 'triple-density' drives). There is also a special version of the J box — a CJ2 — which can be directly attached to a channel, i.e. the control unit function is included in the head-of-string box.

All these boxes can be configured as shown in Fig. 2.4 but, in practice, the illustrated configuration would be inadequate because it only provides a single path from each DASD unit to the channel. As this path is shared by all the devices in the string, this means that only one of them could be connected to the channel at a time, so the data transfer stage of an I/O operation could only be in progress for one of the attached devices at a time. Clearly this is a potential bottleneck, and, in practice, contention for DASD units and paths to them is one of the commonest causes of performance degradation for applications running under MVS. In addition, any failure in any of the components between the head of string and the channel would leave the whole string inaccessible to the processor complex. If the string held any datasets that were critical to the operation of your system (which most strings do!) this would result in your system grinding to a halt until the hardware problem was fixed.

It is therefore normal to configure DASD strings with several paths to the processor complex, and Figs 2.5 and 2.6 show two typical ways of doing this. Both options take advantage of the presence of two separate 'storage directors' in the 3880 control unit, each of which may be attached to a separate channel (or several channels, if the appropriate switches are installed), and of the presence of two interfaces on the head of string which may be attached to separate storage directors.

In Fig. 2.6 further reliability is introduced by cross-configuring 3880s and 3380 strings, so that either of the strings shown can continue to process I/O requests even if one of the control units fails completely.

2.4.2   3390 DASD and 3990 control units

More up-to-date sites will be using 3990 control units with 3390 DASDs, or some mixture of 3990, 3390, and 3380 devices. The issues here are similar, but there are

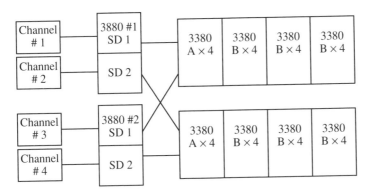

Figure 2.6. Cross-connection of 3880s and 3380s.

many more configuration options. A sample configuration is shown in Fig. 2.7. The 3990 can be attached to up to 16 channels, although only four of these can belong to any one MVS system and only four can be actively transferring data at any one time. It is divided into two 'storage clusters' or multipath storage directors (MPSDs) with two 'storage paths' each, and all four of these paths can be used by a single string of 3390 devices. The 3380 devices shown are attached behind the

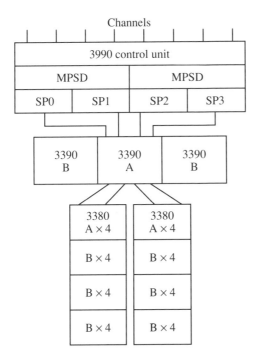

Figure 2.7. 3390s and 3380s mixed behind 3990 control unit.

3390 head of string and have only two paths to each string. There are, however, many possible configuration variations.

3390 devices differ in a number of ways from 3380s:

- Each head of string can be attached to four paths.
- Each A box (containing the head-of-string function) can hold up to 8 actuators, and each B box can hold up to 12. Boxes can be fitted and used while only partially populated with HDAs, then the gaps filled later without disrupting operations on the existing actuators.
- The track size is about 20 per cent larger and the disks revolve faster, with the result that search times are reduced and maximum data transfer rates are increased by about 40 per cent (to 4.2 megabytes per second).
- Cylinders are recorded closer together on a smaller recording surface, so seek times are also reduced (see Sec. 2.4.3 for a description of seek and search operations on disk devices).
- The data capacity of a model 2 device is equivalent to that of a triple density 3380 (i.e. a K device). There are also model 1 and model 3 devices available, with capacities of one-half and one-and-a-half times that of the model 2 respectively.

3390 model numbers are in the format abn where a is A for a head-of-string box and B for other boxes; b is the model number; and n reflects the number of actuators that can be fitted to the box (4, 8, or C — meaning 12). So, for example, an A18 box would be a head-of-string box with capacity for 8 half-capacity drives, and a B2C box would be a non-head-of-string box with capacity for 12 full-density drives.

Let us now turn to the 3990 control units which are now replacing 3880s. These represent a substantial advance over 3880s:

- They support data transfer rates of $4.5\,\mathrm{Mb\,s^{-1}}$, rather than the traditional $3\,\mathrm{Mb\,s^{-1}}$.
- They support four-path strings as well as two-path strings.
- They support 3390 devices as well as 3380s.
- Probably most important of all, they provide vastly improved caching facilities. The 3990 model 3 provides 32 megabytes or 64 megabytes of cache, it allows write caching, and when used with IBM's DFSMS software, it allows caching to be controlled at the dataset level instead of only at the volume level. 3990 caching facilities can make a spectacular difference to DASD I/O performance.

2.4.3 A typical I/O request

We will return to caching shortly, but first, let us discuss briefly the details of how a typical (uncached) I/O request to a DASD device is performed by the hardware.

By the time it reaches the channel cable, any I/O request will have been translated into a channel program consisting of a series of real channel command words.

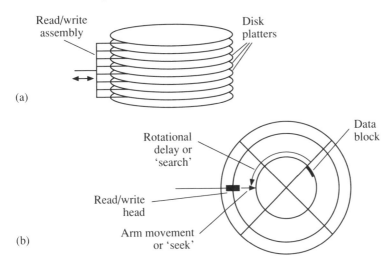

Figure 2.8. Seek and search processes in DASD I/O.

Each channel command word (CCW) specifies the device to be accessed, the operation to be performed on it, and the physical location on the device of the block of data to be accessed. At this point, the request will already have been waiting in the I/O supervisor for the device and channel path required to become free, so there should be no contending requests being sent out or received at this moment by the same operating system (this waiting period is known as IOSQ time). From here, the I/O goes through the following stages:

1   If it finds that the storage director or device is busy (i.e. servicing a request from another system), it will wait again — this is known as pending time.

2   Once the CCW gets through to the device, 'channel end' is presented to the processor complex, meaning that the request has finished with the channel path for the time being. This is because there is now a relatively long wait while the arm carrying the read/write heads moves to position them over the cylinder to be accessed (known as a seek operation). During this wait the channel path is disconnected, so that it can be used by other I/O requests — this is known as disconnect time. Figure 2.8 shows seek and search operations diagrammatically.

3   Once the arm movement is complete, the device uses rotational position sensing (RPS) to determine how much further the disk must spin before the block to be read comes under the read/write heads (known as a search operation or latency). The disk is divided into sectors, each corresponding to a portion of every track, and when RPS indicates that the desired sector is approaching the read/write heads, it attempts to reconnect to a channel path to the system which initiated the I/O request. Modern disk devices have a facility known as dynamic path reconnect, which means they can reconnect to any path to the system concerned, whether or not it is the same one down which the original request was received. However, it is still possible that all the paths from the DASD

device to the system concerned will be busy when the device attempts to
reconnect. If this is the case, then an 'RPS miss' will occur, i.e. when the block
to be read appears under the read/write heads, it will not be possible to send
it to the requesting processor. When this occurs, the I/O must wait until another
revolution of the disk has occurred, when reconnect will be attempted again.
RPS miss delays add to disconnect time.

4 Once the device has reconnected to a suitable channel and the data to be
accessed has come under the read/write heads, the I/O can be completed, and
data transfer occurs through the channel path. This is known as connect time,
and the length of the connect time will depend on how long it takes for the area
of disk to be accessed to pass under the read/write heads.

The processing of I/O requests by MVS will be covered in the next chapter; for
greater detail, see [9] which covers both MVS and hardware processing of a DASD
I/O request.

2.4.4   Disk caching

Caching is the ability to resolve an I/O request out of solid-state storage in the
control unit, rather than by doing a physical read (or write) to the DASD volume.
This is much faster than doing the physical write, as it completely eliminates
disconnect time (seek and search), cuts down the number of elements that have to
be available before a path can be established (i.e. the device need not be available,
as the request need only connect to the control unit), and allows data transfer to
occur at a higher speed than that allowed by disk rotation speeds, as long as the
channel supports higher speeds.

Cached reads and writes can only occur, however, if the data to be accessed is
already present in the cache memory when the I/O request arrives at the control
unit. Caching algorithms are used in the control unit to select tracks of data to be
kept in the cache memory. Their basic principles are as follows:

* When a record is read from disk the track concerned is 'staged' into the cache
  memory, and kept there so that repeat references to this track can be resolved
  from cache.
* When a sequential read is detected, the control unit initiates a 'read ahead'
  operation which loads the next track into the cache before the processor
  complex actually requests it.
* When the cache becomes full, the least recently used tracks are overwritten.

Write caching requires some extra facilities — in particular, it requires non-
volatile storage (NVS) in the cache controller. A write can only be cached when the
track concerned is already in the cache memory; in this case, the control unit does
not complete the I/O operation to disk before returning 'device end' (i.e. notifi-
cation that the I/O operation is complete) to the processor complex. Instead, it
returns 'device end' as soon as the track to be written has been loaded into both

the cache memory and the NVS, and only completes the write to disk at a later time (or never, if the same track is updated again before the first write can be completed, thus making the first write redundant). The NVS is required in case there is a failure in the control unit or any other component which leads to a loss of the data in the cache memory — when this occurs, the updates to the DASD which the processor believes have been completed must not be lost or the integrity of your data will be compromised! In these circumstances, the copy of the updated tracks held in NVS can be used to complete any outstanding updates when the control unit is reactivated — provided that your operators follow the correct procedures.

2.5 Tape devices

By comparison with disk devices, tape devices are stunning in their simplicity! There are two types available: those using open-reel tapes and those using cartridge-type tapes.

2.5.1 Open-reel tape devices

Older-style tapes come on open reels, with nine parallel recording tracks on the tape, so that each byte of information is recorded across the tape, one data bit on each of the first eight tracks and a 'parity' bit on the ninth. Various recording densities are supported by System/370, including 800, 1600, and 6250 bpi (bytes per inch), although more modern tape drives only support the last two of these, or only 6250. The typical modern tape drive is the IBM 3420 series (or functional equivalents).

Tape is an inherently sequential medium, so if you want to access any record on a tape, you must start from the beginning of the tape and read through it until you reach the one you want. This means that the operation of tape drives is inevitably simpler than that of DASD. When a program attempts to allocate a tape dataset, the operating system will assign a tape drive and issue a mount message to the operator, requesting the operator to put the required tape onto the tape drive. The operator puts up the tape, closes the drive door by hitting the READY button, and allows the I/O to start by hitting the START button. From now on, I/O operations continue sequentially until the system has finished with the tape, when a dismount message is issued and the operator removes the tape. Tapes can only be written to if a plastic 'file protection ring' is inserted around the hole in the middle before they are put up on the tape drive.

There are two 'tape marks' at the beginning of the tape which mark the end of the leader tape and the beginning of the first file, which on a standard labelled tape will be the tape header file. At the end of each file there is another tape mark, and on a standard labelled tape, each data file will be preceded by a header file and followed by a trailer file, containing information such as the volume serial number, dataset names, and DCB parameters. Finally, two more tape marks mark the end of the recorded portion of the tape.

Configuration of tape drives is straightforward — a string of them is attached behind a control unit (for 3420 drives this will be an IBM 3803). There can be two channel paths attached to the control unit, and two paths from the control unit to the drives. Multiple tape drives can be active concurrently because the rate at which data is read from the tape is relatively slow (it is limited by the recording density and the speed of the tape transport mechanism, which in turn is limited by the vulnerability of the tape itself to damage) and data is sent to the processor in blocks (these are physically separated on the tape by interblock gaps of a fixed length). This means that the control unit can accumulate the current block of data from each drive in a buffer at the speed at which it is read off the tape, then send it to the processor at (much faster) normal channel speeds, while the interblock gap is passing the read/write heads. The data transfers between the different drives and the processor can therefore be interleaved.

2.5.2   Cartridge drives

Open-reel tapes are rapidly going out of fashion, and most large MVS sites have switched to cartridge tapes for most of their tape media requirements. These have several advantages over open-reel tapes:

1   The tape itself is completely contained within the cartridge, protecting it from damage, dirt, and the danger of being dropped and unwound all over the machine-room floor! It only comes out of the cartridge within the tape drive itself.

2   The cartridges are much smaller than traditional tapes, making for easier handling and less storage space requirements.

3   Data is recorded on 18 tracks at a higher density than on open-reel tapes, resulting in a larger data capacity on one cartridge than on a 2400 feet open-reel tape recorded at the same block size, and faster data transfer times.

These tapes can be read/written on IBM 3480 and 3490 devices or plug-compatible drives. The 3480 serial number refers both to the control unit (3480-Axx) and the tape units themselves (3480-Bxx — one of these boxes actually includes two tape drives). As with 3420s, the typical configuration is fairly simple, with a string of up to eight drives attached to a single control unit with one to four channel interfaces. It is possible, however, to cross-connect two control units and two strings of tape units to minimize contention and increase availability. This is shown in Fig. 2.9. Note that, in addition to the paths from the control units to the tape units, links are established between the control units themselves, giving maximum flexibility in the choice of paths from any one device to the processor.

The organization of data on the 3480 tape and the buffering process in the control unit are similar to those for open-reel tapes, although the 3480 buffer can also be used for read-ahead operations, similar to disk caching for sequential reads. There is a file-protect mechanism — a dial on the corner of the cartridge which is

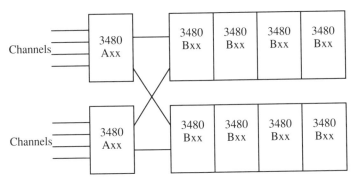

Figure 2.9. Cross-connection of 3480s.

turned, and displays a white dot when write is inhibited. Loading and unloading are similar in principle to open-reel tape drives, but there is a display on the drive which actually shows the volume serial number of the required tape, and there is an optional facility for automatic cartridge loading, which can be very useful, especially for scratch tapes — the operators can fill up a rack with scratch tapes, and the drive will automatically load the next one when it receives a mount request. For volume-specific requests, if the automatically loaded tape is not the right one, the drive rejects it and tries the next one.

3490 drives and control units are very similar to 3480s, the main difference being that twice as many drives can be fitted onto the same floor space. 3490s support Improved Data Recording Capability (IDRC) — a hardware data compression and decompression facility that can increase the amount of data stored on one tape. There is also an upgrade to 3480s available to give them this facility.

2.5.3   Automated tape libraries

Manual tape mounts, like any human intervention, introduce delays and the potential for error into computer operations. The process, however, requires no real decision-making, and so mounting tapes is a prime candidate for automation. Many sites are therefore now introducing automated tape libraries. The market leader in this area is Storagetek's Nearline system, but IBM has belatedly entered the market with its 3495 library system.

The basic principles of both are the same: the tapes within the automated system are kept in an enclosed set of shelves; the system keeps track of which tape is stored where; and whenever a mount request is received a robot retrieves the tape from the shelves and mounts it in a conventional cartridge drive which is under the control of the library system.

2.6   Communications devices

A vast range of communications devices can be attached indirectly to System/370 and System/390 processors, but here we will concentrate on the two types of device that are most commonly attached directly to them: 3x74 cluster controllers and 37x5 front-end processors. Networking as such is beyond the scope of this book, although the basics of starting up a VTAM network are discussed in Chapter 9. You will probably find that your network is a great deal more complicated than the example discussed here, but this section should give you a flavour of how MVS machines connect to networks.

2.6.1   Cluster controllers

Cluster controllers such as IBM 3274s and 3174s (and third-party equivalents) are used to attach local terminals and network printers (up to 32 per 3274) to the processor complex. Terminals on channel-attached cluster controllers are directly addressable by the processor complex, which means that messages can be sent to them without going through the normal telecommunications access methods (i.e. VTAM). Only terminals attached to your processor complex in this way can be used as consoles, so you must have at least one 3274-type control unit attached to your processor complex (strictly speaking, you can manage without one if you are running MVS version 4 or later on an ES/9000). Normally you would have at least two, so that if the 3274 used by the master console failed, an alternate console on a different controller could take over — otherwise your system would grind to a halt.

Both terminals and printers can be attached to 3274s, though JES printers cannot be — they must be directly channel-attached. Printers on 3274s can be used for screen prints from terminals on the same control unit, and also for printed output sent through the network (e.g. using JES328X). It is necessary to configure the 3274 by logging on to a terminal on a special port and entering configuration data, so that the control unit knows which types of device are attached to each port. The configuration is stored on a diskette in the controller and loaded when it is powered on or when the IML button is pressed on the unit. Figure 2.10 shows a typical 3274 configuration.

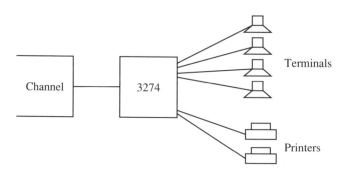

Figure 2.10. Typical channel-attached 3274 configuration.

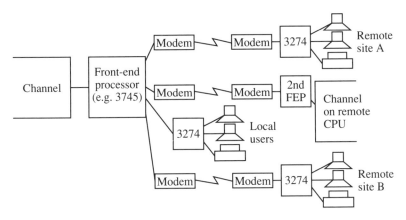

Figure 2.11. Typical FEP configuration.

2.6.2 Front-end processors

These are much larger communications controllers, such as IBM's 3725 and 3745, which are connected to processor channels on one side and longer distance communications lines on the other. Front-end processors (FEPs) run control programs (typically IBM's NCP) which direct messages down the appropriate lines depending on the intended destination, and these control programs must be generated on the processor complex and downloaded into the FEP. The generation and use of an NCP are discussed in Chapter 9.

The lines attached to FEP ports can support local terminals, but usually they are attached, via modems and telecommunications links, to cluster controllers at remote locations, which in turn support a number of terminals or printers at that location. The communication lines can be either dialup lines or permanently connected (leased) lines. FEPs may also have lines which are connected to other FEPs, and in this way complex multinode networks can be built up.

Figure 2.11 illustrates how terminals may be attached to an MVS processor's network through a 3725 or 3745.

2.7 Other devices

2.7.1 Printers

There are two main types of printer that may be channel-attached to System/370 processor complexes: impact printers and laser printers. In addition, there are many printers available that can be attached to your network and so may be available for 'remote printing'.

Impact printers are the traditional type, and they have some specialist uses which lasers find it hard or impossible to replace, such as printing on multipart stationery or security stationery (often used for printing payslips, where the 'printed' surface is inside a sealed envelope). Impact printers are also cheaper than lasers for installations or locations with relatively small print requirements. In most larger installations, however, laser printing is rapidly replacing impact printing — it is faster, quieter, produces a better quality image, and offers opportunities for many additional features, such as compressed printing to save paper, graphics, and double-sided cut-sheet printing.

There is a wide variety of models of impact printers on the market, with typical IBM models being the 3203, 3211, and 4245. Most channel-attached laser printers, however, are based on the IBM 3800 printing subsystem. Numerous third-party suppliers offer 3800 equivalents which emulate the 3800 mode of operation and sometimes offer additional facilities.

Configuration of printers is fairly straightforward — they are usually directly attached to a channel, though some, including the 3211, require an intervening control unit. Several impact printers can easily be daisy-chained on a single channel, as they are very slow relative to channel speeds. Lasers, however, may be better placed on a dedicated channel, especially if they are printing significant amounts of graphics.

Printers require a certain amount of software to be set up. For impact printers, all that is generally required is the provision of suitable FCBs and UCS definitions in SYS1.IMAGELIB, but for lasers which are doing anything more advanced than emulating impact printers, you will need to install and configure one or more of the components of IBM's Advanced Function Printing (AFP) family of software products, or third-party equivalents. To avoid long-term dependence on a single hardware supplier, it is generally best to go with AFP, which is becoming a de facto industry standard, or you may find you have large numbers of applications that will only work with the software supplied to drive your current supplier's printers.

2.7.2   Card readers and punches

These are more or less redundant today, though still remembered with a mixture of hatred and nostalgia by programmers who had to hand-punch their programs, JCL, and test data, then send it round to the operators to be fed into the card reader. No longer can production job failures be blamed on someone 'shuffling' the cards; no longer can operators' life expectancies be radically shortened by the act of dropping an unnumbered deck representing a month's development work in a heap on the floor! If you do have to deal with these museum-pieces (or devices which emulate them) you will probably have to set up a byte-multiplexor channel to handle them. On most modern machines, only a few channels have the capability to be configured as byte-multiplexor channels (usually channel paths 00, 01, 10, 11, etc.), so this can be quite inconvenient. If you have more than one of these devices, however, you should make sure to daisy-chain them all on the same channel, as they are painfully slow by current standards.

2.7.3   Channel-to-channel adaptors

A channel-to-channel adaptor (CTCA) provides the function required to connect a channel belonging to one system to one belonging to another system, thus allowing the two systems to communicate with each other. CTCAs are often used to allow communications between the GRS and/or VTAM subsystems running on different processor complexes, where 'loosely-coupled' processors are in use, and they are used by XCF to establish a sysplex between multiple CPCs. These days they may also be required to perform the same function between systems running on the same processor complex but under different logical partitions, using PR/SM on a 3090 or a similar facility from a plug-compatible supplier.

CTCAs were optional attachments on pre-3090 processor complexes, but if you need one on a 3090 or an ES/9000 you will have to buy a separate box (a 3088). The exception to this occurs when you are using ESCON channels, which can usually attach directly to each other without any intervening CTCA — all you need to do is define one end as a CTC-type channel in your I/O configuration parameters.

Physical configuration of CTCAs is straightforward — each CTCA is attached to one channel on each of the machines concerned. With ESCON, multiple logical device addresses may be defined on the channel, and used by different applications.

2.8   Hardware environments

Most System/370 and System/390 processors capable of supporting MVS require special environments in which to run, as do many of the peripheral devices which can be connnected to them. They need:

- Air-conditioning.
- Chilled water supplies to cool the TCMs in the processor complex of the larger boxes (308x, 3090, and 9021 series). The 4381 and 9121 series, however, are air-cooled — they need extra air-conditioning instead.
- 'Clean' power supplies, and preferably uninterrupted power supply (UPS) devices and backup generators so that they can continue functioning through a power cut.
- Strengthened and raised floors with enough space below them to run very large volumes of channel cables (until you manage to dispense with copper cables by using ESCON).
- Special fire control systems which minimize damage done to your computer equipment by the fire control systems themselves. (Spraying water on your computers is not wise!)

In addition, the machine room should be a secure area with controlled access to minimize the danger of deliberate or accidental disruption — someone just has to hit a power switch on one of the hundreds of devices in your machine room to bring down the whole system. The objective of most operations managers is to keep the processors and DASD in a 'dark room' area as they should hardly ever require attention, to put the printers and tape drives in dedicated paper- and tape-handling areas, and to put the main consoles and monitoring screens in a 'bridge' area which acts as a control point for all the hardware.

References and bibliography

IBM manuals

1. *IBM System/370 XA Principles of Operation*, SA22-7085. This documents the machine instructions and other facilities provided by the System/370 architecture. There are different versions of this manual for ESA and for System/390.

   There are many manuals describing each of IBM's hardware products; you might find it rewarding to review whatever manuals you have for the hardware on your site. Some examples of manuals containing useful introductory material are:
2. *ES/3090 J/JH Models Functional Characteristics & Configuration*, SA22-7135.
3. *Using 3380 DASD in an MVS Environment*, GC26-4492.
4. *3480 Planning & Migration Guide*, GC35-0098.
5. *3725 Model 2 Communication Controller Introduction*, GA33-0021.
6. *3274 Control Unit Description and Programmer's Guide*, GA23-0021.

Other

7. Llana, A. Jr: Mainframe Channel Extenders, *Mainframe Journal*, July 1989, pp. 12–18.
8. Artis, H.P. and Houtekamer, G.E.: 3390s: A Faster Revolution in I/O, *Mainframe Journal*, March 1990, pp. 36–38.
9. Fairchild, W.R.: The Anatomy of an I/O Request, *Enterprise Systems Journal*, May 1991, pp. 119–126.

3
MVS internals

3.1   Introduction

This chapter aims to give a brief overview of the internal workings of MVS, which
it is essential for all systems programmers to understand. There are many courses
on MVS internals, which will go into much more detail than I can cover here, and
I would strongly recommend that any aspiring systems programmer attend a series
of these courses. Perhaps the greatest problem with most of the available courses,
however, is that they go into too much detail too soon. The newcomer can easily
be overwhelmed with the detail, and fail to appreciate the bigger picture to which
the details belong. I hope that my brief overview can show that bigger picture, so
you can then go on to fill in the details more confidently.

In addition to formal courses and IBM manuals, you will find lots of articles on
MVS internals in the technical journals — systems programmers seem to like
nothing more than poking around in the bowels of MVS and telling other systems
programmers about it! Some of these articles are listed in the bibliography at the
end of this chapter. The ultimate source, of course, is the source code of MVS itself.
Once upon a time this was freely available to MVS customers, but IBM is now
implementing an 'object code only' policy, so the source code available is rapidly
shrinking. If you are an accomplished assembler programmer who has grasped the
basics of MVS internals you may find some illumination in the bits of source code
that are still available, but it is more likely that you will have to rely on the written
and spoken word.

There is one concept of general application with which you need to be familiar
before delving into MVS internals, that is, the use of control blocks and control
block chains in MVS. Control blocks are areas of storage in predetermined formats
which are used to describe MVS resources and processes. The formats of all
MVS/ESA control blocks are described in detail in [26], while MVS/XA control
blocks are covered in [27].

Control blocks are linked together in logical chains using pointers. A pointer is
a field in the control block that contains the address of the linked control block.
Most MVS control blocks can be located by following a series of pointers starting

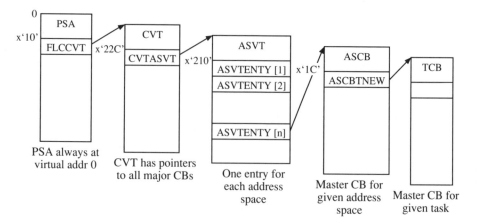

Figure 3.1. Typical MVS control block structure.

from the communications vector table (CVT), which itself is always pointed to by
the address at offset 16 (hex 10) within the PSA. When a chain of control blocks
needs to be constructed (e.g. to represent a queue of outstanding requests for a
resource), each control block in the chain will usually contain a forward pointer to
the next one and a backward pointer to the one before it. Figure 3.1 shows a typical
usage of control block pointers — to find the chain of task control blocks (TCBs)
belonging to a selected address space. Control blocks and chaining are discussed
in more detail in Chapter 6.

The rest of this chapter is divided into sections, each one corresponding to one
functional area of MVS.

3.2   Storage management

3.2.1   Virtual storage and real storage

MVS stands for Multiple Virtual Storage, which is a fair indication of how crucial
the concept of virtual storage is to MVS!

Virtual storage is the ability of units of work to refer to areas of storage using
addresses that are meaningful to the unit of work, but do not correspond to the
actual location of the data concerned in real storage (also known as central
storage). Furthermore, different units of work can use the same virtual address to
refer to different real storage locations. This is one of several aspects of the design
of MVS which allow applications to run as if they had sole use of the machine even
though in reality they are sharing it with other applications.

Each of these units of work, then, has a range of virtual storage locations which
it can address. This range of virtual storage locations is known as an address space.
Each address space can include virtual storage with addresses in the range from 0
to 2 gigabytes (2048 megabytes, or something over 2 billion characters of storage),

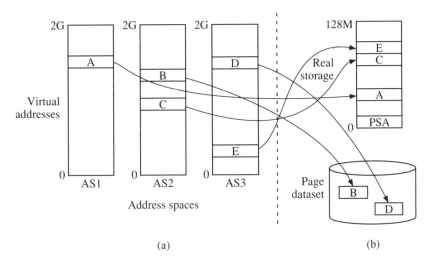

Figure 3.2. Real and virtual storage. (a) Program's view of storage. (b) Real location of referenced areas.

and there can be literally hundreds of address spaces active within MVS at any one time. Most System/370 computers, however, have far less real storage available to them than this—a typical 3090, for example, might have 128 megabytes of real storage.

MVS therefore has to provide a mechanism to translate virtual addresses into real addresses when an item of data needs to be accessed, and another one to extend the amount of storage which can be addressed beyond that physically available in real memory. These two mechanisms are known as Dynamic Address Translation (DAT) and paging respectively. Figure 3.2 summarizes the relationship between real and virtual storage which is implemented by these mechanisms.

Whenever a program makes a reference to a virtual storage address, either to fetch data from it or to store data into it, it is necessary to translate that address into a real storage address before the processor can find and access the area of storage in question. The DAT hardware does this automatically, so that there is no software overhead required for virtual address translation.

In order to make this possible, MVS must maintain tables in storage which relate each address space's virtual storage addresses to real storage addresses, and which are accessible to the DAT routines. The first of these is the 'segment table'. MVS maintains a separate segment table for each address space, at a fixed location in real storage, and loads the address of the current address space's segment table into the segment table origin register, one of the control registers which is inaccessible to application programmers, but is used for system functions. The segment table contains an entry for each 1 megabyte segment of the address space's virtual storage. If the address space is not using that megabyte at all, there is an indicator to this effect, and any attempt to resolve a virtual address in that segment will result

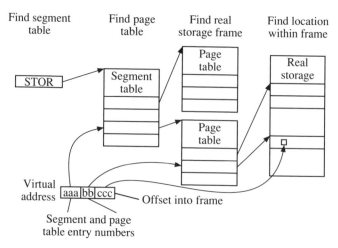

Figure 3.3. Dynamic address translation.

in a protection exception (this will appear to the user as an 0C4 abend). If the segment is in use, however, the segment table entry will contain the address of a 'page table' for that segment. The page table in turn contains an entry for each 4K page in the segment. If the page is unused the corresponding page table entry will contain an indicator to this effect; if it has been paged out a different indicator will be set; and if it is present in real storage it will contain the real storage address of the page. The DAT process is illustrated in Fig. 3.3.

The sizes of a page and a segment are significant because they allow the DAT hardware to do some very simple and therefore very fast table lookups — if we think of a 32-bit address as a string of eight hex digits, then the first three of these represent the segment number of the area being addressed, and can be used as an argument to look up the address of the page table in the segment table; the next two digits then represent the page number within the segment, and can be used as the argument to directly look up the real address of the required page from the page table. The last three digits can then be used simply as the offset into this real page frame of the required address.

To speed up the DAT process even further, the results of recent address translations are stored in the translation lookaside buffer (TLB), which the DAT routines check before attempting the full translation process. The high degree of 'locality of reference' in most programs means that a high proportion of address translations can be resolved from the TLB. The efficiency of these design features means that the DAT hardware can locate the real storage corresponding to any virtual address extremely quickly, thus allowing MVS to implement virtual storage with very little address translation overhead.

Although DAT is a hardware process, MVS has to maintain the environment which DAT relies on. Thus, MVS must:

- For each address space, create and keep up to date the segment table which contains pointers to the page tables for that address space.
- Ensure that the address of the new address space's segment table is stored in the STOR whenever the current address space changes.
- Ensure that the segment table itself is in a fixed area of storage (i.e. it cannot be paged out, or address translation would be impossible).
- Create and keep up to date the page tables.

3.2.2   Paging

In order to provide vastly more virtual storage than the amount of real storage that exists on the machine being used, MVS uses paging. When real storage fills up, and an address space requires another page of virtual storage, the paging process swings into action. Simplifying somewhat, the real storage manager (RSM) component of MVS identifies the 4K pages of storage which have not been referenced for the longest time, invokes the auxiliary storage manager (ASM) component to copy these into 4K 'slots' in paging datasets on DASD (a 'page out' operation), then 'steals' one of the pages which have been made available to satisfy the new requirement. If a program subsequently attempts to reference the stolen page, a 'page fault' occurs, and the ASM is invoked to 'page in' the required page, stealing another page frame to provide the necessary real storage.

In effect, then, the inactive pages of each address space are moved out of real storage onto auxiliary storage, and only the active pages (i.e. relatively recently used ones) are kept in real storage. The real storage which each address space retains is known as its working set. Typically working sets are much smaller than the amount of virtual storage that the address space has initialized with GETMAIN instructions, as a large proportion of each address space's storage is used for routines and data that are very rarely referenced. This means that the amount of paging that is necessary to provide large address spaces to many users in a relatively small amount of real storage can be quite low, as only each user's working set need be kept in real storage, even when many users are active concurrently.

Let us look in a little more detail at the process by which the RSM manages real storage.

Every interval (around a second when the pressure on real storage is high, but lengthened — up to around 20 seconds — when it is not), the RSM checks the status of each frame of real storage. Each frame has a few bytes of control information associated with it (this is not addressable storage in the normal sense), including the 'hardware reference bit'. Whenever a page is referenced, the hardware sets this bit on; if the bit is on when the RSM checks it, it resets the value of the unreferenced interval count (UIC) for this page to zero, and turns off the reference bit; if it is off, the RSM increments the UIC for the page by one. These UICs (held in a table called the page frame table (PFT)) therefore indicate how many intervals it was since each page was last referenced.

The RSM also maintains an available frame queue (AFQ), which is a list of pages available for stealing. When the number of pages on the AFQ falls below a predetermined limit, the RSM scans the PFT for the pages with the highest UICs. It then attempts to add these to the AFQ. If the page has been paged out before and has not been updated since (there is another hardware bit associated with every real frame which is set whenever a page is updated), it can immediately be placed on the AFQ. If it has not been paged out before, or has been updated since it was last paged out, then the RSM will invoke the ASM to page it out again, and when this is complete the frame will be placed on the AFQ. This process is intended to ensure that when a page frame needs to be stolen, there will already be a copy of it on auxiliary storage, so the page in can be started immediately, without waiting for the frame to be paged out first.

A frame may need to be stolen to provide new pages to an address space (in response to a GETMAIN request) or to provide space for a page in. When a frame is stolen, the corresponding entry in the page table is updated, removing the address of the real storage frame it was using, and inserting an indicator that the page is on auxiliary storage. If DAT subsequently attempts to resolve a reference to this page of virtual storage it will encounter this indicator and issue a 'page fault' exception. The ASM will then be invoked to page in the required page.

The RSM and ASM components between them are therefore able to use the paging mechanism to share the available real storage between conflicting requirements for virtual storage in such a way as to minimize the performance degradation that results when a DASD I/O is required to resolve a page fault. If paging becomes excessive, however, this degradation can become unacceptably high, and there is then a requirement for tuning of the system. If this cannot resolve the problem it is then necessary to increase the amount of real storage available to the system.

The pressure on real storage is increased by the ability of MVS to make some pages 'immune' to paging using a mechanism known as page-fixing. This mechanism marks a page so that the RSM will never select it for stealing, with the result that it cannot be paged out. While this runs counter to the basic philosophy of virtual storage, it is essential in some circumstances. When an I/O operation is to be performed, for example, the channel subsystem will read/write data from/to a real storage location, not a virtual storage location (see Sec. 3.4). It is therefore necessary for MVS to prevent the real storage location required by the I/O operation being stolen by the RSM before the I/O operation has completed. It does this by fixing the page(s) concerned for the duration of the I/O operation, then unfixing them after the operation has completed.

3.2.3 Central storage and expanded storage

In 1985, a new type of processor storage called expanded storage was introduced on 3090 machines, and it is now also available on ES/9000s and on machines from the plug-compatible vendors. Expanded storage is cheaper than central storage and much larger quantities of it can be configured on a single machine (in theory up to 16 000 gigabytes, although existing machines do not support anything like this amount). However, access to expanded storage is several orders of magnitude slower than access to central storage, although still several orders of magnitude faster than DASD I/O or even I/O operations which are resolved from cache memory.

On MVS/XA systems, the only use of expanded storage was as a fast paging device. Retrieving a page from expanded storage is almost 1000 times faster than retrieving a page from DASD, with obvious performance benefits on systems which do any significant paging. The paging process works a little differently with expanded storage. A process that takes a page fault and resolves it from expanded storage does not relinquish control of the processor or suffer an I/O interrupt, which also contributes to improving performance.

With MVS/ESA, however, further uses of expanded storage were introduced, notably methods of keeping large amounts of data in expanded storage using dataspaces and/or hiperspaces (these are discussed in more detail in Sec. 3.9.3). These effectively turn expanded storage into a very fast caching device for important or heavily used application data.

Like central storage, expanded storage is likely to fill up at some stage, and MVS must manage this situation. It does this by 'migrating' pages from expanded storage to paging datasets on 'auxiliary storage' (i.e. DASD). Unfortunately, at the time of writing, page migration requires the page to be moved from expanded storage to central storage before it can be paged out to DASD, which clearly imposes an additional bottleneck when page migration is required. However, it seems likely that IBM will address this problem in future developments.

MVS selects pages to be migrated by reviewing the 'old page bit' associated with each page of expanded storage. The process works as follows:

1   It starts initially from the first page in expanded storage and scans forward through the pages.
2   When it finds a page which is allocated, it sets the old page bit (this will be turned off again when the page is referenced).
3   When it finds a page with the old page bit set, it knows that this page has not been referenced since the last time it was scanned, so it steals it.
4   When it has stolen enough pages it stops, but retains a pointer to the last page scanned, and the next time it starts a scan it will start from this point.
5   When it reaches the last page it goes back to the first one again.

This is a simple, fast, and effective process.

3.2.4   *Attributes of virtual storage areas*

Within each address space, different areas of virtual storage have different attributes and uses. The main attributes which vary between different areas are:

- Common versus private
- Above or below the 16 megabyte line
- Storage protection

Common areas are areas in which any given virtual address is translated to the same real address in every address space. This means that the virtual storage at these addresses is shared between all address spaces, and any unit of work can address the data in these areas. Apart from the PSA, the common areas are all in a contiguous area of virtual storage which starts and ends on 1 megabyte boundaries. This is because 1 megabyte is the size of a segment, i.e. the amount of storage described by a single page table, and common storage is implemented by sharing the same page tables between all address spaces. In other words, for the common segments, the entry in each address space's segment table points to the same page table.

Private areas, on the other hand, are areas in which any given virtual address is translated to a different real address in every address space, so any virtual storage at these addresses is unique to the address space concerned and can normally only be addressed by tasks running in that address space. Each address space has its own page tables for its own private areas.

The 16 megabyte line is only significant because of the continuing requirement for compatibility with programs written to run under MVS version 1, referred to below as MVS/370. Under MVS/370, a 24-bit addressing scheme was used, and 16 megabytes was the maximum virtual address that could be referenced with a 24-bit address. Programs written under MVS/370 could therefore only address virtual storage up to this limit. In order to allow such programs to run, MVS/XA and MVS/ESA still support a 24-bit addressing mode, although MVS is also now capable of supporting 31-bit addressing (allowing virtual storage up to 2 gigabytes to be addressed). As many programs still run in 24-bit mode, all storage areas which may need to be referenced by programs running in this mode must continue to be kept below the 16 megabyte line. Most of the storage areas we will discuss are now split into two parts, one above and one below the line, so that they can satisfy this requirement, while keeping as many areas as possible above the line. There is a strong incentive to put data above the line, as the major reason for the introduction of MVS/XA was to relieve the shortage of virtual storage addresses below 16 megabytes, and this shortage can still pose problems for 24-bit programs.

Storage protection restricts the ability of programs to fetch or update storage. Each frame of real storage has a 'key' associated with it, and access to the page is restricted to users with a matching 'storage protect key' in their PSW. If the storage is 'fetch-protected', users without a matching key cannot even read it; if it is not,

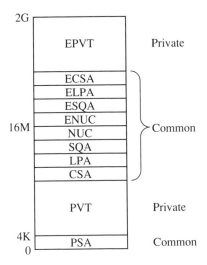

Figure 3.4. MVS/XA and ESA virtual storage map.

users without a matching key can read but not update it. Typically, common areas have a key which prevents ordinary applications from updating them, while private areas are updatable by anyone (but only addressable by work executing within the address space concerned!).

3.2.5 Areas of virtual storage

Figure 3.4 shows the main areas of virtual storage, which are briefly discussed in turn below.

The main areas of virtual storage are:

- *Prefixed save area* (PSA) From 0 to 4K — in a uniprocessor this is fixed in the first 4K of both virtual and real storage, but in a multiprocessor there is a separate PSA for each processor, and a control register called the prefix register contains the address of the processor's PSA. The PSA contains certain areas which are critical to MVS and the hardware, such as the new PSWs to be used for processing interrupts, and the pointer to the CVT control block, from which most of the MVS control block structure can be traced.
- *Private area* The bottom limit of this is at 4K; the top limit is set at IPL time and is determined by deducting the size of the common areas below the 16 Mb line from 16 Mb and rounding down to a megabyte boundary. This is the area available to user programs executing in 24-bit mode, and also includes some system areas that relate specifically to this address space, such as the SWA (scheduler work area, containing control blocks relating to the executing job), and the LSQA (local system queue area, containing control blocks for this address space, including the segment table and private area page tables).
- *Common service area* (CSA) Contains control blocks and data used primarily

for communicating between address spaces. Tasks such as VTAM which must pass data between address spaces often use large amounts of buffer space in CSA. The size of the CSA is specified at IPL time.

- *Link pack area* (LPA) Contains program modules to be shared between address spaces, including many system routines such as SVCs and access methods. Programs in the LPA cannot normally be modified between IPLs. The size of the LPA depends on the number and size of the modules loaded into it at IPL time. It is divided into fixed, pageable, and modifiable areas (FLPA, PLPA, and MLPA), of which the PLPA is usually by far the largest. The LPA is discussed in more detail in Sec. 3.7.
- *System queue area* (SQA) Contains control blocks which need to be shared between address spaces, e.g. the page tables for common areas. The size is fixed at IPL time, but if the system runs out of SQA it will use CSA instead.
- *Nucleus* This contains the core of the MVS control program itself, including certain tables such as the PFT and the unit control blocks (UCBs) for I/O devices. Its size depends on the configuration of your system, but does not vary once it has been loaded at IPL time.
- The extended nucleus, SQA, LPA, CSA, and private area perform the same functions as the corresponding areas below the line, and their sizes are determined in the same way (note that programs in the LPA are loaded above or below the line depending on their 'residency mode', which is determined at assembly or link-edit time). The only difference is that they can only be addressed by programs running in 31-bit addressing mode.

3.2.6   Swapping

Swapping is similar to paging (which is sometimes called demand paging to distinguish it from swapping) in that its objective is to reduce the usage of real storage by moving less used areas of virtual storage out to disk. It can also reduce the size of the queues used by the dispatcher by removing 'swapped-out' tasks from them.

Swapping, however, is unlike demand paging in that it deals with entire address spaces instead of individual pages. When a decision is made to swap an address space physically, all of the virtual storage belonging to that address space is paged out (in large blocks known as 'swap sets') and the frames it was using are added to the available frame queue.

Swapping is controlled by the component of MVS called the system resources manager (SRM); there is a complex set of algorithms used by the SRM which determines when address spaces should be swapped out and in, and selects the address spaces to be swapped. Systems programmers (or members of your performance tuning team) define parameters which are used by the SRM to determine the swap priority of each address space and the conditions in which swapping should occur. The details of these parameters are extremely complex and beyond the scope of this book. The general principles, however, are simple — when the machine is so busy that it cannot provide sufficient real storage to meet the requirements of the most important executing tasks, lower priority tasks should be swapped out, and the machine's resources should be distributed between the competing workloads in accordance with their relative importance. This is what the SRM attempts to achieve.

There is also a form of swapping known as logical swapping, which removes inactive tasks from the dispatching queues and thus speeds up the dispatching process. In this case, the storage belonging to the address space is not swapped out immediately, but if there is pressure on real storage, the logical swap may subsequently be converted to a physical swap. It is normal for TSO users to be logically swapped at the end of each transaction, to minimize the system overhead they cause during the relatively long 'think time' until they next press the Enter key.

3.3 Task management

3.3.1 Dispatchable units of work

The MVS dispatcher is a routine within the supervisor component of the operating system that determines which units of work will be allowed to execute next, i.e. given control of the processor until the next interrupt occurs. It maintains queues of dispatchable units of work, each with an associated priority (dispatching priorities are independent of swap priorities), and whenever the dispatcher is given control it selects the highest priority ready unit of work to dispatch.

Dispatchable units of work are represented by control blocks of two types: task control blocks (TCBs) and service request blocks (SRBs). TCBs represent tasks executing within an address space, such as user programs — but note that there are several TCBs associated with each address space, so more than one task could be running in any one address space at any one time. SRBs represent 'requests to execute a service routine' — they are usually initiated by system code executing from one address space to perform an action affecting another address space.

TCBs are created when a program issues the ATTACH macro to initiate a new task. While it is possible for an application to do this, it is more commonly done by system code. When an address space is created, a chain of TCBs is also created within it. The first of these is the region control task, followed by the dump task and the started task control task. Beyond here, the task structure depends on the type of address space, of which there are three:

1 *Console-started jobs* (commonly known as started tasks) These have a TCB for the started job.
2 *Batch jobs* These run in JES 'initiator' address spaces, with one TCB for the initiator itself and another for the current JOB STEP.
3 *TSO users* These have a TCB for the TSO terminal monitor program — an

address space is created for each TSO user at logon time by the TCAS address space.

SRBs are created using the SCHEDULE macro, but can only be created by units of work running in the supervisor state and key 0 (see Sec. 3.3.3 for further explanation of these terms). There are two types: SRBs with global priority, which have a very high dispatching priority, and SRBs with local priority, which take on the dispatching priority of the address space in which they are scheduled to run.

SRBs are non-preemptive, which means that if they are interrupted, control must be returned to them immediately after the interruption has been processed. In addition, they are subject to a number of restrictions. For example, they can only GETMAIN storage in subpool 245 (SQA), and they cannot issue SVCs, which means, for example, that they cannot open datasets, or issue ENQs. This is to prevent them from going into a wait for any avoidable reason, and means that SRBs usually represent very short pieces of work that complete much more quickly than TCBs.

SRBs have the ability to SUSPEND or RESUME TCBs in their address space, and they can be scheduled by a function in one address space to execute in another address space. They therefore provide a mechanism by which one address space can control the execution of tasks in another address space.

3.3.2   The dispatching process

The dispatching process shares the processor cycles available to the system between the TCBs and SRBs which are waiting to execute at any one time. The key elements of the dispatching process are the PSW, interrupts, and the dispatching queue.

The PSW (or, more accurately, the current PSW) is a special-purpose register within the processor which indicates the address of the next instruction to be executed, along with certain status information such as the current storage protect key, whether the program is running in supervisor or problem state, the addressing mode, and whether the processor is enabled or disabled for certain types of interrupt. After each instruction to be executed has been fetched, the PSW is updated to point to the next one to be executed. If a unit of work is interrupted to allow some other unit of work to run, the PSW must be saved so that when the original unit of work is restarted the processor can pick up where it left off by reloading the PSW that was current at the time of the interruption. Of course, other information must also be restored to its status at the time of the interruption, notably the values in the general-purpose registers being used by the program.

Interrupts are a hardware feature which was introduced in Chapter 2. They are signals to the processor which pre-empt the currently executing unit of work and initiate a different process. Interrupts can be generated by a number of different events, including completion of an I/O request, hardware-detected program errors, and program requests for supervisor services (SVCs). There are six main types of interrupt, and for each of these there is a corresponding first-level interrupt handler

(FLIH) routine, 'old PSW' field in the PSA, and 'new PSW' field in the PSA. When an interrupt occurs, the hardware saves the current PSW in the old PSW field for the type of interrupt concerned, disables the processor for further interrupts of the same type (if possible — some types of interrupt cannot be disabled), and loads the PSW from the new PSW field for the type of interrupt concerned. The new PSW contains the instruction address of the first instruction of the corresponding FLIH, so loading it causes the FLIH to be invoked. The FLIH saves the status (registers and old PSW) of the interrupted unit of work, enables the processor for interrupts again, and determines the action required to process the interrupt. It may then directly invoke the system routines required to process the interrupt, or schedule these for later execution and return control to the dispatcher.

The dispatching queues are chains of control blocks representing address spaces and units of work. The address space control block (ASCB) ready queue is a chain of the ASCBs of those address spaces that are swapped in and contain at least one TCB or SRB which is ready to execute (i.e. not awaiting the completion of any other event). The ASCBs are chained together in priority order, i.e. the ASCB with the highest dispatching priority is at the front of the chain. Each address space then has its own chain of ready SRBs and/or TCBs, pointed to from its ASCB. Whenever an event completes which changes the status of an address space, the relevant MVS function updates the dispatching queues to reflect it.

Whenever control is returned to the dispatcher after a unit of work has terminated or been interrupted, it selects the highest priority unit of work that is ready to execute. There are some special exit routines dealing, for example, with hardware recovery, which will always be dispatched before any other unit of work, but in more usual situations, the dispatcher will first select any SRBs that have global priority, and then will select the ASCB at the front of the dispatching queue (i.e. the one with the highest priority). Any ready SRBs within this address space will be selected, and if there are none of these, any ready TCBs within it will be selected. If there is no work ready to execute, the dispatcher loads an 'enabled wait PSW', otherwise it builds a PSW for the selected unit of work and loads it.

Whatever routine is given control will continue to execute until it is interrupted or relinquishes control (e.g. by ending or issuing an SVC).

3.3.3   *Storage protection and execution states*

The functions a routine can perform are constrained by its execution state, as defined in the control bits of the current PSW, and its storage protect key, which is also part of the PSW.

The storage protect key can take any value from 0 to 8. A function running with storage protect key 0 can update any storage except areas in page-protected pages (these pages cannot be updated by any function). A function running with any other storage protect key (i.e. 1 to 8) can only update pages with a matching storage key (every page has a storage key associated with it which is stored in one of the bytes of non-addressable storage associated with every page, and can also take the values 0 to 8). In addition, a page can be fetch-protected. A page which is not fetch-protected can be read by any function, irrespective of the function's key, though it can only be updated by a function running in key 0 or with a matching key. A page which is fetch-protected can only be read by a function running in key 0 or with a matching key. Any attempt to breach any of these rules causes the function to be abended with abend code 0C4.

The execution state of a unit of work can be either problem state or supervisor state. Problem state is the normal mode of execution for application programs, and in this mode certain machine instructions may not be executed (these are known as privileged instructions), such as those which change the PSW or the storage protect key. This prevents application programs from interfering with the system itself and from bypassing system security products such as RACF. Supervisor state, on the other hand, is the normal mode of execution for system routines, which allows them to execute any System/370 instruction. Most programs running in supervisor state also run in storage protect key 0.

Clearly it is necessary for MVS to provide a mechanism to switch the processor from problem state to supervisor state, and to change the current storage protect key. Equally clearly, it is necessary to restrict the ability of programs to use this mechanism, or there would be no point in making the distinction between problem and supervisor state in the first place, as any clever programmer could switch their code into supervisor state. The mechanism which MVS uses to achieve this is called authorized program facility (APF) authorization. Only an APF authorized program may issue the MODESET macro which is used to switch execution states and change the storage protect key. In order to be APF authorized, the program must have been loaded from an APF authorized library and link-edited with an authorization code (AC) of 1. As anyone can link-edit a program with AC(1), it is one of the systems programmer's responsibilities to ensure that the ability to put programs into APF authorized libraries and execute them from there is strictly controlled (it is usually restricted to the systems programmers themselves).

3.4   I/O management

The previous chapter discussed the various types of I/O devices that can be connected to System/370 processors and some details of how I/O operations are handled at the device level. Here we will look at the processes MVS goes through to initiate a typical DASD I/O request. As with many aspects of MVS, there are several layers to the I/O onion! Figure 3.5 summarizes the overall picture for a typical I/O request. Note that the sequence of events starts at the top left, with the GET/PUT request, then moves diagonally down to the right until the interrupt is received by the channel subsystem to indicate that the device and channel have completed their part in the operation. From here, events move diagonally down

User program	Access method	EXCP	IOS	Channel subsystem
GET/PUT	Create channel program			
	Wait for ECB			
		Translate CP STARTIO		
			Queue request on device	
			SSCH	
				Execute channel program
	⋮			
				Transfer data
				Interrupt
			Process interrupt	
		Post ECB		
		Return control to dispatcher		
	Resume when next dispatched			
I/O complete				

Figure 3.5. MVS/XA I/O processing using EXCP.

back to the left-hand column. Each column from the left to right represents a successively deeper layer of the I/O processing onion!

Before the I/O process can begin, the user program must OPEN the dataset to be accessed. The OPEN process builds the data control block (DCB), which contains various information about the dataset, including the address of the access method to be used to process it. It also builds a data extent block (DEB) containing further information about how the dataset is to be processed, including, for DASD datasets, the device address and the physical addresses of the extents of the dataset. These control blocks are used in the processing of subsequent I/O instructions for the dataset.

When the program subsequently wishes to read or write a record of the dataset, it typically invokes the GET or PUT macro (which may have been generated by a compiler as part of the expansion of a READ or WRITE statement in a high-level language). This results in a branch to the access method routine whose address was saved in the DCB.

There is a variety of access methods available for processing different types of datasets. The most widely used are:

- *QSAM* For logical record processing of sequential datasets and members of PDSs processed as sequential datasets
- *BSAM* For block processing of sequential datasets
- *BDAM* For direct access datasets
- *BPAM* For partitioned datasets
- *VSAM* For VSAM datasets
- *VTAM* For telecommunications I/O

The access method builds more control blocks — the input/output block (IOB) and the event control block (ECB). The IOB contains information required by the next stage of the operation (execute channel program (EXCP) processing), and pointers to all the other control blocks associated with the I/O operation. Most importantly, it points to the channel program. This is also built by the access method, and consists of a series of channel command words (CCWs) which describe the I/O operations to be performed by the channel subsystem, including details such as the address of the area of storage into/from which data is to be transferred and the amount of data to be transferred. Finally, the access method issues the EXCP macro instruction, which invokes an SVC, causing an interrupt, and the interrupt handler passes control to the EXCP processor. The next time the access method is dispatched it will issue a WAIT macro against the ECB representing this I/O request.

EXCP builds a control block called the I/O supervisor block (IOSB), fixes the page containing the storage to be read/written by the I/O operation so that it cannot be paged out before the operation is complete, and translates the addresses in the channel program from virtual to real addresses, as only real addresses are meaningful to the channel subsystem. It then invokes the STARTIO macro instruction to activate the I/O supervisor (IOS) to process the I/O.

EXCP is one of several IOS drivers which may pass instructions to IOS. Although in this example it is invoked from an access method, it may also be invoked directly from JES2 or a user program, although the latter is far more complex than using an access method. Other IOS drivers include the ASM, used for paging requests, the FETCH processor for program loads, and the IOS driver components of VSAM and VTAM.

IOS builds an I/O queue (IOQ) control block and operation request block (ORB) describing the I/O for the channel subsystem, obtains control of the device (i.e. preventing any other concurrent I/O requests to it) by obtaining the relevant unit control block (UCB) lock, and then issues a start subchannel (SSCH) instruction to request the channel subsystem to perform the I/O operation.

The channel subsystem executes the channel program, which causes the requested I/O operation to occur, and it transfers the data being input (output) into (out of) the real storage locations referred to in the channel program. It updates control blocks including the interrupt response block (IRB), which holds the return code from the I/O operation and can be interrogated to check whether completion was successful or not. It then posts an I/O interrupt to indicate the completion of the request.

The I/O interrupt handler schedules an SRB to run the IOS post status routines. These check the status of the completed I/O, invoke error recovery routines if required, and, for successful I/Os, return control to EXCP. EXCP will POST the ECB which was created by the access method to indicate the completion of the I/O; the access method will therefore be made dispatchable, and when it regains control it will resume execution, returning control to the user program. The I/O operation is now complete and the user program can continue processing.

There are many variations on this process for different types of I/O operation, but this example should be enough to make the general principles clear.

The I/O supervisor also deals with other conditions which can arise in the I/O subsystem, most notably:

- Unsolicited interrupts from devices due to a hardware error — when this occurs repeatedly it is known as hot I/O, and the IOS attempts to clear it by issuing a Clear Subchannel instruction. If this is unsuccessful, the IOS will attempt more radical action such as 'boxing' the device — i.e. forcing it offline.
- Failure of a device to respond to an I/O request — known as a missing interrupt. The length of time the IOS should wait before dealing with a missing interrupt condition for each type of device is specified in SYS1.PARMLIB at IPL time. Once this time has elapsed, the IOS will attempt to recover, e.g. by trying to repeat the operation.

3.5   Job management

This section shows how MVS processes jobs by looking at the stages a job goes through, from the time it enters the system until it is finally purged. Strictly speaking, much of the processing of jobs is not done by MVS itself but by a separate piece of software called the job entry subsystem (JES). There are two flavours of this available from IBM, known as JES2 and JES3. Although JES3 was originally intended to replace JES2, it has failed to do so; there are many more MVS sites using JES2 than JES3. Broadly speaking, JES handles the processing of jobs before and after the execution stage, while MVS handles it during execution.

The basic stages of job processing which we shall cover are: job entry, the input queue, execution, the output queue, printing, and purge.

In order to be entered into the system, the job, consisting of a stream of job control language (JCL) statements, must first be created in a machine-readable format. Historically this would have been a deck of punched cards, but these days it will usually be created in a dataset on DASD or in an area of virtual storage.

Job entry is invoked by passing this job stream to a JES reader — either a card reader which is owned by JES, or more usually these days, an 'internal reader', which is a JES2 program. The TSO submit command, for example, invokes an internal reader to pass a job stream stored in a DASD dataset to JES.

The job stream is passed to the JES converter program, which does the following:

- Assigns a job number to the job (only one job with any given number may exist on the job queues at any one time, thus giving a unique identifier to jobs with the same jobname).
- Analyses the JCL statements.
- Merges in any cataloged procedures which the JCL statements reference.
- Converts the JCL into 'internal text', which is meaningful to JES and the MVS job scheduler.
- Checks for syntax errors, and if it finds any, fails the job with a 'JCL error', placing it straight on the output queue without queuing it for execution.
- Invokes various user exits, if they are present, which can do further checking/ modification of the JCL.
- If no errors are found, the converter stores the internal text on the spool dataset and adds the job to the input queue.

JES3 also does interpreter processing at this stage, but we will follow JES2's practice and leave it a little longer. Both JES2 and JES3 store the internal text and output data belonging to jobs on the spool dataset, which frequently extends to multiple volumes of DASD, and can only be accessed by JES itself.

There are two special internal readers called STCINRDR and TSOINRDR. STCINRDR is used to process the JCL for START commands entered at the operator's console, and TSOINRDR is used to process the JCL for TSO LOGON attempts. In both cases, the master scheduler starts up a new address space to execute the command (START or LOGON), then a routine running in the started address space invokes JES to do conversion and interpretation of the corresponding JCL.

Ordinary batch jobs, however, are now placed on the input queue on the spool dataset, where they wait to be selected for execution. Associated with each job there is a number of control fields which JES uses to determine which jobs to execute when and where. The most important of these are the JOB CLASS, usually coded on the JOB card of the JCL, and the priority, which may be coded on a JES control card in the JCL, but is more commonly assigned by JES on the basis of rules set in the initialization parameters by the systems programmer.

Batch jobs run in address spaces in which there is already an initiator task running. These initiator address spaces are started by JES at system initialization time, using the JCL in SYS1.PROCLIB(INIT). Whenever the job running under an initiator completes, the MVS job scheduler asks JES for another job to run. Each initiator has one or more jobclasses assigned to it, and JES will look for jobs on the input queue with the first jobclass assigned to the initiator. If there are any of these, JES will select the highest priority one to run. If there are none, JES will look for jobs in the next jobclass assigned to the initiator, and so on until the list of classes assigned to this initiator is exhausted. If no jobs are selected by this process, the initiator will remain idle until a job appears on the input queue with one of these jobclasses.

Once JES has passed a job to the initiator, the job enters the execution phase. On JES2 systems, the initiator will invoke the JES2 'interpreter' to build control blocks required by the job scheduler. On JES3 systems, this will have been done already at job entry time.

The next action taken by the job scheduler (JES3 may do this at an earlier stage) is to perform device allocation, which:

- Identifies the datasets required by the job
- Locates existing datasets (including issuing volume mount requests to the operator when this is required)
- Allocates new datasets required to suitable volumes
- Invokes MVS serialization services through the ENQ macro (see Sec. 3.6) to prevent other jobs making conflicting requests for the same datasets.

Finally, the initiator attaches a task to perform the program named in the EXEC statement of the first job step. When each step completes, the initiator task checks the completion code and starts the next step whose COND values are consistent with the completion codes of the previous steps.

During execution, jobs may wish to write printed or punched output. To avoid contention for the printers and punches (which can clearly only service one dataset at a time each), and to avoid slowing down jobs by forcing them to wait for relatively slow I/O to these devices, such output datasets are not allocated directly to the ultimate output device. Instead, they are allocated to JES SYSOUT datasets (JES suballocates space for these datasets on its spool dataset). This allows print and punch datasets to be written to disk at relatively high I/O rates, without having to wait for allocation of a real output device, and then spun off to the printer at a later time.

At the completion of the job, then, there will still be an entry on the JES job queue for it, and usually there will also be a group of associated output datasets on the JES output queue. JES usually has a number of printers permanently allocated to it, and it selects output datasets to print off according to various selection criteria. Although these selection criteria are under the control of the systems programmer, they are normally set up in such a way that datasets will only be selected for printing if their FCB, forms id, destination, and output class match those of the available printer. Datasets for the first output class associated with the printer will be selected for printing first, and within output classes datasets with the highest priority will be selected first.

Some output datasets may be 'held' — whole output classes may be held by default — which means that they will not be printed/punched until a JES output command is used to change their status (this is often done through SDSF). On the other hand, some output classes can be defined as 'dummy' classes, which means that as soon as any output dataset written to the class is closed it is deleted from the spool. While this may sound strange, dummy classes are often used to suppress the production of datasets that are never used by anyone but are a by-product of a necessary process (e.g. message datasets for utility programs). JES commands may also be issued to delete (purge) individual datasets without printing them.

Once all the output datasets belonging to a job have been printed/punched or deleted, JES will purge the job, removing all trace of it from its queues, and making its job number and spool space available for reuse.

3.6   Serialization

One potential problem in a multiprogramming operating system (i.e. one which can interleave multiple units of work, running them all concurrently) is the danger of two units of work attempting to update the same resource at the same time, or attempting to use a process which can only handle one requestor at a time. This could lead to serious integrity problems if it were allowed to occur. Imagine, for example, two tasks attempting to update the same record of a dataset at the same time. Each would read the record, update its copy in storage, then write its updated copy back to the dataset. The second updated copy to be written back, however, would overwrite the first one, and the first update would be lost.

MVS provides several mechanisms to prevent such problems. These are:

- Running disabled for interrupts
- The ENQ/DEQ mechanism
- The lock mechanism
- The intersect mechanism

The following sections will cover each of these in turn.

3.6.1   Running disabled

We have already come across this in Chapter 2 and Sec. 3.4. Whenever an interrupt is accepted by a processor, it stores the current PSW in the old PSW location for the interrupt type concerned, moves the corresponding new PSW into the current PSW, and allows execution to resume. It is clear that access to the old PSW must be serialized — if another interrupt came along and overwrote the same old PSW before the interrupt handler had stored it away somewhere more permanent, then the status of the task that was interrupted the first time would be lost forever.

Serialization of the old PSW is achieved by disabling the processor for further interrupts of the same type before allowing the interrupt handler to start executing. This is done by setting a bit in the PSW corresponding to the type of interrupt to be disabled. If any further interrupts of the same type occur while this bit is set, the processor will not accept them until the bit is turned off again. The interrupt handler must store the old PSW along with the rest of the interrupted task's execution environment (registers, etc.) before re-enabling the processor for interrupts of the same type.

Disabling the processor is an effective mechanism for serializing interrupt processing, but it would be impractical for other types of serialization. It is essentially a hardware mechanism which is suitable only for controlling hardware events. It relates to an individual processor, as the PSW bits which it uses to control serialization are kept in a register of the processor concerned, so it is not suitable for serializing resources which are shared between multiple processors. And it requires a dedicated bit in the PSA for each resource requiring serialization, which would be totally impractical for serializing access to resources such as datasets, of which there could be tens of thousands in your installation, and which have unpredictable names — how would the system know which bit related to which dataset?

3.6.2   The ENQ/DEQ mechanism

Serialization on datasets and most other resources used by applications is done using the ENQ and DEQ macro instructions. These invoke the services of the MVS component known as Global Resource Serialization (GRS), which has its own address space running constantly.

The ENQ/DEQ mechanism itself is completely independent of the resource being serialized and of the process of using it. In other words, there is nothing to prevent a user accessing the resource without going through the ENQ/DEQ mechanism, and serialization depends on each user following the conventions governing the use of ENQ/DEQ. In many cases, the MVS routines you use to access a resource will themselves invoke ENQ/DEQ for you, thus preventing the user from accessing the resource outside the serialization mechanism, but it should still be clear that the mechanism is separate from the actual process of accessing the resource. This means that the same mechanism can be used for serializing access to a wide variety of resources which are accessed in many different ways.

The basic convention is that each resource to be serialized has a name associated with it, and every user of the resource must serialize on the same name, using the ENQ macro instruction, and release the resource when it is finished with it, using the DEQ macro instruction. The name of each resource consists of two parts: the queue name (QNAME), which describes the type of resource, and the resource name (RNAME), which relates to the particular resource to be used. So, for example, whenever MVS performs dataset allocation, it serializes access to the dataset by issuing an ENQ with QNAME = SYSDSN and RNAME = datasetname.

GRS builds a set of control blocks corresponding to each ENQ, and uses these to determine whether future ENQ requests for the same resource should be allowed to proceed or not. For each resource with an outstanding ENQ, GRS constructs a queue control block (QCB), containing among other things the QNAME and the

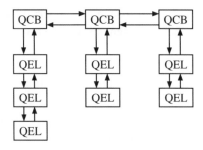

Figure 3.6. GRS control blocks.

RNAME of the resource. For each outstanding requestor of the resource, GRS chains a queue element (QEL) control block behind the corresponding QCB. All these control blocks are held in the GRS's private address space. Figure 3.6 shows the structure of the queues.

Each ENQ request can have a 'scope' of SYSTEMS, SYSTEM, or STEP. SYSTEMS means the resource is to be serialized across all MVS systems known to (and communicating with) the GRS address space on the current system. This is discussed in more detail in Chapter 14. SYSTEM means the resource is to be serialized across all address spaces on the current MVS system, and STEP means the resource is to be serialized only within the current address space. The scope should correspond to the usage of the resource — if a dataset is shared between multiple MVS systems, the scope of an ENQ for it should be SYSTEMS, for example, to ensure that requestors of the same resource on another system sharing the dataset are not able to ignore the first requestor. Similarly, if a control block exists only within a given address space and can only be used by that address space, an ENQ for it should only have a scope of STEP, or the ENQ could hold up requestors of a control block with the same name in a different address space.

Each ENQ must also specify whether the requestor requires SHARED or EXCLUSIVE control of the resource. Usually, requestors who only wish read-type access to a resource will ENQ it as SHARED, while those who need to update it will ENQ it with EXCLUSIVE control. GRS will allow multiple requestors to hold the same resource with SHARED control, but only one to hold it with EXCLUSIVE control. For example, if you specify DISP=SHR on a JCL DD statement for a dataset, MVS will ENQ it for SHARED access at allocation time, but if you specify DISP=OLD, MVS will ENQ it for EXCLUSIVE access at allocation time. As a result, only one job at a time can allocate a given dataset with DISP=OLD, whereas many can allocate it concurrently with DISP=SHR.

The action GRS takes in response to an ENQ macro is as follows:

- Check the existing QCBs in its address space to see if there is an outstanding ENQ for this resource.
- If there is not, create a QCB for the resource and add it to the QCB chain, then

create a QEL for this request and add it to the queue for this QCB, and finally return control to the task issuing the ENQ.

- If there is already a QCB for this resource, add a QEL representing this request to the queue for the resource, then check to see if the request can be satisfied.
- If the request is for exclusive control and there is already a QCB for the resource (and therefore a QEL representing an outstanding ENQ), then the requestor will be suspended, and GRS will not return control to it until the request reaches the top of the queue.
- If the request is for shared control and there is a QCB for the resource and a QEL representing an outstanding ENQ for exclusive control, then this requestor will also be suspended (whether the previous request for exclusive control has been granted yet or not) until all previous requests for exclusive control have been released with DEQ instructions.
- If the request is for shared control and there is a QCB but all QELs on the queue represent requests for shared control, then this requestor will be allowed to proceed, and GRS will return control to it.

When the DEQ macro is issued, GRS will:

- Delete the QEL representing the request.
- If this is the only QEL for the QCB concerned, delete the QCB.
- If there are other QELs for this QCB, rebuild the QEL chain without the deleted QEL.
- If there are other QELs for this QCB which were suspended but now can be released, allow the tasks owning them to resume execution.

This is an effective method of serializing access to a wide range of resources, but there are a couple of potential problems which make it unsuitable for serializing on vital system resources. One is simply the inefficiency of holding up shared requests when there are exclusive requests above the shared request in the queue but all the current holders of the resource are only actually holding shared control. Thus, one user mistakenly specifying DISP=OLD on a widely shared dataset (e.g. an ISPF dataset) can cause many others to grind to a halt, with little hope of the exclusive request ever getting to the top of the queue itself. This can only be dealt with by cancelling the user concerned and ensuring they do not make the same mistake again.

More insidious, however, is the case of the 'deadly embrace'. This can occur if task A gains exclusive control of resource X, then attempts to gain control of resource Y, while task B has already gained exclusive control of resource Y and is now attempting to gain control of resource X. Similar problems can occur with a chain of tasks making interrelated requests, but the two-task, two-resource version is the commonest. In this case it is logically impossible for either task ever to resume as they will both wait indefinitely for each other. The only solution once again is to cancel one of the tasks and try to prevent the recurrence of the problem. In practice, this can usually be done by amending the program code concerned so that all tasks which will attempt to gain control of the same group of resources always do the ENQs for the different resources in the same order. Thus, in our example above, if both tasks attempted to ENQ on X first and then Y, the deadly embrace would never occur.

These problems can be resolved for applications, as there are tools available which will display the contention occurring and allow the cancellation of the guilty tasks. For system code, however, which may bring the whole system to a halt when it is forced to wait, long waits and deadlocks are unacceptable — both because of the impact on other users, and because it may be impossible to recover at all without re-IPLing the system (the tools for diagnosing and solving the problem may themselves be locked out).

3.6.3   Locks

Locks are the serialization mechanism used by MVS for fundamental system modules. They do not suffer from the deadly embrace danger, they have a much shorter path length than ENQ/DEQ (i.e. they use fewer instructions so execute faster), and, unlike the process of disabling the processor for interrupts, they are capable of serializing access to resources that are shared between multiple processors in a multiprocessor CPC. They are used for serializing access to processes and resources (particularly control blocks) used in storage management (real, virtual, and auxiliary), dispatching, the I/O supervisor, and cross-memory services, among others.

Locks differ from ENQs in that the system does not need to search a chain of control blocks to see if a lock can be satisfied. Instead, there is a specific location, known as a lockword, whose contents can be tested to reveal the status of a lock. Lockwords are tested and set by an MVS component known as the lock manager, in response to requests made using the SETLOCK macro. There is one lockword for each type of lock, except for locks that control multiple resources of the same type (e.g. UCBs). These are known as multiple locks and have one lockword for each occurrence of the resource (in the case of a UCB, for example, the lockword for each UCB is found in an area of storage immediately in front of the UCB concerned).

Each CPU also has a group of bits in its PSA which is used to indicate which locks it currently holds. When a requestor issues the SETLOCK macro, the lock manager first checks the bits in the PSA, then accesses the lockword if the bits indicate that the lock can proceed. The lockwords are in storage which is shared between all processors in the complex, and the value in them is either hex zeros (indicating the lock is not held) or an indicator of the CPU-id of the processor holding the lock.

If the lock is not already held by another processor, the lock manager will set the value of the requesting CPU in the lockword, set the relevant lock bit in the PSA,

Table 3.1. Partial hierarchy of MVS locks (highest first)

Lock name	Category	Type	Resource serialized
ASM	Global	Spin	Auxiliary storage management
RSM	Global	Spin	Real storage management
DISP	Global	Spin	Dispatcher (ASVT and dispatching queue)
IOSUCB	Global	Spin	UCB updates
SRM	Global	Spin	SRM control blocks
CMS	Global	Suspend	Cross-memory services
LOCAL	Local	Suspend	Local storage

and return control to the requestor. If the lock is already held, the lock manager will force the requestor to wait.

However, there are different types of lock, and the precise action which the lock manager takes will depend on the type of lock. For a SUSPEND lock, the lock manager will suspend the requestor if the lock is unavailable, which allows other tasks to be dispatched on the processor in the meantime. For a SPIN lock, however, the lock manager will place the requestor in a spin loop and disable it for interrupts if the lock is unavailable. This prevents other work from being dispatched — even interrupts — and ensures the requestor obtains the lock as quickly as possible. The lock manager also disables the requestor for interrupts when it does obtain a SPIN lock, in order to allow it to release the lock again as quickly as possible. One implication of this is that units of work requesting SPIN locks must ensure they will not encounter page faults during the time they hold the lock (since these cannot be resolved without taking an I/O interrupt), by fixing any pages of virtual storage they will require in real storage before asking for the lock.

Locks are also divided into local and global locks, analogous to STEP and SYSTEM scope for ENQs: local locks serialize access to resources within an address space, while global locks serialize across the entire system.

The feature of locks which prevents deadlocks occurring is the existence of a hierarchy. If a task has obtained one lock, it may only obtain other locks which are higher in the hierarchy; if it attempts to obtain a lower lock than one it holds already, it is abended. This enforces the procedure recommended above for preventing deadlocks using ENQ, i.e. it ensures that requests for different resources are always made in the same order, so there is no danger of one task asking for lock A then lock B, while another is asking for lock B then lock A. It is the process of setting and checking the lock bits in the PSA that determines whether a higher level lock is held when a SETLOCK macro is issued.

Table 3.1 shows some of the lock types in hierarchical order. Note that all the global spin locks appear at the top, followed by global suspend locks and finally local suspend locks (there are no local spin locks).

3.6.4   Intersects

Intersects are used in addition to the lock mechanism to serialize access to the queues used by the MVS dispatcher. They are designed to give the dispatcher itself priority in the use of its queues, but to allow other MVS functions to update those queues when the dispatcher is not using them.

Whenever a function other than the dispatcher wishes to use one of these queues, it must first obtain the relevant lock (the local lock if the queue is one that belongs to a specific address space, such as the TCB queue, or the dispatcher lock for a shared queue, such as the ASCB ready queue). This ensures that only one function other than the dispatcher itself can attempt to access a given queue at any one time. It must then request an intersect to find out if the dispatcher is using the queue. If it is, it will have set a bit to indicate this. This bit will be detected by the intersect process, and the requestor will spin until the dispatcher frees the resource by resetting the bit (these bits are in the ASCB for local queues, and the supervisor vector table (SVT) for global queues). Once the requestor can gain control of the resource, it sets the bit itself. Once it has completed, it resets the bit, releasing the intersect, then it relinquishes the lock. Thus the dispatcher need only check/set the intersect bit to obtain control of one of its queues, while any other function must first obtain the relevant lock and then check/set the intersect bit.

3.7   Program management

3.7.1   Program fetch

Wenever you attempt to load a program via an EXEC statement in your JCL, or via a LOAD, LINK, XCTL, or ATTACH macro, the MVS program fetch function is invoked (DFSMS/MVS replaces program fetch with a similar function called the loader — not to be confused with the loader in previous versions of DFP, which did something similar to the linkage editor). This does two jobs: it finds the program you want, then, if it is not already present in the virtual storage addressable by the requesting address space, it loads the program into storage. If fetch was invoked via the LOAD macro, it will then return the address of the program it has loaded; if it was invoked using any of the other interfaces listed above, it will continue by passing control to the fetched program.

Fetch finds the requested program by issuing a BLDL SVC. BLDL searches through a hierarchy of locations and libraries until it finds a program with the requested name. This hierarchy is as follows (in the order of search):

1   The job pack area (JPA) is a notional area of storage within the caller's address space containing programs that have already been loaded and are available for reuse. It is represented by a chain of control blocks known as the JPA queue, consisting of load list elements (LLEs) and contents directory entries (CDEs). There is one LLE for each program that has been loaded, and each LLE has

a pointer to a chain of CDEs — one for each name by which the program may be invoked, including, among other information, the virtual address of the entry point corresponding to that name. If the program is found here, there is no need to reload it, and the fetch process is now complete.

2   Any tasklibs which have been specified for the current task, in order of their concatenation, followed by any STEPLIBs specified in the JCL in concatenation order, or (if there are no STEPLIBs) by any JOBLIBs specified in the JCL in concatenation order. Unless you have used the library lookaside (LLA) facility of MVS/ESA to load the directories of these libraries into virtual storage, BLDL will need to perform physical I/O to read the directories of each of these libraries in order to determine whether the program is there. If the program is found in any of these libraries, it will then be loaded into storage.

3   The link pack area (LPA), starting with the fixed LPA (FLPA) if one is present, then the modified LPA (MLPA), and finally the pageable LPA (PLPA). The PLPA is an area of common storage which is loaded at IPL time (when you do a cold start, i.e. specify CLPA in your IPL parameters) with all the members of SYS.LPALIB and any other libraries that are specified in the active LPALSTxx member(s) of SYS1.PARMLIB. The MLPA is loaded at every IPL with those modules listed in the active IEALPAxx member of SYS1.PARMLIB, and is used for temporary changes to the PLPA. The FLPA is also loaded at IPL time, with those modules listed in the active IEAFIXxx member of SYS1. PARMLIB, and contains (antiquated!) modules which must be kept in fixed storage frames (i.e. cannot be paged out). To speed up the process of finding modules in the LPA, there are two control block chains known as the LPA directory and the LPA queue. The LPA directory contains a link pack directory entry (LPDE) for each module in the PLPA, including its virtual storage address, and the LPA queue contains an entry (a CDE) for each member of the FLPA and MLPA, and each member of the PLPA that is currently in use. If the program is found in the LPA, it need not be loaded in from disk, as the copy in the LPA can be addressed and used by any address space.

4   The last place BLDL looks for the program is in the linklist. This is the list of libraries in the LNKLSTxx member of SYS1.PARMLIB that was selected at the last IPL, concatenated behind SYS1.LINKLIB in the order in which the libraries appear in that list. Since the introduction of MVS/XA, searches of linklist libraries have been speeded up substantially by the use of LLA (linklist lookaside, known as library lookaside under MVS/ESA). LLA is a separate address space, started at IPL time (from IEACMD00), which holds a copy of the directory entries of all the linklist libraries (see Sec. 3.7.3 for more details of how the linklist and LLA operate). BLDL can therefore tell whether a requested module exists in any of those libraries, and, if so, what its physical (CCHHRR) address is on the relevant pack, without performing any I/O to the libraries' directories. Whether or not the directory entries are held in virtual

storage, however, physical I/O will usually be required to load the program into the caller's private address space if it is found in a linklist library (unless you are using VLF to manage your linklist libraries — see Sec. 3.7.3).

5   If the program is not found in any of these, program fetch will abend the caller with system abend code 806.

If the program is found in a tasklib, STEPLIB, JOBLIB, or linklist library, it must now be loaded into virtual storage in the caller's private address space. Fetch has its own IOS driver (see Sec. 3.4) which bypasses EXCP and access methods and optimizes the process of loading in the program. The text of the load module is passed to the relocating loader, which resolves any pointers in the program that are dependent on the virtual address at which the program is loaded into storage. Finally, the JPA queue is updated to reflect the addition of the new module, and control is passed to the fetched program (or back to the caller if the fetch was performed in response to a LOAD macro).

3.7.2   Program modes, attributes, and properties

There are a number of modes, attributes, and properties which programs may possess that affect the way they are handled by program management and other areas of MVS.

Each program has an addressing mode (AMODE) and residency mode (RMODE) associated with it at link-edit time. The AMODE can be 24, 31, or ANY, and determines whether the program runs in 24-bit addressing mode or 31-bit addressing mode when it is executed. Many programs from the days of MVS version 1 still execute in 24-bit mode, but programs which need to address storage above the 16 megabyte line must execute in 31-bit mode. During execution, the mode can be changed using the BSM or BASSM instructions, but it is more common for each program to execute in one mode only — the initial mode is set by the fetch process depending on the AMODE of the program. At any time, the current mode is indicated by the high-order bit of the next instruction address in the PSW, which is 1 in 31-bit mode and 0 in 24-bit mode.

Similarly, each program is assigned a residency mode (RMODE) at link-edit time, which determines whether FETCH will load it below or above the 16 megabyte line. The RMODE can be 24 or ANY. With RMODE = 24, a program will always be loaded below the 16 megabyte line, and with RMODE = ANY, it may be loaded above or below, depending on the AMODE of the caller.

Program attributes are also assigned at link-edit time, and describe the scope for sharing a single copy of a program between concurrent users. Each program can be non-reusable, reusable, re-entrant, or refreshable:

- *Non-reusable* (the default) simply means that a single copy of the program cannot be shared between multiple concurrent users. Thus, if multiple tasks running in the same address space all wish to load and execute the program, each will have to load its own copy, even though there is already a copy loaded into the address space. This is clearly a wasteful use of virtual storage. However, many batch application programs never need to be shared between multiple tasks concurrently, and so there is no real objection to making these non-reusable. The advantage of making them non-reusable is that they do not have to comply with the rules relating to programs with the other attributes — in particular, they may be self-modifying, and may therefore include work areas within the program itself.

- *Reusable* or *serially reusable* progams can be shared between multiple tasks, but only one can use it at a time. If multiple tasks in the address space wish to load such a program, only one copy will be loaded, but if multiple tasks wish to execute it at the same time, only the first will be allowed to proceed. The others will be suspended until the first task completes. Serially reusable programs may be self-modifying, but must restore themselves to their initial state before terminating, so that they perform identically for each task. Programs which modify their own machine code are rare these days (though this used to be a frequent trick when storage was at a premium and execution speeds were highly sensitive to the number of machine instructions executed). However, many programs include their own data areas, buffers, and switches, and it is these that usually have to be reinitialized by serially reusable programs before they terminate.

- *Re-entrant* programs are much more acceptable for serious sharing between multiple concurrent users. These programs allow genuine multithreading — several different tasks can be using the same program concurrently. Because of this, single copies can serve multiple users simultaneously, and such programs are eligible to be loaded into common areas of storage and shared between users in multiple address spaces. They can be used in the FLPA or MLPA, and they can be loaded into the CSA and shared from there (e.g. some third-party systems software products give the appearance of dynamic modification to the PLPA by loading modules into the CSA then updating the LPA directory to point to the copy in the CSA instead of the original version in the PLPA proper). To be re-entrant, modules should generally not modify themselves at all — this means that any data areas, switches, buffers, etc., required by the program must usually be placed in separate work areas which are GETMAINed at the beginning of the program and FREEMAINed at the end. Each task using the program therefore has its own copy of the work area. In theory, self-modifying sections are allowed in re-entrant programs as long as they are preceded by an ENQ, followed by a DEQ, and restore the modified section to its original value before issuing the DEQ. These restrictions ensure that only one user can use the modifying section of code at any one time; however, it introduces potential delays for widely shared programs and is not recommended.

- *Refreshable* programs are very similar to re-entrant ones, but no self-modification whatsoever is allowed. They can be fully shared between multiple tasks in multiple address spaces. Programs to be loaded into the PLPA must be refreshable, because of the way paging works for this area of storage. The copy of the PLPA pages on auxiliary storage (i.e. in the paging datasets) is created at IPL time, and from then on PLPA pages are never paged out. If the RSM decides to steal a PLPA page, it always does it without a page out operation, as these areas are never updated, so the original copy in the page dataset is always considered to be usable. The next page in for the page will always page in the copy which was created at IPL time. As any page of the PLPA could be paged out at any time, it is clear that any modification to it would be lost when it was paged back in. To prevent problems of this sort, PLPA pages are page-protected, so they cannot be updated, and programs to be loaded into the PLPA must be refreshable. If you place non-refreshable programs into the PLPA they will abend 0C4 as soon as they attempt to modify themselves.

Another attribute that can be assigned at link-edit time is APF authorization, though this is only effective if the library into which the program is linked is also APF authorized. This is discussed in more depth in Sec. 3.2.

Properties can also be assigned to programs in the MVS program properties table. This can be used to make programs non-swappable or non-cancellable, or to assign special storage keys to them. Prior to MVS 2.2 you had to reassemble the module IEFSD060 to update this table, but you can now specify these properties in the SCHEDxx member of SYS1.PARMLIB which you select at IPL time.

3.7.3   The linklist and LLA

As was mentioned earlier, the linklist concatenation is established at IPL time. It consists of SYS1.LINKLIB, followed by the libraries specified in the LNKLSTxx member(s) of SYS1.PARMLIB which were selected in the IPL parameters. This happens early in the IPL process, before any user catalogs are accessible, so only datasets whose catalog entries are in the master catalog may be included in the linklist. They are concatenated in the order in which they appear in the LNKLSTxx members, and a data extent block (DEB) is built describing the concatenation. This contains details of each physical extent allocated to the linklist. MVS provides no mechanism for changing this DEB, so you cannot usually add any new linklist libraries except by re-IPLing your system.

More seriously, if any linklist library extends into secondary extents that were not present at IPL time, those members which are placed in the new extents will not be accessible through the linklist until the next IPL. This can cause serious problems if the library extends, existing members are replaced (so the directory now points to the version of the member in the new extent), and then attempts are made to use the program. Now the old version is inaccessible because the directory points to the new one, and the new one is unusable because it is in an extent that is not in the linklist's DEB. The answer is either to ensure that your linklist libraries are always allocated in single extents (i.e. with zero secondary space specified), or to install a third-party software product that allows you to update the linklist DEB without an IPL.

Prior to MVS/XA, linklist datasets were automatically APF authorized, which was a serious security exposure if you wanted to simplify application JCL by placing application program libraries in the linklist. Now, however, it is possible to specify either LNKAUTH = APFTAB in the IEASYSxx member of SYS1. PARMLIB, which means that only linklist datasets that are specified in the APF list (IEAAPFxx) will be authorized. This is highly recommended. Furthermore, update access to all libraries in your APF list should be strictly controlled, as anyone with sufficient knowledge of assembler who can place a program in an APF authorized library will be able to circumvent MVS security (this is discussed further in Chapter 15).

Since the introduction of MVS/XA, there has been an optional MVS facility called linklist lookaside (LLA), which was mentioned above. LLA is initialized at IPL time by a START LLA command in IEACMD00 unless you remove this command. The only good reason for removing it would be if you were running a third-party substitute which provided equivalent function, as LLA gives substantial performance benefits. It does this by keeping copies of the directories of all linklist libraries in its address space, so that when a BLDL is issued against the linklist, the program can be found (or not!) without the need physically to read the directory of each library in the concatenation in turn until the program is found. This eliminates a large amount of I/O against these directories, with performance benefits not only for the task issuing the BLDL but also for all other users wishing to access datasets on packs holding linklist datasets.

One interesting side-effect, which has probably saved the bacon of several systems programmers, is that if you accidentally delete a linklist library, the system will carry on working quite happily, and carry on finding modules in the deleted library! This is because the physical addresses of the members which FETCH uses are still held by LLA even though it is no longer possible to open the directory. This only works, of course, until the space is reused by something else, but at least it gives you a breathing space to wriggle your way out!

In other circumstances, however, this 'advantage' of LLA can seem more like a problem. The fact that LLA's addresses do not reflect changes to the directories of the linklist datasets means that when you change a module in a linklist library, the system continues to use the old version even though the directory entry has been updated to point to the updated version of the module. To update LLA's copy of the directory entries, you must issue the F LLA,REFRESH or F LLA,UPDATE = xx console command.

Another similar problem is that posed by the need to compress a linklist library. Under MVS/XA, the only safe way to do this was to stop the LLA address space with a P LLA command, compress the library, then restart LLA. Otherwise, the directory entries in LLA for every module moved by the compress operation would be invalid, leading to abends whenever a user attempted to load one of these, until a refresh command was issued.

With MVS/ESA, LLA has been renamed library lookaside as it can now be extended to cover non-linklist libraries, and it now uses an ESA facility called the virtual lookaside facility (VLF) to extend its function to include keeping commonly used load modules in virtual storage so that fetches for them can be resolved without any disk I/O at all. Refreshes can now be issued for a single member or a single library, and libraries can be dynamically added to or removed from LLA control.

Probably the most interesting extension to LLA, however, is the use of VLF. ALLA resolves BLDL requests, it keeps a record of the most heavily used load modules, and calculates an index known as the net staging value for each module, which takes account of how often it is loaded, how large it is, and how great the response time saving arising from keeping it in memory would be. It then 'stages' the modules with the highest net staging values into a VLF dataspace, and any future FETCH requests for them will be resolved from here instead of through physical I/O to the dataset on disk. Modules may later be purged from VLF for various reasons, for example, if the dataspace runs short of storage, it will purge the least recently used modules, or if a refresh is issued which covers the module, it will be purged.

LLA now also has two modes: a freeze mode and a nofreeze mode. Freeze mode is the default for linklist libraries, and works as we have described LLA processing above. Nofreeze mode, however, bypasses LLA directory processing and only does VLF staging for the library concerned. This is useful for libraries that are frequently updated, or updated by application programmers, as it means that it is unnecessary to issue refreshes every time a member of the library is updated. When a FETCH request is issued for a module that is already in the VLF dataspace but whose CCHHRR address has changed, LLA detects that the module has been updated, purges it from VLF, and resolves the FETCH request from disk. This does not work if you update a program in place (e.g. using AMASPZAP) so you still need to issue a refresh command when you do this.

3.8   Catalogs

Catalogs are used by MVS to locate datasets when a task attempts to allocate them without supplying their volume serial number; they hold records of the volume(s) on which each cataloged dataset exists. All allocations of VSAM datasets and SMS-managed datasets must go through the relevant catalog, and in this case the catalog also holds other information: for VSAM datasets, for example, this includes the physical location of each extent of the dataset on the disk, DCB-type information, and much more (this information is held in the VTOC entry, also known as the DSCB, for non-VSAM DASD datasets). This section looks briefly at the logical and physical structure of catalogs and how the catalog management process works.

Over the course of MVS's history, catalogs have gone through a number of different structures. The current flavour is known as integrated catalog facility (ICF), and I shall concentrate on ICF catalogs here, though I will make a few comments on the earlier flavours in passing (the predecessors to ICF catalogs were known as VSAM catalogs, and the previous generation as CVOLs).

3.8.1   Logical catalog structure

Each MVS system must have a master catalog, and there will usually also be a number of lower level catalogs known as user catalogs. All catalog searches begin by searching the master catalog, and many major system datasets must be cataloged in it.

Prior to MVS version 4, the master catalog was described in the SYSCATxx member of SYS1.NUCLEUS, where the suffix xx was specified in response to the message IEA3347A SPECIFY MASTER CATALOG PARAMETER at IPL time, and defaulted to LG. This is still a valid option on MVS version 4 systems, but it is also now possible (and simpler) to specify the master catalog parameters in the LOADxx member of SYS1.PARMLIB. The use of LOADxx is discussed in more detail in Chapter 7.

MVS obtains the name of the master catalog and the VOLSER of the disk it is on from the SYSCATxx or LOADxx member, and then opens the master catalog, which it uses to find the other datasets it requires for the early stages of the IPL process. At this stage, the master catalog is the only catalog that is open and usable by the system, which is why any system datasets opened during the IPL process must be cataloged in it. Later in the IPL process, catalog management services are fully initialized, allowing the use of user catalogs.

The physical structure of the master catalog is identical to that of a user catalog; they are defined with the same IDCAMS command, and any catalog can be used as either a master catalog or a user catalog. So it is only the selection of a particular catalog at IPL time that identifies it as the master catalog for the MVS system concerned.

However, once you have established which catalog is your master catalog, it is necessary to define its relationships with its user catalogs, and in practice this will make the entries in a master catalog very different from those in a user catalog. Whenever MVS initiates a catalog search in order to locate a dataset, it starts by looking at the master catalog. The dataset to be located may be cataloged in the master catalog, but more commonly it will be in a user catalog. If the search process is to find it, that user catalog must be defined as such in the master catalog, and there must be an 'alias' entry in the master catalog which relates the high-level qualifier of the dataset's name to the user catalog. When catalog management finds

Master catalog		CATALOG.VOL001			
Alias	Usercatalog	Dataset name	Volume	DEVT	...
USERA	CATALOG.VOL001	USERA.ISPPROF	VOL004	3380	...
USERB	CATALOG.VOL016	SYS3.ISPPLIB	VOL001	3380	...
SYS3	CATALOG.VOL001	USERA.TST.JCL	VOL006	3390	...
⋮		⋮			

Figure 3.7. Relationship between master and user catalogs.

such an alias entry, it interprets this as an instruction to look in the specified user catalog for the catalog entries of all datasets with this high-level qualifier.

Thus there is a two-level hierarchy of catalogs, with most user datasets cataloged in the user catalogs, and the master catalog containing alias entries pointing to the user catalogs, plus catalog entries for system datasets required at IPL time. This is illustrated in Fig. 3.7. It is generally the systems programmer's responsibility to design and enforce this hierarchy.

3.8.2   Physical catalog structure

Physically, the ICF catalog structure consists of two types of datasets: the basic catalog structure (BCS) and VSAM volume dataset (VVDS). When we define a master catalog or a user catalog (using IDCAMS), we are creating a BCS. The BCS is itself a VSAM KSDS, whose cluster name is 44 bytes of binary zeros (as this is used as the key to the dataset, this ensures that the first entry in the data component of the BCS is always its own self-describing entry). The name of the data component is the name you assign in your IDCAMS DEFINE command, and the name of the index component, assigned by IDCAMS, always begins CATINDEX and continues with a timestamp.

The BCS contains entries of various types, such as ALIAS, NONVSAM, USERCATALOG, and CLUSTER, describing the various types of entity which may be searched for by catalog management:

- ALIAS entries were discussed in the previous section. They redirect a catalog search from the master catalog to a user catalog for a given high-level qualifier. Note that DFP version 3 permits multilevel alias structures, but these are still uncommon.
- USERCATALOG entries define user catalogs.
- NONVSAM entries describe non-VSAM datasets. For a non-SMS managed dataset the entry contains only the dataset name and the device type and volume serial number of the volume on which it is cataloged. Further information, e.g. on the DCB and physical location of the dataset on the volume, is found in the volume table of contents (VTOC) for DASD datasets or in the dataset labels for tape datasets.
- CLUSTER entries describe VSAM datasets, and point in turn to DATA entries

describing the data component of the cluster, and (for KSDSs) to INDEX entries describing the index component. This is where ICF catalogs differ most markedly from their predecessors.

In an ICF catalog, the entry in a BCS for a physical component of a VSAM cluster works in a similar way to a NONVSAM entry. The BCS entry only contains minimal information about the component, such as the name, the device type and volume serial number, and all the physical details, such as location of extents, CISIZE, etc., are held on the same volume as the dataset itself, to simplify recovery and space management. For VSAM components, however, this information is not held in the VTOC entry. Instead it is held in the second component of the ICF catalog structure — the VSAM volume data set (VVDS).

The VVDS is a special type of ESDS. It is created automatically whenever a VSAM component (including a BCS) is allocated on a volume which does not yet have a VVDS. The VVDS is always called SYS1.VVDS.Vvolser, where volser is the volume serial number of the volume; you can preallocate a cluster with this name on the volume if you wish to override any of the defaults for VVDS allocation (or control its physical location on the volume).

The first record in every VVDS is known as the VSAM volume control record (VVCR), and it consists of two parts. The first of these lists the BCS catalogs which own (or have owned) VSAM datasets cataloged on this volume — these entries are known as back pointers. The second part maps free space within the VVDS itself, and allows reuse of space within the VVDS (this is the main way in which it differs from a normal ESDS). The second record in the VVDS is a self-describing record, and the rest of the records are either VSAM volume records (VVRs) or non-VSAM volume records (NVRs, a new record type introduced with DFSMS).

There is at least one VVR for each VSAM component on the volume, describing its physical extents, key and record sizes, CI/CA sizes, etc. The physical extent information duplicates information in the VTOC, but the VTOC is only used when the component is being defined, deleted, and extended, while normal read/write accesses to the component use the extent information in the VVR.

It should be clear that in this structure there is a many-to-many relationship between BCS and VVDS datasets. That is, each BCS can own VSAM components on multiple volumes (and therefore use multiple VVDSs), while each VVDS can contain entries for VSAM components owned by multiple BCSs. Just as the BCS entry for each component contains a pointer to the volume it exists on (and therefore to the VVDS), each VVR contains an indicator which connects it to the back pointer in the VVCR which corresponds to its owning BCS.

To complicate the matter just a little more, the introduction of DFSMS has extended the function of the VVDS. Non-VSAM datasets before the days of DFSMS were only represented in the catalog structure by an entry in a BCS, while all other dataset information was held in the dataset's entry in the VTOC. SMS-controlled non-VSAM datasets, however, do also have an entry (an NVR) in the VVDS of the volume on which they are located.

Before we leave catalog structures, let us briefly mention the differences between ICF catalogs and their predecessors, VSAM catalogs, whch you may occasionally come across. (If you do, I strongly recommend getting rid of them as quickly as possible!) The main differences were:

- VSAM catalogs did not use VVDSs — all information was held in the main catalog structure, which was simply known as a VSAM catalog.
- Because this would have made recovery of volumes with VSAM components belonging to different catalogs extremely difficult, there was a concept of 'VSAM volume ownership' — each volume was 'owned' by a VSAM catalog, and VSAM datasets could only be allocated on the volume if they were cataloged in the VSAM catalog which owned it.
- Under ICF catalogs, every VSAM component corresponds to a dataset which has space allocated to it using normal direct access device storage management (DADSM) routines and which appears in the VTOC with the same name as the VSAM component. VSAM catalogs, however, allowed the user to allocate a 'dataspace' (no connection to the MVS/ESA dataspace concept discussed below!) which was then available for VSAM to suballocate to VSAM components without telling DADSM or the VTOC.

3.8.3   The catalog address space

With the introduction of MVS/XA, a catalog address space (CAS) was created, which is started up at every IPL. This is used by the data facility product (DFP) catalog management function to hold most of its program modules and control blocks, which were previously held in the PLPA and CSA respectively. (DFP like JES, is a product which, for all intents and purposes, is part of MVS, though IBM markets it as a separate product.)

Catalog management routines also use CAS to 'cache' records from catalogs, in other words, frequently referenced catalog records, including ALIAS entries from the master catalog, are held in virtual storage in the CAS address space to avoid the need repeatedly to perform real I/O to disk for them. Unfortunately, in pre-ESA versions of DFP, records from catalogs shared with other MVS systems are flushed out when the system attempts to reuse them.

Each request for a catalog management service is handled by a CAS task, which is assigned a task ID, and the status of these tasks can be monitored using the MODIFY CATALOG operator command. The LIST subcommand lists out CAS tasks, showing their task ID, the catalog they are trying to access, and the job on whose behalf they are trying to access it. The END or ABEND subcommand can then be used to terminate the CAS task if necessary.

MVS/ESA versions of DFP also provide commands that allow you to allocate and deallocate user catalogs, enabling certain maintenance functions to be performed more easily.

3.9 Interaddress space communication

The way in which the MVS addressing scheme works is ideal for protection of users from one another. Separate address spaces are unable to address each other's private virtual storage because they cannot access the page and sgment tables that tell them where the real page frames are which back the virtual storage of another address space. In other words, the architecture itself protects the private virtual storage of each address space from tasks executing in other address spaces.

However, this 'advantage' turns into an enormous obstacle when you have a genuine reason for wishing to communicate between two address spaces — and this is an increasingly common requirement in the era of online/real-time computing. Originally, MVS only had one mechanism for communicating between address spaces — the use of common storage. True, the system could schedule an SRB to run in one address space from another one, but this still had to use common storage for any data to be passed between them. But there are disadvantages in using common storage for interaddress space communication:

- There is a limited amount of common storage available, particularly below the 16 Mb line, so using it for frequent tasks passing significant amounts of data can be impractical — indeed, if you try to use more CSA than was allocated at IPL time, your MVS system will fall over!
- By definition, any address space can 'see' what is in common storage, and update it if it is not page-protected, so sensitive or system-critical data is less secure there than in an area of private virtual storage.

So IBM has developed services that allow us to communicate between address spaces without using common storage: cross memory services, introduced with MVS/XA, and dataspaces and hiperspaces, introduced in MVS/ESA.

Each of these mechanisms for interaddress space communication is discussed in a little more detail in the sections that follow. Each of them is complex to use, and it seems unlikely that many users or application programmers will use any of them directly, but they are already in widespread use by writers of packaged software inside and outside IBM.

3.9.1 Common storage and SRBs

We have already covered common storage in Sec. 3.2. Some areas, such as the PLPA, are page-protected, and some, such as the nucleus, have specialized system uses. Others, however, are available for tasks running with storage protect key zero to GETMAIN, update, read, and FREEMAIN as required. In particular, the common service area (CSA/ECSA) and system queue area (SQA/ESQA) are available for the use of tasks wishing to pass data between address spaces.

Indeed, there are several common system tasks that frequently use CSA for this purpose. The main user of CSA on many systems is VTAM, which puts its message buffers there. Thus, when VTAM has received a message from a terminal via an interrupt from the I/O subsystem, it places it in the CSA, determines which address space it is intended for, then schedules an SRB into that address space to inform it that a message has been received and where in virtual storage it can be found. If VTAM were to place the message in its own private area, the receiving address space could not access it; the architecture prevents it from placing it directly into the receiving address space's private area.

SRBs were mentioned above in Sec. 3.3. They are high-priority dispatchable units of work created with the SCHEDULE macro by functions running in supervisor state and storage key zero. Their relevance to this section is that they can be scheduled to run in any specified address space, whichever address space the function that schedules them is running in. Thus, a function in one address space can schedule an SRB to prompt a function in another address space to process some data placed in common storage by the first function.

The use of this mechanism led to increasing requirements for CSA in older levels of MVS. However, since the introduction of the new methods of interaddress space communication, there has been a tendency to reduce the usage of CSA in favour of the new methods, and most installations should now see a decline in the use of CSA.

3.9.2   Cross-memory services

The term 'cross-memory services' refers to a set of machine instructions, and the facilities they invoke, which were introduced in MVS/XA. These instructions provide the ability to address data in two address spaces simultaneously, to move data between these two address spaces, and to invoke programs in one address space from another.

Unlike SRBs, cross-memory services allow synchronous use of data and programs in different address spaces — a function which switches itself into cross-memory mode may access resources in another address space without suffering any interrupts in the process, and without the requirement to initiate another unit of work to access the second address space on its behalf. This is clearly much more flexible, and potentially faster and more efficient, than asynchronous communication using SRBs.

At the heart of cross-memory services is the concept of primary and secondary address spaces. Normally the primary address space will be the 'home' address space of the unit of work that initially invoked cross-memory services, and the secondary address space will be another address space with which communication is required. Control registers are used to hold the real addresses of the segment tables for the primary and secondary address spaces, and this enables a modified version of dynamic address translation to be used to resolve the real storage locations of data in both address spaces for a single cross-memory instruction.

The main facilities supplied by cross-memory services are implemented as follows:

- *Data movement between address spaces* Several instructions are provided which can perform this function. MVCP moves data from the secondary address space to the primary; MVCS moves data in the opposite direction; and MVCK performs a similar function between areas with different storage protect keys. Note that these instructions require that the function knows the addresses of the data areas it wishes to use in both address spaces — finding these can be complicated!

- *Data sharing between address spaces* Address spaces can be set up which act as data servers for a number of other address spaces, then one of several methods used to access the data from the 'clients', without actually moving it into the client address space. For example, programs running in common storage can switch into secondary mode to access data in the shared address space. (In primary mode, ordinary machine instructions are taken to refer to storage in the primary address space, but in secondary mode they are taken to refer to storage in the secondary address space.) Alternatively, the program call mechanism (see next point) can be used to invoke a server program in the shared address space to access data and return a result to the client.

- *Program sharing* The progam call (PC) instruction can be used to transfer control to a program in another address space, and the program transfer (PT) or program return (PR) instructions used to return. This requires the function running in the original address space to know how to find the program to be called, and cross-memory services provides a control block structure containing linkage tables and entry tables to hold this information.

The linkage and entry tables are held in the PCAUTH address space. There is one linkage table for each address space containing an entry for each PC service the address space is authorized to access. Whenever an address space wishes to offer a PC service, it creates an entry for the service in the linkage table of each address space to which it wishes to offer the service. The linkage table entries point to entry tables, which contain more information about the program(s) that can be called as part of this service, including their entry point address(es) and the address spaces in which they will execute. Thus, any given address space can only invoke PC services to which the supplying address spaces have deliberately given it access.

There are a number of restrictions on programs running in cross-memory mode. Some of the most important are:

- They cannot issue any SVCs except ABEND.
- Cross-memory access to swapped-out address spaces is not supported, and any attempt to do so results in an ABEND.
- Only one step of any given job can set up a cross-memory environment.

There is also a separate authorization structure which restricts the address spaces that any one address space can access using cross-memory facilities. This, and many other aspects of cross-memory services, is well documented in [20] (or [21] for XA systems).

It should be clear that use of cross-memory services is highly complex, and is usually only attempted within sophisticated software products. IBM warns that improper use of cross-memory services can cause severe system problems, so most of us would be well advised to leave it to the software suppliers!

A typical use of cross-memory services is in the implementation of multiregion operation (MRO) in CICS. Users log on to a terminal-owning region (TOR), but when they enter a transaction identifier to select the application they wish to use, the TOR uses cross-memory services to 'ship' the processing request to the 'application-owning region' (AOR) corresponding to the application selected. The AOR processes the transaction, then when it has a message to return to the user, it uses cross-memory services to pass this back to the TOR. The TOR is then responsible for sending the response back to the user. Interestingly, CICS is able to run MRO using either cross-memory services or SRBs, and it is at the discretion of the CICS systems programmer which is used.

3.9.3   Dataspaces and hiperspaces

Dataspaces and hiperspaces, introduced with MVS/ESA, are MVS's latest mechanism for interaddress space communication.

A dataspace is a special type of address space which does not include the common areas in its virtual storage (i.e. it has private areas at those addresses which are used for common areas in a normal address space), and from which machine instructions cannot be executed. These restrictions make dataspaces unsuitable for any use other than as a repository for data, hence their name. Although they were ostensibly introduced in order to allow a single address space to address more than the 2 gigabytes of virtual storage allowed by a 31-bit addressing scheme, it seems unlikely that there are many genuine applications yet available which are restricted by this limit. A more important reason for their use is to make it possible to bring large data files into virtual storage in such a way that they are shareable between multiple address spaces.

Dataspaces are much easier to use than previous methods of interaddress space communication, due to a new way of addressing the data in them, called access register (AR) addressing mode or the advanced address space facility (AASF). This uses a new set of 16 access registers which are part of the ESA architecture, and a series of changes to machine instructions to take advantage of them. A function can switch itself into AR mode with a single instruction; once it has done this, familiar instructions such as MVC take on new ways of working.

The MVC instruction, for example, normally uses an offset from a value in a general-purpose register as a 'from' address, and another similarly constructed value as a 'to' address. It moves an area of data from the 'from' address in the virtual storage of the current address space to the 'to' address in the virtual storage of the current address space. In AR mode, however, each general-purpose register has an associated access register. This can contain a token which uniquely describes a dataspace or address space, and if so, the corresponding address will be treated as being in the virtual storage of the dataspace or address space concerned. Thus, for example, a function can move data from the dataspace into its own address space by first switching into AR mode and then executing an MVC instruction with the token of a dataspace in the access register for the 'from' address. By using two different tokens in the access registers for the 'from' and 'to' address spaces, it can move data between two dataspaces.

These tokens provide the processor with a route to the segment tables of the address spaces or dataspaces concerned. As long as an address space knows the token values for the other address spaces it wishes to communicate with, AR mode provides a much simpler and more efficient mode for moving data between two address spaces than cross-memory services. In addition, the ability to have tokens for up to 15 different address spaces simultaneously available in different access registers means that communication involving more than two address spaces becomes feasible without painfully long path lengths. [20] also covers programming with access registers and dataspaces.

A hiperspace is a special type of dataspace (high-performance dataspace) which cannot exist in central storage. There are two types: 'standard', which is created in expanded storage, and paged out to auxiliary storage as necessary; and 'expanded storage only', which can only exist in expanded storage. The latter type is used by a number of MVS/ESA facilities to buffer data in expanded storage which users would otherwise need to perform real I/O to obtain — hence 'high performance'. In both cases, it is necessary to move the data required from the hiperspace to the user's address space (a page at a time) before it can be used, because of the restriction preventing storage belonging to a hiperspace from moving into central storage. A new set of assembler macros has been provided with ESA to read pages from hiperspaces or write them out to them.

Hiperspaces seem to be intended more for system usage than application usage, and IBM has rapidly introduced a series of new facilities which exploit hiperspaces. These include:

- Virtual lookaside facility and library lookaside (discussed in Sec. 3.7)
- Batch LSR for VSAM buffering
- HIPERSORT — a hiperspace for sort work areas
- Hiperbatch — which keeps a single copy of heavily used, sequentially read files in a hiperspace to speed up batch job execution

All of these are intended to improve system performance by eliminating I/O for frequently used data. In essence, they use expanded storage as a clever caching device, and the use of expanded storage to cache large quantities of data seems certain to be a major feature of future MVS systems, since this eliminates the number one bottleneck on most commercial systems today — DASD I/O.

Bibliography

1. *MVS/XA Overview*, GC28-1348. A very readable overview of some aspects of MVS internals.

Storage management

2. *MVS/ESA Initialization and Tuning Guide*, GC28-1634. Detailed discussions of MVS storage management and how SRM controls swapping (this is the version 4 manual — earlier versions of MVS combined the *Initialization and Tuning Guide* and *Initialization and Tuning Reference* which covers SYS1.PARMLIB members in a single manual).
3. Friedman, M.: The Age of a Page, *Mainframe Journal*, September 1989, pp. 16–22. Discusses virtual storage and the paging process.
4. Friedman, M.: MVS Expanded Storage — Big Bang or Bust?, *Enterprise Systems Journal*, May 1991, pp. 71–75. Discusses how expanded storage works and how to monitor usage of it.
5. Jackson, E. and Klein, P.: Common Storage Advantages and Problems, *Candle Computer Report*, October 1989, pp. 1–6.

Task management

6. Sinclair, B.J: The Service Request Block, *MVS Update*, June 1987, pp. 15–20.

I/O management

7. *370/XA Principles of Operation*, SA22-7085. Includes several chapters on fundamental I/O processing.
8. Fairchild, W.R.: MVS/XA I/O Subsystem and DASD Event Traces, *Mainframe Journal*, March 1990, pp. 60–67. Traces a DASD I/O through all the stages of MVS I/O processing.

Job management

9. Bordonaro, B.: Understanding MVS Converter/Interpreter Processing, *Mainframe Journal*, July 1990, pp. 47–54.

Serialization

10. *MVS/ESA SPL: Application Development Guide*, GC28-1852. Detailed programming considerations for system software, including serialization, progam management, etc.
11. *System Macros and Facilities, Volume 1*, GC28-1150. The MVS/XA equivalent of [10].
12. *MVS/ESA Diagnosis: System Reference*, LY28-1011. Includes a chapter on the lock hierarchy and ENQ names used by MVS components, plus coverage of storage subpools and storage protection.

13. Feinstein, A.: Serialization in MVS/XA and MVS/ESA, *Candle Computer Report*, November 1989, pp. 1–3, December 1989, pp. 1–4, and January 1990, pp. 1–3. An excellent explanation of ENQs, locks, and intersects.

Program management

14. *MVS/ESA Linkage Editor and Loader User's Guide*, SC26-4510. Documents program attributes and addressing modes and how to assign them.
15. Johnson, R.H.: MVS Program Management, *Mainframe Journal*, December 1989, pp. 32–42.
16. Brunner, T.A.: Utilizing MVS/ESA's Library Lookaside, *UKCMG 1990 Proceedings*, Glasgow, pp. 19–27 (also USCMG 1989 Proceedings).
17. Goldin, S.: Getting the Most out of Contents Supervision, *Candle Computer Report*, August 1989, pp. 1–2. Explains reusability and re-entrancy.

Catalogs

18. *MVS/ESA Catalog Administration Guide*, SC26-4502.
19. Clark, J.W.: VSAM Catalogs Concepts, *Mainframe Journal*, July 1989, pp. 64–72. A very useful discussion of the structure of ICF catalogs, VVDSs, BCSs, and the old VSAM catalogs.

Interaddress space communication

20. *MVS/ESA SPL: Application Development — Extended Addressability*, GC28-1854. Includes a chapter on cross-memory programming.
21. *System Macros and Facilities Volume 1*, GC28-1150. The XA manual to look at for cross-memory programming techniques.
22. Dimond, S.: Writing a Cross Memory Program, *MVS Update*, October 1987, pp. 17–27.
23. Hollar, R.D.: Inter-Address Space Communications using Cross Memory Services, *Technical Support*, March 1991, pp. 58–60.
24. Haupt, M.: Through the Data Window, *Mainframe Journal*, March 1989, pp. 33–40. Explains dataspaces and hiperspaces.
25. Haupt, M.: IBM Conquers Space, *Mainframe Journal*, June 1989, pp. 39–44. Discusses VLF and other ESA facilities.

General

26. *MVS/ESA Diagnosis: Data Areas, Volumes 1–5*, LY28-1043 to 1047. Documents the layout and characteristics of MVS control blocks.
27. *MVS/XA Debugging Handbook, Volumes 1–6*, LC28-1164 to 1169. XA equivalent of [26].

Part Two
Tools of the trade

4
Basic tools

4.1   Introduction

The aim of this chapter is to introduce you to some of the basic tools that are available to systems programmers; to point you to the tools you might need to do a particular job, and to the manuals which will provide you with further information. It will not cover the most basic tools of all, such as MVS JCL and ISPF/PDF, with which you should already be familiar. Instead it will concentrate on more unusual uses of TSO, the MVS utilities, and the console commands.

These tools provide an enormous range of facilities, which may take many years to master, but familiarity with these facilities can save you an immense amount of time and effort. Just look through the letters columns in a few copies of *MVS Update* or *Technical Support* — time and again you will see that many of the complex assembler routines in earlier issues provided facilities that a single simple command can achieve just as efficiently. So take the time to learn your way round the basic toolset, and you will make life a lot easier in the long run!

4.2   Using TSO

4.2.1   TSO commands

Although it is usually more convenient in an interactive session to use the full-screen facilities provided by ISPF dialogs, there are several good reasons why you should also learn about TSO commands and how to use them in TSO's line mode:

1   If you manage to get your system up with VTAM and TSO active but ISPF is not functional for some reason (e.g. someone has uncataloged a critical ISPF dataset), you must be able to recover using the facilities provided by raw TSO.
2   Many functions are most effectively performed by using TSO commands in CLISTs or REXX EXECs. Note that CLISTs and EXECs can be run in batch as well.
3   If you wish to write ISPF dialogs, you will need to understand CLISTs or

REXX first, and the use of TSO commands in your ISPF CLISTs or EXECs can increase their power enormously.

4   The ability to issue TSO commands from the ISPF command line is often valuable. For example, if you are already using both halves of your split screen and you want to know whether a dataset is cataloged and where, you can type TSO LISTC ENT(datasetname) VOL on the command line rather than exiting the current screen, going into PDF option 3.4, and returning to your original screen when you have got the volume serial number.

Table 4.1 lists some of the more important TSO commands for systems programmers, and what they are used for. These are documented in more detail in [1] and [3]. Writing CLISTs is documented in [5], and writing REXX EXECS in [6] and [7].

Table 4.1. Important TSO commands

Command	Usage
ACCOUNT	To perform TSO user administration, e.g. adding and deleting user ids and changing the logon procedures they can use. See Chapter 10 for more on this command.
ALLOCATE	Dynamically allocates a dataset — old or new. Equivalent to a DD statement in JCL, but can be used at any time during a job step or TSO session.
ALTLIB	Adds user and application CLIST and EXEC libraries to the list of libraries searched by TSO to locate command procedures, in front of SYSPROC and SYSEXEC.
AMS commands	Access method services commands can be used directly at the TSO READY prompt, as well as in IDCAMS batch jobs. See the AMS manual for full details. Commands which are particularly useful in TSO include: • DEFINE — To create a VSAM dataset, a GDG, or an alias, for example, or to catalog a non-VSAM dataset. • DELETE — To delete any of the above, including uncataloging non-VSAM datasets by using the NOSCRATCH operand. • LISTCAT — To show information from a catalog.
CLIST statements	These are not commands as such but can be used in CLISTs to control execution of the CLIST and to provide additional functions which are useful in a programmed environment, for example: • CONTROL specifies processing options for the CLIST, such as what debugging messages are to be written to the terminal. • DO–WHILE–END and DO–UNTIL–END structures are used for loop control. • IF–THEN–ELSE and SELECT structures allow you to perform conditional processing. • OPENFILE/CLOSFILE/GETFILE/PUTFILE allow file I/O to be performed. • WRITE is used to put messages to the terminal.
EDIT	The TSO line editor — this is discussed in some detail in Sec. 4.2.3.
EXEC	Can be used to execute a CLIST or EXEC which is not in your SYSPROC or SYSEXEC concatenation.
FREE	Dynamically deallocates a dataset or concatenation.
HELP	HELP cmdname provides help information on the TSO command specified as cmdname — this also extends to AMS commands.
LISTALC	Displays your current allocations on the screen — very useful when you are debugging clists and ISPF dialogs and you are unsure about which version of a clist/panel/message etc. is in use!
LISTBC	Lists messages from the SYS1.BRODCAST dataset — useful with the NOTICES operand for listing messages of general interest which have been saved in BRODCAST using the SAVE operand of the SEND command.

Table 4.1. (cont.)

Command	Usage
LISTDS	Displays the attributes of a dataset (or a group of datasets) on the terminal. Note that the LISTDSI statement can be used in CLISTs to return similar information in CLIST variables.
OPER	Allows authorized users to view certain console messages and issue certain console commands — but less powerful and less convenient than SDSF, and more hassle to administer and control, so use SDSF instead if you can.
PARMLIB	A systems programmer command which displays data from the active IKJTSOxx parmlib member and allows you to change the active member (see Chapter 10).
Program product commands	Any program in your STEPLIB or linklist which will run in the TSO environment can be executed as a command. Some programs are specifically designed to be used in this way, e.g. HSM commands like HMIG (which migrates a dataset), but many others can also be invoked if you provide the necessary dataset allocations and parameters. For one-off jobs it is usually easier to write a piece of JCL, but it can be useful to call programs in a CLIST when you want to provide the function in a menu-driven system.
RENAME	Renames a non-VSAM cataloged dataset or member of a PDS, or creates an alias for a PDS member (not for load modules, though — use the linkage editor for this!).
SEND	Sends a message to the operator's console, another TSO user, a list of users, or all users. It can send the message immediately, store it in the BRODCAST dataset until the user logs on, or save it in BRODCAST indefinitely to be sent every time a user logs on. The SEND console command is similar but has more functions (e.g. deleting saved messages) — see Sec. 4.4.
STATUS	Shows the current status of jobs on the JES queues — the default IBM STATUS exit restricts the display to jobs with jobnames consisting of the user's user id plus one or more alphameric characters. The exit can be changed, but once again SDSF is far more user friendly and convenient to administer, so stick to that instead!
SUBMIT	Submits a batch job to JES for processing.
SYNC	A systems programmer command which allows you to synchronize SYS1.BRODCAST with SYS1.UADS or the RACF database.
TEST	An interactive debugging tool for programs and CLISTs — clumsy, but then so is reading a dump! Can set breakpoints in programs and check the values of PSW, registers, key areas of storage, etc., at these points.
TIME	Returns date and time information, including elapsed and CPU time used by your session so far, and service units used.
TRANSMIT and RECEIVE	These commands, also known as Interactive Data Transmission Facility (IDTF), provide an e-mail function for communication between users. In a networked environment, they allow users on your system to communicate with users on connected systems, including VM and VSE systems, as well as other MVS systems. To set this up effectively requires customization of both your JES system and TSO — discussed in Chapters 8 and 10 respectively.
VLFNOTE	Removes objects from VLF control.

4.2.2 *Displaying storage with TSO TEST*

Certain TSO commands, including ACCOUNT, EDIT, OPER, and TEST, establish a subenvironment in which you may enter subcommands of the command concerned but not ordinary TSO commands. They replace the READY prompt with their own prompt, they usually provide a HELP subcommand which offers assistance on the use of their subcommands, and you terminate most of them using an END subcommand.

The TEST command has one particularly useful and simple application, which is to display virtual storage in your TSO address space. Normally, you invoke TEST using the TEST command, and specify the program to be debugged as a parameter. You may then use subcommands to set breakpoints, then issue the GO subcommand to start stepping through the program. At any time in the TEST environment, you may issue LIST commands to inspect the contents of registers and storage locations. This last facility, however, can be very useful for inspecting system control blocks even when you are not debugging a program. To do this, specify a dummy program (conventionally SYS1.LINKLIB(IEFBR14)) to get into TEST, then issue the LIST commands to show the control blocks you are interested in. Example 4.1 shows a typical session using TEST in this way.

```
 READY
TEST 'SYS1.LINKLIB(IEFBR14)'
 TEST
EQUATE CVT 10.%
 TEST
EQUATE EXT CVT+4AC%
 TEST
EQUATE LPAT EXT+38?
 TEST
LIST LPAT L(20) C
 LPAT      LPAT.....SYS1.LPALIB
 TEST
END
 READY
```

Example 4.1. Use of TSO TEST to inspect control blocks.

The following points should be noted:

• Lines starting in column 1 are commands entered by the terminal user; lines starting in column 2 are output messages.
• This example displays the beginning of the LPA list table (on an MVS/ESA system), using the LIST subcommand of TEST. The first operand of the LIST command specifies the address of the storage to be listed — in this case we are using a symbolic address which was built up by the previous series of EQUATE commands. The L operand specifies the length of the area to be displayed, and the C operand requests a display in character format.
• Each EQUATE statement associates a symbolic name with an address, using indirect addressing. The % indirect addressing operand means 'the area pointed to by the 24-bit address in the word at this location' — so 10.% means 'the area pointed to by the 24-bit address at virtual address 16 (i.e. hex 10)'. The ? operand is similar but uses a 31-bit address.
• This series of EQUATE statements is a relatively clear representation of how to use TEST to chain through control blocks to get what you want. We could issue the LIST command to show us the same area of storage without going through the EQUATEs, but it is rather less comprehensible:

```
LIST 10.%+4AC%+38? L(16) C
```

The use of control block chains in MVS is discussed at more length in Chapters 3 and 6. The use of TSO TEST is explained in [4], which includes a step-by-step tutorial — but in order to use TEST to examine control blocks, you really only need to get to grips with how to construct indirect addressing chains like those shown in Example 4.1.

4.2.3 TSO EDIT

EDIT is a particularly important command to get to grips with, as this is the one you are likely to have to use when your system comes up but ISPF does not. Unfortunately, it is also rather a painful one to use, for those of us who have become used to the luxury of a full-screen editor. EDIT is an old-fashioned line-editor, which means that in general you can only work with the 'current' line, and you do not work with it by overtyping or amending it directly. Instead, commands are available to display lines from the current dataset, and other commands are available to edit individual lines.

You enter the EDIT environment by issuing the EDIT command, with operands which specify the name of the dataset, certain processing options, and the dataset 'type'. There are a number of standard dataset types, each of which represents a set of defaults for the processing options. You may also create new types yourself, but this is likely to be a waste of time as TSO EDIT is usually only used in

Table 4.2. Selected TSO EDIT dataset types

Type	Usage	LRECL (See note 2)	LRECL overridable	BLKSIZE (See note 2)	Line numbers
ASM	Assembler source	80	No	3120	Last 8 columns
CLIST	Clist code	255	See note 1	3120	See note 1
CNTL	JCL	80	No	3120	Last 8 columns
COBOL	COBOL source	80	No	400	First 6 columns
TEXT	Text and/or DCF controls	255	See note 1	3120	See note 1

Notes:
1   CLIST and TEXT datasets default to variable-length records, with a maximum record length of 255, but if the LINE operand is used to override this length, EDIT assumes they are fixed-length records. Line numbers for these datasets are assumed to be in the first eight characters when they have variable-length records and the last eight characters when they have fixed-length records.
2   When you EDIT an existing dataset, EDIT takes the LRECL and BLKSIZE from the dataset label, as long as they fall within the supported limits for the dataset type. The values shown in the table really only apply to new and empty datasets.

emergencies, and you can override the defaults anyway. Table 4.2 shows some of the IBM-supplied EDIT types.

By default, EDIT attempts to use the dataset type as the low-level qualifier of the dataset name, so you may find it useful when you do have an emergency if you have named and organized your datasets to fit in with the IBM-supplied types. Thus, for example, if you have your JCL in a partitioned dataset with:

- A high-level qualifier equal to your user id
- A middle qualifier of FRED
- A low-level qualifier of CNTL
- LRECL = 80, RECFM = FB; and
- line numbers in the last eight columns

then as long as your prefix is set to your user id in your TSO profile, you can start to edit the member FIXJCL with the simple command

```
EDIT FRED(FIXJCL) CNTL OLD
```

If you have called it something else, e.g. by using JCL as the low-level qualifier, this becomes more complex:

```
EDIT 'userid.FRED.JCL(FIXJCL)' CNTL OLD
```

Keeping to the conventions makes life a little easier. Perhaps the main learning point here, though, is that you should familiarize yourself with how to get into EDIT before you have to do it in an emergency — trying to get to grips with this under pressure is not pleasant.

Once you are into EDIT, the basic subcommands you will need to amend a dataset or a member of a PDS are:

- LIST, to display one or more lines of the dataset on the terminal, e.g. LIST without operands displays the whole dataset; LIST * displays the current line — the asterisk is used to indicate the value of the current line counter; and LIST n1 n2 lists the lines n1 to n2 inclusive. It does not change the current line pointer, so avoid falling into the trap of assuming that the last line you can see on the screen is necessarily the one you are working on!
- UP/DOWN/TOP/BOTTOM are all used to change the value of the current line counter, e.g. DOWN moves it down one line; UP 7 moves it up seven lines.
- FIND changes the current line pointer to point at the next line containing the find string.
- INPUT/INSERT/DELETE allow you to insert and delete lines.
- CHANGE changes either the first occurrence or all occurrences of a string in a given range of lines to a new string.
- COPY/MOVE allow you to copy or move lines within the dataset.
- Insert/replace/delete function — this is invoked by typing a line number followed (optionally) by some data. If you type a line number which does not exist, the line will be created and your data inserted into it; if you type a line number which does exist, your data will replace it; if you type an existing line number with no data, the line will be deleted. Be very conscious of this last point — accidental deletions are all too easy as a result!
- VERIFY activates (or deactivates, if you enter VERIFY OFF) a facility which

displays the current line every time the current line or current line pointer is changed — highly recommended for novice or irregular users!

- SAVE/END do the obvious things, and END prompts you to do SAVE or NOSAVE if you try to END without saving changes.

Example 4.2 illustrates a simple editing session, showing commands entered by the terminal user on lines starting in column 1, and TSO responses on lines starting in column 2.

```
 READY
EDIT 'SYS1.TSOPROC(ISPFPROC)' CNTL OLD
 EDIT
LIST
 0100 //ISPFPROC PROC ....
 0200 //*........
 .
 12700 //SYSPROC DD DSN=SYS9.CLIST,DISP=SHR
 .
 IKJ52500I END OF DATA
 EDIT
VERIFY
 EDIT
TOP
 EDIT
FIND 'SYSPROC'
 12700 //SYSPROC DD DSN=SYS9.CLIST,DISP=SHR
 EDIT
CHANGE '//' '//*'
 12700 //*SYSPROC DD DSN=SYS9.CLIST,DISP=SHR
 EDIT
INPUT *
 INPUT
 12710 //SYSPROC DD DSN=SYS001.ALTPROC,DISP=SHR
 12720
 EDIT
END
 IKJ52555I NOTHING SAVED
 ENTER SAVE OR END-
SAVE
 EDIT
END
 READY
```

Example 4.2. A TSO EDIT session.

Note that in Example 4.2:

- A period at the beginning of a line indicates lines have been omitted from our listing.
- An exception to our rule that terminal input starts in column 1 appears on the line labelled 12710 — after you enter the INPUT subcommand, EDIT responds with INPUT on the next line, then a line number on the following one, and leaves the cursor immediately after the line number. You may then type in a line to be inserted into the dataset at this point, and here the user typed in a

replacement DD statement. When you finish typing in the input line, you press Enter and another input line is presented. Pressing Enter without typing any data on the line (as the user did on the second input line shown here) cancels INPUT mode.

- Here the user comments out a line in a logon procedure (perhaps a deleted dataset which is causing the procedure to fail with a JCL ERROR) and inserts a replacement line.
- The use of the VERIFY subcommand — this causes the following FIND subcommand to display the line it has moved the current line pointer to, and causes the CHANGE subcommand to display the line it has changed. Without VERIFY being on, this would not occur, and editing the dataset would be a slower and more frustrating process!

The EDIT command and all its subcommands are fully documented in [1].

4.3   MVS utility programs

4.3.1   Uilities available

IBM supplies a range of utility programs which you will find useful for a wide variety of tasks. However, the documentation for these is spread over a range of publications, and it is not always obvious which is the most appropriate utility for a given job, or whether there is one available that will do what you need. This section aims to give you an idea of what utility programs IBM provides as part of MVS and the commonest MVS program products (DFP, DFDSS, and DFSORT), and a task-oriented guide to which programs do what. As with TSO and console commands, familiarity with what the utilities can do will save you from wasting valuable time duplicating facilities which IBM has already provided for you. Most systems programmers build up a library of JCL for performing common tasks using these utilities, which avoids the need to go back to the manual every time you need to use them.

Table 4.3 lists the main utilities included in MVS and DFP, with a very short description of each and a pointer to the appropriate manual (the full manual titles for both XA and ESA systems are shown in Table 4.4). Note that:

- Obsolete facilities such as IEHATLAS and IEHMOVE have been omitted from Table 4.3.
- Some of these utilities have commonly used aliases, e.g. IMASPZAP for AMASPZAP, and ICEMAN for SORT.
- Table 4.4 lists the manuals referred to in Table 4.3. See the reading list at the end of the chapter for order numbers.

Table 4.3. IBM utility programs

Program name	Manual	Description
ADRDSSU	DFDSS UG, DFDSS Ref	DFDSS — efficient data movement utility, able to copy/move/backup/restore individual datasets, logical groups of datasets, or whole DASD volumes. Also provides space management facilities such as COMPRESS, DEFRAG and RELEASE for improving the utilization of DASD space.
AMASPZAP (IGWSPZAP from MVS 4.3 on)	Service Aids	SUPERZAP — inspects and modifies in place (zaps) data in PDSs and at any location of a direct access dataset (including VTOC entries). Usual use is for applying fixes directly to load modules without reassembling and relinking them. IGWSPZAP also supports modification of PDSEs.
AMBLIST	Service Aids	Lists and formats the contents of a load module, an object module, the nucleus, or the LPA. Particularly useful for verifying the contents of a load module, e.g. when it was linked, what zaps have been recorded in IDR records, and what link-edit attributes it has.
ICKDSF	DSF UG	DSF — DASD formatting utility, including facilities to change volume serial numbers, create and index VTOCs, inspect packs for bad tracks and assign alternate tracks.
IDCAMS	AMS Ref	IDCAMS is the batch interface to DFP, and provides functions such as creating and deleting VSAM datasets, catalogs, and GDGs, cataloging and uncataloging non-VSAM datasets, copying VSAM datasets, and backing up, moving, merging, and restoring user catalogs.
IEBCOMPR	Utilities	Compares two datasets — but users of recent levels of ISPF will find the SUPERC utility (options 3.12 to 3.14) more powerful and flexible.
IEBCOPY	Utilities	The utility for most PDS administration functions, including complete and selective copies, compressing individual PDSs, unloading PDSs into sequential datasets (e.g. on tape), and reloading these.
IEBDG	Utilities	Generates test data based on parameters supplied in control statements.
IEBEDIT	Utilities	Selective copy facility for sequential datasets containing JCL — allows you to extract selected jobs from a multijob piece of JCL.
IEBGENER	Utilities	Flexible copying facility, with options to create a PDS from sequential input, edit a dataset as it copies it, change LRECLs and blocksizes, and extend these facilities via user exits.
IEBIMAGE	Utilities	Creates IBM 3800 and IBM 4248 printer control modules, including FCBs and character-related tables.
IEBISAM	Utilities	Copy/backup/restore/print utility for ISAM datasets — hopefully now obsolete in most sites, as ISAM datasets should be converted to VSAM KSDSs when possible.
IEBPTPCH	Utilities	Print utility, which can edit records before printing, e.g. omitting or rearranging fields, and showing fields in either hex or character format.
IEBUPDTE	Utilities	Update utility for PDSs — used heavily by IBM to package updates to source modules and macros.
IEFBR14	—	A program which does nothing! But often used to create a 'dummy' step in a jobstream so that JCL statements can be used to allocate or delete a dataset.
IEHINITT	Utilities	Tape initializer — creates tape marks and dummy labels.
IEHLIST	Utilities	Lists OS CVOLS (old-fashioned catalogs!), PDS directory entries, and VTOCs, both indexed and unindexed.

Table 4.3. (cont.)

Program name	Manual	Description
IEHPROGM	Utilities	Originally provided facilities for manipulating OS CVOLs; still useful for scratching and renaming datasets, particularly for renaming datasets on non-SMS-managed volumes when other datasets exist with the same name.
SORT	Getting Started	DFSORT (although OEM alternatives often use the same name and provide identical function) sorts, merges, and copies datasets, with facilities for extracting subsets of the records and reformatting records.

Table 4.4. Manuals for IBM utilities

Manual	MVS/XA version	MVS/ESA version
DFDSS UG	DFDSS User's Guide [8]	Same as XA
DFDSS Ref	DFDSS Reference [9]	Same as XA
Service Aids	MVS/XA SPL: Service Aids [10]	MVS/ESA SPL: Service Aids [11]
DSF UG	DSF User Guide and Reference [12]	Same as XA
Getting Started	Getting Started with DFSORT [14]	Same as XA
AMS Ref	DFP: ICA Access Method Services Reference (for ICF catalogs) DFP: VSAM Access Method Services Reference (for VSAM catalogs)	MVS/DFP V3R2 Access Method Services for ICF [15] MVS/DFP V3R2 Access Method Services for VSAM catalogs [16] (Note that DFP manual titles have changed several times since MVS/ESA appeared)
Utilities	DFP: Utilities	MVS/ESA Data Administration: Utilities [18]

4.3.2 Which utility does which task?

Chapter 1 of [15] provides an alphabetical table of common tasks, showing which AMS command to use for each task, and the second section of [18] (guide to utility program functions) provides a similar table for the programs documented in that manual. Both of these tables are extremely useful, but suffer from some problems, notably, lack of references to utilities documented elsewhere. The 'utilities' table also tends to list obsolete programs against certain tasks, even though it is recommended elsewhere in the manual that you do not use them!

Table 4.5 is intended as a supplement to these tables to remedy these defects. When you need to identify the correct utility for a task, look in this table first. If the task you want to perform is not listed, go to the table in the AMS manual next, and finally to the table in the utilities manual. 'Concatenating' the tables in this order in effect gives you a higher level table showing all the utilities together, with recommended solutions appearing earlier in the concatenation than obsolete ones. Note that this table deals with batch utilities — the PDF SUPERC program is

Table 4.5. Task-oriented guide to MVS utilities

Task	Options	Program/command
ALLOCATE	Non-VSAM dataset	IEFBR14
ANALYZE	A disk for hardware errors	ICKDSF ANALYZE command (but INSPECT command is similar — be sure you understand the differences)
BACKUP	DASD datasets, volumes, or specific tracks	DFDSS COPY or DUMP command (CONCURRENT operand allows instantaneous backup)
CLIP	A DASD volume to a different volume serial number	ICKDSF REFORMAT command
COMPARE	Datasets	PDF SUPERC program (options 3.12–3.14, but can also be run in batch — see below)
COMPRESS	One PDS	IEBCOPY
	More than one PDS	DFDSS COMPRESS command
CONVERT	Volumes to and from SMS management	DFDSS CONVERTV command
CONSOLIDATE	Extents belonging to a dataset	DFDSS — DUMP the dataset with the DELETE PURGE operands, then DEFRAG the disk, then RESTORE the dataset.
COPY	Datasets between like and unlike device types	DFDSS COPY command
	A dataset	DFSORT can be used to do dataset copies, but IEBGENER, IEBCOPY, or AMS REPRO is usually more suitable
CORRECT	Permanent I/O errors on a disk	ICKDSF INSPECT command
CREATE	A VTOC	ICKDSF INIT command
	A VTOC index	ICKDSF BLDIX command
DEFRAGMENT	i.e. reduce free-space fragmentation on a volume	DFDSS DEFRAG command
DELETE	A dataset	IEFBR14 — unless you need to check a return code for successful completion, in which case use IDCAMS DELETE
DUMP	Datasets, volumes, or specific tracks	DFDSS DUMP command (see BACKUP)
EXTRACT	Records from a dataset	DFSORT using INCLUDE/OMIT statement
FORMAT	A DASD volume	ICKDSF INIT command
INDEX	A VTOC	ICKDSF BLDIX command
INITIALIZE	A DASD volume	ICKDSF INIT command
INSPECT	Contents of a load module	AMASPZAP
	A DASD volume for hardware errors	ICKDSF INSPECT command (but ANALYZE command is similar — be sure you understand the differences)
LIST	Contents and attributes of a load module or object module	AMBLIST
MAP	A load module	AMBLIST
	The nucleus or LPA	AMBLIST
MERGE	Datasets	DFSORT using MERGE statement
MOVE	Datasets between like and unlike device types	DFDSS COPY command with DELETE operand
REFORMAT	Records in a dataset	DFSORT using OUTREC statement

Table 4.5. (cont.)

Task	Options	Program/command
RELEASE	Unused space allocated to one or more datasets (or all datasets on a volume)	DFDSS RELEASE command
RESTORE	Datasets, volumes, or tracks dumped using DFDSS	DFDSS RESTORE command
SORT	Datasets	DFSORT using SORT statement
STAND-ALONE RESTORE	Of a whole DASD volume	Stand-alone DFDSS
UNINDEX	A VTOC	ICKDSF BLDIX command with OS operand
UPDATE	An unindexed VTOC	AMASPZAP
	A load module in place	AMASPZAP
	SSI or IDR information for a load module	AMASPZAP
	Data at a known CCHHRR location on a DASD volume	AMASPZAP
VERIFY	Contents of a load module	AMASPZAP
ZAP	A load module, DASD dataset, or VTOC	AMASPZAP

mentioned only because it can be run in batch. Many of the facilities listed in Table 4.5 can also be invoked interactively, via PDF or ISMF options. Note also that:

• If you have a cached DASD controller there are additional IDCAMS commands (SETCACHE and LISTDATA) which allow you to monitor and control use of the cache. These, however, are not documented in the access methods services manuals — instead, see [17].
• The PDF SUPERC utility can be submitted in batch using JCL like that shown in Example 4.3.

```
//SUPERC   EXEC PGM=ISRSUPC,PARM=('L SRCHCMP ANYC')
//NEWDD    DD   DSN=..................,DISP=SHR
//OUTDD    DD   SYSOUT=*
//SYSIN    DD   *
  SRCHFOR 'string'
/*
```

Example 4.3. Use of PDF SUPERC utility in batch.

4.4   Console commands

4.4.1   *Ways of entering console commands*

Perhaps surprisingly, considering how powerful they are, there are rather a lot of possible ways of entering console commands:

- From a real console (i.e. a terminal defined as a console in the CONSOLxx member of SYS1.PARMLIB).
- Under MVS version 4 or later, from a TSO console.
- Using the SDSF LOG facility, if you are authorized to use it by your SDSF authorization exit.
- Using the TSO OPER command, if your SYS1.UADS entry includes the OPER attribute.
- From a jobstream submitted to JES, unless COMMAND=IGNORE has been specified on the JES2 JOBCLASS initialization statement for the jobclass concerned. You should ensure commands are ignored for all jobclasses unless this is impossible for historical reasons, e.g. production jobs are scheduled using in-stream commands, as this facility is a serious security exposure.
- From an APF-authorized assembler program, using SVC 34.
- From various third-party system software products.

It should be clear that access to all these facilities should be carefully controlled to avoid malicious or incompetent users from issuing dangerous commands. As a systems programmer, though, you should have access to at least one of these facilities, giving you the opportunity to use yet another range of useful tools — MVS and subsystem commands.

One level of control on console security is provided by the MVS operator command groups. These group commands fall into several authorization levels:

- INFO — Informational commands, such as DISPLAY, DEVSERV, REPLY, and SEND
- SYS — System control commands, such as CANCEL, DUMPDS, MODIFY, PAGEADD, SET, START, and STOP
- IO — I/O control commands, such as MOUNT and VARY OFFLINE, ONLINE, PATH, and NET
- CONS — Console control commands, such as VARY commands for consoles and some CONTROL commands
- MASTER — Master console commands, such as CONFIG, DUMP, FORCE, VARY GRS, and VARY MSTCONS

The authorization levels of the different facilities for entering commands can be controlled as follows:

- Physical and TSO (MVS V4) consoles — in CONSOLxx member of PARMLIB.
- SDSF — the SDSFPARMS module allows you to control whether console commands can be submitted or not, but not what levels of command can be used.
- In jobstreams — if you allow commands to be used from a jobclass at all, the AUTH parameter of the JOBCLASS initialization statement specifies which command groups are allowed for this jobclass.
- Third-party console emulators usually provide an equivalent authorization

structure which can be specified using their start-up parameters.

- OPER can only use a very restricted set of commands (C U=, DISPLAY, MONITOR, SEND, SLIP, and STOPMN) and this cannot be controlled further
- There is no facility for restricting commands issued by APF-authorized programs using SVC 34.

IBM's direction, however, is to use RACF to control the authority to issue console commands, which will allow each installation to define and enforce its own console command security policy.

4.4.2   MVS commands

Table 4.6 gives a task-oriented guide, along the lines of Table 4.5, to some of the most useful MVS commands, from the systems programmer's point of view. It is intended only to point you to the command you need for a particular task — for

Table 4.6. Useful MVS console commands

Task	Command examples	Comment
Cancel an address space	C jobname C STARTING,A = asid C U = userid,DUMP C cua	Use the U operand for TSO users, the cua operand for MOUNT requests, the STARTING operand for address spaces which have not yet been assigned names, and the A operand to distinguish between multiple address spaces with the same name (do a D A,name command to display the asid values). If CANCEL does not work, see FORCE.
Catalog address space control	F CATALOG,LIST F CATALOG,END(id) F CATALOG,ABEND(id) F CATALOG,CLOSE(cat) F CATALOG,UNALLOCATE (cat)	LIST shows the catalog requests currently being processed. END terminates a selected catalog request (id is the catalog task to be ended — the id is shown by LIST) and allows it to be rerun — useful for resolving contention shown by LIST. CLOSE and UNALLOCATE can be useful when you need to do catalog maintenance. There are lots of other interesting options!
Change limit on number of users who can logon to TSO	F id,USERMAX = nn	Where id is the procedure name of the TSO terminal control address space, or the identifier assigned to it at startup time.

Table 4.6. (cont.)

Task	Command examples	Comment
Change status of devices or channel paths	CF CHP(chp),ON V dev,OFFLINE V PATH(dv,ch),ONLINE	CF CHP configures a channel online or offline; VARY varies either a device or a path to a device. Both can be issued for a group of devices or paths at one time. CF can also be used to change the status of processors, storage, and other resources.
Change a job's performance group	E jobname,PERFORM = n	Very useful if the job is hogging CPU and impacting on other users' performance. Avoid using it to make a job run faster or it will become a habit — and never let anyone outside systems programming have the authority to issue it, or you will lose control of your MVS performance priorities.
Console control	D C K E,1 K S,DEL = RD V cua,MSTCONS V cua,CONSOLE,AUTH = x	D C shows the status of all consoles. The control (K) command controls the display of messages on the current console, e.g. K S,DEL = RD makes non-highlighted messages roll off the screen automatically. The vary command to change the master console can only be issued from the current master console.
Display active jobs, tasks, and TSO users	D A,L D TS,L D TS,SYS*	The A operand shows all address spaces; TS shows just TSO users. Using L for the second operand gives a list of address spaces; specifying a jobname or generic jobname gives more detail on the jobs/users selected.
Display cache status	DS P,dev D SMS,CACHE	The DS command (DFP V3+) shows cache status for the specified device if it is attached to a 3990 controller. The D SMS,CACHE command displays cache statistics for each 3990 controller with at least one SMS-managed device attached.
Display datasets allocated to a device	D U,,ALLOC,cua,1	cua is the unit address of the device — and specify a count of 1, or you will get this for eight devices!
Display ENQs, RESERVEs, and contention	D GRS,,CONTENTION D GRS,RES = (SYSDSN, SYS1.PARMLIB)	The contention operand shows outstanding ENQ conflicts, while the resource operand shows all outstanding ENQs for the named resource.
Display online/ offline devices	D U,DASD,ONLINE D U,TAPE,OFFLINE D U,3390,ONLINE,,256	Note that only the first 16 devices will be displayed unless you specify ,,nnn on the end.

Table 4.6. (cont.)

Task	Command examples	Comment
Display outstanding messages requiring operator action	D R	
Display status of channel paths	D M = CHP(chp) D M = DEV(dev) DS P,dev	The D M command can also display the status of processors, real storage, and other resources. The DS (DEVSERV) command displays the status of each path to each device, and can also display the cache status of devices attached to 3990 controllers.
Display status of a string of DASD	D U,,,cua,16	Displays status of 16 devices starting at unit address cua.
Display SMS information	DS SMS,dev D SMS,CACHE	The DS command shows the volume and storage group status of the selected device(s). The D SMS command can display information on SMS datasets, storage groups, and volumes as well as the cache.
Display VTAM information	D NET,ID = node,E D NET,MAJNODES	The MAJNODES operand lists all active major nodes (e.g. groups of terminals and applications); the ID = operand lists any given major or minor node, and E gives an extended display. Very useful, for example, for displaying what terminals are logged on to a given VTAM application, or what is the status of a given terminal.
Dump an address space	DUMP COMM = text C jobname,DUMP	The DUMP command initiates a dialog in which you must specify the details of the address space and storage areas to be dumped, then writes the dump to a system dump dataset. For most user address spaces, the cancel command is easier and just as effective, as long as the step has a SYSUDUMP DD card.
Dump dataset control	D D,T DD CLEAR,DSN = nn DD ADD,DSN = nn DD DEL,DSN = nn	The display command shows the status of your dump datasets; the T option shows dump titles. The DD commands allow you to clear dump datasets which have filled up, or to change the list of available (cataloged) dump datasets.
Force an address space	FORCE jobname FORCE,jobname,ARM	If you have attempted to cancel an address space and it will not go, FORCE is the last resort — but it can mess up the rest of MVS as well, so only use it if you have no choice! The ARM operand is used for non-cancellable procedures.
Issue a command to a processing task	F procname,command	The modify (F) command is only effective when the address space has a task running which will pick it up and process it.

Table 4.6. (cont.)

Task	Command examples	Comment
LLA control	F LLA,REFRESH F LLA,UPDATE=nn	REFRESH rebuilds the entire LLA directory (this is the only option under XA). UPDATE rebuilds the part of the directory specified in the selected CSVLLAnn member of PARMLIB. For certain operations you may even wish to P LLA, make changes, then S LLA again.
Message processing control	D MPF,MSG T MPF=xx	The display command lists processing defined in the current MPFLSTxx member; the set command changes the current member.
Mount a DASD volume	M dev,VOL=(SL,vol), USE=STORAGE	Mounts a DASD device with the specified volume serial on the specified device with the specified usage attribute. Before MVS 2.2.3, this was required after every V ONLINE instruction for a non-PUBLIC DASD volume — now, however, it is only required when you want to change the usage from that specified in the VATLSTxx member of PARMLIB.
Page dataset control	D ASM PA dsname PD DRAIN,dsname PD DELETE,dsname	The display command shows the type, DSN, device address, % full, and status of each page dataset. The PA (page add) command adds a paging dataset. The PD command deletes one — take care with this, you could cause a shortage of paging space, and you could hit the system with a lot of work moving pages from the dataset to be deleted. If you really must delete a page dataset and cannot wait for an IPL, issue the PD DRAIN command well beforehand to minimize this effect.
Reply to a console message	R nn,replytext	nn is the identifier at the beginning of the outstanding WTOR message. Note that once JES is up you can omit the R, the blank, and the comma.
Send messages to users	SEND LIST SEND 'msg',ALL,SAVE SEND msg-nbr,LIST SEND msg-nbr,DELETE	The SEND console command is similar to the TSO SEND command, but with additional options for the control of 'notices' — messages which are kept in SYS1.BRODCAST and displayed at every TSO LOGON. The ALL,SAVE operand creates notices, the LIST command displays them with their message number, and the DELETE command removes the specified notice.

Table 4.6. (cont.)

Task	Command examples	Comment
SMF control	D SMF I SMF T SMF = xx	The display command displays the current SMF datasets (or options, if the O operand is specified). The I (switch) command switches SMF recording to a different dataset. The T command restarts SMF (useful if it abends!) using the selected SMFPRMxx member of PARMLIB.
SMS control	T SMS = xx SETSMS options V SMS,SG(grp),ENABLE	The set command changes the IGDSMSxx member of PARMLIB currently in effect; the SETSMS changes some of the SMS options without changing the member of PARMLIB (to be avoided!); while the V SMS command changes the SMS status of an individual storage group or volume.
SRM control	D DMN T IPS = nn T ICS = nn T OPT = nn E jobname,PERFORM = n	The display command shows the domain descriptor table (or a specific entry), including the current and target MPL for each domain, and the T (set) commands allow you to change the current SRM parameters by switching to a different PARMLIB member. The E (reset) command can be used to move an individual job into a different performance group (see above). Do not touch the SD command with a bargepole!
Start an address space	S jobname	jobname must be the name of a procedure in the concatenation of procedure libraries for started task control (see Chapter 8).
Stop an address space	P jobname	The stop command is only effective when the address space has a task running which will pick it up and process it. If this is so, always use the stop command as it gives the address space the opportunity to close down cleanly. Otherwise, use the cancel command.
SYSLOG control	W class	The writelog command closes the current SYSLOG segment and writes it to the specified SYSOUT class.
Vary the status of a device or path	V dev,ONLINE CF CHP(chp),ON	See the entry under 'Change status...' for comments.
VTAM control	V NET,ACT,ID = name V NET,INACT,ID = name,I	There are lots of variants of V NET. ACT activates a resource and INACT deactivates one. The I operand on INACT means 'immediate' — an even stronger variant is F — 'force'. Beware: when you deactivate a VTAM resource, all subordinate resources are also deactivated! See [25] for full details.

full documentation of all of these commands, see the appropriate version of [19]. Most of these commands are also summarized in [20].

4.4.3 JES2 commands

An MVS subsystem may define a command identification character, and any console command beginning with this character will be passed to the subsystem. By default, JES2 uses the $ (dollar) symbol as its command character, though you can change it using the CONCHAR operand of the JES2 CONDEF initialization parameter. In the examples below, it is assumed that the default command character is used.

Table 4.7 provides a task-oriented guide to the JES2 commands that are most useful to the systems programmer. JES2 commands are documented in [22], and summarized in [23].

Note that the space between the initial command and the first operand is optional.

The following groups of commands have been omitted from the table:

- Commands which merely duplicate the function of MVS commands.
- Commands which duplicate common SDSF functions but are less user friendly (note that SDSF invokes some of these commands itself), e.g. commands for displaying queues, changing attributes of items on the queues, and deleting items from the queues.
- NJE and RJE commands.

Table 4.7. Useful JES2 commands

Task	Command	Comment
Automatic command scheduling	$T A,ALL $T A,T = 18.00,'$TI4, A' $S A $C A,nnnn	TA,ALL simply displays all the outstanding automatic commands. The second TA command will cause the JES command TI4,A to be issued at 6 p.m. (or immediately, if it is already past this time). Use the $VS command within the quotes if you wish to issue an MVS command using this facility — you cannot do it directly. SA starts the processing of automatic commands.CA cancels the specified automatic command (you find the value of nnnn for any given command from the output of TA,ALL).
Backspace a printer	$B PRTnnn,D	For a stopped printer, goes back to the beginning of the current dataset so it can be reprinted when the printer is restarted.
Change current values of JES2 initialization parameters	$T init-stmt,option e.g. $T BUFDEF, BUFWARN = 90	Only some parms can be changed using $T. [26] tells you which ones.

Table 4.7. (cont.)

Task	Command	Comment
Display current values of JES2 parameters	$D init-stmt e.g. $D CONDEF	Most of the current settings can be displayed this way.
Display status of JES-controlled devices	$D U,dev $D U,ACT $D U,STA	The ACT and STA variations show all active and started devices respectively — very useful when you are trying to close down JES cleanly for an IPL and it refuses to come down because some devices are still active!
Delete held output	$O Q,Q = x,CANCEL,A = nn	This example deletes all class x held output over nn days old. It is vital to issue commands like this for all your held output classes on a regular, automatic basis to prevent your spool filling up.
Delete non-held output	$P Q,Q = x,A = nn	The non-held equivalent of $O Q,CANCEL — and just as important to do on a regular basis.
Display status of members of a multi-access spool	$L SYS	
Display usage of the spool volumes	$D SPOOL	
Initiator control	$T In,xxxx	Assigns the jobclasses xxxx (up to 36) to initiator n. A useful one to have in your automatic commands, unless your initiator structure is controlled by a job-scheduling package.
Interrupt a printer	$I PRTnnnn	Useful when you want to stop a printer in the middle of a long-running print (e.g. to IPL). It does, however, lead to an unsightly break in the middle of the user's print, though the print can be restarted from the beginning using the backspace command.
Issue an MVS command	$VS,'command'	Not necessary if you can issue the MVS command direct, but useful for automatic command scheduling.
Release a held job	$A jobname	
Reset the checkpoint lock	$E SYS,RESET = sysid	Releases the lock held by the specified system — useful when one system in a multi-access spool complex has gone down while holding the lock. Until you issue this command all the other members of the complex will wait for all JES services!
Start a JES2 device	$S devname	Most devices come up with an initial status of active, but some may require a JES start command before you can use them, depending on your initialization parameters.
Start JES activity	$S	This is required after JES2 has been started from MVS's point of view, unless you specify NOREQ in the parameters of the EXEC statement in the JES2 procedure.

Table 4.7. (cont.)

Task	Command	Comment
Stop a JES device (including printers, punches, offload devices, network devices, and even spool volumes)	$P devname	This will change the status of the device to DRAINING until it has finished processing the current dataset — then it will become DRAINED. All devices must be drained before JES will come down cleanly — see the comment above on interrupting printers!
Stop JES	$P $P JES2 $P JES2,ABEND	$P on its own will suspend JES processing (except active devices), so be careful not to specify it by mistake! $P JES2 will bring it all the way down, but only if all devices have been drained. $P JES2,ABEND is more drastic! See Chapter 8 for details.

References and bibliography

TSO/E manuals

Note the order numbers depend on which version of TSO/E you have; those shown here are for version 2.

1. *TSO/E V2 Command Reference*, SC28–1881. Guide to the generally available TSO/E commands.
2. *TSO/E V2 Command Reference Summary*, GX23–0015. A mid-sized ring-bound reference book.
3. *TSO/E V2 Systems Programmers Command Reference*, SC28–1878. Covers restricted commands such as ACCOUNT, OPER, and PARMLIB.
4. *TSO/E V2 Programming Guide*, SC28–1874. Includes useful explanation of how to use TSO TEST and a TEST tutorial.
5. *TSO/E V2 CLISTS*, SC28–1876. Guide to writing CLISTs and documentation on CLIST statements.
6. *TSO/E V2 REXX User Guide*, SC28–1882. Guide to writing REXX EXECs.
7. *TSO/E V2 REXX Reference*, SC28–1883. Documentation of REXX statements.

Utilities manuals

8. *DFDSS User's Guide*, SC26–4388.
9. *DFDSS Reference*, SC26–4389.
10. *MVS/XA SPL: Service Aids*, GC28–1159.
11. *MVS/ESA SPL: Service Aids*, GC28–1844.
12. *DSF User Guide and Reference*, GC35–0033.
13. *DSF: Primer for the User of 3380 and 3390 DASD*, GC26–4498. Short and highly readable description of DASD I/O error processing — recommended!
14. *Getting Started with DFSORT*, SC26–4109.
15. *MVS/DFP V3R2 Access Method Services for ICF*, SC26–4562.
16. *MVS/DFP V3R2 Access Method Services for VSAM catalogs*, SC26–4570.
17. *Cache Device Administration*, GC35–0101. Documents the AMS LISTDATA and SETCACHE commands.
18. *MVS/ESA Data Administration: Utilities*, SC26–4516.

Console commands manuals

19. *MVS/ESA Operations: System Commands*, GC28–1826. Chapter 1 is a task-oriented guide to the commands, Chapters 2 and 3 deal with console control, and Chapter 4 is an alphabetical reference guide to the commands.
20. *MVS/ESA Operations: System Commands Reference Summary*, GX22–0013. Reference booklet, showing commands in alphabetical order.
21. *MVS/XA Operations: System Commands*, GC28–1206. The XA version.
22. *MVS/ESA Operations: JES2 Commands*, SC28–1039. Commands are gathered together into functionally-related chapters.
23. *MVS/ESA Operations: JES2 Command Syntax Booklet*, SX22–0011. Reference booklet showing commands in alphabetical order.
24. *MVS/XA Operations: JES2 Commands*, SC23–0064. XA version of [22].
25. *VTAM Operation*, SC31–6408. Documents the D NET, F NET, and V NET commands.
26. *MVS/ESA SPL: JES2 Initialization and Tuning*, SC28–1038. Documents which JES2 initialization parameters can be modified by an operator command.

5
SMP/E

5.1   SMP/E fundamentals

5.1.1   Introduction to SMP/E

System modification product/extended (SMP/E) is a product supplied by IBM to control the application of maintenance and upgrades to your software portfolio. Its main functions are:

- To provide a controlled process for building new product libraries.
- To protect the integrity of your system software libraries by preventing the application of updates which are inconsistent with your existing software (e.g. because you have not applied other updates which are prerequisites to this one).
- To provide facilities which enable you to enquire on the status of your software (e.g. what fixes have been applied already), and to back out changes which prove to be in error.

All modifications to your MVS system should be made using SMP/E, or your SMP/E database (known as its consolidated software inventory, CSI) will cease to reflect the true status of your product libraries, and SMP/E will no longer be able to protect the integrity of your software. Because suppliers depend on SMP/E to protect the integrity of their software, you should always use SMP to install a product if the supplier provides the necessary input for you to do this; and you must apply any maintenance to SMP-installed products using SMP. Likewise, any inhouse modifications to SMP-installed products must be done using SMP.

This makes SMP/E a key tool for the systems programmer, and although it is a complex and sometimes confusing one, you will get to appreciate all the things that SMP/E does for you. Any time you devote to learning how it works, how to maintain your SMP environment, and how you should use it will be time well spent.

This chapter begins by discussing the basic terms and concepts of SMP, then looks at the standard SMP processes you will use frequently — RECEIVE, APPLY, and ACCEPT — and goes on to deal more briefly with problem resolution, special SMP processes, and customizing SMP. Note that throughout this chapter I use the terms SMP and SMP/E interchangeably. This is normal practice, though in theory the term SMP only refers to older releases of the product.

5.1.2   Basic SMP terminology

For SMP's purposes, all of the software it controls and all changes to it are packaged as system modifications (SYSMODs), of which there are various types:

- FUNCTIONS are the closest to our idea of 'products', although one product often contains multiple FUNCTIONs.
- PTFs are permanent fixes
- APARs are problems and also temporary fixes for them
- USERMODs are modifications made by the user site (you!) or any third party.
- A SYSMOD consists of (a) modification control statements (MCSs), and (b) the text of the module(s) or modification itself. The MCSs describe the modification and the module(s) concerned to SMP, including characteristics such as the format of the text supplied (object module, source code, etc.), where to find/put the modules concerned, what function the SYSMOD belongs to (its function modification identifier, FMID), and its dependencies on other SYSMODS.

We tell SMP what to do with these SYSMODs by running batch jobs that invoke the SMP program and supply it with an input stream of SMP commands. These often do large amounts of validity checking and invoke other programs to perform installation functions. As a result they can run for long periods of time — major product installations can literally take hours to run. SMP can also be invoked from ISPF dialogs, which provide a subset of the functions available in batch.

SMP keeps a record of the SYSMODs under its control in a VSAM dataset (or group of datasets) known as a consolidated software inventory (CSI). Each CSI consists of multiple zones, and each zone contains logical groups of records describing SYSMODs, modules, datasets, options, etc. The group of records describing a given entity is known as an entry, and it may consist of various subentries describing different aspects of the entity.

There are three types of zone: global, target, and distribution. The global zone (of which there is only one per CSI) acts as an index to the zones themselves and controls as yet uninstalled SYSMODs. Each target zone controls SYSMODs installed into one set of target libraries (TLIBs) — in theory the libraries from which the product is to be executed, though in practice it is sometimes executed from copies of the target libraries. Each distribution zone controls SYSMODs installed into one set of distribution libraries (DLIBs). These libraries contain all the elements (source code, object code, macros, etc.) required to build any or all of the modules in the target libraries, and therefore provide the input required to rebuild the target libraries from scratch or back out any changes to the target libraries if they prove to be in error.

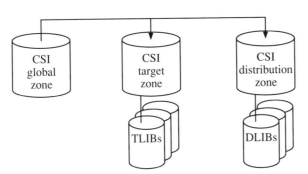

Figure 5.1. CSI zones and product libraries.

Figure 5.1 illustrates the relationships between the CSI zones and the main product libraries they control. Arrows indicate that the 'pointing' zone contains entries describing elements in the dataset or zone pointed to.

5.1.3   SMP processes

The key SMP processes are those invoked by the RECEIVE, APPLY, and ACCEPT commands. The normal procedure for installing a SYSMOD is to RECEIVE, APPLY, and then ACCEPT it. This procedure is illustrated in Fig. 5.2 and each of these processes is outlined briefly below. We will go into much more detail on all three of them in Sec. 5.2.

The RECEIVE process takes SYSMODs from a dataset outside SMP's control, moves them into SMP-controlled libraries, and builds the CSI entries to describe them, so that they are available for querying and then for input into subsequent processes. The source of the SYSMODs is often a product tape or fix tape from

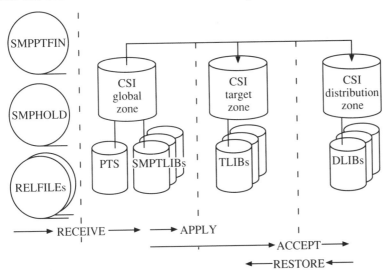

Figure 5.2. SMP/E processes.

IBM or a third-party software supplier. The work done by the RECEIVE process includes:

- Checking that the construction of the SYSMODs is valid (e.g. the syntax of the modification control statements) and that they relate to products installed in the CSI.
- Building entries in the global zone describing the SYSMODs.
- Loading the SYSMOD into SMP-controlled libraries, such as the 'PTF temporary store' library.
- By default, also reading in HOLDDATA, which is a series of modification control statements used to tell SMP about problems with previously or concurrently supplied SYSMODs.

As with all the SMP commands, there are many optional parameters on the RECEIVE command, most notably a number which allow you to select specified SYSMODs or groups of SYSMODs to be RECEIVEd out of all those available in the input dataset. The APPLY process can then be invoked to take selected SYSMODs from the global zone and attempt to install them into the target libraries in the selected target zone. The work it does includes:

- Checking the relationship of the new SYSMODs with others already installed into the zone concerned. For example, if the CSI entry for the new SYSMOD states that another SYSMOD is a prerequisite of this one, SMP will only proceed to install the new one if the prerequisite is already installed.
- Invoking the appropriate utility to install the SYSMOD into the target library. The utility selected will depend on the type of input text supplied and the type of target module being modified. For example, if the SYSMOD's text consists of assembler source and the target module is a load module, SMP will invoke the assembler and linkage editor. The target library's DDNAME will be found in the CSI entry of the target module being updated, or will be supplied in the CSI entry of the SYSMOD for a new target module. SMP will allocate a dataset to this DD name, either using a DD statement supplied by you in the JCL for the current SMP run, or more commonly using its own CSI entries (known as DDDEFs) which describe datasets to be dynamically allocated.
- Modifying the CSI entries of the updated modules to show they were updated by the SYSMOD, and creating an entry for the SYSMOD itself in the CSI. Any type of failure will be reported in the printed output.

Once a SYSMOD has been installed into its target library and tested satisfactorily it can be ACCEPTed. This process takes the selected SYSMODs and attempts to install them into the associated distribution libraries in a similar manner to the APPLY process. The ACCEPT process:

- Checks the target zone CSI entries for the modules and SYSMODs concerned in the same way as APPLY, to ensure the updates you are making to the distribution libraries are consistent with the elements already present there.

- Creates or rebuilds the elements affected by the SYSMOD(s) in the distribution libraries, using the text of the SYSMOD as input and invoking the appropriate utilities, depending on the format of the input text and of the element to be modified.
- Updates the CSI entries of affected elements in the distribution zone in the same way as APPLY does in the target zone.
- Cleans up various items which should no longer be required, deleting, for example, the global zone CSI entries, PTS members, and SMPTLIBs for the SYSMODs concerned.

Should the SYSMOD prove to be in error, however, you should not ACCEPT it — instead, you use the RESTORE process, which takes the modules updated by the selected SYSMOD and rebuilds the copies in the target libraries, using the related modules in the distribution libraries as input. RESTORE also updates the target zone CSI entries to reflect the removal of the SYSMOD. Once you have ACCEPTed a SYSMOD, it is no longer possible to back it out using RESTORE.

5.1.4   SMP datasets

In addition to its CSIs (to which we return in the following sections), SMP uses numerous other datasets, both permanent and temporary. The key ones are listed in Table 5.1, by DDNAME, showing their functions and key attributes. For a full list of SMP datasets and their functions, see the chapter 'SMP/E datasets' of [1].

Usually most of these datasets are dynamically allocated by SMP, and it will be part of your job to ensure the definitions SMP uses to do its dynamic allocation are correct. These definitions are in different places for different DDNAMEs. Most SMP datasets are defined by DDDEF entries in the CSI zone, which can be queried and updated either in batch or using the ISPF dialogs. However, for some files, dynamic allocation information can be supplied in the GIMMPDFT table, which you must code and assemble as part of SMP customization, and for some, there is also default allocation information defined in the SMP programs which will be used if neither DDDEF nor GIMMPDFT data is available. Finally, the CSI zones themselves can be dynamically allocated on the basis of the CSI=dsname parameter in the PARM field of the JCL EXEC statement (for the global zone) or the dataset names held in the global zone's GLOBALZONE ZONEINDEX subentry.

There are lists of the files required for each command at the end of the chapter on the command in [1], but most of the time you will be able to leave most of the datasets to be dynamically allocated and specify only the bare minimum in your JCL.

Table 5.1. Major SMP/E datasets

DDNAME	Function of dataset	Dataset attributes
SMPCSI	Consolidated software inventory — a database of SYSMODs, datasets, etc., under SMP's control	One or more VSAM clusters
zonename	Target or distribution zone of the CSI — zonename is defined by the user	Either a VSAM cluster or a logical subset of one cluster for the whole CSI
tlib	Target library — contains the code of one or more of the software products under SMP's control — DDNAME generally corresponds to low-level qualifier of dataset name	Partitioned dataset
dlib	Distribution library — contains components required to rebuild members of target libraries if a change to the target library needs to be backed out. DDNAME generally corresponds to low-level qualifier of dataset name	Partitioned dataset
SMPCNTL	Input dataset containing SMP commands to be executed	Card-image dataset. Always required.
SMPPTFIN	Input dataset containing SYSMODs to be RECEIVEd	Card-image dataset
SMPHOLD	Input dataset containing HOLDDATA to be RECEIVEd	Card-image dataset
SMPOUT	SMP message printfile (RPT and LIST output also comes here if SMPRPT and SMPLIST are not separately defined)	SYSOUT dataset
SMPRPT	SMP report printfile	SYSOUT dataset
SMPLIST	Printfile for output from the LIST command	SYSOUT dataset
SYSPRINT	Printfile for output from utilities invoked by SMP (e.g. IEBCOPY and the assembler)	SYSOUT dataset
SMPPUNCH	SMP command file punched out by the UNLOAD, GENERATE, and REPORT commands	Card-image output file
SMPLOG	History log	Sequential dataset. Always required.
SMPLOGA	Alternate history log	Sequential dataset. Always required.
SMPPTS	PTF temporary store used to hold RECEIVEd SYSMODs	Card-image partitioned dataset
SMPMTS	Macro temporary store — intermediate library for storage of macros which are updated or replaced by an APPLY but do not reside in a target library	Card-image partitioned dataset
SMPSTS	Source temporary store—like SMPMTS, but for source which is updated/replaced by an APPLY and does not reside in a target library	Card-image partitioned dataset
SMPTLIBs	Temporary libraries used to hold SYSMODs RECEIVEd from RELFILEs on tape	Partitioned datasets
SYSUT1–4 SMPWRK1–5	Work and scratch datasets used by utilities invoked by SMP	Temporary files

Key	Entry	Subentry
0000...	GLOBALZONE	ZONEINDEX

Zonename	Type	Datasetname
GLOBAL	G	CSI.MVS
TGT1	T	CSI.MVS
DST1	D	CSI.MVS

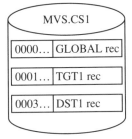

Figure 5.3. Single dataset CSI.

5.1.5   *CSI structures*

There are two main questions to be answered when configuring a CSI:

1   Will it be held in one VSAM cluster for all zones, or will some zones be in separate clusters of their own?
2   Will there be single or multiple target and distribution zones in the CSI? (There can only be one global zone.)

The CSI can be configured as either a single VSAM cluster, with all zones contained within it, or with a separate cluster for one or more of the zones. The GLOBALZONE ZONEINDEX subentry includes the dataset name of each zone, and when a cluster is divided between multiple zones SMP manages the logical division of the cluster transparently to the user. In fact, the two high-order bytes of the key of each record in the CSI indicate which zone it belongs to, so when a CSI is shared, each zone is represented by a separate key range. Figures 5.3 and 5.4 show the two options.

If you are installing a CBIPO and follow the defaults, the CBIPO jobs will set up a CSI with multiple datasets, putting the target zone dataset on the same volume as your target libraries, and the distribution zone dataset on the same volume as the distribution libraries. This is a great configuration for backup/restore purposes: if you backup the volumes regularly and then make an error in your installation, you can restore the pack concerned and still be confident that the libraries you have restored are accurately reflected in the corresponding CSI zone — they were backed up together and therefore should have been consistent at the time of the backup. For simpler installations, however, it is common to have all zones of your CSI in a single dataset.

Key	Entry	Subentry
0000...	GLOBALZONE	ZONEINDEX

Zonename	Type	Datasetname
GLOBAL	G	CSI.GLOBAL.MVS
TGT1	T	CSI.TGT1.MVS
DST1	D	CSI.DST1.MVS

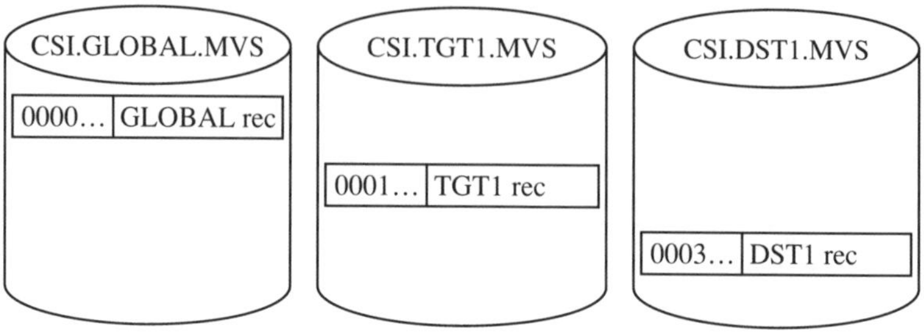

Figure 5.4. Multiple dataset CSI configuration.

The other configuration option is to include multiple target and distribution zones in your CSI. One reason for doing this might be to maintain two copies of a piece of software, both of them under SMP's control: for example, a testing and a production version of MVS, where fixes were APPLIED to the test zone, tested, then APPLIED to the production zone if they tested out satisfactorily. Personally I do not favour this approach — see Chapter 11 where I outline an SMP/backout strategy for your MVS system datasets.

Another reason for using multiple target and distribution zones might be to use the single global zone in the CSI as an index to all the SMP-controlled software on your system, by connecting up all new target and distribution zones to the same CSI. Though this sounds superficially attractive, I would not recommend this either. The normal process with new CBIPOs is to set up a new CSI every time and throw away your old ones after implementing the new system. If instead you had connected the new target and distribution zones to the old global zone, you would either be left with redundant zones lying around, and redundant entries in your global zone for SYSMODs in the redundant zones, or be faced with the tedium and risk of deleting these redundant zones and entries from your global zone. As in many other areas of systems programming, then, the trick is to keep things as simple as possible — keep one CSI for each CBIPO product group (MVS, NCP, CICS, and IMS/DB2, if you have all of these), and one or more for third-party software. The only disadvantage of this approach is that you will have to remember a number of CSI names, and remember to change your SMP JCL depending on which product you are working with. You should minimize this problem by documenting your CSI names in your inhouse system manual.

5.1.6 CSI entries

The groups of records in your CSI describing libraries, SYSMODs, modules, and other SMP entities are known as entries. There are three types: CONTROL, STATUS, and STRUCTURE entries.

CONTROL entries describe:

- Zones — pointers from the global zone to the rest, self-describing entries in all zones, and pointers to the associated distribution zone in each target zone.
- Datasets to be dynamically allocated by SMP (DDDEF entries).
- Processing options such as what program name to use for copy, assemble, and link operations (OPTIONS and UTILITY entries).
- Logical groupings of FUNCTIONs (FMIDSET entries).

These, and the other types of entry, are discussed in more detail in the chapter 'SMP dataset entries' of [1]. Some of them can be modified from the SMP/E dialogs, and they can all be modified using the UCLIN command. The control entries will generally be created for you by CSI initialization jobstreams supplied with a new product, so you are more likely to need a detailed understanding of the STATUS and STRUCTURE type entries.

STATUS entries describe SYSMODs and the relationships between them. They also describe the type of input text and the module(s) to which it is to be applied. They are created in global zones by the RECEIVE command, in target zones by the APPLY command, and in distribution zones by the ACCEPT command. Ordinary SYSMOD entries will list:

- prerequisite SYSMODs — SYSMODs which must be installed before this one can be
- corequisite SYSMODs — SYSMODs that must be installed before or at the same time as this one
- PTFs and APARs which are superseded by this one
- conditional requisites (meaning in effect 'if you have function x installed you must apply fix y as well as this one')

In the global zone only, there may also be HOLDDATA entries, which describe SYSMODs that SMP will HOLD (i.e. prevent you installing) until you have taken some other action. This is used in two main ways:

1 To stop you installing PTFs which were sent out and subsequently found to be in error
2 To force you to check documentation and take any necessary actions when the PTF requires other changes in the system

STRUCTURE entries, of which there are five types, describe the modules making up your products:

1 LMOD entries describe load modules.

2   MOD entries describe object modules.

3   SRC entries describe source modules.

4   MAC entries describe macros.

5   Data element entries describe other modules, e.g. clists or procedures.

The description of each module includes information about which library it is in and what relationship it has with other modules. In effect, this is information like: 'load module x is created by assembling and linking together source modules y and z with the following link-edit control statements ...' or 'macro a is used in source modules b and c' — though it is not held in quite such a comprehensible form as this! SMP needs information like this so that when source module y or macro a is changed by a PTF, SMP knows what to do with the supplied text to produce the correct effect on the load modules that were built using the module being changed. If you need to construct a SYSMOD yourself, you will also need to know how to code modification control statements that will be translated by SMP into structure entries like these.

5.1.7   SYSMOD construction

As was said earlier, SYSMODs consist of two parts: the modification control statements describing them, and the text, which is the source, control statements, or object module to be installed. The MCSs are 80-byte records distinguished by keywords beginning with the characters '+ +', while the text itself can be supplied instream with the MCS (the normal method for maintenance SYSMODs), held in a library and pointed to by the MCS (a common method for USERMODs), or supplied in separate files on the installation tape known as RELFILEs (usually only used when a whole product is being installed or reinstalled).

The first record in any SYSMOD must be a header modification control statement, which identifies the type of SYSMOD and its individual name. The header will be a + +FUNCTION, + +PTF, + +APAR, or + +USERMOD statement, depending on the type of SYSMOD. In the case of function-type SYSMODs, the name on this statement is known as the function modification identifier (FMID). The header is followed by statements identifying the relationship of the SYSMOD with others:

*   The + +VER statement (required) specifies the system release (SREL) to which the SYSMOD applies (always Z038 for MVS CSIs), the FMID of the function being modified (unless this is a FUNCTION SYSMOD) and any prerequisite/corequisite/superseded PTFs.
*   Conditional requisites are identified at this stage with + +IF statements.
*   Any hold reasons are represented with + +HOLD statements.
*   Statements can also be included which instruct SMP to move, rename, or delete existing modules to make way for the new one, though these are rarely used.
*   Element control statements define the elements to be modified, which libraries

Table 5.2. SMP/E element modification control statements

Modification control statement	Nature of associated text
++MAC	A macro replacement
++MACUPD	A macro update (IEBUPDTE control statements)
++SRC	A source replacement
++SRCUPD	A source update (IEBUPDTE control statements)
++MOD	An object module
++ZAP	IMASPZAP control statements
Data element	Data of various types, e.g. TSO clists
MCS statements, e.g. ++CLIST or ++PROC	(++CLIST) and procedures (++PROC)

they are in, and their relationship with other modules.

• The information in the element control statements can be added to using ++JCLIN statements, which are discussed further in Sec. 5.1.8.

Table 5.2 lists the element control statements. Note: some data element types can be supplied in various languages, and in these cases the last three characters of the MCS name indicate the language, e.g. ++PNLENU (for ISPF panels in US English) or ++MSGESP (for ISPF message members in Spanish). See the section on data elements in the MCS chapter of [1] for a full list of data element MCS statements.

Example 5.1 illustrates the method of constructing a SYSMOD — this is the SMPPTFIN input to define a USERMOD which will zap a piece of IBM code. Note: this USERMOD is modifying module IFG0194F, which belongs to function HDP2210 (a component of DFP release 2 version 2). It supersedes an earlier mod (TMS0001) and has as a prerequisite the fix UZ84798. The control statements for the zap are instream, following the ++ZAP element modification control statement (do not confuse the VER statement, which is to be an input to AMASPZAP when it is invoked at APPLY time, with the ++VER statement, which is an MCS for SMP's internal use!).

```
++USERMOD (UMOD005) .
++VER (Z038)   PRE(UZ84798) SUP(TMS0001) FMID(HDP2210) .
++ZAP (IFG0194F) .
  NAME   IFG0194A IFG0194F
  VER    0962   D501A01A3E17,472039C0
  REP    0962   1BFF,47F03F7E,47000000
/*
```

Example 5.1. SMP/E modification control statements.

```
//SMPPTFIN DD DATA,DLM=QQ
++USERMOD (UMOD024) .
++VER (Z038) FMID(HHM2402) .
++JCLIN .
//SYS006A JOB (DXSYSUMOD),'UMOD024'
//LINK    EXEC PGM=IEWL
//SYSLMOD  DD  DSN=SYS1.LINKLIB,DISP=SHR
//SYSLIN   DD  *
  INCLUDE SYSPUNCH(ARCBDEXT)
  NAME ARCBDEXT(R)
/*
++SRC(ARCBDEXT) DISTLIB(ASAMPLIB) .
QQ
//         DD DSN=INSTALL.UMOD.SOURCE(UMOD024),DISP=SHR
```

Example 5.2. ++JCLIN.

5.1.8   ++JCLIN modification control statements

In addition to the element modification control statements discussed in the
previous section, a ++JCLIN statement may be supplied (before the element
control statements). The ++JCLIN statement indicates that the lines following it
are sample JCL from which SMP is to extract additional information about the
modules concerned. The JCL supplied with a ++JCLIN statement is not executed
at any time — instead, SMP reads it in and interprets it, extracting the implicit
relationships and adding the information to its CSI entries. Example 5.2 shows the
++JCLIN input for a ++MOD element which supplies linkage editor control
statements to define the relationship between the object module and a load module.

Note that SMP ignores anything in the JCLIN jobstream that is not meaningful
to it, so there is little point in supplying jobclasses, region sizes, or numerous other
parameters, and it is vital to use the PGM names which SMP recognizes. Note also
that although these jobstreams are never supposed to be executed, they will be if
you forget your basic JCL and fail to code DD DATA,DLM=xx on the instream
input file. This could have very nasty consequences — you could easily update live
system libraries. This is another good reason for leaving off parameters which SMP
ignores but which JES requires on valid jobstreams!

The JCLIN process and its implications are somewhat complex, but very
important to a practical understanding of SMP processing. Example 5.2, again an
SMPPTFIN input stream, illustrates a typical usage of ++JCLIN. Note that this
USERMOD is updating function HHM2402 (DFHSM version 2 release 4) by
adding a new load module, ARCBDEXT, which is supplied in source format
(technically instream, although in fact the source itself is in the concatenated
dataset INSTALL.UMOD.SOURCE(UMOD024)). The ++JCLIN input will
be interpreted by SMP to mean that at APPLY time, after the supplied source has
been assembled into the work file SYSPUNCH, it should be link-edited using the
link-edit statements supplied here into the target library with the DDNAME
LINKLIB. Note that the target library DDNAME is taken from the low-level

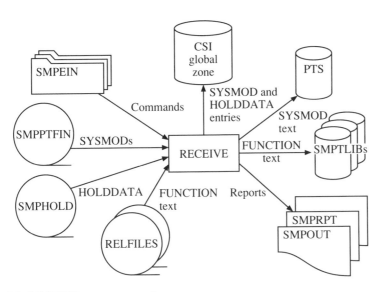

Figure 5.5. RECEIVE process overview.

qualifier of the dataset name in the SYSLMOD statement — so you could have obtained the same effect by coding anything. LINKLIB, and the library used at APPLY time will be whatever library is allocated by SMP to the DDNAME LINKLIB. The + +JCLIN is terminated when SMP encounters the next modification control statement, in this case the + +SRC statement. The + +SRC statement names the source module and the distribution library into which it should be copied if and when the SYSMOD is ACCEPTed.

5.2   Standard SMP processes

We are now ready to discuss how you will use SMP in practice, looking in turn at the RECEIVE, APPLY, and ACCEPT processes, and at the normal ways of dealing with service, taking IBM's methods of supplying service as a model. For more detail on the commands discussed in this section see the chapters relating to each command in [1]. The reports they produce are documented in a separate chapter (Chapter 26 in the release 5 version).

5.2.1   RECEIVE processing

The main function of RECEIVE is to load SYSMODs from suppliers' datasets into the SMP environment. This includes copying the text of the SYSMOD into the PTS, creating a CSI entry for the SYSMOD in the global zone, and loading any RELFILES into temporary files known as SMPTLIBs. The SMPTLIBs usually have dataset names like SMPETLIB.fmidname.Fn, where fmidname is the name of the function being installed, and n is a numeric character. Figure 5.5 summarizes the inputs and outputs to the RECEIVE process.

One of the most important processing considerations is the question of which SYSMODs to process. By default, the RECEIVE command will process every SYSMOD in your SMPPTFIN dataset whose SREL and FMID match with an SREL and FMID already present in the global zone (only the SREL has to match for FUNCTION type SYSMODs). It will also process every + +HOLD and + +RELEASE statement in your SMPHOLD dataset whose FMID matches one already present in the global zone. In some cases, this may be exactly what you want to do (e.g. when a new product is RECEIVEd from a product tape) but in others it would lead to you filling up your global zone, PTS, and DASD space with data you will never use (e.g. when attempting to install a single fix from a preventative service tape). In cases like this, you must use the various selection operands available for the RECEIVE command. If you only wish to RECEIVE SYSMODs, use the SYSMODS operand; if you only wish to RECEIVE HOLDDATA, use the HOLDDATA operand. If you only wish to receive specific SYSMODS, use the SELECT keyword to specify these (the EXCLUDE keyword can be used to give the opposite effect). If you only wish to receive SYSMODs relating to specific FMIDs or FMIDSETs, use the FORFMID operand.

Two other operands can also be particularly useful in certain circumstances. The LIST operand lists the MCS of the SYSMODs being RECEIVEd, which is extremely useful if you need to understand what modules the SYSMODs are going to affect and in what way (but LIST generates more data than you can review productively when you are installing a large number of SYSMODs, e.g. a new product). The SOURCEID operand assigns a name that can be used to identify the group of SYSMODs being RECEIVEd in future SMP commands — so, for example, if you specify a long SELECT list with your RECEIVE statement and also specify a SOURCEID, you can select this group of SYSMODs on your APPLY command simply by specifying the SOURCEID without repeating the SELECT list.

As with all SMP processing, you must review the output from your RECEIVE command carefully to check whether it has had the desired effect, as there are a multitude of things that can go wrong. It is not enough to check the job step return code or even the return code for the RECEIVE command listed in the SMPOUT dataset, as these could indicate successful completion when in fact SMP did something completely different from what you intended!

This means you need to familiarize yourself with the format of the SMPOUT and SMPRPT output. The SMPRPT listing consists of a number of reports for each SMP command you have used. Each command which invokes dynamic allocation produces a dynamic allocation report, listing which datasets on which volumes have been allocated to each DDNAME; RECEIVE also produces a 'RECEIVE summary report' and a 'RECEIVE exception SYSMOD data report', which summarize the action taken for SYSMODs and HOLDDATA respectively.

The main points to look for will usually be:

- Non-zero return codes and associated messages in SMPOUT.
- Check the reports in SMPRPT to ensure that the SYSMODs or HOLDDATA you wanted were received, and those you did not were not.
- Check the HOLDDATA listed to see if any SYSMODs you need have been held.
- Look at the MCS listings of the SYSMODs you are interested in to see what they will do (if required).

Common problems are:

- Selection criteria wrongly specified, leading to the wrong SYSMODs (or none at all) being RECEIVEd.
- SYSMODs required not in SMPPTFIN dataset.
- SYSMODs selected not received because there is already an old SYSMOD with this name in the global zone (more common with USERMODs).

Most of these errors are simple to correct and the RECEIVE can then be rerun. If you need to re-RECEIVE a SYSMOD with a given name, you will have to remove the old one from the global zone first using the REJECT command, and if the old version had already been APPLYed, you will have to specify the BYPASS(APPLYCHECK) operand when you rerun the RECEIVE.

5.2.2   APPLY processing

The main purpose of APPLY processing is to install SYSMODs into your target product libraries (your live product libraries will either be the target libraries themselves or copies of them). APPLY processing can be divided into three stages, which we shall call selection, validation, and installation.

Selection

As with RECEIVE, the APPLY command will, by default, attempt to process all apparently eligible SYSMODs in its input dataset. For APPLY, this means all SYSMODs in the global zone which have been RECEIVEd but not yet APPLYed to the target zone you are processing (the name of this zone must be specified in a SET BOUNDARY command before the APPLY command). This is a dangerous default and you should never leave an APPLY step to take this path; otherwise you risk installing, for example, fixes that other people have RECEIVEd in the past and then decided not to APPLY — presumably for a good reason! Instead, use one or more of the selection operands available on the APPLY statement. The SOURCEID, FORFMID, EXCLUDE, and SYSMOD type (FUNCTION, PTF, APAR, and USERMOD) operands cumulatively restrict the SYSMODs to be selected, in other words, only SYSMODs which satisfy all of these criteria will be selected. IBM adopted a different rule for the SELECT statement — any SYSMODs explicitly specified on the SELECT operand will be added to those selected as above, whether or not they satisfy the other criteria. And if you use the SELECT operand without any of the others, only the SYSMODS which you explicitly select will be APPLYed.

The sensible approach is to use only one of these criteria on a single APPLY statement if you can possibly get away with it: e.g. SELECT to specify a small list of fixes to be APPLYed together; SOURCEID to specify a longer list of fixes which you RECEIVEd using the SOURCEID parameter; or FORFMID to install a new product you have just received from a product tape. In addition, you should always use the CHECK operand, which causes APPLY to do the SYSMOD selection and validation process without actually attempting to install the selected SYSMODs, so you can find out what SYSMODs your APPLY command would actually install before you run it in anger.

Validation

The other reason for always running an APPLY CHECK before a full APPLY is that your SYSMODs, once they have wormed their way through your selection criteria, then have to pass a series of validation checks before they can be installed, and APPLY CHECK will also reveal any problems at this stage.

Validation is intended to protect the integrity of your software, and a SYSMOD will fail at the validation stage if any of the following are true:

- The + + VER FMID value (except for FUNCTION SYSMODs) does not match one already present in the target zone, or being installed concurrently.
- Any PRE or REQ SYSMODs specified on the + + VER statement are missing from the target zone (unless they are being installed concurrently, in the case of SYSMODs named on the REQ operand).
- SYSMODs specified on a + + IF statement are missing from the target zone, but the FMID on whose presence the + + IF requirement depends is present in the target zone.
- A previously installed SYSMOD (or one being concurrently installed) supersedes it. This restriction is intended to prevent older fixes from backing out more recent ones if an attempt is made to install them in the wrong order.
- It is attempting to replace or update a target element (e.g. a load module) but does not PRE or SUP the SYSMODs which have previously replaced or updated it (these SYSMODs are identified by the RMID and UMID values for the element). This is also intended to prevent older fixes from backing out more recent ones.
- There is an outstanding (unresolved) + + HOLD statement for this SYSMOD.
- It has been previously APPLYed to this target zone or ACCEPTed into the associated distribution zone.

Given the length of this list, you will probably find that many of your APPLY CHECKs reveal validation problems. So how should you deal with them?

Let us take HOLD problems first. There are three types of hold reasons — ERROR, SYSTEM, and USER — though the third is rarely used. ERROR holds indicate that the SYSMOD is in error, and the reason-id is generally an APAR number. When a fix is available to resolve the error it will either have this APAR number as its SYSMOD-id, or it will SUP this APAR number. This automatically 'resolves' the reason-id, and SMP will validate the old fix OK once you have RECEIVEd the new one and as long as you APPLY both together. So the normal resolution for an ERROR hold is to obtain the resolving fix from the supplier. Alternatively, after consultation the supplier may advise you to put on the original fix without waiting for the resolution of the APAR (e.g. if the original problem has serious consequences but the error in the fix does not) and then you will have to use the BYPASS(HOLDERROR) operand on your APPLY command to force SMP to ignore the reason-id. Take care to check the syntax of this operand, and code the version that releases only specific reason-ids, or you risk inadvertently releasing other held fixes at the same time.

SYSTEM hold reasons are much simpler to deal with. The reason-id here can be:

- DOC Indicates you should check the documentation for points that need to be noted or sometimes modify a manual that is inaccurate after the application of the SYSMOD, due to a change it makes in the way the product functions.
- ACTION Indicates there is some other action you need to take at the same time as applying the SYSMOD.
- USER Someone on your site has held it.

In either of the first two cases, you must LIST the corresponding ++HOLD statement to display the associated text, take whatever action it recommends, then bypass the reason-id with the BYPASS(HOLDSYSTEM) operand on your APPLY command. In the third, you must find out who held it and why!

Other validation errors tend to fall into four groups:

1 Coding errors in your APPLY command.
2 Attempts to re-APPLY a SYSMOD which is already applied. This will usually only be valid for USERMODs — once you have checked that it is valid, you can use the REDO and/or BYPASS(APPLYCHECK) operands to force SMP to APPLY the SYSMOD.
3 Failure to find prerequisite or corequisite SYSMODs in the target zone. You must usually resolve this by finding or obtaining these other fixes and applying them as well. The GROUP and GROUPEXTEND operands of the APPLY command can be very useful here. GROUP has the effect of adding any corequisite SYSMODs to those selected, as discussed in the previous section. This automatically resolves errors due to missing corequisites, as long as the corequisite fixes have been RECEIVEd. GROUPEXTEND takes this a step further by adding SYSMODs which supersede requisite SYSMODs — usually this makes GROUPEXTEND the better option. As a last resort, the

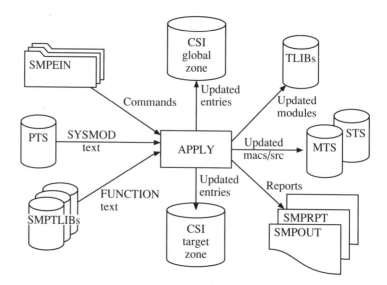

Figure 5.6. APPLY process overview.

BYPASS(ID) operand can also be used to force SMP to APPLY a SYSMOD which fails these checks, but you should never do this unless specifically advised to do so by the supplier of the SYSMOD, or you could seriously compromise the integrity of your software.

4   Failure to PRE or SUP one or more target elements. If this occurs with a SYSMOD from a software supplier, they have either made an error in the MCS, or you are trying to APPLY a SYSMOD out of logical sequence. In either case you must call the supplier and follow their advice to resolve the problem. More interesting is the case where you are trying to APPLY a new USERMOD: here you will have to REJECT the USERMOD (i.e. reverse the RECEIVE command for it); modify the MCS by adding suitable PRE or SUP operands to the + +VER statement; then re-RECEIVE and APPLY the USERMOD.

Installation

Once your SYSMOD has successfully passed through the selection and validation stages of an APPLY CHECK, it is time to run the APPLY itself. This will repeat all the processing in the first two stages, then attempt to install the SYSMOD by invoking the appropriate utility programs. Figure 5.6 gives an overview of the installation stage.

There are still things which can go wrong at this stage! The most common are:

• Failure of the utility due to errors in the text of the SYSMOD, e.g. AMASPZAP VER statements which are inaccurate, or assembler statements which generate assembly errors.

• Failure of the utility due to errors in your SMP setup, e.g. SYSLIB DDDEF does not include the macro libraries required to resolve references in an assembler source module.
• Out-of-space conditions in target libraries.

The first two of these may sometimes be confused, but should not be if your problem determination is up to scratch. All will produce high return codes for the APPLY statement, and any failures in utilities should be diagnosed by referring to the SYSPRINT output produced by the utility. If the failure is due to the supplied text being wrong, you should contact the supplier (fixing it yourself may sometimes seem feasible but could easily lead to disaster!); if the SMP setup is wrong, you should alter it — e.g. by amending the DDDEF using the SMP administration dialog — then rerun the APPLY.

Out-of-space conditions are often avoided by using the RETRY(YES) operand on the APPLY command. This is the default. Its effect is to tell SMP to compress automatically any eligible target library running out of space and retry the installation. Eligible datasets for RETRY are defined in the RETRYDDN subentry of the current OPTIONS entry in the CSI zone being used. This will normally be initialized to the correct values by the supplier, but you may need to amend it if you have defined new target datasets, using the UCLIN command, discussed in more detail in Sec. 5.3.4. Of course, this will not work if the library is still out of space after compression, and you will then be compelled to reallocate the target library with more space (amending the corresponding DDDEF if it specifies the volume serial number and you have had to move the library to a different volume), then rerun the APPLY.

As with RECEIVE, the various reports in the SMPRPT dataset provide useful diagnostic information, and you should familiarize yourself with their formats. Messages in the SMPOUT dataset should always be reviewed — watch out for the word REGRESS which can indicate that a fix has wiped out one of your USERMODs!

5.2.3   ACCEPT processing

ACCEPT processing works in a very similar fashion to APPLY processing, with the same three stages and very similar operands on the ACCEPT command to those on the APPLY command. Once you have successfully applied a group of SYSMODs it is generally a simple process to ACCEPT them — you may need to do nothing more than change the zone in the SET BOUNDARY command, change APPLY to ACCEPT in the command text, and rerun your APPLY job. Figure 5.7 summarizes the processing done by the ACCEPT command.

Potential problems and their resolution are in theory similar to those in the APPLY stage, but in practice you will have resolved most of these during the APPLY stage so there should be little risk of them recurring. Out-of-space problems can of course occur, and are resolved as for APPLY, and problems can

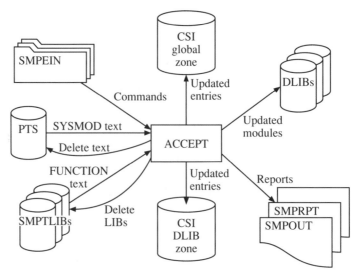

Figure 5.7. ACCEPT process overview.

occur if you attempt to ACCEPT SYSMODs when you have APPLYed but not ACCEPTed their prerequisites.

If anything, the biggest problem with ACCEPT is that it is too easy. Too easy because you could do it almost without thinking, when often you should delay doing it, or not do it at all! ACCEPTing a SYSMOD makes it impossible to back it out using SMP, so you should only do it when you are confident you will not need to back it out. In particular:

- Do ACCEPT base functions and 'integrated service' which comes with them on the product tape, so you have the basic product components in your distribution libraries and hence the ability to back out later updates made by APPLY.
- Avoid ACCEPTing USERMODs
- If you need to apply service to the base module which your USERMOD amends, you may need to remove the USERMOD using RESTORE before applying the service. The USERMOD should then be modified if necessary and re-applied.
- Avoid ACCEPTing additional service until you are confident that it is stable — usually I would recommend waiting until it has proved satisfactory for at least a month in a production environment. You can only use SMP RESTORE to back out to the level of service you have ACCEPTed into your DLIBs, so when you wish to apply more service to the elements that the previous service modified, you should consider raising your distribution libraries to the current level of your target libraries to provide a backout option should the new service cause problems.
- Avoid ACCEPTing some of the fixes on a product but not others. Try to keep

the version in your distribution libraries in line with a known working version of the product as a whole.

5.2.4   APARs, PTFs, and PUTs

Having covered the main SMP processes, it seems appropriate to discuss briefly some of the more common situations in which you may want to use them — those involving the application of IBM maintenance. Third-party maintenance follows similar principles.

When IBM receives information about a problem which it acknowledges to be due to a bug in its software or documentation, it creates an authorized problem analysis report (APAR). If you are one of the earlier sites to experience such a problem, you may be asked to send diagnostic material to your local APAR coordinator, who will forward them to the 'change team' responsible for the product in error. The APAR is allocated a number, and if it was caused by a service SYSMOD, that SYSMOD may be marked 'PE' (program error). IBM does this by issuing a + + HOLD statement for the causing SYSMOD, with the APAR number as the reason-id, in the HOLDDATA on the next program update tape (PUT).

PUTs are maintenance tapes that are issued fairly regularly by IBM, and yours will include fixes for all functions included in your site profile (IBM's record of the products you have installed). PUTs are assigned numbers in the form *yynn*, where *yy* is the last two digits of the year of issue and *nn* is a sequence number — there are usually 6 to 12 of them per year. Once the change team has developed a fix for your APAR, it will be included on a PUT as a program temporary fix (PTF) — in this case 'temporary' means 'until integrated into the base product', or in other words, permanent! If you need a quick fix before this, it may be sent out as an APAR fix — this really is a temporary one, and will usually be replaced by a PTF in due course. Whether or not there is an APAR fix, the PTF will SUP the APAR number, thus releasing the HOLD on the earlier service (it may also SUP the earlier service itself, in which case it will never be applied, but instead is replaced by the new PTF).

From the systems programmer's point of view, there are two types of service: corrective and preventative. Corrective service fixes problems you are actually experiencing, and unless the problems are trivial (i.e. acceptable to your users), you will normally want to apply this. Preventative service fixes problems you are not experiencing, and can sometimes introduce worse problems than those it solves! There is a strong argument against applying preventative service at all, and I recommend you not to do it every time a PUT arrives.

If you are worried that you could miss a potentially serious problem this way, you should order a regular preventative service planning (PSP) tape from IBM, which tells you about high-impact problems you should consider applying fixes for. In practice, though, if there is a problem which affects you, will probably know about it before the PSP arrives anyway. But there is one case when you should always order and check it — when you are installing a new product or a new level of a product. In this situation it is a must to find out about other sites' high-impact problems and how you can avoid them.

In practice, then, you should not APPLY the fixes from a PUT *en masse*, and I would recommend that you do not RECEIVE them *en masse* either, to minimize the danger of inadvertently installing fixes you do not want, and to keep down space utilization in your global zone and PTS. Instead, keep a library of PUTs extending back to the PUT level of the earliest installed piece of software still on your system, and pick off fixes as and when you need them for corrective service. On the other hand, you *should* routinely RECEIVE the HOLDDATA from every PUT when it arrives — this will prevent you from applying a fix that is known to be in error.

When you receive HOLDDATA, you should also make use of the REPORT ERRSYSMODS command — a new feature of release 5 — which will list SYSMODs you have already APPLYed or ACCEPTed which are now in error according to the HOLDDATA in your global zone. As well as listing the SYSMODs in error, this command punches APPLY and ACCEPT statements to put on the corrective fixes, if these fixes have also been RECEIVEd. However, you should beware of gaily slapping these fixes onto your production system! In practice, many of the 'fixing' fixes turn out to be in error themselves, a few PUTs later, and if the error in the new fix has worse consequences than the original one, you will be in trouble. The most sensible approach is to run the REPORT then 'eyeball' the output and determine whether any of the errors are high impact. If you decide that any of them are important enough to you to be worth fixing, check with IBM first, in case there are more problems with the new fixes that have not yet reached the HOLDDATA on the PUTs.

There are SMP dialogs designed to help you RECEIVE and APPLY preventative or corrective service, HOLDDATA, products on product tapes, etc., but I find them very unhelpful, except for generating a sample piece of JCL which you can then copy into your own CNTL library and amend yourself as required.

The downside of not routinely installing preventative service is that when you do need to apply corrective service, you may have to RECEIVE a long chain of prerequisite fixes from a series of different tapes. If you do need to do this, ask the supplier to research all the prerequisites between your current level and the desired PTF and tell you which tapes they are on — otherwise you could spend a very long time running unsuccessful APPLY CHECKs, tracking down the next missing PTF in the chain, then repeating the process until you have completed the chain. The way to keep this problem to a minimum is to reinstall all your products or upgrade them to a reasonably recent maintenance level every 6 to 12 months (or a little longer for very stable third-party products). This is very much simplified by using IBM's CBPDO or CBIPO process to upgrade or install a large group of products *en masse* (see Chapter 7).

5.3   Problem resolution

5.3.1   Querying and listing CSIs

When SMP does not do what you expect, or you need to know what SMP has done in the past (e.g. the last fix applied to a given target element), the first weapons in your armoury are those that tell you what information SMP has in its CSI. There are two of these, the LIST command, and the QUERY dialogs.

The LIST command can list entries from other SMP datasets, such as the PTS, but this can be browsed just as easily using ISPF, so its main value is for interrogating the CSI. It can list the entries describing the zones themselves, and indeed any other entry in the CSI, but the most useful operands tend to be those that list selected SYSMODs or selected elements in the target or distribution zones. For example:

- LIST USERMODS — To list all USERMODs in the zone specified in the preceding SET BOUNDARY statement
- LIST PTF NOACCEPT — To list PTFs in a target zone which have not been ACCEPTed into the related distribution zone
- LIST SOURCEID(aaaaaaaa) ERROR MCS — To list PTFs in error that were assigned the given SOURCEID at RECEIVE time and their associated modification control statements
- LIST FUNCTION — To list all the FMIDs in the zone
- LIST LMOD(aaaaaaaa) XREF — To list the given LMOD entry and show the MOD entries which are linked or copied to this load module
- LIST SYSMOD(aaaaaaaa) XREF — To list the given SYSMOD and all related SYSMODs in the zone

Whatever requirement you have for listing information from the CSI, it is worth checking to see if there is a variant of the LIST command that will do the job.

In some cases, though, the query dialogs are quicker and easier to use — especially when you need more information on one particular entry. I prefer to use option 3.2, the cross-zone query option, which gives a summary of the status of the requested entries across all the zones in the CSI; for a SYSMOD, this gives an at-a-glance picture of whether it has been RECEIVed, APPLYed, and ACCEPTed. Beware, though, of the similarity of two messages: a single asterisk against a zone indicates the SYSMOD is not present (i.e. has not been RECEIVed, APPLYed, or ACCEPTed into the zone, depending on the type of zone); but a double asterisk means the dialog failed to allocate the zone. Once you correct the allocation problem, the SYSMOD may well be there! Another peculiarity is that if you want to find a FUNCTION/FMID, PTF, APAR, or USERMOD, you cannot use these terms on the query entry screen but must enter SYSMOD.

The dialogs are particularly useful for answering questions like:

- What is the status of a given SYSMOD, i.e. which zones is it present in and

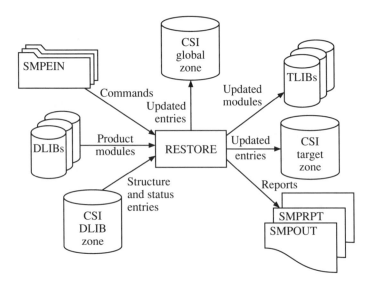

Figure 5.8. RESTORE process overview.

when was it RECEIVed/APPLYed/ACCEPTed?

- What were the last SYSMODs to replace/update a given target element (its RMID and UMID)?
- What link-edit statements and parameters are required to create a given load module? (Query the LMOD entry and continue selecting the line you want until the link-edit information — usually from JCLIN — is displayed.)
- What load module is a given module contained in? (Query the MOD element.)

5.3.2   Backing out changes

SYSMODs can be removed from the global zone using the REJECT command, which effectively reverses the RECEIVE command. Selection operands similar to those used on the APPLY command (but with some additional options) are available. Usually the only time you should need to use this command is to modify a SYSMOD you have already RECEIVEd. Here you will need to REJECT it, modify your input text or MCS, and RECEIVE it again. If you have already APPLYed the SYSMOD you will need to code BYPASS(APPLYCHECK) on the REJECT command.

The RESTORE command is used to reverse the APPLY command, by rebuilding the target elements updated by the SYSMOD being RESTOREd, using the associated elements in the distribution libraries as input (e.g. link-editing object modules from the DLIBs to create a load module in the target library). Figure 5.8 gives an overview of the RESTORE process.

Although this process sounds straightforward, it is actually very dependent on what you have done before: you can only RESTORE the versions of target elements which can be rebuilt from the elements in the distribution libraries, i.e. those at the level of the most recently ACCEPTed SYSMODs. This was discussed in some detail in Sec. 5.2.3, but there are three points worth clarifying here:

1 If you have never ACCEPTed the base product and any integrated service, there may be nothing in the distribution libraries to restore from!
2 If you have already ACCEPTed SYSMODs which prove to be in error, there is no way SMP can back them out using RESTORE.
3 If you have APPLYed multiple SYSMODs to any of the target elements to be RESTOREd since the last ACCEPT which affected them, you will not be able to RESTORE the SYSMODs individually — you will have to RESTORE all of them together. This is not necessarily disastrous, as you should then be able to re-APPLY the good SYSMODs. However, it can lead to some complex recovery situations which are best avoided.

You should avoid getting into any of these situations by following my advice in Sec. 5.2.3. With careful planning, however, there is another recovery option which should get you out of even these holes. It goes like this:

1 Put all your target libraries, the target zone of your CSI, and preferably nothing else, on a single DASD pack.
2 Put all your distribution libraries, your distribution zone, and preferably nothing else, on another single pack.
3 Take backups of these packs after every change and keep these on a cycle of tapes so several versions are available.
4 Now, if any changes need to be backed out, you can simply restore the pack concerned to its state before the change was made — and because the CSI zone and associated libraries were backed up at the same time, they will still be in step after the restore.

As we noted earlier, the CBIPO process makes this dedicated-pack approach straightforward to implement, as by default it allocates the CSI zones on the same pack as the associated libraries. When the pack is shared by other datasets, recovery is still possible, as you can do a selective dataset restore from your pack dump to avoid overwriting the non-SMP-controlled libraries with an out-of-date version.

You can even extend this to the situation where your libraries are spread around a number of packs, by making logical backups of the groups of datasets concerned, though this is more complex and poses maintenance problems for your backup jobs if datasets are moved around (or much more serious problems if you do not do the maintenance then attempt to restore from these backups).

The pack-restore option is probably not one you will wish to use very often, but there may be cases when it is very useful. For example: you have updated your MVS target libraries, tested your updated system, copied the updates to your live system libraries, and now you are experiencing a serious system problem as a result of your updates; you would probably be happier doing a quick restore from a backup to get your system back to a known stable state than trying to construct and run an SMP RESTORE job.

In Chapter 11, we will see how this option can be used as part of various SYSRES maintenance and recovery strategies.

5.3.3   Administration dialogs

The SMP administration dialogs allow you to view, amend, add, and delete certain types of CSI entries — specifically DDDEF entries and entries related to zone definitions and options. DDDEFs are the most likely of these to require amendment once you have completed the initial setup of your SMP zones. Whenever you move an SMP-controlled dataset, rename one, or install a new product that uses libraries not previously controlled by SMP, you should review the DDDEF entries and possibly amend them or add new ones. If you do not, you will encounter problems the next time you try to use SMP on these libraries. The administration dialogs are fairly self-explanatory, so we will not go into more detail here.

5.3.4   UCLIN

The UCLIN command is the ultimate weapon for seeing off problems related to your SMP CSI. There are numerous options for adding, amending, and deleting CSI entries and subentries of all kinds. However, the danger of this command is directly proportional to its power — you can easily destroy the integrity of your CSI, and therefore of the software it controls, by misguided use of UCLIN, for example by altering the relationships SMP believes to exist between modules and then applying related service. It is very important, then, that you carefully research the structure and meaning of any entries you wish to change using UCLIN, and the exact command you propose to use, before attempting it (see the chapter entitled 'CSI entries' in [1] for detailed explanations of these). Even UCLIN recommended by software suppliers should be reviewed and understood before running it.

You should always back up your CSI and LIST out the relevant entries before running any UCLIN, then LIST them again afterwards and check that the effect was as expected.

Finally, before developing any UCLIN of your own, spend some time researching alternative ways of solving your problem — you may find a solution which is cleaner. Using UCLIN is generally an admission of defeat; the option exists because SMP and the environments it controls are far too complex for standard solutions always to work, but it breaks the unwritten rule of SMP — that changes to CSIs should always be simultaneous with equivalent changes to the product libraries they reflect.

5.4   Special SMP processing

5.4.1   Unusual installation processes

Although the RECEIVE–APPLY–ACCEPT sequence is the normal method of installing functions and service using SMP/E, it is possible to use other methods in certain circumstances. This should only be done on the recommendation of the software supplier, i.e. if a different process is outlined in the installation documentation. The various alternative processes are outlined in the chapter 'Installing a new function' of [2].

We will discuss only one of the alternative methods here, which is of particular interest to us as it is used by the CBIPO process to build MVS systems. Prior to version 4, MVS installation included a process known as system generation, which had to be integrated into the CBIPO installation process. System generation (SYSGEN) begins with the assembly of a stage 1 macro, on which you specify operands describing certain aspects of the MVS system you want to generate. The output from this is a jobstream known as the stage 2 deck, consisting of the assembly and link-edit JCL and control statements required to create the core MVS product modules. In the past, this jobstream would then be submitted to create these modules. This process does not fit easily into the RECEIVE–APPLY–ACCEPT sequence, as it requires user input after the RECEIVE type process and a two-step process thereafter to create the 'target' modules. Furthermore, SYSGEN applies only to the core products — known as the SYSGEN-supported products — and does not generate the many other products usually supplied on the MVS CBIPO tapes.

The CBIPO process for MVS installation therefore uses a very different sequence of SMP commands from the usual one. This is documented in [4]. The sequence used is as follows:

1   It builds the distribution libraries which contain all the elements required to create both the SYSGEN-supported and non-SYSGEN-supported products in your CBIPO order. At this stage it also copies the distribution zone from the CBIPO tapes. This already includes all the entries and JCLIN required to build the non-SYSGEN-supported products — in effect, these have already been RECEIVEd for you and ACCEPTed with the BYPASS(APPLYCHECK) operand.

2   The target zone is built by copying the distribution zone, renaming it, and adding other required entries, such as DDDEFs.

3   If you are building a pre-version 4 system, you create the stage 1 SYSGEN input deck, including parameters describing the products, access methods, etc., to be generated, and run it.

4   The jobstreams produced as the output from stage 1, instead of being executed, are input to SMP as JCLIN data, which SMP uses to construct CSI entries describing how the target modules for SYSGEN-supported products should be constructed.

(Steps 3 and 4 are not required when building a version 4 system.)

5   The SMP/E GENERATE command is then used to create the jobs to build the target libraries. The command analyses the entries in the target zone created by reading in the stage 1 output (for the SYSGEN-supported products), and also those copied previously from the distribution zone (for the others), and uses this information to create jobs which will copy, assemble, and link all the required products from the distribution libraries to the target libraries.

6   The jobs created by GENERATE are then executed.

7   The system modules that are dependent on your I/O configuration are then created by running the MVS configuration program. (Prior to MVS 2.2, this was done by including the I/O definitions in your stage 1 deck, so this additional step was unnecessary — but it meant you had to run a partial SYSGEN every time your I/O configuration changed.)

This should be the most complex installation process you ever come across, but it illustrates the point that you will need a sound understanding of SMP to understand what is going on inside processes like this — and a sound understanding will make it a lot easier to avoid mistakes and correct them when they occur.

Fortunately, IBM is gradually simplifying its installation processes, and two major strides forward have been taken with MVS version 4 (elimination of SYSGEN) and SMP/E release 6, which provides ISPF dialogs for managing the CBIPO process.

5.4.2   USERMODs

We have touched on USERMODs occasionally in the chapter so far, but, as the only type of SYSMOD routinely constructed by systems programmers at user sites, they deserve a section to themselves.

There are numerous ways in which USERMODs can be constructed, and you will find many samples supplied by IBM and other suppliers on which to model your own (see the CBIPO MVS Customisation Guide [5] for numerous examples). IBM's supplied samples, however, are not always suitable examples for what you need to do, and their construction is rarely explained in detail.

Normally, your own USERMODs (as opposed to any from third-party suppliers, such as 'hooks' that have to be inserted in IBM modules to make third-party products work) will consist of source decks which need to be assembled or linked, either into stand-alone load modules (usually exits), or along with IBM modules to replace IBM versions of load modules. The principles of constructing a USERMOD are discussed in the chapter 'Building a user modification' of [2], although this is not very helpful for USERMODs consisting of source to be assembled and link-edited. Example 5.3 illustrates the principles involved.

```
//UMOD     EXEC IPOSMPE,CSI='SMPE220.GLOBAL.CSI'
//SMPEIN   DD    *
  SET BOUNDARY(GLOBAL).
  REJECT    SELECT(UMOD024) BYPASS(APPLYCHECK).
  RESETRC.
  RECEIVE  SELECT(UMOD024) SYSMODS.
  SET BOUNDARY(M220TAA).
  APPLY     SELECT(UMOD024) REDO.
  LIST      SYSMOD(UMOD024).
/*
//SMPPTFIN DD DATA,DLM=QQ
++USERMOD (UMOD024).
++VER (Z038) FMID(HHM2402).
++JCLIN .
//SYS006A JOB  (DXSYSUMOD),'PGMR NAME'
//LINK    EXEC  PGM=IEWL
//SYSLMOD  DD   DSN=SYS1.LINKLIB,DISP=SHR
//SYSPRINT DD   SYSOUT=*
//SYSLIN   DD   *
 INCLUDE SYSPUNCH(ARCBDEXT)
 NAME ARCBDEXT(R)
/*
++SRC(ARCBDEXT) DISTLIB(ASAMPLIB) .
QQ
//          DD DSN=INSTALL.UMOD.SOURC(UMOD024),DISP=SHR
/*
```

Example 5.3. USERMOD to add a stand-alone exit.

Note that:

- This jobstream installs an HSM exit from a source file.
- You should make your jobstreams for installing USERMODs rerunnable, as they are unlikely to work perfectly first time, and even if they do, you may later want to change the modification and replace it. The commands used in SMPEIN in this example achieve this: REJECT removes the previously RECEIVEd version of the mod from the global zone; RESETRC resets the return code to zero so the following commands will be attempted even if the REJECT fails (usually because the mod is not in the global zone anyway); and REDO on the APPLY command allows a new version of the same mod to be APPLYed even though an earlier version has been APPLYed before.
- The JCLIN defines the load module to be created from the source. The source is automatically assembled into an object module of the same name in the SYSPUNCH dataset, then SMP uses these link-edit control statements to create a load module and put it in the library whose DDNAME is defined by the low-level qualifier of the SYSLMOD DD statement in our JCLIN.
- The source is packaged using the instream method, although it is actually in a PDS member which is concatenated to the SMPPTFIN file.

There are many different ways of constructing USERMODs, and you should choose the one which is most appropriate to the modification you need to make.

Before leaving USERMODs, I should point out that because they tend to be fairly stable across releases of software (particularly if you have adhered to IBM's recommended programming interfaces), and because they are your own code as opposed to IBM's, you need to keep the source code and JCL for them separate from IBM's libraries — you will throw away IBM's libraries when you upgrade the products concerned, but your USERMODs will need to be kept much more permanently. To make it easy to apply the correct set of USERMODs when you create a new version of your operating system, you should keep the source and JCL for all your USERMODs together, in libraries dedicated to the purpose, and ensure you keep adequate documentation of your USERMODs — some sites, for example, have an ISPF table documenting them, and a dialog to interrogate and update the table.

5.5   SMP implementation and customization

The installation of the SMP/E programs is done in exactly the same way as any other MVS-related product — either through the CBIPO process, or by running SMP RECEIVE, APPLY, and ACCEPT steps (using your previous level of SMP!) against a product tape or CBPDO tape. Note that CBIPO is not dependent on having a copy of SMP on your 'driving' system as it downloads a limited function version to IPO1.LINKLIB before performing the SMP-driven parts of the installation process.

Once the SMP programs have been installed, there are a number of implementation steps you need to perform:

1   Allocate the SMP CSI dataset(s) and 'prime' them by REPROing in the contents of SYS1.MACLIB(GIMZPOOL).
2   Allocate the other permanent SMP datasets.
3   Define the control entries in your CSI. This is usually done by using the UCLIN command to add the required entries, notably the ZONE, OPTIONS, UTILITY, FMIDSET, and DDDEF entries.
4   Modify the default values in the GIMMPDFT CSECT if required. These define the defaults for dynamic allocation of SYSOUT datasets. It is common to zap GIMMPDFT (make it a USERMOD!) to set the SYSOUT classes according to your installation standards.
5   Modify the default values in the GIMUTTBL CSECT if required. These allow you to restrict the utility programs to be invoked by SMP. Usually you can leave this alone, as the default allows you to use any programs.
6   If you need to change the list of assembler instructions which SMP regards as opcodes and those which it regards as macros (listed in SYS1.PARM-LIB(GIMOPCDE)), you must define your own PARMLIB member to override GIMOPCDE — see the chapter 'SMP/E PARMLIB Member Control statements' in [1]. This is rarely required!
7   Modify your ISPF allocations and menus to include the SMP dialogs.

All this is documented in some detail in [3], particularly the chapter 'Initializing the SMP/E system' — and if you install SMP as part of a CBIPO, most of it will be handled for you.

References bibliography

IBM manuals

1. *SMP/E Reference*, SC28–1107. Describes all the SMP commands, datasets, CSI entries, modification control statements, etc.
2. *SMP/E User's Guide*, SC28–1302. A task-oriented guide to SMP.
3. *Installing SMP/E*, SC23–0130.
4. *MVS Custom Built Offerings Planning and Installation*, SC23–0352. An overview of the CBIPO and CBPDO processes.
5. *CBIPO MVS Customization Guide*. (No order number as it is supplied in *IPO1. RIMLIB* on the CBIPO tapes.) Describes CBIPO sample USERMODs.

Other sources

6. Shein, D.: SMP/E for Managers *Enterprise Systems Journal*, February 1991, pp. 100–101. A clear high-level survey of the objectives of SMP/E and how it is used.
7. Eshom, T.: SMP/E part III: APPLY, *Technical Support*, April 1990, pp. 57–60. One of a series of helpful articles on the main SMP processes.

6
Assembler programming for systems programmers

6.1   Introduction

Although systems programming is only occasionally concerned with programming as such, to be fully effective as a systems programmer you will need to become a competent assembler programmer — and one of the most interesting and challenging parts of the job is coding modules and exits which interact with MVS itself.

There are many books and courses available which will teach you the more basic assembler coding principles, and you should follow these up with some practical programming experience to give you a good grasp of these principles. However, there are a number of assembler programming techniques which are unlikely to be covered in application-oriented assembler courses but are essential to systems programmers. The objective of this chapter is to introduce these techniques, and it is therefore assumed throughout that the reader is familiar with the basics of assembler coding.

The coding of exits is discussed further in Chapter 12, which focuses on the range of exit points available and some common uses of them.

Finally, this chapter looks briefly at implementation and customization of the assembler itself. This is an essential systems programming task as many other products rely on the assembler to perform their own installation processes.

6.2   Accessing MVS control blocks

We have already seen, in Chapter 3, that control block chains are fundamental to the functioning of MVS, and Fig. 3.1 illustrated a typical control block chain. Tracing through these chains to find the piece of information you want is equally fundamental to the coding of many system-oriented assembler programs. In order to do this sort of thing you need to know a little about the structure of these chains and how to find their starting points.

Control blocks are chained together by the process of maintaining pointers in each control block to related control blocks. A pointer is an address field holding the virtual storage address of the control block to which it points. You can therefore find a control block from an assembler program if you know: (a) the address of another control block containing a pointer to the block you want; and (b) where in the second control block that pointer is held. More commonly, you will have to trace through several pointers in several different control blocks to find the block you want.

Clearly, you need sources of information concerning: (a) the structure and expected contents of each control block; (b) how to find any given control block; and (c) which control block contains the piece of information you need to locate. Fortunately, IBM provides the answers to (a) and (b) in [3], currently in five fat volumes (prior to ESA this manual was known as the *Debugging Handbook* [4]). For each control block, [3] provides you with the following information:

- The name, function, size, and acronym of the control block.
- The name of the macro which can be used to generate DSECTs for the control block, including symbolic names and offsets for all the fields, and sometimes symbolic names for some of the values which can be assigned to those fields.
- The storage subpool in which the block resides and its storage key.
- Pointers to the control block in other control blocks.
- Rules for serializing access to the block.
- The offset, field type (e.g. bitstring, address, signed decimal, or character), length, name, and usage of each field in the control block.
- Which fields are recognized by IBM as 'programming interfaces', and are therefore likely to remain stable in position and usage across MVS releases. Other fields are documented in these manuals purely for diagnostic purposes, and you should be wary of using them in your programs.

Unfortunately, IBM does not provide you with the answer to (c)! This is one reason for the large numbers of articles by systems programmers in journals like *MVS Update* and *Technical Support* which aim to show how to find and process useful items of information in the MVS control blocks (a particularly useful example is [21]). Some third-party vendors help fill the gap by publishing wallcharts which show the overall structure of the main control block chains (Circle Education does an excellent one on CICS control blocks). Nevertheless, finding out which control block contains the data you need is often still the most difficult part of specifying a program that has to access MVS system information.

Once you have decided which control block you need to access, you will need to work out the route to take to find it. Clearly you must start from a known point, and usually you will have two main choices for your starting point:

1   An address supplied to your program by its caller. It is common for exits in particular to be supplied with the addresses of control blocks they may wish to access, and the documentation for the exit point may explain how to find other relevant control blocks if required.
2   The communications vector table (CVT) is the starting point for most of MVS's control block chains. Its address is always held at offset 16 (hex 10) into the

PSA, and since the PSA can always be found at virtual storage address zero, this provides a fixed point from which to start tracing a chain.

The route from your starting point to your target control block may be short and easy to find, or extremely obscure, but there are various sources which may help you identify it:

- The pointers to your target control block listed in [3] (and the pointers to the blocks containing those pointers, and so on until you get back to a known address!).
- A control block structure diagram, if you can get hold of one.
- Documentation on functions related to your program. For example, if you are coding an exit, the exit point should be documented in the supplier's manuals, and this documentation may include information on how to access relevant control blocks.
- Sample exits and programs provided by IBM and other vendors which provide similar functions to those you are aiming to provide.
- Articles in journals such as *MVS Update* often give examples which show the routes to useful control blocks.

The coding required to scan through a control block chain to find the information you need is illustrated in Example 6.1. Note:

- Gaps in this extract are shown by lines with a period in position 1.
- This example shows the code required to: (a) find the ASCB for each currently active address space in turn; and (b) determine whether the address space is currently occupied by a TSO user. It uses the fact that each active address space has an entry in the chain of command scheduling control blocks (CSCBs) to identify the active address spaces, then uses the address space identifier (ASID) of each of these in turn to index into the address space vector table (ASVT) to the entry for the address space concerned, which supplies a pointer to its address space control block (ASCB). From the ASCB we can then locate various other control blocks which give more information on the address space, and we look for one of these — the terminal status block (TSB). If the address of the TSB is present, then the address space is occupied by a TSO user. If it is not (i.e. it is equal to zero), then it is a batch job or console-started task.
- Beware of assuming you can follow all the pointers from an ASCB which does not belong to your current address space! The ASCBs for address spaces other than its own are accessible to your program because they reside in common storage; but some of the blocks to which they point reside in the private storage of the address space associated with the ASCB. For example, the address space's TCBs reside in its own private virtual storage, so if you attempt to use the pointer to a TCB from another address space's ASCB you will end up pointing not to the TCB you want, but to the area of virtual storage in your own address space with the same virtual storage address. Confusingly, this area

```
*********************************************************************
*     LOCATE CSCB CHAIN (COMMAND SCHEDULING CONTROL BLOCK–       *
*                   ONE FOR EACH ACTIVE AS)                  *
*********************************************************************
       L      R3,CVTPTR        I.E. HEX 10–OFFSET OF CVTPTR IN PSA
       USING  CVTMAP,R3        CVT ADDRESSABILITY
       L      R4,CVTMSER       ADDRESS MSTR SCHED RESIDENT DATA
       USING  BASE,R4          BASEA ADDRESSABILITY
       L      R4,BACHN         POINT TO 1ST CSCB
       USING  CHAIN,R4         CSCB ADDRESSABILITY
       SPACE  2
*********************************************************************
*     MAIN PROCESSING LOOP                                   *
*         - FOR EACH CSCB:                                   *
*         - FIND ASID THEN ASCB AND DETERMINE IF TSU           *
*         - ...                                              *
*********************************************************************
LABL0200 EQU    *
       LH     R5,CHASID        LOAD ASID OF CURRENT AS
       SLL    R5,2             MULTIPLY BY 4
       L      R6,CVTASVT       POINT TO AS VECTOR TABLE
       USING  ASVT,R6          ASVT ADDRESSABILITY
       L      R6,ASVTENTY-4(R5)  INDEX INTO ASVT TO FIND ASCB ADDRESS
       USING  ASCB,R6          ASCB ADDRESSABILITY
       ICM    R7,B'1111',ASCBTSB  POINT TO TERM STATUS BLOCK
       BZ     LABL0300         IF ASCBTSB IS ZERO, THIS IS NOT A TSU
.
.(code to extract info for each TSO user goes here)
.
*******************************    LOOP TO NEXT CSCB ENTRY *******
LABL0300 EQU    *
       L      R4,CHPTR             NEXT CSCB ADDRESS
       LTR    R4,R4                END OF CHAIN?
       BZ     LABL0400             YES–NORMAL TERMINATION
       B      LABL0200             NO–LOOP
.
.
.
       PRINT  NOGEN
       CVT    DSECT=YES,LIST=NO
       IEEBASEA             MSTR SCHED RESIDENT DATA
       IEECHAIN             CSCB
       IHAASVT              ASVT
       IHAASCB              ASCB
```

Example 6.1. Tracing through a control block chain.

may also contain a TCB, since the process by which TCBs are created tends to give them the same addresses in many address spaces but, if so, it will be one of the TCBs for your own address space, not one belonging to the address space you wanted to find out something about! If you are unsure whether you will encounter this effect with a control block, check the entry for it in [3] to find out what subpool it is allocated in. There is a table in [2] that tells you which subpools are in common and which in private storage areas.

• The code starts by loading the address of the CVT — note that CVTPTR actually represents an EQU statement which sets this symbol to an absolute value of decimal 16, while all the other control block mapping symbols used in the example represent base-displacement addresses which depend on: (a) the starting address for the control block concerned being loaded into a register; (b) a USING statement establishing addressability for the control block using that register as a base; and (c) a macro being coded to generate the DSECT referred to in the USING statement.

- The last five lines of this example are the mapping macros used to generate the DSECTs referenced in the extract. With the exception of the CVT macro, which is in SYS1.MACLIB, these macros are found in SYS1.MODGEN (SYS1.AMODGEN prior to MVS/ESA), which therefore needs to be included in your SYSLIB concatenation for your assembly step. The PRINT NOGEN statement prevents some very large DSECT listings appearing in your assembly output, and these listings merely duplicate the information you can find in [3] — omit this statement if you want to see the DSECTs which are generated.
- To appreciate the example fully, you should refer to the descriptions of the CVT, BASEA, CSCB, ASVT, and ASCB control blocks in [3].

Whenever you write code which deals with MVS control blocks, you must also remember that MVS is both a multiprogramming and a multiprocessing operating system. 'Multiprogramming' implies that your task can be interrupted and other tasks executed on the same processor in between one instruction and the next in your program, while 'multiprocessing' implies another task can be executing on another processor simultaneously with your task. Clearly both of these make it possible that the control blocks you are looking at could change while your program is executing. Even worse, any updates you make to these control blocks could be reversed out by another task which is updating the same control block concurrently (or vice versa — your code could reverse out another task's updates). In either case, you could obtain unpredictable results or abends in your code, and if you inadvertently interfere with updates being made by other tasks you could cause all sorts of problems in those tasks as well.

The most obvious way to deal with this problem is to serialize access to the control blocks. Some of the serialization mechanisms which MVS provides, such as locks and intersects, are specifically designed to protect critical control blocks (these were discussed in Chapter 3). Many other control blocks, however, are not protected by locks and intersects, and other programming techniques are available to help you access these safely.

One of the most useful of these is the compare and swap (CS) instruction. The description of this instruction in [1] explains exactly how it can be used to update a control block safely, and there are coded examples in the same manual's appendices. The basic idea is that CS can compare an area of storage with the value it had when you read it originally, and only update it if it has not changed since. Furthermore, while CS is executing, the storage area being (conditionally) updated is protected from updates by tasks running on other processors. Of course, if CS finds that the area has changed since you read it, your code will have to redo the procedure it used to determine the change to make to the control block, and then make another attempt to update it using CS.

Before we leave the subject of control blocks, we must devote a few words to a new direction which seems to be tentatively emerging from IBM in this area. If you wish to access a unit control block (UCB) under MVS/XA or higher levels of MVS, IBM has provided a new service known as the UCB scan routine (IOSVSUCB — documented in [10] and [12]). This is intended to be used instead of the traditional process of chaining through control blocks yourself, and could be seen as the first step in a process of declaring control block chains 'out of bounds' for user systems programmers — just as IBM's 'object code only' policy declared the source code of MVS out of bounds. If so, it will take a very long time to weed out the many fields in control blocks which are regarded by IBM as acceptable 'programming interfaces' at the moment.

MVS/ESA took another small step in this direction by providing similar routines for accessing scheduler work area (SWA) control blocks, including the job control table (JCT), step control table (SCT), accounting control table (ACT), and job file control block (JFCB). These are the SWAREQ and IEFQMREQ services, also documented in [10]. These services may make access to control blocks easier and more stable across changing levels of MVS, but if they do represent a trend towards outlawing direct access to control blocks, this — like the object code only policy — would inevitably reduce both the range and flexibility of system interfaces available to the systems programmer and also the scope for systems programmers to learn about MVS internals at first hand. However, where programming interfaces like this are provided, it will be essential for systems programmers wishing to access these resources to use them to ensure their code continues to work across successive levels of MVS.

6.3   Using system macros

If you are familiar with application programming using assembler, you should already be familiar with using IBM-supplied macros such as OPEN, CLOSE, GET, PUT, READ, WRITE, WAIT, LOAD, LINK, XCTL, DELETE, ENQ, DEQ, GETMAIN, FREEMAIN, etc. The macros which are available for general use (i.e. by unauthorized programs) are documented in [6] and [8] (or [9] for XA systems).

When you start writing system-oriented code, however, you have additional macros available to you, and additional variants of the general-use macros. These are documented in [11] (note the 'SPL' for systems programming library, which distinguishes this from the unauthorized version). This was [13] for XA systems. This volume lists:

- Macros which require the issuer to be APF authorized.
- Additional parameters on the general-use macros which can only be used when

Table 6.1. Selected system macros and authorized parameters

Macro	Authorized parameters	Authorized usage
ASCRE		Create a new address space.
ASDES		Destroy an address space.
ATTACH	SM and KEY	Attach a task which will execute in supervisor state or key zero.
BLS*		IPCS macros — for use in IPCS exits for analysing dumps.
CHANGKEY		Change the key or fetch protect bit for a page of virtual storage.
CMDAUTH		Verify with RACF if a console command is authorized.
COF*		VLF macros.
DPSERV		Create/delete/control a dataspace or hiperspace.
HPSERV		Read or write to a hiperspace.
IOS*		Obtain information from the I/O supervisor (e.g. on UCBs).
LXRES		One of many cross-memory services macros.
MGCR		Issue console commands.
MODESET	MODE and KEY	Change execution state or key of program.
PGFIX/ PGFREE/ PGSER		Fix, free, page in, or page out a page of virtual storage. Note that PGSER is the preferred interface.
RACROUTE		Interface to RACF, e.g. to verify authorization of caller to access a resource. There are many variants of this macro which perform different functions.
SCHEDULE		Start an SRB.
SYSEVENT		Interface to SRM, e.g. to notify it a transaction has completed or control swap status of a unit of work.
TESTAUTH		Test the authorization of a calling program.

the issuer is APF authorized

● Other system-oriented macros which are of little interest to application programmers

Table 6.1 lists some of these additional macros and facilities. See the manuals referred to above for further details of any of them.

In addition to the system macros provided by MVS itself, the systems programmer may wish to use macros and services provided by other system components and program products, such as JES2 macros (documented in [17]) and TSO/E macros and services (documented in [16]).

6.4   31-bit addressing

Since the introduction of MVS/XA, MVS has been able to run in either of two addressing modes: 24 bit or 31 bit. In 24-bit mode, only the low-order 24 bits of address fields are used as addresses by the processor, and the highest virtual storage

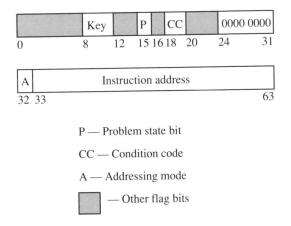

P — Problem state bit

CC — Condition code

A — Addressing mode

☐ — Other flag bits

Figure 6.1. Selected fields from the program status word.

location that can be addressed is therefore one byte short of 16 megabytes (as we start at byte zero!). MVS/370 programs, however, started to run out of virtual storage, so IBM introduced 31-bit addressing. In 31-bit mode, the low-order 31 bits of address fields are used, and the highest virtual storage location that can be addressed is therefore raised to one byte short of 2 gigabytes.

Although the use of 31-bit addressing mode is not confined to system-oriented code, it is unusual for applications to include 31-bit code, simply because most application programmers find it easier to stick with traditional 24-bit code and unnecessary to use 31-bit code. Systems programmers, however, cannot get away with this — more and more of the control blocks used by MVS and other products are moving above the 16 megabyte line, and so can only be accessed by 31-bit code.

During program execution, the current addressing mode is determined by the value of bit 32 in the current PSW (which corresponds to the high-order bit of the next sequential instruction address — see Fig. 6.1). If this bit is set to 1, the processor is running in 31-bit mode; if it is set to 0, it is running in 24-bit mode. So how is the value of this addressing mode bit set?

Every program which executes under MVS/XA or MVS/ESA is assigned an AMODE attribute and an RMODE attribute, both of which can be specified using the linkage editor or assembler. The AMODE determines the addressing mode of the program if it is invoked using ATTACH, LINK, or XCTL, and can be given the values 24, 31, or ANY. ANY indicates that the program can receive control in either addressing mode, and the actual addressing mode will be determined at invocation time. The RMODE (residency mode) determines where the program will reside in virtual storage, and can take the values 24 or ANY. 24 indicates that the module must be loaded below the 16 megabyte line, while ANY indicates that it may be loaded either above or below it. The combination of AMODE 24 with RMODE ANY is invalid, as the program would be unable to address itself if it was loaded above the 16 megabyte line!

You should note that the AMODE of a program will only determine its addressing mode if it is entered via one of the 'supervisor-assisted linkage macros' listed in the previous paragraph. If you enter a program by issuing the LOAD macro then the CALL macro (which uses BALR), for example, the addressing mode will remain as it was in the calling program.

There are, however, other ways of changing the addressing mode (see [14] for a full list of these). The most important is the use of the mode-setting machine instructions branch and save and set mode (BASSM) and branch and set mode (BSM). BASSM is an RR format instruction, which saves the current PSW instruction address, including the high-order bit determining the addressing mode, in R_1, and loads the new instruction address, again including the addressing mode bit, in R_2. This results in a branch to the second address, a change of addressing mode to that specified in the high-order bit of the second register, and the saving of the original PSW address and addressing mode so that they can be returned to later. The BSM instruction (another RR instruction) is used to make this return. The full version of this instruction inserts the high-order bit determining the addressing mode in R_1, and loads the new instruction address, again including the addressing mode bit, in R_2. The normal usage, however, is to set the first register to zero, in which case only the branch and addressing mode switch occurs.

What this means in practice is that in a mixed addressing-mode environment, BASSM and BSM can be used to replace the traditional usage of BALR and BR to call a subprogram and return from it. They perform branching in the same way, but also set the correct addressing mode corresponding to the high-order bit of the branch address. Thus, both 31-bit and 24-bit programs should invoke subprograms using the BASSM instruction, which stores the original addressing mode along with the return address, and all subprograms should return control to their callers using the BSM instruction, which restores the caller's addressing mode.

Note that the MVS/ESA linkage stack provides an alternative linkage mechanism that preserves the addressing mode of the caller on return. This facility is simple to use and provides a number of other benefits, so you should use it in preference to the other approaches described here as long as you are writing code which will only run on MVS/ESA or higher level systems.

The BSM and BASSM instructions can also be used to change the addressing mode within a program: for example, in a predominantly 24-bit program you might switch into 31-bit mode in order to read a control block above the 16 megabyte line, then switch back into 24-bit mode. Example 6.2 shows a piece of code which uses BSM in this way. Note that the sequence in this example does not preserve the original addressing mode — it returns to AMODE 24 irrespective of the original mode. If there is any doubt about the original addressing mode, or if the code might at some time in the future change to a different addressing mode, it is clearly preferable to save and restore the original addressing mode. This can be achieved easily and flexibly by putting the code requiring a different addressing

```
        .
        .
        .
        LA   1,LAB31
        O    1,=X'80000000'  SET HIGH-ORDER BIT OF R1 TO 1
        BSM  0,1             BRANCH AND SET AMODE 31
LAB31   EQU  *
        .
        .
        .
31-bit code
        .
        .
        .
        LA   1,LAB24         N.B. LA CLEARS HIGH-ORDER BIT
        BSM  0,1             BRANCH AND SET AMODE 24
LAB24   EQU  *
        .
        .
        .
```

Example 6.2. Changing addressing mode using BSM.

mode in a subroutine, branching to this subroutine using BASSM, and returning using BSM, as in Example 6.3.

There are a number of cautions, conventions, and restrictions relating to the use of 31-bit addressing with which you must be familiar:

- A program should return control in the same addressing mode in which it received control.
- It is the programmer's responsibility to ensure that a program does not attempt to use a 31-bit address in 24-bit mode — if this occurs, you may experience a protection exception (usually resulting in an 0C4 abend), or end up accessing the wrong area of virtual storage. Equally, if you attempt to use a 24-bit address in 31-bit mode you may experience problems; the high-order byte of a register containing a 24-bit address may be used to hold flag bits which will be inter-

```
        .
        .
        .
        LA    15,SUBRTN       LOAD SUBROUTINE ADDRESS
        O     15,=X'80000000' SET AMODE 31 FOR SUBROUTINE
        BASSM 14,15           BRANCH, SAVING AMODE & RETURN ADDR
        .
        .
        .
SUBRTN  EQU   *
        .
        .
        .
        BSM   0,14            RETURN TO CALLER & RESTORE AMODE
```

Example 6.3. Changing AMODE using BASSM and BSM.

```
***********************************************************************
*   ENSURE ADDRESS IN R2 IS 31-BIT                                    *
***********************************************************************
        STCM  R2,B'1000',R2HIBYTE  EXTRACT HI BYTE FROM R2
        TM    R2HIBYTE,HIBIT       TEST HI-ORDER BIT
        BO    PARMDONE             IF ONE, ADDRESS ALREADY 31-BIT
        ICM   R2,B'1000',=X'80'    IF ZERO, CONVERT 24-BIT ADDRESS
PARMDONE EQU  *
.
.
.
HIBIT    EQU  B'10000000'
R2HIBYTE DS   CL1
.
```

Example 6.4. Validating a parameter address for a 31-bit program.

preted as part of the address if it is used in 31-bit mode. You must therefore validate addresses passed from other programs and if necessary clean them up before using them (see Example 6.4). You must also take care when using addresses obtained from system control blocks: 24-bit programs may find they have to cope with 31-bit addresses relating to control blocks held above the line, and 31-bit programs may find they have to cope with 24-bit addresses with other information held in the high-order byte.

- DFP access methods other than VSAM do not support 31-bit addresses, nor do some older MVS services such as SPIE and STAE (the ESPIE and ESTAE macros provide 31-bit versions of these services).

- Some machine instructions behave differently in 24-bit and 31-bit modes, notably BAL, BALR, and LA. In 24-bit mode, BAL and BALR return the instruction-length code, the condition code, and the program mask in the high-order byte of the register which is used to save the return address, while in 31-bit mode they do not. You must therefore check any code containing BAL and BALR instructions which is to be converted to 31-bit mode to ensure that it does not make any use of this information. The BAS and BASR instructions, new with MVS/XA, do not save this information in either mode, and should be used in place of BAL and BALR in new code. The LA instruction clears the high-order byte of the register being loaded in 24-bit mode, but only the high-order bit in 31-bit mode.

- Beware of converting any code to 31-bit mode if it uses the high-order byte of address fields for non-addressing information!

6.5   Re-entrant coding

If you wish to share one copy of a load module between multiple concurrent users (i.e. allow multithreading through the module), you must code it as a re-entrant module. This means that in most circumstances the program may not modify its own code, including data areas held within the program, and any data areas it requires must therefore reside outside the load module. In other words, each concurrent user must have its own copy of the data areas, or the different users will interfere with each other's data. Re-entrancy was discussed in more detail in Sec. 3.7; this section discusses the special coding techniques that are necessary for the coding of re-entrant programs.

In theory, sections of a re-entrant program can be self-modifying if access to the code segment concerned is serialized. However, if you wish to place a program in the PLPA or any page-protected area of storage, not even serialized self-modifying sections are allowed. There is therefore a more stringent standard for these programs (known as refreshable programs). In practice, you should avoid self-modifying sections in all re-entrant programs, i.e. make them fully refreshable, as they are bound to form a bottleneck and also restrict your ability to place the program in the LPA.

If modifiable data areas cannot be held in the program itself, where can they be held? There are two typical answers to this question: either the program which calls the re-entrant program must provide a work area and supply the re-entrant program with its address; or the re-entrant program must obtain a work area (sometimes called a dynamic work area) using the GETMAIN macro and release it at termination time using the FREEMAIN macro (on ESA systems, the new STORAGE macro can be used instead). Either of these options results in each concurrent user having an individual copy of the work area, addressed via a register. In either case, it is normal to use a DSECT to describe the work area so that symbolic addresses can be used to reference data in it.

One complication here is that standard linkage conventions require each module to create a register save area for use by called programs, and maintain the chain of save area pointers by storing the address of the higher save area in its own save area. This also requires a modifiable work area, which must be available while the program is still in the process of establishing addressability within itself. Unless your program's caller has thoughtfully provided a save area for you to use (in addition to its own!), it is therefore necessary to modify the standard entry linkage by inserting a GETMAIN for the save areas, and the exit linkage by inserting a FREEMAIN for them. Re-entrant versions of the standard entry and exit linkage are shown in Example 6.5. Note that:

- The GETMAIN during the entry linkage can obtain as large an area as you need for all your work areas. There is no need to code one GETMAIN in the entry linkage for your save areas and another later on for other work storage. This is achieved here by defining a DSECT for the work area which includes all the fields required, and using the length of this DSECT as the length operand of the GETMAIN macro.
- If a parameter address is supplied in register 1, we must save this in another register before executing the GETMAIN for the work area, as GETMAIN corrupts this register.

```
**********************************************************************
*     RE-ENTRANT ENTRY LINKAGE                                      *
**********************************************************************
     STM    R14,R12,12(R13)      SAVE CALLER'S REGS IN HIS SAVE AREA
     BASR   R12,R0               LOAD NEXT SEQ INSTR ADDRESS
     USING  *,R12                ESTABLISH MODULE BASE REGISTER
     LR     R2,R1                SAVE PARM ADDRESS BEFORE R1 CORRUPTED
     GETMAIN RU,LV=WORKALEN      GET WORKAREA
     LR     R11,R1               WORKAREA ADDR RETURNED IN R1
     USING  WORKAREA,R11         ESTABLISH WORKAREA ADDRESSABILITY
     ST     R13,SAVEAREA+4       SAVE HIGHER SAVE AREA POINTER
     LA     R15,SAVEAREA         GET OUR SAVE AREA ADDRESS
     ST     R15,8(R13)           SAVE OUR SA POINTER IN HIGHER SA
     LR     R13,R15              SET STANDARD SA POINTER TO OUR SA
.
.(main section of executable code goes here)
.
**********************************************************************
*     RE-ENTRANT EXIT LINKAGE                                       *
**********************************************************************
     L         R13,4(R13)        LOAD ADDRESS OF HIGHER SAVE AREA
     FREEMAIN RU,LV=WORKALEN,A=(R11) FREE THE WORKAREA
     LR     R15,R10              LOAD RETURN CODE
     L      R14,12(R13)          RESTORE CALLER'S REG 14
     LM     R0,R12,20(R13)       RESTORE CALLER'S REGISTERS 0-12
     BSM    R14                  RETURN TO CALLER
.
.(rest of main CSECT goes here)
.
WORKAREA DSECT
         DS     0F
SAVEAREA DS     18F
.
.(other fields required in work area defined here)
.
WORKALEN EQU    *-WORKAREA    WORKAREA LENGTH (FOR USE IN GETMAIN)
```

Example 6.5. Re-entrant entry and exit linkage.

- If a return code is to be returned in register 15, we must set it up in a different register (register 10 in this case), then load it into register 15 after the FREEMAIN of the work area as FREEMAIN corrupts register 15. We must also avoid overwriting it again with the LM instruction which restores the caller's registers!

If you are writing re-entrant code which will only execute under ESA or higher levels of MVS, you can simplify your entry linkage enormously by using the new linkage stack facility, which uses an MVS-provided area to save not only the general-purpose registers but also the PSW, the access registers used by some of the new cross-address-space services such as dataspaces and hiperspaces, and other control information. The article by Edward Williams [25] provides a good overview of this facility, which is documented more fully in [15].

Another area where care is required in coding re-entrant programs is the use of macros, because the standard forms of many IBM macros generate self-modifying

```
************* EXECUTABLE SECTION *****************
.
        MVC     WTOPARMS,WTOLIST     MOVE PARMLIST TO WORKAREA
        WTO     MF=(E,WTOPARMS)      EXEC FORM—PARMS IN WORKAREA
.
*************  CONSTANTS SECTION *****************
.
WTOLIST WTO     'TEXT OF MESSAGE',ROUTCDE=(11),DESC=(6),MF=L
LISTLEN EQU     *-WTOLIST               LENGTH OF GENERATED PARMLIST
.
*************   WORKING STORAGE  *****************
WORKAREA DSECT
.
WTOPARMS DS     CL(LISTLEN)             AREA TO HOLD WTO PARMLIST
.
```

Example 6.6. Use of LIST and EXECUTE macro forms.

code. If you need to use one of these macros in a re-entrant program, you will usually have to use the LIST and EXECUTE forms of the macro instead of the standard form.

The LIST form of the macro generates those parts of the parameter list which are known at coding time, and the EXECUTE form completes the parameter list at execution time. Since this entails modifying the parameter list, it must be in your work area when you come to execute the macro. In order to achieve this, you must: (a) code the LIST form of the macro in a data area within the program to generate the parameter list at assembly time; (b) copy the list generated by the LIST form into a (modifiable) work area at execution time using MVC; and then (c) issue the EXECUTE form, referencing the copy of the parameters in your work area, to complete the parameter list and execute the macro. Example 6.6 shows what is required to issue the WTO macro from a re-entrant program. Note that:

- This example assumes that the WORKAREA DSECT has been made addressable by loading its address into a register and coding a suitable USING statement.
- The LIST form of the macro is identified by the parameter MF=L, and the EXECUTE form by the parameter MF=(E,listaddr), where listaddr is the base-displacement address of the parameter list to be completed at execution time.
- You can even go a step further and copy a parameter list generated using the list form into a work area, then modify the parameters before using them to execute the macro. For example, you could code a list form of the WTO macro with a skeleton message, copy it into the work area, move the actual message text over the top, and then invoke the execute form of WTO. In this way, a single parameter list can be used for several different WTO messages.

If you intend to open a dataset in a re-entrant program, you must remember that the DCB macro essentially generates a parameter list for OPEN and the

```
************** EXECUTABLE SECTION *****************
          MVC    SAMPOUT,DCBSKEL        MOVE SKELETON DCB TO WORKAREA
          MVC    OPENLIST,OPENSKEL      MOVE LIST FORM OF OPEN
          OPEN   (SAMPOUT,OUTPUT),MF=(E,OPENLIST)  EXEC FORM OF OPEN
.
**************   CONSTANTS SECTION *****************
.
DCBSKEL   DCB    DSORG=PS,DDNAME=SAMPOUT,RECFM=FB,LRECL=80,MACRF=PM
DCBLEN    EQU    *-DCBSKEL
OPENSKEL  OPEN   (,),MF=L
OPENLEN   EQU    *-OPENSKEL
.
**************   WORKING STORAGE   *****************
WORKAREA  DSECT
.
.
.
          DS     0F
SAMPOUT   DS     CL(DCBLEN)            SPACE FOR DCB
OPENLIST  DS     CL(OPENLEN)          SPACE FOR LIST FORM OF OPEN
.
.
.
```

Example 6.7. Opening a dataset from a re-entrant program.

subsequent I/O macros, and that OPEN will modify that parameter list. Your DCB therefore needs to be treated in exactly the same way as the LIST form of a macro — code it in your re-entrant program, but copy it into a work area before using it, and reference the copy in the work area on your OPEN macro and all subsequent I/O macros relating to this file. Example 6.7 illustrates the coding required to open and process a dataset from a re-entrant program.

One final problem you may encounter is the need to pass information from one invocation of a re-entrant program to another. This is a problem because it is conventional to FREEMAIN all work areas related to any one invocation of the program at termination of that invocation. This is an important convention to follow, particularly if you are GETMAINing work areas in common storage, as there is otherwise a danger of unused areas accumulating. In CSA, 'creep' of this sort can bring MVS to a halt!

One approach to this problem might be to ask callers of your program to: (a) make an initial call during which you will GETMAIN storage to be kept from call to call; (b) make one or more 'processing' calls; and (c) when all processing is complete, make a final call during which you will FREEMAIN the storage you obtained in step (a). The calling programs could be asked to supply a parameter indicating what type of call was being made. This approach, however, suffers from some obvious drawbacks:

• 'Badly behaved' callers might fail to issue the final call.
• Abending callers would only issue the final call if the programmer had coded their own termination routine to do so, and although the MVS termination

routines are able to clean up GETMAINed storage obtained by an abending program, they may not identify and free storage obtained by other programs on behalf of the abending program.

- Your program needs to know the address of the work area to access for any given processing call, and it has no way of keeping this address from call to call, so it can only be kept if you return it to the calling program after the initial call and ask the calling program to supply the work area address for each subsequent call.

If you are going to require the calling program to keep track of the work area address, you may as well ask the calling program to GETMAIN the work area itself, and simply supply its address with each processing call, thus eliminating the need for 'initial' and 'final' calls altogether. This is a much more practical method, and allows you to store information in the work area which may be required in subsequent calls.

This method is only practical, however, if you are in a position to specify the interface to your program yourself — this is not true if you are coding an exit routine for an IBM or third-party product, for example. It also assumes the calling program is actually able to GETMAIN storage in the area where your program needs it, which may not always be true, and that you do not wish to store information relating to multiple callers (e.g. to keep a count of how many times your program was called and by whom).

When this method is not practical, you need to GETMAIN your storage in an initial call (or a separate initialization program), and store its address in a readily accessible location which is not already used. Unfortunately, there are not many of these lying about in the MVS control blocks! Traditionally, the CVTUSER field of the CVT was used for this sort of thing — but this was not very practical when a second application wanted to use the same field (as some sites found out the hard way when a third-party product tried to use it!).

The more practical approach is to create an entry in the subsystem communications vector table (SSCVT) for your application, and use this to store the address of your storage area. This is relatively straightforward — you simply place an entry for your application in the IEFSSNxx member of PARMLIB which is referenced at IPL time, and use that entry to invoke an initialization routine which GETMAINs your permanent work area and then stores its address in the SSCTSUSE field. This can be located by later tasks using code like that shown in Example 6.8. If you then wish to obtain further work areas to be kept across multiple calls, you can save their addresses in turn in your permanent work area. Note that:

- The piece of code in Example 6.8 finds the SSCVT, which contains an entry for each subsystem that has been initialized (usually at IPL time via an entry in IEFSSNxx), and scans through it until it finds our subsystem (whose four-character identifier is assumed to be stored in the field named OURSYS). Each

```
        L     R2,CVTJESCT              JES COMMON TABLE
        USING JESCT,R2                 MAKE IT ADDRESSABLE
        L     R3,JESSSCT               SUBSYSTEM CVT
        USING SSCT,R3                  MAKE IT ADDRESSABLE
FINDSSCT EQU  *
        CLC   SSCTSNAM(4),OURSYS       IS THIS OUR SUBSYSTEM?
        BE    FOUNDIT                  YES—GO TO GET ADDRESS
        CLC   SSCTSCTA(4),=X'00000000' IS THIS LAST SUBSYS IN CVT?
        BE    NOTFOUND                 YES—OURS NOT INITIALIZED
        L     R3,SSCTSCTA              ADDRESS NEXT SUBSYS ENTRY...
        B     FINDSSCT                 . . .  AND CHECK IT
FOUNDIT EQU   *
        L     R4,SSCTSUSE              LOAD ADDR FROM USER FIELD
```

Example 6.8. Locating an area of storage anchored in the SSCVT.

subsystem has a fullword user field associated with it, and we load the value from this field into a register. For this to be of value, the user field must have been set to something meaningful by the initialization routine — here we assume that an initialization routine has been coded which GETMAINs an area of storage and saves its address in the user field.

- Descriptions of the JES common table (JESCT) and the subsystem communications vector table (SSCVT) can be found in [3].
- You can do much more than this with MVS subsystems, of course. See the chapter on subsystems in [18] and the articles by Wiedemann [24] and Bordonaro [23] for more information on using the subsystem interface.

6.6   Authorized functions

Protecting the system against accidental or malicious corruption and maintaining the privacy of confidential data are vital functions of any serious operating system. MVS contains many facilities designed to do this, and many of them depend on the concept of 'authorized' and 'unauthorized' programs. MVS considers a program authorized if it is executing in any of the following states:

- Supervisor state, as opposed to problem state, which is the normal state for application programs. MVS considers a program to be in supervisor state if bit 15 of the PSW is zero.
- System key, i.e. bits 8–11 of the PSW indicate that the program has access to page frames whose storage key is zero.
- As part of an APF-authorized job step task, i.e. the program was loaded from an APF-authorized library and was link-edited with AC = 1. See [10] for further discussion of APF authorization. APF authorized programs can issue the MODESET macro instruction to put themselves into supervisor state and/or system key.

An unauthorized program cannot:

- Issue privileged instructions, e.g. the LPSW instruction which modifies the

PSW, and all I/O instructions. These can only be issued by programs in supervisor state.

- Store into pages with a storage protect key of zero.
- Read (fetch) from pages with a storage protect key of zero and the fetch-protect bit turned on.
- Issue the MODESET SVC to make itself authorized, or any other restricted SVC. The chapter on SVCs in [2] documents which SVCs require their callers to be authorized.

By contrast, authorized programs *can* perform these functions (obtaining supervisor state or system key via MODESET if necessary). Thus they can bypass the security and integrity mechanisms that protect MVS and your organization's data against accidental or malicious damage or exposure. So restricting the ability to create and run APF-authorized programs is an important component of an effective MVS security policy. We will return to this in Chapter 15.

Of more immediate relevance to this chapter, the unlimited power conferred by authorization also means that extreme care should be exercised when writing authorized code! If you need to go into supervisor state or key zero in order to access a privileged instruction or a protected control block, minimize the potential for serious system damage by doing the following:

- Only give yourself the privileges you need to do the job.
- Relinquish those privileges as soon as possible after completing the job, so that you do not, for example, inadvertently authorize yourself to write all over an important control block with an MVC instruction that does not need to execute in key zero.
- Double desk-check bits of code that will run in supervisor state or key zero.
- Get the rest of your program working properly before you add in the bits that need to be authorized.

Now that you know what not to do, let us look at what you do need to do to run in an authorized state.

First of all, you must link-edit your program into an authorized library with an authorization code of 1. At execution time, your program must be loaded from a concatenation which does not include any unauthorized libraries, or MVS will make the whole concatenation unauthorized for the purposes of your job step. No unauthorized modules must be loaded by your program or its subprograms, or MVS will revoke your authorization and abend the job step with an abend code of S306. Other types of authorization failure are characterized by abend codes S047 (attempting to execute a function that requires APF authorization), S0C4 (attempting to access storage which your key does not give you access to), and S0C2 (attempting to use a privileged instruction while in problem state).

Secondly, if your program receives control in problem state and a user key, you will need to issue the MODESET macro to switch into supervisor state and/or

```
MODESET KEY=ZERO        TSB FETCH PROTECTED—SET KEY ZERO
MVC    COMTERM,TSBTRMID MOVE TERMID TO  BUFFER
MODESET KEY=NZERO       BACK TO USER KEY
```

Example 6.9. Use of the MODESET macro.

system key. Example 6.9 shows how to use this macro (see [11] for full documentation on MODESET). Note that:

- This piece of code accesses a fetch-protected control block in key zero storage and therefore requires to execute in key zero. For clarity, it uses the standard form of the MODESET macro, but you can do exactly the same thing using the list and execute forms.
- If we wished to change the execution state of the program instead of (or as well as) the key, we would use the MODE keyword on the MODESET macro.

6.7   Dynamic allocation

One facility that is often required in system-oriented assembler code is to allocate datasets dynamically, i.e. during program execution, rather than during job setup, via DD statements in JCL. This is performed using the DYNALLOC macro, which invokes SVC 99 to perform dynamic allocation. There are various restrictions on the use of SVC 99, for example, it does not work in cross-memory mode, and you must take care not to serialize any resources it requires. These restrictions are documented in the chapter on SVC 99 in [10].

SVC 99 must be supplied with a parameter list, including:

- A request block, indicating the function you want SVC 99 to perform (e.g. allocation or deallocation by dsname, concatenation, or deconcatenation).
- An optional request block extension, containing message processing information.
- Text pointers, which point to the text units.
- Text units, which contain keys and parameters. Each text unit is equivalent to a parameter you could code on a JCL DD statement.

Figure 6.2 shows the structure of the required parameter blocks. IBM provides mapping macro IEFZB4D0 to generate DSECTs for each of these control blocks, and macro IEFZB4D2 to generate symbolic names for the keyword values used in the text units.

Example 6.10 shows how to use DYNALLOC to perform a simple dynamic allocation. Perhaps the most obvious thing about dynamic allocation is that it is a lot more complicated than coding a DD statement in your JCL — so it is well worth while using a DD statement instead if you can get away with it! Note that:

- This particular allocation is a very simple one — it allocates an existing dataset with a disposition of old, and does not use the request block extension. The only

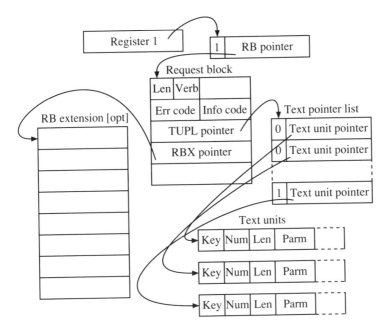

Figure 6.2. Structure of SVC 99 parameters.

complication is that the dataset name is not supplied until execution time, so the text unit for the dataset name must be built in the dynamic work area rather than being supplied as a list of constants. Most of the coding is concerned with building the parameter lists for the DYNALLOC macro in the work area.

- Text units for SVC 99 are documented in detail in [10].
- The request will be failed if another user has allocated the dataset with DISP=OLD, unless this program is authorized, in which case it will wait in the same way as an allocation requested in a JCL DD statement.
- You must check the return code in register 15 to see if the allocation was successful. Error and information codes are returned in the S99ERROR and S99INFO fields of the parameter list (named DYNERROR and DYNINFO in our example), and you may check or display these to assist in diagnosis. These codes are also documented in [10].
- If you do not specify a DDNAME in your allocation request, SVC 99 assigns a default name of SYSnnnnn, where nnnnn is numeric.
- You can request SVC 99 to return information such as DDNAME, dsname, vol ser, and DSORG by including the appropriate text units in your parameter list.
- You also use SVC 99 to deallocate datasets dynamically. In general you should ensure that you clean up prior to program termination by deallocating any datasets you allocated using SVC 99. Deallocation is much simpler than allocation and you can reuse some of the same parameter lists.

```
          .
          .
          .
          LA    R4,DYNRBLN           ADDRESS REQ BLOCK
          ST    R4,DYNRBPTR          AND STORE IN RB PTR
          OC    DYNRBPTR(1),HIBIT    AND SET ON HI-ORDER BIT
          XC    DYNRBLN(20),DYNRBLN  ZEROIZE REQ BLOCK
          MVI   DYNRBLN,20           STORE RB LENGTH
          MVI   DYNVERB,1            REQUEST ALLOCATION BY DSNAME
          LA    R4,DYNTUPL           ADDRESS TEXT UNIT POINTER LIST
          ST    R4,DYNTXTPP          AND STORE IN TXTPP
          LA    R4,DDNTUNIT          ADDRESS DDNAME TEXT UNIT
          ST    R4,DYNTUPL           AND STORE IN 1ST WORD OF TUPL
          LA    R4,DSNTUKEY          ADDRESS DSNAME TEXT UNIT
          ST    R4,DYNTUPL+4         AND STORE IN 2ND WORD OF TUPL
          LA    R4,DSPTUNIT          ADDRESS DISP=OLD TEXT UNIT
          ST    R4,DYNTUPL+8         AND STORE IN 3RD WORK OF TUPL
          OC    DYNTUPL+8(1),HIBIT   AND SET ON HI-ORDER BIT
          LH    R4,=H'2'             KEY FOR DSN TEXT UNIT
          STH   R4,DSNTUKEY
          LH    R4,=H'1'             NUM OF PARMS IN TEXT UNIT
          STH   R4,DSNTUNUM
          STH   R3,DSNTULEN          LENGTH OF DSN IN TEXT UNIT
          BCTR  R3,R0                DECREMENT R3 TO GIVE EXECUTE LENGTH
          EX    R3,MOVEDSN           MOVE DSN TO TEXT UNIT
          LA    R1,DYNRBPTR          LOAD ADDRESS OF RB POINTER
          DYNALLOC                   AND INVOKE SVC 99 TO DO THE DEED
          LTR   R15,R15              WAS RETURN CODE ZERO?
          BNZ   ALOCFAIL             NO — ALLOCATION FAILED
          .
          .
          .
          DS    OF
DDNTUNIT  DC    AL2(1)               SVC 99 DDNAME TEXT UNIT
          DC    AL2(1)
          DC    AL2(7)
          DC    CL7'SAMPOUT'
          SPACE
          DS    OF
DSPTUNIT  DC    AL2(4)               SVC 99 DISP=OLD TEXT UNIT
          DC    AL2(1)
          DC    AL2(1)
          DC    AL1(1)
          .
          .
          .
WORKAREA  DSECT
          .
          .
          .
DYNRBPTR  DS    F                    REQ BLOCK POINTER
          SPACE
DYNRBLN   DS    XL1                  REQ BLOCK
DYNVERB   DS    XL1
DYNFLAG1  DS    XL2
DYNERROR  DS    XL2
```

Example 6.10. Dynamic allocation of a dataset.

```
DYNINFO  DS    XL2
DYNTXTPP DS    F
DYNRBXAD DS    F
DYNFLAG2 DS    XL4
         SPACE
DYNTUPL  DS    3F              TEXT UNIT POINTER LIST
         SPACE
DSNTUKEY DS    H               DSN TEXT UNIT
DSNTUNUM DS    H
DSNTULEN DS    H
DSNTUPAR DS    CL44
.
.
.
```

Example 6.10. (cont.)

6.8   More advanced techniques

Though you may never need to use them, you should be aware of the requirement for other techniques in certain circumstances. Some important examples are:

• Using cross-memory services to communicate with other address spaces, and exploiting dataspaces and hiperspaces via the use of access registers. These techniques are discussed in detail in [15].

• Coding I/O programs which do not use standard access methods but instead build their own channel programs then use the EXCP macro to execute them (see [19]). This is not recommended unless it is absolutely essential, partly because it represents a potential security exposure, and partly because the standard access methods provide numerous facilities such as device independence, error handling, security interfaces, and exploitation of performance features, which it would be difficult and extremely time-consuming to attempt to duplicate in your own code.

• Writing your own SVCs. Again, this is not recommended, for security reasons. Some journals, for example, have published code for an 'APF authorization' SVC, which allows programs that are not authorized to make themselves so. Although some users of this code have modified it to include calls to a security package to validate the user's authority to invoke the SVC, there must still be serious question marks over the security of such facilities. I do not believe there is any valid requirement for such an SVC which outweighs this exposure.

• If you start writing very sophisticated system code, you may need to use locks and intersects to serialize on access to certain system resources (see Sec. 3.6 for a discussion of these). You should certainly familiarize yourself with the system resources that use locks for serialization, and ensure that if you wish to access these you follow the conventions relating to lock usage. Failure to do so could hang and/or corrupt MVS.

These last two areas are documented in more detail in [10], and the serialization required for each control block is shown in its entry in [3].

6.9   Assembler installation and customization

The assembler program (the current one is known as the H level Assembler) is a prerequisite for the installation of almost all software products, including MVS itself, so it is part of the systems programmer's job to ensure that a fully functional copy of the assembler is available on the system. The basic installation steps are very simple, and are handled for you automatically by the CBIPO process, if you use it. Indeed, CBIPO installs the assembler twice — once by copying an untailored version into IPO1.LINKLIB early in the installation process, so it can use this copy to install the rest of the products on the CBIPO, and again during the main product installation process, this time into SYS1.LINKLIB. If, on the other hand, you install the assembler from a product tape, the basic installation involves nothing more than ensuring the necessary target and distribution libraries are available and running an SMP RECEIVE and APPLY job.

Two further tasks may then be required. The first is to copy and optionally customize the standard assembler procedures ASMHC, ASMHCG, ASMHCLG, and ASMHCL. Both the CBIPO and the non-CBIPO install processes place these in SYS1.SAMPLIB, and you must copy them into one of your procedure libraries from there. You may also wish to customize them, e.g. by adding libraries to the SYSLIB concatenation, but it simplifies future upgrades if you do not!

The second optional customization task is the definition of your assembler options. These are held in load module IEV60, and if you wish to modify the IBM-supplied versions, e.g. in order to change the default output produced by the assembler, or the DDNAMEs it uses, then you will need to modify and reassemble this module. This should be done using an SMP/E USERMOD to modify and reassemble source module IEV61, and an example is supplied in [20] — and also in IPO1.JCLLIB(ASMUMOD) if you use CBIPO. As with the cataloged procedures, it is generally wisest not to change the IBM defaults unless you need to do so to maintain compatibility with earlier modifications.

References and bibliography

IBM manuals

1. *IBM System/370 XA Principles of Operation*, SA22-7085. The 'bible' of System/370 machine instructions, with descriptions of every instruction and important information about how System/370 processors handle execution of programs (including address translation, the PSW and control registers, instruction formats and interrupts). Note there are different versions for different variations of the architecture, e.g. ESA, System/390, etc.
2. *MVS/ESA Diagnosis: System Reference*, LY28-1011. Information on lock and system ENQ names, storage subpool numbers, MVS SVCs, and an index of common acronyms.
3. *MVS/ESA Diagnosis: Data Areas Volumes 1 to 5*, LY28-1043 to 1047. Gives the layout

of all MVS control blocks, and documents mapping macros, storage keys, pointers to each control block, etc.

4. *MVS/XA Debugging Handbook Volumes 1 to 6*, LC28–1164 to 1169. Volume 1 is the XA version of *System Reference*, while volumes 2 to 6 are the XA version of *Data Areas*.

5. *MVS/ESA Data Administration Guide*, SC26–4505. Describes use of access methods other than VSAM.

6. *MVS/ESA Data Administration: Macro Instruction Reference*, SC26–4506. Documents macros used by access methods other than VSAM.

7. *MVS/ESA Application Development Guide*, GC28–1821. General guidance for the coding of unauthorized assembler programs, including linkage conventions and subtask creation.

8. *MVS/ESA Application Development Macro Reference*, GC28–1822. Macro instructions available to unauthorized assembler programs.

9. *MVS/XA Supervisor Services and Macro Instructions*, GC28–1154. The XA version of both the *Application Development Guide* and *Application Development Macro Reference*.

10. *MVS/ESA SPL: Application Development Guide*, GC28–1852. General guidance for the coding of authorized assembler programs, including security, SVC 99, exit routine and user SVC considerations, and using VLF.

11. *MVS/ESA SPL: Application Development Macro Reference*, GC28–1857. Macro instructions available to authorized assembler programs, parameters of unauthorized macros which are only available to authorized programs, and macros of more interest to the systems programmer than the applications programmer.

12. *MVS/XA SPL: System Macros and Facilities, Volume 1*, GC28–1150. XA version of *SPL: Application Development Guide*.

13. *MVS/XA SPL: System Macros and Facilities, Volume 2*, GC28–1151. XA version of *SPL: Application Development Macro Reference*.

14. *MVS/ESA SPL: Application Development 31-bit Addressing*, GC28–1852. Covers 31-bit addressing, AMODEs and RMODEs, and rules, conventions, and techniques for writing 31-bit programs.

15. *MVS/ESA SPL: Application Development Extended Addressability*, GC28–1854. Covers the use of cross-memory services, dataspaces, and hiperspaces from Assembler programs, and also the use of the linkage stack.

16. *MVS/ESA TSO/E Programming Services*, SC28–1875. How to access TSO/E services from assembler programs.

17. *MVS/ESA SPL: JES2 Customization*, LY28–1010. Includes documentation of JES2 macros.

18. *MVS/ESA SPL: System Modifications*, GC28–1831. Includes several chapters on the subsystem interface.

19. *MVS/DFP: Systems Programming Reference*, SC26–4567. Includes a chapter on writing and executing channel programs.

20. *Assembler H Installation*, SC26–4030.

Other

21. Bowler, R.: Some Useful Fields in MVS Control Blocks, *MVS Update*, July 1988, pp. 18–23.

22. Goldin, S.: Getting the Most out of Contents Supervision, *Candle Computer Report*, August 1989, pp. 1–2. Describes 're-entrant', 'refreshable', and other program attributes.

23. Bordonaro, B.: Understanding the Subsystem Interface Component of MVS, *Mainframe Journal*, March 1989, pp. 69–76.
24. Wiedemann, W.: Development of an MVS subsystem, *MVS Update*, October 1991, pp. 13–21, and November 1991, pp. 15–26.
25. Williams, E.: MVS/ESA Linkage Stack Saves Program Status, *Candle Computer Report*, May 1991, pp. 1–3.

Part Three
Creating a working system

7
MVS initialization and implementation

7.1 Introduction

This chapter and the three which follow it address the question of how to create a usable MVS system. In this chapter we will look at creating the MVS system itself, while the following chapters will deal with creating working versions of the essential subsystems and non-MVS software which you need in order to do practical work on your new system. These are JES, which must be started before any user work can be submitted, and VTAM and TSO (including ISPF), which are required in order to do online work.

To create a working MVS system, we must provide all the datasets (and their contents) that required during the MVS initialization process. The first step towards understanding what we are doing, therefore, is to understand the initialization process itself, and this is where this chapter begins. We will then look in a little more detail at the factors to be considered when we are providing each of the datasets required by MVS. The last part of the chapter will cover the standard installation processes which IBM makes available to simplify the process of creating a new or updated system.

7.2 MVS initialization

7.2.1 Background

MVS initialization is normally referred to as 'IPLing', although strictly speaking initial program load (IPL) is only the first stage of the initialization process. IPL is initiated by an operator command entered on the system or hardware console (the console attached to the processor complex itself, not one of the MVS consoles), and may be performed, for example, because:

- You are bringing up a system on a new processor for the first time.
- You have made a change to the hardware or software configuration which requires re-initialization of MVS to become effective.
- The processor is being restarted after scheduled maintenance, or

- The system requires re-loading to overcome a problem which has locked up MVS.

In the second and third of these cases, the initialization will be preceded by an orderly closedown of the system. In the last, we may have to IPL 'over the top' of a running system. It is important to have written procedures in place for both of these types of situation, as the IPL process will normally be handled by your operators and should be dealt with as quickly and efficiently as possible to minimize the downtime experienced by users.

7.2.2   Prerequisites

Before an IPL can take place, certain conditions must exist:

- The processor complex must be powered up and its microcode loaded; the latter is done by the IML process when the complex is powered up, and also when a power-on-reset process is initiated from the hardware console.
- The processor complex must be configured to use the central storage, expanded storage, processors, and channels required by your system. The configuration is saved across power up sequences, but if you need to change it you must first use commands on the hardware console to select the resources to be configured, then perform a power-on-reset to implement the change.
- Any I/O devices required during initialization must be powered up. In most installations, all channel-attached devices and the processor complex itself are kept permanently powered up.
- If you are using PR/SM or an equivalent feature, the logical partition you wish to IPL must be defined and enabled.
- The current I/O configuration dataset (IOCDS) must define the I/O devices your system needs and the channel paths to them, and the devices themselves must be attached to the processor in a way which is consistent with the IOCDS. The systems programmer must create the IOCDS and write it to the service processor's disk storage using the I/O configuration program (IOCP) before it can be selected and made current. The service processor keeps several alternative IOCDSs on internal disk storage, and to make a new one current, it must be selected from the hardware console, and a power-on-reset performed.

Note that if you have the PR/SM feature installed on your processor complex, the IOCDS will define whether you are running in LPAR mode or not, and will determine which channels belong to which partitions. If you are running under VM, you will still need an IOCDS to define the real devices in use, and this may be created either from MVS or from a CMS machine. The addresses by which MVS knows devices may, however, differ from their real addresses. This complication is ignored in the rest of this chapter. The use of PR/SM and VM to run multiple MVS systems is discussed in Chapter 13.

7.2.3   *Steps in the initialization process*

Step 1

The operator selects the correct frame on the hardware console (OPRCTL or SYSCTL on most IBM machines), amends the load address if required (i.e. the unit address of the SYSRES pack), and selects the load function. This initiates MVS initialization.

The operator may also add or modify a field containing parameter information to be passed to MVS, before initiating the load. On pre-MVS version 4 systems, the first character of the load parameter could be used to specify the suffix (one numeric character) of an alternate version of the nucleus module IEANUC01, for example in order to test a new version with a PTF on it (or an alternate I/O configuration on an MVS/370 system). The second and third characters could be used to specify the suffix of an alternate version of the MVS I/O configuration modules, and the remaining five characters were ignored.

The format of the loadparm has, however, been changed for MVS version 4. Now the first four characters specify the device number of the volume containing the new LOADxx IPL control member; the next two specify the suffix of the LOADxx member to be used to control this IPL; the seventh controls message suppression during IPL; and the last character can be used to specify the suffix of an alternate nucleus, which is used in the same way as the first character of the old loadparm.

Systems programmer must provide: valid IOCDS.

Step 2

In response to the load command, the service processor initiates an I/O operation to read the IPL bootstrap program from track 0, cylinder 0 of the device at the load address. This 'bootstrap' module is loaded into storage at real storage location zero, and control is passed to it. The bootstrap then reads in the IPL control program (IEAIPL00) and passes control to it. The device at the load address is known as the system residence (SYSRES) pack, and it must hold a valid and up-to-date copy of the bootstrap and IEAIPL00 (known as the IPL text) at the correct location. Note that this track is always reserved on MVS-format DASD devices for IPL text, and cannot be used for normal MVS datasets.

Systems programmer must provide: bootstrap records and IPL text.

Step 3

IEAIPL00 prepares an environment for the programs which are invoked in step 4, as normal MVS services cannot be used until the modules providing them have been loaded and the control block structures they require have been built and initialized. It clears all online real storage (except the part it occupies itself!) to hex zeros; it maps virtual storage required for the master scheduler address space to real storage locations; it sets up service routines for the use of the programs in step 4; then it finds the dataset SYS1.NUCLEUS on the SYSRES pack.

Systems programmer must provide: SYS1.NUCLEUS.

Step 4

IEAIPL00 invokes a series of programs called IPL resource initialization modules (IRIMs), which it loads from SYS1.NUCLEUS. These begin the process of constructing the normal environment of modules and control block structures which make up a working MVS system. Some of the functions the IRIMs perform include:

- Read the loadparm information entered at IPL time on the hardware console.
- On MVS version 4 systems, search the volume whose device number was specified in the loadparm for the LOADxx member. The IRIM will look first for a library called SYS0.IPLPARM, then SYS1.IPLPARM, and so on up to SYS9.IPLPARM, and if it does not find any of these it will look for SYS1. PARMLIB. When it finds one of these, it will open the LOADxx member, where xx is the suffix supplied in the loadparm. The format of this member is discussed in more detail in Sec. 7.5, but it can include information on the I/O configuration to be used, the nucleus suffix to be used (unless this was overridden on the last character of the loadparm itself), the master catalog to be used, and the suffix of the IEASYSxx member of PARMLIB to be used later in the initialisation process.
- Load the MVS nucleus. Note that this includes both the DAT-on nucleus, which is the part that appears in the virtual storage map of all address spaces (by virtue of being loaded at this time into a common area of the master scheduler address space), and the DAT-off nucleus, which does not appear in virtual storage at all, but is placed in real storage at the highest possible address.
- Initialize or reserve virtual storage in the master scheduler address space for the SQA, extended SQA, extended LSQA, and PSA. By the end of the IPL phase of MVS initialization, the PSA has replaced IEAIPL00 at real storage location zero, where it stays from here on. Figure 7.1 illustrates the state of virtual and real storage at the end of this phase. Note that the size of real storage depends on the physical storage available on your processor complex, and how much of this is online (and configured to the current logical partition, in a PR/SM environment). Also, you should note that the areas shown in the middle of real storage are not necessarily contiguous or in the order shown — each may consist of pages in scattered locations, intermixed with other areas. But this is not true of the DAT-off nucleus, which consists of contiguous frames at the highest available real storage addresses, or of the PSA, which consists of a single frame at real storage address 0.
- Start to initialize real storage management, including the segment table for the

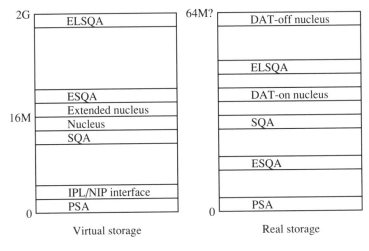

Figure 7.1. Storage at end of IPL phase of MVS initialization.

master scheduler address space — which includes the segment table entries for common storage areas — and the page frame table.

If there is an unrecoverable failure during any part of the IPL phase of system initialization, the IPL program places an error code in the low-order 12 bits of the PSW, displays this on the system console, and puts the system into a disabled wait state. The possible wait codes and the appropriate recovery actions are documented in [15].

On version 4 systems, the systems programmer must provide: IPLPARM or PARMLIB library and LOADxx member.

Step 5

The last of the IRIMs loads the first part of the nucleus initialization program (NIP), which begins the next phase of the system initialization process. NIP also invokes programs to do resource initialization, known simply as resource initialization modules (RIMs). One of the earliest of these starts up the communications task which controls console communications and opens communication with the first available NIP console (defined in the MVS I/O configuration modules in SYS1.NUCLEUS). This becomes the MVS console for the remainder of the NIP phase. Many of the other RIMs require parameter input from either the operator or SYS1.PARMLIB, so we will return to these in step 10.

Systems programmer must provide: NIP console definitions in MVS I/O configuration generated using MVSCP.

Step 6

On pre-MVS version 4 systems, and on version 4 systems where the loadparm has been set to indicate that the operator should be prompted for the system parameters and master catalog suffix, NIP issues the message:

        IEA101A   SPECIFY SYSTEM PARAMETERS

on the NIP master console.

Step 7

If this message is issued, the operator replies either by pressing Enter, which causes NIP to use the parameters specified in SYS1.PARMLIB(IEASYS00), or by entering details of any overrides which are required to the values specified there. On version 4 systems where the prompt has been suppressed, the suffix of the IEASYSxx member to be used will be taken from the LOADxx member. We will discuss the processing of some individual PARMLIB parameters in more detail later in the chapter, but we should touch on some general principles here:

- The operator may specify SYSP=xx, which will result in the values in IEASYSxx overriding those in IEASYS00 (except the PAGE parameters, where values in IEASYSxx are used as well as those in IEASYS00, not instead of them).
- The operator may also specify any of the individual parameters that may appear in IEASYSxx, which will result in these overriding the values in both IEASYSxx (if specified) and IEASYS00 — except for the PAGE parameter, which is once again additional and not a replacement.
- Many of the parameters in IEASYSxx in turn specify suffixes of other members of PARMLIB. For example, the parameter LNK=01 in IEASYSxx instructs the linklist RIM to use the list of linklist libraries in member LNKLST01 of PARMLIB. In most cases, multiple suffixes can be specified, and the entries in the later members referred to will be concatenated behind those in the earlier members.

Systems programmer must provide: SYS1.PARMLIB, IEASYS00 member, any other members to be specified via operator overrides, any other members referred to in IEASYSxx members, and a catalog entry for SYS1.PARMLIB in the master catalog.

Step 8

On pre-MVS version 4 systems, and on version 4 systems where the loadparm has been set to indicate the operator should be prompted for the system parameters and master catalog suffix, NIP issues the message:

        IEA437A   SPECIFY MASTER CATALOG PARAMETER

on the NIP master console.

Step 9

If this message is issued, the operator replies either by pressing Enter, or by entering a two-character suffix. If the operator presses Enter without typing in a suffix, NIP will read the member SYSCATLG of SYS1.NUCLEUS, which should hold the master catalog pointer to be used by MVS — this includes the name and volume serial number of the master catalog. If a suffix is entered, this replaces the LG in the member name of the pointer – in other words, NIP searches for member SYSCATxx, where xx is the suffix entered. On version 4 systems where the prompt has been suppressed, the LOADxx member supplies the master catalog pointer information directly, without the need for a SYSCATxx member in SYS1.NUCLEUS.

Systems programmer must provide: SYSCATLG or SYSCATxx member of SYS1.NUCLEUS, unless LOADxx is being used to supply the catalog pointer.

Step 10

Once it has received these replies, NIP can proceed to invoke the rest of its RIMs. The processing these perform includes:

- Initialize the UCBs and other I/O supervisor control blocks for available I/O devices, test their accessibility by requesting an I/O operation to them and, for DASD devices, determine the volume serial number and put this in the UCB. At this stage you may receive the console message:

```
IEA120A DEVICE ddd VOLID NOT READ. REPLY 'CONT' OR
                        'WAIT'
```

where ddd is the device address, if any of the DASD volumes is currently reserved by another system. If the volume is one you require for system initialization, you must reply WAIT, and the IPL will wait until the volume is released. Otherwise you may reply CONT, in which case the volume will be left offline and the IPL will continue. You must then remember to vary the volume online later. You may also receive the message:

```
IEA212A  DUPLICATE VOLUME 'vvvvvv' D, xxx or yyy. REPLY
                    DEVICE ADDRESS.
```

This is issued when the two DASDs with addresses xxx and yyy both have volumes labelled vvvvvv mounted on them. Be careful when replying to this one, as the logic is counterintuitive — the device you specify in your reply will be demounted and varied offline, and the one you do not specify will be kept online.

- Open and initialize the master catalog
- Open SYS1.PARMLIB and read the members to be used to control the processing done by the RIMs.
- Open the page datasets and initialize the auxiliary storage manager.
- Build the LPA, either by fetching the contents of SYS1.LPALIB and all the other libraries specified in the selected LPALST member(s) of SYS1.PARMLIB, or by reloading it from the PLPA page dataset (and if necessary the COMMON page dataset). The former process occurs if the PLPA page datasets are unusable, or if the CLPA parameter is specified in the selected IEASYSxx member of SYS1.PARMLIB or by the operator. This is known as a cold start of MVS. The alternative — reloading from the page datasets — is known as a warm start or quick start, depending on whether VIO datasets are also preserved across the IPL.
- Allocate the other common areas of virtual storage, including the CSA, whose size is determined by the CSA parameter in IEASYSxx, then rounded up to take the overall size of the common area up to a megabyte boundary.
- Initialize the linklist, reading the libraries to be used from the LNKLSTxx member(s) of PARMLIB specified in IEASYSxx.
- Perform limited-function starts of the PCAUTH, GRS, DUMPSRV, and TRACE address spaces.

Systems programmer must provide: SYS1.LOGREC, SYS1.SVCLIB, various members of PARMLIB, page datasets, lpalist libraries, linklist libraries, other datasets referred to in the selected PARMLIB members, master catalog, entries in catalog for all datasets required during initialization. (Note that user catalogs are not available during system initialization, so all datasets referred to during it must be cataloged in the master catalog, except those which MVS requires to be located on the SYSRES pack itself.)

Step 11

If the processor time-of-day (TOD) clocks are not set, or if the OPERATOR parameter is specified in the selected CLOCKxx member of SYS1.PARMLIB, the reconfiguration RIM issues message IEA888A, asking the operator to set the TOD clocks. You should use the OPERATOR parameter to force the operators to check the clocks at this point.

Systems programmer must provide: CLOCKxx member of PARMLIB.

Step 12

The operator replies "R 00,U" to confirm the TOD clocks are already set correctly, or if they are not, replies in the format:

```
R 00,DATE=yy.ddd,CLOCK=hh.mm.ss,GMT
```

to change the time. Depending on the model of processor you are using, the operator may then be asked to hit the TOD button on the system console to confirm the time change. The RIM re-issues the IEA888A message showing the new time after each reply until the operator replies U. Note that the system keeps two clock values, one known as GMT and the other known as the LOCAL time. The LOCAL time is calculated by adjusting GMT by the amount specified in the TIMEZONE parameter in CLOCKxx. However, the LOCAL date is not obtained in the same way! This means that if you have to set or adjust the GMT date using the above command, you will also have to set the LOCAL date, using the format:

```
R 00,DATE=yy.ddd
```

before you reply U.

Systems programmer must provide: CLOCKxx member of PARMLIB.

Step 13

The NIP phase ends when the NIP control module invokes IEEVIPL, the first of the routines used in the third and final phase — master scheduler initialization. This performs various initialization functions for the master scheduler address space, then loads the JCL for the address space from the MSTJCLyy member of SYS1.LINKLIB, where yy is supplied by the MSTJCL parameter in IEASYSxx. This JCL is passed to an initiator, which starts the module IEEMB860. IEEMB860 completes initialization of the address space and invokes IEEVWAIT, the permanent system task which is generally known as the master scheduler.

Other processes performed during this phase include:

- Full-function starts of the SMF, CONSOLE, and ALLOCAS address spaces. Note that during initialization of the CONSOLE address space, the MVS console definitions in the CONSOLxx and PFKTABxx members of PARMLIB come into force, and the message:

```
IEE152I ENTER CANCEL D C,K
```

is issued on the console selected as the MVS master console. This may be a different device from that used as the NIP console, but you should aim to keep your NIP console definitions in line with your CONSOLxx definitions to avoid the confusion that can occur when messages appear in unexpected places! In addition, SYSLOG processing is started during this phase. If you look at the SYSLOG for an IPL, you will find that it starts during the master scheduler initialization phase, but after a few pages of messages from this phase there is a break, and the messages from earlier in the IPL phase (lacking details such as the timestamps) are then printed out. This is because these messages are kept in buffers until SYSLOG initialization is complete, then recorded on the SYSLOG in a 'catch up' exercise.

- invoke RACF initialization if RACF is in use.

- Process the automatic commands in the IEACMD00 and COMMNDxx members of PARMLIB — though those which depend on JES, for example to start address spaces from JCL in PROCLIBs, will wait for JES initialization to complete before they will be processed.
- Set up the subsystem interface control blocks, then initialize the subsystems in the subsystem name table (including those in the IEFSSN00 member of PARMLIB), using the initialization modules named in the table.

Systems programmer must provide: MSTJCLxx member in SYS1.LINKLIB, SYS1.PROCLIB, SYS1.UADS and SYS1.BRODCAST datasets specified in the master JCL, various members of PARMLIB including automatic commands, SYS1.MANx datasets for recording SMF data, SYS1.STGINDEX which keeps track of VIO pages, RACF datasets if RACF is in use, full catalog structure, subsystem initialization modules.

Step 14

One of the last steps of the master scheduler initialization stage is to kick off the initialization of the job entry subsystem, which now normally happens as part of the subsystem initialization processing. Since MVS 2.2, the subsystem initialization process has been modified to include the creation of the primary subsystem, which is the job entry subsystem, and JES can now be started automatically by defining it as the primary subsystem in IEFSSN00. Previously, it was usually started by an S JES2 command at the end of MSTJCLxx, though it could be started simply by including it in the automatic commands, or even by operator command from the console. JES2 initialization is covered in more detail in Chapter 8; JES3 initialization is beyond the scope of this book.

Systems programmer must provide: JES parameters, JES procedure in SYS1.PROCLIB, other procedure libraries allocated in the JES procedure, spool and checkpoint datasets.

Step 15

Once MVS and JES initialization is complete, user-submitted jobs and started tasks using JCL procedures can be started. This will normally include various tasks started as a result of your automatic commands, such as DFHSM, third-party security products, and LLA. Of particular interest to us will be VTAM and (TCAS), the terminal control address space which controls logons to TSO. These are discussed in Chapters 9 and 10 respectively.

Systems programmer must provide: procedures, programs, parameters, and datasets used by all started tasks and jobs in the automatic commands.

If you have reached this point without any catastrophic errors, you now have a usable system. However, an error in almost any of the components required during the above process could prevent your MVS system from starting successfully. If this is a test system, that is embarrassing. If it is a production system, it is going to get you into trouble. If it is the only system you have, you may find it impossible to fix the problem because you need the system up in order to correct the mistake, and your career in systems programming could be in danger of coming to a premature end!

Clearly, getting MVS initialization to work right is one of the most vital (and most complicated) parts of a systems programmer's job. The following sections will discuss how to do it.

It should be equally clear that being able to recover whenever things do go wrong is a high priority for the career-conscious systems programmer. One extremely sensible precaution is to create an MVS system which contains everything required to bring up MVS, JES, VTAM, and TSO/ISPF on a single DASD pack, so that it is not dependent on anything which could conceivably go wrong with your live systems or your normal test systems. A one-pack system is one of your most valuable assets in many potentially disastrous situations, and we will discuss how to create one (and other emergency recovery facilities) in Chapter 19.

7.3   The SYSRES pack

Successful MVS initialization requires that the SYSRES pack contains the correct versions of the IPL bootstrap module, the IEAIPL00 module (the IPL text), SYS1.NUCLEUS, and SYS1.SVCLIB. In addition, it is normal practice to keep all the program libraries and other run-time libraries for MVS and associated IBM products on this pack, for example, SYS1.LINKLIB, SYS1.LPALIB, SYS1.CMDLIB, and the ISPF, PDF, and SDSF program, clist, panel, message, skeleton, and table libraries. This is the way the CBIPO process configures the SYSRES pack, and it has several advantages when it comes to maintaining/ upgrading your system. I would recommend a slightly modified version of the CBIPO configuration, which is explained in Chapter 11. In this section, we will discuss the setting up of the key datasets and groups of datasets which normally reside on the SYSRES pack.

7.3.1   The IPL program

As we have seen, this must reside on track 0, cylinder 0 of the SYSRES pack, and this area is reserved on every MVS-format DASD pack for IPL text by the simple expedient of making it impossible to allocate space on this track using MVS allocation services. We therefore require a special process to install the IPL text itself, and this is supplied by the ICKDSF (device support facilities) program. The JCL to install IPL text on a pack called SYSRS1 is shown in Example 7.1.

The BOOTSTRAP and IPLDD operands of the REFORMAT command in the SYSIN dataset instructs DSF to install the bootstrap records and IPL text contained in members IPLRECS and IEAIPL00 of SYS1.SAMPLIB in the correct

```
//STEP1     EXEC PGM=ICKDSF
//SYSPRINT DD SYSOUT=*
//IPLVOL    DD DISP=SHR,VOL=SER=SYSRS1,UNIT=3380
//IPLTEXT   DD DISP=SHR,VOL=SER=XA313R,UNIT=3380,
//             DSN=SYS1.SAMPLIB(IPLRECS)
//          DD DISP=SHR,VOL=SER=XA313R,UNIT=3380,
//             DSN=SYS1.SAMPLIB(IEAIPL00)
//SYSIN     DD *
  REFORMAT   DDNAME(IPLVOL)                -
             IPLDD(IPLTEXT)                -
             NOVERIFY                      -
             BOOTSTRAP
/*
```

Example 7.1. Creating IPL text on a DASD volume.

location on the volume. The rest of the volume is untouched. It is also possible to install the IPL records at the same time as formatting the entire volume, by using these operands on the DSF INIT command instead.

7.3.2 SYS1.NUCLEUS

As noted above, this dataset must reside on the SYSRES pack. It contains the IRIMs, NIP, and RIMs used in MVS initialization, the permanently resident (after NIP) modules of both the DAT-on nucleus and the DAT-off nucleus, and the master catalog pointer module. These modules are created by the MVS installation process. Included in the DAT-on nucleus, however, are some modules which can be altered to reflect changes in your I/O configuration — the processes for amending these are discussed in the next section.

Other than the I/O configuration modules, the only member of SYS1.NU-CLEUS you are likely to want to tailor is the master catalog pointer. If you want to change your master catalog, or set up an alternate master catalog (e.g. for use in disasters or when you are performing maintenance on the production master catalog), you will need to set up an alternate version of the SYSCATLG member. CBIPO provides an IEBDG job in IPO1.INSTLIB(CATPTR) which can be used to generate this (and also documents the meaning of each field in the catalog pointer record). Alternatively, you can copy the SYSCATLG member to create a new member with a name in the format SYSCATxx, then edit the new member, substituting the new master catalog's name and volume serial number for the old one. This cannot be done using the ISPF editor, which will not edit members in load module format, but it can be done using AMASPZAP, or some third-party online editors.

7.3.3 SYS1.SVCLIB

This load library must also reside on the SYSRES pack, as it contains service modules used in the early stages of system initialization. It is also set up by the

```
ISF.V1R3M0.ISFLPA,
SYS9.CA7.LPALIB,
SYS9.CICS210.LPAMODS,
SYS1.COB2LPA,
SYS9.OEM.LPALIB
/* LIB:  SYS1.PARMLIB(LPALST00)
/* DOC:  LPA LIBRARIES CONCATENATED BEHIND SYS1.LPALIB
/*       WHEN LPA IS LOADED AT A CLPA IPL
```

Example 7.2. LPALSTxx member of SYS1.PARMLIB.

MVS installation process, and you will normally never have to touch it yourself. The only modules in SYS1.SVCLIB in which you may have to take an interest are I/O appendages, used by some products which perform I/O without using the standard access methods.

7.3.4   SYS1.LPALIB and the lpalist libraries

These load libraries may reside on any DASD volume, but must be cataloged in the master catalog, as the user catalogs are not available at the time when the NIP RIM rebuilds the LPA. It is normal to leave SYS1.LPALIB itself, and any other LPA libraries built by the CBIPO process, on the SYSRES pack. Third-party or inhouse LPA modules should be kept in libraries on other packs, as these will be kept from one release of MVS to another, while all the SYSRES datasets will be discarded when you upgrade.

The usage of the LPA was explained in Sec. 3.7 — it is an area of common storage containing programs which can be shared between all address spaces. The RIM which builds the LPA finds the LPALSTxx member(s) of PARMLIB selected as a result of your specification of the LPA = xx parameter in IEASYS00 (or in any overrides to IEASYS00). If you have specified CLPA in your IEASYSxx member (i.e. requested a cold start of the LPA), it then concatenates the libraries listed in these members behind SYS1.LPALIB, and builds the LPA by loading the library members from this concatenation (i.e. it loads everything in SYS1.LPALIB, followed by everything in each succeeding library in the lpalist which does not duplicate a module it has already loaded). Example 7.2 shows an example of an LPALSTxx member of SYS1.PARMLIB.

If you want to change a module in the lpalist without reloading the whole LPA, you can provide a temporary replacement in the modified LPA (MLPA). The MLPA is reloaded at every IPL, irrespective of whether it is a cold, warm, or quick start. It is loaded with modules listed in those IEALPAxx members of PARMLIB which are selected by the MLPA = xx parameter in IEASYS00 (or overrides to IEASYS00). The IEALPAxx members list modules to be loaded and the libraries from which to load them. Note, however, that on pre-version 4 systems, you can only specify SYS1.LINKLIB, SYS1.LPALIB, or SYS1.SVCLIB as the source of an MLPA module. Also, on pre-version 4 systems, SYS1.LINKLIB is taken to

```
SYS1.LINKLIB,                /* SYSTEM LINK LIB              */
SYS1.MIGLIB,                 /* IPCS LINKLIB                */
SYS1.CMDLIB,                 /* TSO COMMANDS                */
ISF.V1R3M0.ISFLOAD,          /* SDSF                        */
ISR.V2R3M0.ISRLOAD,          /* ISPF/PDF                    */
ISP.V2R3M0.ISPLOAD,          /* ISPF                        */
SYS1.DGTLLIB,                /* DFDSS         VER 2 REL 4   */
SYS9.TSS.LOAD,               /* TSS                         */
SYS1.JSX.LOAD,               /* JES328X                     */
SYS1.COB2COMP,               /* VS COBOL II    VER 3        */
SYS1.COB2LIB,                /* VS COBOL II    VER 3        */
BLM.V4R2M0.BLMMOD1,          /* INFO..                      */
BLG.V4R2M0.BLGMOD1,          /* INFO..                      */
SYS9.LINKLIB,                /* IN-HOUSE LINKLIB            */
SYS9.CA.CAILIB,              /* CA PRODUCTS                 */
SYS1.GDDMLOAD                /* GDDM                        */
/*                                                          */
/* LIB: SYS1.PARMLIB(LNKLST00)                              */
```

Example 7.3. LNKLSTxx member of SYS1.PARMLIB.

mean the linklist concatenation, and SYS1.LPALIB to mean the lpalist concatenation. Version 4 allows the MLPA to be loaded from any authorized load library cataloged in the master catalog, and only searches the named library for a given module. Take care not to confuse the functions of the LPALSTxx and IEALPAxx members of SYS1.PARMLIB.

Another important point about the LPA is that all libraries in the lpalist must be APF authorized. SYS1.LPALIB itself is automatically considered authorized when it is opened as part of the LPALST concatenation, while APF authorization of other libraries is determined by the IEAAPFxx member of PARMLIB, discussed in Sec. 7.5.

7.3.5   SYS1.LINKLIB and the linklist libraries

Like the lpalist libraries, the linklist libraries may reside on any DASD volume, but must be cataloged in the master catalog. Again, it is normal to keep SYS1.LINK-LIB itself and any other libraries built by the CBIPO process on the SYSRES pack, and other libraries on other packs.

The linklist consists of the libraries specified in the LNKLSTxx members of PARMLIB selected at IPL time using the LNK = xx statement in IEASYS00 (or overrides to it). The libraries are concatenated in the order in which they appear in those members, except that SYS1.LINKLIB is placed at the front of the concatenation irrespective of whether, and where, it is coded. On MVS/ESA systems, the first library after SYS1.LINKLIB in the linklist concatenation must be SYS1.MIGLIB, the load library for the IPCS dump management product. Example 7.3 shows an example of a LNKLSTxx member of SYS1.PARMLIB.

Unlike the LPA, the members of these libraries are not actually loaded into storage during system initialization — instead, the system builds a BLDL table which records the physical locations of all the libraries in the concatenation, including details of each physical extent of each library, and when attempts are made to fetch a program from the linklist, this table is used to avoid catalog and VTOC searches. One important implication of this is that if a linklist library goes to an additional extent after system initialization, any modules placed in the new extent will not be accessible via the linklist. Traditionally, the solution to this has been to allocate all linklist libraries with zero secondary space allocations, so that they never go to additional extents. There are now third-party products which allow you to add additional extents to the linklist after an IPL if necessary. However, given the chaos which could occur in the gap between extending a dataset and adding the new extent to the linklist (especially as the extend could occur as a result of a change made by a non-systems programmer and could result in problems being experienced by many users which are not perceived as system problems for some time), it seems advisable to stick to the traditional rule, particularly for datasets which are not totally under the systems programmer's control.

Until MVS/XA, linklist datasets had to be APF authorized by naming them in the selected IEAAPFxx members. Now, however, it is not necessary for all linklist datasets to be APF authorized, which means that you can give application programmers the benefits of using the linklist, without creating the security exposure of allowing all and sundry to create and run APF-authorized code. If you do wish to authorize all linklist datasets, you can specify the LNKAUTH = LNKLIST parameter in IEASYS00 (or overrides), which will automatically authorize all linklist datasets, whether or not they appear in the selected IEAAPFxx members. The alternative is to specify LNKAUTH = APFTAB, which means that only those linklist datasets specified in your IEAAPFxx members will be authorized.

7.3.6   SYS1.DCMLIB

If your MVS system is at level 2.2 or higher, you will not have SYS1.DCMLIB on your system. Before this level, however, SYS1.DCMLIB was a required dataset on your SYSRES pack. It held definitions of MVS consoles, including the commands assigned to PF keys on the consoles. The dataset was set up automatically by the CBIPO jobs, and updated by the SYSGEN process, which could be irritating, as any operator modifications to the PF key definitions for their consoles were wiped out by every IOGEN. To save these modifications it was necessary to copy them out of DCMLIB before the IOGEN and back in again afterwards. Other than this, there should be no need for you to modify this dataset.

7.3.7   Catalog entries for SYSRES datasets

One feature which is particularly useful for SYSRES datasets is the ability to catalog a dataset with an indirect reference instead of a specific volume serial

```
//LIST      EXEC PGM=IDCAMS,REGION-512K
//STEPCAT    DD   DSN=CATALOG.VSYSCAT,DISP-SHR
//SYSPRINT   DD   SYSOUT=*
//SYSIN      DD   *
  DELETE              (SYS9.PLI.PLILINK    ) NONVSAM NOSCRATCH
  DEF NVSAM  ( NAME(SYS9.PLI.PLILINK    ) VOL(******) DEVT(0000))
```

Example 7.4. Recataloging a dataset to the SYSRES pack.

number. This is interpreted as meaning that the dataset will be found on the current
SYSRES volume at the time the catalog search is performed. Thus you can use the
same master catalog to IPL a system from any one of several SYSRES packs,
simply by ensuring that all your SYSRES datasets are cataloged using indirect
references. This is highly recommended—it gives you considerable operational
flexibility, and is a crucial aspect of my recommended strategy for system maintenance (see Chapter 11). Example 7.4 shows how to recatalog a dataset with an
indirect reference.

7.3.8   Master JCL

The JCL for the master scheduler address space is kept in the MSTJCLxx member
of a linklist library (usually SYS1.LINKLIB), where xx is specified by the
MSTRJCL = xx parameter in the IEASYS member of PARMLIB selected at IPL
time. Example 7.5 shows the typical JCL from an MSTJCLxx member for an
MVS/ESA system. On MVS/370 systems, there is usually an additional statement
which starts the job entry subsystem at the end of the JCL.

The master JCL is kept in load module format, which means that you cannot
amend it simply by using the ISPF editor. If you need to amend statements in it
(or remove statements by converting them to comments), you should take a copy
of your MSTJCL module, giving it a different suffix, and use AMASPZAP to
change it. If you need to add statements, you must reassemble and relink the
module from scratch — on CBIPO systems, the source is usually provided in
SYS1.SAMPLIB(SAMPMJCL), and the job in IPO1.JCLLIB(SYSADDM) is an
example of how to modify it.

```
//MSTJCL05 JOB MSGLEVEL=(1,1),TIME=1440
//         EXEC PGM=IEEMB860,DPRTY=(15,15)
//STCINRDR DD SYSOUT=(A,INTRDR)
//TSOINRDR DD SYSOUT=(A,INTRDR)
//IEFPDSI  DD DSN=SYS1.PROCLIB,DISP=SHR
//IEFPARM  DD DSN=SYS1.PARMLIB,DISP=SHR
//SYSUADS  DD DSN=SYS1,UADS,DISP=SHR
//SYSLBC   DD DSN=SYS1.BRODCAST,DISP=SHR
/*
```

Example 7.5. Master scheduler JCL.

7.4   Creating an I/O configuration

In order to communicate with the I/O devices attached to the channels, both MVS and the processor complex itself need to know what devices are attached to each channel, the names (addresses, subchannel numbers, or device names, depending on the context) by which they are known, and what protocols to use in communicating with them. MVS uses control blocks known as unit control blocks (UCBs) to store this sort of information, while the processor complex itself uses unit control words (UCWs). The information stored in these control blocks is known as the system's I/O configuration. In this section we will discuss the generation of these control blocks in general terms, then look at a practical example.

The UCBs are completed by the RIMs during NIP processing, and reside in the MVS nucleus. They are built from the MVS I/O configuration modules. These can be built in different ways and held in different places depending on your version of MVS:

- Prior to MVS 2.2 it was necessary to do a partial SYSGEN, known as an IOGEN, in order to build a new version of the nucleus whenever the configuration changed, and the configuration was part of the nucleus module itself (IEANUC0x).
- From MVS 2.2 onwards, the I/O configuration was built independently of the SYSGEN process using the MVS configuration program (MVSCP). MVSCP creates four separate modules in SYS1.NUCLEUS, called IOSUCBxx, IEANCTxx, IEFEDTxx, and IOSIITxx, where xx is the I/O configuration suffix. MVSCP is supported up to level 4.3 of MVS.
- From version 4 of MVS, the I/O configuration can be built using the new hardware configuration definition (HCD) facility, an ISPF dialog. HCD creates the configuration in a VSAM linear dataset called the I/O definition file (IODF).

The following discussion describes the creation of an I/O configuration using MVSCP. Given the limited lifespan of MVSCP, most sites should now be aiming to migrate to HCD, but many of the basic principles discussed below will still hold good.

The UCWs are built from the information held in the current IOCDS and kept in the hardware save area (HSA), an area of real storage which is not mapped onto any MVS virtual storage. The systems programmer must create the IOCDS using the I/O configuration program (IOCP) for the processor complex (this can be invoked by HCD on your behalf). The information required by IOCP overlaps considerably with your MVS I/O configuration data, and these must be kept in line. IBM has helped us to do this by allowing the same input to be used to generate both your IOCDS and your MVS I/O configuration, whether you are using MVSCP or HCD.

If you are using MVSCP, it automatically ignores the bits which are required only by IOCP, and IOCP can be instructed to ignore the bits which are required only by MVSCP by coding the IGNORE=YES parameter on the EXEC statement. It is highly advisable to take advantage of these features by creating a combined input deck for MVSCP and IOCP — changes to your configuration then only need to be coded in one place, and the risk of making two inconsistent changes is minimized (though you still have to remember to run both programs and bring the new MVS configuration and IOCDS into effect at the same time!).

7.4.1   I/O configuration for shared DASD

If you are sharing DASD between two systems, you can also share the same MVSCP/IOCP input deck between both systems. This is simplest if you ensure: (a) that any given device is given the same address on both systems; and (b) that you code all the channel paths attached to each control unit from either system on its CNTLUNIT macro. When you bring a system up using the shared configuration, the paths which do not actually exist on the current system will appear 'offline', and those that do exist will work normally. This has the advantage of minimizing the amount of change required when your configuration changes. It also gives you operational flexibility, as it is easy to IPL either system from the same SYSRES pack (though this can also be achieved by keeping two separate I/O configurations with different suffixes on the SYSRES pack, one for each system, and changing the loadparm to point to the one you want before you IPL).

Unfortunately, the 3990 control unit makes this a little more difficult, as it is possible to define more than four channels to a 3990, and MVSCP will not allow you to do this (no more than four can be used from the same MVS system). However, you can get round this by specifying each real device with two different addresses, one for use on each of your systems, with separate sets of CTLUNIT macros for each set of addresses, and only the CHPIDs used on the appropriate system defined on the CTLUNIT macros for that system. Although this sounds complicated, in practice it is safer than trying to keep two different MVSCP/IOCP decks in line. The example we discuss below shows just such a combined input deck.

7.4.2   IOCDS implementation

Each processor complex has a number of IOCDS 'slots', typically four or eight of them, each of which is identified by a two-character name, such as A1 or B3. The system console on the processor complex usually has a frame for IOCDS management, and from this frame you can write-protect or unprotect any of the available slots (except the one currently in use). When you are syntax-checking an IOCDS change, it is normal to code the WRTCDS=NO parameter to avoid overwriting an existing IOCDS; but once you have completed this stage, you should take the following steps to implement your new I/O configuration:

- Unprotect the IOCDS slot you plan to use using the system console.
- Run the IOCP with the WRTCDS = xx parameter, where xx is the name of the IOCDS to be overwritten.
- Protect your new IOCDS using the system console.
- When you can get a testing slot, select your new IOCDS on the system console, and perform a power-on reset to make it 'current'.
- IPL using a version of the MVS I/O configuration data which also reflects the changes you have made.

The HCD ACTIVATE command also updates the IOCDS, and if you have MVS 4.2 or later and an ES/9000 machine, you can even update the hardware configuration 'in-flight', using the dynamic reconfiguration management feature.

7.4.3   A combined MVSCP/IOCP input deck

We now turn to a detailed example of the creation of an I/O configuration. Example 7.6 shows sections of a typical combined input deck for MVSCP and IOCP which also combines the channel definitions required by two separate systems, in this case two logical partitions of a 3090 called TEST and PROD. Note that:

- This is part of a combined MVSCP/IOCP deck, with the location of missing sections shown by an ellipsis (. . .)
- Non-existent control units and devices can be included in this deck — MVS will check for their existence at IPL time, not find them, and mark them as offline. This allows new control units and devices to be added later without needing to run a new IOGEN and IOCDSGEN and perform a power on reset.
- Your I/O configuration can be made more easily comprehensible through the use of naming conventions. In this deck, the convention of using the CHPID number as the first two characters of the CU number of each control unit attached to the CHPID helps to keep things clear and simple. The labels in columns 1–8 are also purely for documentation purposes.
- If you have any devices on your system which are not documented in your MVSCP and IOCP manuals, you will usually find that they emulate a device which is. Solid-state DASD, for example, will usually be defined in your IOCP/MVSCP deck as disk devices, such as 3380s. The supplier of any non-standard device should provide you with documentation on the MVSCP/IOCP statements required to configure it.
- There is usually an element of redundancy and resilience built into the channel subsystem of modern processors. For example, on a 3090, channels are divided into blocks of four, there are two power supplies, and alternate blocks of channels are attached to alternate power supplies (i.e. channels 00–03, 08–0B, 10–13, etc., are on one power supply, while channels 04–07, 0C–0F, 14–17, etc.

```
******************************************************************************
IOCONFIG IOCONFIG ID=00                                   -- Note 1 --
*
IOCPHEAD ID    MSG1='PRD-CDS 28/11 FOR 3090-300E'     -- Note 2 --
******************************************************************************
*
*    3090 CHANNEL/DEVICE CONFIGURATION                    -- Note 3 --
*
*      CHPID     TYPE       PARTITION    ATTACHED DEVICE
*       00       BLOCK        PROD       3274-41D
*       01       BLOCK        PROD       3380
*       02       BLOCK        PROD       3380
*       03       BLOCK        PROD       3380/3390
*       04       BLOCK        TEST(R)    3380
*       05       BLOCK        PROD       3380/3390
*       06       BLOCK        PROD       3725   COMMS CONTROLLER
*       07       BLOCK        PROD       CTC LINK TO 3084Q
.
.
.

******************************************************************************
*    CHANNEL/PATH  DEFINITIONS                          -- Notes 4 & 5 --
******************************************************************************
PATH00    CHPID PATH=00,TYPE-BL,PARTITION=(PROD)
PATH01    CHPID PATH=01,TYPE=BL,PARTITION=(PROD)
PATH02    CHPID PATH=02,TYPE=BL,PARTITION=(PROD)
PATH03    CHPID PATH=03,TYPE=BL,PARTITION=(PROD)
PATH04    CHPID PATH=04,TYPE=BL,PARTITION=(TEST,REC)
PATH05    CHPID PATH=05,TYPE=BL,PARTITION=(PROD)
PATH06    CHPID PATH=06,TYPE=BL,PARTITION=(PROD)
PATH07    CHPID PATH=07,TYPE=BL,PARTITION=(PROD)
.
.
.

******************************************************************************
*   CHPID 00   -  3274-41D,  LOCAL COMMS          -- Notes 6 & 7 --   *
******************************************************************************
CU000    CNTLUNIT CUNUMBR=000,PATH=(00),PROTOCL=D,SHARED=YB,          +
              UNIT=3274,UNITADD=((A0,16))
DEVAA0   IODEVICE ADDRESS=(AA0,14),CUNUMBR=000,UNIT=3278,MODEL=2,     +
              FEATURE=(UKCHAR,EBKY3277,KB78KEY,SELPEN,NUMLOCK,AUDALRM)
DEVAAE   IODEVICE ADDRESS=(AAE,2),CUNUMBR=000,UNIT=3286,MODEL=2,      +
              FEATURE=(UKCHAR)
******************************************************************************
*   CHPID 0D   -  3274-41D, LOCAL COMMS                               *
******************************************************************************
CU0D0    CNTLUNIT CUNUMBR=0D0,PATH=(0D),PROTOCL=D,SHARED=YB,          +
              UNIT-3274,UNITADD=((40,32))
DEVB40   IODEVICE ADDRESS=(B40,29),CUNUMBR=0D0,UNIT=3278,MODEL=2,     +
              FEATURE=(UKCHAR,EBKY3277,KB78KEY,SELPEN,NUMLOCK,AUDALRM)
DEVB5D   IODEVICE ADDRESS=(B5D,3),CUNUMBR=0D0,UNIT=3286,MODEL=2,      +
              FEATURE=(UKCHAR)
.
.
.
```

Example 7.6. Extracts from a combined MVSCP/IOCP input deck.

```
**********************************************************************
*   CHPIDS  OE  19  25  &  29        3380 'E'      -- Notes 8 & 9 --   *
**********************************************************************
CU190    CNTLUNIT CUNUMBR=190,PATH=(19,OE),PROTOCL=S,SHARED=N,         +
             UNIT=3880,UNITADD=((30,16))
CU290    CNTLUNIT CUNUMBR=290,PATH=(29,25),PROTOCL=S,SHARED=N,         +
             UNIT=3880,UNITADD=((30,16))
DEV430   IODEVICE ADDRESS=(430,16),CUNUMBR=(190,290),UNIT=3380,        +
             FEATURE=(SHARED)
**********************************************************************
*                                         -- Notes 10 & 11 --   *
*   CHPIDS  03  05  OB  &  27        3390 & 3380 'E'      PROD    *
*   CHPIDS  OF & 23                  3390 & 3380 'E'      TEST    *
**********************************************************************
CU030    CNTLUNIT CUNUMBR=030,PATH=(03),PROTOCL=S4,SHARED=N,           +
             UNIT=3990,UNITADD=((40,64))
CU050    CNTLUNIT CUNUMBR=050,PATH=(05),PROTOCL=S4,SHARED=N,           +
             UNIT=3990,UNITADD=((40,64))
CUOBO    CNTLUNIT CUNUMBR=OBO,PATH=(OB),PROTOCL=S4,SHARED=N,           +
             UNIT=3990,UNITADD=((40,64))
CU270    CNTLUNIT CUNUMBR=270,PATH=(27),PROTOCL=S4,SHARED=N,           +
             UNIT=3990,UNITADD=((40,64))
CUOFO    CNTLUNIT CUNUMBR=OFO,PATH=(OF),PROTOCL=S4,SHARED=N,           +
             UNIT=3990,UNITADD=((40,64))
CU230    CNTLUNIT CUNUMBR=230,PATH=(23),PROTOCL=S4,SHARED=N,           +
             UNIT=3990,UNITADD=((40,64))
DEV140   IODEVICE ADDRESS=(140,32),CUNUMBR=(030,050,OBO,270),UNIT=3390,+
             FEATURE=(SHARED)
DEV160   IODEVICE ADDRESS=(160,16),CUNUMBR=(030,050,OBO,270),UNIT=3380,+
             FEATURE=(SHARED)
DEV170   IODEVICE ADDRESS=(170,16),CUNUMBR=(030,050,OBO,270),UNIT=3380,+
             FEATURE=(SHARED)
DEV240   IODEVICE ADDRESS=(240,32),CUNUMBR=(OFO,230),                  +
             UNIT=3390,FEATURE=(SHARED)
DEV260   IODEVICE ADDRESS=(260,16),CUNUMBR=(OFO,230),                  +
             UNIT=3380,FEATURE=(SHARED)
DEV270   IODEVICE ADDRESS=(270,16),CUNUMBR=(OFO,230),                  +
             UNIT=3380,FEATURE=(SHARED)
.
.
.

**********************************************************************
*   CHPIDS 06 & 10  -  3725, COMMS CONTROLLER      -- Note 12 --   *
**********************************************************************
CU060    CNTLUNIT CUNUMBR=060,PATH=06,PROTOCL=D,SHARED=N,              +
             UNIT=3705,UNITADD=((40,2))
CU100    CNTLUNIT CUNUMBR=100,PATH=10,PROTOCL=D,SHARED=N,              +
             UNIT=3705,UNITADD=((40,2))
DEV640   IODEVICE ADDRESS=(640,2),CUNUMBR=(060,100),ADAPTER=CA1,       +
             UNIT=3705
**********************************************************************
*   CHPID  07       CHANNEL-TO-CHANNEL ADAPTORS     -- Note 13 --   *
**********************************************************************
CU070    CNTLUNIT CUNUMBR=070,PATH=(07),SHARED=N,UNIT=CTC,             +
             UNITADD=((00,4))
         IODEVICE ADDRESS=(400,4),CUNUMBR=070,UNIT=CTC,TIMEOUT=N
```

Example 7.6. (cont.)

```
*******************************************************************
*   CHPID 08  -  4248 PRINTER                       -- Note 14 --    *
*******************************************************************
CU080    CNTLUNIT CUNUMBR=080,PATH=(08),PROTOCL=D,SHARED=N,          +
              UNIT=4248,UNITADD=90
DEVC90   IODEVICE UNIT=4248,ADDRESS=C90,CUNUMBR=080
*******************************************************************
*   CHPID 03  -  3480, TAPES                        -- Note 15 --    *
*   CHPID 07  -  3480, TAPES                                         *
*******************************************************************
CU090    CNTLUNIT CUNUMBR=090,PATH=(09,1A),PROTOCL=S4,SHARED=N,      +
              UNIT=3480,UNITADD=((A0,16))
CU260    CNTLUNIT CUNUMBR=260,PATH=26,PROTOCL=S4,SHARED=N,           +
              UNIT=3480,UNITADD=((A0,16))
DEV6A0   IODEVICE ADDRESS=(6A0,16),CUNUMBR=(090,260),UNIT=3480,      +
              FEATURE=(SHARABLE)
.
.
.


*******************************************************************
*   DUMMY DEVICE FOR VIO                            -- Note 16 --    *
*******************************************************************
DEVFE0   IODEVICE UNIT=2305,ADDRESS=(FE0,1),CUNUMBR=***
*******************************************************************
*   UNITNAMES FOR           DEVICES                 -- Note 17 --    *
*******************************************************************
USYSSQ UNITNAME NAME=SYSSQ,VIO=NO,                                   +
              UNIT=((100,16),(140,64),(240,64),(430,16),(650,16))
USYSDA UNITNAME NAME=SYSDA,                                          +
              UNIT=((100,16),(140,64),(240,64),(430,16),(650,16))
UWORK  UNITNAME NAME=WORK,VIO=YES,                                   +
              UNIT=(14D,14F,240,24F,436)
UDISK  UNITNAME NAME=DISK,                                           +
              UNIT=(104,108,10A,434,437)
UTSO   UNITNAME NAME=TSO,                                            +
              UNIT=(105,433)
USYST  UNITNAME NAME=SYSTEM,VIO=NO,                                  +
              UNIT=(101,102,103,10C,146,14A,160,163,166,167,170,176, +
              246,24A,260,263,266,267,270,276,432,43A,43B,           +
              650,652,653,65A,65B,65E,65F)
UCTAPE UNITNAME NAME=CTAPE,UNIT=((6A0,16))
.
.
.


VIO    UNITNAME NAME=VIO,VIO=YES,UNIT=(FE0)
*******************************************************************
*  NIP CONSOLES FOR 3090                            -- Note 18 --    *
*******************************************************************
          SPACE 2
NIPCONS NIPCON DEVNUM=(AA0,AA2,B40,B42)            /*IPLCONS*/
          SPACE 2
*******************************************************************
*   DO NOT PLACE AN END STATEMENT HERE                              *
*******************************************************************
```

Example 7.6. (cont.)

are on the other). Where this is the case, you should take advantage of it, ensuring for example that where there are two paths to a string of DASD they are on separate power supplies, and that the paths to the 3274s with your master and alternate master consoles are on separate power supplies.

The following notes relate to particular sections of Example 7.6:

1 The IOCONFIG macro is used to specify a two-character identifier which will be used as the suffix of the I/O configuration modules to be created by MVSCP in SYS1.NUCLEUS.

2 The ID macro is used to specify header information for reports produced by both MVSCP and IOCP.

3 The table describing CHPIDs is a good example of internal documentation.

4 The CHPID macro is used by IOCP to define a channel path. The TYPE parameter identifies this as either a BLOCK multiplexor or a BYTE multiplexor channel. The latter type is rarely used these days, but may be required for devices such as card punches and readers, and front-end processors running EP or PEP.

5 The PARTITION parameter on the CHPID macro defines which logical partition a channel belongs to in a PR/SM environment. The REC keyword indicates that the channel is dynamically reconfigurable. PR/SM is discussed further in Chapter 13.

6 The CNTLUNIT macro is used by IOCP to define a control unit. It identifies the type of control unit, the channel path(s) to which it is attached, the unit addresses of devices which may be attached to it, and various aspects of the protocols to be used to communicate with it. Most of these protocol values are fixed for each type of control unit, and these will be documented in your IOCP manual.

7 The IODEVICE macro is used by both MVSCP and IOCP to define an I/O device or, more commonly, a group of similar I/O devices at contiguous addresses. It identifies the device type, address(es), the control unit(s) to which it is attached, and any device-specific features which MVS may need to know about. These features will be documented in your MVSCP manual. In this example, we see fourteen 3278-type terminals and two 3286-type printers attached to a 3274 control unit. Note that the 'address' of a device is, strictly speaking, referred to as the 'device address' on processors in S/370 mode, but as the 'device number' in XA and ESA modes, as the channel subsystems use addresses in quite a different way on post-370 systems. The number-of-units part of the ADDRESS parameter should always be explicitly coded, as the defaults sometimes differ between MVSCP and IOCP!

8 This group of statements defines a string of 3380 DASD connected to two 3880 storage directors. Note that a separate CNTLUNIT macro is coded for each storage director, whether they are part of the same 3880 or not. We have defined two channels to each storage director, one from each of the logical

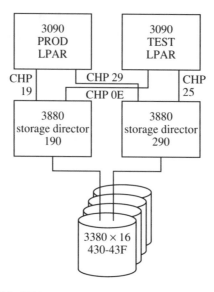

Figure 7.2. 3880 configuration in stage 1 example.

partitions, so this configuration can be used to generate not only the IOCP for
the complex but also an MVSCP configuration which will work on either
partition. When this configuration is used on the PROD partition, CHPIDs
0E and 25 will appear to be offline, and when it is used on the TEST partition,
CHPIDs 19 and 29 will appear to be offline. Figure 7.2 illustrates the configuration represented by this group of statements.

9   The FEATURE = SHARED parameter on the IODEVICE macro is used for
shared DASD to indicate to MVS that it should enable RESERVE/RELEASE
processing for these devices (see Chapter 14 for more details on sharing
DASD). Do not confuse this parameter with the SHARED = parameter on
the CNTLUNIT macro.

10 This group of statements defines a string of 3390 DASD and two strings of
3380 DASD connected to a single 3990 control unit. As with the 3880 defined
earlier, both PROD and TEST CHPIDs are included. However, in this case
there are more than four channels to each device, so we have been forced to
adopt the solution discussed in the last section, where each device appears in
two separate places. In this case, control unit number 0B0 is the same device
as control unit 0F0, control unit 270 is the same device as control unit 230, and
the DASD 140–17F are the same devices as the DASD 240–27F. This enables
this configuration to be used by either the TEST or the PROD partition. When
PROD is using it, CHPIDs 0F and 23, control units 0F0 and 230, and the
DASD 240–27F will appear to be offline, and when TEST is using it, CHPIDs
03, 05, 0B, and 27, control units 030, 050, 0B0, and 270, and DASD 140–17F
will appear to be offline. Figure 7.3 shows the configuration represented by

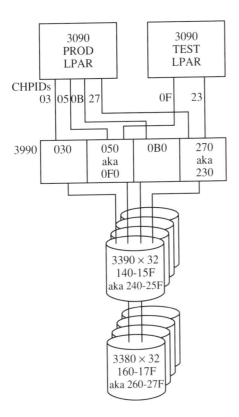

Figure 7.3. 3990 configuration in stage 1 example.

this group of statements.

11 Note the use of PROTOCL=S4 on the CNTLUNIT macros for the 3990. This indicates the use of 4.5 megabyte per second channel speeds.

12 This group of statements defines a 3725 front-end processor. This device is running NCP rather than EP or PEP, and can therefore be attached to a block multiplexor channel.

13 This group defines a channel-to-channel adapter. While multiple addresses are defined on the notional control unit, you should only actually use one address on each channel. ESCON CTC links, however, do support the use of multiple addresses on a single channel.

14 This group defines a 4248 printer. Note that the CNTLUNIT macro is included, even though the control unit function is actually integral to the printer, i.e. there is only one box, which requires both a CNTLUNIT and an IODEVICE macro to define it.

15 This group defines a string of 3480 tape drives.

16 This IODEVICE macro represents a non-existent device which is referred to later in the deck when we define the esoteric device name for VIO. It is used to define features of allocations made with UNIT=VIO such as the track

geometry of the device simulated by VIO, and the maximum size of a dataset (this is limited to the size of a single volume of the simulated device). As it does not exist and will never exist, there is no need to define a channel path or control unit for it, but we must code the CUNUMBR parameter with a value of *** to avoid a syntax error. VIO is discussed in much more detail later in Sec. 7.4.6.

17 This group of UNITNAME macros defines the eligible device table (EDT). The coding and use of the EDT is covered in Sec. 7.4.5. Note that where the same device appears in this deck with more than one address, both are coded on the UNITNAME macros for the esoteric groups to which it belongs.

18 The NIPCON macro defines the console addresses which may be used during the NIP stage of MVS initialization (see Sec. 7.1 for more on NIP processing). NIP will go through the devices at these addresses until it finds one which is a valid device type, powered on, and with an available path, and it will then use that device as its console. Later in the initialization process, the console parameters in the CONSOLxx member of SYS1.PARMLIB will replace these definitions.

7.4.4   The hardware configuration definition facility

HCD is a new facility of MVS version 4 which is designed to simplify the process of defining I/O configurations for MVS systems. It runs as an ISPF dialog, and allows the systems programmer to create or update an I/O configuration interactively. It provides selection lists of alternatives whenever choices have to be made, and validates the options you enter at data entry time, thus eliminating many potential errors later in the configuration process.

As we mentioned earlier, I/O configurations created using HCD are stored in VSAM linear datasets known as IODFs. When you create or update a configuration, it is placed in a 'work IODF', with a name like hlq.IODFnn.workname, where you select the values of hlq, nn (numeric), and workname. You also assign a name to the configuration itself, as you can have multiple configurations in the same IODF (e.g. old and new configurations, or configurations for different machines or partitions). There is also an option to migrate an existing MVSCP/IOCP deck into an IODF.

Once you are satisfied with your configuration, you can translate it into a format that can be used by the IPL process to build your MVS UCBs, etc. When you translate your configuration you also move it into a production IODF, which will have a name like hlq.IODFnn, where nn is numeric. Your configuration can then be selected at IPL time by naming the configuration, and the values of hlq and nn which define your IODF datasetname, on the IODF card in the LOADxx member. Note, however, that the IODF used at IPL time must be on the same device as the LOADxx member which refers to it (i.e. the device whose device number was entered as the first four characters of the loadparm on the hardware console).

You can also instruct HCD to submit a batch IOCP job which will build a new IOCDS from your configuration.

If you have MVS 4.2 or higher, and are running on an ES/9000 machine with the appropriate hardware feature, you can take this all a stage further by using dynamic reconfiguration management to change your hardware configuration while your system is up and running. With this option, the HCD ACTIVATE command or the new ACTIVATE console command can be used to take the configuration in an IODF and use it to: (a) modify the IOCDS; (b) modify the MVS UCBs; and (c) modify the UCWs in the HSA. Thus, for example, a new string of DASD could be installed on a new control unit and a group of new (ESCON) channels, then added to the configuration dynamically and varied online, all without bringing down your MVS system. Only certain types of device, however, can be dynamically reconfigured — these are known as dynamic devices, while those which can not be reconfigured dynamically are known as static devices.

7.4.5 The eligible device table

One part of the MVS I/O configuration is the eligible device table (EDT), which defines which devices on the system are eligible to be used to satisfy requests for any given esoteric device name. Thus, for example, if you code a JCL DD statement requesting allocation of a dataset on UNIT=WORK, MVS will go to the EDT to determine which devices are associated with the esoteric name WORK, and may therefore be used to satisfy this request.

As with the rest of the I/O configuration, the location and means of creation of the EDT depends on your level of MVS:

- On a pre-MVS 2.2 system, the EDT is part of the nucleus module IEANUC0n, and can only be modified by doing a partial SYSGEN known as an EDTGEN.
- If you are using MVSCP to generate your I/O configuration, the EDT is created in the IEFEDTxx member of SYS1.NUCLEUS. You can generate a new EDT independently of the rest of the I/O configuration by running MVSCP with PARM=EDT on the EXEC statement. By default, the version of IEFEDTxx selected at IPL time will be the one with the same suffix as the rest of the MVS I/O configuration modules. It is possible to override this, however, by specifying an alternate EDT suffix on the EDT statement of the SCHEDxx member of SYS1.PARMLIB.
- If you are using HCD to generate your I/O configuration, the EDT will be part of the configuration stored in the IODF. The configuration selected will depend on the IODF card in the LOADxx member, and an alternate EDT identifier can also be selected from here.

If you are using MVSCP, e.g. as in Example 7.6, the EDT is generated from the

UNITNAME macros in the MVSCP input deck (exactly the same macros were used in the old SYSGEN, and the same principles still apply using HCD). Each macro represents a pool of DASD or tape devices, and you should also have a special entry for VIO (see Sec. 7.4.6 for more on VIO). It is essential to keep the definitions in your EDT in line with your DASD pooling rules, otherwise you will experience numerous problems — datasets being allocated on wrong volumes, security violations when allocation on wrong volumes is attempted, and possibly mount messages being issued for non-existent volumes. See Chapter 16 for further discussion of DASD pooling.

You will note that device names such as 3380 and 3390 do not appear in the EDT — these 'generic device names' are handled by MVS automatically. The esoteric device name SYSALLDA is also generated automatically, so you should not code a UNITNAME macro for this in your EDT. On the other hand, there are some standard entries that you should ensure are there, as many IBM and third-party products assume they will be. Other than VIO itself, SYSDA, SYSSQ, and WORK are generally used. SYSDA usually covers all DASD, though you may find that this can cause problems when a job specifies UNIT=SYSDA and MVS then tries to allocate the dataset on a volume which the user is not authorized to use. If you use security products to control allocation on DASD, it is wise to restrict SYSDA to devices which are freely available to all demand users. SYSSQ is sometimes used as an equivalent to SYSDA which is not eligible for VIO. WORK is generally used to represent freely available work packs where temporary datasets can be allocated.

There is one important caution which anyone changing an EDT must be aware of. When a dataset is cataloged using IDCAMS or IEHPROGM and the device type is specified as an esoteric device type instead of a generic device type (e.g. with UNIT=WORK instead of UNIT=3390), the device type field of the catalog entry for the dataset (which usually corresponds to the UCBTYP value for the device on which the dataset is cataloged) will simply specify the lookup value (in effect the sequence number) for the relevant UNITNAME in the EDT. If you subsequently change the EDT in such a way as to alter the sequence number of that UNITNAME, then attempts to allocate datasets cataloged on that UNITNAME may fail.

The classic symptoms of this (which I have seen in three different sites!) are console messages which:

- Ask the operator to vary online a DASD device on which MVS wishes to mount a tape volume
- Say there are no devices available with a given DASD unit name on which to mount the tape volume; or
- Say the unit field in a dataset's catalog entry specifies an incorrect device type

To understand how this can happen, imagine that the fifth entry in your EDT is a group of tape devices, then you insert a group of DASD in the fifth position.

Now, if you attempt to allocate a tape dataset which was cataloged with the old esoteric device type, MVS will find that it is cataloged on the fifth esoteric device group, identify this as the new DASD group, and ask the operators to mount the tape volume on one of the DASD units in the new group! The simple way to avoid problems of this nature is never to disturb the sequence of the existing entries in your EDT — if you wish to add a new entry, add it at the end, and if you wish to delete an entry, don't! (You can simply define it with a non-existent device, or alternatively replace it with an entry for a DUMMY device type.)

Incidentally, EDTs are now starting to become less important, as the preferred method for pooling DASD volumes has now become SMS storage groups. However, this will no doubt create the temptation on many sites to start deleting UNITNAME macros from the EDT as the DASD pools they represent become SMS storage groups!

7.4.6 *Virtual I/O*

Virtual I/O (VIO) is also controlled from the EDT — if a DASD esoteric device type is made eligible for VIO by coding VIO = YES on its UNITNAME macro, then MVS may allocate certain datasets assigned to that device type to VIO instead. When this occurs, the dataset is not allocated on a real device in the pool. Instead, MVS emulates I/O operations to it as if they were going to disk, but actually moves the data to and from a 'window' of virtual storage, later backing it on paging datasets when the auxiliary storage manager decides to page out this virtual storage. This eliminates a number of overheads associated with allocation of real datasets, and for small datasets whose pages are unlikely to be stolen it can eliminate real I/Os when the data is rereferenced.

MVS selects VIO for datasets which are: (a) defined with temporary dataset names (or no dataset names); (b) assigned to VIO-eligible device names; and (c) not kept beyond the end of the current job. Although this sounds terribly clever, on storage-constrained systems VIO datasets of any size are likely to suffer page-stealing, which means you are saving very little I/O and placing a strain on your paging system to boot. Very large datasets going to VIO can actually fill up your page datasets and bring your entire system to a halt.

You should therefore control VIO carefully, particularly by preventing large datasets from using it (on typical storage configurations at the time of writing, anything over about 10 cylinders of 3390 is too large for VIO — this works out around 8 megabytes). If you are using DFSMS, you can control VIO allocations using this. However, if you are not, you will have more difficulty — JES exits can be used to prevent large allocations from JCL, but dynamic allocation is far more difficult to control. Some products allow you to specify options which control their dynamic allocations, and where the product is causing problems through its use of VIO you should use these options to direct dynamic allocation to an esoteric device group which is not eligible for VIO. Sort programs in particular are notorious for soaking up VIO space, so you should ensure that dynamically allocated sort work areas are directed to a non-VIO device group.

A broad-brush approach is possible by specifying a 'simulated device' for VIO (like the device with address FE0 in the stage 1 example earlier) with a relatively small data capacity (e.g. a 2305), as MVS will not allocate a dataset to VIO if it requires more space than is available on one volume of the simulated device. Note, however, that support for many of these older devices, including the 2305, is not available in DFSMS/MVS, so this option will only be possible for those at lower levels of DFP.

Another option is to use directed VIO. This means dividing your paging datasets between those which are eligible for VIO (slower speed devices can be used for these, as system performance is not so critically dependent on a fast response for VIO paging as it is for demand paging), and those which are not. The system will direct VIO paging to the eligible datasets and demand paging to the others when possible. However, if the non-VIO datasets are too small, demand paging will also use the VIO-eligible ones, and if the VIO-eligible ones are too small, VIO paging will use the others, but in single-page mode rather than block-paging mode, which degrades performance for all I/O to the dataset. If you choose to implement directed VIO you must therefore monitor the usage of your paging datasets carefully.

Directed VIO also does not impose any definite limit on VIO usage, and it is therefore questionable whether it is of value unless you have paging datasets spread across higher and lower speed devices and wish to improve the performance of demand paging by concentrating it all on the higher speed devices at the expense of VIO.

7.5   SYS1.PARMLIB

As we saw in Sec. 7.2, the master parameter list controlling MVS initialization is held in the IEASYS00 member of SYS1.PARMLIB. Unless you have an MVS version 4 system and are using the LOADxx member to control system configuration, parameters specified in IEASYS00 can be overridden individually by the operator at IPL time. Alternatively, the operator can specify SYSP=xx as part of the list of override parameters, which will result in the contents of IEASYSxx overriding the equivalent parameters in IEASYS00 (this is like concatenating IEASYSxx in front of IEASYS00 — any parameters which are not coded in IEASYSxx will be taken from IEASYS00). If you are using the LOADxx member, the SYSPARM card can be used, and has the same effect as replying SYSP=xx.

IBM recommends that you keep only the parameters which never change from one IPL to another in IEASYS00, and keep other parameters in alternative IEASYSxx members, which can be selected depending on the type of IPL required. However, for simplicity's sake, I would recommend that you avoid using different types of IPL for different situations, and keep all your IEASYS parameters in

IEASYS00. If you do have a parameter you need to change in an emergency, do it using operator overrides, and when bringing up a test system (or an emergency recovery 'one-pack' system like that described in Chapter 19), use a completely separate copy of SYS1.PARMLIB.

SYS1.PARMLIB is allocated by CBIPO on the SYSRES pack, but I recommend you move it onto another system pack, such as the master catalog pack. The reason is to enable you to use the same copy of PARMLIB on a given system at all times, while switching between SYSRES packs (see Chapter 11 on maintenance strategies for further discussion of this point). PARMLIB must be allocated in a single extent, as the RIMs which read it cannot process multiple extents. If you are still running MVS/370, you must allocate it as an unblocked dataset, though this is not necessary under more recent versions of MVS.

You should set a standard for amendment of PARMLIB members which ensures that a backup of recently changed members as they were before they were changed is always available in case you need to back out the change. In extreme cases, your system may not IPL unless you back out the change, so you should ensure that the backup members can be selected using operator overrides instead of the changed members. For example, your standard could be:

- Always use the suffix 00 for the live version of any member and 99 for the backup version. You may have multiple live versions of some members, such as the IPS and ICS used by SRM — in these cases, use suffixes starting with a 0 for the live version and suffixes starting with a 9 for the backup.
- Before changing any member of PARMLIB, check carefully whether or not it is the current live one. If so, take a backup before changing it.

The danger of this standard is that two people could each change the same member, and the second person's backup could overwrite the first, so that the 'backup' version becomes one that has never been tested in a real IPL. To avoid this, you must check that the backup was taken earlier than the most recent IPL. An alternative standard is to use your initials as the suffix of backup members. This, however, tends to fill up PARMLIB with out-of-date backups until you have a backup of every member taken by every member of the systems programming team! To avoid this, you must regularly remove obsolete backups.

In any case, you should review your SYS1.PARMLIB after major upgrades and remove any obsolete members and obsolete parameters in current members. This minimizes confusion when making changes. However, you must exercise caution when 'cleaning up' PARMLIB, as many members are used in situations other than IPLs, such as MPFLST members, which can be invoked by command, or ERBRMF members, which are used by various components of RMF, and it may not be immediately clear which are in use and which are not. To be on the safe side, take a backup of any you delete.

Note that the syntax used differs between PARMLIB members: comments, for example, must be coded in different ways in different members; and continuation

```
IODF      01 SYS1      PROD9201 03
NUCLEUS   2
SYSCAT    SYSCAT113CCATALOG.VSYSCAT
SYSPARM   00
*
*   SYSTEM CONFIGURATION MEMBER FOR PROD SYSTEM
*
```

Example 7.7. LOADxx member of PARMLIB.

from one line to another follows different rules in different members. You must take great care with your syntax when changing PARMLIB members — it is all too easy, for example, to 'lose' part of a member by missing out a continuation requirement from a line halfway through it. [8] documents the parameters that are valid in all the members of PARMLIB, as well as the syntax of each member, and you should check it whenever you are unsure of what you are doing.

7.5.1   LOADxx

The LOADxx member was introduced in MVS version 4 to eliminate the need for operators to make major decisions at IPL time. It makes it possible to eliminate the messages which ask the operator to specify the system parameters and the master catalog pointer suffix, and also makes it easier to specify the I/O configuration to be used at IPL time.

The member need not be in SYS1.PARMLIB itself; it may be in a SYSn. IPLPARM dataset instead. In either case, the dataset containing the LOADxx member must be on the volume whose device number was specified in the first four characters of the loadparm on the hardware console at IPL time. You should note that this makes it possible for two different versions of SYS1.PARMLIB to be used during the same IPL — the one on the loadparm device, which contains LOADxx (and NUCLSTxx, if used), and the one pointed to by the master catalog, which contains all other IPL parameters. It is probably wise to avoid this potential for confusion by putting your LOADxx members in an IPLPARM dataset instead.

The format of the LOADxx member is illustrated in Example 7.7. Note that:

- The parameters in LOADxx are all positional, and the meaning of the characters in each position is documented in [8].
- The IODF statement here indicates that the I/O configuration is to be taken from configuration PROD9201 in SYS1.IODF01, and that the EDT with identifier 03 is to be used. There is an MVSCP statement which can be used in place of the IODF statement if you are still using MVSCP to generate an I/O configuration in SYS1.NUCLEUS.
- The NUCLEUS statement supplies the suffix of the alternate nucleus to be used if you do not wish to use IEANUC01. This can be overridden from the loadparm.
- The SYSCAT statement replaces the master catalog pointer in member

SYSCATxx of SYS1.NUCLEUS, and the format of the parameters is essentially the same as that of the old SYSCATxx member. It specifies the master
catalog's volume serial number and dataset name, plus a number of other
indicators. If the SYSCAT statement is not coded, the operator will be
prompted to supply a value for the SYSCATxx suffix as on pre-version 4
systems.

- The SYSPARM statement allows you to specify the suffix of the IEASYSxx
member to be used as the master parameter list for this IPL, instead of
prompting the operator with the SPECIFY SYSTEM PARAMETERS
message. If SYSPARM is not coded, the operator will be prompted anyway.

7.5.2   *IEASYSxx*

A typical IEASYS00 member is shown in Example 7.8. This and all the remaining
examples in this section were taken from an MVS 3.1.3 system. In Example 7.8 note
that:

- Internal comments are used to good effect, so many of the parameters should
be self-explanatory.
- Many of the parameters specify suffixes for other parameter lists; of these, the
LNKLSTxx and LPALSTxx members have already been discussed in Sec. 7.3,
and the others used in this example are discussed in more detail in the rest of
this section. Some of the suffixes default to 00, but you should specify them
anyway in your IEASYSxx member, so that: (a) it is immediately apparent to
anyone reading the member how your system is configured, and (b) if you need
to change the suffix, the change is very easy to make.
- When the NIP routines scan the IEASYSxx parameters, they always stop after
the first parameter which is not followed by a comma — it is therefore vital to
ensure that when you are modifying any parameter except the last one you
include the comma! Failure to do so can lead to many types of problem with
your IPL, e.g. messages on shortage of paging space, because the scan stopped
before the PAGE parms were reached, or failure of critical subsystems to start
because their LPA libraries were not loaded into the LPA.
- Again, any of the parameters in IEASYS00 can be overridden, except the
PAGE parameter. Any PAGE parameters specified in operator overrides
(either directly, or indirectly through use of the SYSP=xx override parameter
to invoke an additional IEASYSxx member) are treated as ADDITIONAL to
those in IEASYS00. This can be confusing until you are used to it. However,
if a page dataset specified in the IPL parameters is not found, the system will
attempt to continue without it.
- Although there are many circumstances that will bring the IPL to a halt, the
system does attempt to recover from many types of error, or continue the IPL
process using defaults. In some cases, it issues messages to give you the
opportunity to specify replacement parameters. If you are bringing up a test

```
APF=00,                                  AUTHORIZATION LIST—IEAAPF00
CLOCK=00,                                TIME OF DAY PARMS—CLOCK00
CLPA,                                    RELOAD LPA AT EVERY IPL
CMB=(UNITR,COMM,GRAPH,CHRDR),            ADDITIONAL CMB ENTRIES
CMD=00,                                  AUTO COMMANDS—COMMND00
CON=00,                                  CONSOLE PARMS—CONSOL00
CSA=(2100,4000),                         MINIMUM CSA AND ECSA SIZES
DUMP=DASD,                               PLACE SVC DUMPS ON DASD DEVICES
GRS=NONE,                                NO COORDINATION OF GRS REQUESTS
ICS=00,                                  SRM CONTROL SPECS—IEAICS00
IPS=00,                                  SRM PERF SPECS   - IEAIPS00
LNK=00,                                  LINK LIST—LNKLST00
LNKAUTH=LNKLST,                          MVS/XA DEFAULT, APFTAB IS ALT
LOGCLS=L,                                SYSOUT=L FOR SYSLOG
LOGLMT=999999,                           LINES OF SYSLOG BEFORE AUTO SPIN OFF
LPA=00,                                  LPA LIST—LPALST00
MAXUSER=250,                             (SYS TASKS + INITS + TSOUSERS)
MSTRJCL=00,                              MASTER JCL—MSTJCL00
PAGTOTL=(16,4),                          ALLOW TOTAL OF 16 PAGE D/S AND 4 SWAP D/S
OPI=YES,                                 ALLOW OPERATOR OVERRIDE TO IEASYS00
OPT=00,                                  SRM TUNING PARMETERS—IEAOPT00
PAGE=(PAGE.VSYSCAT.PLPA,                 PLPA PAGE DATA SET
      PAGE.VSYSCAT.COMMON,               COMMON PAGE DATA SET
      PAGE.VSYSPG2,                      LOCAL PAGE DATA SET
      PAGE.VSYSPG3,                      LOCAL PAGE DATA SET
      PAGE.VSYSPG4,                      LOCAL PAGE DATA SET
      PAGE.VSYSPG6,                      LOCAL PAGE DATA SET
      PAGE.VSYSPG7,                      LOCAL PAGE DATA SET
      PAGE.VSYSPG8,L),                   LOCAL PAGE DATA SET
REAL=128,                                128K MAX FOR V=R JOBS (76K REQD FOR OLTEP)
SCH=00,                                  SCHEDULER PARMS—SCHED00
SMF=00,                                  SMF PARAMETERS—SMFPRM00
SQA=(8,128),                             SQA (8 X 64K) + 256K; ESQA (128 X 64K) + 8M
SSN=00,                                  SUBSYSTEM NAMES—IEFSSN00
SVC=00,                                  USER SVC LIST—IEASVC00
SYSNAME=SYSA,                            ID OF SYSTEM IN GRS COMPLEX
VAL=00,                                  VOLUME ATTRIBUTE LIST—VATLST00
VRREGN=64                                DEFAULT REAL-STORAGE REGION SIZE
/*                                       */
```

Example 7.8. A typical IEASYSxx PARMLIB member.

system or need to bring up the system to fix the problem, it can be worth while getting out the messages manual, responding to the messages, and continuing the attempt to bring up the system. If, however, you are bringing up a production system and have an alternative method of fixing the problem (e.g. from a test system running on another logical partition), it is usually not worth continuing, as a system which has not come up 100 per cent correctly will usually not be 100 per cent functional.

7.5.3 CLOCKxx

This member specifies parameters relating to the system time. A typical member (for a site in the UK) is shown in Example 7.9. Note that:

• The PROMPT parameter of the OPERATOR statement indicates that the

```
OPERATOR PROMPT
TIMEZONE W.00.00.00
/*                                                        */
/*LIB: SYS1.PARMLIB(CLOCK00)                              */
/*                                                        */
```

Example 7.9. CLOCKxx member of SYS1.PARMLIB.

operator should be prompted to check the TOD clocks at IPL time, whether or
not they are already set. The alternative is NOPROMPT.

• The TIMEZONE statement indicates how far east (E) or west (W) of GMT
  your timezone is. This determines the difference between the GMT and
  LOCAL times used by MVS.
• On MVS version 4 systems there are also several statements relating to the
  external timer reference (ETR, also known as the sysplex clock).

7.5.4   COMMNDxx

This member lists commands to be executed automatically at IPL time, in addition
to the IBM-supplied commands in IEACMD00. Note that any commands that
require services that are unavailable at this point in the initialization process will
be delayed, in particular, commands requiring JES services, such as START
commands. Also, there is no guarantee that they will be completed in the order in
which you specify them, so you should avoid using them for any type of inter-
dependent scheduling of commands. You can avoid some of these problems by
putting some or all of your automatic commands in different places. JES
commands, for example, can be placed in the JES parameters, which will cause
them to be automatically executed whenever JES is started; some other software
products offer similar facilities. These commands will, however, be executed every
time the product concerned is started, not just at IPL time! They also suffer from
the disadvantage that a future systems programmer, or one who is not familiar with
your site, may find it difficult to trace the origin of automatic commands which they
need to modify. It is sensible, therefore, to document where other such commands
can be found within your COMMNDxx member. Example 7.10 shows a typical
COMMNDxx member. Note that:

```
COM='CONFIG MEMBER(00)        DISPLAY OFFLINE RESOURCES '
COM='SET MPF=01               MESSAGE PROCESSING OPTIONS'
COM='S TSS                    START TOP SECRET          '
COM='S MIM                    START MIM/MII             '
COM='S DFHSM                  START HSM                 '
COM='D MPF                    MESSAGE PROCESSING OPTIONS'
COM='D T             **** OTHER AUTO CMDS ARE ISSUED BY    ****'
COM='D T             **** TSS FROM SYS1.PARMLIB(TSSAUT00) ****'
```

Example 7.10. COMMNDxx member of SYS1.PARMLIB.

```
INIT PFK(00) MONITOR(DSNAME) MLIM(1500) RLIM(10) UEXIT(N) CMDDELIM(:)
DEFAULT ROUTCODE(ALL)
/*                                                                           */
/* LIB: SYS1.PARMLIB(CONSOL00)                                               */
/*                                                                           */
CONSOLE DEVNUM(840) ALTERNATE(060) ROUTCODE(ALL) /*IBM MCONS-840            */
        PFKTAB(PFKTAB1)
        AUTH(MASTER)
        UNIT(3277-2)
        MONITOR(JOBNAMES-T)
        CON(N) SEG(19) DEL(RD) RNUM(19) RTME(1) MFORM(J,T) AREA(NONE)
/*                                                                           */
CONSOLE DEVNUM(060) ALTERNATE(841) ROUTCODE(ALL) /* IBM SECONS 060          */
        PFKTAB(PFKTAB1)
        AUTH(ALL)
        UNIT(3277-2)
        MONITOR(JOBNAMES-T)
        CON(N) SEG(19) DEL(RD) RNUM(19) RTME(1) MFORM(J,T) AREA(NONE)
/*
```

Example 7.11. CONSOLxx member of SYS1.PARMLIB.

- The member is essentially self-explanatory — partly because of clear internal comments.
- There is no provision for comments in the syntax of this member, but you can get round this, as here, by including your comments within the commands to be issued, and in this case extra, relatively trivial commands have been included simply in order to allow an extra comment to be included.

7.5.5   CONSOLxx and PFKTABxx

These members control the use of consoles by MVS after the completion of the NIP stage of initialization. Example 7.11 shows part of a CONSOLxx member. Note that:

- The primary and alternate consoles are on different controllers (and different channels, though this is not obvious from the PARMLIB member) for the sake of maximizing system resilience in the event of hardware failure.
- The PFK parameter of the INIT statement specifies the suffix of the PFKTABxx member of SYS1.PARMLIB containing PF key definitions to be used by consoles defined in this member. Within each PFKTABxx member, multiple PF key tables may be specified, and the PFKTAB parameter on each CONSOLE statement specifies the name of the table to be used for this console. Example 7.12 shows the PFKTABxx member referenced here.

  Note that in Example 7.12:

- This member contains two sets of definitions, though only the first set is referenced in the CONSOLxx member shown in Example 7.11, and the second set defines only two PF keys.
- The commands associated with each PF key are not executed immediately

```
/*LIB: SYS1.PARMLIB(PFKTAB00)                                              */
/*DOC: THIS MEMBER CONTAINS THE CONSOLE PFKEY DEFINITIONS                  */
/*                                                                         */
PFKTAB TABLE(PFKTAB1)
PFK(01) CMD('K E,1        ERASE ONE LINE')
PFK(02) CMD('$DSPL        DISPLAY SPOOL')
PFK(03) CMD('D A,L        LIST ACTIVE JOBS AND TSO USERS')
PFK(04) CMD('K S,DEL=RD,SEG=19,CON=N,RNUM=19,RTME=01,MFORM=T;K A,NONE')
PFK(05) CMD('S CICSLOG,C=_XXXXXX,J=X') CON(Y)
PFK(06) CMD('S CICSSOD,J=_XXXXXX') CON(Y)
PFK(07) CMD('S DRDR,J=_XXXXXX') CON(Y)
PFK(08) CMD('S NONLOAD,JOURNAL=_XXXXXXXX,CLASS=X,TAPE=XXXXXX') CON(Y)
PFK(09) CMD('$SPRT2')
PFK(10) CMD('$SPRT2')
PFK(11) CMD('R 'XX,WAIT;R XX,NOHOLD')
PFK(12) CMD('D U,,ALLOC,6A0')
PFK(13) CMD('D U,TAPE,ONLINE')
PFK(14) CMD('D U,DASD,ONLINE')
PFK(15) CMD('D GRS,LINK')
PFK(16) CMD('D U,,,400,4')
PFK(17) CMD('D GRS,SYSTEM')
PFK(18) CMD('D GRS,LINK')
PFK(19) CMD('D GRS,CONTENTION')
PFKTAB TABLE(PFKTAB2)
   PFK(01) CMD('D J,L')                    /*DISPLAY ALL JOBS */
   PFK(02) CMD('D C')                      /*DISPLAY CONSOLES  */
```

Example 7.12. PFKTABxx member of SYS1.PARMLIB.

when the PF key is pressed; instead they are displayed on the command line of the console, where they can be executed by pressing Enter, or modified then executed. An underscore in the command assigned to a PF key indicates that when the command is displayed, the cursor should be positioned under the character following the underscore.

- Before MVS 2.2 the CONSOLxx and PFKTABxx members of PARMLIB were not used; instead, consoles and PF key usage on them were defined at SYSGEN time, and PF key tables were stored by the SYSGEN process in SYS1.DCMLIB. See Sec. 7.3 for more details.

On MVS V4 systems additional console options can be specified, including:

- Names can be assigned to consoles.
- Consoles can be assigned to groups (using yet another PARMLIB member, called CNGRPxx), and failing consoles can be switched to any console in an alternate console group, rather than a specific alternate console.
- The hardware console can be defined as an MVS console (on ES/9000s only).
- There are also some additional options relating to Sysplex console support.

Some of the implications of the console changes in Version 4 are quite far-reaching:

- TSO sessions can be defined as 'consoles'.
- Consoles attached to other systems in a Sysplex can receive messages from your system.

```
ACFNCP.NCPLIB SYST01,
ACFNCP.SSPLIB SYST02,
IP01.LINKLIB SYSBKP,
ISF.V1R3M0.ISFLOAD SYSBKP,
ISF.V1R3M0.ISFLOAD SYSR01,
ISF.V1R3M0.ISFLOAD XA223R,
ISF.V1R3M0.ISFLPA SYSBKP,
ISF.V1R3M0.ISFLPA SYSR01,
ISF.V1R3M0.ISFLPA XA223R,
SYS1.CMDLIB SYSBKP,
SYS1.CMDLIB SYSR01,
SYS1.CMDLIB XA223R,
.
.
.
SYS9.SAS.LPALIB SYST10,
SYS9.TSS.LOAD SYST09,
SYS9.UCC1.LINKLIB SYST09,
SYS9.VSAMTUNE.LOADLIB SYST09
/*
/*   LIB:  SYS1.PARMLIB(IEAAPF00)
/*   DOC:  THIS MEMBER CONTAINS A LIST OF PROGRAM
/*         LIBRARY NAMES AND VOLUME SERIAL NUMBERS
/*         THAT REQUIRE APF AUTHORIZATION.
```

Example 7.13. IEAAPFxx member of SYS1.PARMLIB.

- An MVS system can be IPLd on an ES/9000 without a local non-SNA controller and a console attached to it, since the early IPL messages can be sent to the hardware console and later messages can be sent to either a TSO console or a Sysplex console on another system.

7.5.6   IEAAPFxx

This member controls the APF authorization of load libraries (see Sec. 3.7 for more details of APF authorization). Note that if you specify LNKAUTH = LNKLST in your IEASYSxx member, the list of APF-authorized libraries will automatically be extended to include all libraries in the linklist. APF authorization is crucial for many components of MVS and a number of other system software products, so you must exercise great care to ensure that the necessary libraries are included in your APF list. All LPA libraries, for example, must be included in it, as must the libraries in the VTAMLIB, NCPLIB, and SSPLIB concatenations in your VTAM procedure; otherwise, vital system components may be unstartable! Prior to MVS 4.3 and DFSMS/MVS, dynamic additions to the APF list were not possible without an IPL, unless you had a third-party product which provided this facility. If you have neither MVS 4.3 nor any of these third-party products, you will have to modify your APF list and re-IPL to solve problems of this nature. Example 7.13 shows a section of an IEAAPFxx member. Note that:

- As with many other members of PARMLIB, the use of commas after each entry but the last one is crucial — if you miss the comma off a line, MVS regards that line as the last valid entry and ignores all following lines!

- I would advise keeping your entries in the APF list in alphabetical order — it can easily become very long and if it is not sorted it will become confusing and difficult to maintain.
- SYS1.LINKLIB and SYS1.SVCLIB are automatically included in the list, so you need not code them explicitly.
- Where you have multiple versions of the same library which could be used (e.g. depending on which SYSRES pack or which set of IPL parameters you use), you should keep them all in your APF list, so you only need to maintain one version of the list and do not need to vary your IPL parameters to change the APF list in use in different circumstances. Note that under MVS V4 you can code ****** in the volume serial number field to indicate that the dataset is to be APF authorized if it is on the current SYSRES pack. This should eliminate much of the need for duplication of datasets in this PARMLIB member.
- Remember that sophisticated assembler programmers with access to an APF-authorized library can bypass standard security products and procedures — so ensure that libraries in your APF list are subject to strict access controls (this is discussed further in Chapter 15).

7.5.7   IEAICSxx, IEAIPSxx, and IEAOPTxx

These members define the parameters for the system resources manager (SRM) and dispatcher components of MVS, which control the dispatching and swapping of units of work. This is a highly complex area which is beyond the scope of this book, though those who are interested will find a detailed discussion in the later chapters of [8] (these chapters have become the *Initialization and Tuning Guide* for MVS V4). These members of PARMLIB are generally controlled by performance specialists, though in small and medium-sized shops these may be members of the systems programming team. Broadly speaking, the ICS controls the assignation of units of work to performance groups, the IPS determines the dispatching and swapping priorities of work in the different performance groups, and the OPT sets SRM options of general applicability.

7.5.8   IEASVCxx

This member lists the user SVC routines which MVS is to include in its table of valid SVCs. This includes not only any inhouse SVCs you may have but also any SVCs supplied by third-party products, and SVCs supplied by IBM products which are not part of MVS itself (e.g. CICS, IMS). On MVS/370 systems, this member of PARMLIB was not used, and instead it was necessary to code the descriptions of user SVCs in the stage 1 deck and perform an IOGEN to modify the SVC table (to avoid the need to do this for every new SVC, it was normal to

```
/*LIB: SYS1.PARMLIB(IEASVC00)                                       */
/*DOC: THIS MEMBER CONTAINS THE MVS USER SVC TABLE                  */
/*                                                                  */
SVCPARM 254,REPLACE,TYPE(2),APF(NO)                 /*DBMS          */
SVCPARM 248,REPLACE,TYPE(3),EPNAME(IGC0024H)        /*TMS           */
SVCPARM 241,REPLACE,TYPE(4),APF(NO)                 /*SCHEDULER     */
SVCPARM 237,REPLACE,TYPE(3),EPNAME(IGC0023G)        /*TMS           */
SVCPARM 226,REPLACE,TYPE(2),APF(NO)                 /*CICS(CSVC)    */
SVCPARM 225,REPLACE,TYPE(6),APF(NO)                 /*CICS(HPSVC)   */
SVCPARM 217,REPLACE,TYPE(4),APF(NO)                 /*VSAM OPT'R    */
SVCPARM 214,REPLACE,TYPE(4),APF(NO)                 /*STATS PACK    */
```

Example 7.14. IEASVCxx member of SYS1.PARMLIB.

define spare SVCs of each type in the SVC table). Example 7.14 shows a typical IEASVCxx member. Note that:

- User SVCs must use SVC numbers in the range 200 to 255.
- Different types of SVC receive control in different states. The differences are explained in [10] or [9].
- Before they can be used, SVCs listed in this table must also exist as executable routines which are loaded at IPL time. Types 1, 2, and 6 SVCs must be CSECTs link-edited into the nucleus (member IEANUCxx of SYS1.NUCLEUS) — you should create an SMP/E USERMOD to do this. Types 3 and 4 SVCs (type 5 is obsolete) must exist as load modules in SYS1.LPALIB.
- The EPNAME parameter specifies the entry point name for the SVC, though this is only required if the name differs from the IBM standard. The standard CSECT name for types 1, 2, and 6 SVCs is IGCnnn, where nnn is the SVC number. The standard module name for types 3 and 4 SVCs is in the format IGC00nna, where nna is the SVC number in zoned decimal format — in effect, this means nn is the first two characters of the SVC number, and a is derived from the last character of the SVC number as shown in Table 7.1.
- The APF parameter specifies whether or not programs invoking the SVC must be APF authorized.

Table 7.1. Format of SVC types 3 and 4 module names

Last character of SVC number	Last character of module name
0	}
1	A
2	B
3	C
4	D
5	E
6	F
7	G
8	H
9	I

```
JES2,,,PRIMARY
CICS
UCC1,U01SSNIT,'X=248,Y=237'
DB,DBSSIPR
CNMP
```

Example 7.15. IEFSSNxx member of SYS1.PARMLIB.

7.5.9   IEFSSNxx

This member lists the subsystems which MVS will initialize at IPL time. An entry is reserved for each subsystem in the subsystem communications vector table (SSCVT), and if an initialization routine is specified for the subsystem in the PARMLIB member, that routine is invoked to initialize the subsystem. Example 7.15 shows an IEFSSNxx member. Note that:

* Each line represents a different subsystem. The first parameter on the line is the subsystem name; the second, if present, is the subsystem initialization module, which will be invoked at subsystem initialization time (the system attempts to LINK to the initialization module, so you must ensure it exists in either the LPA or linklist); and the third, if present, is a parameter which will be passed to the initialization routine. In the example, the UCC1 subsystem is passed a parameter which specifies the SVC numbers that have been assigned to its SVC routines.

* The fourth parameter is used to identify the primary subsystem, which must be your job entry system. Prior to MVS/XA, there was no PRIMARY parameter, and the job entry subsystem was usually started from the master JCL. If for any reason you wish to start JES from the master JCL, from your automatic commands, or even by asking the operator to enter the start command on a console, you must use the NOSTART parameter on the IEFSSN entry for JES to prevent the subsystem being started twice. See Chapter 8 for further discussion of JES2 initialization.

7.5.10   SCHEDxx

This member contains parameters for the master scheduler address space, including:

* The suffix of the EDT module to be selected at IPL time (if the EDT was placed in SYS1.NUCLEUS using MVSCP)
* The size of the system trace table
* Additions and subtractions from the default list of abend codes eligible for automatic restart
* The user-defined entries for the MVS program properties table (PPT)

The PPT assigns attributes such as 'non-swappable' and 'non-cancellable' to specified programs. Prior to MVS/XA, the PPT could only be changed by

```
EDT ID(09)                              /* SUFFIX FOR IEFEDT          */
MT SIZE (64K)                           /* MASTER TRACE TBL SIZE      */
 /*******************************************************************/
 /*              PROGRAM PROPERTIES TABLE ADDITIONS                 */
 /*******************************************************************/
 /*                     ALTERNATE JES2                              */
PPT PGMNAME(HASJES2A)                   /* PROGRAM NAME               */
    NOCANCEL                            /* CAN NOT BE CANCELLED       */
    KEY(1)                              /* PROTECTION KEY             */
    NOSWAP                              /* NON-SWAPPABLE              */
    PRIV                                /* PRIVILEGED                 */
    NODSI                               /* NO DATA SET INTEGRITY      */
    PASS                                /* NO PASSWORD BYPASS         */
    SYST                                /* SYSTEM TASK , NOT TIMED    */
    AFF(NONE)                           /* NO PROCESSOR AFFINITY       */
 /*                     CICS                                        */
PPT PGMNAME(DFHSIP)                     /* PROGRAM NAME               */
    CANCEL                              /* CAN BE CANCELLED           */
    KEY(8)                              /* PROTECTION KEY             */
    NOSWAP                              /* NON-SWAPPABLE              */
    PASS                                /* NO PASSWORD BYPASS         */
    NOPREF                              /* NO PREFERRED STORAGE REQD  */
    AFF(NONE)                           /* NO PROCESSOR AFFINITY      */
 .
 .
 .

 /*               NETWORK PERFORMANCE MONITOR                       */
PPT PGMNAME(FNMMAIN)                    /* PROGRAM NAME               */
    NOSWAP                              /* NON-SWAPPABLE              */
    PRIV                                /* PRIVILEGED                 */
    KEY(6)                              /* PROTECTION KEY             */
    AFF(NONE)                           /* NO PROCESSOR AFFINITY      */
```

Example 7.16. SCHEDxx member of SYS1.PARMLIB.

modifying the CSECT IEFSDPPT in load module IEFSD060. This was generated by the SYSGEN process from the SGIEF0PT macro. It could be modified using an IBM-supplied SMP/E USERMOD, though it was more common (and a lot simpler!) to generate extra dummy entries at SYSGEN time and use AMASPZAP to modify these as required. Note that some IBM programs may require to be included in these 'user-defined' entries, e.g. RMF and CICS. Example 7.16 is an extract from a SCHEDxx member. Note that:

- The PPT entries defined here are additional to those for MVS programs — the latter entries are included automatically by MVS.
- Programs must be APF authorized at execution time in order to inherit the properties defined for them in the PPT.

7.5.11 SMFPRMxx

This member defines the parameters to be used by the system management facility (SMF). This is the component of MVS which records audit-type records for events such as I/O activity, TSO transaction completion, and many other event types. The

```
    ACTIVE                          /* ACTIVE SMF RECORDING*/
    DSNAME(SYS1.MAN1,SYS1.MAN2,SYS1.MAN3)
    NOPROMPT                        /* DO NOT PROMPT OPERATOR FOR OPTIONS*/
    REC(PERM)                       /* TYPE 17 PERM RECORDS ONLY*/
    MAXDORM(3000)                   /* WRITE AN IDLE BUFFER AFTER 30 MIN*/
    STATUS(010000)                  /* WRITE SMF STATS AFTER 1 HOUR*/
    JWT(0030)                       /* 522 AFTER 30 MINUTES*/
    SID(SYSA)                       /* SYSTEM ID IS SYSA          */
    LISTDSN                         /* LIST DATA SET STATUS AT IPL*/
    SYS(NOTYPE(4:5,16:19,40,62:69,150),EXITS(IEFU83,IEFU84,
            IEFACTRT,
            IEFUJV,IEFUSI,IEFUJI,IEFUTL,IEFU29),INTERVAL(010000),
            DETAIL)
    SUBSYS(STC,EXITS(IEFU29,IEFU83,IEFU84,IEFUJP,IEFUSO))
/*
/* NB.  TYPE 14,15,26,30 MUST NOT BE REMOVED—USED BY SCHEDULER
/*      ALSO TYPE 128—USED BY DBMS
```

Example 7.17. SMFPRMxx member of SYS1.PARMLIB.

data recorded by SMF can subsequently be interrogated to give reports on system performance, resource usage by users, etc. It is very widely used for performance analysis and accounting/chargeback. Example 7.17 shows an SMFPRMxx member. Note that:

- The DSNAME parameter specifies the datasets in which SMF will write its records. The first of these is the primary SMF dataset, and the rest are the secondary datasets (these are discussed further in Sec. 7.7). They must all have names in the format SYS1.MANx, where x is any alphanumeric character.

- The JWT parameter specifies the length of time a job or TSO user is allowed to wait without doing any processing. When this limit is exceeded, control is passed to the IEFUTL exit (if it is active), which will normally cancel the job or user with an abend code of 522.

- The SID parameter specifies the SMF ID of the system. Note that this need not be the same as the GRS system name or the JES system id, but it makes life a lot simpler if you keep these three identifiers in line so that any one MVS system is always referred to by the same name.

- The SYS statement allows you to specify which SMF records are to be written, using the TYPE or NOTYPE parameter, and which SMF exits will be valid. The NOTYPE parameter used in this example specifies SMF records to be excluded. Some system software depends on the creation of certain SMF record types to function correctly, particularly job scheduling packages. To prevent a future systems programmer inadvertently removing a vital record type, it is worth placing comments in your SMF parameters indicating which records are used and by what.

- The SUBSYS statement allows you to specify a different set of records and/or exits for a subsystem from the system defaults defined with the SYS statement.

```
VATDEF IPLUSE(PRIVATE) SYSUSE(PRIVATE)
WORK*  ,0,0,*       ,N        WORK PACKS      STORAGE
TSO*   ,0,0,*       ,N        TSO PACKS       STORAGE
PFIN*  ,0,0,*       ,N        FINANCE         STORAGE
ADEV*  ,0,0,*       ,N        ACCEPTANCE      STORAGE
DDEV*  ,0,0,*       ,N        DEVELOPMENT     STORAGE
DBASE2,0,0,3390     ,N        DATABASE
DBASE3,0,0,3380     ,N        DATABASE
PFINO1,0,2,3390     ,N        FINANCE
PFINO2,0,2,3390     ,N        FINANCE
DDEVOB,0,2,3380     ,N        DEVELOPMENT
```

Example 7.18. VATLSTxx member of SYS1.PARMLIB.

SMF recognizes STC as a subsystem for work started from the operator console (i.e. started tasks), and TSO as a subsystem for TSO users.

7.5.12 VATLSTxx

This member (the volume attribute list) is used to specify the default mount and use attributes for all DASD volumes on the system. The mount attribute may be permanently resident, reserved, or removable, although only the first two of these can be selected in the VATLST. Mount attributes of reserved and removable are only meaningful for devices where the storage medium is removable, so all modern DASDs should be given mount attributes of permanently resident. The use attribute may be private, public, or storage, and controls the types of allocation request for which a volume may be assigned. Private volumes may only be assigned to datasets which request them specifically by volume serial number. Public volumes may also be assigned to temporary datasets which request allocation to a generic device type or esoteric device group. Storage volumes may be assigned in either of these cases and also to permanent datasets which request allocation using a generic or esoteric name.

Until MVS 2.2.3, the VATLST could only be used to specify attributes for individual volumes identified by their whole volume serial number, and the use attributes specified in it were only used when MVS mounted the volumes at IPL time. If a volume was varied online at any other time it was automatically given the use attribute of 'public'; if this was not suitable, you had to issue an appropriate MOUNT command to alter the volume's use. Since MVS 2.2.3, however, it has been possible to specify your own defaults for the use attribute, both for devices varied online during IPL and for those varied at other times, using the VATDEF parameter. In addition, the coding of statements for volumes which do not conform to the general defaults has been simplified by allowing you to code generic defaults for volumes whose names share the same pattern. A sample VATLSTxx member (using the new options) is shown in Example 7.18. Note that:

- The VATDEF statement here is used to make the default use attribute PRIVATE, both during IPL (the IPLUSE parameter), and afterwards (the

Table 7.2. Meaning of VATLSTxx parameters

Columns	Meaning	Valid values
1–6	Volume serial number, or pattern for generic volume serial number using % and/or * wildcard characters	Alphanumeric characters, %, and *
7	S indicates the entry is a specific volume serial number, not a generic, even though it contains the % and/or * characters; otherwise this is merely a field separator	S or ,
8	Mount attribute: 0 for permanently resident, or 1 for reserved	0 or 1
9	Field separator	,
10	Use attribute: 0 for storage, 1 for public, or 2 for private	0, 1, or 2
11	Field separator	,
12–19	Device type, e.g. 3380 or 3390. Note that an * in column 12 can be used to specify a generic device type, i.e. any DASD	* or a device type defined in the MVS I/O configuration
20	Field separator	,
21	N indicates mount messages should not be issued at IPL time if the volume is not already mounted; any other character indicates they should be issued	Any character
22	Field separator	Blank
23–80	Optional comment	Any characters

SYSUSE parameter). Note also that this must be the first statement in the VATLST member, and if multiple members are used, it must be the first statement in the first member listed in the VAL parameter of IEASYSxx.

- Before MVS 2.2.3, VATLST members needed one entry for every DASD volume on the system, and so were typically rather large. Now, however, you can define a large configuration with relatively few VATLSTxx statements, by judicious use of the defaults. Here, the general default is PRIVATE, but some pools are given a default of STORAGE, and it is then only necessary to define individual volume statements for volumes whose mount attributes differ from the default for their pool.
- The format of the volume statements is position sensitive. Table 7.2 lists the position, meaning, and use of each parameter. Note that wherever a parameter is shorter than the columns available for it, it must be left-justified and padded to the right with blanks.

7.5.13 COFVLFxx

The COFVLFxx member of PARMLIB is used to define the resources managed by the virtual lookaside facility (VLF). VLF is introduced in MVS/ESA, and it provides a facility for keeping objects in virtual storage that are likely to be reused

```
CLASS NAME(CSVLLA)
      EMAJ(LLA)
      MAXVIRT(256)
CLASS NAME(IKJEXEC)
      EDSN(SYS8.CLIST)
      EDSN(ISR.V3R2M0.ISRCLIB)
      EDSN(SYS1.CMDPROC)
      MAXVIRT(256)
```

Example 7.19. COFVLFxx member of SYS1.PARMLIB.

in the reasonably near future — in effect, an intelligent caching facility. IBM has supplied three implementations of VLF so far, which use it to store load modules, TSO clists, and catalog records. The load module implementation and, to a lesser extent, the clist implementation can deliver significant performance benefits. At the time of writing, however, there are a number of bugs in the catalog implementation, and people who have tried recommend you do not use it. In theory, you can write your own VLF implementations for other resources, but this could be a major undertaking and it is unlikely that many user sites will do this.

VLF must be started explicitly using the S VLF,SUB = MSTR,NN = xx command, where xx is the suffix of the COFVLFxx member holding the VLF resource definitions to be used. If you decide to implement it, you should place this command in your automatic commands executed at IPL time (e.g. in COMMND00). Example 7.19 shows a typical COFVLFxx member. Note that:

- VLF-managed resources are divided into resource classes, and within each class resources are assigned major names and minor names. VLF will only manage resources with class names and major names which are defined in the COFVLFxx member.
- There are two types of class: PDS-type classes, and non-PDS-type classes. PDS-type classes use the EDSN keyword to define valid major names, while non-PDS-type classes use the EMAJ keyword. The practical difference between them is that MVS notifies VLF of changes made to any PDS which VLF is managing via a PDS-type class, thus enabling it to maintain the integrity of its in-storage copy. For non-PDS-type classes, the VLF implementation must itself detect changes in order to protect the integrity of the data VLF is managing for it.
- The two classes defined here are those used by the load module (CSVLLA) and clist (IKJEXEC) implementations provided by IBM. Both have been assigned maximum virtual storage of 256 4K pages, i.e. one megabyte.
- The major name supplied for CSVLLA serves no purpose other than to satisfy the VLF calling requirements, since LLA determines what objects to manage without any assistance from VLF. The major names for IKJEXEC, however, are used by VLF to determine which clist libraries it should manage — only

clists in the libraries named in these EDSN statements will be staged into VLF's virtual storage.

7.6   The catalog structure

Prior to DFP version 3, MVS catalogs had a tree structure restricted to two levels. The top level was the master catalog, and there were user catalogs at the lower level. For any given high-level qualifier: *either* all datasets with that HLQ were cataloged in the master catalog; *or* there was an ALIAS entry in the master catalog relating that high-level qualifier to a given user catalog, and all datasets with that HLQ were cataloged in that user catalog.

DFP version 3 now allows the use of multilevel aliases, but this is not commonly used and suffers from certain implementation problems.

The workings of catalog management are discussed in more detail in Chapter 3; here we will look a little further at how catalogs are set up and configured.

Both master catalogs and user catalogs are created using the IDCAMS utility program, with the DEFINE command. In theory, any catalog can be defined as a master catalog, simply by specifying its name and volume serial number in the SYSCATxx member of SYS1.NUCLEUS (or the LOADxx member of PARMLIB under V4). In practice, however, master catalogs contain quite a different set of entries from user catalogs. A master catalog must contain catalog entries for all system datasets required during the IPL process up to the point where normal catalog management services become available, and it should also contain ALIAS entries for the high-level qualifiers used for other datasets. User catalogs, by contrast, will contain entries for the datasets whose high-level qualifiers correspond to the ALIAS entries related to this catalog.

Those datasets which must be defined in the master catalog include all datasets in the lpalist and linklist, SYS1.PROCLIB, SYS1.PARMLIB, SYS1.UADS, SYS1.BRODCAST, any other datasets referred to in the master JCL (e.g. RACF datasets), all page and swap datasets, SYS1.STGINDEX, SMF datasets, and DUMP datasets. Conventionally, the IBM-supplied datasets in this list will use the high-level qualifier SYS1 (except the page and swap datasets, which usually use PAGE). To keep your usage of the master catalog simple and clear, it is wise to reserve another high-level qualifier to use for all non-IBM datasets which require to be in the master catalog (e.g. non-IBM lpalist and linklist datasets), such as SYS2. The CBIPO process also catalogs target libraries with a variety of high-level qualifiers (e.g. AMS, GIM, ICQ, ISF, ISP, ISR, and others depending on your product profile). It is simplest to leave these in the master catalog. In addition, all user catalogs must be defined in the master catalog, and you should reserve another high-level qualifier for these (the CBIPO default is CATALOG, which seems remarkably sensible).

All other datasets should be cataloged in user catalogs, with ALIAS entries in the master catalog for their high-level qualifiers. This rule has several advantages:

- It optimizes the performance of catalog management, as it must scan the master catalog as part of every catalog search, and the fewer entries there are in it the quicker you can expect this to happen.
- It enables you to restrict update access severely to the master catalog using your security package, as only the systems programmers and the administrator who creates new aliases should ever need update access. The user catalogs, by contrast, must allow update access to anyone who might need to catalog a dataset in them.
- It makes the process of migrating from one master catalog to another relatively simple, as the ALIAS entries can simply be copied across, and only the SYS1, PAGE, CBIPO, CATALOG, and (in this example) SYS2 datasets require any special action.
- It makes it easier to implement shared DASD across multiple MVS systems, because master catalogs cannot be shared, but each system's master catalog can have ALIAS entries pointing to the same user catalogs. In this way the same catalog entry for a dataset on a shared DASD volume can be shared between multiple systems, and any cataloging or uncataloging done on one system will automatically be reflected on the others. The headache of keeping multiple catalog entries in line for the same dataset is then restricted to those system datasets which are actually shared between the systems (and most of your SYS1 and PAGE datasets will not be shared anyway).

You (or your data management group) will also need to specify some other rules to make the catalog structure work well. In particular, you will need some rules which tell you which HLQs should go in which user catalogs. One sound option is to have a user catalog for each DASD pool or SMS storage group (see Chapter 16 for a detailed discussion on DASD pooling), and then assign HLQs to the catalog for the storage group they belong to. If your storage groups are very large, however, you may need to have more than one catalog for each storage group.

Implementing your catalog structure is done using the IDCAMS (access method services) utility program, which has commands for various catalog administration functions, including creating catalogs and aliases, and connecting a user catalog to a master catalog. Examples 7.20–7.22 illustrate some of the key functions.

In Example 7.20:

- Many of the parameters shown are defaults, but are included explicitly for clarity.
- You should aim to place your master catalog (and indeed any user catalog) where it will suffer the minimum head movement for a typical I/O. It is normally considered that this is achieved by placing the VTOC and VTOC index in the middle of the pack, and the catalog and catalog index next to these. However, IDCAMS does not allow you to specify an absolute track address when you are defining an object, and automatically allocates it in the first available extent which is large enough to accommodate it. To place a catalog

```
//CATALC1 EXEC PGM=IDCAMS,REGION=1024K
//SYSPRINT DD SYSOUT=*
//CATVOL   DD VOL=SER=SYSCAT,UNIT=3380,DISP=OLD
//SYSIN    DD *
  DEFINE   MCAT                                                  —
  ( ICFCAT                                                       —
NAME(CATALOG.MASTER.VSYSCAT)                                     —
FILE(CATVOL)                                                     —
VOL(SYSCAT)                                                      —
TRK(90 7)                                                        —
FOR(9999)                                                        —
SHR(3 4)                                                         —
NWCK                                                             —
IMBD                                                             —
REPL                                                            —
BUFSP(6144)                                                      —
STRNO(2)                                                         —
BUFND(3)                                                         —
BUFNI(3)                                                         —
  )                    /*END OF CLUSTER-LEVEL PARAMETERS    */—
  DATA                                                           —
  (  TRK(85 6)                                                   —
CISZ(1024)                                                       —
  )                    /*END OF DATA-LEVEL PARAMETERS       */—
  INDEX                                                          —
  (  TRK(5 1)                                                    —
CISZ(1024)                                                       —
  )                                                              —
                       /*THE CATALOG TO RECEIVE THE CONNECTOR */—
                       /*ENTRY FOR THE NEW CATALOG.          */—
CAT(CATALOG.MASTER.VOLDCAT/PWUPDATE)
  /*
```

Example 7.20. Defining a master catalog.

in a particular location you therefore need to allocate datasets in all the available extents up to the location where you wish to place the catalog, which you must ensure is large enough to take both the catalog and its index. If the pack is heavily fragmented you may find it is worth running a DFDSS DEFRAG first, or you may have to allocate hundreds of datasets to fill the gaps! You should also ensure the volume you are using is mounted as private, and stop other people allocating on it while you are working, or other allocations will interfere with your plan.

• You should ensure the first extent is large enough to avoid any need to go to secondaries, or the catalog could become fragmented, impacting catalog

```
//DEFINE  EXEC PGM=IDCAMS
//SYSPRINT DD  SYSOUT=*
//SYSIN    DD  *
 IMPORT CONNECT OBJECTS ( (CATALOG.VBKPRES DEVT(3380) VOL(BKPRES) ) )
 IMPORT CONNECT OBJECTS ( (CATALOG.VSYST01 DEVT(3380) VOL(SYST01) ) )
 /*
```

Example 7.21. Connecting a user catalog to a master catalog.

```
//DFALIAS  EXEC PGM=IDCAMS,REGION=512K
//STEPCAT   DD DSN=CATALOG.MASTER.VXA220C,DISP=SHR
//SYSPRINT DD SYSOUT=*
//SYSIN     DD *
   DEF ALIAS ( NAME (ABCDEF) RELATE (CATALOG.VSYST01 ) )
/*
```

Example 7.22. Defining an ALIAS for a user catalog.

management performance. (Use your old master catalog as the starting point
for estimating the space required.)

● Although the DEFINE statement specifies MCAT to indicate that this is a
  master catalog, the processing and parameters are identical to those for a user
  catalog, and it will be defined as a user catalog connected to the current master
  catalog or to the catalog specified in your STEPCAT or the CATALOG
  parameter of your DEFINE command. When you are defining a new master
  catalog, it can be useful to have it connected as a user catalog to your existing
  master catalog, as it is then easier to use IDCAMS commands to customize it.

When you create a user catalog, you will define it in a master catalog (just as the
master catalog in Example 7.20 was defined as a user catalog to another master
catalog). If, however, you need to reference the user catalog from any other master
catalog, you will need to define a connector entry in the additional master catalog
first. This is done with the IMPORT CONNECT command shown in Example
7.21.

Example 7.22 defines an ALIAS entry for the high-level qualifier ABCDEF.

7.7   Major system datasets

In this section we will look briefly at the role and creation of the more important
system datasets which have not yet been discussed.

7.7.1   Page and swap datasets

Page datasets are required by MVS to hold copies of areas of virtual storage that
cannot presently be backed by real storage (and copies of certain common areas
at all times). You must define one PLPA page dataset, one common page dataset,
and at least one local page dataset (used to back all private virtual storage) for use
by MVS at IPL time.

Swap datasets are used to hold copies of the working sets of tasks that are
swapped out by SRM; they are not mandatory, but if they are not present
swapping will still occur, being directed to the page datasets instead. There have
been long debates between performance specialists over the question of whether
separate swap datasets improve your system's performance or not. The lack of any
clear conclusion means you can decide for yourself — personally I do not use them,
as they add an extra layer of complexity with no apparent justification.

It is more important that you place your page datasets carefully. Page datasets should always reside on dedicated DASD volumes, or volumes with extremely low activity datasets on them (and there is a school of thought which says there is no such thing as a 'low activity dataset' — even rarely used datasets suffer occasional bursts of high I/O activity). Paging activity is most heavily concentrated on the local page datasets, and you must allocate a number of these, each on a different pack, to spread the burden of this I/O. Paging datasets should never be allocated on packs which are shared with another system, as a RESERVE issued by the other system could cause the system waiting for paging I/O to grind to a halt.

Furthermore, you should take care to ensure that each paging dataset can be simultaneously accessed down a separate path. It is acceptable for paging I/O to contend with non-paging I/O for channels and control units (up to a point), but not for multiple paging or swapping I/Os to contend with each other — this is likely to lead to serious performance degradation. This is most clear in the case of swapping — when MVS decides to swap out an address space, it will divide the pages to be swapped between the available page/swap datasets, and concurrently initiate a chain of long I/O operations to each of these datasets. If two page/swap datasets are contending for a single path, then the swap operation will take twice as long as it should. A similar effect will occur with ordinary demand paging at times when paging is heavy, simply because page faults tend to be fairly evenly spread across available paging datasets. And when paging is slow, every user of the system suffers! You should therefore ensure that the number of paging datasets behind a given control unit does not exceed the number of channel paths available or the number of internal paths available.

The number and size of local page datasets you need is a matter for trial-and-monitor — this is not a question where trial-and-error is acceptable! Increasing the number of page datasets allows you to spread paging I/O more widely and therefore do it faster, on average, but on the other hand most of us are subject to financial pressures which restrict the number of dedicated packs we can use. Increasing the size of page datasets allows more virtual storage to be backed by them, but it can slow down paging by increasing the head movement required to locate any given page. RMF or an equivalent product can be used to monitor how full your page datasets are and how quick I/O to your paging packs is. If your page datasets are more than about 70 per cent full at peak usage periods, you would be wise to make them bigger or get more; decisions on paging speed, on the other hand, are best left to performance experts. Unless you are starting a green-field site from scratch, you should be able to work from your performance stats and existing configuration to move towards the right configuration for your situation. If you are starting from scratch, you should get some advice from a supplier or someone running an installation with a comparable hardware configuration and workload, use that as a starting point, then apply the trial-and-monitor approach.

Note that common and PLPA page datasets can overflow into each other (i.e. if one becomes full and the other is not, it will overflow — but note that the PLPA

```
//SYSA      EXEC PGM=IDCAMS
//STEPCAT   DD   DSN=CATALOG.MASTER.VXA220C,DISP=SHR
//SYSPRINT  DD   SYSOUT=*
//SYSIN     DD   *
 DEF PGSPC(NAME(PAGE.VSYSPG2) CYLINDERS(150) VOLUMES(DISKOM))
/*
//SYSB      EXEC PGM=IDCAMS
//STEPCAT   DD   DSN=CATALOG.MASTER.VSYSCAT,DISP=SHR
//SYSPRINT  DD   SYSOUT=*
//SYSIN     DD   *
 DEF PGSPC(NAME(PAGE.VSYSPG2) CYLINDERS(150) VOLUMES(DISKOM) RCTLG)
//
```

Example 7.23. Defining a page dataset.

is written to its paging dataset at IPL time and effectively becomes read-only thereafter, so any overflow after IPL time will be from common to PLPA). It is often said that it is all right to allow PLPA to overflow into common (but not vice versa) in order to economize on unused space in these datasets, but IBM now recommends making both the PLPA and common datasets large enough to ensure that overflow never occurs.

Setting up page datasets is done using the IDCAMS DEFINE PAGESPACE command. Example 7.23 shows how to create a page dataset (in step SYSA), and also how to define an already existing page dataset into a different master catalog (in step SYSB). You may wish to do the latter if you are migrating to a new master catalog, or if you are setting up (or maintaining) an alternative master catalog for use in emergencies or when performing maintenance on the regular master catalog. If a page dataset is defined in more than one master catalog, however, you must take care to ensure that you never attempt to IPL two systems alongside each other which are attempting to use the same page datasets.

7.7.2   SYS1.PROCLIB

This is a required dataset containing cataloged procedures used during MVS initialization, including the JES2 (or JES3) procedure. Further PROCLIBs can be defined in the JES2 procedure itself and the JES2 parameters (see Chapter 8), and it is wise to keep all inhouse procedures in these additional procedure libraries. This is because each new CBIPO will supply you with a new SYS1.PROCLIB, and some of the members in it are sensitive to levels of MVS — so if you have all your inhouse procedures elsewhere, you can simply throw away your old SYS1.PROCLIB and use the new one whenever you implement a new CBIPO — or almost. In practice you will have to modify the JES procedure itself, and perhaps one or two others.

SYS1.PROCLIB must be cataloged in the master catalog. It is created by the CBIPO process and you should not need to recreate it, though as with PARMLIB, I recommend moving it off the SYSRES pack. If you do, be sure to catalog it properly, or your system will not IPL.

```
//LREC    EXEC PGM=IFCDIP00
//SERERDS  DD DSN=SYS1.LOGREC,DISP=(NEW,KEEP),
//            VOL=SER=SYSCAT,
//            SPACE=(TRK,(20),,CONTIG),UNIT=3380
```

Example 7.24. Allocating and initializing SYS1.LOGREC.

7.7.3   SYS1.LOGREC

This mandatory dataset is used by MVS to record details of hardware errors and some software errors. It is placed by the CBIPO process on the SYSRES pack, but personally I feel happier with it on a different system pack, e.g. the master catalog pack, for the same reasons as for SYS1.PARMLIB. It must be initialized using the IFCDIP00 program (a version of it at the same level as the system which is going to be writing to LOGREC), as shown in Example 7.24. Regular housekeeping jobs should be set up to archive the data recorded in SYS1.LOGREC and print off reports using the EREP program (see Chapter 17). These reports are an important source of diagnostic information for hardware engineers.

7.7.4   SYS1.DUMPxx datasets

These are used by MVS error-handling routines to record dumps (known as SVC dumps) of virtual storage when system tasks fail. They can be on DASD or tape, but the use of tape dump datasets slows down the dump process, and as the entire system may wait on the completion of an SVC dump, this is highly undesirable. It is therefore wise to allocate your dump datasets on DASD. In theory, you may do without dump datasets altogether, but this would result in the loss of important diagnostic information for many serious system problems, so this is not a sensible option. You should have a number of dump datasets, so that dumps can be created for multiple problems — MVS keeps track of which dump datasets are empty, and therefore available for use, and which are full, and if all dump datasets are full, it will discard the dump data.

MVS keeps an ordered list of dump datasets, based on the DUMP parameter in the IEASYSxx member of PARMLIB, and you should ensure that at least the first one or two datasets are large enough to take a full dump. The size of a full dump depends on a number of factors, so there is an element of trial and error in getting this right, but you can be sure of one thing — the DUMP datasets set up by CBIPO are too small! A reasonable size to start with on an MVS/ESA system would be around 30 cylinders on a 3380. Obviously, a large number of datasets of this size could be costly in terms of disk space, so you may wish to compromise by setting up, say, two datasets of this size, then a number of much smaller ones. If you put regular dump housekeeping procedures in place (see Chapter 17), so that dump datasets are offloaded and made available for reuse frequently, you should still get full dumps for most problems, and by keeping a number of smaller dump datasets at the end of the list, you will at least get dump titles for the other problems you

```
//DMPALC   EXEC PGM=IEBGENER
//SYSPRINT DD   SYSOUT=*
//SYSUT1   DD   DUMMY,
//              DCB=(RECFM=F,BLKSIZE=4104,LRECL=4104)
//SYSUT2   DD   DSN=SYS1.DUMP00,DISP=(,KEEP),
//              UNIT=3380,VOL=SER=SYSCAT,
//              SPACE=(4104,4500),DCB=(RECFM=F,BLKSIZE=4104,LRECL=4104)
//SYSIN    DD   DUMMY
//
```

Example 7.25. Creating a SYS1.DUMPxx dataset.

do not get full dumps for. Dump status can be displayed and altered, and titles displayed, using console commands which are discussed in Chapter 4, and dump analysis is discussed in Chapter 18.

CBIPO places SYS1.DUMPxx datasets on the SYSRES pack, but I would recommend you move them onto another of your system packs, so that you always use the same dump datasets on a given system, irrespective of which SYSRES pack you are using. They must be cataloged in the master catalog, as this is where MVS looks to determine what dump datasets are available and where they are. If you wish to set up additional or replacement datasets, Example 7.25 gives an example of the JCL required.

7.7.5   SYS1.STGINDEX

This dataset is used to map VIO datasets onto the slots in the page datasets which hold the corresponding pages of virtual storage. It is used to reconstruct VIO datasets across job steps and when you IPL without the CLPA or CVIO option. It is created by the CBIPO process on the master catalog volume, and can be allocated as shown in Example 7.26. If you IPL without SYS1.STGINDEX,

```
//STGALC   EXEC PGM=IDCAMS
//SYSPRINT DD   SYSOUT=*
//STGVOL   DD   UNIT=3380,VOL=SER=SYSCAT,DISP=OLD
//SYSIN    DD   *
  DEFINE   CLUSTER -
              ( BUFFERSPACE(20480) -
                CYLINDERS(4) -
                FILE(STGVOL) -
                KEYS(12,8) -
                NAME(SYS1.STGINDEX) -
                RECORDSIZE(2041,2041) -
                REUSE -
                VOLUME(SYSCAT) ) -
           DATA -
              ( CONTROLINTERVALSIZE(2048) ) -
           INDEX -
              ( CONTROLINTERVALSIZE(4096) ) -
                CATALOG(CATALOG.MASTER.VSYSCAT/PWUPDATE)
```

Example 7.26. Creating SYS1.STGINDEX.

```
//SMFALC    EXEC PGM=IDCAMS
//SYSPRINT  DD SYSOUT=*
//SYSIN     DD *
  DEFINE    CLUSTER -
                ( CONTROLINTERVALSIZE(4096) -
                  CYLINDERS(40) -
                  NAME(SYS1.MAN1) -
                  NONINDEXED -
                  RECORDSIZE(4086,32767) -
                  REUSE -
                  SHAREOPTIONS(2) -
                  SPANNED -
                  SPEED -
                  VOLUME(SYSCAT) ) -
                  CATALOG(CATALOG.MASTER.VSYSCAT/PWUPDATE)
  DEFINE    CLUSTER -
                ( CONTROLINTERVALSIZE(4096) -
                  CYLINDERS(10) -
                  NAME(SYS1.MAN2) -
                  NONINDEXED -
                  RECORDSIZE(4086,32767) -
                  REUSE -
                  SHAREOPTIONS(2) -
                  SPANNED -
                  SPEED -
                  VOLUME(SYSCAT) ) -
                  CATALOG(CATALOG.MASTER.VSYSCAT/PWUPDATE)
  DEFINE    CLUSTER -
                ( CONTROLINTERVALSIZE(4096) -
                  CYLINDERS(10) -
                  NAME(SYS1.MAN3) -
                  NONINDEXED -
                  RECORDSIZE(4086,32767) -
                  REUSE -
                  SHAREOPTIONS(2) -
                  SPANNED -
                  SPEED -
                  VOLUME(SYSCAT) ) -
                  CATALOG(CATALOG.MASTER.VSYSCAT/PWUPDATE)
```

Example 7.27. Creating SMF datasets.

journalling of VIO pages is disabled, which means that VIO datasets cannot be saved across job steps or IPLs, but otherwise the system will work as usual.

7.7.6 SYS1.MANx datasets

These datasets are used to record SMF data, and are required if you are going to use SMF to do any recording, which most sites do, for a variety of purposes, including accounting and performance monitoring. They are VSAM ESDSs, placed on the master catalog volume by CBIPO, and can be reallocated using JCL similar to that shown in Example 7.27. SMF starts recording on the first dataset listed in its parameters (see Sec. 7.5), then when this fills up it 'switches' to the next one, and so on until all the SMF datasets are full. At this point, it will either stop recording SMF records, or bring your entire system grinding to a halt, depending on your SMF parameters. If your SMF records are being used for anything important, which they usually are, either of these two situations is disastrous. You must therefore ensure that there is always an SMF dataset available. This is usually achieved by:

- Setting up at least two and preferably three SMF datasets so switches can occur.
- Making the first SMF dataset relatively large — at least large enough to hold several hours' worth of SMF data at peak usage periods — but the others much smaller, so that most recording occurs on the first dataset, and the others are only used for relatively short periods while the first is being dumped off.
- Setting up automatic housekeeping jobs to dump off and clear down SMF datasets whenever they fill up (see Chapter 17 for further discussion of SMF housekeeping).

7.7.7   SYS1.UADS and SYS1.BRODCAST

In theory these two datasets are optional, but in practice you will always find them necessary, as they are both required by TSO. SYS1.UADS holds details of all TSO userids authorized to use the system, and details of their logon procedures, account numbers, etc. If you have RACF version 1.8 or higher, you can use RACF to perform these functions instead of SYS1.UADS, but I would recommend that even if you use this for day-to-day operation, you keep a copy of UADS with at least your systems programmers' ids in it which you can use in an emergency if RACF is unusable.

SYS1.BRODCAST holds broadcast messages (e.g. NOTIFY messages) for TSO users which cannot be delivered at the time of their creation.

If you are using them, both of these datasets are usually allocated in your MSTJCLxx member, so it is crucial to the initialization of the master scheduler that they exist and are correctly cataloged in the master catalog. They are placed by CBIPO on the SYSRES pack, but I recommend moving them onto another system pack, for the same reasons as for PARMLIB. These datasets are discussed in a little more detail in Chapter 10.

7.7.8   SYS1.IMAGELIB

This is a required load library, which contains various 'images' used by printers, including universal character sets (UCSs), forms control buffer modules (FCBs), and various modules used by the 3800 laser printing subsystem. You can install IBM-supplied UCSs and FCBs using the IEBIMAGE utility documented in [16], or by using the processes documented in [17]. One important action during a system upgrade is to copy any modules which are in use in your old IMAGELIB but not supplied in the CBIPO one across to the new library. Unfortunately, there is no way to keep user images in a separate library and concatenate this with SYS1.IMAGELIB.

7.8 MVS installation processes

By far the simplest and commonest installation process for MVS these days is the custom built installation process offering (CBIPO), and this is discussed in some detail in Sec. 7.8.1. However, you may come across other installation processes, depending on your circumstances, including driver systems, CBPDOs, and traditional product tapes, and these are discussed briefly in Sec. 7.8.2.

7.8.1 The CBIPO process

A CBIPO is a set of tapes supplied by IBM which contains:

- All the object code, macros, parameters, etc., required to build the products you have asked IBM to include in the CBIPO, including all stable maintenance for those products available at the time of preparation of your tapes.
- A set of JCL libraries containing all the jobs required to build a working MVS system from these components.
- A set of documentation libraries describing how to run these jobs and in what order, as well as giving advice on further customization required and system design considerations, and the program directories (softcopy documents describing installation requirements) for the products you have ordered.
- Some samples of PARMLIB members, USERMODs for common requirements, etc.

A CBIPO tape costs nothing, although IBM will of course only supply products on it for which you are paying licence fees. To determine what products you can order and what levels are current, you need to ask your IBM SE (SE stands for systems engineer — although 'engineer' is rather a strange term for someone whose main job is to manage IBM's relationship with you as a client) for a 'CBIPO shopping list'.

The shopping list shows four different CBIPO features you can order, which means that separate CBIPO tapes are available for four different product groups: MVS, CICS, NCP, and IMS/DB2. However, the MVS feature can include a large variety of other IBM software products, such as compilers, INFOMAN, VTAM, Netview, and a host of others, as well as products like DFP and JES2 which are virtually part of MVS anyway.

CBIPO is probably the most widely used process for upgrading MVS, including major upgrades such as going from XA to ESA. It is common to re-install all of the products on the MVS CBIPO at the same time, thus keeping them all up to recent levels of maintenance. This also avoids the need to maintain multiple SMP/E CSIs; each CBIPO creates a new CSI for your new MVS system, and if you have replaced all the products from the last CBIPO, you can throw away your old MVS CSI when you have finished the MVS upgrade.

Installing a new version of MVS using CBIPO includes the following steps.

Preparation phase

1   Use IEBCOPY to load the userid.IPO1.INSTALL dataset from the RIM tape onto DASD, as documented in the *MVS CBIPO Memo to Users* supplied in hardcopy with your CBIPO tapes.

2   Run the DOCLOD job from the INSTALL dataset to load the documentation library (IPO1.DOCLIB) from the RIM tapes onto DASDs. Note that you can order the documentation libraries without the CBIPO by asking your SE for the *CBIPO Process Aids* [14] for the 'feature' (i.e. MVS, CICS, NCP, or database) which you want. This is a useful way to start preparing for a CBIPO if you have not done one before.

3   Read the documentation — particularly the *Memo to Users Extension* in IPO1.DOCLIB(MEMOEXT), which describes the products on your tape, the *CBIPO MVS Installation Guide* [14] in IPO1.DOCLIB(MVSINST), which describes the jobs you must run later, and the *CBIPO System Design Reference* [14] in IPO1.DOCLIB(SYSDSGN), which describes some of the configuration choices you must make at this stage and the usage of the IPOUPDTE job which will tailor the rest of the installation JCL.

4   Determine how much DASD space you require for the installation process, and ensure that you have this available to you for the duration of the upgrade project. The minimum depends on your software configuration, but most installations now require at least a double-density 3380 for the SYSRES pack to be built and the equivalent of at least three single-density 3380s for the other datasets (divided logically into those which CBIPO expects to place on a DLIB pack and those it expects to place on a master catalog pack).

5   Determine your migration strategy. For example, which datasets do you want to end up on which packs and what CSI structure do you want for your SMP/E datasets? You must understand clearly what your endpoint will be before you start the process of implementing it, or confusion and problems will result, so think these issues out carefully at this stage. One of the key decisions you must make is whether to reuse the existing master catalog or to convert your CBIPO master catalog into the new production master catalog. Both options are feasible, but both require a certain amount of work and a lot of care! Reusing the existing master catalog requires setting up a process for switching it between the old and new levels of your system, whereas making the CBIPO catalog into a production one requires copying all aliases from the old catalog, and also moving certain dataset entries across at the cutover point to your new system. Personally I prefer the former option, but I would adopt the latter in some situations, e.g. if the format of the master catalog changed in any way, or if

there were any problems with the DASD volume on which the existing one was located.

6 Determine as far as possible what customization will be required for each of the products you are upgrading. There is likely to be a long list of these, so you should aim to 'contract out' some of this to other people! You need to know what customization is required for each product and how long it will take before you can go into the next step.

7 Prepare a detailed plan of what you are going to do and when, ensuring that you include at least two weeks for customization, even if you have several people helping you, at least two weeks for testing of the customized system, and some contingency for fixing problems before your scheduled implementation date. Obtain management approval for your plan, and management commitment to provide the staff required for testing (see below), and ensure you put your intended changes through any change authorization processes used at your site. Once the work starts, check up regularly to ensure the people helping you are keeping to the planned schedule.

8 Determine the values you will use as parameters for the IPOUPDTE program. This program tailors the JCL in IPO1.INSTLIB and other IPO1.* libraries which you will then run to perform the rest of the CBIPO installation process. Once IPOUPDTE has tailored the JCL for you, inserting your own jobcard parameters and volume serial numbers, for example, you should be able to run most of the CBIPO jobs without further modification.

9 Review the contents of IPO1.REPORTS(INSTINFO) and (PTFCLTRS) which contain important information about the service on your CBIPO, and call IBM to ask if there are any known problems with the CBIPO level you are using. It is a good idea to order your CBIPO to arrive a month before you need it, so that when you make this call somebody else has already installed this level and found out what is wrong with it!

Installation phase

1 Run the RESBLD job from the INSTALL dataset, which allocates many of the IPO1 and target datasets to be built by CBIPO, downloads the IPO1 datasets from the CBIPO tapes, and invokes IPOUPDTE to tailor the jobs in IPO1.INSTLIB and other IPO1 libraries.

2 Run the jobs in IPO1.INSTLIB in the order specified in *CBIPO MVS Installation Guide* [14], following the instructions there carefully, and avoiding making any changes to the CBIPO jobs if at all possible — changes which seem sensible in one place can have unfortunate consequences later on in the process. These jobs will build your system from scratch, including:

a Initializing the DASD to be used
b Building the master catalog and user catalogs for CBIPO datasets
c Building the SMP datasets and CSI entries for your new system

d   Allocating all required system datasets
e   Copying pregenerated modules into these datasets from the tapes
f   For pre-MVS V4 systems, running the stage 1, JCLIN, GENERATE, and
    system build steps described in Sec. 5.4.1; for V4 systems, simply running
    the GENERATE and system build steps
g   Running MVSCP or HCD to create your I/O configuration
h   Creating IPL text and the master catalog pointer
i   Initializing system datasets such as SYS1.LOGREC
j   Providing skeleton procedures and parameters for IPLing your system and
    bringing up VTAM, JES, and TSO

3   At key points in this process, back up your packs so you do not have to start
    again from scratch if you make a mistake.
4   You should now have a working MVS system. Ensure you also have working
    versions of JES, VTAM, TSO, ISPF, and PDF (see Chapters 8–10), and obtain
    a testing slot or use of a PR/SM partition.
5   Modify COMMND00 to vary offline all DASD except your dedicated CBIPO
    packs immediately after IPL (so you are not in any danger of damaging any
    other data if you have somehow generated a dodgy system!).
6   IPL your system, if you can!
7   Solve any problems which appear.
8   Run the installation verification procedures (IVPs) to test some basic functions
    of your system.

Customization phase

You must now depart from the well-defined path laid down by the CBIPO
documentation and transform your new system into one which not only works, but
also works in exactly the same way as the old one as far as the applications running
on it are concerned.

1   Begin by performing the necessary product customization you identified in the
    preparation phase; this will probably include the application of any
    USERMODs required by inhouse or third-party software (if you have
    previously collected the JCL and source for these together in one place, as
    recommended in Chapter 5, this will be a lot easier).
2   You will also need to perform other customization to turn your IPLable
    system into a production-quality system (see the *CBIPO MVS Customisation
    Guide* [14] in IPO1.DOCLIB). Thus, for example, the CBIPO-created page
    datasets are not likely to be large enough to support a production system, so
    you must either create new ones in suitable locations and with enough space
    allocated to them, or you must prepare to use the existing page datasets. The
    issue of which versions of major system datasets you should use at each stage
    of the CBIPO process is discussed at the end of this section.

3 Create the PARMLIB members you will use for testing your customized system, which should be as close to the live parameters as possible, after taking account of parameter changes due to the new software levels, and the need to use testing versions of certain datasets (e.g. PAGE and SMF datasets). Also prepare the versions you will use when you put the new system into production, which will be largely the same as your testing versions, but using the live versions of these datasets.

4 Tidy up the master catalog entries for CBIPO datasets other than the target libraries. CBIPO creates separate user catalogs for the distribution libraries and each of the CSI zones. The DLIB catalog can be ignored, as most of the DLIBs need never be referenced through the catalog — the SMP DDDEFs should be all that is required. However, one or two of your DLIBs may be required as SYSLIBs for assemblies, such as SYS1.AMODGEN and SYS1.HASPSRC, so you should ensure these are cataloged in whichever master catalog you are going to use. Also, the CSIs must be accessible through the catalog structure, so if you are going to use the existing master catalog, you must ensure the user catalogs for the CSIs are connected to it, and suitable ALIAS entries are defined.

5 If you intend to make the CBIPO master catalog your new production master catalog, you will have to copy all aliases from the existing master catalog and recatalog any PAGE and VSAM datasets in it which you intend to reuse (e.g. SMF datasets). This must be carefully timed and coordinated with parameters defining which system datasets are in use, or you risk interfering with the operation of the existing production system, e.g. by attempting to use a production SMF dataset from a test system sharing DASD with the production system. (See the discussion on the use of datasets during CBIPO at the end of this section for more detail on this issue.) CBIPO provides a master catalog conversion job to help you copy existing master catalog entries into your new catalog.

6 If you intend to reuse your existing catalog, you will need to create a suitable SYSCATxx member pointing to it in SYS1.NUCLEUS (see Sec. 7.3.2 on how to do this).

7 Whichever catalog is going to be the production one eventually, you should produce full LISTCATs of the CBIPO and production catalogs, compare them carefully, and confirm that you understand what is to happen to each and every non-ALIAS entry when you go live with your new system.

8 Ensure both the old and the new levels of all stand-alone utilities (dump, DSF, and DFDSS) are available prior to migration.

9 Ensure you have adequate machine time available for testing your new system. Ideally, you want a dedicated machine or a dedicated partition for full-time testing. If you cannot have this, you will need to schedule as many dedicated test slots as possible on the production machine itself. Even if you do have the use of a dedicated machine or partition, you need to schedule some test slots

on the production machine/partition, to ensure that those things which differ between the production and test machines are also tested. For example, the I/O configuration is likely to be different, and even if both machines are using the same I/O configuration modules, they are likely to be using different definitions within the modules. Also, it is unlikely that every resource available on the production machine is available on the test one, e.g. large amounts of storage, specialized (and/or unsharable) devices such as laser printers, solid-state paging DASD, or open-reel tape drives, and software which drives such devices.

10 Test your customized system. This is an area in which you cannot afford to take short-cuts! The systems programmers doing product customization must check the basic function of each product, including each third-party product on your system, whether it is being changed or not. In addition, you should ensure you obtain the assistance of a sample of the users/developers of the key applications on your system, both batch and online, and have them do some testing. As a minimum, they should test at least one example of each major application technology in use at your site.

11 Fix any problems revealed by your testing and retest the affected products from scratch.

Migration phase

1 Check with IBM that there have been no more HIPER problems reported for your level of CBIPO.
2 Plan how to back out if things go wrong.
3 Do a dummy 'cutover' the week before to test your plans, if possible.
4 Immediately before starting, ensure your old system is properly backed up, including performing a spool offload if you are going to cold-start JES.
5 Last thing before closing down the old production system, run a job to make any necessary master catalog changes which could not be done before this point.
6 Bring up your new system, cold-starting JES if necessary.
7 Do a little last-minute testing of anything which you are implementing for the first time (e.g. full-size spool).
8 Reload the job queues if you offloaded the spool, then allow production work to start, reloading the output queues alongside the normal workload.
9 Stand by to deal with problems!

Even if you have followed the CBIPO process scrupulously, checked with IBM when required, checked every return code carefully and followed up any discrepancies, ensured every necessary piece of customization has been performed, and tested every changed function, you will almost certainly still have some problems. But your objective should be zero defects, and if you do all of these things, you stand a good chance of migrating to your new level of MVS with few problems,

Table 7.3. Dataset usage during CBIPO testing

Dataset	Version to use up to IVPs	Version to use during parallel testing	Version to use during dedicated testing	Version to use after cutover	Notes
Target libraries not mentioned below	CBIPO	CBIPO	CBIPO	CBIPO	
SYS1.PARMLIB	CBIPO	CBIPO	CBIPO	Existing	Prepare PARMLIB members for testing and cutover carefully
Spool	CBIPO	CBIPO	CBIPO	Existing	If spool does not need to be reformatted you can use existing one earlier
Master catalog (if you plan to make the CBIPO one your new master catalog)	CBIPO	CBIPO	CBIPO	CBIPO	Requires you copy all aliases from the existing master catalog and recatalog any VSAM datasets you will reuse, e.g. SMF datasets. CBIPO provides a catalog conversion process to help with this
Master catalog (if you plan to reuse the existing one)	CBIPO	CBIPO	Existing	Existing	Requires some catalog changes when swapping between live and testing systems — see Example 7.28
LOGREC, page and SMF datasets	CBIPO	CBIPO	Existing	Existing	
User libraries	Copies	Copies, then existing	Existing	Existing	

and hopefully only minor ones! Nevertheless, you should expect a few things to go wrong; you should warn your users of the possibility of some disruption (e.g. unscheduled IPLs) for a few days after the cutover, and you should ensure that the cutover is done at a time when such disruption is not going to be disastrous to your users.

Use of datasets during the CBIPO process

Normally, if you are upgrading an existing system you will wish to reuse its existing resources, but you will not be able to while you are testing your new system alongside the existing one (e.g. on another PR/SM partition). When you do testing in dedicated slots on the production 'machine', you can use more of the existing resources, but you will then need to switch back to the 'parallel test' situation until you go live. Table 7.3 summarizes which versions of which datasets you are likely to use at different stages in the CBIPO process, but you will have to consider each major system library separately and make a decision on which version to use at each stage. The issues to be considered include:

• Can the dataset be shared between the two systems if they are sharing DASD?

```
//RECAT1   EXEC  PGM=IEHPROGM
//STEPCAT  DD  DSN=CATALOG.MASTER.VSYSCAT,DISP=SHR
//SYSPRINT DD  SYSOUT=*
//DD5      DD  UNIT=3380,VOL=SER=XA313D,DISP=SHR
//DD6      DD  UNIT=3380,VOL=SER=XA313C,DISP=SHR
//SYSIN    DD  *
UNCATLG DSNAME=SYS1.AMODGEN
CATLG DSNAME=SYS1.AMODGEN,VOL=3380=XA313D
UNCATLG DSNAME=SYS1.HASPSRC
CATLG DSNAME=SYS1.HASPSRC,VOL=3380=XA313D
UNCATLG DSNAME=SYS1.PARMLIB
CATLG DSNAME=SYS1.PARMLIB,VOL=3380=XA313C
UNCATLG DSNAME=SYS1.PROCLIB
CATLG DSNAME=SYS1.PROCLIB,VOL=3380=XA313C
/*
```

Example 7.28. Amending the master catalog when switching MVS systems.

If not, you will not be able to use this dataset until the 'dedicated test' stage.

● Is there any danger of the CBIPO system corrupting the live dataset? You should assume there is in the early stages of testing, and not start using any live system datasets until you are satisfied the CBIPO system is reliable.

● Does the format of the dataset change between the two software levels? The JES spool often does, and other datasets may — in these cases you will probably have to reformat the datasets concerned, and you must not reformat the live ones until the cutover to the new system, so you will not be able to use these for your CBIPO system until that time.

● Do you need to modify the dataset to support the cut-down environment used in the early stages of testing your CBIPO system? This is likely for VTAMLST and ISPF clist libraries—in cases like this you will have to take copies of the live libraries, modify them, then migrate to the live ones at a later stage of testing.

For those planning to reuse an existing catalog, Example 7.28 illustrates the type of modifications to the catalog required when switching between your existing MVS system and your CBIPO system. It assumes that the SYSRES datasets for both levels are already cataloged using indirect references. This job should be run last thing before closing down the system, to set up the catalog entries for the other system when it is IPLd. The job to switch back should be essentially the same, but pointing to the other system's volumes.

Note that if you intend to do any assemblies during your test you must switch the catalog entries for any distribution libraries used in your SYSLIB concatenations. This JCL is merely an example — you will have to decide in each situation which datasets' catalog entries need to be changed.

SMP release 6 supplies new dialogs for managing MVS CBIPO installations, which should make the process simpler and faster, but even if you plan to use these it is still important that you understand and plan for all the issues discussed in this section.

7.8.2 *CBPDO*

A custom-built product delivery offering (CBPDO) is a set of tapes containing the files required to install a single IBM product or a group of products, plus the service required to bring them (and the rest of the products on your system) up to a recent level, the program directories for the products to be installed, and some of the JCL required to carry out the installation process. You may also order a service-only CBPDO, if you wish to install only cumulative service for the products already on your system. As with CBIPO, there are four 'features', MVS, CICS, NCP, or database, and the MVS feature includes the same products as for CBIPO. CBPDO is therefore a convenient way to add products to an existing MVS system, to upgrade individual products, or to install preventative service.

As with CBIPO:

- You specify what products you want using a 'shopping list', and return this to your SE.
- When you receive your CBPDO tapes, you will also receive a 'CBPDO memo to users', telling you how to start the installation process.
- The documentation files on the tapes include a 'CBPDO memo to users extension' with further details of what is included in your order.
- You should go through preparation, installation, customization, and migration phases as part of the process of implementing your CBPDO, and many of the issues in each of these phases are similar to those for a CBIPO process.

Unlike CBIPO, however, CBPDO does not provide a full set of installation jobs to carry out the installation phase for you, though there is an SMP/E dialog which is designed to handle the SMP steps of a CBPDO installation. Overall, the installation process should be much simpler than for CBIPO, without the need for DASD initialization, setting up catalog structures and MVS system datasets, the GENERATE process which performs the function of an MVS SYSGEN, etc.

Typically, the sequence of actions required to implement a CBPDO will be something like this:

1 Print and review the 'memo to users extension' and the program directories; review the installation and customization guides for the products to be installed.
2 Prepare your plan, ensure you have DASD space available, and satisfy change control requirements.
3 Backup anything you are going to change, including the SMP CSIs into which you plan to RECEIVE the products.
4 RECEIVE what you want from the tape (you may choose, for example, to RECEIVE the products to be installed plus the service relating to them, but exclude the preventative service for other products).
5 Review any HOLDDATA on the tape and ask IBM if there is any further PSP information about the tape you have received.

6   Allocate any new target libraries and review space allocations for any old libraries into which modules will be installed (the documentation with the CBPDO should specify how much additional space is required in each of these). If necessary, reallocate old libraries with more space (and allow enough for reruns of your APPLY step in case you have problems with the first run).
7   Review the DDDEFs in your SMP zones and revise them as required.
8   APPLY CHECK and APPLY each of your new functions and any required maintenance.
9   Re-APPLY any regressed USERMODs.
10 Create/revise any parameters and new datasets required for the products to function.
11 Perform any other customization required for the products.
12 Test the products carefully, including their impact on other areas of the system, and if they are existing products which are being upgraded involve users in this.
13 Implement the change in your production system.
14 Deal with any problems.
15 ACCEPT the base products and initial service.

The CBPDO process is well structured and systematic, which should minimize the risk of problems with your installation, though it still requires a proper understanding of SMP and other products used in the installation process, and proper attention to the customization and testing of the products being installed. It is an attractive option for adding new products to your system or upgrading individual products between CBIPOs.

7.8.3   Other installation processes

Driver systems

If you do not have an MVS system in place already, you will not be able to use the CBIPO process, as it requires a 'driving' system on which to run the CBIPO jobs. This situation is common when an installation is starting up from scratch (a 'green-field site'), or when a conversion from another operating system (typically VSE) is being started. In cases like this, you will need to order a pregenerated MVS system from IBM. The simplest of these is an MVS CBIPO driver. This is a very basic MVS/370 system with enough function to be used as the driving system for a full CBIPO installation, but not enough for practical use as a production system. It is supplied with standard addresses for a restricted range of hardware devices (these are documented in [13]), so you must physically configure the hardware required by the driver system to conform with the standard configuration in the driver system. The actual installation of the driver system is simply a question of running stand-alone utilities to initialize the two DASD volumes required and restore the driver system onto them from the supplied tapes.

Other pregenerated systems

At a price, IBM is also prepared to supply you with pregenerated systems which have been tailored to your I/O configuration, including all the products you want from the MVS feature, and are production-quality systems with the latest service integrated. These systems will have been built and tested on an IBM machine, and will simply be downloaded from tape onto your DASD, tested, and handed over to you — all in the space of a single day. Currently this service is known as MVS/Express (though it may be superseded by a service called SystemPac), and is available from the 'customer engineering' side of IBM. No systems programmer is likely to opt for a deal like this — after all, putting in a CBIPO is one of the most exciting parts of the job! But on a site with a shortage (or absence) of systems programmers, it is an option which managers will consider. An Express system will also include considerably higher maintenance levels than a basic CBIPO system delivered at the same time.

Product tapes

Traditionally, systems software was supplied on product tapes without any of the assistance provided by the modern installation process offerings. You had to follow the instructions in the machine-readable program directory supplied on the product tape, and/or the product installation manual to install or upgrade a product. This process relied on your knowledge and experience as a systems programmer to avoid the many potential pitfalls in the installation process; in addition, it imposed a very large workload on systems programmers who needed to keep a wide range of products up to date. By contrast, CBIPO and CBPDO make installations much simpler, safer, and quicker, especially when you wish to upgrade/install a wide range of products at the same time. However, the traditional option is still available — for non-CBIPO-supported software products it is still the only option. Occasionally there may be other good reasons for using product tapes, but I suspect that some systems programmers who choose them in preference to CBPDOs are motivated more by plain old-fashioned Ludditism than a balanced assessment of their relative advantages.

Other product installation options

IBM also offers 'load-and-go' product tapes along the lines of MVS/Express, called MVS/ProductPac. Essentially this is a CBPDO which IBM has installed, brought up to a more recent maintenance level, and then downloaded onto a tape. Once again, they will charge you for the extra work they have done beyond generating the CBPDO.

References and bibliography

IBM manuals

1. *MVS/XA Overview*, GC28–1348. Contains a chapter on initializing the system.
2. *MVS/XA System Initialization Logic*, LY28–1200. The introduction is quite readable!
3. *MVS/ESA Operations: System Commands*, GC28–1826. Documents console commands and the operator's role in system initialization.
4. *DSF User's Guide and Reference*, GC35–0033. Covers DASD initialization, including creation of IPL text.
5. *MVS/ESA SPL: System Modifications*, GC28–1831. Includes sections on customizing the EDT, VATLST, PPT, master JCL, and subsystems.
6. *MVS/ESA MVS Configuration Program Guide and Reference*, GC28–1817.
7. *3090 IOCP: User's Guide and Reference*, SC38–0038. Note that there is a different IOCP manual for each type of processor.
8. *MVS/ESA SPL: Initialization and Tuning*, GC28–1828. Documents all of the PARMLIB parameters, as well as outlining the system initialization process, real and virtual storage management, the SRM, and guidelines on sizing and placing page datasets. For MVS V4 the PARMLIB parameters have been split from the rest: the parameters are documented in *Initialization and Tuning Reference*, GC28–1635, while the rest is in *Initialization and Tuning Guide*, GC28–1634.
9. *MVS/ESA SPL: Application Development Guide*, GC28–1852. Documents use of MVS facilities for assembler programmers, including rules on the creation of SVCs.
10. *MVS/XA SPL: System Macros and Facilities Volume 1*, GC28–1150. The XA version of *SPL: Application Development Guide*.
11. *MVS/DFP V3R2 Access Method Services for ICF*, SC26–4562. Documents the use of IDCAMS, e.g. for creating catalogs and catalog entries.
12. *MVS/ESA System Generation*, GC28–1825. Documents the SYSGEN process, including a description of each of the MVS system datasets.
13. *MVS Software Manufacturing Offerings: Planning and Installation*, SC23–0352. Describes the CBIPO, CBPDO, and CBIPO driver processes and how to prepare for them.
14. *CBIPO MVS Installation Guide, CBIPO System Design Reference*, and *CBIPO MVS Customization Guide*. These do not have order numbers as they are only supplied in machine-readable form as part of a CBIPO. You can order just the manuals and related installation material by asking for the *CBIPO Process Aids*.
15. *MVS/ESA Message Library: System Codes*, GC28–1815. Documents wait codes.
16. *MVS/ESA Data Administration: Utilities*, SC26-4516. Includes coverage of IEBIMAGE.
17. *MVS DFP System Programming Reference*, SC26-4567.

Other

18. Bordonaro, B.: Understanding the MVS/ESA System Initialization Process, *Enterprise Systems Journal*, January 1991, pp. 30–36. Detailed coverage of the early stages of the initialization process.
19. Stanislawski, L.: Defining MVS/ESA SP V4 Hardware Configuration, *Enterprise Systems Journal*, May 1991, pp. 99–102. Covers HCD, IODFs, and dynamic reconfiguration.
20. Waterhouse, P.S.: Adventures in ESA: Part II, *Technical Support*, September 1991,

pp. 22–28. Describes major MVS V4 changes to SYS1.PARMLIB members and migration considerations from MVS V3.

21. Kidd, C.L: Using VLF to Reduce the I/O Bottleneck, *Mainframe Journal*, April 1990, pp. 14–22. Comprehensive coverage of how to use VLF.

8
JES2 implementation

8.1 Introduction

8.1.1 JES2 and JES3

JES is the batch interface and print spooler for the MVS operating system. It handles the input, preparation for execution, queueing for execution, and output processing for all batch work, TSO sessions, and all console-started tasks which are begun after MVS initialization is complete. The job management functions of JES have been discussed already in Chapter 3, and JES2 commands have been covered in Chapter 4; in this chapter we will look at how to implement a JES2 subsystem.

IBM offers two flavours of JES, called JES2 and JES3, each of which has been evolving separately (though in gradually converging directions) for around 25 years. IBM estimates that around 90 per cent of MVS sites use JES2, although the 10 per cent which use JES3 account for 40 per cent of IBM's MVS revenues. This reflects the existence of features in JES3 which in the past have made it more suitable for sites using multiple processor complexes, such as the 'single-system image' it presents.

JES3 also offers some powerful scheduling features, which JES2 sites often buy third-party packages to provide. However, JCL statements for the two are not compatible, so the costs of conversion to JES3 outweigh any potential benefits for most JES2 sites. Furthermore, the announcement of Sysplex suggests there will be alternative ways of providing a single-system image in the future. It is not inconceivable that JES2 and JES3 might at some time be combined. As most sites still use JES2 and are likely to continue to do so in the near future, this chapter confines itself to JES2.

8.1.2 Summary of JES2 processing

JES2 processing for a unit of work occurs in six stages:

1 *Input* Jobs can be input to JES2 from various sources, including dedicated card

readers and remote RJE terminals, but these days they are usually input through special datasets called internal readers. MVS uses two specialized internal readers, called the STCINRDR and the TSOINRDR. STCINRDR is used by the started task control routine to submit the JCL for started tasks and mount processing, while TSOINRDR is used by the TSO logon processor to submit the JCL for TSO sessions. There is also a pool of generally available internal readers which can be used by other tasks to submit batch jobs (e.g. the TSO SUBMIT command). During the input stage, JES2 assigns a job number to the unit of work, and saves its JCL and input data on the JES spool.

2 *Conversion* During this stage JES2 merges in any JCL from procedure libraries and checks for syntax errors. If no errors are found, the JCL is converted into internal text (the format required by MVS), placed back on the spool, and queued for execution (JES2 keeps an input queue for each job class, ordered according to job priority). If any errors are found, the JCL is written straight back to the output queue with diagnostic messages, skipping the execution stage altogether.

3 *Execution* Started tasks, mount commands, and TSO logons are passed immediately to MVS for execution, and MVS creates a dedicated address space for each one. Batch jobs, however, must wait on the input queue for an initiator to become free which is then assigned to their jobclass. When an initiator does become free, JES2 selects the highest priority job in the first jobclass assigned to this initiator and passes it to the initiator for execution. Processing at this stage now becomes MVS's responsibility. JES2, however, continues to provide services to the executing job — any writes to datasets defined in the job's JCL as SYSOUT will be passed to JES, and JES will write it to output datasets on the JES2 spool.

4 *Output* Once the job has completed, JES2 creates work elements in the job output table. A work element is created for each group of SYSOUT datasets with common output characteristics (output class, hold status, destination, FCB, etc.). From now on, any manipulation of output datasets (e.g. changing output class or hold status) must be done at the work element level.

5 *Hardcopy* JES2 queues the output datasets for hardcopy processing — usually printing, but possibly punching, or transmission to another JES system in an NJE network. There is a separate queue for each output class, and there are numerous other criteria which affect the selection of work for printing, such as the destination, output priority, and forms id associated with each work element. Output datasets may be 'held', in which case they will not be printed until the work element is explicitly released using a JES command (either entered at the console or generated from a facility such as SDSF — IBM's online viewing facility for spool datasets). Once a work element has been selected for printing, JES2 writes it to the output device concerned and marks it as deleted from the spool.

6 *Purge* When the last output dataset belonging to a job is deleted, JES2 purges

the job. Purge processing removes all traces of the job from the spool, releasing the space it has used and making its job number available for reuse.

8.1.3 Starting JES2

This was discussed in Chapter 7. Briefly, there are three ways in which JES2 may be started:

1 On MVS/XA and MVS/ESA systems, JES2 must be defined as the PRIMARY subsystem in the IEFSSNxx member of SYS1.PARMLIB. This will automatic-ally lead to JES2 being started at the end of the master scheduler initialization phase of the IPL process, unless the NOSTART parameter is also coded.

2 On MVS/370 systems, JES2 was normally started by a START JES2 command on the last record of the master scheduler JCL (in the MSTJCLxx member of SYS1.LINKLIB).

3 JES2 can also be started by operator command at any time after master scheduler initialization has completed — this could be done from your automatic commands, or by an operator using the console. If JES2 abends for any reason, it can be restarted in this way.

Whichever of these methods is used, the start command for JES2 is processed by the master scheduler itself. It must invoke a cataloged procedure in SYS1.PRO-CLIB, which is the only procedure library available before JES2 itself is started up. A typical JES2 procedure is shown in Example 8.1. Note that:

* The procedure is heavily parametrized to maximize your chance of starting it when there is a problem. If, for example, one of the PROCLIBs in the sample procedure were deleted, JES2 would fail at startup time with a JCL error. With this procedure, you can start JES2 by substituting one of the other PROCLIBs for the missing one using a parameter override in the START command. True, your PROCLIB structure will be wrong, but at least you can get JES up so that you can fix the problem, then restart it with the right procedure libraries later.

* By default, JES2 will use the HASPPARM DD statement to allocate its parameter dataset. However, by specifying HASPPARM=ddname in the PARM field (or in an override to the PARM field in your START command), you can instruct JES2 to use a different DD statement for its parameters. The ALTPARM DD statement is coded here to provide an alternative version of the JES2 parameters, which can be invoked in this way if the primary version is unusable for some reason.

* Sec. 8.2.2 discusses the way procedure libraries are defined in this example.

* The NOREQ parameter in the PARM field saves the operator from having to enter the $S JES2 command to start JES processing. If you do not specify this parameter, JES2 will issue the message:

```
$HASP400 ENTER REQUESTS
```

```
//JES2     PROC VERSION=20,MEMBER=JES2PRM0,ALTMEM=JES2PRM9,
//              N1='SYS1.PARMLIB',
//              N2='SYS1.PROCLIB',
//              N3='SYS9.STCPROC',
//              N4='SYS9.TSOPROC',
//              N5='SYS9.DEVPROC',
//              N6='SYS9.ACTPROC',
//              N7='SYS9.PRDPROC',
//              N8='SYS9.GENPROC'
//*
//*   JES2 PROCEDURE FOR SYSA
//*
//IEFPROC EXEC PGM=HASJES&VERSION,DPRTY=(15,15),TIME=1440,PERFORM=9,
//              PARM='WARM,NOREQ',
//              ACCT='JESPRDSYSA'
//*PROC00   **   STARTED TASKS ONLY   **
//PROC00   DD   DISP=SHR,DSN=&N2
//         DD   DISP=SHR,DSN=&N3
//*PROC01   **   TSO LOGONS ONLY   **
//PROC01   DD   DISP=SHR,DSN=&N4
//*PROC02   **   DEVELOPMENT   **
//PROC02   DD   DISP=SHR,DSN=&N5
//         DD   DISP=SHR,DSN=&N8
//*PROC03   **   ACCEPTANCE   **
//PROC03   DD   DISP=SHR,DSN=&N6
//         DD   DISP=SHR,DSN=&N8
//*PROC04   **   PRODUCTION   **
//PROC04   DD   DISP=SHR,DSN=&N7
//         DD   DISP=SHR,DSN=&N8
//HASPPARM DD   DISP=SHR,DSN=&N1(&MEMBER)
//ALTPARM  DD   DISP=SHR,DSN=&N1(&ALTMEM)
//HASPLIST DD   DDNAME=IEFRDER
```

Example 8.1. JES2 procedure.

once it has completed initialization, and it will not start up any of its facilities until the $S JES2 command has been issued.

There are three types of JES startup, known as cold, warm, and hot. A hot start occurs automatically when you restart JES2 after it has abended (see Sec. 8.1.2). A warm start is the normal type of startup, requested by coding PARM = WARM on the EXEC statement of the JES2 procedure, as in Example 8.1. A cold start is requested by specifying PARM = FORMAT, normally as an override on the START command. This causes the spool dataset to be reformatted, destroying in the process all data remaining on the spool, including both output queues and job queues. You must therefore take care to avoid inadvertently cold-starting any JES system.

Various problems may occur during initialization. For example:

- If JES2 is unable to open the parameter dataset, it will issue the messages:

```
$HASP450   OPEN FAILED FOR JES2 PARAMETER LIBRARY
$HASP441   REPLY Y TO CONTINUE INITIALIZATION OR N TO
           TERMINATE
```

If you have an alternative version of the parameters in another member or library, it is simplest to reply N and restart JES2 using the symbolic parameters or the HASPPARM = ddname PARM statement to allocate the alternative version. If you have made an error in your specification of the library name or member name reply N, then restart JES2 using the appropriate symbolic parameters to override these values. Creative use of the symbolic parameters should even enable you to handle the situation where your parameter library is uncataloged. Using the JCL in Example 8.1, you could specify N1 = 'YOUR.PARMLIB(YOURMEM), UNIT = 3380,VOL = SER = YOURVL' (note the space at the end, which turns the (&MEMBER) part of the DD statement into a comment, preventing a JCL error). If you are unable to deal with the problem in any of these ways, you should bring up a different system using a different JES2 procedure (or an alternative JES2 procedure on your existing system if you have one), and fix the problem from there. In the very worst case, where you cannot do even this, you may specify the CONSOLE parameter on your START command, which will cause JES to prompt you to enter all the initialization parameters at the console. However, this will be a long and painful process, even if you just enter enough parameters to get a working version of JES up so you can fix the problem.

• If JES2 finds a syntax error in any of the initialization parameters, it will display the first line of the statement in error, then go into CONSOLE mode, issuing the message:

    $HASP469   REPLY PARAMETER STATEMENT, CANCEL, OR END

Your reply to this message should specify the corrected parameter statement. The message will be re-issued after each of your replies, until you specify CANCEL, in which case JES2 will be terminated, or END, in which case JES2 will carry on processing the next initialization parameter. Once all the initialization parameters have been processed, JES2 will issue the messages:

    $HASP451   ERROR ON JES2 PARAMETER LIBRARY
    $HASP441   REPLY Y TO CONTINUE INITIALIZATION OR N TO
    TERMINATE

If you are happy you have respecified the parameters adequately, reply Y, otherwise reply N and start again!

• If you have changed a JES2 initialization parameter which can only be changed on a cold start, but specified a warm start in the PARM field, the action JES2 takes will depend on whether or not this system is part of a multi-access spool with other members active. If it is, JES2 will simply issue a message and terminate; if it is not, JES2 will assume you do want a cold start, and issue a message ($HASP436) asking the operator to confirm this. Your operating instructions should state clearly that the operators must *never* reply Y to this message unless instructed to the contrary by a systems programmer — or all output on the spool could be lost as a result of your parameter change.

Some other problems which can occur at startup time are discussed in Sec. 8.2.1.

8.1.4   Stopping JES2

A normal closedown of JES2 can only occur after all activities using JES facilities
have been closed down. This includes all batch jobs, TSO users, and started tasks
(other than those started without the use of JES, i.e. those which start before JES
during system initialization), plus all JES2 devices (printers, RJE and NJE sessions,
offloads, etc.). JES2 devices can be closed down (drained) by issuing the $P
command, though you will have to wait for each device to finish processing the
current dataset before it will be stopped. Therefore a normal JES closedown
(performed with the $P JES2 command) is usually one of the last actions in a
planned closedown of your MVS system before a scheduled IPL.

   However, JES2 can be stopped at any time using the $P JES2,ABEND
command. JES2 will respond by issuing the messages:

```
$HASP095  JES2 CATASTROPHIC ABEND.   CODE=$PJ2
$HASP098  ENTER TERMINATION OPTION
```

You should reply PURGE or EXIT to abend JES without a dump. You may then
restart it when you wish. This sounds rather drastic, but in fact abending JES is a
feasible option for implementing certain sorts of emergency change, as it has only
a limited impact on online users. While JES is down, jobs may not be submitted,
TSO users may not log on, started tasks and jobs may not start, and output may
not be written out, but work which is not using JES services will continue normally.
Since this includes most TSO and CICS users, abending JES may be a preferable
alternative to an emergency IPL, for example. It is wise to stop all printing before
abending JES, but if you do not, JES2 will merely simulate a $I command when
it restarts for each device that was active at the time JES2 was brought down. Note
that most JES parameters either require at least a warm start to effect a change,
or can be changed by operator command anyway, so abending JES is not a useful
option for implementing parameter changes, but there are circumstances when it
is useful, e.g. to change the procedure or parameter libraries allocated in the JES2
procedure.

8.2   JES2 datasets

8.2.1   JES2 parameters

Apart from the allocation of the procedure libraries, all the facilities provided by
JES are defined and configured by coding statements in the JES2 parameter
dataset. The parameters may be held in any card-image partitioned dataset, but the
logical place to keep them is in SYS1.PARMLIB. However, the parameter deck
often runs to many hundreds, if not thousands, of lines, and so it was usual on

MVS/370 systems to keep them out of SYS1.PARMLIB. Under MVS/370, PARMLIB was an unblocked dataset and the space used by keeping the JES parms there was prohibitive. SYS1.PROCLIB was often used instead.

The parameter dataset is allocated by the HASPPARM DD statement in the JES2 procedure (but see the comments in Sec. 8.1.3 about the use of the HASP-PARM=ddname statement when starting JES2). It is usual to use symbolic parameters to allow substitution of alternative members at JES2 startup time. This gives you the opportunity to test out new versions of the parameters while keeping older versions around to fall back to if you have problems. You should exploit this facility by adopting a similar set of standards for maintaining JES parameters to those for maintaining other members of PARMLIB (see Chapter 7). For example, you could make a rule that the current live parameters will always be suffixed 0, and before changing them you must make a backup with the suffix 9. Now, if you have modelled your JES2 procedure on the IBM-supplied one you can fall back to the old version by starting JES2 with:

```
S  JES2,MEMBER=memname9
```

where memname is your member name prefix.

The parameters themselves are documented in the current version of [1]. The rest of this chapter gives many examples of extracts from a JES2 parameter deck, taken from a JES2 version 3.1.3 system. IBM has a habit of making rather radical changes to the syntax and structure of the JES2 parameters, so if you are working with a different level of JES2 you must check the correct version of the manual carefully before using any of these examples as models.

As we noted earlier in connection with starting and stopping JES2, different parameters require different types of JES2 startup to effect a change to them. Some require a cold start (i.e. complete reformat of the JES2 spool) because they affect the format of the spool; others can be changed on a warm start; and still others can be changed by operator command. [1] documents for each parameter what type of start is required to change it.

JES2 commands may also be included among your initialization statements. Wherever they appear in the statements, they will be saved up and executed after JES2 initialization has completed.

8.2.2   Procedure libraries

Procedure libraries are the libraries that contain the cataloged procedures which may be referenced in JCL EXEC statements (and merged into JCL during the conversion stage of JES processing). You may define several alternative concatenations of procedure libraries to be used in different circumstances. Each concatenation is defined using a //PROCnn DD statement in the JES2 procedure, where nn is a numeric identifier (see Example 8.1 for a number of illustrations). The default concatenation for each job class is then specified using the PROCLIB=nn keyword on its JOBCLASS initialization statement. Similarly, the default concatenation for started tasks is specified on the STCCLASS initialization statement, and the default for TSO logon procedures is specified on the JES2 TSUCLASS initialization statement. The defaults for batch jobs may be overridden by coding a /*JOBPARM PROCLIB=PROCnn statement in the job's JCL [6].

You should aim to keep your procedure library structure as simple as possible — my ideal is three concatenations, one each for batch jobs, TSO users, and started tasks. However, your application developers, security administrators, and applications analysts may require separate procedure libraries for development, acceptance testing, and production versions of applications procedures. It is then a simple matter to make the production PROCnn concatenation the default for production job classes, the development PROCnn the default for development job classes, etc. You will usually also want to have a general-purpose procedure library for procedures which are common across all of these environments (e.g. procedures supplied with third-party software products). This is the structure illustrated in Example 8.1.

You may also wish to enforce standards about who can use which PROCnn concatenations. The simplest way to do this is to use a JES exit (see Chapter 12) to prevent or restrict the use of the /*JOBPARM PROCLIB statement, thus forcing unauthorized users to use the default concatenation for their jobclass.

8.2.3 JES2 spool dataset

The spool dataset is used by JES2 to store input and output for all the jobs on its queues, including converted JCL. It is typically very large, often covering several complete DASD volumes. All space management functions for the spool dataset are handled by JES2 itself, including the suballocation of space to the input and output 'datasets' belonging to executing jobs. These datasets appear to the executing program as ordinary sequential datasets, but they are actually logical subdivisions of the spool rather than MVS datasets, and I/O operations to them are done by JES2 routines rather than the appropriate access method.

The purpose of the spool dataset is to make the input of control information and the output of print into asynchronous operations. In other words, executing jobs need not read their control information directly from a card reader or terminal when it is entered by the user, and at the I/O rates this implies, but, instead, control information can be read by executing jobs at any time and at DASD I/O rates. Similarly, instead of having to wait to allocate a printer and then write out print datasets at printer I/O rates, the job can write print output at any time (and many jobs can write print output at the same time, however few printers you have), and it can write it at DASD I/O rates. Print datasets are 'spooled' by JES2, then 'spun off' to a printer later, when JES2 decides to allocate them to an available printer.

The characteristics of the spool datasets are defined to JES2 using the

```
SPOOLDEF BUFSIZE=3992,         /* MAXIMUM BUFFER SIZE         CS*/
         DSNAME=SYS1.HASPACE, /*SPOOLDATA SETS' NAME          CS*/
         FENCE=NO,            /* DON'T FORCE TO MIN.VOL.      OC*/
         SPOOLNUM=32,         /* MAX. NUM. SPOOL VOLS         CS*/
         TGBPERVL=5,          /* 5  TG BLOCKS PER VOL         WS*/
         TGSIZE=30,           /* 30 BUFFERS/TRACK GROUP       OC*/
         TGNUM=32576,         /* FITS TGMS INTO 2 x 4K PAGE   CS*/
         TGWARN=90,           /* WARNING THRESHOLD %          OC*/
         TRKCELL=3,           /* 3 BUFFERS/TRACK-CELL         CS*/
         VOLUME=SPOOL         /* SPOOL VOLUME SERIAL #S       CS*/
```

Example 8.2. JES2 SPOOLDEF parameters.

SPOOLDEF statement in the JES2 initialization deck. Example 8.2 shows a typical SPOOLDEF definition. Note that:

- CBIPO supplies skeleton JES2 parameters with comments that show which parameters can be changed by operator command (OC), which by a warm start (WS), and which can only be changed on a cold start (CS). It is useful to leave these in as a reminder, as in this example.

- Quite a few of the SPOOLDEF parameters can only be changed on a cold start, so think ahead when you are defining them. SPOOLNUM, for example, which determines the maximum number of spool volumes you can use, should be set higher than your current requirements (although JES2 rounds up the value you specify to a multiple of 32, so you will not need to worry about it until you get to your 33rd spool pack!).

- The BUFSIZE parameter determines the size of each JES2 buffer. Physical records written to the spool consist of a buffer of this size, accompanied by an IOB of 88 bytes. The value specified here (3992) is the maximum, which makes best use of real and virtual storage.

- Spool space is allocated to jobs in track groups. The number of records in a track group is determined by taking the TGSIZE parameter and rounding up to the number required to make it a whole number of tracks. The simplest possible job requires 13 records on the spool, so the value should be larger than this to avoid excessive track-group allocation overhead. On the other hand, many units of work (notably TSO users), produce very little output, and so you will be wasting spool space if you make track groups very large. The default, 30, when combined with the default BUFSIZE, corresponds to three tracks of a 3380, which is a reasonable compromise.

- The TGNUM parameter determines the maximum number of track groups on the spool. To estimate the required value, work out how many you need for your current spool volumes, add a generous amount for future growth because you need a cold start to change this parameter too, and round up to the nearest multiple of 16 288.

- Track-celling is used with fast printers (i.e. lasers). When it is in use, output is read from the spool and placed in print buffers a track cell at a time, instead

```
//ALLOC    EXEC PGM=IEFBR14
//HASPACE  DD   DISP=(,CATLG),DSN=SYS1.HASPACE,
//              SPACE=(CYL,884),
//              UNIT=3380,VOL=SER=SYST11
```

Example 8.3. Allocating a spool dataset.

of a record at a time. The TRKCELL parameter determines how many records there are in a track cell. Note that in certain circumstances, records which are left over after a track has been subdivided into track cells may be unusable, so you should aim to ensure that the value you specify for this parameter is exactly divisible into the number of records on a track (and if you have spool volumes on mixed device types, you should ensure that this is true whatever the device type).

● JES does not use the catalog to locate spool datasets. Instead, when it starts up it searches all DASD volumes whose volume serial number starts with the characters specified in the SPOOLDEF VOLUME parameter for datasets with the name specified in the SPOOLDEF DSNAME parameter. All such datasets become part of the spool. In this example, all datasets called SYS1.HASPACE on volumes SPOOL1, SPOOL2, etc., would become part of the spool. In addition to specifying your SPOOLDEF parameters, therefore, you must preallocate the spool datasets on the spool volumes before you attempt to add them to your spool. All that is necessary is to allocate the space using IEFBR14, as shown in Example 8.3. Each time JES starts, it checks that the datasets available for it to use as part of the spool are the same as at the previous closedown. If any active spool volumes are missing, or any new ones have been added, it will force a cold start to occur (prompting the operator first, as outlined in Sec. 8.1.3). If you wish to add or remove any spool datasets, you should therefore follow the procedures discussed in the spool control chapter of [2], rather than simply deleting or allocating datasets on spool volumes.

Other than setting the values of the SPOOLDEF parameters, the main spool issue you will have to address is how large it should be. Given that you usually allocate space to your spool in increments of whole DASD volumes, the real cost of increasing the size of your spool is quite considerable, and you will therefore be under pressure to ensure that it is no bigger than necessary. However, when your spool fills up JES2 grinds to a halt, and most of your batch jobs with it — and gradually all your TSO users too, when they request JES services, e.g. by invoking SDSF or trying to submit a job. So the cost of letting your spool fill up is even less acceptable than that of increasing it!

The answer to this dilemma comes in two stages: (a) ensure that you keep no more output on your spool than absolutely necessary; and (b) once you have reached this level, ensure you have enough spool volumes so that you never run out of space. The second stage is simply a question of monitoring how much space is

```
$PQ,Q=A,A=04,R=LOCAL
$PQ,Q=A,A=07,R=R1-R99
$PQ,Q=B,A=02
$PQ,Q=F,A=03
$OQ,Q=S,CANCEL,A=01
$OQ,Q=X,CANCEL,A=02
```

Example 8.4. Automatic commands to clear down JES2 spool.

used and doing a little capacity planning; the first stage is a little more interesting, and involves a variety of activities, for example:

- Ensure that the settings of the SPOOLDEF TGSIZE and TRKCELL parameters optimize the usage of spool space for the typical mix of output dataset sizes found on your spool. See the discussions of this issue in [1] and [8].
- Ensure that unnecessary output is not kept on the spool at all, for example:
  - Define a dummy output class, and set an installation standard which requires that all output datasets that will never be read are written to this class.
  - Specify the CONDPURG=YES parameter (new with JES 2.2.0) on the TSUCLASS parameter statement, so that TSO message output is automatically purged at logoff time if the TSO session ended normally and produced no other SYSOUT datasets.
  - Many installations find it possible to set the message class for all started tasks to a dummy output class, as the messages from these tasks are hardly ever referred to. If you need to see the messages, e.g. because you have a problem starting a task, you can usually start it as a batch job in order to put the messages to a class where you can read them. However, the CONDPURG= YES parameter may now be a better option for started class output too.
- Create a set of automatic commands which runs every day and deletes old output from the spool. Most installations find they can delete output from testing output classes after three days (enough so that the output from Friday's jobs is still there on Monday until the delete command runs!), and from production classes after a little longer. You will have to set a standard requiring any needed production output to be removed from the spool within this period of time. Example 8.4 shows a typical set of commands to do this. Note that the $PQ commands clear down non-held output classes after the number of days specified by the A= parameter, while the $OQ...CANCEL commands do the same for held output classes.
- Regularly offload output from the spool which is only required for possible reference — such as the message class output from production jobs, which can usually be offloaded in bulk at the end of your batch cycle. It is possible to set up procedures to do this using JES2 offload devices, but most installations will find it worth while to purchase a third-party print management package to handle this function. This should not only save spool space but also enable you to eliminate printing of huge numbers of unread reports.

```
CKPTDEF  CKPT1=(DSN=SYS1.HASPCKPT,   /*FIRST CHECKPOINT DATASET   CS*/
         VOLSER=SYST05,              /*FIRST CHECKPOINT VOLSER      */
         INUSE=YES),                 /* USE THIS DATASET            */
         CKPT2=(DSN=SYS1.HASPCKP2,   /* SECOND CHECKPOINT D/S     CS*/
         VOLSER=SYST08,              /* SECOND CHECKPOINT VOLSER    */
         INUSE=YES),                 /* USE THIS DATASET            */
         NEWCKPT1=(DSN=SYS1.HASPCKPT,  /* NEW CHECKPOINT D/S      CS*/
         VOLSER=SYST07),             /* NEW CHECKPOINT VOLSER       */
         NEWCKPT2=(DSN=SYS1.HASPCKP2,  /* NEW CHECKPOINT D/S      CS*/
         VOLSER=SYST10),             /* NEW CHECKPOINT VOLSER       */
         MODE=DUAL,                  /* FLIP-FLOP DATASETS          */
         LOGSIZE=1,                  /* NO. OF 4K PAGES FOR CH LOG */
         APPLCOPY=COMMON             /* KEEP COPY FOR SDSF IN ECSA */
```

Example 8.5. JES2 CKPTDEF parameters.

- Have dumps written to a special output class, which is offloaded as quickly as possible (but remember the spool space will not be released until the whole of the offending job's output has gone and it is purged from the queues — so if possible, offload all datasets belonging to dumping jobs together).
- Review the use of spool space from time to time to identify any large users of spool space which could be trimmed somehow.

8.2.4 JES2 checkpoint dataset

The checkpoint dataset holds a copy of the job and output queues which JES2 maintains in virtual storage, so that these can be preserved across JES2 closedowns and restarts. In effect, these queues are the index to the spool dataset, and without them the spool dataset itself is useless. One consequence of this is that if you lose your checkpoint dataset while JES2 is down and cannot recover it, you also lose the contents of your spool dataset — JES2 will force a cold start if it cannot obtain a valid copy of the checkpoint dataset.

In a multi-access spool (MAS) environment, the checkpoint is also used to communicate information about the MAS environment and changes in the job and output queues between different members of the MAS complex. Multi-access spool configurations are discussed in more detail in Sec. 8.5.

The checkpoint datasets are defined to JES2 using the CKPTDEF statement in the JES2 parameter dataset. Example 8.5 shows a typical specification of the CKPTDEF statement.

The process of writing to the checkpoint dataset is known as checkpointing. There are three alternative checkpointing modes: DUPLEX without backup, DUPLEX with backup, or DUAL (DUAL mode was introduced with level 2.2.0 of JES2).

You select DUPLEX checkpointing without backup by specifying MODE= DUPLEX,DUPLEX=OFF in your CKPTDEF statement. This option means there is only one active checkpoint dataset at any time. In the event of an I/O error which damages the primary checkpoint dataset and brings down JES2, it will be impossible to recover without cold-starting JES and therefore losing the entire contents of the spool. If the error does not bring down JES2, and you have spare checkpoint datasets available, you may be able to recover from the in-storage checkpoint information using the checkpoint reconfiguration dialog (see the discussion of this at the end of this section). You might think that in this day and age the chances of any given dataset of a couple of cylinders experiencing an I/O error are small, but in my experience JES2 checkpoint datasets have a fatal attraction for I/O errors out of all proportion even to the amount of I/O performed on them! You should therefore avoid DUPLEX checkpointing without backup.

You select DUPLEX checkpointing with backup by specifying MODE= DUPLEX,DUPLEX=ON on your CKPTDEF statement, and defining both CKPT1 and CKPT2 datasets (preferably on different volumes). In this case, the CKPT1 dataset is the primary dataset, which is used to record all checkpoint information, but once for every 10 writes to the primary, the CKPT2 or duplex dataset will also be updated with the checkpoint information. In the event of an I/O error to the checkpoint dataset, the checkpoint reconfiguration dialog should be able to recover from either the in-storage copy of the checkpoint (if JES2 is not brought down by the error) or the duplex checkpoint dataset. IBM recommends duplex checkpointing with backup for single-member spool complexes.

DUAL checkpointing is selected by specifying MODE=DUAL on your CKPTDEF statement, and defining both CKPT1 and CKPT2 datasets. With DUAL checkpointing, JES2 flip-flops between two checkpoint datasets. Each time a system obtains control of the checkpoint, it does its initial read from the most up-to-date checkpoint, then writes to the other (duplexing every tenth write to the first dataset). The next time a system obtains control, the second checkpoint is now the most up-to-date, so it will read it, and write to the first. As with duplex processing with backups, you should always be able to recover from I/O errors using the checkpoint dialog, using either the in-storage copy of the checkpoint from the most up-to-date member of the multi-access spool complex, or the surviving checkpoint dataset. DUAL checkpointing is recommended if you have a multi-access spool configuration, or DASD contention problems with a DUPLEX checkpoint dataset.

Note that in Example 8.5:

- As with the spool, JES2 does not use the catalog to locate its checkpoint datasets; instead, the DSN and VOLSER keywords of the CKPTn parameters are used to tell it where to find them.
- The NEWCKPTn parameter defines a checkpoint dataset which may be used to replace CKPTn using the checkpoint reconfiguration dialog, in both error and non-error situations. This is known as forwarding the checkpoint dataset. If you do forward CKPTn, the definition of CKPTn used by JES2 will be modified to reflect the DSN and VOLSER of NEWCKPTn, and even though your initialization deck contains the original definitions, JES will use these as

```
//ALLOC    EXEC  PGM=IEFBR14
//CKPT     DD    DSN=SYS1.HASPCKP3,UNIT=3380,VOL=SER=SYSTO3,
//               DISP=(,CATLG),SPACE=(CYL,4)
```

Example 8.6. Allocating a checkpoint dataset.

pointers to the new definitions, and thus honour the forwarded definitions across a hot or warm start (unless the RECONFIG option is specified).

- You may tell JES to keep a copy of the checkpoint in virtual storage for use by SDSF, in order to reduce I/O to the checkpoint datasets and improve SDSF response times. This is specified using the APPLCOPY parameter (new with JES2 2.2.0). With recent releases of SDSF, no further action is required to tell SDSF to use the in-storage copy. Older releases, however, may require additional action to force SDSF to use the APPLCOPY. Use of APPLCOPY is recommended.

- In DUAL mode, JES2 uses a change log to cut down I/O to the checkpoint dataset. The size of this log is controlled by the LOGSIZE parameter, and you can minimize I/O to the checkpoint dataset by specifying a value for this which allows a typical checkpoint operation to complete with only a single I/O. See the chapter on the checkpoint dataset in [1] for a detailed explanation of this.

You should preallocate any checkpoint datasets which you intend to use, using JCL similar to that shown in Example 8.6. Checkpoint datasets should be allocated as a single extent on a cylinder boundary (using the ABSTR or CYL subparameter of the SPACE parameter), and you should aim to place them where they will experience minimal delay due to head movement — usually next to the VTOC, with the VTOC placed near the middle of the pack. The space required will depend on the maximum size of the queues which JES will be keeping, and this in turn depends on the values you specify for the SPOOLNUM, TGNUM, JOBNUM, and JOENUM parameters (these determine the maximum number of spool datasets, track groups, jobs, and output datasets which JES will support). The amount of space needed can be calculated exactly from the values of these parameters using the formula given in the checkpoint chapter of [1]. However, you would be wise to allocate a bit extra, or one day you may cold start JES2 with a new value for one of these parameters and find JES2 refuses to start because the checkpoint dataset is too small.

Note that the checkpoint dataset is usually one of the most heavily accessed datasets on the system, and because virtually all units of work use JES services, poor response times on the checkpoint dataset will tend to contribute to poor responses throughout your system. You should therefore consider the placement of your checkpoint datasets very carefully. They must not be placed on a spool volume; they must be placed on high-speed devices; and they must be placed on otherwise lightly used volumes (ideally, dedicated volumes for the primary checkpoint in DUPLEX mode and for both checkpoints in DUAL mode). If you have write caching available (e.g. using 3990 extended functions), the checkpoint dataset is normally an outstanding candidate for write caching. You should also ensure that backup checkpoint datasets (e.g. the secondary checkpoint in a DUAL checkpoint configuration, or alternative checkpoints in a DUPLEX configuration) are on separate volumes (and HDAs) from the dataset they are backing up, and preferably also on separate strings, channels, and control units, for maximum redundancy.

JES2 uses the RESERVE instruction to serialize access to the checkpoint volume, so if you are sharing DASD you must ensure there are no other datasets on the checkpoint volume which are likely to be serialized using RESERVEs — this can lead not only to dreadful JES performance but even to total system lockouts due to deadly embraces (see Chapter 14 for more on RESERVEs).

In addition to RESERVE/RELEASE, JES2 also uses a mechanism called the checkpoint lock to serialize access to the checkpoint dataset. The first record on the checkpoint dataset is known as the lock record, and when a system gains control of the checkpoint by issuing a RESERVE, the first thing it does is to update the lock record to indicate that it holds the checkpoint lock. After completing any other writes it wishes to do to the checkpoint, the system will update the lock record to indicate that it no longer holds the lock, then issue a RELEASE instruction. In a multi-access spool, other members of the complex may then access the checkpoint.

Superficially, the lock process is redundant, in that the hardware RESERVE will normally always prevent access by another system until after the lock has been relinquished anyway. However, the lock process deals specifically with serialization of the checkpoint across JES failures and system failures. When JES abends, the MVS recovery/termination manager will automatically RELEASE the RESERVEs JES held as part of its cleaning-up process; similarly, when you IPL 'over the top' of a failed MVS system, it automatically RELEASEs all the RESERVEs the failed system held. In such circumstances, the lock prevents other systems from taking control of the checkpoint without attempting to recover from the consequences of the failure.

In a multi-access spool, if one member (i.e. one system's JES2) goes down without relinquishing the checkpoint lock, the other members will wait for a time then issue the message:

```
$HASP264   WAITING FOR RELEASE OF CHECKPOINT LOCK BY
sysname
```

If the member called sysname actually has failed, you can reset the lock by issuing the command:

```
$E SYS,RESET=sysname
```

In a single-system spool (or a MAS complex where no other members are

active), if JES2 goes down without relinquishing the checkpoint lock, it will issue
the message:

```
$HASP479   UNABLE TO OBTAIN CKPT DATA SET LOCK
$HASP454   SHOULD JES2 BYPASS THE MULTI-SYSTEM
           INTEGRITY LOCK?
```

when it is restarted. You must reply Y to reset the checkpoint lock and continue.

As we noted above, I/O errors on the checkpoint dataset can cause serious
problems to JES2. If one occurs, you are likely to be thrown into the checkpoint
reconfiguration dialog, either immediately (if the error does not bring down JES2),
or when you restart JES2 (if it does). This dialog consists of a series of console
messages and your replies to them. It is used to: (a) respecify the CKPTDEF
NEWCKPTn parameters, if required, and (b) replace the failing CKPTn dataset
with the corresponding NEWCKPTn dataset. If JES2 is still up, the in-storage
copy of the checkpoint data will then be forwarded to the NEWCKPTn dataset,
which will be used in place of the CKPTn dataset until the next reconfiguration (or
the next cold start). If JES2 is not up, the checkpoint data to be placed in
NEWCKPTn will be obtained from the alternate checkpoint dataset (unless you
are running without an alternate, in which case you will have to cold start JES2).
You can even enter the checkpoint reconfiguration dialog voluntarily (e.g. in order
to move the checkpoint so hardware maintenance can be performed on a checkpoint volume), by entering the $T CKPTDEF,RECONFIG command. The dialog
is complex and potentially confusing, so you should familiarize yourself with it
before a crisis occurs. There is a detailed discussion of it in the checkpoint chapter
of [1], and some examples of the whole dialog in the appendices to [3]. You should
also ensure that you have some spare checkpoint datasets preallocated with names
and volsers corresponding to your NEWCKPTn definitions — once you have
entered the dialog it is too late to do this!

8.3   Defining JES2 facilities

8.3.1   Input classes

Work on the JES2 input queues is divided into input classes. Each input class
represents a separate queue of work awaiting execution. Two special classes are
defined for: (a) console-started tasks and mount commands; and (b) TSO logons.
In addition, you can define up to 36 job classes. Example 8.7 shows some typical
input class definitions. Note that:

- The JOBDEF statement specifies values which relate to all types of input class.
  The JOBNUM parameter specifies the maximum number of jobs which can
  exist on the spool at any one time, including jobs at all stages of processing. If
  you hit this limit, no new jobs will be accepted from the internal readers. You
  can clear down jobs from the spool to get your system moving again, but

```
JOBDEF    ACCTFLD=OPTIONAL,  /* ACCT'G FIELD OPTIONAL              OC*/
          JCLERR=YES,        /* TERMINATE JOBS WITH JCL ERRROR     OC*/
          JOBNUM=9999,       /* JOB QUEUE SIZE                     CS*/
          JOBWARN=80,        /* WARNING THRESHOLD %                OC*/
          PRTYHIGH=10,       /* UPPER LIMIT FOR AGING              OC*/
          PRTYJECL=NO,       /* PRIORITY JECL NOT ALLOWED          OC*/
          PRTYJOB=YES,       /* PRTY= ON JOB IS ALLOWED            OC*/
          PRTYLOW=5,         /* LOWER LIMIT FOR AGING              OC*/
          PRTYRATE=1,        /* PRTY AGING RATE X/DAY              OC*/
          RANGE=(1,9999)     /* LOCAL JOB NUMBER RANGE             OC*/
                             /*                                      */

JOBCLASS(A) ACCT=YES,        /* ACCT CODE REQUIRED                 WS*/
          PGMRNAME=YES,      /* PGMR NAME REQUIRED                 WS*/
          TIME=(0001,01),    /* MAX JOB STEP TIME (MMMM,SS)        WS*/
          REGION=999,        /* DEFAULT REGION SIZE                WS*/
          COMMAND=VERIFY,    /* VERIFY COMMANDS                    WS*/
          BLP=NO,            /* IGNORE BLP PARM                    WS*/
          AUTH=ALL,          /* ALLOW ALL CMDS                    WS*/
          MSGLEVEL=(1,1),    /* JOB, ALL MSGS                      WS*/
          COPY=NO,           /* NOT TYPRUN=COPY                    WS*/
          HOLD=NO,           /* NOT TYPRUN=HOLD                    WS*/
          IEFUJP=YES,        /* TAKE SMF JOB PURGE EXIT IEFUJP     WS*/
          IEFUSO=YES,        /* TAKE SYSOUT EXCESS EXIT IEFUSO     WS*/
          JOURNAL=NO,        /* DO NOT JOURNAL THIS JOB CLASS      WS*/
          LOG=YES,           /* PRINT JES2 JOB LOG                 WS*/
          OUTPUT=YES,        /* PRODUCE OUTPUT FOR JOB             WS*/
          PERFORM=000,       /* DEFAULT SRM PERF GROUP             WS*/
          PROCLIB=02,        /* USE //PROCO2 DD FOR PROCLIBS       WS*/
          RESTART=NO,        /* NO REQUEUE (XEQ) ON IPL            WS*/
          SCAN=NO,           /* NOT TYPRUN=SCAN          NOSCAN    WS*/
          TYPE6=YES,         /* PRODUCE SMF 6 RECORDS     TYPE6    WS*/
          TYPE26=YES         /* PRODUCE SMF 26 RECORDS    TYPE26   WS*/
                             /*                                      */

STCCLASS TIME=(0060,00),     /* MAX JOB STEP TIME (MMMM,SS)        WS*/
          REGION=999,        /* DEFAULT REGION SIZE IN K           WS*/
          COMMAND=EXECUTE,   /* EXECUTE COMMANDS                   WS*/
          BLP=YES,           /* IGNORE BLP PARM                    WS*/
          AUTH=ALL,          /* ALLOW ALL CMDS                    WS*/
          MSGLEVEL=(1,1),    /* JOB, ALL MSGS                      WS*/
          IEFUJP=YES,        /* TAKE SMF JOB PURGE EXIT IEFUJP     WS*/
          IEFUSO=YES,        /* TAKE SYSOUT EXCESS EXIT IEFUSO     WS*/
          LOG=YES,           /* PRINT JES2 JOB LOG                 WS*/
          OUTPUT=YES,        /* PRODUCE OUTPUT FOR JOB   OUTPUT    WS*/
          PERFORM=000,       /* DEFAULT SRM PERF GROUP             WS*/
          PROCLIB=00,        /* USE //PROCOO DD FOR PROCLIBS       WS*/
          TYPE6=YES,         /* PRODUCE SMF 6 RECORDS     TYPE6    WS*/
          TYPE26=YES,        /* PRODUCE SMF 26 RECORDS    TYPE26   WS*/
          MSGCLASS=S         /* DEFAULT MESSAGE CLASS              WS*/
                             /*                                      */

TSUCLASS TIME=(0060,00),     /* MAX JOB STEP TIME (MMMM,SS)        WS*/
          REGION=999,        /* DEFAULT REGION SIZE                WS*/
          COMMAND=EXECUTE,   /* EXECUTE COMMANDS                   WS*/
          CONDPURG=YES,      /* CONDITIONALLY PURGE TSO OUTPUT     OC*/
          BLP=NO,            /* IGNORE BLP PARM                    WS*/
          AUTH=ALL,          /* ALLOW ALL CMDS                    WS*/
          MSGLEVEL=(1,1),    /* JOB, ALL MSGS                      WS*/
          IEFUJP=YES,        /* TAKE SMF JOB PURGE EXIT IEFUJP     WS*/
```

Example 8.7. JES2 input class parameters.

```
IEFUJP=YES,       /* TAKE SMF JOB PURGE EXIT IEFUJP   WS*/
IEFUSO=YES,       /* TAKE SYSOUT EXCESS EXIT IEFUSO   WS*/
LOG=YES,          /* PRINT JES2 JOB LOG              WS*/
OUTPUT=YES,       /* PRODUCE OUTPUT FOR JOB          WS*/
PERFORM=0,        /* DEFAULT SRM PERF GROUP          WS*/
PROCLIB=01,       /* USE //PROC01 DD FOR PROCLIBS    WS*/
TYPE6=YES,        /* PRODUCE SMF 6 RECORDS    TYPE6   WS*/
TYPE26=YES,       /* PRODUCE SMF 26 RECORDS   TYPE26  WS*/
MSGCLASS=X        /* DEFAULT MESSAGE CLASS    TSUMCLAS WS*/
                  /*                                  */
```

Example 8.7. (cont.)

increasing JOBNUM itself requires a cold start of JES2. It is therefore wise to set this to the maximum value, as we have in this example.

- Several of the JOBDEF parameters are used to define the priority aging process. If you use this facility, it causes the priority of any item on the input queue to be increased by 1 (on a scale of 0 to 15) after each time period. The PRTYLOW and PRTYHIGH parameters determine the limits of priority aging, while the PRTYRATE parameter determines how many times per day a job's priority will be raised.

- The JOBCLASS statement is used to define one or more jobclasses (you can have up to 36, one for each letter of the alphabet and one for each digit), while the STCCLASS statement defines the input class for started tasks, and the TSUCLASS statement defines the input class for TSO users. They share many of their subparameters, but not all (see [1] to check the usage of any particular parameter).

- The TIME, REGION, PERFORM, MSGCLASS, and MSGLEVEL keywords specify default values of these parameters for work in the class concerned. These may be overridden in JCL unless you prevent this using your JES exits (but remember that started tasks and TSO users do not have JOB cards so there is nowhere to override the default message parameters for these). 999 is the highest value which may be specified for the REGION parameter in your JES parameters, and there is little point in coding a smaller value in these days of abundant virtual storage. The PERFORM value in both the JES parameters and JCL is meaningless when the IEAICSxx and IEAIPSxx members of PARMLIB are used to control SRM. Note also that long-running started tasks usually require TIME=(1440,00) to be specified, either in this parameter or on the EXEC statement of their JCL.

- The BLP keyword specifies whether bypass label processing is allowed for tape datasets in this class. You may wish to prohibit BLP as a general rule, to protect the security of tapes — security packages which protect tape datasets generally depend on standard label processing being performed.

- The COMMAND keyword specifies whether instream commands can be included in the JCL submitted in this class. I recommend prohibiting instream commands by coding COMMAND=IGNORE for all input classes — also for security reasons, as you can then restrict the ability to issue console commands to selected users, as discussed in Chapter 15. If you use started tasks to schedule automatic commands, however, you may have to code COMMAND= DISPLAY, which causes instream commands to be executed and written to the SYSLOG. Avoid COMMAND=EXECUTE, the default for STCCLASS and TSUCLASS, which does not write the command to the SYSLOG and therefore makes it difficult to work out where any given command came from. The AUTH parameter further controls the types of command which may be entered in any given class.

- The PROCLIB parameter determines which //PROCnn DD statement in the JES2 procedure is used by default when resolving references in JCL to cataloged procedures (see Sec. 8.2.2). This can be overridden by coding a JES2 /*JOBPARM PROCLIB=PROCnn statement in the job's JCL.
- The LOG and OUTPUT parameters determine whether a job log and other output respectively will be produced for jobs in that class.
- The CONDPURG parameter (new with JES2 2.2.0) on the JOBCLASS, TSUCLASS or STCCLASS statement allows you to specify that message output for all units of work (jobs/sessions/tasks) in the specified class which end normally and produce no other SYSOUT will be purged automatically at job end/logoff/task end. Setting this parameter to YES for TSUCLASS is a virtually painless way of economizing on spool space, and so is highly recommended. It is less likely to be useful for jobclasses, as very few jobs finish without producing some non-message output.
- The JOURNAL parameter controls whether JES2 job journalling will be performed for all work in the class, or only for jobs with RD=R or RD=RNC on the JOB statement in their JCL. Journalling is required for jobs which are to use checkpoint/restart facilities.

Most installations will define a range of jobclasses so they can segment batch jobs into different classes depending on their characteristics, and then control the types of work using the system by controlling the corresponding jobclasses. The main considerations used to separate work into different jobclasses are as follows:

1 Is it production, acceptance, or development work? Production work will normally receive higher priority, particularly during overnight processing. The JOBCLASS definitions may differ, e.g. different PROCLIB values, different default MSGCLASS and MSGLEVEL, and banning of TYPRUN parameters for production and acceptance work.

2 Are there jobs which need to be turned around particularly quickly, because they are doing work which is time-critical for your organization? These will receive the highest priority of all. Note that SRM can use jobclasses to determine a job's swapping and dispatching priority, as well as JES using it to prioritize jobs for execution.

3 Is the job going to require tape processing? You will normally wish to restrict

Table 8.1. Typical jobclass structure

Class	Type of work	Tapes allowed?	Max. execution time
A	Fast production	No	10 mins
B	Normal production	Yes	Unlimited
C	Normal production	No	Unlimited
D	Acceptance	Yes	Unlimited
E	Acceptance	No	Unlimited
F	Development	Yes	2 hours
G	Development	No	2 hours
H	Development	No	20 mins
I	Development	No	1 min
J	Special — BLP jobs	Yes	Unlimited

the number of tape jobs running at any one time to less than the number of tape drives available (remember some jobs may use more than one tape drive at a time), so that you do not have tape jobs using up system resources while they are waiting for drives. You can use your JES exits to prevent tape jobs from running in non-tape classes.

4   How quickly is the job likely to run? It is common, particularly for testing and daytime work, to give short jobs preference over longer running jobs in order to minimize average turnaround time for batch processing. If you do this, you must prevent users sneaking long-running jobs into classes reserved for short jobs — normally by using your JES exits to prohibit coding of the TIME parameter on batch jobs.

5   You may also wish to define a special class, restricted by the JES exits to certain users, with special facilities such as BLP.

Combining these factors, we could end up with a jobclass structure like that shown in Table 8.1.

To understand how we could implement the restrictions and priorities discussed above, we also need to consider the allocation of jobclasses to initiators. The next section discusses this question, and completes this example.

Other factors may be advanced as valid reasons for creating additional job classes (e.g. 'let's have a jobclass for each major application so we can use the initiators to control which applications go through quickest'). On the whole these should be firmly resisted. Jobclasses and initiators do not offer fine enough control to be effective scheduling devices, and the proliferation of similar jobclasses simply leads to confusion in the end (and a shortage of jobclasses when you really do need some new ones).

8.3.2   *Initiators*

Initiators are address spaces in which batch jobs can be executed (see Sec. 3.5 for further details on how they work). Initiators are started at JES startup time, and the number to be started is determined by the JES2 INITDEF parameter

```
INITDEF   PARTNUM=20    /* NUMBER OF INITIATORS    WS*/
                        /*                            */
INIT001   NAME=1,       /* INITIATOR NAME          WS*/
          CLASS=AB,     /* INITIAL JOBCLASS        OC*/
          DRAIN         /* DRAINED INITIALLY       OC*/
INIT002   NAME=2,       /* INITIATOR NAME          WS*/
          CLASS=CDE,    /* INITIAL JOBCLASS        OC*/
          DRAIN         /* DRAINED INITIALLY       OC*/
INIT003   NAME=3,       /* INITIATOR NAME          WS*/
          CLASS=Z,      /* INITIAL JOBCLASS        OC*/
          DRAIN         /* DRAINED INITIALLY       OC*/
```

Example 8.8. Defining initiators to JES2.

statement. Determining the total number of initiators is a question for your performance analyst, and will depend on the capacity of your processor complex — it should be enough to keep your machine busy given the online workload, but not so many as to degrade the total amount of useful work done on the system by causing excessive amounts of swapping and paging. The SRM parameters and number of initiators will need to be kept in line with each other — there is little point in increasing the number of initiators from 20 to 30, for example, if the number of batch jobs which can be swapped in at one time stays at 20.

The initial status of each initiator is determined by the JES2 INITnnn parameter statement, where nnn is the sequence number of the initiator. Example 8.8 shows some typical INITDEF and INITnnn statements. Note that:

- The INITDEF PARTNUM parameter defines the number of initiators.
- Each INITnnn statement describes the initial state of one initiator, that is, what jobclasses should be assigned to it, and should it be made active immediately at JES2 startup or should it be left 'drained' so that the operators can start it when they are sure the system is ready for batch work to run. I recommend you have your initiators come up as drained, or you may find that batch work starts to run when you do not want it, e.g. when you bring up a test system, or when a system startup is only partially successful but you want to bring JES up to enable you to fix the problem. It must then be part of the operators' written IPL procedures to start up the initiators as soon as they are confident a production system has come up correctly.
- Up to 36 jobclasses (i.e. all of them!) can be assigned to any one initiator, and the sequence in which they are assigned determines which class of jobs is selected first when the initiator becomes available. So for initiator one, for example, jobs from class A will be selected for execution first, and if there are none of these awaiting execution, jobs from class B may be selected.

You use the assignation of jobclasses to initiators to control variables like:

- How many jobs of each class can run at any one time
- How many jobs in any given group of classes (e.g. development classes, or classes eligible to use tape drives) can run at any one time

Table 8.2. Typical initiator structure

Initiator	Jobclasses assigned during daytime	Jobclasses assigned overnight
1	AC	AC
2	AC	AC
3	AC	AC
4	AC	AC
5	AC	AC
6	ABC	AB
7	ABC	AB
8	AB	AB
9	AE	AE
10	AE	AC
11	AE	AC
12	ADE	AB
13	AIHG	AIHG
14	AIHG	AC
15	AIHG	AC
16	AIHG	AC
17	AGIH	AC
18	AHGI	AC
19	AFIHG	AB
20	AFJ	AB

- Which job classes receive priority when the opportunity arises for a new job to be executed

Defining the assignation of jobclasses to initiators is therefore part of the process of defining your jobclass structure, and we will now continue the example we started in Table 8.1.

Say we wish to ensure that:

- The fast production class is always executed ahead of any other.
- No more than six tape jobs can run at any one time (because we have eight drives and around a third of our tape jobs use two at a time).
- Up to eight development jobs and four acceptance jobs can run at any time during the day, but only one of each can run at any time overnight, and overnight they may not use tapes, as all drives are needed for production work.
- Jobs in short development classes should usually be executed ahead of others, but longer classes should also have a chance to execute when the machine is busy.

We might therefore end up with an initiator structure which looks something like Table 8.2. Note that:

- Initiators 6–8, 12, 19, and 20 are always the tape-class initiators. This prevents tape-drive shortages when the switch between daytime and overnight structures occurs. If the tape-class initiators changed, then we could end up with six long-running tape jobs which started up during the daytime holding all the tape drives, with six new tape jobs coming in when we switched to the overnight structure. This illustrates a general problem — because jobs can run for a long time, changes in initiator structure may not change the mix of executing jobs for some time. It also illustrates the general solution — keep the usage of initiators as stable as possible during changeovers.

- During the day we have allowed non-tape production jobs to share initiators 6 and 7 with the tape jobs, so that the number of production jobs that can run is not artificially restricted when none of them happen to be tape jobs. On the other hand, to prevent all production tape-class initiators from being tied up by long-running non-tape jobs, we have avoided allowing class C to run on initiator 8 as well. Where to draw the line on questions like this will depend entirely on the pattern of work in your installation.

- We have deliberately placed the tape-class initiators at the end of each group of initiators. When there are a number of free initiators, any new job on the input queue will be assigned to the first one which is free. By putting the tape-class initiators at the end of each group, we therefore minimize the prospect of non-tape-class jobs using them when other non-tape-class initiators are free. If we were to put them at the front, we could find that class B jobs were unable to execute because class C jobs were using the tape-class initiators, even though there were plenty of other class C initiators sitting idle.

- The reasons for the rest of the structure should be fairly easy to work out!

An initiator structure like this, however, cannot be implemented solely using your JES parameters, as these control only the initial setup. To switch to a different structure at a different time of day, you will have to schedule a set of JES2 commands to reset the initiators automatically, using the $TI command. You may use the JES2 command scheduling facility to do this, or alternatively have the commands issued from a scheduling or console automation package.

Unfortunately, however, systems programmers are not the only people who can issue the $TI command. Every junior operator thinks they can improve on the initiator structure you have spent days getting right (including hours of consultation with the ops manager and shift leaders), and with the $TI command they have the tools to do it! Within half an hour the overnight initiator structure could bear absolutely no resemblance to your target one. The easiest approach to this problem is to set up your automatic commands to run not just twice a day but every five minutes! This does not prevent short-term modifications to the structure, but your junior ops should soon get sick of changing things only to see them changed back a few minutes later.

8.3.3   Output classes

Output classes are used by JES to assign characteristics to output datasets and to control the selection of datasets to be 'spun off' to available output devices. They are defined by the OUTDEF and OUTCLASS parameter statements. Example 8.9 illustrates these statements. Note that:

```
OUTDEF     BRODCAST=YES,     /* BRODCAST AND UADS SHARED    OC*/
           COPIES=255,       /* MAX. NUM OF COPIES          OC*/
           DMNDSET=NO,       /* NO DEMAND SETUP             WS*/
           JOENUM=9999,      /* MAX. NUM OF OUTPUT ELEMENTS CS*/
           JOEWARN=80,       /* WARNING THRESHOLD %         OC*/
           PRTYHIGH=255,     /* CEILING FOR PRTY AGING      OC*/
           PRTYLOW=0,        /* FLOOR FOR PRTY AGING        OC*/
           PRTYOUT=YES,      /* PRTY= OK ON // OUTPUT       OC*/
           STDFORM=STD,      /* DEFAULT FORMS ID            WS*/
           USERSET=NO        /* NO USER DEMAND-SETUP        WS*/
                             /*                              */
OUTCLASS(D) HOLD=YES         /*                             WS*/
OUTCLASS(X) HOLD=YES         /*                             WS*/
OUTCLASS(Z) OUTPUT=DUMMY     /*                             WS*/
```

Example 8.9. Defining JES2 output classes.

- Parameters on the OUTDEF statement specify values which apply to all output classes, and to output classes as a whole. JOENUM, for example, specifies the maximum number of output datasets that can be accommodated on the spool at any one time. This is another parameter which should be set high, as it can only be changed on a cold start.
- There are three main types of output class: print, punch, and dummy. It is very useful to have a dummy output class for output which will never be looked at or spun off; output written to this class is discarded immediately without taking up space on the spool dataset. Punch classes were used for spinning off datasets to punched cards. They are more or less obsolete these days, though they may be emulated by file transfer processes. Most of your usable output classes will therefore be print classes.
- To keep control of output classes, you should define unused ones as DUMMY; otherwise they will default to PRINT, and someone will start using them. This will cause problems when you need to use the class for something else.
- Print and punch datasets may be held or non-held, depending on the value of the HOLD keyword for their output class and any overrides coded in their DD statement. Non-held output datasets may be selected for printing/punching by JES at any time, and once they have been printed they are deleted from the spool dataset. Held output datasets will not be selected for printing/punching until they have been explicitly released using a JES or SDSF command. Output in a held class is made available for printing by transferring it to a non-held class.

As with jobclasses, it is wise to avoid an excessive proliferation of output classes. Possible reasons for defining a separate output class might include the following:

- You should have at least one held class to which the vast majority of testing output should be sent, as it is usually unnecessary (and wasteful of paper and printer time) to print this output.
- It may be useful to have a separate held class for production output (including

message output) which must be available for viewing but need not be printed. This class should normally be archived using a print management package. You may even have two such classes: one to be archived for a relatively short period and one to be permanently archived.

- You may wish to define a held class for output to be microfiched — again to save on unnecessary printing.
- Sometimes separate classes are defined for printing on different types of stationery (e.g. two-part, three-part, payslips, special forms, etc.). However, it should not be necessary to define a different class for each type of stationery; instead, you should use the forms control parameters on your output datasets to define the type of stationery to be used, and ensure that these parameters are used to control the selection of work for printing (see Sec. 8.3.4).
- Where you have a mixture of printing technologies available, it may be useful to use classes to separate work which can only be printed using one type of technology. In other words, you may define a laser-printing class and an impact-printing class, so that prints using AFP graphics only go to the former, and prints requiring multipart stationery only go to the latter. You could then have a third class for work which can use either type of technology.
- It is normal to have separate classes for production and development output, to make it easy for the operators to ensure that production printing receives the priority it needs, when it needs it.

8.3.4   Printers

JES2 uses two types of printers, known as local and remote printers. Local printers are channel-attached devices which are dedicated to JES2. Remote printers may be physically identical to local printers, but they are usually attached through the network, they may be shared between JES2 printing and other VTAM applications, and they are usually not controlled directly by JES2 itself. Instead, software is used which takes print datasets from JES2, usually by emulating RJE remote workstations, and establishes a VTAM session with the remote printer to send the print to it. IBM's remote printing software for JES2 is known as JES328X. In this section we shall confine our attention to local printers.

General print parameters are defined using the PRINTDEF statement, and individual local printers with PRINTERn statements. Some typical instances are shown in Example 8.10. Note that:

- Each printer is known to JES by the number used to suffix the PRTn statement.
- The UNIT parameter on the PRTn statement defines the address (strictly speaking the device number, on XA and ESA systems) of the printer to be used.
- The CLASS, FCB, and FORMS parameters specify the initial settings of these work selection criteria for the printer concerned (CLASS refers to the output class of work which may be selected for printing on this device).
- The only difficult thing here is the use of the WS parameter. This determines

```
PRINTDEF CCWNUM=100,          /* NUM CCW'S/PRINT BUFFER     WS*/
         DBLBUFR=YES,         /* DOUBLE BUFFER LCL PRTS     WS*/
         FCB=6,               /* INITIAL FCB LOADED         WS*/
         LINECT=66,           /* 66 LINES/PAGE              OC*/
         RDBLBUFR=NO,         /* SINGLE BUFFER RMT PRTS     WS*/
         RSEPLINE=50,         /* 50 LINES ON RMT SEPRTR     OC*/
         SEPLINE=60,          /* 60 LINES ON LCL SEPRTR     OC*/
         TRANS=NO,            /* PN-XLATE FOR 1403/RM.PR    WS*/
         UCS=0                /* BYPASS UCS-LOADING         WS*/
PRT1 WS=(R,Q,PMD,LIM/F,T,C,P),      /*   4245 PRINTER         */
        CLASS=A1,FCB=STD2,
        FORMS=SINGLE,UNIT=480
PRT2 WS=(R,Q,PMD,LIM/F,T,C,P),      /*   4245 PRINTER         */
        CLASS=A1,FCB=STD2,
        FORMS=DUAL,UNIT=580
PRT3 WS=(R,Q,PMD,LIM/F,T,C,P),      /*   SPARE PRINTER        */
        CLASS=1A,FCB=STD2,
        FORMS=SINGLE,UNIT=584
```

Example 8.10. Defining local printers to JES.

the work selection criteria to be used for this device; in other words, what variables should JES take into account when selecting output datasets for printing on this device? The WS parameter value consists of two lists of criteria, enclosed in parentheses, and separated by a slash. The list before the slash specifies selection criteria which must be matched exactly before output can be selected for printing on this printer. The list after the slash specifies criteria which will be used to determine the sequence of selecting output. So, for example, if we specify WS=(R,Q/F,T), then only work which matches the routcode (R) and output class(es) (Q) currently assigned to the printer can be selected for printing on it. In addition, work which matches the forms id (F) currently assigned to the printer will be selected first, and within this, work which matches the current print train (T) will be selected first. See [1] for a list of all the criteria which may be used in a work selection list. You should avoid specifying unnecessary criteria to the left of the slash, or your operators will have to issue frequent commands to reassign the printer. Also, it is sensible to keep the value of the WS parameter the same for all of your printers, or your operators are liable to become extremely confused!

It is often useful to group printers logically and assign a destination id to the group using the DESTID statement, as this enables users to direct prints to a group of printers, so that they can be printed on whichever device becomes available first. By default, print is assigned the DESTID of LOCAL, which is associated with all printers defined by PRINTERn statements (i.e. excluding remote printers).

8.3.5   Internal readers

Internal readers are JES 'devices' which can be allocated by a unit of work wishing to submit a job. They are not real devices, but rather logical devices used to pass

```
INTRDR    AUTH=0,        /* ALLOW SYSTEM,DEVICE & JOB CMDS OC*/
          CLASS=A,       /* DEFAULT JOB CLASS                WS*/
          HOLD=NO,       /* DO NOT HOLD JOBS READ            OC*/
          PRTYINC=0,     /* DO NOT PRTY AGE JOBS             WS*/
          PRTYLIM=15,    /* LIMIT JOB PRTY TO 15             WS*/
          RDINUM=32      /* NUMBER OF INTERNAL RDRS          WS*/
```

Example 8.11. Defining internal readers to JES2.

card images to JES. As far as the submitting program is concerned, they appear as sequential datasets, but, like SYSOUT files, output written to them is passed to JES rather than being sent to an MVS dataset. A job may allocate an internal reader using a JCL statement like this:

```
//ddname   DD SYSOUT=(x,INTRDR)
```

where x is the default message class to be assigned to jobs submitted via this internal reader.

Internal readers are defined to JES2 using the INTRDR parameter statement. A case is shown in Example 8.11. Note that: the main parameter you are likely to have to adjust here is the RDINUM, which defines the number of internal readers available for concurrent use. Internal readers called STCINRDR and TSOINRDR are permanently allocated by the master scheduler for the submission of JCL for started tasks and TSO logons respectively (these are allocated in the master JCL). You may also find that each of your CICS regions, for example, permanently allocates one or more internal readers from its startup JCL, if you allow the submission of batch jobs from CICS. On top of this, whenever a TSO user attempts to submit a job for execution, the SUBMIT command dynamically allocates an internal reader, so you must have enough internal readers left over to have a realistic number of TSO users concurrently submitting jobs. You should find out all uses of internal readers at your installation and set the RDINUM parameter high enough to cover them all, allowing a generous margin for error.

8.3.6   Offload devices

Offload devices are another sort of 'virtual' JES2 device. In this case, they are used both for writing output from JES2 out to an MVS dataset, and the other way round — for loading JES2 datasets which have been previously offloaded back onto the spool. Before the introduction of offload devices, programs called external writers were the only way of offloading data from the JES2 spool. These, however, were difficult to control — they were only able to select work to be offloaded by specifying an output class. Offload devices are much more flexible and much more powerful. Some important uses are:

- For preserving spool data across cold starts (e.g. when upgrading to a new release of JES which requires the spool to be reformatted) — you offload everything on the spool, cold start JES2, then reload it.

```
OFFLOAD1 DSN=BACKUP.SPOOL.DMPLOD1
OFF1.JR   CLASS=,NOT=NO,SYS=ANY
OFF1.JT   CLASS=,NOT=NO,SYS=ANY
OFF1.SR   HOLD=NO,NOT=NO,DS=ANY
OFF1.ST   DS=ANY,HOLD=YES,NOT=NO,QUEUE=
OFFLOAD2 DSN=BACKUP.SPOOL.DMPLOD2
OFF2.JR   CLASS=,NOT=NO,SYS=ANY,MOD=(HOLD=YES)
OFF2.JT   CLASS=,NOT=NO,SYS=ANY
OFF2.SR   NOT=YES,DS=ANY,MOD=(HOLD=YES)
OFF2.ST   DS=ANY,HOLD=YES,NOT=YES,QUEUE=
```

Example 8.12. Defining JES2 offload devices.

- To offload data for transfer to another site's spool (e.g. dumps to send to software suppliers).

Offload devices are defined to JES2 using the OFFLOADn parameter statement, and various OFFn substatements. These are illustrated in Example 8.12. Note that:

- Each offload device consists of four elements: a job receiver, for loading jobs (i.e. anything on the input queue) onto the spool; a job transmitter, for offloading datasets from the input queue; a SYSOUT receiver, for loading output datasets onto the spool; and a SYSOUT transmitter, for offloading output datasets. These can be controlled separately, though only one can be active at any one time for any given offload device.
- Each offload device must be assigned to a real dataset before it can be used, using the OFFLOAD DSN parameter. If the dataset to be used already exists and is cataloged, this is all that is required. If not, other parameters must be specified in addition. This dataset can be assigned in the JES parameters, as here, or using the $TOFFLOADn command. If it is preallocated, it must have RECFM = U and BLKSIZE = 4042.
- The parameters on the OFFn.* substatements define the attributes of each receiver and transmitter belonging to the offload device OFFLOADn. They include work selection parameters, which control what datasets can be received or transmitted using the device, and parameters which control how datasets are processed (e.g. the NOT= parameter controls whether NOTIFY messages are to be sent to the owner of the job when its input/output datasets are received or transmitted).

Offload devices are rather complex to use until you have got the hang of them. Offloads can also lead to a security exposure due to passwords appearing in the input streams of offloaded jobs — ensure that offload datasets containing input datasets are carefully protected using your security package.

```
LOAD(JESEXIT1)
LOAD(JESEXIT2)
LOAD(JESEXIT3)
LOAD(JESEXIT4)
LOAD(RDJESX01)
EXIT(1)    ROUTINES=(USER01,UEXIT1),STATUS=ENABLED,TRACE=NO
EXIT(2)    ROUTINES=UEXIT2,STATUS=ENABLED,TRACE=NO
EXIT(3)    ROUTINES=UEXIT3,STATUS=ENABLED,TRACE=NO
EXIT(4)    ROUTINES=UEXIT4,STATUS=ENABLED,TRACE=NO
```

Example 8.13. Defining JES exits to JES2.

8.4   Defining JES exits

As at JES2 level 2.2.0, there are 27 exit points defined in JES2 by IBM, each identified by an exit number. Several of these exit points are in widespread use, including JESEXITs 2 and 4 which allow you to review and modify the JOB card and JCL statements respectively of all jobs submitted to JES, and reject any jobs which do not adhere to your standards.

We have already mentioned some reasons you might wish to do this, including:

- Preventing jobs which allocate tape devices from running in non-tape classes
- Restricting access to production classes to production jobs, acceptance classes to acceptance jobs, and development classes to development jobs
- Restricting use of BLP-eligible jobclasses to certain users
- Banning the use of the TIME parameter in JCL in order to enforce the defaults set in the JES parameters

In addition, many other JCL standards can be enforced using exits at these exit points, for example:

- Restricting jobnames and account codes depending on the id of the submitter
- Preventing development users from using production output classes
- Restricting the names of datasets which are being allocated for the first time

Ideally, most of these functions should be performed by security products such as RACF, but many of them are not yet explicitly supported by these products. Even where they are, you may find that for historical reasons you are still maintaining JES exits to enforce standards which RACF could not enforce when the standard was created.

We will discuss the JES exit points available in Chapter 12, but here we will briefly cover the process of defining JES exits to JES2. Example 8.13 shows the parameter statements which must be coded to define exits to JES. Note that:

- The LOAD statement here instructs JES2 to issue an MVS LOAD macro for the load module of this name. JES2 will scan the load module for the correct format and for entry points defined using the $ENTRY macro.
- The EXIT statement is used to activate a given EXIT point and associate it with the entry point names defined in the ROUTINES parameter. When this exit is

invoked, control will be passed to each of the routines in the order they appear in the list (here, for example, calls to exit 1 will be passed first to the routine USER01 and then to UEXIT1).

8.5   JES2 communications facilities

8.5.1   Multi-access spool

A multi-access spool (MAS) complex is a group of JES2 systems that share the same spool and checkpoint datasets, and therefore the same set of input and output queues and datasets. Each system is known as a 'member' of the complex, and the members take turns to use the spool, serializing their access to it using the RE-SERVE/RELEASE process to enqueue the checkpoint dataset, and also the check-point lock for 'belt and braces' (as discussed above in Sec. 8.2.4).

Sharing your JES2 spool between multiple systems can be extremely useful. It allows you to view output from one system on another, print output from one system on another, submit jobs on one system to execute on another, all with the minimum complexity for the user. This ease of scheduling work efficiently and flexibly across multiple systems makes a multi-access spool the preferred option whenever you have MVS systems sharing DASD. There are only a few exceptions:

- When one system is unstable, e.g. a testing system for new software
- When the systems are at levels of JES which require incompatible formats for the spool dataset
- When the systems are being deliberately segregated, e.g. in a bureau running work for different customers on the different systems

In order to share your JES spool between any two systems (it can be shared between up to seven), the following conditions must be satisfied:

1   Each system must have access to all of the spool and checkpoint volumes in use.
2   Their JES2 initialization parameters must be consistent (particularly those on the MASDEF statement, which defines the multi-access spool configuration).
3   Their time-of-day clocks must be synchronized (the degree of accuracy of synchronization required is dependent on the MASDEF SYNCTOL parameter).

The MASDEF parameters provide the key to understanding how JES shares the spool. Example 8.14 shows a sample of the MASDEF statement. Note that:

- SID(1), SID(2), ..., SID(7) Up to seven SID parameters can be specified, each defining the name of a system which may participate in the MAS complex. Although you can dynamically add these (i.e. when a new system is warm-start-ed and wishes to join the complex, it can simply use an unassigned SID number to define a 'slot' for its name), clarity and simplicity are best served by defining

```
MASDEF    DORMANCY=(100,500),  /* MIN/MAX DORMANCY TIME (1/5 SECS) */
          HOLD=85,             /* MINIMUM HOLD TIME (0.85 SECS)    */
          LOCKOUT=1000,        /* LOCK-OUT WARNING TIME            */
          OWNSID=SYSA,         /* SYSTEM IDENTIFIER                */
          SHARED=CHECK,        /* CHECK FOR SHARED DASD            */
          SID(1)=SYSA,         /* IDS OF ALL MAS MEMBERS—SYSA      */
          SID(2)=SYSB,         /* IDS OF ALL MAS MEMBERS—SYSB      */
          SYNCTOL=120          /* SYNCH. TOLERANCE (SECS.)         */
```

Example 8.14. Defining a multi-access spool configuration to JES2.

an identical list of the potential SIDs in each of the participating systems' JES parameters.

- OWNSID This defines the system's own SID. This is the one parameter which must be different in each system's initialization deck. It is wise to use the SMF IDs of your systems as their JES2 SID names as well. This avoids the potential confusion caused by referring to one MVS system by several different names in different contexts.

- SHARED=CHECK/NOCHECK This is the parameter which tells JES whether or not it is sharing the spool. The default (CHECK) implies that you are sharing it, and the JES manuals emphasize the need to code NOCHECK if you are not.

- DORMANCY and HOLD These specify respectively how long JES is to wait before attempting to recover the checkpoint lock after releasing it (to give other systems a chance to obtain it and use the spool), and how long it will keep it once it has it. The best values to specify will depend on several factors, including the number of systems in the complex and the types of workload they are running. This is discussed in some depth in the 'Checkpoint dataset definition and configuration' chapter in [1]. What is perfectly clear, however, is that you must not allow HOLD to take its default value in a shared spool configuration — if you do, the second system to start will have to wait $11\frac{1}{2}$ days before it will be given a chance to use the spool!

These and the other MASDEF parameters are discussed in more detail in the chapter 'Initialization statement definitions' of [1]. They can all be changed in-flight (at least with recent releases of JES) using the $T MASDEF command, documented in [2].

Note, as we discussed in Sec. 8.2.4, that JES uses the RESERVE instruction to preserve the integrity of the checkpoint dataset once it has obtained control of it, which could drastically affect the performance of another system attempting to access another dataset on this pack. However, if your MASDEF parameters have been specified correctly, the RESERVE should be so short and so frequent that it would be an unacceptable overhead on JES to convert it into a global enqueue using either GRS or MII. You should therefore ensure that this RESERVE is included in your SYSTEMS exclusion RNL if you are using GRS. Otherwise, GRS will convert it to a global enqueue as well as issuing the RESERVE. Even more important, you must ensure that no RESERVEs will be issued for any other dataset on this pack or JES2 will be unable to gain access to the checkpoint dataset, which will lead to serious performance degradation and the possibility of deadly embraces. As with a single-system spool, the ideal is to give your checkpoint dataset a dedicated pack (preferably two dedicated packs for dual checkpoints). If you cannot, an MVS DLIB pack is usually a good alternative. RESERVE processing and GRS RNLs are covered in Chapter 14.

Although only some of the other initialization statements need to be identical between the sharing systems (see 'Initializing the multi-access spool configuration' in [1] for a list of these), it is best as a rule to keep as many as possible of your JES2 parameters identical between all systems in the MAS complex. This makes it easier to understand and maintain your initialization decks and also gives you more operational flexibility: for example, if all your remote devices are defined identically on all systems, you may be able to move them from one system to another and continue using them even when the system to which they are usually attached is down.

In an MAS configuration you should also use your JES parameters to control which work is to be executed on which system. For example, you could set up the same jobclasses on multiple systems, assign them all to initiators on all of the systems, and avoid the use of SYSAFF statements on the JES2 /*JOBPARM card. In this case, a job in one of these classes will run on whichever system in the complex has an initiator available to service the appropriate jobclass when it gets to the front of the queue.

However, if you wish to run different classes of work on different systems in the complex, you will have to establish a method for enforcing this. Perhaps the obvious method is to use the /*JOBPARM SYSAFF statement in each jobstream to identify which system in the complex you want to run each job on, but this is a very inflexible solution, requiring JCL changes to every job whenever you change the division of workloads between systems. Much better is to use different jobclasses for different categories of work, and assign classes to initiators in such a way as to run only the jobclasses required on each system. For example, class A could be defined to run only on system A, and class B only on system B. Now, if you decide to combine these workloads on system A, you can simply redefine the assignment of jobclasses to initiators, so that both jobclasses can run on the required system A and neither on system B. This is a good example of how to set standards which allow for flexibility and reduce the cost of system changes in the future.

8.5.2 *Remote job entry*

Remote job entry (RJE) in its native form is rather an archaic method of submitting JCL to JES2 from a remotely attached card reader and receiving the printed or punched output back at the remote location. This was done from a remote

```
TPDEF     BUFNUM=150,          /* NUMBER OF TP BUFFERS         WS*/
          BUFSIZE=400,         /* TP BUFFER SIZE               WS*/
          BUFWARN=70,          /* WARNING THRESHOLD %          OC*/
          MBUFSIZE=400,        /* M/L BUFFER SIZE              WS*/
          RMTMSG=100,          /* MAX NUM MSGS Q'D TO RMT      OC*/
          SESSION=100          /* MAX NUM ACTIVE VTAM SESSIONS OC*/
                               /*                                */
LOGON1    APPLID=JESNSYSA,LOG=NO,TR=NO
                                            /* RMT6 */
LINE6     UNIT=SNA,LOG=NO,TR=NO
RMT6      DEVTYPE=LUTYPE1,BUFSIZE=256,LINE=6,NUMRDR=0
R6.PR1    CLASS=AR9,NOSEP,LRECL=132
                                            /* RMT7 */
LINE7     UNIT=SNA,LOG=NO,TR=NO
RMT7      DEVTYPE=LUTYPE1,BUFSIZE=256,LINE=7,NUMPUN=1,LUNAME=T0240000
R7.PU1    CLASS=B,START,NOSEP
R7.RD1    CLASS=K,MSGCLASS=X,START
R7.PR1    CLASS=Q,NOSEP,LRECL=132
```

Example 8.15. JES2 remote job entry parameters.

'workstation' consisting of a card reader, card punch, and printer. Before the days of full-screen terminals, TSO, ISPF, and such things, this was quite a useful facility — it meant that programmers at remote locations did not have to send their job streams into the central site in the form of card decks. These days, however, even the most basic online edit-and-submit facility is better than true RJE!

As you might expect, then, true RJE devices have virtually disappeared off the face of the earth. However, RJE lives on in the shape of numerous facilities which emulate RJE. This is because:

1   It is a relatively easy way to get jobs into an MVS system from another MVS system or a non-MVS system, and return the output to the originating system.
2   It is a relatively easy way to send output through the network to VTAM printers.

RJE has therefore evolved into the most commonly used network interface to JES2. JES328X, which was mentioned in Sec. 8.3.4, emulates RJE printers to provide remote JES printing facilities. And many file transfers to and from MVS systems use RJE emulation as well. You therefore need to be familiar with the definition of RJE devices using the JES2 TPDEF, LINEnnn, RMTnnn, and Rnnn.* statements. Example 8.15 shows a typical set of these. Note that:

● The TPDEF statement specifies general networking defaults, such as the number and size of buffers and the maximum number of concurrent sessions, which apply to both RJE and NJE taken together.
● The LOGONn statement is used to define the VTAM application name(s) used by JES2 for networking. Note that JES328X uses the application named on the LOGON1 statement, but conventional RJE usually uses the application named on the LOGON2 statement.
● The LINE statement is used in conjunction with the RMTnnn statement to

identify the address of the remote device. If it is an SNA device, the LINE statement will merely specify UNIT = SNA, as here, and the LUNAME parameter of the RMTnnn statement will specify the network address (this is omitted from RMT6 because this printer is accessed via JES328X, which supplies the network address itself). If it is a BSC device, the UNIT parameter will specify the unit address of the device.

- The RMTnnn statement also identifies the device type of BSC devices and the LU type of SNA devices, plus the number of each type of 'associated device' and whether there is an associated console.
- Each associated device is described by a RMTnnn.aan statement, where aa identifies the type of device (PR for a printer, PU for a punch, and RD for a card reader), and n identifies its sequence number within the RMT definition. This supplies information such as the output classes assigned to output devices, whether separator pages are to be written to output devices, and default jobclasses and message classes for jobs submitted via card readers.
- In this example, RMT6 is actually a remote printer controlled by JES328X, while the RMT7 definition is used for communications with a remote machine which is emulating an RJE device.

Routeing of output to remote printers can be accomplished via various JCL statements, including the JES2 /*ROUTE statement and the DEST parameter on the DD or OUTPUT statement. By default, output from jobs submitted from an RJE device will be routed back to the same device, though this can be altered with the PRDEST and PUDEST parameters on the Rnnn.RDn statement. Symbolic destination identifiers can also be associated with RJE devices using the DESTID statement.

8.5.3 Network job entry

Network job entry (NJE) is a much more modern and sophisticated facility for communication between IBM's mainframe job entry systems over a network, including both RSCS and POWER systems (IBM's job entry systems for the VM and VSE operating systems respectively) as well as JES2 and JES3 systems. It can be used to move jobstreams, SYSOUT datasets, job-oriented commands, and messages between networked systems (including messages and datasets transmitted using TSO IDTF (interactive data transmission facility, better known as the TRANSMIT and RECEIVE commands).

Processors in an NJE network are referred to as nodes. A node consists of a set of spool/checkpoint datasets and the JES system(s) using them. A MAS complex therefore constitutes a single node, though with multiple members of the node. The links between nodes are referred to as connections — including the implicit link via the spool between multiple members of the same MAS node. NJE communication can be carried across an SNA network, in which case the nodes using SNA services must define the VTAM ACBs they are using; alternatively, they can be carried

```
NJEDEF    OWNNODE=1,NODENUM=15,LINENUM=4
APPL(JESNSYSA) NODE=1,COMPACT=00,REST=10
APPL(JESRSYSA) NODE=1,COMPACT=00,REST=10
LOGON1    APPLID=JESNSYSA,LOG=NO,TR=NO
NODE1     NAME=OURSYS,SNA,COMPACT=0
NODE3     NAME=INTSYS,PASSWORD=INT,SNA
NODE4     NAME=FARSYS,NONETATH,SNA
CONNECT   NODEA=1,MEMBA=1,NODEB=1,MEMBB=2        /* MAS CONNECTION */
/* */
/*    THESE ARE THE JES2 DEFINITIONS FOR THE FARSYS LINK ***/
/* */
APPL(JESNINTA) NODE=3,COMPACT=00,REST=10
CONNECT   NODEA=1,MEMBA=1,NODEB=3,MEMBB=1,REST=200
CONNECT   NODEA=3,MEMBA=1,NODEB=4,MEMBB=1
LINE69    UNIT=SNA
```

Example 8.16. JES2 network job entry definitions.

across BSC lines or channel-to-channel adapters, in which case JES2's own comms access method, called RTAM, is used.

Each node participating in the network must use a consistent set of NJE definitions. JES2 systems must have these defined for them in their initialization parameters. Example 8.16 shows a sample set of NJE definitions for a JES2 node using SNA to communicate with the neighbouring system in the network. Note that:

- The OWNNODE parameter of the NJEDEF statement identifies which number will be used to define this system's node, i.e. the suffix of the NODEn statement relating to this system. The NODENUM and LINENUM statements define the maximum numbers of lines and nodes which may be defined on this system (LINENUM may only be changed at a warm start and NODENUM at an all-systems warm start so it is wise to make them large enough to accommodate potential additions to the network). Each member system creates a node information table (NIT), which contains an entry for each node defined to it with a NODEn statement, and the NODENUM parameter determines the size of this table.
- There must be an APPL statement which defines the VTAM ACB name used by each job entry system which could participate in an SNA session with this member, as well as one for each VTAM ACB which could be used by this member itself. This ACB name must match that used by VTAM in the APPL statement which defines the application to VTAM (see Chapter 9 for a quick outline of VTAM resource definition statements).
- There must be a LOGONn statement for each VTAM ACB which this member might wish to open — and the name must match that of an APPL statement relating to this member's node. The LOGON1 statement defines the ACB to be used for NJE communications.
- There must be a NODEn statement describing every node in the NJE network with which, or via which, this member intends to communicate. The name

assigned to any given node must be the same on every member of the network. The PASSWORD parameter is used to check that a system is the system it claims to be! The NONETATH parameter can be used to prevent a user at another node issuing console commands for your system, except display commands and commands relating to jobs belonging to the originating node.

- When JES2 nodes talk to each other over NJE links, they identify themselves to each other dynamically, and use the network path manager component of JES2 to broadcast information about available links in the network to other nodes. However, non-JES2 nodes do not support this level of functionality, and connections between them must be predefined using CONNECT statements. Notional links between members of MAS complexes must also be defined using CONNECT statements.

- Every comms line to be used for NJE communication must be defined using a LINEnnn statement; this is exactly equivalent to the LINEnnn statement used to define RJE lines.

Example 8.16 therefore represents the NJE definitions for a member of a MAS complex (the first CONNECT statement defines a link to a second member of the same node), which will engage in NJE sessions over SNA links to two other nodes. This member is to be known as OURSYS (this may make this example clearer, but it would actually be quite confusing in a real situation, as of course our system would also have to be known as OURSYS when it was defined on other people's nodes!), and it will engage in NJE comms with systems known as INTSYS and FARSYS. These are non-JES2 systems (we need to define the links to them with CONNECT statements), and our only connection with FARSYS is via INTSYS. We therefore do not need to define the FARSYS VTAM ACB, as all of our system's VTAM sessions will be with INTSYS, using the VTAM ACB named JESNINTA.

It should be clear that these definitions are slightly incomplete, as there is nothing to connect the SNA line we have defined to the session with JESNINTA. In fact, the definitions will be completed when we start networking over the link to INTSYS using a command sequence like this:

```
$S LGN1
$S LNE69
$S N,LNE69,A=JESNINTA
```

The first command causes our JES2 system to establish a session with VTAM (a LU-SSCP session, in SNA terms). The second activates one of JES2's SNA LINE definitions: note that this LINE is purely a logical concept, for use by JES2 internally, as communication with VTAM is via control blocks in virtual storage, and VTAM itself will determine what physical line is to be used to make the connection to the other application. The third command causes JES2 to 'start networking', i.e. to establish a session with the application JESNINTA (an LU–LU session) and associate the session with its control blocks for line 69.

For a non-SNA link, there would be no need to specify the application on the $S N command, as the line being used would be a real one. In both SNA and non-SNA environments, any given link must be started from both ends before a connection can be established. Once a connection has been established, job and SYSOUT transmitters and receivers are automatically started at each end (analogous to those used on offload devices). These can be controlled using further JES commands.

Jobs can be routed for execution from one node to another in a number of different ways:

- By the user coding /*ROUTE XEQ, /*XEQ, or /*XMIT statements in jobstreams
- Using the $R XEQ command to route a jobstream from this node to another one
- Using the $G R nodename,XEQ command to route a jobstream from another node
- Automatically for all jobs submitted from a given reader by coding the XEQNODE parameter on the READERn or Rn.RDn statement describing it in the JES2 initialization parameters

SYSOUT data will, by default, be sent back to the node which submitted the original job. It can, however, be rerouted in various ways:

- By the user coding /*ROUTE PRINT or DEST=nodename (on DD or OUTPUT statements) in jobstreams
- Using the $R ALL/PRT/PUN command to route output from a job on the input queue from this node to another one
- Using the $TO ...,D=nodename command to route an output dataset from this node to another one
- Using the $G R Nnnn,OUT command to route an output dataset from another node
- Automatically for all jobs submitted from a given reader by coding the PRNODE and/or PUNODE parameter(s) on the READERn or Rn.RDn statement describing it in the JES2 initialization parameters

The use and control of NJE is discussed in more detail in dedicated chapters of [1] and [2].

References and bibliography

IBM manuals

1. *MVS/ESA SPL: JES2 Initialization and Tuning*, SC28–1038. Describes all the JES2 initialization statements, and discusses various aspects of JES2 implementation including SPOOL and checkpoint dataset considerations, and NJE implementation.
2. *MVS/ESA Operations: JES2 Commands*, SC28–1039. Describes all the JES2 commands,

in chapters relating to functional areas, e.g. chapters on controlling jobs, output, and networks, and including how to start, stop, and restart JES2.
3. *MVS/ESA Message Library: JES2 Messages*, SC28–1040. Describes JES2 messages and responses to them, and gives examples of the checkpoint reconfiguration dialog.
4. *MVS/ESA JES2 Customization*, LY28–1010. Describes all the JES exit points and all the JES macros you may wish to use in them.
5. *MVS/XA SPL: JES2 User Modifications and Macros*, LC23–0069. The XA version of *JES2 Customization*.
6. *MVS/ESA JCL Reference*, GC28–1829. Documents all JCL statements and JES2 control language statements.

Other

7. Pearkins, J. E.: JES3: Is it Worth the Conversion Costs?, *Mainframe Journal*, March 1989, pp. 77–79.
8. McSweeney, A.: Relieving spool congestion, *MVS Update*, May 1988, pp. 27–34.
9. Bordonaro, B.: The JES2 Checkpoint Dataset Mechanism, *Enterprise Systems Journal*, October 1991, pp. 21–29.

9
Basic network configuration

9.1 Introduction

9.1.1 The bare essentials

Networking is an enormous subject, and even if you work at a 'true blue' IBM site, the full complexities of configuring your network are well beyond the scope of this book. However, every MVS systems programmer bringing up a test system needs to know enough about networking to make a TSO terminal work. The network is one of those critical components you have to get up before you can fix what has gone wrong with your test, so if you do not know how to do it you will always be dependent on someone else to make your system work. This chapter aims to give you enough knowledge to bring up the essential components of an existing network, without attempting to go any further.

The two products you need to understand to bring up a typical IBM mainframe network (or at least the bits you are likely to need) are VTAM and NCP.

VTAM (virtual telecommunications access method) is the software product which runs on your mainframe and handles all network I/O. Some sites may still use BTAM or TCAM, the forerunners to VTAM, but this is becoming rare, and usually these products are used in addition to VTAM, to support old applications, rather than instead of it.

NCP (Network Control Program) is the software which runs in your front-end processor — typically a 3725 or 3745. The role of the front-end processor is to take network output from a single mainframe channel and split it out to the appropriate comms lines, and to concentrate the input from the many physical lines onto the single mainframe channel. The NCP is effectively the operating system for the front-end processor — a sophisticated device which takes an active role in regulating and routeing I/O operations. Communications protocols are required which set out the rules these semi-autonomous devices must use when communicating with each other.

9.1.2   Systems network architecture and binary synchronous communication

VTAM implements two alternative sets of communications protocols: systems network architecture (SNA) and binary synchronous communication (BSC). SNA is IBM's strategic choice for future communications processes, and IBM has developed a considerable number of products which implement it. SNA consists of published standards and interfaces for a wide range of communications functions, and these have become the de facto standard for communications in the IBM-dominated sectors of the communications market, including communications for midrange and even personal systems as well as the mainframe arena. As a result, a large number of other vendors also offer products which implement SNA.

BSC is an altogether humbler sort of beast. It is a relatively antiquated protocol for connecting channel-attached 3270-type devices to IBM mainframes. It describes a limited range of communications functions by comparison with SNA, in fact, it covers an area roughly similar to the synchronous data link control (SDLC) protocol, which implements only one of the seven layers of the SNA model. Although BSC is supported by NCP for remotely attached 3270-type devices, it is clear that the long-term future of IBM communications lies with SNA. However, for the moment, many older cluster controllers still require BSC, so it is often still used for this type of device. More modern cluster controllers, on the other hand, can be configured to support either BSC or SDLC. You therefore need to know how to deal with both of these protocols.

9.1.3   A typical configuration

One area of MVS terminal I/O is completely outside the control of VTAM — I/O to devices used as MVS consoles. MVS requires its consoles to be devices on channel-attached cluster controllers, and it handles I/O to them directly. However, other terminals on the same cluster controller may be controlled by VTAM, so most sites make use of the spare ports on the 3x74s supporting their consoles to provide VTAM screens. Channel-attached devices are restricted in location by the length of a channel cable, so these will be found on the same site as the mainframe to which they are attached (the announcement of ESCON has extended these lengths, but still only to a few kilometres). 3x74s are also restricted in the numbers of terminals they can support (IBM devices currently support a maximum of 64). As a result, sites supporting significant numbers of users at remote locations generally use the more sophisticated front-end processors to handle the network traffic to remote users.

A typical MVS mainframe network configuration therefore includes one or more 37x5 front-end processors running NCP (which implements SNA protocols), and two or more 3x74 channel-attached cluster controllers (one for the master console and one for the alternative console as a minimum), using BSC or SDLC protocols for non-console terminal I/O. The front-end processors will in turn be connected

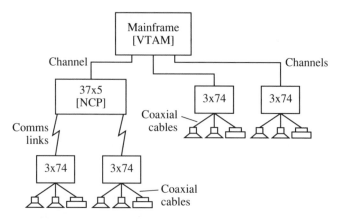

Figure 9.1. Typical IBM mainframe network configuration.

to communications lines, which may run across the public telephone network (via modems or equivalent digital devices) to remote sites, and at the end of these lines we usually find remotely attached 3x74 cluster controllers (using either BSC or SDLC protocols), or devices emulating them. Whether local or remote, each 3x74 will then have up to 64 3270-type terminals and/or printers attached to it. There are endless variations and improvements on this basic pattern, but the pattern itself is very widespread. Figure 9.1 shows the basic pattern.

It is worth noting that this network is a hierarchical one. Although there is a certain degree of independent function in the front-end processor, and even in the cluster controllers, ultimately they all dance to the tune played by VTAM in the mainframe. Modern networks are moving away from this pattern, as increasingly intelligent devices (notably PCs, midrange systems, and even other manufacturers' mainframes) start to participate in mainframe networks, but traditional mainframe terminals still fit nicely into the hierarchical mould. If your network consists of multiple mainframe hosts and front-end processors, you will find that each host has hierarchical control over its own part of the network, and it is only when the hosts speak to each other that communication occurs on an equal (peer-to-peer) basis.

What the typical MVS systems programmer needs to know is how to set up VTAM and NCP to run TSO on a 3270-type terminal attached to either a local or remote 3x74 controller. This is the main question this chapter addresses.

9.1.4   SNA concepts

It will help you to understand VTAM if you familiarize yourself with some of the basic concepts used by SNA.

An SNA network consists of one or more system services control points (SSCPs), and many physical units (PUs), logical units (LUs), and links between them. An SSCP is responsible for owning and controlling a section of the network known as a domain. A PU provides services controlled by the SSCP, and an LU

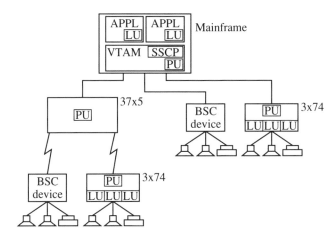

Figure 9.2. SNA components in typical configuration.

is a user of the services controlled by the SSCP. The object of communication across an SNA network is to send messages between two LUs, but before this can occur, various components of the network must establish logical connections with each other, known as sessions.

SSCPs, PUs, and LUs are all logical concepts, and in theory any one of them can be implemented by hardware, software, or a combination of both. In practice, the SSCP is typically a piece of software, PUs are typically hardware devices, and LUs are either terminals (including virtual terminals) or applications. Note that application LUs are known as primary LUs, and terminal LUs as secondary LUs, as application LUs have more control over the establishment of sessions. In Fig. 9.1, for example, the SNA part of the network is a single domain controlled by an SSCP which is implemented as part of VTAM (note that VTAM does more than supply the SSCP function — for example, it also supports BSC communications). Another part of VTAM, along with the mainframe itself, performs the role of a PU (a type 5 PU); the front-end processor and the NCP together implement the function of a PU (type 4); and the remote cluster controllers also implement the function of a PU (type 2). Each terminal attached to a cluster controller (along with the corresponding terminal-controller functions of the cluster controller itself) implements the function of a secondary LU, and each application on the mainframe which could participate in a session with a terminal is performing as a primary LU. Figure 9.2 shows this configuration.

When the SSCP function in VTAM starts up, it starts sessions with each PU (an SSCP–PU session) and LU (an SSCP–LU session) specified in the list of resources to be configured at startup time (see Sec. 9.2 for details of how this list is defined). Before the SSCP can establish a session with any LU, it must establish one with each PU on the route to the LU. So, for example, before a session can be established with a remote terminal LU, a SSCP–PU session must be established by

VTAM with the host processor PU, another one with the NCP PU, and another with the cluster controller PU.

During the process of establishing a session, the SSCP sends a message defining the parameters it intends to use for communication during the session (e.g. when establishing a session with a terminal LU it will specify the screen size it intends to use and whether or not it will use 3270 extended datastreams to send messages which will appear on the terminal in colour). This is known as the bind message. If the other partner in the session is able to accept these parameters, it sends a message confirming that the session can be bound; if not, it sends a negative response and communications cannot be established. This is why VTAM must have detailed resource definition information about the PUs and LUs with which it is expected to go into session.

Once VTAM has established a session with an LU, the LU can request a session with another LU. Typically, this occurs as a result of a user on a terminal entering a logon command. A VTAM logon command is translated by VTAM into a request to start a session with the application named in the command. If VTAM already has an SSCP–LU session with the application it will pass the request on to it. If the application is prepared to accept the request, it will issue a BIND request to the secondary LU, and if this is successful, an LU–LU session will be established. Messages can then pass between the LUs; typically, screens of data from the application to the terminal and keyboard input in the opposite direction. If any part of this process fails, VTAM will issue an information message to the terminal user (this is often the rather obscure SESSION NOT BOUND message you may have experienced when trying to logon to a VTAM application).

We have noted already that there can be more than one SSCP in a network, and that each is in charge of an area of the network called its domain. Each domain can be further divided into subareas. There is one subarea for each host and one for each NCP in the network. An NCP subarea consists of the network components under the control of that NCP, and a host subarea consists of the components under the direct control of the SSCP without any intervening NCP. Each subarea has a subarea number assigned to it, which is used in the process of addressing components of the network. Figure 9.3 illustrates the concepts of domains and subareas. Note that cluster controllers and terminals attached to the various mainframes and front-end processors are not shown for the sake of simplicity.

9.2   Basic VTAM implementation

9.2.1   Starting VTAM

VTAM runs on an MVS system as a started task. It is usually started automatically at IPL time, with a command like:

```
S VTAM.NET,,,(LIST=AA)
```

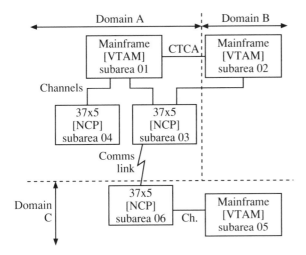

Figure 9.3. Multi-domain VTAM network.

In this case, VTAM is the name of the VTAM cataloged procedure, NET is an optional identifier by which VTAM is to be referred in operator commands (the stop (P) and modify (F) commands), and AA is a suffix to be used by VTAM in selecting its startup parameters. You must be familiar with the format of this command so that you can start up your own version of the procedure with your own version of the startup parameters when you are doing system testing.

Example 9.1 shows a typical VTAM cataloged procedure. Note that:

- The data sets referenced by the STEPLIB, VTAMLIB, NCPLIB, and INITEST DD statements must be APF authorized or your VTAM startup will fail.
- The STEPLIB, NCPLIB, NCPDUMP, and INITEST statements can, however, be omitted if you are not using NCP, i.e. if you can manage using only terminals on channel-attached cluster controllers.
- The VTAMLST DD statement defines the dataset(s) containing the VTAM

```
//VTAM     PROC
//*
//VTAM      EXEC PGM=ISTINM01,
//          TIME=1440,REGION=4096K
//STEPLIB  DD DSN=NCP.SSPLIB,DISP=SHR
//VTAMLST  DD DSN=SYS8.USER.VTAMLST,DISP=SHR
//         DD DSN=SYS1.VTAMLST,DISP=SHR
//VTAMLIB  DD DSN=SYS8.USER.VTAMLIB,DISP=SHR
//         DD DSN=SYS1.VTAMLIB,DISP=SHR
//NCPLIB   DD DSN=NCP.NCPLIB,DISP=SHR
//NCPDUMP  DD DSN=NCP.NCPDUMP,DISP=SHR
//INITEST  DD DSN=NCP.SSPLIB,DISP=SHR
//SYSABEND DD SYSOUT=*,HOLD=YES
```

Example 9.1. VTAM cataloged procedure.

```
SSCPID=01,NOPROMPT,LIST=AO,                                             X
MAXSUBA=7,SUPP=INFO,                                                    X
LPBUF=(64,,0,,1,1),                                                     X
SFBUF=(163,,0,,1,1)
*/*
*/*    MEMBER ATCSTR00
*/*
SSCPNAME=M01,SSCPID=01,NETID=OURSYS,                                    X
TNSTAT,                                                                 X
CONFIG=00,PPOLOG=YES,                                                   X
CRPLBUF=(325,,15,,1,16),                                                X
IOBUF=(300,512,19,,1,20),                                               X
LFBUF=(300,,0,,1,1),                                                    X
WPBUF=(1250,,0,,1,1),                                                   X
HOSTSA=1,                                                               X
HOSTPU=DV01311
*/*
*/*    MEMBER ATCSTRAA-OVERRIDES FOR ATCSTR00
*/*
```

Example 9.2. VTAM startup parameters.

resource definition parameters, and the VTAMLIB DD statement defines the dataset(s) containing VTAM resource definition tables. VTAM parameter and table definitions are discussed in Sec. 9.2.2.

- We are concatenating some user libraries in front of the IBM-supplied SYS1.VTAM* libraries. This is in order to preserve our inhouse parameter and table definitions when we replace the SYS1 libraries as a result of installing a new version of VTAM (e.g. through the MVS CBIPO process).

VTAM interprets the LIST parameter on the START command as the suffix to be used to identify the ATCSTRxx member of VTAMLST containing its startup parameters. This member is used in addition to member ATCSTR00 and can override values specified there, so you may code stable startup parameters in ATCSTR00 and less stable ones in suffixed versions. Alternatively, you may find it less confusing to simply include a comment line in ATCSTR00, and keep all your startup parameters in the current suffixed member. Example 9.2 shows samples of ATCSTR00 and ATCSTRxx members. Note that:

- The CONFIG parameter supplies the suffix for member ATCCONxx, which contains a list of network resources to be activated at VTAM startup. Note also that the CONFIG = xx parameter can also be coded on the START command, along with the LIST parameter, in which case it overrides the value in ATCSTRxx. Example 9.3 shows an ATCCONxx member.
- The other parameters here relate mainly to the various names by which this VTAM system will be known and the resources used by the SSCP itself, notably buffer allocations. We will not go into these as you are unlikely to have to change them simply in order to get your network working.
- A continuation character must be coded in column 72 as well as a comma after the last item of the line to indicate continuation of the parameters.

```
A01TS01,A01TS02,A01TS03,        TSO APPLS                         X
A01J328X,                       JES328X                           X
A01WEST1,                       SESMGR                            X
PATH0103,                       PATH TO 3725 (NCP)                X
LCL060,LCL840,                  LOCAL TERMINALS (NON SNA)         X
A01NVIEW,A01NPM,                NETVIEW / NPM                     X
A01CICP,                        PROD CICS SERVICES                X
A01CTCA,                        CTCA TO 2ND MACHINE               X
PATH0102,                       PATHS TO 2ND MACHINE              X
CDRMA0,A01ADJ,                  CDRM AND ADJ SSCPS FOR 2ND M/C    X
A01JES,                         JES RJE & NJE                     X
DN03420                         NCP
```

Example 9.3. VTAM configuration member (ATCCONxx).

Note that in Example 9.3:

- The names listed in this member are simply the names of the other members of VTAMLST containing the definitions of resources to be activated at VTAM startup. See Sec. 9.2.2 for further discussion of the types of member referenced here.
- As with ATCSTRxx, a continuation character must be coded in column 72 as well as a comma after the last item of the line to indicate continuation of the parameters.

In order to simplify VTAM startup during testing of basic MVS systems, you may wish to set up and use an alternative version of ATCCONxx, leaving out the resources you are not going to need. This also has the advantage of making it impossible for users to attempt to log on from terminals you have not included, or to applications you have not included. In the simplest case of all, you will need to include only one TSO application member and one local terminal member in the list in your ATCCONxx member.

9.2.2 VTAM resource definition

Both SNA and BSC require that the software controlling a communications session has detailed information about the resources participating in the session. VTAM will not start a session unless it has this information available to it, and so we must supply it in advance with definitions of the resources in the network. In SNA terms, we must supply it with definitions of all the SSCPs, PUs, and LUs with which or for which it will be expected to establish sessions.

Most of VTAM's resource definitions are held in the form of source members in the libraries in your VTAMLST concatenation. We have already seen that the ATCSTR00 and ATCSTRxx members contain VTAM's startup parameters, and that the ATCCONxx member contains a list of resources to be activated at startup time. Most of the other members of VTAMLST contain definitions of VTAM 'major nodes' — groups of resources. These in turn may refer to VTAM tables to define certain aspects of resources, and these tables exist in load module format in the VTAMLIB concatenation.

Each major node defines a group of resources of a given type. Each resource in the major node is known as a minor node, and will be described by a definition statement. The statement used depends on the type of resource being defined, e.g. the APPL statement is used to define an application and the LOCAL statement is used to define a local non-SNA terminal. The following sections show how major nodes describing local terminals and VTAM applications are defined.

You should define naming conventions for your major nodes. In Example 9.3, for example:

- Each application node name is in the form Annxxxx, where nn is the subarea number of the host on which the application executes and xxxx is descriptive.
- Each local terminal node name is in the form LCLcua, where cua is the unit address (i.e. device number) of the first terminal in the node.
- Each PATH name is in the form PATHaabb, where aa is the subarea number of the VTAM host using the definition, and bb is the number of the subarea at the other end.

The use of subarea numbers in node names is particularly useful in large and complex networks.

9.2.3   Defining BSC terminals

Example 9.4 shows a section of a major node definition for a group of local BSC terminals. This is member LCL060 of our sample VTAMLST library, referred to in the ATCCONxx listing of Example 9.3. All of the VTAM resource definition statements and parameters for each type of major node are documented in detail in [3].

Note that in Example 9.4:

- This major node defines the terminals and printers on a local cluster controller. The LBUILD statement identifies this as a local non-SNA major node.
- There is a LOCAL statement for each device attached to the controller (except 061), in address order. The statements for devices 063–07D are identical to that for 062 so have been omitted to save space, and that for 07E is identical to that for 07F.
- Note, however, that these statements need not have been grouped together in this way — we could have divided the terminals on this controller between multiple major nodes, or combined terminals on multiple controllers in a single major node. Similarly, the terminals need not have been coded in address sequence. It is sensible, however, to group and sequence your definitions this way, as this makes your configuration more easily comprehensible and easier to control using operator commands.
- The terminal at address 060 is normally a console, and so is not normally under

```
LCLO60    LBUILD
*
LT060     LOCAL CUADDR=060,                                              X
                MODETAB=MT3270L,                                         X
                USSTAB=USSLOCL,                                          X
                ISTATUS=INACTIVE,                                        X
                TERM=3277
*
LT062     LOCAL CUADDR=062,                                              X
                MODETAB=MT3270L,                                         X
                USSTAB=USSLOCL,                                          X
                ISTATUS=ACTIVE,                                          X
                LOGAPPL=SESMGR,                                          X
                TERM=3277
.

.

.
*
LP07F     LOCAL CUADDR=07F,                                              X
                MODETAB=MT3270L,                                         X
                DLOGMOD=DSILGMOD,                                        X
                ISTATUS=ACTIVE,                                          X
                TERM=3286
```

Example 9.4. Extract from a major node for BSC local terminals.

VTAM's control, but the definition provided here allows it to be varied offline as a console then varied active as a VTAM terminal. The terminal at address 061 is always a console, so it has not been defined to VTAM at all.

- The terminals at addresses 062 through 07D are typical 3277-type terminals (note that many OEM terminal devices emulate these devices). When this major node is activated, these devices come up as active because of the ISTATUS parameter, and are automatically logged on to the application SESMGR because of the LOGAPPL parameter. In fact, SESMGR is the name of a 'network front end' application, which provides network security by requiring users to enter a password before they can use an application. It also makes the network more user-friendly by providing personalized menus of available applications, newsflashes, and other helpful facilities. Most VTAM networks use an application of this kind to improve the user interface to the network.
- The devices at addresses 07E and 07F are 3286-type printers.
- Naming conventions have been defined for these terminals and printers to make it easy for network operators and systems programmers to connect the VTAM name of a device with its physical address.
- The MODETAB and USSTAB parameters name tables in VTAMLIB which further define the characteristics of sessions with the terminal concerned. The MODETAB parameter names the logmode table to be used for this terminal, and the DLOGMOD parameter names the default entry to be used from this table. The logmode entry used for a terminal specifies many of the session parameters to be used when establishing a session with the terminal — these

```
LCS840   VBUILD  TYPE=LOCAL
*
LPU840   PU     CUADDR=840,                                    X
                MODETAB=MT3270S,                               X
                USSTAB=USSLOCL
*
LST840   LU     LOCADDR=2,                                     X
                LOGAPPL=SESMGR
.
.
.
*
LSP85F   LU     LOCADDR=33,                                    X
                DLOGMOD=SPRLGMOD
```

Example 9.5. Extract from SNA local terminal major node.

parameters define attributes such as the character set used by the terminal and the maximum message size it can handle.

- The USSTAB parameter specifies the unformatted system services table to be associated with the terminal. The main function of this is to define the messages VTAM sends to the terminal when it is not owned by any application. Message 10 in the USS table, for example, is the dormant screen message that will be sent to the terminal when VTAM comes up, or after the user has logged off an application. Other messages in the table are sent in various error situations (the cryptic SESSION NOT BOUND message mentioned earlier is one of these from the IBM default USS table). If you use the LOGAPPL parameter to assign a front-end application to the terminal automatically, however, you will only see the messages from the USS table when the front-end application is down.

9.2.4   Defining SNA local terminals

More modern channel-attached 3x74 controllers can be configured to support SNA protocols instead of BSC. Example 9.5 shows part of a major node defining an SNA local controller and the attached terminals. For the sake of comparability with Example 9.4, this example defines similar devices (except that we have not reserved any terminals for use as consoles).

Note that in Example 9.5:

- The VBUILD TYPE=LOCAL statement indicates that this is an SNA local node.
- Each cluster controller in the local node must be defined with a PU statement. The CUADDR parameter identifies the address of the controller. Most of the other parameters you can specify on this statement simply name defaults for the LU statements which follow.
- Each terminal or printer attached to the controller must be defined with an LU statement. The LUs attached to a given cluster controller must all be defined

```
AO1CICP  VBUILD TYPE=APPL
*
AO1CP1O APPL  ACBNAME=DCICP1O
AO1CP3O APPL  ACBNAME=DCICP3O
AO1CP5O APPL  ACBNAME=DCICP5O
```

Example 9.6. Major node defining CICS applications to VTAM.

together, immediately after the PU statement for the controller. You must therefore specify all the devices attached to a given controller within a single major node. You may define more than one controller and their attached devices in a single major node, but it is easier to understand your configuration if you specify only one controller per node.

- The LOCADDR parameter specifies the port address of the device on the controller.
- The first LU defined is a terminal which is to be automatically logged on to the network front-end application SESMGR.
- Again, we have left out repetitious definitions from the middle of this example.
- The last LU defined is a printer, which will use a different logmode table entry from the default entry used by the terminals.

9.2.5 *Defining VTAM applications*

Although the main objective of this chapter is to show you how to get a TSO-only system working, we will start our look at VTAM application definition with a non-TSO example. This is because non-TSO applications are easier to define to VTAM and therefore provide an easier introduction to some of the principles involved.

Example 9.6 shows a major node defining a group of CICS applications. Note that:

- The TYPE=APPL parameter on the VBUILD statement defines this as an application major node. The name used in the label is optional and is used purely for documentation purposes.
- Each APPL statement defines and names an application minor node.
- Each CICS region you define requires only one APPL statement, even though multiple users could be logged on to it simultaneously. Most non-TSO VTAM applications can be defined in this way.

The name used in the label on the APPL statement (referred to below as the APPL name) and the name specified in the ACBNAME parameter can both be used to reference this minor node, for example in network commands. If the ACBNAME parameter is coded, it must specify the name the application uses to identify itself to VTAM (i.e. the APPLID operand on the ACB macro instruction which it uses to request an SSCP–LU session). If the ACBNAME parameter is not

```
A01TS01 VBUILD TYPE=APPL                    APPLICATION MAJOR NODE
*
A01TS0    APPL   AUTH=(NOACQ,NOBLOCK,PASS,NOTCAM,NVPACE,TSO,NOPO),           X
                 EAS=1,ACBNAME=TSO
A01TS001 APPL    AUTH=(NOACQ,NOBLOCK,PASS,NOTCAM,NVPACE,TSO,NOPO),           X
                 EAS=1,ACBNAME=TS00001
A01TS002 APPL    AUTH=(NOACQ,NOBLOCK,PASS,NOTCAM,NVPACE,TSO,NOPO),           X
                 EAS=1,ACBNAME=TS00002
A01TS003 APPL    AUTH=(NOACQ,NOBLOCK,PASS,NOTCAM,NVPACE,TSO,NOPO),           X
                 EAS=1,ACBNAME=TS00003
A01TS004 APPL    AUTH=(NOACQ,NOBLOCK,PASS,NOTCAM,NVPACE,TSO,NOPO),           X
                 EAS=1,ACBNAME=TS00004
A01TS005 APPL    AUTH=(NOACQ,NOBLOCK,PASS,NOTCAM,NVPACE,TSO,NOPO),           X
                 EAS=1,ACBNAME=TS00005
```

Example 9.7. Major node defining TSO applications to VTAM.

coded, the APPL name must be the name used as the APPLID operand on the ACB macro.

The APPL name must be unique within the entire network if this application is to be available for cross-domain sessions (i.e. accessible by users at terminals belonging to different domains from that in which the application runs). By contrast, the ACBNAME need only be unique within the domain where the application is running. This may seem confusing, but it allows multiple applications with the same local name to run on networked hosts and still be accessible to cross-domain users using cross-domain names. In this situation, each local application uses the same APPLID on its ACB macro, and links up with a locally defined minor node which specifies this name on its ACBNAME parameter. However, each minor node definition specifies a different APPL name (e.g. one prefixed by the local subarea number, as here). Thus a user at a terminal in host subarea 02, for example, can access DCICP10 on the host in subarea 01 by specifying A01CP10 on the logon command, even though there is an application called DCICP10 running on the host in subarea 02 as well.

The VTAM definitions required for TSO are rather more complex. Example 9.7 shows how they are coded. Note that:

- The first APPL statement here defines an application with the ACBNAME of TSO. This is the APPLID used by the VTAM application running in the TCAS address space. When a user attempts to logon to TSO, their logon command specifies this application and their terminal goes into session with TCAS.
- Once TCAS has validated the sign-on request, it creates a separate address space for the user, and initiates a session between the terminal and the VTAM application running in the new address space. It therefore requires a different APPLID to refer to this application, and it will use one in the format TSOnnnn. The additional APPL definitions specified in this member are for this purpose.

TCAS regards the TSOnnnn applications as a pool, and assigns the next available ACB from its pool whenever it needs one. It only includes in its pool

ACBNAMES in the correct format, starting with one numbered 0001 and continuing sequentially until there is a break in the sequence numbers available. Your TSOnnnn applications need not all be included in the same major node, though it will usually be simpler if they are. In Example 9.3, we have assumed that the TSOnnnn applications are divided between several major nodes (A01TSO1, A01TSO2, and A01TSO3). The subsequent major node definitions will each contain their own VBUILD statement, but the APPL statement for TSO itself must not be repeated.

Because any TSOnnnn application definition that is missing from the sequence will determine the end of the pool of TSO ACBNAMEs, and therefore the size of the pool, this can place a constraint on the number of simultaneous TSO sessions VTAM will support, independent of the TSO USERMAX limit (USERMAX is discussed in Chapter 10). Fortunately, you can add applications dynamically by defining additional major nodes and varying them active (see the next section).

9.2.6 Controlling a VTAM network

We have seen that the major nodes comprising a VTAM network can be activated automatically at VTAM startup by naming them in the ATCCONxx member. However, VTAM also provides extensive facilities for dynamic control of the network. Any given major or minor node, for example, can be activated at any time using the vary network command:

    V NET,ACT,ID=nodename

or deactivated when not in use:

    V NET,INACT,ID=nodename

and we can add ,F to the latter command to force the deactivation even when the resource is in use. This version will result in any sessions dependent on the resource being broken, so it must be used with care.

The ability to issue these commands at the level of the major node as well as at the level of the minor node gives us the opportunity to save a lot of work, as long as we define our major nodes with this in mind. If, for example, you lump all your local terminals into one major node instead of defining a separate major node for each logical group, you will lose the ability to vary logical groups of them using a single vary command for the major node.

When the V NET,ACT,... command is issued for a major node (unless the node definition has been checkpointed by VTAM and the WARM operand is coded on the command), VTAM rereads the definition for the major node from VTAMLST, so by varying a major node inactive and then active again we can change the definitions in force. This must, however, be used with care: an application whose APPL is varied inactive, for example, may be unable to reactivate its SSCP–LU session once you have reactivated the APPL except by closing down and restarting the application. Other variants of the V NET command allow us to change certain attributes dynamically (e.g. the LOGMODE in force for a given terminal).

Before issuing any vary commands, it is useful to be able to display the status of a resource, and VTAM provides the D NET command for this purpose:

```
D NET, ID=nodename
```

gives a display of the status of a resource, and for major nodes:

```
D NET, ID=nodename, E
```

gives an extended display, including a one-line display of the status of each subsidiary minor node.

Most sites use network management products, such as IBM's Netview, to control the network. Netview can be used to issue V NET commands rather than entering them at the console, but it also provides other network management functions, including, for example, automatic responses to network error messages, fault monitoring, and, with the addition of Netview performance monitor (NPM), capacity monitoring and response-time monitoring.

9.3 Basic NCP implementation

9.3.1 The NCP generation process

NCP is the software which runs in SNA front-end processors. If you have older, non-SNA communications access methods running on your mainframe, you may find other software running in your FEP. If you run BTAM instead of VTAM, you will need to run the emulation program (EP) instead of NCP; if you are running both BTAM and VTAM, you need to run both EP and NCP, and these are combined in the form of a partitioned emulation program (PEP). BTAM and the associated emulation software is, however, dying out now, so we shall ignore them here.

In order to install the NCP software onto your front-end processor, you must 'generate' the NCP load module on your mainframe, then load it into your FEP via the channel attaching it to the mainframe. The libraries from which your NCP will be built will usually have been installed using the NCP CBIPO. As well as this program code, the NCP loaded into your front-end processor includes tables defining the resources which it is going to use, such as the lines and devices attached to it, its channel connections to host systems, and the FEP's own hardware configuration. You must supply an input deck at generation time describing these resources.

However, the copy of VTAM on the host processor which owns the NCP must also know what resources are attached to the NCP, so that it knows what network I/O requests to route to the front-end processor. Fortunately, IBM has allowed us to combine the two sets of definitions required in a single PDS member, which can serve both as the input deck to the NCP generation process, and also as the VTAM major node definition for the NCP. Note that VTAM uses this member in source format, whereas NCP only uses it when it has been converted into a load module which is part of the NCP itself. Some of the definition statements in the deck are used only by VTAM, some only for NCP generation, and some for both.

You must ensure that the deck VTAM is using to define the major node is the same one which was used to generate the NCP currently loaded in the FEP, or chaos will result! The easiest and safest way to do this is to adopt some simple standards on the naming and location of your NCP definition decks:

1 Keep several versions of your NCP deck, with member-name suffixes reflecting their version numbers, and, in large networks with multiple FEPs, second-level suffixes reflecting their subarea numbers. For example, you could name your decks NCPaavv, where aa is the subarea number and vv the version. At any one time, you should have a 'current' and 'previous' version, and possibly a 'next' version, for each FEP.
2 Never change an NCP deck once it has been 'genned' and loaded for production use. Once you have done this it becomes your current version and any changes should be applied after copying it to create your next version.
3 Keep these decks in your VTAMLST library and nowhere else (except backups of course!), so that there is no danger of multiple copies of the same 'version' of your NCP getting out of step.

Once you have coded your definition statements, you must run them through the NCP/EP definition facility (NDF) to create the NCP load module. The JCL for this is rather complex — if you really need to gen an NCP, talk to your VTAM systems programmer. Alternatively, if your NCP software was installed using the CBIPO process, look in hlq.IPO1.INSTLIB(NCPASM), where hlq is the high-level qualifier of your NCP libraries (the default is ACFNCP). This job is explained in detail in the COMGUIDE member of hlq.IPO1.DOCLIB.

The NCP load module must be created in the library defined in the NCPLIB DD statement in your VTAM procedure, with the same name as the corresponding major node in VTAMLST. To load it into the FEP, first deactivate the current NCP, using the command:

```
V NET,ID=oldncp,INACT,F
```

Note that this will break all users' sessions which are currently routed through the FEP and so should only be done during scheduled or emergency system downtime. Complete the process with the command:

```
V NET,ID=newncp,ACT,LOAD=YES
```

The NCP will usually take several minutes to load. VTAM will switch to using the major node definitions in the newncp member of VTAMLST as well as loading the NCP load module in the newncp member of NCPLIB into the FEP.

```
*****************************************************************************
*       PATHS FROM   SUBAREA 1 TO 3 (HOST TO NCP)                          *
*****************************************************************************
PATH0103 PATH   DESTSA=3,ERO=(3,1),VRO=0,                                  *
                VRPWS00=(50,255),VRPWS01=(50,255),VRPWS02=(50,255)
```

Example 9.8. PATH definitions for paths to NCP.

Note that in our start-up configuration for VTAM, we included both the major node for the NCP and the path to it (PATH0103, shown in Example 9.8). This will result in the node being activated without reloading the NCP at each VTAM startup.

9.3.2   NCP resource definition

Example 9.9 shows an extract from an NCP input deck which serves both as the input to the NCP generation process and the major node definition used by VTAM. This is a very restricted extract, intended to give a flavour of a typical NCP deck, and to show the statements used to define cluster controllers and terminals attached to your FEP. Further detail on the statements used in the NCP generation deck can be found in [6].

Although Example 9.9 may seem rather large, it is in fact only a tiny fraction of a typical NCP deck — you will typically find dozens of lines attached to a FEP, each with one or more terminal controllers attached, and each of these with up to 64 terminals attached to it. In addition, there can be many hundreds of lines of definitions describing connections with other subareas in connected networks. Even some of the statements we have shown have been simplified and cut down (as shown by the ... in column 1). Because the typical NCP is so complex, it is well worth setting and following clear conventions for resource naming, and including extensive documentation within the source. Even this small section of an NCP shows several examples:

- A table has been created at the front of the listing describing in detail each line attached to the FEP. Note that this is structured to reflect the internal structure of the FEP: this consists of several modules known as line attachment bases (LABs), each supporting a number of line interface couplers (LICs). Each LIC supports up to four lines, depending on their line speeds, and the port numbers (or line addresses) on the FEP are assigned sequentially, starting with the lines on LAB 1, LIC 1, then the lines on LAB 1, LIC 2, etc.
- The NCP line names are in the format Lnnnxxxx, where nnn is the address of the FEP port to which the line is attached, and xxxx is descriptive of the location served.
- Controller names are in the format Pnnnxx, where nnn is the number of the line they are attached to and xx is their sequence number within the group of controllers attached to the line.

```
DN03420 TITLE '-- NCP GENERATED ON DD/MM/YY --'
*************************************************************************
* LINE ADDRESS TABLE LEGEND :                                          *
*                                                                      *
* CS  - COMMUNICATIONS SCANNER                                         *
* CON - CONNECTION TYPE : M - MODEM, D - DIRECT, K - KILOSTREAM,       *
*                         E - MODEM-ELIMINATOR, C - MULTIPLEX CHANNEL  *
* MDE - MODE           : F - FULL DUPLEX, H - HALF DUPLEX              *
* DIS - DISCIPLINE     : B - BSC, S - SDLC, A - SS                     *
*                                                                      *
*--------------------------------------------------------------------- *
*                                                                      *
*  LAB POSITION 1 (TYPE A)                                             *
*  ----------------------                                              *
*--------------------------------------------------------------------- *
*LINE]  I/F  ]HEX  ]NCP LINE]LIC]CS ]LIC]CON] SPEED ]MDE]DIS]WGT ]WGT *
*ADDR]  ADDR ]ADDR ]NAME    ]POS]NO.]TYP]   ] BITS/S]   ]   ]    ]SUM *
*----]-------]-----]--------]---]---]---]---]-------]---]---]----]----*
* 00 ]000/001]00/01]L000AAAA] 1 ] 1 ] 1 ] K ]  9600 ] H ] S ] 12 ] 12 *
* 01 ]002/003]02/03]L001BBBB]   ]   ]   ] K ]  9600 ] H ] S ] 12 ]    *
* 02 ]004/005]04/05]L002CCCC]   ]   ]   ] K ]  9600 ] H ] S ] 12 ]    *
.
.
* 07 ]094/095]5E/5F]L007DDDD]   ]   ]   ] K ] 19200 ] H ] B ] 25 ]    *
*----]-------]-----]--------]---]---]---]---]-------]---]---]----]----*
.
.
*--------------------------------------------------------------------- *
*                                                                      *
*  LAB POSITION 3 (TYPE B)                                             *
*  ----------------------                                              *
*--------------------------------------------------------------------- *
*LINE]  I/F  ]HEX  ]NCP LINE]LIC]CS ]LIC]CON] SPEED ]MDE]DIS]WGT ]WGT *
*ADDR]  ADDR ]ADDR ]NAME    ]POS]NO.]TYP]   ]       ]   ]   ]    ]SUM *
*--------------------------------------------------------------------- *
* 64 ]128/129]80/81]L064EEEE] 1 ] 1 ] 3 ] K ] 48000 ] H ] S ] 25 ] 25 *
* 65 ]130/131]82/83] N/A   ] ] ] ] ] ] ] ] ] ] *
.
.
* 80 ]160/161]A0/A1]L080FFFF] 5 ] 2 ] 1 ] C ] 19200 ] H ] S ] 25 ] 25 *
.
.
.
*************************************************************************
* PRODUCTION PARTITION PCCU STATEMENT
*************************************************************************
DXV01311 PCCU  AUTODMP=YES,         TAKE AUTOMATIC NCP DUMP            *
               AUTOIPL=YES,         AUTO REIPL AFTER FAILURE           *
               CUADDR=640,          CHANNEL DEVICE ADDRESS             *
               DUMPDS=NCPDUMP,      DDNAME=NCPDUMP FOR NCP DUMPS       *
               VFYLM=YES,           PROMPT AT RELOAD                   *
               MAXDATA=4864,        UNITSZ*MAXBFRU ROUNDED MULT OF 128 *
               GWCTL=ONLY,          *** IBM IE CHANGE ***              *
               NETID=OURSYS,        *** SNI PARM CHANGE ***            *
               SUBAREA=1            HOST SUB AREA OF 1
```

Example 9.9. Extracts from NCP definition statements.

```
                .
                .
                .
          BUILD MAXSUBA=7,            ALLOW 7 SUBAREAS                          *
                MODEL=3725,          3725                                       *
                SUBAREA=3,           THIS NCP IS SUBAREA 3                       *
                TYPGEN=NCP,          CHAN/LINK ATTACH,NO EMULATION              *
                BFRS=128,            100 BUFFERS EACH 128 BYTES                 *
                MAXSSCP=4,           4 VTAM IN COMMUNICATION                    *
                NEWNAME=DN03420,     NCP NAME                                   *
                VERSION=V4R3.1,      ------- V4 CHANGE --------                 *
                PUNAME=DN03420,      ------- V4 CHANGE --------                 *
                NETID=OURSYS,                                                   *
                .
                .
                .
*******************************************************************************
* PRODUCTION PARTITION HOST STATEMENT
*******************************************************************************
          HOST  INBFRS=16,           16 NCP BUFFERS FOR HOST SEND               *
                NETID=OURSYS,                                                   *
                MAXBFRU=20,          MAX VTAM BUFFERS FOR RECEIVE               *
                UNITSZ=240,          VTAM BUFFER SIZE                           *
                SUBAREA=1,           SUBAREA=01                                 *
                BFRPAD=0             ACF/VTAM REQUIREMENT
                .

                .
                .
*******************************************************************************
* PATHS TO PROD AND TEST PARTITIONS
*******************************************************************************
          PATH  DESTSA=(1),ERO=(1,1),ER1=(1,1),ER2=(2,1),ER3=(1,1),            *
                VRO=0,VR1=1,VR2=2,VR3=3
          PATH  DESTSA=(2),ERO=(2,1),ER1=(1,1),ER2=(2,1),ER3=(2,1),            *
                VRO=0,VR1=1,VR2=2,VR3=3
                .
                .

                .
*******************************************************************************
* GVBSC192- GROUP BSC LINES AT SPEEDS UP TO 19.2K
*******************************************************************************
*
GVBSC192 GROUP LNCTL=BSC,            BI-SYNC                                    *
                TYPE=NCP,            NETWORK CONTROL MODE                       *
                PU=YES,              BSC 3270 TREATED AS PU                     *
                SPEED=19200,         LINE OPERAND—MAX LINE SPEED                *
                CLOCKNG=EXT,         LINE OPERAND—MODEM CLOCKS                  *
                DUPLEX=FULL,         LINE OPERAND—HOLD RTS                      *
                CODE=EBCDIC,         DOES NOT ACCEPT ASCII.                     *
                DLOGMOD=S3270,       DEFAULT LOGMODE                            *
                MODETAB=MT3270B,     DEFAULT MODE-TABLE                         *
                SSCPFM=USS3270,      NEEDED FOR 3271                            *
                USSTAB=USSBSC,       DEFAULT USS-TABLE                          *
                RETRIES=(7,10,3),    LINE/PU OPERAND                            *
                INHIBIT=SUBBLOCK,    DONT ALLOW SUBBLOCKS (APAR IR66242)        *
                CUTOFF=1,            CUTOFF AT 1 (APAR IR66242)                 *
                ITBMODE=(NO,NO)      NO INS IF ITB MODE.                        *
*-----------------------------------------------------------------------------*
*                                                                             *
*         LINE : LOO7DDDD                                                      *
*                                                                             *
```

Example 9.9. (cont.)

```
* DESTINATION : DDDDDDDD                                                        *
*         TEL : 0123 456789                                                     *
*     CONTACT : AARON USER                                                      *
*        LINK : K/S KXBF123456                                                  *
*         DTE : CASE DCX/860                                                    *
*                                                                               *
*-----------------------------------------------------------------------------*
*                                                                               *
L007DDDD LINE   ADDRESS=(07,HALF),POLIMIT=(1,QUEUE),POLLED=YES,                 *
                SESSION=33,NPACOLL=YES
*
P007S0    SERVICE ORDER=(P00700,T0070000,T0070001,T0070002,T0070003,           *
                T0070004,T0070005,T0070006,T0070007,T0070008,T0070009,          *
                T0070010,T0070011,T0070012,T0070013,T0070014,T0070015)
          SERVICE ORDER=(T0070016,T0070017,T0070018,T0070019,T0070020,         *
                T0070021,T0070022,T0070023,T0070024,T0070025,T0070026,          *
                T0070027,T0070028,T0070029,T0070030,T0070031)
P00700    CLUSTER CDATA=NO,GPOLL=40407F7F,FEATUR2=(MODEL2),                     *
                ISTATUS=ACTIVE,NPACOLL=YES
T0070000 TERMINAL TERM=3277,LOGAPPL=SESMGR,ADDR=60604040,POLL=40404040
T0070001 TERMINAL TERM=3277,LOGAPPL=SESMGR,ADDR=6060C1C1,POLL=4040C1C1
T0070002 TERMINAL TERM=3277,LOGAPPL=SESMGR,ADDR=6060C2C2,POLL=4040C2C2
T0070003 TERMINAL TERM=3277,LOGAPPL=SESMGR,ADDR=6060C3C3,POLL=4040C3C3
 .
 .
 .

T0070030 TERMINAL TERM=3284,ADDR=60605E5E,POLL=40405E5E,BFRDLAY=13,             *
                DIRECTN=OUT,USSTAB=USSPRT
T0070031 TERMINAL TERM=3284,ADDR=60605F5F,POLL=40405F5F,BFRDLAY=13,             *
                DIRECTN=OUT,USSTAB=USSPRT

 .
 .
 .

*******************************************************************************
* GV2419K2 LINE GROUP 2 — V24, 19.2 KB/S
*******************************************************************************
*
GV2419K2 GROUP LNCTL=SDLC,                                                      *
                TYPE=NCP,                                                       *
                SPEED=19200,        LINE OPERAND — LINE SPEED                   *
                CLOCKNG=EXT,        LINE OPERAND — MODEM CLOCKS                 *
                DUPLEX=FULL,        LINE OPERAND — HOLD RTS                     *
                NRZI=YES,           LINE OPERAND                                *
                RETRIES=(7,5,5),    LINE/PU OPERAND                             *
                ANS=STOP,           PU OPERAND — STOP ON AUTO NET SHUT          *
                PUTYPE=2,           PU OPERAND — TYPE                           *
                DLOGMOD=M32702S,    LU OPERAND—DEFAULT LOGMODE                  *
                MODETAB=MT3270R     LU OPERAND—MODE TABLE                       *
*                                                                              *
*-----------------------------------------------------------------------------*
*                                                                              *
*         LINE : L080FFFF                                                       *
*                                                                              *
* DESTINATION : FFFFFFFF                                                        *
*         TEL : 012 345 6789                                                    *
*     CONTACT : FRED USER                                                       *
*        LINK : K/S KXBF654321                                                  *
*         DTE : 3274                                                            *
*                                                                              *
```

Example 9.9. (cont.)

```
*-----------------------------------------------------------------------*
*                                                                       *
L080FFFF LINE  ADDRESS=(80,HALF)
*
         SERVICE ORDER=(P08000)
P08000   PU    ADDR=01
T0800000 LU    LOCADDR=02,LOGAPPL=SESMGR,                                *
               USSTAB=USSREMT
T0800001 LU    LOCADDR=03,LOGAPPL=SESMGR,                                *
               USSTAB=USSREMT
T0800002 LU    LOCADDR=04,LOGAPPL=SESMGR,                                *
               USSTAB=USSREMT
    .
    .

    .
T0800030 LU    LOCADDR=32
T0800031 LU    LOCADDR=33
    .

    .

    GENEND
    END
```

Example 9.9. (cont.)

- Terminal names are in the format Tnnnnnxx, where nnnnn is the number of the controller they are attached to and xx is their sequence number within the group of terminals on the controller.
- A descriptive panel is included for each line with information on the location and equipment it serves and who is the network contact at the site.

Note that in Example 9.9:

- The BUILD statement specifies general parameters for this NCP gen, of which only a few are shown here. Note in particular the NEWNAME parameter, which will determine the name given to the load module to be created in NCPLIB at generation time — this is the first thing you should change when starting to create the 'next' version of your NCP!
- The PCCU, HOST, and PATH statements define attached hosts and paths to them.
- Numerous other statements have been omitted from this example for the sake of simplicity.
- Line and device definitions follow a hierarchical pattern. Lines with similar characteristics are grouped together under a single GROUP statement. This is followed by a group of definitions for each line in the group. Each line definition in turn consists of a LINE statement, followed by a group of definitions for each cluster controller in the group. Each BSC controller is defined by a CLUSTER statement, followed by a TERMINAL statement for each device attached to it. Each SNA controller is defined by a PU statement, followed by a LU statement for each device attached to it. SNA and BSC

BSC group   SNA group

GROUP	GROUP
LINE	LINE
CLUSTER	PU
TERMINAL	LU
TERMINAL	LU
CLUSTER	PU
TERMINAL	LU
TERMINAL	LU
LINE	LINE
CLUSTER	PU
TERMINAL	LU

Figure 9.4. Structure of NCP terminal definition statements.

devices cannot be mixed in the same group, so you will end up with two types of GROUPs, with structures like those shown in Fig. 9.4.

- One nice feature of this hierarchy of definitions is the concept of filtering. This means that any relevant attributes defined on a higher level statement are automatically inherited by the associated statements below it in the hierarchy. So, for example, the DLOGMOD and MODETAB values specified on the GROUP statement labelled GV2419K2 in our example will be inherited by all the T08* LUs which belong to this group.
- In addition, SERVICE ORDER statements can be coded for each LINE to define the order in which devices on the line should be polled (for BSC devices, the individual terminals are given a service order, while for SNA devices, the various PUs attached to the line are given a service order).
- The definitions for line 07 service a third-party device emulating a remotely attached BSC-protocol 3274. (However, these particular devices have some unusual connections, so I would not recommend using these definitions as a model for a real BSC 3274.)
- The definitions for line 80 are for a more standard SNA connection to a 3274 device, servicing some terminals (the devices shown with LOGAPPL and USSTAB entries) and printers (the others). The PU and LU statements used here are very similar to those for locally attached SNA cluster controllers.

The purpose of this example is to help you feel comfortable enough with the structure of an NCP deck to make simple modifications to the definitions of remote cluster controllers and terminals. More substantial changes should be left to network experts. The previous section should have made clear that the process required to make even simple modifications to your NCP is far from simple and quick, so you should not contemplate updating your NCP on the spur of the moment to help you log on to your test system. Instead, consider other options, such as:

- Change your terminals around to match the NCP.

- Modify a locally attached terminal instead, by simply modifying the local major node and reactivating it (or even by a simple VTAM command, depending on the type of change).
- If you have a spare port on a local controller, plug your terminal into this and create the VTAM definitions required.
- Activate a cross-domain link to another system and log on to your test system from there.

References and bibliography

IBM manuals

1. *SNA Network Concepts and Products*, GC30–3072. Describes SNA concepts and the IBM hardware and software products which implement it.
2. *Network Program Products — Planning*, SC30–3351. Gives an overview of network configuration issues for VTAM and NCP.
3. *VTAM Installation and Resource Definition*, SC23–0111. Describes the definition of major nodes in VTAMLST, VTAM start options, etc., for releases up to 3.2.
4. *VTAM Resource Definition Reference*, SC31–6412. Describes definition of major nodes, tables, start options, etc., for release 3.3 onwards.
5. *NCP and SSP Resource Definition Guide*, SC30–3349. Describes the NCP generation process and how to define various types of resource to NCP.
6. *NCP and SSP Resource Definition Reference*, SC30–3254. Describes the NCP definition statements in detail.
7. *3725 Model 2 Introduction*, GA33–0021. Describes internal structure and other aspects of 3725 front-end processor.

Other

8. Weaver, B. J.: Getting Acquainted with the Network Control Program, *Mainframe Journal*, September 1989, pp. 26–32.
9. Ranade, J. and Sackett, G. C.: *Introduction to SNA Networking — A Guide for using VTAM/NCP*, McGraw-Hill, New York, 1989. A comprehensive introduction for those who need to know this subject in more depth.

10
TSO, ISPF, and ISPF/PDF implementation

10.1   Introduction

TSO, ISPF, and ISPF/PDF (abbreviated to PDF in this chapter) are essential tools for systems programmers, and indeed for most MIS staff and many end users. The installation and customization of these products will certainly be part of the MVS systems programmer's job. They are particularly important to the systems programmer, however, because the online browse-and-edit function they provide is essential for identifying and fixing most system problems. This means that as well as IPLing MVS and starting JES and VTAM, you must be able to use TSO, and preferably also ISPF and PDF, before you can recover from an MVS disaster. So it is essential for the systems programmer to understand how these products work and how to implement them.

TSO (Time sharing option) is a component of MVS which comes as part of the MVS base product. For a number of years, however, enhancements to TSO have been delivered as part of the licensed product TSO/E, which now includes so much of the function of TSO that it is virtually inseparable from the base product. Throughout this chapter I assume that you have TSO/E as well as base TSO, and refer to the two products interchangeably as 'TSO'.

Even TSO/E, however, provides an environment rather than a user friendly online service. For example, it is possible to perform browse-and-edit functions using the TSO EDIT line-editor (as discussed in Chapter 4), but this is an extremely cumbersome process. It is therefore necessary to add ISPF and PDF to provide a usable facility. ISPF provides the services necessary to build full-screen applications, and PDF is a ready-made application which uses ISPF services to provide program development facilities, such as browse, edit, and dataset utilities. The ISPF programs run in the environment provided by the user's TSO address space, and ISPF applications such as PDF in turn run in the environment provided by ISPF, using ISPF services to present screens, messages, etc., to the user. The PDF user is therefore sitting on top of a pyramid of environments, with MVS itself as the foundation, TSO on the ground floor, ISPF on the next level, and PDF at the apex. In this chapter we will start with TSO and work our way up!

```
//TSO       PROC MBR=TSOKEY00
//STEP1     EXEC PGM=IKTCAS00,TIME=1440
//PARMLIB    DD  DSN=SYS1.PARMLIB(&MBR),DISP=SHR,FREE=CLOSE
//PRINTOUT   DD  SYSOUT=*,FREE=CLOSE
```

Example 10.1. TCAS cataloged procedure.

10.2   TSO implementation

10.2.1 Starting up TCAS

TSO may use either TCAM or VTAM to handle terminal I/O. TCAM, however, is more or less obsolete now, and I therefore assume throughout this chapter that you will be using the VTAM version of TSO. To log on to TSO/VTAM, a user will enter a VTAM logon command from a terminal (or may simply select an option from a menu provided by a network front-end product, which will itself generate the logon command). This command will be passed by VTAM to the terminal control address space (TCAS), which will verify the sign-on attempt, including prompting the user for a password. Once it has done this, it will set up a separate address space for the sole use of this user. The logon procedure selected by the user will be used to define the initial allocation of datasets to this TSO session, the initial clist, and various startup parameters, and TCAS will initiate a VTAM session between the new address space and the user's terminal.

TCAS must therefore be available before any user can log on to TSO, and most installations will start it at IPL time by automatically issuing the command

```
S TSO
```

where TSO is the name of the TCAS cataloged procedure (you may use a different name in your installation, but I will assume you use TSO in the examples which follow). This cataloged procedure is very simple — see Example 10.1. You will probably never need to change the procedure supplied by IBM.

TCAS is normally not started until shortly after VTAM. If it is started too soon relative to VTAM, it will reach the point where it is ready to open its VTAM ACB before VTAM has activated the major node containing the TSO application. If this occurs, TCAS issues a console message and waits for a reply from the operator. To avoid this you should start up VTAM first, put the TSO major node early in the VTAM configuration list so it is activated quickly, and start TCAS after a short delay, when the ACB is likely to be available.

As should be clear from the cataloged procedure, the startup parameters for TCAS are normally held in member TSOKEY00 of SYS1.PARMLIB, although you may create alternative parameters and use the &MBR symbolic parameter to select them when you start TSO, e.g. by specifying:

```
S TSO,MBR=TSOKEY01
```

```
USERMAX=80,
RECONLIM=9,
BUFRSIZE=132,
HIBFREXT=6600,
LOBFREXT=3300,
CHNLEN=4,
SCRSIZE=1920
```

Example 10.2. TSOKEYxx member of SYS1.PARMLIB.

The TSOKEYxx member contains parameters relating to buffer sizes, screen sizes, etc. A typical member is shown in Example 10.2.

The USERMAX parameter specifies the maximum number of TSO users that will be allowed to log on concurrently — this can be overridden at TSO startup time by specifying the USERMAX parameter on the start command, for example:

```
S TSO,USERMAX=90
```

Alternatively, it can be changed dynamically using the modify command, for example:

```
F TSO,USERMAX=95
```

Note that the number of TSO users that can log on concurrently is also restricted by the number of TSOnnnn ACBs defined to VTAM, as discussed in Chapter 9. You may therefore have to add or activate an extra major node containing additional TSOnnnn minor nodes as well as raising USERMAX if you wish to raise the maximum number of users.

10.2.2 Requirements for user logons

Once TCAS has started, users may attempt to log on. For this to be successful, there are a number of requirements that must be satisfied:

1 There must be a VTAM ACB with a name in the format TSOnnnn available for them to connect to.
2 The user must specify a valid userid, either in the initial logon command, or when prompted for it by TCAS.
3 The user will then be presented with a full-screen logon menu, which asks them to enter a password, logon procedure, and various other parameters. Apart from the password, these parameters are saved from one session to the next, to minimize data entry. The user may only enter authorized values.
4 The selected logon procedure must be available in the TSO procedure library and be in a valid format. Any datasets the procedure attempts to allocate must be available.
5 If the procedure invokes an initial clist or REXX EXEC, this too must be present in the right library and be in a valid format.

We will consider each of these requirements in turn (except the VTAM ACBs,

```
//TSOPROC   PROC
//TSO       EXEC PGM=IKJEFT01,DYNAMNBR=50,TIME=1440
//SYSPROC   DD   DSN=SYS2.CLIST,DISP=SHR
//SYSPRINT  DD   TERM=TS,SYSOUT=*
//SYSTERM   DD   TERM=TS,SYSOUT=*
//SYSIN     DD   TERM=TS
```

Example 10.3. Basic TSO logon procedure.

which were discussed in Chapter 9). Note that the logon process can be modified using exits, and if this has been done, the process may not appear exactly as described above.

Userids and their logon authorizations are held in the UADS dataset (unless you take advantage of the facility offered by recent releases of RACF and third-party equivalents to replace UADS partially or completely for logon processing). An entry must be created in UADS for each user who is to be authorized to log on to TSO, and it must define various attributes of the users, including the logon procedures they are authorized to use. Defining entries for users in UADS is not generally part of the systems programmer's job, but there will be times when you need to do it, so you should understand the structure of UADS entries and the use of the ACCOUNT command to update them. These are discussed in Sect. 10.2.4.

At logon time, the user may select any of the procedure names defined in their UADS entry (or RACF profile), and TCAS will then pass this procedure name to JES. JES will search for this cataloged procedure in your TSO procedure library (see Sec. 8.2.2) and use this procedure when it starts up the address space for the TSO user.

Defining logon procedures is another part of the systems programmer's job. The contents of a logon procedure depend on what facilities you choose to make available to the users of the procedure, and on how you choose to implement them. Most of the potential complexities, however, are a result of introducing ISPF and products which run under it, and logon procedures for users who will only use 'raw' TSO are relatively simple. Example 10.3 is typical. Note that:

- The EXEC statement invokes the main TSO program, specifies TIME=1440 to prevent the user from abending S322 when an arbitrary time limit is reached, and uses the DYNAMNBR parameter to specify how many datasets may be dynamically allocated at any one time by the user. If you wish to execute an initial command or command procedure at logon time, you can specify this by using the PARM field to pass the command and parameters to TSO.
- The SYSPROC DD statement defines the default command procedure library to be used in this session — this is the concatenation which is searched for CLISTs or REXX EXECs when you enter a command procedure name at the TSO READY prompt. To make this logon procedure as robust as possible (i.e. to stop it failing with a JCL error if this library is uncataloged or deleted), you

could exclude this DD statement and use the TSO ALLOCATE command to allocate SYSPROC once you have logged on.

- The remaining DD statements define terminal datasets (the logical files corresponding to your keyboard input and screen output).

Once a user has succeeded in logging on with this logon procedure, they will be presented with the familiar READY prompt of raw TSO.

10.2.3 Customizing TSO commands

Raw TSO enables you to use command processors (compiled programs which may make use of TSO services) and command procedures (CLISTs and REXX EXECs), by typing the command name at the READY prompt. An experienced user can perform a vast range of activities using these fundamental facilities, some of which were described in Chapter 4. There are, however, some command customization tasks the systems programmer must perform to make certain commands work, and to control the usage of others.

IBM supplies a wide selection of command processors in SYS1.CMDLIB and SYS1.LINKLIB, and these libraries must therefore be available to the user's address space. In theory, this can be achieved by allocating them at logon time as part of the STEPLIB concatenation. It is far more efficient, though, to ensure that CMDLIB appears in the linklist as well as LINKLIB. Other TSO commands may be found in the LPA, as this avoids the real storage (or paging) overhead caused when many TSO users each load the same command module into the private area of their own address space.

Some command processors need to be APF authorized, and TSO uses a group of tables to determine which command processors are to be given control in an authorized state. These tables are in CSECTs IKJEFTE2, IKJEFTE8, and IKJEFTAP of the load module IKJTABLS in SYS1.LPALIB. Until TSO/E version 2.1 it was necessary to modify these tables with SMP/E USERMODs if you wished to change the IBM-supplied versions — this is documented in [4]. With 2.1 or later versions of TSO/E, however, you may use the IKJTSO00 member of SYS1.PARMLIB to specify user additions to these tables. This member is selected automatically at IPL time, and its function has gradually been extended to cover other parameters, including default values for various TSO commands. It is also used to list commands which are not supported in the background, another function which could previously only be performed by modifying IKJTABLS (CSECT IKJEFTNS in this case).

A typical IKJTSO00 member is shown in Example 10.4. Note that:

- As the example shows, a significant number of IBM-supplied commands need to be authorized via IKJTSO00 or they will not work!
- The SEND statement allows you to specify defaults for the TSO SEND command, including whether messages sent using this command should be

```
/* LIB: SYS1.PARMLIB(IKJTSO00)                                       */
/*                                                                   */
AUTHCMD NAMES(          /* AUTHORIZED COMMANDS        */    +
   RECEIVE             /* TSO COMMANDS               */    +
   TRANSMIT XMIT       /*                            */    +
   LISTB    LISTBC     /*                            */    +
   SE       SEND       /*                            */    +
   RACONVRT            /*                            */    +
   SYNC                /*                            */    +
   LISTD    LISTDS     /*                            */    +
   IKJEHDS1            /*                            */    +
   TESTAUTH TESTA      /*                            */    +
   PARMLIB  IKJPRMLB   /*                            */    +
   ALTER               /* DFP COMMANDS               */    +
   DEF      DEFINE     /* DFP COMMANDS               */    +
   IMP      IMPORT     /* DFP COMMANDS               */    +
          )            /*                            */
                       /*                            */
AUTHPGM NAMES(         /* AUTHORIZED PROGRAMS        */      +
   IEBCOPY             /*                            */      +
          )            /*                            */
                       /*                            */
NOTBKGND NAMES(        /* COMMANDS WHICH MAY NOT BE  */  +
                       /* ISSUED IN THE BACKGROUND   */  +
   OPER     OPERATOR   /*                            */  +
   TERM     TERMINAL)  /*                            */
                       /*                            */
AUTHTSF NAMES(         /* PROGRAMS TO BE AUTHORIZED  */  +
                       /* WHEN CALLED THROUGH THE    */  +
                       /* TSO SERVICE FACILITY.      */  +
   IEBCOPY             /*                            */  +
   IKJEFF76)           /*                            */
                       /*                            */
SEND                   /* SEND COMMAND DEFAULTS      */  +
   OPERSEND(ON)        /*                            */  +
   USERSEND(ON)        /*                            */  +
   SAVE(ON)            /*                            */  +
   CHKBROD(OFF)        /*                            */  +
   LOGNAME(SYS1.BRODCAST)  /*                        */
ALLOCATE               /* ALLOCATE COMMAND DEFAULT   */  +
   DEFAULT(OLD)        /*                            */
TRANSREC NODESMF((NODENAME,SMF)) /* XMIT/RECEIVE DEFAULTS */  +
   CIPHER(YES)         /*                            */  +
   SPOOLCL(B)          /*                            */  +
   OUTWARN(50000,15000) /*                           */  +
   OUTLIM(5000000)     /*                            */  +
   VIO(SYSALLDA)       /*                            */  +
   LOGSEL(LOG)         /*                            */  +
   LOGNAME(MISC)       /*                            */  +
   DAPREFIX(TUPREFIX)  /*                            */  +
   USRCTL(NAMES.TEXT)  /*                            */  +
   SYSOUT(*)           /*                            */
```

Example 10.4. IKJTSO00 member of SYS1.PARMLIB.

stored in SYS1.BRODCAST (the default), or whether each user should have their own message log dataset. If you find that SYS1.BRODCAST is being heavily accessed and this is causing performance problems, you should consider setting up user message logs — otherwise stick with SYS1.BRODCAST.

- The TRANSREC statement allows you to specify defaults for the TRANSMIT and RECEIVE commands (also known as interactive data transmission facility — IDTF). These defaults could formerly only be overridden by modifying the IBM-supplied version of the INMXPARM CSECT of load module IKJTABLS (see [4] for more details on doing this). If you are activating TRANSMIT and RECEIVE for the first time on your system, [3] contains a useful list of the customization actions (including possible JES changes) required.
- If you have MVS/ESA and TSO/E version 2 or higher, you can change the version of IKJTSOxx in force using the TSO PARMLIB command.

You may also have to set up other TSO/E facilities such as the information centre facility or the session manager if your users require them. Installation and customization actions for these products are also documented in [3] and [4].

10.2.4 TSO user administration

Although user administration is not generally a systems programming function, you will need to know how to set up TSO userids in order to allow yourself and other users to log on to test systems. You must therefore familiarize yourself with the structure of the UADS dataset, which contains details of authorized TSO users, and the TSO ACCOUNT command, which is provided to administer changes to UADS. If your site has replaced UADS with RACF or an equivalent product, you should also learn how to administer TSO userids using the security product. But remember, you will still need to use the ACCOUNT command to set up userids in UADS for use when the security system is unavailable. You should also be familiar with the other activities required when setting up new TSO users. This section deals with these issues; it does not, however, cover the wider questions of security policy, which are picked up in Chapter 15.

The UADS dataset contains one entry for each user who is authorized to log on to TSO. These entries may, however, be very simple or quite complex, depending on the range of facilities which are to be made available to the user. Each user may have one or more passwords defined; for each password they may have one or more account numbers defined; for each account number they may have one or more procedure names defined; and for each procedure they will usually have a set of other attributes defined.

In theory, this tree structure could become very complex. However, in practice, it should not. For example, if you use RACF or an equivalent product the user will have to specify their RACF password to log on to TSO rather than the password in the UADS, so there is no point in specifying multiple passwords for users.

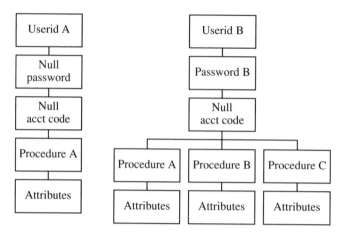

Figure 10.1. Structure of typical UADS entries.

Indeed, there is no point in specifying any password at all, unless you anticipate using TSO when RACF is not available, e.g. on an emergency recovery system. TSO therefore allows you to make the password a null field. Likewise, it is usually possible to avoid multiple account codes for one user, and if you do not perform any accounting activities on your TSO users, you may make the account code a null field as well.

If you can keep the number of passwords and account codes down to one per user, you are therefore left with a relatively simple structure, like that illustrated in Fig. 10.1. Here we have two types of user: users with one logon procedure (like userid A) and users with more than one (like userid B). The vast majority should fall in the former group, but a few users will require multiple logon procedures. Systems programmers themselves are the most likely group to need more than one; in addition to their standard logon procedure, they may need one which they can use to test changes to the logon procedure, and one with minimal facilities which they can use in emergencies (see Example 10.6).

User definitions in UADS are created, listed, modified, and deleted using the TSO ACCOUNT command, with which you should become familiar. Like the EDIT and TEST commands discussed in Chapter 4, once you have entered the ACCOUNT command the READY prompt is replaced with the ACCOUNT prompt, and instead of entering TSO commands, you may now only enter ACCOUNT subcommands.

The main subcommands are:

- HELP Used to obtain descriptions of the other subcommands
- LIST Lists the contents of one or more UADS entries (see Example 10.5)
- ADD Used to add entries to UADS, or additional passwords, account codes, or procedures to existing entries
- CHANGE Changes existing entries

```
   SYS001     USER ATTRIBUTES:  NOOPER    ACCT   JCL  NOMOUNT    RECOVER
              INSTALLATION ATTRIBUTES, IN HEX: 0000
              MAXSIZE:     3072K BYTES
              USER PROFILE TABLE:
              000000000000000000000000A3000000 SYS001
              DESTINATION  =  CENTRAL SITE DEFAULT
              HOLD MSGCLASS=  (DEFAULT)
              JOB CLASS    =  (DEFAULT)
              MESSAGE CLASS=  (DEFAULT)
              SYSOUT CLASS =  (DEFAULT)
              NO PERFORMANCE GROUPS
      SYS001
        SYSTSOELDERVASS
          SYSPROC   PROCSIZE=    3072K, UNIT NAME= WORK
          CRISIS    PROCSIZE=    1024K, UNIT NAME= WORK
          TESTPROC  PROCSIZE=    2048K, UNIT NAME= WORK
IKJ56590I LISTED
```

Example 10.5. Output from LIST subcommand of ACCOUNT.

- DELETE Used to delete whole entries, or individual passwords, account codes, or procedure names from entries

The ACCOUNT subcommands are fully documented in [6].
Note that in Example 10.5:

- The output from the LIST (SYS001) subcommand is given, which shows the UADS entry for userid SYS001. This user has one password (SYS001) and one account code (SYSTSOELDERVASS), with three logon procedures (SYSPROC, CRISIS, and TESTPROC).
- MAXSIZE determines the maximum region size the user is allowed to request at logon time, and the PROCSIZE for each procedure determines the default region size when the user selects the procedure concerned — although this will be overridden by any value the user codes on their sign-on screen, up to the limit set by MAXSIZE.
- The UNIT NAME you assign for each procedure determines what default unit name TSO will use when it attempts to allocate datasets for the user. This unit name is often used for allocating temporary datasets, and it is important to set it to a value which conforms to your DASD allocation policy. If you do not, you may find TSO users' datasets cropping up in all sorts of unexpected places, or, if you use security products to prevent this, TSO users will experience repeated security violations which they cannot resolve without your assistance.
- Some of the other attributes determine whether the user can use certain TSO commands — JCL, for example, allows them to use the SUBMIT command (also required if they are to submit jobs using the SUBMIT command in PDF EDIT), while NOJCL would prevent this. OPER allows them to use the OPER command, which permits them to emulate a system console, while ACCT allows them to use the ACCOUNT command itself. It is good security practice to restrict the use of the ACCOUNT command to systems programmers and

security administrators; it is probably unnecessary for anyone to have OPER now that SDSF provides more powerful and user friendly console-like facilities to selected users.

If you are using RACF version 1.8 or higher, you may dispense with the ACCOUNT command and do all your TSO user administration from RACF instead, using the ADDUSER, ALTUSER, and LISTUSER commands. This has the great advantage of keeping all your user security information in one place, so that it is: (a) always mutually consistent; and (b) easier to maintain. You will still, however, have to assign the same types of attributes to users, and I would advise keeping a very basic copy of UADS around so systems programmers can bring up a system without RACF and log on to it in an emergency. Administration of TSO users from RACF is documented in [7] and [8].

Alternatively, if you have activated the information centre facility (ICF), you may use the ICF ENROLL option to add and amend TSO user definitions. This allows you to define users to both TSO/E and RACF at the same time, and also do some of the supplementary user setup activities discussed next. The ENROLL option is documented in [5].

However you set up a new TSO user, you will need to ensure that certain resources are available to them when they first try to log on.

Many products assume that you will follow the normal convention of providing an alias in your master catalog for each TSO user, with the same name as the userid, so that each user can set up their own datasets using their userid as the high-level qualifier. To keep life simple, I recommend you follow the convention, and ensure that your procedure for setting up new users also includes the creation of a corresponding alias.

Some products assume that the prefix defined for the user in their TSO profile will also be equal to their userid — this prefix is automatically attached to dataset names entered without quotes in numerous TSO commands and on many ISPF panels. The default prefix is the user's userid for foreground sessions and null for background sessions (i.e. TSO in batch), and can only be changed by logging on to the userid and issuing the TSO PROFILE PREFIX command — a tedious process if you are setting up lots of new users. This is another good reason for using the userid as the high-level qualifier for the user's own datasets.

Users who will use ISPF (the vast majority in most installations) will need an ISPF profile dataset, which you may choose to create at user setup time. It is common, however, to set this up automatically in the ISPF logon clist if it is not already present (see Example 10.8).

This leads us nicely on to the issue of providing ISPF services to TSO users, the subject of our next section.

10.3   ISPF and PDF implementation

There are few things more infuriating than IPLing your test system, watching JES2, VTAM, and TSO come up smoothly, and logging on to TSO successfully, only to find that you cannot get into ISPF and PDF. Of course, it should be possible to locate the datasets you need, allocate them dynamically from the READY prompt, and start up ISPF or, having found the datasets, to use TSO EDIT to set up a suitable logon procedure or clist. But in practice that is a long, painful, process, and one you will want to avoid.

To ensure you can get into ISPF first time, you need to:

1 Find or create (and catalog) the datasets that ISPF needs.
2 Set up a logon procedure which allocates these datasets, or which invokes a logon clist to allocate them, and then starts ISPF.
3 Create a menu structure for your ISPF session which gives you access to the facilities you require.

To implement ISPF for your users, there is one other significant step that may be required:

4 Make any necessary additions to the ISPF TSO command table (ISPTCM).

There are other optional customization processes for ISPF and PDF, but these four are the essentials. The rest of this section covers these four processes.

10.3.1 ISPF datasets

ISPF provides the facility for TSO users to engage in full-screen dialogs with applications. The application must provide the various components of the dialog in the correct ISPF datasets, and it is these datasets which must be allocated before you can go into ISPF. The main components of an ISPF dialog are: CLISTs or REXX EXECs, programs, panels, messages, skeletons, tables, and profiles.

CLISTs or REXX EXECs

These usually control the dialog at the highest level, invoking screens and passing control to various subroutines depending on the processing selected by the user. They can also be invoked as subroutines. CLISTs must exist in the SYSPROC concatenation found in normal ISPF processing, and REXX EXECs must be in either the SYSPROC or the SYSEXEC concatenation (you have to modify the REXX CSECT IRXTSPRM to activate searching of SYSEXEC). While it makes more sense in some way to keep your EXECs in SYSEXEC libraries, as these are searched first and are dedicated to EXECs, note that TSO does not currently support the use of VLF for SYSEXEC, although it does for SYSPROC. There is therefore a performance benefit from keeping EXECs in SYSPROC and using VLF. If you have TSO/E version 2.1 or higher and MVS/ESA, you may also use the ALTLIB command to concatenate 'user' and 'application' CLIST and EXEC libraries in front of the standard concatenations.

Programs

These can also perform the functions of high-level control or of subroutines within a dialog. It is generally much simpler to code an ISPF CLIST or an EXEC than to create an ISPF program, but programs can perform considerably faster than these alternatives and can carry out more complex processing than might otherwise be possible. You may therefore find them being used for ISPF functions which must give a rapid response, or which are highly complex. ISPF programs should normally be placed in the ISPLLIB concatenation, though they may also be found in linklist libraries or the LPA.

Panels

Each ISPF panel describes a screen which is to be presented to the user, and some of the initial processing of the data entered by the user. For example, data validation rules can be included in the panel definition, as well as statements which select the next process to be performed on the basis of the user's response. There are several types of ISPF panel:

- MENU panels, which allow the user to select the next ISPF function to be performed
- Data entry panels
- Table display panels, which may allow scrolling and updating of the table
- Information-only panels, such as help screens

Panels must exist in the ISPPLIB concatenation to be used by ISPF.

Messages

ISPF messages are held in members of datasets in the ISPMLIB concatenation.

Skeletons

An ISPF skeleton is a file containing partially completed data and formatting instructions for the inclusion of data to complete the file. It is used by the file-tailoring services of ISPF to create completed files at execution time. The most typical use is to create and submit pieces of JCL. Say, for example, you wish to submit a job to backup a dataset from an ISPF dialog, but the name of the dataset to be backed up is to be entered by the user on a panel. You would create a skeleton containing the backup JCL, with a variable at the location where the dataset name was required. File-tailoring services could then be used to combine the skeleton with the dataset name entered by the user to create the correct JCL for the backup job at invocation time. Skeletons are held in the ISPSLIB concatenation.

Table 10.1. Typical ISPF library names

Product	Library names
ISPF	ISP.VaRbMc.ISPxLIB
PDF	ISR.VaRbMc.ISRxLIB
SDSF	ISF.VaRbMc.ISFxLIB
DFP(ISMF)	SYS1.DGTxLIB
DFHSM	SYS1.DFQxLIB
DFSORT	SYS1.ICEISPx
SMP/E	GIM.SGIMxyyy

Tables

ISPF tables are permanent or temporary pseudo-direct-access files which may be created, updated, and deleted by ISPF dialogs. Tables are loaded from the ISPTLIB concatenation and saved by default in the ISPTABL dataset.

Profiles

Each user must have an ISPF profile dataset, which is used to store details of their personal defaults. Examples include:

- The default dataset for PDF BROWSE and EDIT
- PDF EDIT profiles
- PF key setup

The profile dataset must be allocated to the DDNAME ISPPROF.

Typically, each product which uses ISPF to provide an application to TSO users will have a SYSPROC, an ISPPLIB, an ISPMLIB, and perhaps also a SYSEXEC, an ISPLLIB, an ISPSLIB, an ISPTLIB, and a table output dataset with its own DDNAME. In addition, ISPF itself provides libraries for most of these DDNAMEs. To provide a number of alternative applications to a user, you must therefore concatenate their ISPF libraries together. Some of the IBM products which include ISPF facilities, and their typical ISPF library names, are listed in Table 10.1. (Lower case characters are variables, with x indicating the usage of the library: P for panel, M for message, etc.).

The following section illustrates how to allocate the necessary libraries to each concatenation.

10.3.2 Logon procedures and clists for ISPF

Once you have established what ISPF libraries you are going to need, you must allocate them to your TSO session, then invoke ISPF. The slow way to do this is by using the ALLOCATE command at the READY prompt, then issuing the ISPSTART command, but you will not want to do this unless you have to! The alternatives are to allocate the datasets you need in your logon procedure then use

```
//PDFPROC  PROC
//PDFPROC  EXEC PGM=IKJEFT01,DYNAMNBR=180,TIME=1440
//*-----------------------------------------------------------------*
//*   TSO DATASETS                                                  *
//*-----------------------------------------------------------------*
//SYSPRINT DD  TERM=TS,SYSOUT=*
//SYSTERM  DD  TERM=TS,SYSOUT=*
//SYSIN    DD  TERM=TS
//SYSLBC   DD  DSN=SYS1.BRODCAST,DISP=SHR
//SYSUADS  DD  DSN=SYS1.UADS,DISP=SHR
//*-----------------------------------------------------------------*
//*   ISPF  DATASETS                                                *
//*-----------------------------------------------------------------*
//ISPPROF  DD  DSN=SYS001.ISPF.ISPPROF,DISP=OLD
//SYSPROC  DD  DSN=ISR.V3R2M0.ISRCLIB,DISP=SHR
//SYSEXEC  DD  DSN=ISP.V3R2M0.ISPEXEC,DISP=SHR
//ISPPLIB  DD  DSN=ISR.V3R2M0.ISRPENU,DISP=SHR
//         DD  DSN=ISP.V3R2M0.ISPPENU,DISP=SHR
//         DD  DSN=ISF.V1R3M0.ISFPLIB,DISP=SHR
//ISPMLIB  DD  DSN=ISR.V3R2M0.ISRMENU,DISP=SHR
//         DD  DSN=ISP.V3R2M0.ISPMENU,DISP=SHR
//ISPSLIB  DD  DSN=ISR.V3R2M0.ISRSENU,DISP=SHR
//         DD  DSN=ISP.V3R2M0.ISPSLIB,DISP=SHR
//ISPTLIB  DD  DSN=ISP.V3R2M0.ISPTENU,DISP=SHR
//         DD  DSN=ISR.V3R2M0.ISRTLIB,DISP=SHR
//         DD  DSN=ISF.V1R3M0.ISFTLIB,DISP=SHR
```

Example 10.6. Minimal ISPF, PDF, and SDSF logon procedure.

the PARM field on the EXEC statement to invoke ISPF, or to put both the allocation and the startup into a CLIST or EXEC which is invoked from the PARM field. We will look at these two alternatives in turn.

Example 10.6 shows a logon procedure which allocates the bare minimum of datasets required to use ISPF, PDF, and SDSF. Note that:

- A logon procedure like this is handy for emergencies, or initial testing of a CBIPO system, as it provides the essential PDF facilities with the minimum of dataset allocations — and therefore the minimum risk of JCL errors.
- The ISPPROF allocation here is personal to the user concerned, which means that this logon procedure can only be used by one user. This is highly impractical for most purposes, so it is almost universal to allocate ISPPROF from an initial EXEC or CLIST instead. A clist can use the &SYSUID variable to supply the current userid, which is then used as the high-level qualifier for the ISPPROF dataset allocation (see the logon clist shown in Example 10.8).
- Note also that no ISPLLIB libraries have been allocated. This is not because ISPF, PDF, and SDSF do not use programs — they use them heavily — but the program libraries for these products should be in the linklist (and some of their programs in the LPA) for best performance.
- Some of the 'LIB' extensions have been replaced by 'ENU' extensions — this simply indicates that there are different national language versions of these libraries available and we are using the US English version. Remember that

```
//ISPINIT  PROC
//ISPINIT  EXEC PGM=IKJEFT01,DYNAMNBR=150,TIME=1440,
//         PARM='%ISPINIT'
//SYSPROC  DD  DISP=SHR,DSN=SYS9.CMDPROC
//SYSPRINT DD  TERM=TS,SYSOUT=*
//SYSTERM  DD  TERM=TS,SYSOUT=*
//SYSIN    DD  TERM=TS
```

Example 10.7. Logon procedure invoking ISPF startup clist.

  MENU in these dataset names means 'US English message library' rather than
  the more obvious interpretation!
- SDSF is an unusual ISPF application, which uses programs heavily and in a
  non-standard way. This is the reason it does not use a message library.
- This procedure will leave the user at the TSO READY prompt. At this point
  the user may start ISPF and go straight into the main PDF menu by entering
  the PDF command. This command could, of course, have been supplied in the
  PARM field of the EXEC statement instead. The default PDF menu does not
  include an option for SDSF, but SDSF can be invoked by entering TSO SDSF
  on the command line.

Most TSO users will require more facilities than we have allocated libraries for
in this logon procedure. We could provide them by adding further datasets to the
concatenations, and setting up different logon procedures for users with different
requirements. This, however, can easily get out of control, so I recommend you use
a CLIST or EXEC instead to allocate ISPF datasets for all circumstances other
than emergencies.

Example 10.7 shows a logon procedure which invokes a clist to start ISPF, and
Example 10.8 shows the clist it uses. Note that in these examples:

- The ISPINIT procedure here allocates the minimum number of permanent
  datasets, i.e. one, the SYSPROC dataset containing the initial clist. This
  minimises the risk of a JCL error due to missing datasets. The PARM field of
  the EXEC statement is then used to issue an initial command, which invokes
  the ISPINIT clist. This clist then performs all the allocations required by ISPF,
  including deallocating and reallocating the SYSPROC dataset itself.
- If an ISPF profile dataset does not already exist for the user, it will be created
  by the clist. ISPF assigns default values to the profile variables when it finds the
  profile dataset is empty, and the user may then customize these to their own
  personal taste. You may prefer, however, to pre-allocate the ISPF profile
  dataset for a user when you set the user up. This simplifies the logon clist a little,
  although it does mean that if a user's profile dataset is deleted their next logon
  attempt will fail. If you wish to set up site-specific defaults in new profile
  datasets, e.g. for PF keys, you can do this by copying in an existing profile
  dataset immediately after creating the new one. This should be equally simple
  whether the dataset is pre-allocated or created in the logon clist.

```
PROC 0
/*------------------------------------------------------------------*/
/*  ISPINIT - ISPF STARTUP CLIST                                    */
/*------------------------------------------------------------------*/

    CONTROL MAIN NOFLUSH NOMSG NOSYMLIST NOCONLIST NOLIST

/*------------------------------------------------------------------*/
/*  ALLOCATE ISPPROF                                                */
/*------------------------------------------------------------------*/

    FREE FILE(ISPPROF)
    FREE FILE(ISPCTL1,ISPCTL2,ISPCTL3)
    SET &DSNAME = &SYSUID..ISPF.ISPPROF
    ALLOC FI(ISPPROF) SHR  DA('&DSNAME.')
    IF &LASTCC NE 0 THEN +
      DO
      FREE FI(ISPCRTE)
      CONTROL MSG
      ATTRIB ISPCRTE DSORG(PO) RECFM(F B) LRECL(80) BLKSIZE(23440)
      ALLOC DA('&DSNAME.') SP(2,1) TRACKS DIR(2) USING(ISPCRTE) +
          FI(ISPPROF) VOLUME(TSOVOL) UNIT(3380)
      IF &LASTCC = 0 THEN +
        WRITE *** ISPF PROFILE DATA SET '&DSNAME.' HAS BEEN CREATED
      ELSE +
        DO
        WRITE  *** UNABLE TO ALLOCATE PROFILE DATA SET '&DSNAME.'
        GOTO CEND
        END
      CONTROL NOMSG
      END
/*------------------------------------------------------------------*/
/*  ASSIGN USERTYPE AND INITIAL PANEL                               */
/*------------------------------------------------------------------*/

    IF &SUBSTR(1:3,&SYSUID) = &STR(SYS) THEN +
      DO
      SET &USERTYPE = SYS
      SET &FIRSTPAN = SYSPANEL
      END

    IF &SUBSTR(1:3,&SYSUID) = &STR(DEV) THEN +
      SET &FIRSTPAN = DEVPANEL

    IF &SUBSTR(1:3,&SYSUID) = &STR(DPC) THEN +
      SET &FIRSTPAN = DATPANEL
/*------------------------------------------------------------------*/
/*  SPECIFY COMMON DATASETS                                         */
/*------------------------------------------------------------------*/

    SET &P1 = 'SYS2.PANEL'              /* IN-HOUSE APPLS   */
    SET &E1 = 'SYS2.REXX'              /* IN-HOUSE APPLS   */
    SET &C1 = 'SYS2.CLIST'            /* IN-HOUSE APPLS   */
    SET &M1 = 'SYS2.MLIB'            /* IN-HOUSE APPLS   */
    SET &S1 = 'SYS2.SLIB'            /* IN-HOUSE APPLS   */
    SET &T1 = 'SYS2.TLIB'            /* IN-HOUSE APPLS   */

    SET &M2 = 'ISR.V3R2M0.ISRMENU'     /* PDF             */
    SET &S2 = 'ISR.V3R2M0.ISRSENU'     /* PDF             */
    SET &C2 = 'ISR.V3R2M0.ISRCLIB'     /* PDF             */
    SET &P2 = 'ISR.V3R2M0.ISRPENU'     /* PDF             */
```

Example 10.8. ISPF startup CLIST.

```
    SET &T2 = 'ISP.V3R2M0.ISPTENU'            /* ISPF               */

    SET &M3 = 'ISP.V3R2M0.ISPMENU'            /* ISPF               */
    SET &S3 = 'ISP.V3R2M0.ISPSLIB'            /* ISPF               */
    SET &P3 = 'ISP.V3R2M0.ISPPENU'            /* ISPF               */
    SET &E3 = 'ISP.V3R2M0.ISPEXEC'            /* ISPF               */

    SET &T3 = 'ISR.V3R2M0.ISRTLIB'            /* PDF                */

    SET &L4 = 'SYS1.DFQLLIB'                   /* HSM                */
    SET &M4 = 'SYS1.DFQMLIB'                   /* HSM                */
    SET &P4 = 'SYS1.DFQPLIB'                   /* HSM                */
    SET &T4 = 'SYS1.DFQTLIB'                   /* HSM                */

    SET &P5 = 'ISF.V1R3M0.ISFPLIB'            /* SDSF               */
    SET &T5 = 'ISF.V1R3M0.ISFTLIB'            /* SDSF               */
/*-----------------------------------------------------------------*/
/*   SPECIFY RESTRICTED DATASETS                                   */
/*-----------------------------------------------------------------*/
    IF &USERTYPE = SYS THEN +
    DO
    SET &T6 = 'SYS3.SMPXA.OTABLES'            /* SMPTABL
    SET &L7 = 'GIM.SGIMLMDO'                   /* SMP/E
    SET &M7 = 'GIM.SGIMMENU'                   /* SMP/E
    SET &P7 = 'GIM.SGIMPENU'                   /* SMP/E
    SET &S7 = 'GIM.SGIMSENU'                   /* SMP/E
    SET &T7 = 'GIM.SGIMTENU'                   /* SMP/E
    END
/*-----------------------------------------------------------------*/
/*   ALLOCATE ISPXLIBS                                             */
/*-----------------------------------------------------------------*/
ALLOC1: +
    FREE F(SYSPROC,ISPPLIB,ISPMLIB,ISPSLIB,ISPLLIB,ISPTLIB,ISPTABL)
/*
/* ALLOCATE SYSPROC
/*
    ALLOC F(SYSPROC) BLKSIZE(9040) SHR +
        DA(&C1,&C2,&C3,&C4,&C5,&C6,&C7,&C8,&C9)
    IF &LASTCC > 0 THEN +
        DO
        WRITE CLIST FAILURE ALLOCATING SYSPROC. CONTACT SYSTEMS
        GOTO CEND
        END
/*
/* ALLOCATE SYSEXEC
/*
    ALLOC F(SYSEXEC) BLKSIZE(9040) SHR +
        DA(&E1,&E2,&E3,&E4,&E5,&E6,&E7,&E8,&E9)
    IF &LASTCC > 0 THEN +
        DO
        WRITE CLIST FAILURE ALLOCATING SYSEXEC. CONTACT SYSTEMS
        GOTO CEND
        END
  .
  .
  .
(here allocate ISPLLIB, ISPPLIB, ISPMLIB, ISPSLIB, and ISPTLIB with
code similar to that for SYSPROC and SYSEXEC above)
  .
  .
  .
```

Example 10.8. (cont.)

```
/*------------------------------------------------------------*/
/*   ALLOCATE SYSHELP                                         */
/*------------------------------------------------------------*/
    FREE F(SYSHELP)
    ALLOC F(SYSHELP) SHR  DA('SYS1.HELP')
    IF &LASTCC > 0 THEN +
       DO
       WRITE CLIST FAILURE ALLOCATING SYSHELP. CONTACT SYSTEMS
       GOTO CEND
       END
/*------------------------------------------------------------*/
/*   ALLOCATE EXTRA FILES FOR SYSPROGS                        */
/*------------------------------------------------------------*/
    IF &USERTYPE = SYS THEN +
       DO
       ALLOC F(ISPTABL) DA('SYS2.TLIB') SHR
       IF &LASTCC > 0 THEN +
          DO
          WRITE CLIST FAILURE ALLOCATING ISPTABL. CONTACT SYSTEMS
    GOTO CEND
    END
    .
    .
    .
(here allocate SMPTLIB, SYSUADS, and SYSLBC with code similar to
that for ISPTABL above)
    .
    .
    .
       END
/*------------------------------------------------------------*/
/*   START ISPF AND RETURN                                    */
/*------------------------------------------------------------*/
 ISPSTART PANEL(&FIRSTPAN) NEWAPPL(ISR)
CEND: +
 WRITE *--------------------------------------------*
 WRITE *   HAVE A NICE DAY                          *
 WRITE *--------------------------------------------*
 EXIT
END
```

Example 10.8. (cont.)

- This clist also addresses the issue of allocating different libraries and menu structures to different types of user, without the need to maintain many different but partially duplicated logon procedures or logon clists. It is much easier to maintain a single logon clist than several, particularly when a product upgrade leads to a change in the names of the libraries which must be allocated for ISPF applications. In this example, the dataset and initial menu allocation are based on the first three characters of the userid, which keeps the logic simple and the amount of conditional processing down (hence speeding up execution). If you cannot do this, though, there are other alternatives. For example, you could maintain one logon clist but invoke it from several logon procedures, each identical to ISPINIT in Example 10.7, except for a parameter passed to the ISPINIT clist. The clist could then use this parameter to determine what datasets and initial menus to allocate. This option still averts the need to maintain several similar procedures and clists (the procedures are so simple they should never need to change), but allows you to assign different logon options to users simply by assigning different logon procedures. It also offers an easy migration path when you start off with many different logon procedures and wish to consolidate them to simplify maintenance.

• Symbolic parameters for dataset names help to keep the clist relatively simple and well structured, again for easy maintenance.

• Inline documentation is essential for the same purpose — if your allocation of options to different user groups becomes at all complex, it is worth document-ing this in a comment box at the front of the clist.

• The SYS2 libraries allocated here are used for inhouse-developed applications. You should definitely create inhouse libraries for this purpose, which can then be migrated easily across upgrades of the operating system and externally supplied ISPF applications.

• Note also the use of the PANEL parameter on the ISPSTART command to control the selection of the initial menu panel.

The major disadvantage of allocating large numbers of datasets in a clist like this (and using lots of conditional logic) is that logging on to ISPF can become dreadfully slow. Up to a point, you can argue that this delay is not serious, as it only occurs once per user session. However, this excuse cannot be stretched too far, so you should also make an effort to keep down the logon time. The easiest approach is to keep the clist as simple as possible, with the minimum amount of allocations and the minimum amount of conditional logic, but there are other alternatives. For example, you could use VLF to keep the logon clist in a dataspace, cutting out the I/O required to load it from disk and the first phase of clist processing (tokenizing of the clist). Or you could try using REXX instead (this may be fractionally faster than clist — but a better reason to move to REXX is the long-term future guaranteed for it by its place in IBM's SAA strategy). Replacing your logon clist with a program which does the same processing is not recommended, although this would undoubtedly be faster, because of the greater difficulty of maintaining programs.

Ultimately, however, the component of the logon process which usually takes most time is the allocation (and opening) of the datasets required, and this will not be a great deal faster with any of these approaches. The most extreme way to speed this up is to slash the number of allocations by combining all the panel libraries into one dataset, all the clist libraries into one, and so on for all the ISPF datasets. I am not enthusiastic about this approach, because of the difficulty of managing software upgrades with such a configuration. Perhaps better is to tackle the problem indirectly, by speeding up the components of the allocation and open processes. Caching volumes containing ISPF datasets, for example, could make a spectacular difference here, as could action to speed up security authorization at open time (e.g. caching your RACF datasets and/or using global access checking to eliminate accesses to the RACF database altogether).

10.3.3 ISPF menu structures

In our discussion of logon clists, we saw that the PANEL parameter of the ISPSTART command can be used to select the initial menu (the default is ISP@MSTR if you use the ISPSTART command and ISR@PRIM if you use the ISPF or PDF command). The member with this name will be loaded from the ISPPLIB concatenation and used to construct the menu presented on the user's screen. Example 10.9 shows a typical ISPF main menu definition. Note that:

- The BODY section of the panel definition describes what is to be presented to the user on the screen. Most of what you enter in this section appears exactly as you enter it here on the user's screen, although variables (strings beginning with &) are substituted with their current values before displaying them, and certain special characters are used to define the nature of the fields that follow. By default, for example, the % character defines a highlighted protected field (i.e. an output-only field); the + character defines a normal protected field; and the _ character defines an unprotected field (i.e. an input field). When you define an input field, the characters following the _ define the name of the field, so that you can use this as a variable in the processing sections of the panel definition.
- The INIT section initializes panel variables and does other processing required before the panel is displayed. As long as you do not change the name of the variable used to hold the user's selection you should never need to change this on a menu panel.
- The PROC section does the processing required after the user has entered their input. Once again, you need not be familiar with all the details of this as you can leave the complicated bits unchanged for any menu panel. The important part of the processing on a menu panel is the statement:

```
&ZSEL = TRANS (&GENVAR1 . . .
```

This statement uses the function TRANS (translate) to set the value of the variable &ZSEL depending on the value of the variable &GENVAR1. The processing which precedes this ensures that &GENVAR1 contains the text entered by the user, up to the first period (.), and the pairs of values on the lines which follow the TRANS keyword are interpreted as meaning: 'if &GENVAR1 contains the value to the left of the comma, set &ZSEL to the value to the right of the comma'. Thus, for each menu option which the user could have selected, we specify the name of an ISPF service which will be inserted into the variable &ZSEL. ISPF automatically selects the service in &ZSEL for execution when we reach the end of the processing in the PROC section. This service may be a program, a command, or another panel — note that the panel option allows us to create a hierarchy of menus if we have too many applications available to fit onto one menu.

- This particular menu follows the common practice of not only allowing the user to select the PDF services and their more heavily used applications from the main menu, but also providing submenus for less heavily used applications.

Although menu panels follow the format shown here fairly closely, non-menu ISPF panels can also be created, which vary significantly in format and function. The syntax for defining panels and the facilities available are documented in [10], as are the other main ISPF facilities (i.e. ISPF clist commands, messages, table services, and file-tailoring services) and how to use them.

```
)BODY
%----------------- TECHNICAL SERVICES PRIMARY OPTION PANEL -------------
%OPTION  ===>_ZCMD
%                    WELCOME TO THE XXXXXXXXXX XXXXXXXX
%                              MVS/ESA SYSTEM
%
%
%        0 +ISPF PARMS                    %USERID   -   &ZUSER
%        1 +BROWSE                        %PREFIX   -   &ZPREFIX
%        2 +EDIT                          %TIME     -   &ZTIME
%        3 +UTILITIES                     %DATE     -   &ZDATE
%        4 +FOREGROUND                    %             &ZJDATE
%        5 +BATCH
%        6 +COMMAND
%        7 +DIALOG TEST
%        8 +SDSF
%        9 +SMP/E
%        A +OEM MENU
%        B +DFP MENU
%        C +INFOMAN
%        D +RMFWDM
%
+ENTER%END+COMMAND TO TERMINATE ISPF.
%
)INIT
   IF (&PMGTERM = ENTER) &ZCMD = X      /* RESTORE ORIGINAL X COMMAND.  */
   &PMGTERM = &Z                        /* SET TERMINATION FLAG NULL    */
   .HELP = ISR00003
   &ZPRIM = YES          /* ALWAYS A PRIMARY OPTION MENU      */
   &ZHTOP = ISR00003     /* TUTORIAL TABLE OF CONTENTS        */
   &ZHINDEX = ISR91000 /* TUTORIAL INDEX – 1ST PAGE           */
   VPUT (ZHTOP, ZHINDEX) PROFILE
)PROC
   &PMGTRL = TRUNC(&ZCMD,'.')          /* TRUNCATE ZCMD.               */
   IF (&PMGINIT NE &Z)                 /* IF WE HAVE INITIALIZED,
*/
      IF (&PMGTRL = X)                 /* AND ''X'' ENTERED ...        */
        &PMGTERM = ENTER               /* ... SET ''ENTER'',           */
      IF (.RESP = END) &PMGTERM = END  /* OR''END''ENTERED SET''END''. */
      IF (&PMGTERM NE &Z)              /*  IF WE ARE TERMINATING,
*/
        .RESP = ENTER                  /*     SIMULATE ENTER.          */
        &ZCMD = '&P'                   /*     AND INVOKE PMGLTERM.      */
      &PMGTRL = .TRAIL                  /* SET TRAIL VARIABLE TO .TRAIL  */
```

Example 10.9. Typical main menu panel for ISPF.

```
&GENVAR1 = TRUNC (&ZCMD,'.')
&GENVAR2 = .TRAIL
&GENVAR3 = TRUNC (&ZPREFIX,4)
&ZSEL = TRANS( &GENVAR1
               0,'PANEL(ISPOPTA)'
               1,'PGM(ISRBRO) PARM(ISRBR001)'
               2,'PGM(ISREDIT) PARM(P,ISREDM01)'
               3,'PANEL(ISRUTIL)'
               4,'PANEL(ISRFPA)'
               5,'PGM(ISRJB1) PARM(ISRJPA) NOCHECK'
               6,'PGM(ISRPTC)'
               7,'PGM(ISPYXDR) PARM(ISR) NOCHECK'
               8,'PANEL(ZSDSFOP2) NEWAPPL(ISF)'
               9,'PGM(GIMISCV) NEWAPPL(SMPE) NOCHECK'
               A,'PANEL(OEMPAN)'
               B,'PANEL(DFPPAN)'
               C,'CMD(%IIFV4)'
               D,'CMD(%RMFWX)'
               ',' ',' '
               X,'EXIT'
               *,'?' )
   IF (&ZCMD = '8')
      &ZSEL = 'PGM(ISFISP) NOCHECK NEWAPPL(ISF)'
   &ZTRAIL = &GENVAR2
)END
```

Example 10.9. (cont.)

10.3.4 Controlling the use of TSO commands from ISPF

If you attempt to execute a TSO command under ISPF, by using the ISPF
SELECT command in a dialog, by entering TSO cmd on the ISPF command line
(where cmd is the command and parameters), or from PDF option 6, then ISPF
will be responsible for 'attaching' the command. You can control the way in which
ISPF does this by creating an entry for the command in the ISPF TSO command
table (ISPTCM), and in certain circumstances you will find it is necessary to do
this.

The factors which ISPTCM can control include:

- Whether the command requires a 'function pool' for ISPF dialog variables.
- Whether the command requires an authorization check — the flag bit for this
  must be turned on for programs which will require APF authorization.
- Whether the command is: (a) a command procedure (CLIST or REXX EXEC);
  (b) a command processor (i.e. a program); or (c) if ISPF is to determine which
  it is for itself, by issuing a BLDL for it first, then attaching the EXEC processor
  to handle it if the BLDL fails. Note that programs in the LPA must be specified
  as command processors — if you choose option (c) above, the BLDL will be
  issued without checking the LPA first. This is the default as supplied by IBM.
- Whether the command is allowed under ISPF at all (commands like ISPF and
  LOGON are not).
- How much of the screen is to be cleared if the command goes into TSO line
  mode.

If you wish to change or add to the IBM-supplied version of ISPTCM, you will need to modify, rename, reassemble and relink the source supplied in SYS1. SAMPLIB(ISPTCMA). This should always be done as an SMP/E USERMOD. You may well find, however, that you and your users can manage quite well without changing the IBM-supplied version of ISPTCM at all. If this is so, keep life simple by leaving it well alone!

Example 10.10 shows an extract from the source code for the IBM-supplied version of the table. Note that:

- The meanings of the various bits of the flag byte are documented in [9].
- It should be clear from the example that many IBM-supplied commands must be included in this table. You should avoid changing the IBM-supplied entries.

10.4 Extending ISPF

10.4.1 Adding products and dialogs

Once you have established a basic ISPF environment, there will be many opportunities and demands for you to extend it. Given that ISPF is essentially an environment for the development of online applications, the most obvious way to extend it will be to develop dialogs of your own and add these to the options available from users' menus. You will also find that an increasing number of IBM and third-party products include ISPF interfaces, and a regular part of the systems programmer's job is to add these to the list of applications on users' menus.

Writing ISPF dialogs is beyond the scope of this book, but if you wish to learn

```
ISPMTCM HEADER
.
.
.
      ISPMTCM  FLAG=02,ENTNAME=IMPORT    AMS COMMAND, CMD PROCESSOR
      ISPMTCM  FLAG=02,ENTNAME=IMPORTRA  AMS COMMAND, CMD PROCESSOR
      ISPMTCM  FLAG=08,ENTNAME=ISPF      PP  COMMAND, INVALID
      ISPMTCM  FLAG=08,ENTNAME=ISPSTART  PP  COMMAND, INVALID
.
.
.
      ISPMTCM  FLAG=02,ENTNAME=OUTPUT    TSO COMMAND, CMD PROCESSOR
      ISPMTCM  FLAG=22,ENTNAME=PARMLIB   TSO CMD, CMD PROC, AUTHCK
      ISPMTCM  FLAG=04,ENTNAME=PASCALVS  PP  COMMAND, CLIST
      ISPMTCM  FLAG=08,ENTNAME=PDF       PP  COMMAND, INVALID
      ISPMTCM  FLAG=02,ENTNAME=PLI       PP  COMMAND, CMD PROCESSOR
.
.
.
      ISPMTCM  END
```

Example 10.10. Extract from ISPTCM.

how to do it, you should refer to [10, 11] and/or one of the books available on the subject.

Adding prewritten dialogs to users' menus, however, is relatively simple. All that is usually required is to add the ISPxLIB and related libraries containing the elements of the dialog to the list of datasets being allocated for the user, ensure they have RACF access to them, and add an option to one of the user's menus which allows them to invoke the application. The installation documentation for the product should list the libraries required and the command to use in the menu panel definition to invoke the application.

10.4.2 Adding command-line options

In addition to ISPF dialogs themselves, you can provide extra facilities to ISPF users in a number of other ways. For example, you can make it easier to invoke commands from the command line by creating customized command tables for your ISPF applications. Usually, if the user wishes to enter a TSO command from the command line, they must enter TSO cmd, where cmd is the full text and parameters of the command they wish to issue. However, each ISPF application keeps a command table in ISPTLIB, which can be used to provide abbreviations for commonly used commands. For example, I often find myself using the AMS LISTCAT command to find out where a dataset is cataloged. This normally requires me to enter TSO LISTCAT ENT('datasetname') VOL on the command line, which is not only cumbersome, but can exceed the space available when the command line is short and the dataset name is not! By creating a suitable entry in the current ISPF command table, I can shorten the command to LCA dataset-name.

If you wish to modify ISPF command tables, you need to understand ISPF's concept of 'applications'. As far as ISPF is concerned, a user is in one application at any one time (or two if in split-screen mode, one for each logical screen). Each application is identified by a one-to-four character code, which is used as the prefix when ISPF attempts to locate certain parameter tables:

- The current user profile, which is member xxxPROF of your ISPPROF dataset
- The current edit profile, which is member xxxEDIT of your ISPPROF dataset
- The current command table, which is member xxxCMDS of your ISPTLIB concatenation

where xxx is the application identifier. The initial application when you start ISPF is ISP, unless you override this using the NEWAPPL parameter on your ISPSTART command. The current application can then be changed by selecting a menu entry which invokes a service using the NEWAPPL parameter. In Example 10.9 above, for example, we change the application when the user selects either the SDSF or the SMP/E application. When the user exits this application, they will automatically be returned to the application they were in before they entered it.

```
COMMAND TABLE - XYZCMDS -------------------------------- ROW 22 OF 27
COMMAND ===>                                          SCROLL ===> PAGE
INSERT, DELETE, AND CHANGE COMMAND ENTRIES. UNDERSCORES NEED NOT BE
BLANKED. ENTER END COMMAND TO SAVE CHANGES OR CANCEL TO END WITHOUT
SAVING.
        VERB      T  ACTION
                     DESCRIPTION
'''  PFSHOW    O  SELECT PGM(ISPOPF) PARM(&ZPARM) NOFUNC
                     DISPLAY PF KEY DEFINITION LINES ON PANEL
'''  ISPPREP   O  SELECT PGM(ISPPREP) NEWAPPL
                     INVOKING PREPROCESSED PANEL UTILITY
'''  LCA       O  SELECT CMD(LISTCAT ENT('&ZPARM') ALL)
                     DO LISTCAT ALL
'''  LCV       O  SELECT CMD(LISTCAT ENT('&ZPARM') VOL)
                     DO LISTCAT VOL
'''  LVL       O  SELECT CMD(LISTCAT LEVEL('&ZPARM') )
                     DO LISTCAT LEVEL
'''  LVV       O  SELECT CMD(LISTCAT LEVEL('&ZPARM') VOL )
                     DO LISTCAT LEVEL VOL
```

Example 10.11. ISPF command table amendment screen.

Note that PDF will use ISR as an application identifier, but if there is no ISRxxxx member for any of the tables listed above, it will use the ISPxxxx member instead.

You can use PDF option 3.9 to amend a command table as long as you have a table dataset allocated to the ISPTABL DDNAME. You may not, however, amend the current command table (i.e. ISRCMDS or ISPCMDS) using this option. If you wish to amend the current table, you must: (a) copy it into your ISPTABL dataset (e.g. using option 3.3), giving it a new name in the format xxxxCMDS; (b) amend this new member using 3.9; (c) copy the amended table back over the original; and (d) exit ISPF and re-enter it to make the change effective. Example 10.11 shows an amendment screen from option 3.9 with a few of the IBM-supplied entries (avoid changing these), and some entries which have been added to provide convenient command abbreviations. Note that:

- The VERB column indicates the short command the user may enter on the command line; the T column indicates the minimum length to which this command may be truncated (0 indicates truncation is not allowed); the ACTION column indicates the full command to be invoked when the user enters the short command; and the DESCRIPTION entry is merely for documentation. Note also that if the user enters a parameter after the short command, it will be inserted by ISPF into the &ZPARM variable.
- Although all the user-defined entries shown here invoke IBM-supplied commands, you could equally well use the command table to provide easy ways for users to invoke IBM-supplied clists, or inhouse commands or clists.

One disadvantage of modifying your command tables is that IBM sometimes changes the default table for ISPF (ISPCMDS) from one release to another. If you

```
/*****************************************************************/
/*    CLIST FOR USE UNDER TSO OPTION 3.4 TO UNCATALOG TAPE DS'S  */
/*****************************************************************/
PROC 1 &TAPEDS
DELETE &TAPEDS NONVSAM NOSCRATCH
```

Example 10.12. Clist to uncatalog datasets from PDF 3.4 dataset list.

continue to use your old (modified) command table, you may find that some of the IBM-supplied bits do not work any more, and if you use the new one, your modifications will be missing. This means you must re-apply all your modifications whenever the supplied version of any table changes.

10.4.3 Invoking commands from PDF 3.4

Since the introduction of ISPF/PDF version 2.3, it has been possible to use the line command field in a PDF 3.4 dataset list display to invoke any command or clist to process the dataset concerned. You can take advantage of this by coding your own clists for users to invoke from here. For example, the u line command will not allow the user to uncatalog a tape dataset. TSO-literate users can get round this by typing DEL / NVSAM NSCR in the line command field, which invokes the AMS delete command to uncatalog the dataset, and uses the / symbol as a place marker which ISPF will replace with the dataset name on the current line (if the '/' is not coded, it will insert it at the end of the command). You can simplify this, however, by creating a clist which does it for the user. Example 10.12 shows a clist for this purpose. Note that:

- Assuming you have placed this clist in member TU of your SYSPROC library, the user can invoke it by simply typing TU against the dataset to be uncataloged. ISPF inserts the name of the current dataset at the end of the command, which the clist picks up as a positional parameter and inserts in the relevant place in the AMS DELETE command.
- Although this is a very simple example, much more complex ones can be coded. [16], for example, describes a clist which is used to allocate a new dataset using the attributes of the current dataset as a model. This uses the TSO LISTDSI command to obtain the attributes of the current dataset, then invokes an ISPF panel to display these attributes and give the user an opportunity to change them and enter the new dataset name, and finally creates the new dataset using the ALLOCATE command.

10.4.4 Providing edit macros

Edit macros are a type of clist which can be invoked from the command line in PDF EDIT, and they use EDIT subcommands to automate repetitive or complex tasks. Learning to code them is a skill in itself, and IBM dedicates a large part of

```
/*-----------------------------------------------------------------------*/
/* JCLBOX: EDIT MACRO TO INSERT JCL FORMAT COMMENT BOX                    */
/*-----------------------------------------------------------------------*/
    CONTROL NOFLUSH NOMSG

    ISREDIT MACRO NOPROCESS (NUMBER)
    ISREDIT PROCESS RANGE A
    ISREDIT (COPY1) = LINENUM .ZFRANGE
    SET &COUNTER = 1
SET &J1 = &STR(//*-------------------------------------------------)+
    &STR(---------------*)
SET &J2 = &STR(//*                                                 )+
    &STR(               *)
SET &J3 = &STR(//*-------------------------------------------------)+
    &STR(---------------*)
      ISREDIT LINE_AFTER &COPY1 = ''&J1''
      SET &COPY1 = &COPY1 + 1
      DO WHILE &COUNTER LE &NUMBER
      ISREDIT LINE_AFTER &COPY1 = ''&J2''
      SET &COUNTER = &COUNTER + 1
      SET &COPY1 = &COPY1 + 1
      END
      ISREDIT LINE_AFTER &COPY1 = ''&J3''
    END
END
```

Example 10.13. PDF edit macro.

a manual [13] to documenting them. I will therefore not attempt to explain them
in detail here, but Example 10.13 (courtesy of Duncan Painter) shows a simple
example, which should give you a flavour of what an edit macro can do. Note that:

- This edit macro is held in member JCLBOX of a library in the SYSPROC
  concatenation. It can be invoked by the user entering JCLBOX n on the
  command line while in PDF EDIT (where n is a numeric value), and entering
  an A line command on the line after which the box is desired. It inserts a
  comment box in JCL format into the member being edited, with n lines
  available for the user to enter comments.
- The ISREDIT MACRO statement identifies this as an edit macro and assigns
  the value passed in the positional parameter to the variable &NUMBER.
- The ISREDIT PROCESS statement causes the label .ZFRANGE to be
  associated with the line on which the user entered the A.
- The next statement assigns the line number of .ZFRANGE to the variable
  &COPY1.
- The ISREDIT LINE_AFTER statements insert lines into the member being
  edited.

Once again, this is a relatively simple example, but it should serve to illustrate
the potential for providing quite sophisticated extensions to the facilities available
in PDF EDIT using edit macros.

```
    PROC O L
/********************************************************************/
/*  NEST:  INVOKE ISPF MAIN MENU TO PROVIDE ANOTHER ISPF SESSION */
/********************************************************************/
    CONTROL NOLIST NOMSG
    ISPEXEC VGET (SPLNUM) SHARED
    IF &SPLNUM =    THEN SET &SPLNUM = O
/********************************************************************/
/*  IF POSITIONAL PARM L SPECIFIED, JUST DISPLAY THE CURRENT LEVEL*/
/********************************************************************/
    IF &L = L THEN DO
      SYSCALL PUTLEVEL &SPLNUM
    END
/********************************************************************/
/*  OTHERWISE PROVIDE ANOTHER SESSION AT NEXT LEVEL              */
/********************************************************************/
    ELSE DO
      SET &SPLNUM = &SPLNUM + 1
      SYSCALL PUTLEVEL &SPLNUM
      ISPEXEC SELECT PANEL(ISR@PRIM)
      ISPEXEC VGET (SPLNUM) SHARED
      SET &SPLNUM = &SPLNUM - 1
      SYSCALL PUTLEVEL &SPLNUM
    END
    EXIT
/********************************************************************/
/*  PUTLEVEL SUBROUTINE CAUSES LEVEL TO BE DISPLAYED IN SHORT MSG */
/********************************************************************/
    PUTLEVEL: PROC 1 SPLNUM
      ISPEXEC VPUT (SPLNUM) SHARED
      SET &ZEDSMSG = &STR(LEVEL IS &SPLNUM)
      SET &ZEDLMSG = &STR(NEST CLIST HAS BEEN INVOKED )
      ISPEXEC VPUT (ZEDSMSG)
      ISPEXEC VPUT (ZEDLMSG)
      ISPEXEC SETMSG MSG(ISRZOOO)
    END
```

Example 10.14. Clist to nest levels of ISPF.

10.4.5 Nested ISPF

Finally, here is a handy little clist which comes to the rescue when two logical
screens are not enough! It takes advantage of the fact that although you cannot
issue the ISPF, PDF, or ISPSTART commands from within ISPF, you can
SELECT the normal main menu at any time, which effectively gives you a new
ISPF session while saving your old one for you to return to when you exit the new
main menu. In effect, then, you can have multiple 'nested' levels of ISPF.
Obviously, this is not quite as good as a split screen, because you can not swap
between the nested sessions — you can only get back to any given session by
terminating the lower level sessions. It can, however, be very useful. The clist also
provides a check on how many levels you have currently nested to, in case you lose
track of where you are. Example 10.14 shows the clist. Note that:

- If this clist is placed in the SYSPROC concatenation in a member called NEST,
  it can be invoked from the command line by entering TSO NEST to provide

a new level of ISPF, or TSO NEST L to display the current level of nesting. This can be simplified further by providing an abbreviation for this command via an ISPF command table entry.

- If you use a different main menu than ISR@PRIM, just substitute its name in the PANEL operand of the ISPEXEC SELECT PANEL command.
- The PUTLEVEL subroutine makes use of the message definition ISRZ000 supplied by PDF version 3, which uses the variable &ZEDSMSG as the short message text and the variable &ZEDLMSG as the long message text.

References and bibliography

IBM manuals

1. *MVS/ESA Operations: System Commands*, GC28–1826. Includes descriptions of the start and modify commands for TSO.
2. *MVS/ESA SPL: Initialization and Tuning*, GC28—1828. Documents the TSOKEYxx and IKJTSO00 members of SYS1.PARMLIB.
3. *TSO/E Program Directory*, GC28–1901. Describes the installation process for TSO/E.
4. *TSO/E Customization*, SC28–1872. Explains how to customize all features of TSO/E.
5. *TSO/E Administration*, SC28–1873. Describes user administration functions for TSO and administration functions for the information centre facility.
6. *TSO/E System Programming Command Reference*, SC28–1878. Documents restricted TSO commands, including ACCOUNT and PARMLIB.
7. *RACF Security Administrators Guide*, SC28–1340. Describes RACF resources (including TSO users) and how to define them.
8. *RACF Command Language Reference*, SC28–0733. Describes RACF commands, including those used to create and amend TSO userids.
9. *ISPF and ISPF/PDF Planning and Customizing*, SC34–4257. Explains how to customize ISPF and PDF, including lots of optional customization.
10. *ISPF Dialog Management Guide and Reference*, SC34–4266. How to write an ISPF dialog.
11. *ISPF Dialog Management Examples*, SC34–4265.
12. *ISPF/PDF Services*, SC34–4259. How to invoke PDF services (e.g. edit and browse) from within ISPF dialogs.
13. *ISPF/PDF Edit and Edit Macros*, SC34–4253. How to use PDF edit and write edit macros.

Other

14. Little, D.: Using the ALTLIB command, *MVS Update*, December 1990, pp. 33–36. Explains how to use the new ALTLIB command to make 'user' and 'application' CLIST and EXEC libraries available.
15. Kidd, C.L.: Using VLF to Reduce the I/O Bottleneck, *Mainframe Journal*, April 1990, pp. 14–22. A good introduction to VLF and how to use it to speed up catalog, load module, and TSO clist processing.
16. Shein, D.: Raising your IQ (ISPF Quotient), *Mainframe Journal*, October 1989, pp. 13–18. Lots of useful tips on extending ISPF and using some of the more advanced facilities.

Part Four
Maintaining and enhancing MVS

11
Maintaining your MVS system

11.1   Introduction

Once you have created a production MVS system, you will have to modify it from
time to time. This may include putting on fixes to correct and prevent problems,
and upgrading components of the system to provide new functions required by
your users. This chapter deals with some key questions raised by the need to update
your system:

- When should you put on maintenance and upgrades, and which of IBM's
  service delivery options should you use?
- How should you structure and 'clone' your system to make the maintenance
  process as painless and effective as possible?

11.2   When and how to put on maintenance and upgrades

11.2.1   The issues

IBM provides a bewildering array of offerings for the provision of service, service
information, and product upgrades, including:

- PUTs — Tapes of all PTFs for your product profile, sent out automatically
  around once a month. These also include 'cover letters' describing key PTFs
  and the problems they resolve, and HOLDDATA describing PTFs on previous
  PUTs which were in error.
- CBIPOs — Installation tapes integrating a whole range of products with stable
  service up to a given PUT level. These are created in response to a specific
  customer order.
- CBPDOs — Installation tapes integrating PTFs for your product profile from
  several PUTs, and additional products if required. Again, these are put
  together in response to a specific customer order.
- Electronic download of PTFs from DIAL-IBM (known as IBMLINK in the
  USA).

- Delivery of individual PTFs on tape on request.
- PSP tapes — Tapes offering information about high-impact problems relevant to your product profile.
- Product tapes — Individual products ordered by a customer.
- Cumulative service tapes — Tapes including service from a series of PUTs for a single product or group of products (often supplied along with a product tape to bring the product up to a reasonably current level).
- Problem records on INFO/MVS and DIAL-IBM (IBMLINK), describing indvidual problems and their resolving PTFs.

Given this array of sources of information, fixes, and product upgrades, which ones should you use and when? To some extent, the answer will depend on your circumstances and personal preferences. But let us start with a few certainties:

- All IBM service and product upgrades are packaged in SMP/E format and should always be applied using SMP/E.
- When you are experiencing a problem with a significant impact on your users and IBM informs you that there is a PTF or a series of PTFs which will correct it, you should apply them — this is known as corrective service.
- When you are installing or upgrading a product, you should obtain the relevant PSP information. If this tells you there are any high impact and pervasive (HIPER) problems outstanding for the product you are installing, you should apply the fixes for these.
- Whenever you receive a PUT, you should RECEIVE the HOLDDATA from it — this will prevent you from inadvertently applying fixes which are known to be in error.

Beyond these few certainties, you will have to apply your judgement. Broadly speaking, there are two options, though you can 'mix and match' these options when it suits you. The options are:

1 Keep reasonably up to date with your preventative maintenance by applying the fixes from PUTs regularly, and upgrade products using product tapes and cumulative service tapes.

or

2 Ignore all preventative service except at product installation time, and bring your whole system up to date in a 'big bang' by installing a CBIPO or CBPDO on a less frequent basis — say once a year.

The rest of this section discusses these two options in detail.

11.2.2 *Option 1: PUTs and product tapes*

Few systems programmers would advocate installing all the service on every PUT as soon as it arrived, but quite a few do seem to favour installing PUT service on a regular basis (there is a fascinating selection of comments on this question in [2]). Typically, they install the service from two or three PUTs every three months, but avoid putting on the service from the most recent couple of tapes.

The reason for avoiding the most recent service is simple — if it has errors in it and you install it, you will experience problems. If, on the other hand, you wait for a while before putting on the service, other installations will find the errors, and the following PUTs will include HOLDDATA for the PTFs in error. As long as you observe the advice above and RECEIVE all HOLDDATA from PUTs as soon as you get them, you will have the benefit of other users' experience when you install the service from slightly older PUTs, as SMP/E will automatically HOLD the PTFs in error as a result of the HOLDDATA from the more recent tapes.

When these systems programmers wish to install a new product or upgrade a product, they typically order a product tape from IBM and a cumulative service tape to go with it, which will bring the product up to the most recent PUT level. As with the PUTs themselves, they will avoid installing cumulative service right up to the current PUT level. Instead, they will bring the product up to the level of service of, say, the last PUT but two, and avoid putting on the more recent service until they have received HOLDDATA from the next two PUTs (once you have added a product to your profile, future service for it should be automatically included in your PUTs).

If you decide to adopt this approach, you will have to go through the following processes whenever you install the service from a group of PUTs:

1 RECEIVE the SYSMODs from the tapes (you should already have RECEIVEd the HOLDDATA from them and from any subsequent tapes you have on site).
2 Ask IBM for any PSP information relating to these PUTs.
3 Obtain any additional fixes for HIPER problems indicated by the PSP information.
4 Perform an APPLY CHECK to show you what fixes will be applied, and more importantly, what fixes will be HELD and why.
5 Investigate any SYSTEM-type HOLDs; often these are merely informational and you can release them without any ill effect (either by specifying BYPASS-(HOLDSYSTEM(...)) when you come to APPLY your service, which will release all SYSTEM-type HOLDs of the specified types, or by coding up + +RELEASE statements for the PTFs concerned and RECEIVEing these).
6 APPLY the service.
7 Bring up a test system with these fixes on and test it thoroughly, paying particular attention to those products and system functions to which you have applied service.
8 Migrate your updated system into production (see Sec. 11.2 for discussion of this process).

When you wish to install or upgrade a product using a product tape and cumulative service tape, you will need to go through a similar series of processes:

1 RECEIVE, APPLY, and ACCEPT the base product.
2 RECEIVE the cumulative service.
3 Research the cumulative service (i.e. the same steps as required for a PUT between RECEIVE and APPLY).
4 APPLY the service.
5 Test the new/upgraded product thoroughly.
6 Migrate into production.

There are three main advantages of this approach:

1 By keeping reasonably up to date with service, you should, in theory, prevent some avoidable problems.
2 If you are reasonably up to date with service and you do experience problems, the 'chain' of PTFs and prerequisite PTFs required to fix them should be short.
3 By keeping all products up to a current level without reinstalling the whole system, it avoids regularly repeating much of the 'customization' and 'restructuring' activity required to migrate a CBIPO system into production.

However, there are some serious disadvantages:

- The PTF research phase of the process is time consuming and tedious, particularly if you have to repeat it every few months—and there is therefore a temptation to skimp on it, which is risky!
- The number of problems prevented by 'preventative service' is often less than the number of new problems it introduces, even if you use HOLDDATA as effectively as possible.
- There is a dangerous temptation when putting on regular service to regard this as a 'minor change', assume that SMP/E HOLDs will prevent any problems, and neglect the requirement for thorough testing before going into production. On the other hand, if you do test thoroughly every time, this will be a time-consuming exercise, both for you and for the other people you will have to involve.
- Upgrading core products such as MVS itself and JES2 is more complex using a product tape than using a CBIPO.
- Many sites have a large selection of IBM program products, and most of these require an upgrade every couple of years, so if you are going to keep up to date by this process you are going to have a full-time job just upgrading program products.

You can, of course, deal with the last two problems by combining the PUT approach with the CBIPO/CBPDO process, rather than with the product tape approach — or use product tapes for some upgrades and CBIPO/CBPDO for others. Personally, however, I prefer to ignore PUTs and product tapes altogether (except as sources of HOLDDATA and corrective fixes), and do all my main-tenance and upgrades using option 2.

11.2.3 *Option 2: CBIPO and CBPDO*

The alternative approach to keeping up to date with PUTs and product tapes is to bring your system up to a stable current level less frequently using CBIPO and/or CBPDO.

Installing an MVS CBIPO involves rebuilding your entire system from scratch and reinstalling almost every IBM product you have (other than CICS, NCP, and IMS/DB2). The CBIPO process is discussed in detail in Chapter 7, but for the sake of comparison with the PUT/product tape approach, we will repeat a few key points here:

- The CBIPO comes with integrated service which has been researched by IBM and brought up to a relatively stable level.
- Because IBM has already done PTF research on your order, you should not have to do as much as on a PUT installation.
- The CBIPO process steps you through all the jobs needed to build a 'base' copy of your MVS system and all the other products included in your order, but once this is complete you must customize your system to make it functionally equivalent to your existing production system and restructure it as discussed in Sec. 11.3 to provide a suitable environment for future maintenance.

Installing a CBPDO is much simpler. The simplest type of CBPDO is known as a service-only CBPDO. This merely integrates service from several PUTs (up to two years' worth) with additional fixes indicated by IBM PTF research. IBM automatically starts building the CBPDO from the point to which your last CBIPO or CBPDO brought your system, unless you request otherwise. As with a CBIPO, you must still request and follow up PSP information, but because IBM has already integrated the results of their own PTF research, less research should be required than for a PUT, and the level of service represented by the CBPDO should be more stable than that on a recent PUT. CBPDO therefore has all the advantages of CBIPO—relatively little PTF research and a relatively stable level of service —without the disadvantage of having to rebuild your system from scratch.

You may also order a CBPDO which combines the service found on a service-only CBPDO with additional/upgraded products. This provides an easy way of installing additional products, or upgrading a group of products, at the same time as putting on preventative service. The CBPDO installation process where new/upgraded products are involved is:

1 RECEIVE the products and service on the CBPDO.
2 Order the PSP information and any additional fixes indicated by it.
3 APPLY the products and service.
4 Perform any customization required for the new/upgraded products.

5   Test the new products thoroughly and any functions which appear to be affected by service.

6   Migrate to production.

CBPDO therefore provides a method of upgrading your maintenance level and installing new/upgraded products with less work overall than using PUTs and product tapes.

MVS and JES upgrades, however, are really too complex to do using CBPDO, so you should order a CBIPO to do one of these. And MVS and JES upgrades are becoming ever more frequent — to the point where you are likely to need a major upgrade every year, so many sites simplify their upgrade workload still further by installing all product upgrades and new products as part of an annual MVS upgrade. The next logical step is to cut out preventative maintenance in between CBIPOs and bundle that in with your annual CBIPO as well. I have followed that line for many years with few problems. The advantages are clear:

- Each upgrade is a major upgrade and so is thoroughly tested before implementation.
- Each upgrade takes you to a relatively stable level.
- No unnecessary fixes are put on which can lead to unpredictable problems when the fix turns out to be in error.
- Product upgrades and preventative maintenance take you a couple of months each year, leaving the rest of the year free for more varied and productive work.
- Time spent on PTF research is minimized.

The disadvantages mirror the advantages of option 1:

- If you do have problems, you could have to apply a long chain of PTFs from a series of PUTs to fix them.
- A CBIPO or CBPDO usually represents a less recent level of service than a PUT you could have obtained at the same time, because: (a) it may have been built up to three months ago; and (b) chains of PTFs in error are excluded at build time.
- A major effort is required to recustomize and restructure the system every year.

If these problems worry you, you can always take an intermediate approach. For example, install a CBIPO every 1–2 years, but use CBPDO every six months to keep up to date with preventative maintenance and install any new products or upgrades which cannot be put off until the next CBIPO.

The suitability of option 2 also depends on how likely you are to need recent service to be applied to your system. If yours is a 'leading edge' site — one which regularly introduces new hardware or software before it has been widely proven on other user sites—you are more likely to need recent fixes to deal with the problems this is likely to cause. In this situation, you might find it necessary to keep up to relatively recent service levels by adopting a variant of option 1.

11.3   Cloning and the MVS maintenance process

11.3.1   The issues

Cloning is an essential stage in the process of implementing maintenance on an MVS system. In order to test fixes and upgrades before they go into production, the systems programmer must first apply them to a testing version of the MVS system. Once testing has been completed successfully, the maintenance must be migrated onto the production version of the system. Either at the stage of creating the test system or at the stage of migrating into production, this process almost always involves cloning — copying one version of the system to create another, functionally identical version.

Your approach to cloning and applying maintenance can be defined by a set of policies and procedures addressing questions like:

- Into which set of libraries will maintenance be installed?
- How will the maintenance be tested?
- How will maintenance be migrated into the production libraries?
- How will you regress back to the previous level if you have problems with the maintenance?

IBM offers little advice on these questions, so over the years systems programmers have evolved a broad selection of answers. This section describes three of the options I have seen in use, with the object of making clear the principles involved and recommending a preferred technique.

11.3.2   Restructuring your MVS system

All the options involve some degree of 'restructuring' your system after you have installed a CBIPO (or built your system in some other way), in order to simplify the process of migrating between the live and target versions of your system. The CBIPO process places all MVS target libraries on the SYSRES pack (assuming that you combine all the 'logical' SYSRES packs on a single physical one, as you should); this is also the normal configuration for other installation processes. However, some of the datasets placed on the SYSRES by CBIPO cause difficulties for most cloning strategies. The process of restructuring your system therefore typically includes a tidy up of the SYSRES pack.

Although there are varying approaches to what should be left on the SYSRES pack and what should be taken off, all the options I discuss below use a similar approach: only target libraries which are updated by SMP/E (and SMP/E alone) should be left on the SYSRES pack. The only exception to this rule is the SMP/E target zone—this is the only dataset whose location varies between the different options, and in some of these it resides on the SYSRES. Thus, datasets such as SYS1.LOGREC, SYS1.DUMPnn datasets, ISF.HASPINDX, and SYS1.BROD-CAST, which are updated by MVS itself or by other system components, should be moved elsewhere. Datasets such as SYS1.PROCLIB, SYS1.PARMLIB, and SYS1.UADS, which are updated by system support staff, should also be moved off the SYSRES pack. By moving these datasets off the SYSRES pack, you ensure that:

1 If you copy one version of the SYSRES pack over the top of another you do not overwrite data placed in these datasets by the system or the systems programmers.

2 You can IPL off any one of several alternative SYSRES packs and still use the same copy of these datasets.

As at MVS/ESA 3.1.3, the datasets mentioned above are the only ones placed on the SYSRES pack by CBIPO that you need to move off, but you should be able to check for yourself which datasets need moving by identifying those updated by the system itself or by staff working on the system. The master catalog pack is a very suitable alternative location for all of the datasets listed above.

Restructuring your system may also involve setting up different SMP/E target zones corresponding to the live and target versions of your system. In addition, in order to be able to IPL your system at will from any one of two or more SYSRES packs, you must ensure that all MVS datasets on the SYSRES packs are cataloged with indirect volume references (i.e. as being on DEVTYPE(0000) and VOLUME(******)).

11.3.3 SYSRES backups

Another issue we need to address is the question of SYSRES backups. Again, I feel there is a definite 'best' approach to this, and I have assumed this approach in all three options discussed below. This is to back up the maintenance SYSRES pack after you have put on maintenance and tested it thoroughly, but before migrating your maintenance into production. The associated SMP/E target zone should be backed up along with the MVS target libraries, so that if you need to restore the MVS libraries you can also recreate an SMP/E environment which is in step with them. These backups should be kept on a GDG with a fairly large cycle (I keep 10 generations), so that you always have copies of a series of versions of your SYSRES pack, as it was when it was put into production at each maintenance upgrade. Option 1 actually integrates this backup into the migration process, which is a useful way of ensuring it is carried out, and this could also be done for the other options.

11.3.4 The options

Given that you need two SYSRES packs to make your system maintainable, there are two possible approaches to using these:

1 Designate one the permanent live SYSRES and the other the permanent maintenance SYSRES.

or

2   Alternate the usage of the two packs (i.e. flip-flop the packs).

The flip-flop approach creates the problem of how to keep the SMP/E target zone(s) in step with the target volumes themselves, and there are at least two approaches to dealing with this problem too.

  These permutations give us the three options which will be discussed below:

- *Option 1: stable SYSRES configuration* — One pack is always the live SYSRES, another is always the target SYSRES, and there is only one SMP/E target zone, which relates to the target SYSRES pack.
- *Option 2: SYSRES flip-flop with two SMP/E target zones* — Both the new target SYSRES and the new target SMP/E zone are rebuilt from the old target SYSRES and SMP/E zone at the end of each maintenance cycle.
- *Option 3: SYSRES flip-flop with one SMP/E target zone* — The new target SYSRES is rebuilt from the old target SYSRES at the end of each cycle, but the target zone is never rebuilt.

As you will see, my preference is for option 1, primarily because it avoids any possible confusion over which is the current live SYSRES pack and which the current target pack. Such confusion could lead an operator to IPL the target pack on your production machine, or a systems programmer to apply maintenance to the live pack, with potentially disastrous consequences in either case. Option 2 also suffers from the considerable overhead involved in rebuilding the SMP/E target zone.

  I should point out that the three options selected are slightly arbitrary combinations of various factors, and you should be able to combine these factors in different ways to get other viable combinations. My selection of combinations is justified only on the grounds that I have seen each of them working in practice.

11.3.5 *Option 1: stable SYSRES configuration*

Option 1 keeps your usage of SYSRES packs stable and consistent at all times. A pack with a given volume serial number, on a given device address, is always the live SYSRES, and another fixed pack is always the maintenance SYSRES. Figure 11.1 illustrates this option.

  The maintenance cycle for option 1 goes like this:

- *Stage 1* — We start with two SYSRES packs in step with one another (i.e. each contains an identical set of MVS target libraries). The maintenance pack (SYSRST on device number 211) also contains an SMP/E target zone TGTT which is linked by its DDDEFs to the MVS libraries on the same pack, while the live pack (SYSRSP on device number 210) does not contain any SMP/E environment.
- We then apply maintenance to SYSRST, using the TGTT target zone.

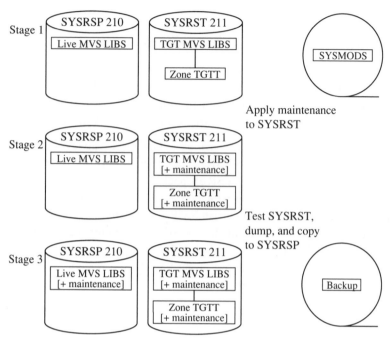

Figure 11.1. SYRES copy via tape cycle.

- *Stage 2* — Now both the MVS libraries and the TGTT target zone on SYSRST reflect the new maintenance.
- It is now necessary to test the maintenance on SYSRST. Because the datasets on here are cataloged with indirect references and are independent of PARMLIBs, LOGRECs, etc., we can use the production versions of the latter libraries (by using the production master catalog) and test SYSRST during a stand-alone test slot on the production machine or partition, simply by IPLing with a load address of 211 instead of 210. Alternatively, we can use testing versions of PARMLIB, LOGREC, etc. (via a test system master catalog), and IPL SYSRST on a test machine or test partition while SYSRSP is in use on the production one.
- Once we are happy that the maintenance has been adequately tested, we dump it to a backup tape, then restore the MVS libraries (but not the SMP/E target zone) from the backup tape to the live SYSRES SYSRSP. We then hand the system back to the operators for them to IPL, as usual, from load address 210. The JCL for the backup and restore jobs, using DFDSS, is shown in Example 11.1. Note that we exclude the CSI from the restore simply by excluding all VSAM datasets — this shortcut will only be valid as long as there are no MVS target datasets using VSAM.

The simplicity of this option is its greatest virtue:

- The production SYSRES is always the same volume on the same device, so

```
//........ JOB ........
//*-----------------------------------------------------------------------
//*      DUMP TARGET SYSRES TO CTAPE
//*-----------------------------------------------------------------------
//DUMP    EXEC PGM=ADRDSSU,REGION=4096K
//SYSPRINT DD SYSOUT=*
//INDD     DD VOL=SER=SYSRST,UNIT=3380,DISP=OLD
//OUTDD    DD UNIT=3480,DSN=DSYSSC.SYSRST.BK(+1),
//            DISP=(,CATLG,DELETE),LABEL=EXPDT=99000,
//            DCB=(DUMMY,RECFM=U,BLKSIZE=32760)
//SYSIN    DD *
 DUMP FULL INDD(INDD) OUTDD(OUTDD) OPT(4)
//*

//........ JOB ........
//*-----------------------------------------------------------------------
//*      RELOAD LIVE SYSRES FROM LATEST DUMP OF TARGET SYSRES
//*-----------------------------------------------------------------------
//*      N.B. BACK OUT A CHANGE BY RELOADING FROM AN OLDER GEN
//*           OF THE GDG-E.G. (-1) INSTEAD OF (0)
//*-----------------------------------------------------------------------
//REST    EXEC PGM=ADRDSSU,REGION=4096K
//SYSPRINT DD SYSOUT=*
//INDD     DD DSN=DSYSSC.SYSRST.BK(0),DISP=OLD
//OUTDD    DD VOL=SER=SYSRSP,UNIT=3380,DISP=OLD
 REST DS( EXCLUDE (                        -
                   SYS1.SMP*,              -
                   SYS1.VTOCIX.*           -
                   )                       -
         BY (DSORG,NE,VSAM) )-
    INDD (INDD)                -
    TOL (ENQF)                 -
    REPLACE                    -
    OUTDD (OUTDD)
//*
```

Example 11.1. JCL to backup and restore SYSRES for option 1.

there is no scope for the operators to be confused about which volume to IPL.

- The maintenance SYSRES is always the same volume accessed via the same target zone, so there is no scope for the systems programmers to be confused about which volume to put maintenance on.
- There is no need to engage in convoluted procedures to rebuild SMP/E target zones after each migration of maintenance onto the live system, and as a result, no discrepancies should arise between the global and target zones.
- Since we always build the live SYSRES from the backup cycle, we can be confident that the backup cycle does actually consist of a series of usable backups, each of which should represent an IPLable system at the time it was migrated into production, and that each recent version of the live SYSRES is available on the backup cycle.

The cost of this simplicity is a little less flexibility than we have with either of the flip-flop options:

- Unlike options 2 and 3, the old SYSRES pack is not available for a quick backout during an intermediate period between going live and completing the cycle. If you do need to backout the upgrade, you will have to restore the SYSRES from an earlier generation of the backup cycle.

- Unlike option 2, there is no SMP/E environment connected to the live SYSRES pack, so no possibility of putting maintenance directly onto the live SYSRES.

However, I believe that neither of these is a serious drawback. I actually prefer my live SYSRES to be insulated from the possible application of maintenance. I would rather have the security of knowing that no one can inadvertently put fixes on my live system than the option of putting them on in an emergency—in practice, there is always a way of putting them onto the maintenance system then migrating them across. The lack of a quick backout path, on the other hand, is a real disadvantage, but the loss of time involved in restoring the live SYSRES from the backup cycle before re-IPLing is bearable as long as you do not have to do it too often. My experience is that you hardly ever have to do it.

11.3.6   Option 2: SYSRES flip-flop with two SMP/E zones

Option 2 is illustrated in Fig. 11.2. In this option, we use two SYSRES packs, volume serial SYSRSA (on device number 210) and SYSRSB (on device number 211), and in addition to a set of MVS libraries, each of them contains an SMP/E target zone which relates to the set of MVS target libraries on the same pack. The maintenance cycle goes as follows:

- *Stage 1* — Pack A is the live SYSRES pack and is exactly in step with pack B. In other words, the contents of the MVS libraries are identical and the contents of the SMP/E zones are identical other than the zone names and the volume serial numbers in the DDDEFs for the MVS libraries. It is these volume serial numbers which link the SMP/E zone to the libraries on this pack rather than any other copy of them.
- Maintenance may now be applied to SYSRSB, which is currently the target SYSRES pack. This is done using the SMP/E SET BOUNDARY statement to select target zone TGTB when APPLYing maintenance.
- *Stage 2* — After the application of maintenance, SYSRSB is now out of step with SYSRSA, in that both the libraries on it and the SMP/E zone reflect the application of the new maintenance.
- We must now test the updated SYSRSB by IPLing it, just as in option 1. Once we are happy that the maintenance has been adequately tested and should be migrated into production, we take a backup of it to tape and inform the operators that the live load address has changed to 211.
- *Stage 3* — Once the operators have brought up the live system from SYSRSB, we are left with SYSRSB representing the new production level, and SYSRSA the previous level. We can leave SYSRSA like this for a few days, so that if

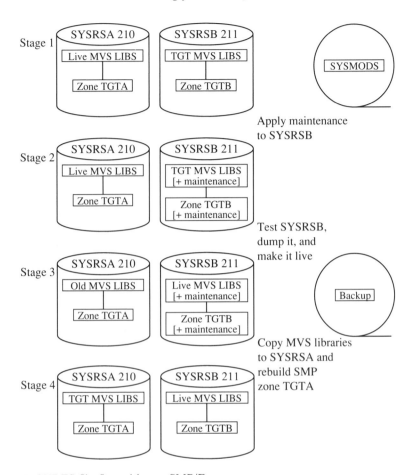

Figure 11.2. SYRES flip-flop with two SMP/E zones.

there are problems with SYSRSB we can re-IPL immediately from 210 to back
out our changes.

- Once we are happy that the changes will not need to be backed out (or earlier,
  if we are happy to settle for a backout which requires a restore from tape), we
  must bring SYSRSA up to the same level as SYSRSB before any further
  maintenance can be applied. The laborious way to do this would be to
  re-APPLY all the maintenance we applied to SYSRSB, but to specify a target
  zone of TGTB in our SET BOUNDARY statements.
- However, this would be a long and messy process if we had put on more than
  a few fixes, so instead we rebuild SYSRSA by cloning it from SYSRSB, either
  copying the MVS libraries directly or reloading them from the dump we took
  to tape between Stages 2 and 3 (using DFDSS or an equivalent third-party
  product in both cases). The SMP target zone, however, cannot be reconstructed
  by a simple DFDSS copy and rename of the CSI dataset, because the internal
  record of the zone name itself needs to be changed to TGTA, and the volume

serial numbers in the DDDEFs for the target libraries need to be changed to
SYSRSA. We must therefore rebuild this zone using SMP/E zone management
commands. Example 11.2 shows one method for doing this, using ZONE-
DELETE, ZONECOPY, and ZONEEDIT commands.

```
///SMPE     EXEC SMPEPROC
//*
//SMPCNTL  DD *
 SET BOUNDARY ( TGTA )    .
 ZONEDELETE TARGETZONE( TGTA )    .
 SET BOUNDARY ( GLOBAL  )    .
 UCLIN .
 ADD GZONE ZINDEX( (TGTA,SYS2.TGTA.CSI,TARGET) ) .
 ENDUCL   .
 SET BOUNDARY ( TGTA ) .
 ZONECOPY ( TGTB ) INTO( TGTA )    .
 ZONEEDIT DDDEF .
 CHANGE VOLUME(SYSRSB SYSRSA) .
 ENDZONEEDIT .
/*
```

Example 11.2. Cloning an SMP/E target zone.

- Note, however, that even this approach does not leave the SMP/E zones
  perfectly aligned — the APPLY ZONE subentries of the SYSMOD entries in
  the GLOBAL zone will not reflect the fact that SYSMODS which were
  APPLYed to SYSRSB are now also on SYSRSA. After a few flips, these entries
  will cease to bear any resemblance whatsoever to the actual state of the zones
  concerned. Fortunately, SMP/E keeps these entries for reporting purposes
  only, so APPLY processing is not affected, and online cross-zone queries use
  the information in the target zone on SYSMOD status rather than that in the
  GLOBAL zone, so these will still provide an accurate reflection of the state of
  the zones. There is, however, scope for confusion if anyone LISTs the status of
  SYSMODs from the GLOBAL zone.
- *Stage 4* — We are now back where we started, with two SYSRES packs in step
  with each other, except that both now include the new maintenance and the live
  pack is SYSRSB instead of SYSRSA. The flip-flop is complete, and the cycle
  can restart, except that now maintenance must be applied to SYSRSA instead
  of SYSRSB, by specifying TGTA in the SET BOUNDARY command for our
  SMP/E APPLY jobs.

Although it is a little laborious, this process works in practice. It has two
significant advantages:

- The old version of the live SYSRES can be kept around for a few days to
  provide a quick and easy backout route.
- There is always an SMP/E environment corresponding to the live system as well
  as one corresponding to the maintenance system. This means, for example, that

if you have an urgent need to apply a simple fix to the live system you can do it without backing out half-complete or half-tested upgrades which you may have spent a great deal of time putting on the maintenance system. Of course, you will have to remember to put the fix on the maintenance system as well, or you will inadvertently back it out when you implement your more complex change.

However, there are also some problems with this approach:

1   If you adopt the version in which fixes are re-APPLYed to the second zone rather than rebuilding the SYSRES as recommended above, there is a considerable amount of work involved in completing the flip-flop, and a danger that the re-APPLY may be left incomplete before you start putting on new maintenance.

2   If you adopt the other (definitely preferable!) version, in which the target zone is copied using the ZONECOPY command, the target zone cloning process is still a potentially unnecessary overhead, and there is some scope for confusion as a result of the discrepancies which arise between the target zones and the APPLY ZONE subentries of the SYSMOD entries in the GLOBAL zone.

3   In either version, there is a major risk of putting maintenance on the live pack by mistake. The operators could IPL off the wrong pack (as they are constantly changing the live load address there is lots of scope for confusion here); or a systems programmer could run an SMP/E job with the wrong zone name in the SET BOUNDARY statement—particularly as each time there is a flip they will actively have to change this statement in each piece of APPLY JCL they use. This can lead to corruption of the live system, and confusion over what maintenance has been applied where, with potentially disastrous results.

11.3.7   Option 3: SYSRES flip-flop with one SMP/E zone

This is a simpler version of the flip-flop approach. It is illustrated in Fig. 11.3. The process is as follows:

●   *Stage 1* — Again we start with two SYSRES packs in step with one another, SYSRSP (P for production), which is currently the live SYSRES on device number 210, and SYSRST (T for target or test) on device number 211. Neither of them, however, includes an SMP/E zone. There is, in fact, only one SMP/E target zone (TGTT), on another volume altogether, which is linked (again via DDDEFs specifying the volume serial numbers of the target libraries) to the MVS libraries on SYSRST.

●   When we wish to put on maintenance, we apply it to SYSRST, specifying TGTT as the target zone name in the SET BOUNDARY statement in our APPLY job.

●   *Stage 2* — SYSRST has now been updated with the new maintenance, and the SMP zone TGTT reflects its updated state.

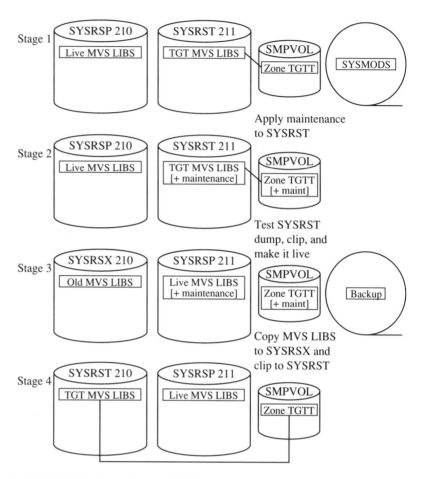

Figure 11.3. SYRES flip-flop with one SMP/E zone.

- We must now test the maintenance by IPLing with load address 211, exactly as in the other two options, and back it up to tape once it has been adequately tested.
- When we are satisfied we are ready to move the maintenance into production, we now depart from the path taken under option 2. We clip the volume on device number 210 to SYSRSX (i.e. relabel it using ICKDSF), to indicate that it is now the old SYSRES, and the volume on device number 211 to SYSRSP, to indicate it is now the live SYSRES. We then inform the operators that the live load address has changed to 211, and hand the system back to them.
- *Stage 3* — Now 211, relabelled to SYSRSP, has become the live SYSRES. 210 is available for a quick backout, which can be done by simply clipping it back to SYSRSP (in theory this step can be left out, though it is tidier to perform it), then using it as the load device at an IPL. The SMP zone TGTT, however, has been sadly bereaved — it is no longer connected to any MVS target

libraries, as all its DDDEF statements point to SYSRST, which no longer exists.

- We must therefore do some more work to get back to the point where we can start applying more maintenance. What is required is to clip 210 to SYSRST and clone the new live MVS libraries from either SYSRSP or the backup tape. Because zone TGTT already reflects the state of the libraries on SYSRSP and already points to SYSRST, we do not need to modify it at all to bring it into line with the new SYSRST.
- *Stage 4* — We have now completed the flip, with SYSRST and SYSRSP in line, though at a higher maintenance level, and SYSRSP is still the live SYSRES, although it has now exchanged device addresses with SYSRST. The maintenance cycle can begin again, with further maintenance being put on SYSRST using target zone TGTT, as before.

Option 3 is perhaps a little more elegant than option 2, and has several advantages:

- Once again, a copy of the old SYSRES can be kept on hand for a few days for a quick backout in case of problems.
- There is no need to rebuild any of the SMP/E target zones at any stage, or indeed to modify them at all (except through the APPLY process itself!), and consequently the global and target zone records will remain in step.
- Because the target zone name is always the same, and always points to the maintenance SYSRES (except when there is no maintenance SYSRES because the second SYSRES is the backout one) there is no danger of systems programmers putting maintenance on the wrong pack by mistake.

However:

- There is never a target zone corresponding to the live system, so there is no facility to put fixes directly onto the live system.
- Although the volume serial number of the production SYSRES is always the same, the device number still alternates, and because this is what the operators must specify as the load address, the potential for errors here still exists.

11.3.8 Conclusion

I can therefore confidently recommend option 1 — it is the one I use and it has never let me down! Either of the other two options, however, is feasible, and there are other variations which are equally feasible, and possibly even better. If you do decide to try a different way, the discussion above should give you a good picture of the factors you must bear in mind when you are designing your process.

References and bibliography

IBM manuals

1. *SMP/E Reference*, SC28–1107. For details on all SMP commands, including the zone management commands.

Other

2. Soucy, J., Shourbaji, R., Hanson, P. et al: Nascom Highlights, *Technical Support*, September 1990, pp. 6–10. Views from a number of systems programmers on the PUTs versus CBIPO/CBPDO question.
3. Krause, R.: An MVS System Software Management Methodology, *Technical Support*, February 1991, pp. 35–37. Recommendations on several of the issues discussed in this chapter and a few more besides.
4. Eshom, T.: SMP/E Part VI: UCLIN and Zone Commands, *Technical Support*, September 1990, pp. 67–73. A useful introduction to the zone management commands and some uses of them.

12
Enhancing your MVS system

12.1   Making system modifications

This chapter discusses how to extend the functionality of your MVS system beyond that supplied by IBM. Its main focus is on the use of exit points provided by IBM, and the later sections of the chapter will describe some of the more commonly used exit points and examples of what you might use them for. We will begin, however, by looking at the options available for modifying your system and recommending some policies on their use.

Once upon a time, the whole of MVS was supplied to you in source code format, and enterprising systems programmers would decipher sections of code and improve upon them when they decided they wanted an additional feature that MVS did not provide. Sadly for these enthusiasts, IBM is gradually restricting the amount of source code distributed with MVS and related products, and delivering its software instead in object-code-only format. While this removes opportunities for learning about your MVS system from the inside and for making innovative modifications, it also removes the nightmare of having to rework someone else's changes whenever maintenance is applied to the affected modules — or when the amended module is completely rewritten for a new release.

However, this does not mean it is becoming impossible to extend and enhance your MVS system. On the contrary, there is an ever-increasing range of options for doing this through IBM-approved interfaces — and these should be much more stable than modifications to source code. Typically, these interfaces are standard exit points which allow you to insert additional processing at well-defined points in system processing, though there are also other types of modification which you may make, e.g. modifying tables used by your system.

Exit points may be subdivided into a number of categories. With its ESA manuals, IBM appears to be using the terms 'user exists' and 'installation exits' in a new way to describe one of these subdivisions. User exits now seem to be exit points which may be used by the application programmer — such as SORT exits or exits to handle I/O errors. Installation exits, on the other hand, seem to be those exit points which apply to the system as a whole, and are therefore under the control of the systems programmer. This chapter will concentrate exclusively on the latter group.

Installation exits can be further subdivided according to how they are invoked:

- *Exit points* are places in the code of your MVS system where an exit may be invoked, depending on an initialization parameter. JES2 exits, for example, will only be invoked if the exit module is loaded using the JES2 LOAD initialization statement, and the exit point is activated using the EXIT initialization statement. Usually you may give the module to be invoked whatever name you wish.
- *Exit name lists* are lists of user exit routine names. When no exits are to be used, the list is blank, but if you wish to use exits, you may modify the list by inserting the names of the routines you wish to call. Again the names of the modules are under your control.
- *replaceable modules* are modules supplied by IBM as part of your system which you may replace in order to provide exit functions. Here you must give the module the same name as the IBM-supplied version. Perhaps the most important point to be borne in mind here is that there are two types of replaceable modules. Most replaceable modules are supplied by IBM as dummy CSECTS which simply return immediately to their caller. However, some are not, and if you replace a module which actually does some processing already, you must take great care to replicate that processing in your replacement module, unless you have good reason not to!

All exit points are documented in the manuals, and you should read this documentation carefully before attempting to use any exit. In addition to telling you whether a replaceable module contains any default processing, the documentation will usually tell you what environment the exit runs in:

- Whether it is APF authorized, and whether it runs in system key or supervisor state
- What parameter lists and register values are passed to it
- What register values it must save and restore (if this is not stated, you must assume that all registers are to be restored before returning control)
- Residency and addressing modes
- Whether the exit may use all MVS services or not (some may not issue SVCs, for example)
- Whether any locks are held during the exit processing
- How the exit may influence processing done by your MVS system, e.g. sometimes a return code may be used to tell the exit's caller what to do next

The manual to turn to will depend on the product you are attempting to modify. [1] ([2] for MVS/XA) documents most of the MVS base exits and includes a useful table (organized by product in the ESA version) of exits in other MVS products (JES2, JES3, DFP, RACF, RMF, TSO/E, TCAM, and VTAM), showing the manual to turn to for each exit. It excludes some major program products, however, such as DFDSS and DFHSM, which we will cover later in this chapter (and the XA version contains only a subset of the DFP exits). See the reading list at the end of this chapter for full titles and order numbers for the main manuals.

In addition to standard exit points, there are some other IBM-approved ways in which you may wish to modify your system:

- Modifying IBM-supplied tables, e.g. the tables containing the PPT and the TSO authorized program lists — although these two can now be modified using SYS1.PARMLIB members instead, which is preferable (see [4]).
- Replacing IBM-supplied tables, e.g. the ISFPARMS table which is used to control who can do what in SDSF (see [15]).
- Supplementing IBM-supplied tables with user tables, e.g. using the JES2 table pairs facility which was introduced with MVS/ESA (see [6]).
- Writing unit information modules (UIMs) to allow MVSCP to recognize and process non-standard I/O devices (see [4]).
- Writing resource managers to clean up resources at task and address space termination. These must be added to the list of resource managers used by MVS — this is an example of an exit name list, held in this case in module IEAVTRML (see [4]).
- Occasionally, IBM will recommend a change to source or object code if you have a particular problem to deal with, e.g. on MVS/XA systems it was sometimes necessary to zap the values of the GVTCREQ and GVTCREQA fields of CSECT ISGGRS00 in IEANUC01 to increase the limit on the number of concurrent ENQs from the default of 4K.

For all system enhancements, whether they are exits or not, there are some golden rules you should try to observe:

1   Do not do it unless you really have to! Systems programmers love writing exits and systems modifications, which often leads them to close their eyes to the real costs these impose. The coding and debugging time itself is always substantial; exits are highly vulnerable to IBM code changes and therefore lead to a continuing maintenance overhead; and the close tie-in between exits and system code can make them difficult to test thoroughly and dangerous when they go wrong.
2   If you have to do it, keep it as simple as possible — to minimize the risk and make it as easy as possible to rework the change if this becomes necessary.
3   Document your changes clearly and comprehensively.
4   Always apply your enhancements as SMP/E USERMODs and save the USERMOD source and JCL in a standard shared library, so that it is easy to identify what changes have been made, back them out if necessary, and find the source code if the change needs to be reapplied, e.g. due to an upgrade of the base product.
5   IBM provides samples of many exits, and frequently articles in journals like

MVS Update give examples of others. You should always attempt to find such a sample before starting to code an exit — this can reduce your coding and debugging time enormously. The following sections include references to samples where I am aware of them.

There are also special techniques for testing exits. One of the most useful is to create a 'front end' for the exit, which can run in key zero and reside in the LPA, but loads the main code for your exit from a non-LPA library and runs it in a user key. This allows you to change the current version without an IPL when the exit would normally have to reside in the LPA, and prevents you from inadvertently overwriting system storage during debugging. The front-end module could also restrict the calling of your exit code to valid testing situations, e.g. only for jobnames starting with your userid.

The remainder of this chapter will look at some of the more commonly-used exit points in MVS, JES2, the data management products, and TSO/E.

12.2   Commonly used MVS exits

The exits discussed in Table 12.1 are a subset of those documented in [1]. For XA, they are documented in [2], except the SMF exits, which are documented in [3]. [16] also contains a useful section on SMF exits, including pointers to sample source in IPO1.SAMPLIB, and JCL to create SMP/E USERMOD using this source, in IPO1.JCLLIB.

12.3   JES2 exits

12.3.1 Commonly used JES2 exit points

These exits are documented in [6]. For XA systems, they are documented in [7].

As at MVS 3.1.3. there is a total of 40 predefined exit points available in JES2, and you may also create additional exit points yourself by coding the $EXIT macro in a modification to JES code, though this is not to be recommended if a standard exit is suitable. Table 12.2 shows some of the most commonly used exit points.

12.3.2 Coding JES2 exits

The JES2 customization manual stresses that JES2 exit points, though they will be kept relatively stable by comparison with JES2 code itself, are not guaranteed to provide an unchanging interface to JES2 across different levels of the software. IBM still supplies the source code for JES2, which means that you can also amend the base product itself, but this should be avoided if at all possible — it is much more risky, both because the lack of specific documentation for the point at which you are inserting code makes it more difficult to get it right, and because the code you are changing is less stable. Even to write a JES exit requires quite detailed

Table 12.1. Commonly used MVS exit points

Exit	Description and use	Examples
CSVLLIX1	LLA module fetch exit — called whenever LLA fetches a module. Its main use is to monitor and collect fetch statistics. Typically, it will obtain storage in CSA (or preferably ECSA) on its first invocation to store statistics, then update them on each subsequent call. A batch program or REXX routine can then be written to interrogate these statistics. At present this is the only way of monitoring LLA.	SYS1.SAMPLIB (CSVLLIX1) contains a version of the exit which does no processing but includes lots of useful comments (also listed in [1]).
CSVLLIX2	LLA module staging exit — called whenever LLA is about to make a decision on staging a module. It can be used to direct that the module be staged, prevent it from being staged, or influence the decision by altering weighting factors. See [17].	Again SYS1.SAMPLIB (CSVLLIX2) contains a commented skeleton version of the exit which is also listed in [1].
IEALIMIT and IEFUSI	Region size limitation exits: IEALIMIT enables you to limit the region size a user may obtain below the 16 megabyte line; IEFUSI (the SMF step initiation exit, available only on XA and ESA systems) can limit the region size both below and above the 16 megabyte line. Unless you are still running MVS/370, IEFUSI is preferable. On storage-constrained systems, this may be useful for preventing users from obtaining so much storage that system performance is degraded. Alternatively, you could enforce such a limit through your JES parameters and JES exits, which gives you more scope for relating region size limits to jobclasses, for example. On ESA systems, IEFUSI can also be used to limit the number and size of dataspaces and hiperspaces an address space can own.	[4] documents region size limitation in some detail.
IEAVM-XIT and user-named exits	WTO/WTOR exits. If you supply an IEAVMXIT in SYS1.LINKLIB, MVS will invoke it for each message issued to the console, except for messages for which you have supplied a specific user exit. Specific message exits are invoked for any given message by coding a statement for the message id in the current MPFLSTxx member of SYS1.PARMLIB and including the USEREXIT(name) operand. These exits can selectively suppress messages, automatically issue replies to selected messages, modify a message's text, or change its routeing code. For example, in a shared DASD environment with some devices offline to some processors, you may wish to automatically cancel non-production jobs which issue messages IEF247I and IEF238D asking the operator to mount offline DASD.	[1] contains a number of very useful examples. Note that these exits are also discussed in [4] and under the MPFLSTxx section of [5]. Also see [18].

Table 12.1. (cont.)

Exit	Description and use	Examples
IEECVXIT and IEFACTRT	IEECVXIT is a WTO exit which can only alter the routeing code of the WTO, and IEFACTRT is the SMF step-end exit. IBM supplies samples of these which work together to write step-end messages to the JOBLOG of the job concerned, giving the completion code and counts of EXCPs (i.e. physical I/Os), TCB time and SRB time used by the step. Job accounting software often uses these exits to calculate, store, and display charges for the step, based on the resources it used. An innovative suggestion by Randy Brack [19] is to trap steps with S222 abend codes, write a WTOR asking the operator why they cancelled the job, then put the reply in a joblog message.	SYS1.SAMPLIB (SMFEXITS) includes a basic IEFACTRT, but the CBIPO version, with the accompanying IEECVXIT, is far superior — see [16] for details.
IEFDB401	Dynamic allocation input validation exit — called for all dataset allocation requests using SVC 99 (this does *not* include JCL allocation). It may approve or deny the request depending on the allocation parameters, or modify the parameters (see Sec. 6.7 for an explanation of SVC 99 parameters). It could be used, for example, to prevent test datasets being allocated with more than a certain amount of DASD space, or to prevent SORTWKxx datasets being allocated to VIO-eligible devices.	[20] gives an example of this exit.
IEFUSO	SMF SYSOUT limit exit — receives control when the number of records written to a SYSOUT dataset exceeds the output limit for the dataset. If you do not supply an IEFUSO exit, the job is cancelled when it hits this limit. Perhaps its best use is to (a) cancel test jobs which exceed SYSOUT limits; and (b) allow production jobs to continue but issue a message to the operator in case the job is looping and filling up the spool with rubbish. Note that JES exit 9 performs a similar function to this and may be more suitable in some cases.	One of the few SMF exits not to be found in SYS1.SAMPLIB or IPO1.SAMPLIB.
IEFUTL	SMF time limit exit — receives control when a job exceeds the job or step CPU time limit, or the continuous wait time limit. It may cancel the job, write a message to the operator, and/or extend the time limit which has been exceeded. The version in SYS1.SAMPLIB extends the step/ wait time three times then cancels the job on the fourth call. (On the whole, I do not approve of extending time limits, as this simply leads to abuse of 'short' jobclasses.)	The sample referred to here is in SYS1.SAMPLIB (SMFEXITS). CBIPO supplies another sample in IPO1.SAMPLIB — see [16] for details.

Table 12.1 (cont.)

Exit	Description and use	Examples
ISGGREX0	GRS resource name list scan exit. This routine scans the GRS RNLs when the cross-system component of GRS is in use (see Chapter 14 for a discussion of GRS RNLs). This is an example of a replaceable module where the supplied module actually does do some important processing, so if you replace it you must ensure your replacement module replicates the original processing, or deliberately replaces it. You might wish to replace it to exclude temporary datasets from cross-system serialization, or to allow the specification of generic dataset names in your RNLs.	IBM supply source in SYS1. ASAMPLIB (ISGGREXS); this is not the same as the default module, as it does cater for temporary datasets. See [21] for a discussion of how to add support for generic dataset names.

knowledge of JES2 programming conventions (which is obtainable from [6]) and JES2 internals (which is not!). In this section there will only be room to give you a very brief flavour of these subjects.

For instance, JES2 exits run in several different programming environments, depending on the exit, and you must be familiar with these and the conventions relating to the environment in which you are working. Exits running in the 'JES2 main task' environment, for example, (this includes exits 1 to 5) must not issue an MVS WAIT, or invoke any instruction or system routine which might do so, because this causes the whole of JES to stop processing. If they need to wait, they must use the JES2 $WAIT macro, which does not return control to MVS, but instead invokes JES2's internal work dispatching routine. This allows JES to continue dispatching other JES2 processes (such as printing and reading in new jobs) while your process is waiting.

There are over 100 JES2 macros available to coders of JES2 exits, which provide a wide range of services, including:

- Equivalent services to those provided by MVS macros but modified to run in the appropriate JES2 environment (e.g. $WAIT, $GETMAIN, $FREMAIN)
- Module structure definition and save area implementation (e.g. $MODULE, $MODEND, $ENTRY, $EXIT, $SAVE, and $RETURN)
- JES2-specific services, such as checkpointing a JES2 element ($CKPT), or adding a JQE to the job queue ($QADD)
- Print services, such as producing block letters on print separator pages ($PBLOCK)

These macros are also documented in [6].

Clearly, coding JES exits requires a whole new set of skills and experience on top of that required to code a normal MVS exit — and I have only touched on the knowledge you need. You should therefore become thoroughly familiar with the contents of [6] and with JES2 internals before starting to code a JES exit.

Table 12.2. Commonly used JES2 exit ponts

Exit	Description and use	Examples
JESEXIT1	Print/punch separator exit — used to create separator pages between the printed output for different jobs or output dataset groups. It can produce installation-created separator pages as well as, or in addition to, the standard separator pages irrespective of the settings of the SEP/NOSEP parameter for the current printer.	A very simple example is provided in Chapter 2 of [6]. See also SYS1.SAMPLIB (HASX01A).
JESEXIT2	JOB statement scan exit — taken whenever JES2 reads a JOB statement or JOB continuation statement. It allows you to cancel jobs (with explanatory messages), modify their JOB statement parameters, modify fields in JES control blocks related to the job, and even supply additional continuation statements for the JOB statement. Because this is usually the first exit encountered by a job, it is an ideal place to control which other exits will be taken by the job by amending the job exit mask in the JCT. The commonest use is to enforce installation standards relating to the JOB statement, e.g. valid jobnames, valid jobclasses for a given jobname, and whether the REGION and TIME parameters can be coded on the JOB statement.	SYS1.SAMPLIB (HASX02A). [22] also includes an example.
JESEXIT3	JOB statement accounting field scan exit — can supplement or replace the JES2 routine for validating the accounting information supplied on each job's JOB statement. It is widely used to enforce standards for account codes — e.g. a standard requiring a certain relationship between the jobname and the account code—by cancelling jobs which do not adhere to the standard.	SYS1.SAMPLIB (HASX03A) and (HASX03B).
JESEXIT4	JCL and JES2 control statement scan exit — taken for each JCL statement and each JES2 control statement (such as /*JOBPARM statements) in a jobstream. It allows you to modify the statement, add continuation statements or even additional JCL statements, or cancel the job. The typical usage is to enforce JCL coding standards, though more ambitious usages are also possible, e.g. you can create your own installation specific JES2 control statements and use this exit to process them.	SYS1.SAMPLIB (HASX04A). [22] also includes an example.

Table 12.2. (cont.)

Exit	Description and use	Examples
JESEXIT5	JES2 command preprocessor exit — receives control every time JES receives a console command. It may validate the command and if necessary reject it. More interesting, though, is the possibility of creating your own installation-specific JES commands and using this exit to perform the processing required by the command.	SYS1.SAMPLIB (HASX05A) and [23] — an example of JES exit 5 which creates a JES command to reload JES exits.
JESEXIT6	Internal text scan exit — called for each JCL statement after it has been converted into JES internal text. It allows you to perform any processing which JESEXIT4 can do, plus processing on statements which are not available to JESEXIT4, such as JCL which has been merged into the job as a result of resolving references to cataloged procedures, and SYSIN data, though modifying SYSIN data is not a recommended use of this exit. The format of internal text is documented briefly in [1], and in more detail in the source of the macros IEFVKEYS and IEFTXTFT in SYS1.AMODGEN. The SMF job validation exit IEFUJV can also be used to process internal text at this stage. Which of these is more suitable depends on whether you have more need to access JES2 or SMF control blocks from the exit.	SYS1.SAMPLIB (HASX06A) and (HASX06B).

12.3.3 JES2 table pairs

With MVS/ESA, a new facility for making JES2 modifications has been added. This is the concept of table pairs. JES2 uses tables to define many of its services, including, for example:

- $SCAN tables for specifying the processing required to parse and syntax check initialization statements, commands, parameters, and options
- MPS tables to describe the JES2 initialization statements and their parameters
- Message tables defining JES2 messages

The table pairs facility allows you to supply a user table to supplement the supplied JES2 table for each of these functions. The JES2 master control table (MCT) holds the addresses of all the JES2 tables, and null entries for the corresponding user tables. By creating a user table and inserting its address into the appropriate MCT entry, you can therefore extend and/or modify the facilities defined by any of these tables without touching the JES2 tables themselves. The insertion of the address into the MCT is usually accomplished using JES exit 0, and an example of the coding required is supplied by IBM in members HASPXIT0 and HASPXJ00 of SYS1.SAMPLIB. This is further documented in the Washington Systems Center manual [8].

Table 12.3. Commonly used data management exits

Exit	Description and use	Examples
IGGPRE00	DADSM (direct access device storage management) preprocessing exit — invoked before DADSM processing for all DADSM functions (allocate, extend, scratch, partial release, and rename). Can reject the request altogether, reject it for the current volume, or allow it. Often used to enforce DASD pooling in a pre-SMS environment by rejecting allocation and rename requests for volumes to which the job or datasetname concerned should not have access.	See [24].
IGGPOST0	DADSM postprocessing exit — invoked after DADSM processing for all DADSM functions. Can be used, for example, to write SMF records relating to allocation/release of DASD space so that you can charge users accurately for it.	
ADRUENQ	DFDSS enqueue exit — invoked during certain DFDSS operations to determine how long DFDSS should ENQ on the VTOC of the volume being processed. If you wish to allow other jobs, or another processor in a shared DASD environment, to access the volume while DFDSS is processing it, then you should implement this exit. For certain operations, the default is to ENQ on the VTOC for the entire operation, but simply by setting a return code of 4 in ADRUENQ you can reduce the ENQ to the period of time during which the VTOC itself is being processed. You need to consider data integrity carefully if you are doing this, but it can prevent system deadlocks in a shared DASD environment.	
ADRUPSWD	DFDSS authorization exit — allows you to bypass authorization checking at the dataset level for most DFDSS functions. This may be considered desirable for performance reasons, particularly when performing routine dumps on volumes with large numbers of datasets, and particularly at sites using RACF. It does, however, create a potential security exposure unless the exit itself checks that the current user has a suitable level of authorization (e.g. at the volume level) before bypassing authorization at the dataset level.	
ARCBDEXT	DFHSM dataset backup exit — taken by DFHSM when it selects a dataset for backup. Can be used to prevent certain datasets from being backed up — on pre-SMS systems, for example, this was a convenient way of preventing GDG datasets on DASD from being backed up by DFHSM. On SMS systems, management classes can be used to perform similar functions and should be preferred where possible.	HSM.SAMPLE.CNTL (ARCBDEXT) — created by running the JCL in SYS1.SAMPLIB (ARCSTRST) during HSM installation.

Table 12.3 (cont.)

Exit	Description and use	Examples
ARCMDEXT	DFHSM dataset migration exit — taken by DFHSM when it selects a dataset for migration from a primary volume. Can be used, for example, to prevent certain datasets from being migrated, or to route certain datasets straight to migration level 2. Note that DFHSM parameters and/or SMS management class parameters can perform similar functions.	
ARCMVEXT	DFHSM space management volume exit — taken by DFHSM after it finishes space management for a primary volume. The data supplied to the exit includes a fragmentation index for the volume, which makes this an ideal point to schedule DEFRAGs for badly fragmented volumes.	HSM.SAMPLE.CNTL (ARCMVEXT)—created as above.

Note
[1] DFP exits are generally linked into SYS1.LPALIB as replacement load modules.
[2] DFDSS exits must be link-edited into ADRDSSU, the main DFDSS load module.
[3] DFHSM exits are generally placed in a linklist dataset, and activated and deactivated using the EXITON and EXITOFF parameter of the DFHSM SETSYS command.

Table pairs are not intended to replace JES exits; rather, they provide a complementary way of customizing certain aspects of JES2. Nor do they simplify JES2 customization — implementing a table pair is just as complex an exercise as coding a JES exit, and the first one you do will probably seem considerably more difficult. The use of table pairs should therefore be treated just as warily as any other customization facility — in other words, do not do it unless you really have to.

12.4 Common data management exits

Table 12.3 covers exits belonging to DFP, DFHSM, and DFDSS. The DFP exits are documented in [9], the DFHSM exits in [10], and the DFDSS exits in [11]. Note that the DFHSM and DFDSS exits are not included in the directory of exits in [1].

Also note, that with the introduction of SMS, many facilities previously implemented using data management exits can now be implemented using standard SMS facilities. IBM recommends that you conduct an audit of any such exits, and aim to remove any which can be replaced using SMS facilities.

All three products allow a range of other exit points — consult the appropriate manual if you suspect there might be one which can be of use to you.

12.5 Common TSO exits

The TSO/E exits listed in Table 12.4 are documented in [12] (see [13] in the unlikely event that you do not have TSO/E).

TSO/E supplies many other exit points, most of which relate to individual TSO

Table 12.4. Commonly used TSO exits

Exit	Description and use	Examples
IKJEFLD	Logon preprompt exit — invoked after the user enters the LOGON command but before the prompt for password, procname, etc. Can be used to replace the usual prompt processing with your own. More useful, perhaps, is the ability to prevent a user logging on to TSO at all, for example, you could check in the exit how many users are already logged on, compare this with the current USERMAX, and if the difference is less than x, issue a message and deny the logon unless the user has a systems programmer's userid. This guarantees you the ability to log on to deal with a crisis even when TSO usage is very heavy. Version 2 of TSO/E allows you to replace this exit with IKJEFLD1, which has more potential power, and a new logoff exit, IKJEFLD2.	
IKJEFF10	SUBMIT exit — invoked whenever TSO encounters a JOB statement in a piece of JCL submitted using the TSO SUBMIT command (including jobs submitted using ISPF/PDF EDIT SUBMIT, which invokes TSO SUBMIT). It can validate and modify the submitted JCL, issue messages to the user and obtain responses, and/ or cancel the SUBMIT request. This exit is often used to restrict the jobname on jobs submitted from TSO, e.g. only allow users to submit jobs with jobnames beginning with their userid, unless they are systems programmers. If other parts of your standards restrict what jobs can do depending on the jobname, then controlling the jobnames available to a user is an essential component of enforcing them! The SMF job validation exit (IEFUJV) performs similar processing, but for all jobs, not just those submitted from TSO.	
IKJEFF53	OUTPUT, STATUS, and CANCEL command exit — invoked whenever a TSO user issues one of these commands. The default exit prevents a user from cancelling a job unless its jobname consists of the user's userid plus one character, and prevents the use of the OUTPUT command unless the jobname begins with the user's userid. CBIPO provides an alternative version which allows users with OPER authority to use OUTPUT and CANCEL on any job, and creates a STATUS TSO command to display currently logged-on TSO users. If, like most installations, you use SDSF in place of these commands, there is little point in changing the default. JES exit 22 performs similar processing, though it is rarely used.	Source for the default exit is provided in SYS1.SAMPLIB (IKJEFF53) and for the CBIPO version in IPO1.SAMPLIB (IKJEFF53). CBIPO also supplies a module to test this exit, in member DRIVER53 of the same library. See [16] for details.

commands. Note that there are many other facilities for customizing TSO, which are also documented in [12]. In addition, there is significant overlap between some of the TSO customization facilities and customization facilities in other parts of MVS, as we can see even with the few examples shown in Table 12.4. This overlap is well documented in [12] in the chapter 'Overview of facilities for customizing TSO/E'.

ISPF and PDF also supply a number of exit points, though these are rarely used. These are documented in [14], and examples of many of the ISPF/PDF exits are supplied in SYS1.SAMPLIB.

References and bibliography

IBM manuals

1. *MVS/ESA SPL: Installation Exits*, GC28–1836. Documents MVS exits, including SMF exits, and includes a directory listing most other MVS-related exits and the manuals in which they are documented.
2. *MVS/XA SPL: User Exits*, GC28–1147. The XA version of *Installation Exits*, but it does not include SMF exits and the exit directory is less comprehensive.
3. *MVS/XA SPL: SMF*, GC28–1153. Includes the XA documentation for the SMF exits
4. MVS/ESA SPL: System Modifications GC28–1831. Includes useful chapters on the use of IEALIMIT and IEFUSI to limit region sizes, using IEECVXIT, IEAVMXIT, and user-named WTO/WTOR exits, and writing MVSCP UIMs and MVS resource managers.
5. *MVS/ESA SPL: Initialization and Tuning*, GC28-1828. Includes discussion of exits invoked from SYS1.PARMLIB (MPFLSTxx).
6. *MVS/ESA SPL: JES2 Customization*, LY28–1010. Documents JES exit points, macros available to JES2 systems programmers, and the use of table pairs.
7. *MVS/XA SPL: JES2 User Modifications and Macros*, LC23–0069. The XA equivalent of *JES2 Customization* — but note that table pairs are not covered as these were only introduced with ESA.
8. *Extending JES2 Using Table Pairs*, GG66–0282. A widely recommended Washington Systems Center manual.
9. *MVS/DFP: Customization*, SC26–4560. Documents both user and installation exits associated with DFP.
10. *DFHSM Installation and Customization Guide*, SH35–0084. Includes documentation of all DFHSM exits.
11. *DFDSS Reference*, SC26–4389. Includes documentation of DFDSS exits.
12. *TSO/E V2 Customization*, SC28–1872. Documents TSO/E exits and many other ways of customizing TSO/E.
13. *MVS/XA SPL: TSO*, GC28–1173. Includes documentation of exits available with the base TSO product.
14. *ISPF and ISPF/PDF Planning and Customizing*, SC34–4257. Covers all aspects of customizing these two products, including exits.
15. *SDSF Guide and Reference*, SC23–0408. Includes documentation on modifying the SDSF authorization parameters module.
16. *CBIPO MVS Customization Guide* (supplied in IPO1.DOCLIB on CBIPO-built systems). Describes CBIPO samples of SMF exits and IKJEFF53.

Other

17. Jackson, B.: Monitoring and Influencing LLA's use of VLF, *UKCMG Proceedings*, Birmingham, 1991, pp. 15–22. An extremely useful article on VLF and the use of CSVLLIX1 and 2 to monitor and control it.
18. Carson, G.W.: IEF238D Revisited, *MVS Update*, July 1991, pp. 42–47. An example of a WTO processing exit.
19. Brack, R. The SMF Job/Step Termination Exit, *Enterprise Systems Journal*, January 1991, 69–71. A good discussion of IEFACTRT.
20. Dynamic Allocation Dataset Diversion, *MVS Update*, March 1988, pp. 19–25. Includes an example of an IEFDB401 exit.
21. Odom, R.W. Jr: Adding Masks to Your GRS RNL, *Technical Support*, March 1991, pp. 68–70. Shows how to use the ISGGREX0 exit to allow the coding of wildcard characters in GRS RNLs.
22. Cornman, J.: JES2 Exits to Control JOBCAT/STEPCAT Use, *MVS Update*, March 1988, pp. 28–33. Includes examples of JES exits 2 and 4.
23. Barnett, S.: Dynamic reload of JES2 Exits, *MVS Update*, April 1991, pp. 36–45. An example of JES exit 5, used to reload other JES exits.
24. Rohwer, E.: Volume Pooling Using IGGPRE00, *MVS Update*, October 1987, pp. 33–40. Includes a fully coded example of IGGPRE00.
25. Reaugh, D.: Volume Pooling and DASD Budgeting using the DADSM Exits, *Technical Support*, April 1990, pp. 40–42.

13
Multi-image environments

13.1   Introduction

What is a multi-image environment? Why would you want one? How can you provide such an environment? What does the systems programmer have to do to set it up? What is the most appropriate way of doing it in different circumstances? These are the questions this chapter will address. Let us start with the first one.

An image in this context is a copy of an operating system, so a multi-image environment exists when you are running more than one MVS system. Usually, this also implies sharing resources between the systems, such as processor cycles, processor storage, I/O devices and paths to them, and even datasets. It is the complexities introduced by the need to control the sharing of these resources that make supporting a multi-image environment more interesting and difficult than running a single MVS system.

There are several ways in which a multi-image environment may be set up, and the following sections of this chapter will consider each of these in turn, covering its advantages and disadvantages and outlining the contribution it requires from the systems programmer. The alternatives are:

1   More than one physical processor complex (also known as a central processor complex, CPC).
2   Physical partitioning of a single processor complex.
3   Logical partitioning of a processor complex using a hardware/microcode feature. Each manufacturer of MVS-capable mainframes has their own product to provide this facility: PR/SM from IBM; MDF from Amdahl; and MLPF from Hitachi.
4   Using VM as a 'hypervisor'.

Resource sharing raises a number of issues, which we will go into in more detail as we discuss each type of multi-image environment:

- How are the resources divided between the systems?
- How readily can they be reassigned between them?

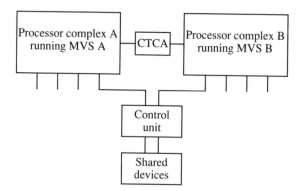

Figure 13.1. Running MVS on multiple processor complexes.

- What mechanisms are required to control the sharing of the resources and protect their integrity?

The need to control resource sharing introduces an additional overhead for the systems involved, i.e. a cost, and for this to be worth doing there must be some benefits from running multiple systems. The most important are:

- *Resilience* — To protect important applications from software failures which impact the operating system, by isolating less reliable applications under a different copy of MVS.
- *Performance* — To protect the performance of important applications against resource demands of less critical ones.
- *Systems testing* — To provide a permanent facility for systems programmers to perform complete system tests on new software, maintenance, etc.
- *Economics* — Your management may decide it is more cost-effective to supply a required increase in capacity by buying an extra machine than by buying a bigger one.

A new development in the multi-image area is IBM's new Sysplex feature, which allows separate MVS systems to be closely coupled — in effect to appear as if they were a single system in some respects. At the time of writing this is still at an early stage of development, but it is clearly going to become increasingly important for large sites, and the final section of the chapter is devoted to Sysplex.

Chapter 14 will discuss sharing of I/O devices and system datasets between multiple MVS images.

13.2   Multiple processor complexes

The most obvious way to provide the ability to run more than one MVS system is to buy more than one box to run it on, and then share resources such as DASD and the communications network between them. This option is illustrated in Fig. 13.1. Note:

- If you are sharing I/O devices between two CPCs, each complex must have its own channel path to the control units concerned (this is discussed in more detail in Chapter 14).
- If you need to communicate between the systems running on the two complexes, you are likely to need a channel-to-channel adaptor (usually a separate piece of hardware), plus channels linking it to each of the systems. ESCON channels, however, support channel-to-channel links (CTCs) without the need for a separate CTCA. CTCs are commonly used for intersystem communication by GRS, VTAM, and JES3.

Multiple processor complexes are quite a common choice, and they have a number of advantages:

1 Resilience is at a maximum — the two (or more) systems are completely independent of each other in hardware terms.
2 The total processing capacity can be greater than that obtainable from any single processor complex.
3 The overhead of resource sharing is at a minimum. There is nothing intervening between MVS and the machine, and the only overhead is that caused by whatever mechanism is used to control DASD sharing — usually GRS or MII (discussed in detail in Chapter 14).
4 The additional skills needed to support the multi-image environment are at a minimum. The systems programmers will have to do some work to set up DASD sharing, connect the new machine with the network, and other device sharing, but the operators will require virtually no additional skills.

On the other hand:

1 Flexibility of resource allocation between the systems and control of resource allocation is also at a minimum. You can only change the allocation of memory or processor cycles between the systems by buying more!
2 The running costs of this option tend to be high. Two machines usually require significantly more floor space, power, and air conditioning than one more powerful one.

In summary, then, this option will certainly be chosen when your site requires more processing power than the largest available processor complex can provide. It may also be chosen when it is important to minimize capital expenditure in the short run or to maximize the resilience of one or more of the systems, but in most other circumstances its lack of flexibility makes it an inferior choice.

From a systems programmer's point of view, this is the simplest multi-image environment to support — but you do still need to deal with DASD sharing and dataset sharing, which are covered in Chapter 14.

The manageability and flexibility of this option is likely to increase over time as IBM extends the implementation of Sysplex. Sysplex, discussed in Sec. 13.9, seems intended primarily to make it easier to use multiple MVS images as if they were a

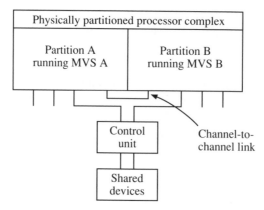

Figure 13.2. MVS on a physically partitioned processor complex.

single image, and to increase resilience in a multi-image environment by allowing one MVS image to act as a backup to another.

13.3   Physical partitioning

Physical partitioning of a CPC is only possible on a two way complex. In effect, this is a machine that consists of two smaller machines bolted together plus the microcode required to make the two halves function as a single CPC. Examples are the 3084 (equivalent to two 3081s), the 3090–280 series (like two 180s), and the 3090–400 series (like two 200s). On these machines, each side has its own processors, storage, channels, service console, and power supply. The two sides can be separated logically and MVS can be IPLed on each side separately, which gives us a configuration like Fig. 13.2. Note that although the CTCA is not shown in this diagram, we still require one if we wish to set up channel-to-channel links between the two partitions (unless we use ESCON channels).

   Once the complex has been partitioned, the only real difference between this option and the previous one is that the two 'processor complexes' are in the same box. Not surprisingly, therefore, this option has pretty much the same advantages and disadvantages as running two separate machines:

- *Flexibility is zero.* Only two systems can be brought up simultaneously, each controlling one side, and each side can use only resources on its own side.
- *Control over resource allocation is minimal.* This is determined at hardware purchase and configuration time. Note that the two sides can be asymmetrically configured, but this still leaves you with less flexibility to alter the configuration of either processor complex, even compared with the option of running two separate machines.
- *Resilience is maximum.* This is effectively the same as for two separate machines, as one MVS system can survive any failure of the other, including a power failure to the other side of the processor complex.

- *Overhead is minimum.* This is the same as for two separate machines.
- *Systems programming input is minimal.* It is just like running two separate machines.
- *Operator input is minimal.* It is just like running two separate machines, except for the process of separating or recombining them, which would normally be done extremely rarely, as it requires an IML of the whole machine as well as some work on the service consoles.

With the advent of logical partitioning, discussed in the next section, the option of physical partitioning is becoming less and less attractive.

As with separate machines, all the issues for systems programmers are covered in Chapter 14 — with the exception of I/O device configuration. With a partitionable box, you will need to develop a configuration which can function for either a single system running unpartitioned, or two systems running in partitioned mode. So each side must have paths to every device which it will need in partitioned mode. This introduces an element of redundancy when operating in unpartitioned mode; the combined halves may, for example, have two paths to your network front-end processor and four to 3880 DASD controllers. In addition, you may need to define and purchase channel-to-channel links from one half of the machine to the other to support GRS and VTAM connections — these will be unused in unpartitioned mode.

13.4   Logical partitioning

Logical partitioning can be implemented on some types of processor using a hardware/microcode feature — PR/SM from IBM, MDF from Amdahl, or MLPF from Hitachi. MDF has been around the longest, and most Amdahl machines now support it, while PR/SM was introduced in 1988 and is only available on 3090s from the E series onwards, and ES/9000s.

All these implementations of logical partitioning are fairly similar in practice; here I will concentrate on PR/SM, but much the same arguments apply to MDF or MLPF. Their basic function is to allow separate copies of MVS to be IPLed and run in separate logical partitions on the same physical processor complex, and to share the complex's resources between those partitions in a relatively flexible way. The resources to be shared are: processors, channels, central storage, and expanded storage. Figure 13.3 illustrates logical partitioning. Note that:

- The dashed lines separating the partitions indicate that the allocation of processor resources between the partitions is not fixed as it was in the case of physical partitioning, but can vary dynamically. Each channel, on the other hand, belongs to one and only one partition at any one time.
- Again, channel-to-channel connections between partitions require CTCAs, which are not shown here for the sake of simplicity.

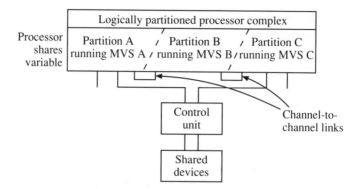

Figure 13.3. MVS on a logically partitioned processor complex.

By comparison with the 'separate machine' and 'physical partitioning' options we considered earlier, logical partitioning has the following characteristics:

- Flexibility in dividing processor power between partitions is high as this is varied dynamically based on rules set by the systems programmer and demands of the partitions (analogous to the way SRM shares cycles between competing units of work within MVS). Each physical processor is defined either as dedicated or shared; dedicated physical processors always belong to a given partition, while shared processors are dynamically assigned to different partitions by PR/SMs equivalent of the MVS dispatcher. You can define partition weights to control the priorities given to different partitions when processor usage approaches 100 per cent, and these can be changed inflight via the system console.
- Flexibility in allocating storage and channels between partitions is medium. Each channel is defined in the IOCDS as belonging to a given partition, but channels can be defined as reconfigurable, and reconfigurable channels can be moved between partitions 'inflight'. Storage allocations are made when defining partitions, and normally reconfiguration requires reactivation of PR/SM — this is similar to a power-on-reset, so the systems in all of the logical partitions then have to be re-IPLed. However, dynamic storage reconfiguration is possible in restricted circumstances, i.e. when you have allowed for it in your storage definitions and when the storage to be reconfigured is contiguous with the storage of the partition you wish to move it to. Dynamic storage reconfiguration is not available on E series 3090s or some smaller S models.
- Control over the allocation of resources is quite fine: granularity of division is one channel or 1 M of storage, and processors can be either dedicated or shared. Logical processors are scheduled onto physical processors using a combination of time-slicing and 'event-driven' SRM-like algorithms, and the relative priorities of partitions are controlled by partition weights which can be modified inflight. Resource capping can also be used to limit the maximum

processor usage of a partition.

- Resilience is high. Each MVS system is independent of failures in other partitions, though all are dependent on the common hardware.
- Overhead is medium: estimated at 5–10 per cent.
- Operator and systems programmer input is medium. Both are likely to be involved in occasional reconfiguration.
- Hardware is restricted to 3090E and above for PR/SM; all current Amdahl processors support MDF.

Systems programming input to support PR/SM again revolves mainly around defining the I/O configuration — as with a physically partitioned machine, you will have to ensure that each logical partition has channels to every device it needs to use, and CTCs to the other logical partitions if these are needed to support GRS and VTAM. In addition, you will probably be involved in determining how resources such as memory and processor cycles (via partition weights) are to be shared between the machines — although if there is a separate capacity planning and performance team, this may fall in their province. The reconfiguration of resources is technically an operator process, but you may also be involved in doing this (via the processor console). Finally, of course, you will have to resolve all the same device-sharing and data-sharing issues as with physical partitioning or multiple machines.

13.5 Implementing PR/SM

Assuming you have a machine with the PR/SM feature installed, there are three main phases of the process of implementing PR/SM:

1 Creating and activating an IOCDS which defines the logical partitions and the channels attached to them.
2 Using the hardware system console to define further attributes of the logical partitions.
3 Activating the PR/SM configuration and IPLing the systems in each partition.

We will look at each of these in turn.

If you have a PR/SM-capable processor complex, it is the active IOCDS which will determine whether or not it is running in logically partitioned (LPAR) mode, and which will provide the initial definitions of the partitions. When you are generating an IOCDS, you can make it either an LPAR mode IOCDS (by specifying LPAR = Y in the PARM field of the JCL EXEC statement for IOCP), or a basic mode IOCDS (by specifying LPAR = N). If a basic mode IOCDS is activated, then the machine will run as a single image with no partitioning; if an LPAR mode IOCDS is activated, PR/SM will be used to partition the machine.

When you create an LPAR mode IOCDS, you must also define the names of the logical partitions which can be activated, and assign each channel path to a partition. This is accomplished using the PARTITION operand on the CHPID statement. (On older versions of IOCP partitions are not named explicitly — IOCP simply assumes that each different name you have coded on a CHPID statement will be a partition. If you are using the newer IZPIOCP, however, you will need to define the partition names on a separate input statement.) Example 13.1 shows

```
PATH00    CHPID PATH=00,TYPE=BL,PARTITION=(PROD)
PATH01    CHPID PATH=01,TYPE=BL,PARTITION=(PROD)
PATH02    CHPID PATH=02,TYPE=BL,PARTITION=(PROD)
PATH03    CHPID PATH=03,TYPE=BL,PARTITION=(TEST)
PATH04    CHPID PATH=04,TYPE=BL,PARTITION=(TEST,REC)
PATH05    CHPID PATH=05,TYPE=BL,PARTITION=(TEST)
PATH06    CHPID PATH=06,TYPE=BL,PARTITION=(PROD)
PATH07    CHPID PATH=07,TYPE=BL,PARTITION=(PROD)
PATH08    CHPID PATH=08,TYPE=BL,PARTITION=(PROD,REC)
```

Example 13.1. LPAR definition statements from an IOCP deck.

statements from an LPAR mode IOCP input deck. Note that the minimum I/O configuration for a partition consists of a dedicated 3×74 control unit with an attached terminal which can be used as a console, plus a channel path to a DASD controller with an attached disk which can be used as your SYSRES device.

Note also that in Example 13.1:

- The REC keyword on the CHPID statement defines the channel path concerned as reconfigurable, i.e. it can be moved between partitions using operator commands.
- If you specify LPAR = YES on your EXEC statement PARM operand, these CHPID statements will result in an LPAR mode IOCDS being generated with two logical partitions called PROD and TEST.

Having generated your LPAR mode IOCDS, you must activate it in the usual way (see the discussion on IOCP and IOCDSs in Chapter 7) — this is equivalent to performing a power-on-reset, so all systems must be down before you can do this.

The next stage is to use the hardware system console to complete the definitions of your logical partitions. First, you must select the LPDEF frame and enter the amounts and locations of the central and expanded storage to be assigned to each partition. Then you must select the LPCTL frame and enter the processing weights for each partition (and whether or not each partition is to be resource-capped). Next, you will need to activate each of the partitions from the LPDEF frame. Once you have more than one active partition, many of the frames on the hardware console will now relate to only one partition — the current or 'target' logical partition (TLP). You can change the TLP from any frame using the SETLP partitionname command. You should make sure that both you and the operators get into the habit of checking which partition is the current TLP before entering any commands on the hardware console. The OPRCTL frame used for IPLing a partition is one rather vital example of a frame which relates to the TLP — if you

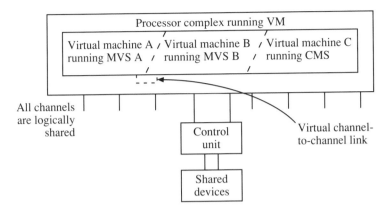

Figure 13.4. Running MVS under a VM hypervisor.

do not establish an iron rule that the current TLP is checked before entering any commands on this frame, there is a serious danger of someone IPLing the wrong partition, which could be disastrous.

Now you are in a position to IPL the systems which will run on each partition, by first using SETLP to set the target partition, then IPLing as normal. All the PR/SM facilities on the hardware console are documented in the appropriate processor manual, e.g. [3] for 3090 machines.

13.6   Software partitioning

In effect, your machine can also be partitioned at the software level, using IBM's VM (Virtual Machine) operating system as a 'hypervisor'. VM runs as the 'host' operating system and shares resources between multiple 'virtual machines' running 'guest' operating systems (MVS, VSE, VM, CMS, or even UNIX). The guest operating system behaves very much as if it were running on a real machine. This is illustrated in Fig. 13.4. Note that:

- This time the channel-to-channel links between the different MVS systems do not require physical CTCA devices, as VM can provide 'virtual CTCs' between the MVS systems under its control.
- Now channels are shared dynamically between the different guests as well as other processor resources.

One virtual machine can be nominated as a 'preferred guest' or V = R machine, which substantially reduces the VM overhead for that guest, especially for MVS I/O when the SIE assist feature is available on the hardware platform and DASD volumes are dedicated to the guest. On some machines there is also a hardware/ microcode feature called multiple preferred guests (MPG) available, which allows more than one virtual machine to acquire the privileges of a preferred guest — one of these is said to run V = R, and the rest V = F. However, the MPG feature requires PR/SM to be installed.

Running MVS under VM we have the following characteristics:

- Flexibility is very high. Processor power is shared dynamically between guests depending on parameters specified by the systems programmer and the demands of the guests; storage is allocated between guests in a similar way to MVS's own sharing of real storage between address spaces (i.e. RSM and paging), except for the preferred guest, whose storage is dedicated; channels belong to VM not individual guests and so are effectively shared between the guests; DASD can be shared between MVS guests if defined as full-pack minidisks, but not if they are dedicated to one virtual machine (e.g. to a preferred guest to take advantage of SIE assist).
- Control over resource allocation is left to VM, within broad parameters set by the systems programmers (e.g. the number of processors on which a guest can execute simultaneously) — except for those resources (DASD and memory) which are dedicated to the preferred guest.
- Resilience is good, with multiple guests isolated effectively from each other, but all guests are now dependent on VM as well as the hardware.
- Overhead is relatively high, and depends on the processor, workload, and whether the guest is using SIE assist (only available to the $V = R$ guest, unless MPG is installed, in which case it is also available to up to five $V = F$ guests). Some typical figures are:

  5 per cent for preferred MVS guests using SIE assist on a 3090
  12 per cent for preferred MVS guests using SIE assist on a 3084
  20 per cent for preferred MVS guests without SIE assist on a 3090
  50 per cent for $V = V$ MVS guests

- Operator input is medium. Operators are likely to be involved in occasional reconfiguration and may be required to move tape drives between guests on a fairly regular basis.
- Systems programmer input is medium if only MVS guests are involved, as there will be little need to change the VM set up after initial installation. On the other hand, it will be quite high if you also intend to support other guest operating systems, particularly CMS — in these circumstances, your site is quite likely to need the services of a specialist VM systems programmer.
- Hardware is unrestricted, though SIE assist and MPG are available only on certain models.
- Unlike all the other options discussed above, it is not necessary for each MVS system to have dedicated channels to each I/O device it needs to access, nor is it necessary for each MVS system to have access to a dedicated 3 × 74 control unit for its master console. This can make it cheaper to set up (e.g. other options may force you to install extra features on your DASD control units to support channels to more than one system), and it is an advantage if you have a channel shortage. However, the costs of providing these additional channels and a

dedicated 3 × 74 are relatively low by comparison with the real cost of, say, an additional 5 per cent CPU overhead.

The performance overheads of VM are quite a strong disincentive to those inclined to run MVS under it. Although these can be alleviated by using PR/SM's multiple preferred guest support, it is obvious that if you have PR/SM you do not need VM anyway — unless you want it for some other reason than to support MVS systems. Such a reason might be the ability to run other guest operating systems. This can be immensely beneficial to some organizations, e.g. those with a community of experienced CMS users, or those in the process of migrating from VSE to MVS.

The input required from the systems programmer to support VM is discussed in the following section.

13.7 Implementing VM

VM is a far simpler operating system to support than MVS, and VM systems programmers have the benefit of an excellent set of manuals — it is probably fair to say that you could sit down and read through them and come out at the end capable of running a VM system. With the benefit of a short course to give you an overview, most MVS systems programmers should therefore be able to support a VM system themselves, once the initial installation and customization has been done. It is, however, highly advisable to have an expert do that initial installation and customization for you. This section is intended only to give you a flavour of what is involved.

Until recently there were several 'flavours' of VM, but IBM has now combined these all into VM/ESA, and all sites running MVS under VM should expect to migrate to VM/ESA. There is a standard installation tape available (called system delivery option (SDO) — a sort of VM equivalent of CBIPO) which will install your entire VM system. It will provide you with a set of skeleton definitions for production and test MVS systems, as well as the 'CMS machines' you need to run and maintain the VM system. This can be installed and tailored to your needs by an expert in a few days.

VM will need a few local terminals for these CMS machines to use. Each CMS user has their own virtual machine, and CMS is its operating system. One CMS machine will be defined as the operator, and will be automatically logged on at VM IPL time; its screen will then effectively become the console for VM, and you will be able to IPL your MVS guests from here. There is a standard CMS user called MAINT which has the authority necessary to perform any maintenance and administration functions you may need. You will generally use this CMS machine to configure your MVS guest machines.

There are two key VM files which will control the configuration of your MVS guests, and to maintain these you will have to edit the source in these files (using the CMS editor, XEDIT) then use VM commands to implement them.

The first of these is the directory, usually called USER DIRECT. This contains the definitions of all the virtual machines which are allowed to log on to VM as guests, including both the CMS users and the MVS guests. These definitions include details of all the resources the guest is allowed to use, including DASD, processors, and other I/O devices. It also defines which machines have attributes such as being a preferred guest or being automatically started after VM is IPLed. After updating the source for this module you can implement it inflight by issuing the DIRECTXA command. This file must be treated with a great deal of respect, as VM does not check it for internal consistency, and it is quite possible to destroy your VM system by updating it wrongly.

The second key file depends on the version of VM you are running. Prior to VM/ESA release 2, the file is called HCPRIO ASSEMBLE, and contains the definition of the I/O devices known to VM and their addresses. This is a good deal simpler than an MVSCP input deck, but note that not all devices supported by MVS are supported by VM. If you wish to use such a device, it must be dedicated to the MVS machine which is going to use it. Once you have updated this file, you need to assemble it then re-IPL your VM system. Under VM/XA, the whole procedure for doing this is outlined in the steps 'Update HCPRIO and HCPSYS' and 'Generate the new CP nucleus' of the 'Installing the system' sections of [4]. The equivalent ESA manual is [5].

On VM/ESA release 2, however, the VM configuration process has been simplified further, and both HCPRIO ASSEMBLE and the related file HCPSYS ASSEMBLE have been replaced by a new file called SYSTEM CONFIG. Like MVS's SYS1.PARMLIB, this file is kept in English-like text form and is interpreted at IPL time, rather than requiring reassembly every time a change is made. From June 1993, VM also now includes its own version of the HCD facility. This allows VM hardware definitions to be changed online and dynamically (i.e. while VM is running), although at the time of writing it cannot change the HSA (i.e. run-time version of the IOCDS) in-flight, unlike the MVS version of HCD.

Probably the main complication in supporting multiple MVS guests under VM is the definition of DASD devices in USER DIRECT. Dedicated devices are fairly easy to define, but in order to share a pack you must define it as a VM minidisk. Minidisks are virtual devices used (usually) to divide up real disks between CMS machines. Each CMS machine behaves as if it has access to a number of small disk devices, and in the directory each of these is mapped onto an area of real disk. One real disk pack, therefore, can be divided up into a large number of minidisks, each occupying a number of cylinders on the real disk. Unfortunately, the only way VM can share DASD volumes is by defining them as minidisks. To share whole packs between two MVS systems, therefore, you have to define them as full-pack minidisks in the directory. Note that you will have to include the alternate cylinders on the pack in the range of cylinder addresses, or some software (e.g. third-party disk housekeeping software) will not work as it addresses these directly. None of the IBM manuals include the alternate cylinders in their sample definitions of full-pack minidisks.

Even more unfortunately, I/O to minidisks must go through VM's address translation routines. This means that shared minidisks lose the performance benefits of using SIE assist to speed up the I/O done by your preferred guest.

To share a pack in this way, you will need to define the pack in the directory statement for the primary machine as an MDISK with an access mode of MWV. The V causes VM to invoke virtual RESERVE/RELEASE processing, which ensures that a RESERVE issued by one guest will lock out I/O from another guest to the pack concerned, even though the control unit will perceive them as both coming from the same system (i.e. the VM control program). The other machine(s) sharing the pack must contain LINK statements for this minidisk in their directory entries. Packs to be used as minidisks must also be listed on the SYSUVOL statement in HCPSYS ASSEMBLE, and the CP nucleus regenerated as for changes to HCPRIO ASSEMBLE.

If your MVS systems running under VM are also sharing their DASD with MVS systems running on other processor complexes, or in other physical or logical partitions, you will also have to ensure that real RESERVE/RELEASE processing is performed (see Sec. 14.5 for more details on this process). As with a native MVS system, you will have to specify FEATURE=SHARED on the IODEVICE macros for the devices to be shared when you are generating your I/O configuration using MVSCP. However, VM tends to assume that its guests are not sharing DASD with any other real machines and so suppresses real RESERVE channel commands by default, using virtual RESERVE/RELEASE processing instead. To prevent this happening, you must specify SHARED=YES on the RDEVICE macros for the devices to be shared in HCPRIO ASSEMBLE, then regenerate the CP nucleus.

While all this makes DASD sharing under VM potentially rather traumatic, VM does have one compensation to offer. This is the ability to define virtual CTCAs — in other words, your MVS guests can talk to each other, believing they are communicating through channel-to-channel links (notably for GRS), even though no such links exist, except by virtue of VM simulating them.

Let me conclude this little peek into the world of VM with a couple of warnings:

1   Like any other data, changes to your VM definitions should be backed up. This means you need to familiarize yourself with VM's backup and recovery procedures, including how to recover your VM packs in stand-alone mode. Failure to do this exposes you to complete loss of your VM system in the event of a disaster such as a head crash or a directory error (overlapping minidisks!) leading to corruption of your system files.

2   Before you start editing files from CMS, spend some time learning how to use CMS and XEDIT, and in particular be sure you understand which minidisks

your files are on and how the CMS process of concatenating minidisks using the ACCESS command works.

13.8   Which option should you choose?

The most appropriate type of multi-image environment for your installation will depend very much on your circumstances. In general the choice should be:

- *Two separate machines* if two partitions only are required *and* the division of resources required is very stable *and* two machines are more economic than one *or* you need more processing power than one machine can provide.
- *Physical partitioning* if two partitions only are required *and* the division of resources required is very stable *and* there is a need to run a single-image system sometimes.
- *Logical partitioning* if flexibility/control of resource allocation is required *and* suitable hardware is available.
- *VM* if flexibility of resource allocation is required *and* relatively high overhead is acceptable *or* other guests are required, e.g. CMS.

In practice, more and more sites are using PR/SM, especially to provide a systems programming test environment which can be used without bringing down the 'production' system; and large sites will continue to run multiple physical processor complexes. The physical partitioning option, on the other hand, seems destined to die out, and although VM will survive for other reasons, its use as a hypervisor for MVS systems seems likely to decline.

13.9   Sysplex

Sysplex is IBM's strategy for providing a 'single-image view' of multi-image environments. A Sysplex (SYStems comPLEX) consists of several MVS systems linked together by channel-to-channel links and sharing a common timer. Communication between the participating systems is established by the cross-system coupling facility (XCF), a component of MVS which was introduced in MVS version 4, and a GRS 'ring' must also be established to control serialization between the participating systems. GRS has been improved with MVS version 4 to make this more feasible; in particular, it can use XCF links for communication instead of dedicated CTCs, and GRS RNLs can be modified without the need to re-IPL all the participating systems (GRS is discussed in more detail in Chapter 14).

Figure 13.5 shows a Sysplex configuration. Note that:

- The Sysplex timer (a 9037 device, with a PS/2 for a console, also known as an external time reference or ETR) is not attached to a channel but to a special ETR port on the processor controller on 3090 and 9000 series CPCs. Each CPC has two ports on each side; to prevent the 9037 becoming a single point of failure

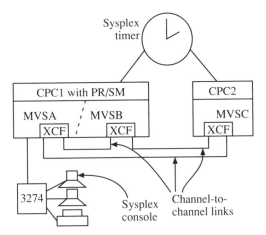

Figure 13.5. A Sysplex.

for the Sysplex, you should ask for the 9037 extended recovery feature which provides a second timer connected to the second port on each machine.
- If the Sysplex consisted entirely of MVS systems running on a single CPC, under either PR/SM or VM, it would not be necessary to use an ETR as these systems would share a common timer anyway. There is a new parameter (SIMETRID) in the CLOCKxx member of PARMLIB which tells MVS to simulate the ETR in these situations.
- Each system in the complex must be connected to every other system in it, and XCF requires two separate paths between each pair of machines: an in path and an out path. With ESCON channels, however, you can define multiple CTC links across a single physical link, so only one physical link is required between each pair if you are using these.
- CTCA devices are not shown on the CTC links, but will be required if you are not using ESCON channels.
- XCF is configured using a new member of PARMLIB — COUPLExx.

MVS version 4 also delivered the first group of Sysplex functions; the ability to use a single terminal as the console for all the systems in the Sysplex, and the ability to recover dynamically from system failures by reassigning work from the failing system to another system in the Sysplex. The former facility merely duplicates the Multi-Image Console facility which has been available from Legent for many years, but the latter is an indication of the true potential of the Sysplex idea.

The dynamic recovery facility allows you to specify that when a given system fails, another system will take on its workload (though this requires the subsystems and/or applications to be recovered to contain the code required to support dynamic recovery). Furthermore, this feature can be combined with the dynamic reconfiguration facilities of PR/SM to reassign resources belonging to the failing system automatically to the recovering system under certain conditions (i.e. storage can be reconfigured if it is contiguous with the storage of the recovering system). When combined with suitable subsystem code (e.g. the XRF facility in CICS), this provides the facility to recover virtually instantaneously from system failures, with no outage for the user. Clearly this could make a major contribution to the goal of providing 100 per cent availability to our users.

There is considerable speculation, though, that Sysplex will go much further. Critical applications such as job schedulers and TP systems could dynamically assign work to whichever system in a Sysplex was least busy, for example. Or, if central storage could be shared between CPCs in a Sysplex, this trend could be taken to its logical conclusion and give us the facility to run a single copy of MVS across multiple CPCs. Perhaps more likely in the foreseeable future is shared expanded storage, which could make a vital contribution to I/O elimination — the fundamental performance requirement for most commercial systems today. Whatever facilities Sysplex delivers in the future, one thing is clear — the facilities delivered in MVS version 4 are just the beginning.

Practical experience of Sysplex is still rare at the time of writing, but some details of the practical issues can be found in [7] and [13].

References and bibliography

IBM manuals

1. *IBM 3090 PR/SM Planning Guide*, GA22–7123. A useful overview of PR/SM and how to implement it.
2. *IBM 3090 IOCP User's Guide and Reference*, SC38–0038. Includes coverage of how to generate an LPAR mode IOCDS.
3. *IBM ES/3090 Operator Tasks for the System Console*, SC38–0069. Step-by-step instructions for using the hardware console, including a chapter on setting up and operating logical partitions.

Each model of processor has its own set of PR/SM manuals, and you should familiarize yourself with those for your processor(s).

4. *VM/XA SF Installation, Administration, and Service*, GC19–6217. Covers most aspects of VM systems programming, although this version of VM is now obsolete.
5. *Installation Guide for VM/ESA*, SC24–5526. A step-by-step guide to VM installation.
6. *VM/ESA Running Guest Operating Systems*, SC24–5522. Guidelines on defining MVS (and other) virtual machines to run under VM.
7. *MVS/ESA Planning: Sysplex Management*, GC28–1260.

Other

8. Sherkow, A. M.: PR/SM Capabilities, *Enterprise Systems Journal*, March 1991, pp. 17–24. An excellent description of PR/SM.
9. Sherkow, A. M.: Implementations of Logical Partitioning, *Enterprise Systems Journal*, April 1991, pp. 98–101. Describes MDF and MLPF.
10. Wright, F.: PR/SM and MDF: A Comparison, *Technical Support*, November 1991, pp.

25–30. Illuminating for users of both; she concludes that MDF is still more flexible than PR/SM.

11. McDonald, J.: Implementing PR/SM, *Technical Support*, January 1992, pp. 48–50. A useful practical guide.
12. Carlson, P.: Sharing DASD Under VM, *DSI Times*, vol. 8, no. 1, pp. 1–2, 1988.
13. Waterhouse, P. S.: Adventures in ESA, Parts 1, 3, and 4, *Technical Support*, August 1991, pp. 43–46, January 1992 pp. 75–79, and February 1992 pp. 29–32. Good coverage of both the theory and the practicalities of Sysplex, from someone who has done it.

14
Sharing I/O devices

14.1 Introduction

The previous chapter discussed various ways of establishing multi-image environments, and some of their implications for resource sharing. Sharing of resources such as processor cycles and memory is very much dependent on the particular method you have chosen to partition your workload, but this is less true for peripheral devices (although there are extra issues to be considered if you are using VM). It is to these devices that we now turn.

Shared peripherals can be divided into those which are switchable and those which are fully sharable. Switchable devices can really only be online to one system at a time, although they can be physically connected to more than one. Fully sharable devices can be online to more than one system and can interleave I/O requests from the sharing systems. I will discuss switchable devices first, as this is the simpler case, then turn to shared communications processors. Most of my attention in this chapter, however, will be devoted to sharing DASD — the most difficult type of device to share but one of the most valuable. The last part of the chapter will discuss how and when to share system datasets between systems which are sharing DASD.

14.2 Switchable devices

Switchable devices include printers, cluster controllers (3274s), and tape drives (both open reel and cassette drives). Each of these behaves somewhat differently, but all share the characteristic that they can only be used by one system at a time, for extended periods.

With some of these the reason is obvious — you could hardly allow two systems to talk to the same printer at the same time or you could end up having to disentangle your pay slips from your sales report line by line! Likewise, two systems attempting to write to the same tape drive simultaneously could be disastrous. The common factor is that these devices are inherently sequential, so the smallest unit of work which must be allowed to complete before allowing the device to service another one is a dataset, whichever system it comes from.

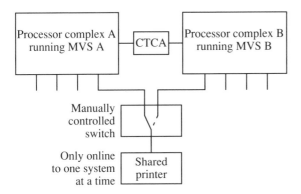

Figure 14.1. Manual switching of devices between systems.

It is less obvious why 3274s should not be fully sharable. While it may be arguable that an application on one system should not be able to interrupt a session which an application on another system is conducting with a logical unit (in effect a single terminal on the 3274), there is no obvious reason why different terminals should not be in session with applications on different systems. Indeed, this is possible at a logical level through VTAM cross-domain services even when the terminals on the 3274 are all physically connected to one host. The real reason for 3274s only being sharable via switching is therefore a limitation in their physical design, and the most recent 3174s appear to have overcome this limitation.

The method of switching between host systems also varies between devices. For printers and 3274s, there is only one channel interface on the device, so switching is only possible by inserting a physical switch between the device and the connected systems, such as a 2914, a 3814, or a T-bar two-channel switch. To move the device from one system to another you must: (a) vary it offline from the first system; (b) throw the switch; and (c) vary it online to the second system. This fairly awkward process is obviously not the sort of thing you would want to do on a routine basis, so it tends to be used only for recovery situations, e.g. to be able to continue printing your output from system B when system A, which usually does all your printing, is down. Manual switching of devices between systems is illustrated in Fig. 14.1.

Open-reel tape drives move us a step closer to full sharability. Here, your controller can have multiple channel interfaces, each of which can be attached to a channel on a different system — one system can be performing I/O to one device on the string while another is performing I/O to another device. Somewhat confusingly, the hardware in the controller which makes this possible is also known as a channel switch. Unfortunately, although it is perfectly clear that it is logically inconsistent to allow two systems to interleave I/O to the same tape device, there is no facility in traditional tape drive controllers to enforce this. It is therefore possible for system A to attempt to allocate a dataset to a device when system B is half way through writing another dataset to it, causing the tape to be rewound

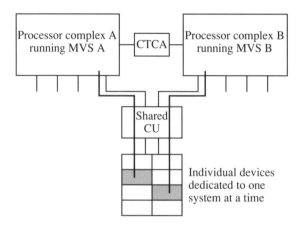

Figure 14.2. Sharing tape devices between MVS systems.

and all hell to break loose! If you intend to share tape drives in this way, then you must ensure that your operators have an absolutely watertight procedure which prevents them from varying the same tape drive online to more than one system at the same time. Given that manual systems are inherently not watertight, it is generally a better idea to buy Legent's Multi-Image Allocation software product, which is. Figure 14.2 illustrates the sharing of tape devices.

Cassette drives such as the 3480 and 3490 are fortunately a little more intelligent. While it is still possible for a drive to be online to both systems, the hardware allows drives to be 'assigned' to systems — once a drive has been assigned to a system, the controller will not allow any other system to use it until the first one 'unassigns' it. MVS will issue the channel command to assign a drive when it allocates it to a task, and the command to unassign it when it deallocates it. This means that multiple MVS systems sharing a 3480 drive will never interfere with each other's I/O. For simplicity's sake, it is best to avoid situations where the drive appears to be online to both systems anyway, but at least you can be sure that the consequences of an operator oversight will not be disastrous.

From the I/O configuration point of view, switchable devices are fairly simple — you simply define the device in each system's IOCDS and MVSCP on whichever channel it will be attached to when the two-channel switch is set to connect the device to this system. To minimize operator confusion, it is preferable to give the device the same address on each system.

For tape drives you wish to share between two systems, you must ensure that the FEATURE=SHARABLE parameter is coded on the MVSCP IODEVICE macro.

14.3   Sharing communications controllers

With devices such as 3725s and 3745s, we move at last into the realm of full sharability. These devices can be supplied with two or more channel adapters, each

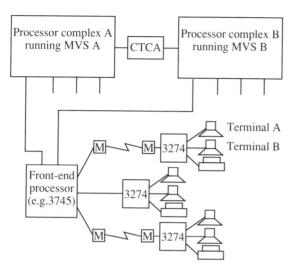

Figure 14.3. Sharing a comms FEP between two MVS systems.

of which can be attached to a channel from a processor complex. I/O requests can be sent independently down these channels at any time for any of the attached lines, and the control program in the comms controller (usually NCP in an SNA environment) will queue these up where necessary and send them down the required lines. Thus in Fig. 14.3, for example, which illustrates the sharing of an FEP between two systems, terminal A can be in session with an application on system A while terminal B is in session with an application on system B. The comms controller is actually an independent processor complex with the specialized function of routeing and scheduling I/O requests to networked devices, and the NCP software is capable of handling messages from multiple sources whenever and however often they arrive.

As with switchable devices, the IOCP and MVSCP definitions for each connected processor and system are no different from those we would code if the device were dedicated to the processor or system concerned. In this case, though, the device will be online to both systems simultaneously, and will handle I/O requests from both simultaneously.

The configuration of the NCP within the comms controller will have to take account of the multiple channel adapters in use, and special VTAM definitions are required to support a multiple-host network. You will need to ensure the node describing the NCP is defined in each of the VTAM configurations for example, but the NCP can only belong in the 'domain' of one of the hosts. This is the one which will initially load the NCP and control it thereafter. Both hosts, though, will be able to communicate to the network and to each other through the comms controller.

Chapter 9 discussed basic VTAM and NCP configuration but the details of how to set up multiple domain definitions are beyond the scope of this book.

14.4   Shared DASD integrity

DASD devices can be fully shared between multiple systems, with each system
concurrently performing I/O to different datasets on the same device. This is
logically possible because of the direct access nature of the device — it can update
a record in one area of the device, move to a completely different area to service
a request for another dataset, then return to the first area to update the next record
in the first dataset. Given that DASD behaves in this fashion in a non-shared
environment anyway, it is not too radical a departure to do the same in a shared
environment. Multiple channels from different systems or processors can be
attached to the DASD controller (e.g. 3880 or 3990), which will then pass on one
I/O at a time to any one attached DASD device, interleaving requests from
multiple systems when required.

However, extending the interleaving of I/O for a given device from one system
to two or more introduces a new problem. When only one MVS system is involved,
it can protect the integrity of the data on the device by preventing multiple
requestors from updating the same dataset at one time, using a mechanism internal
to the MVS system (GRS); but this internal mechanism will no longer be effective
if there are multiple MVS systems which could be updating the same dataset
concurrently. This is because it uses chains of control blocks in the private virtual
storage of the GRS address space to control serialization of requests for control of
any given resource, and this virtual storage is not accessible to the GRS running
on another MVS system.

We can therefore only share DASD between multiple systems if we take some
additional measures to extend the provisions MVS makes to protect the integrity
of DASD datasets. There are three ways of doing this:

- The RESERVE/RELEASE mechanism
- The multi-system component of GRS
- The Multi-Image Integrity software product from Legent

I shall discuss each of these in turn in the following sections, looking at how to use
them and determining which is the most appropriate to your circumstances.

14.5   RESERVE/RELEASE

The RESERVE/RELEASE mechanism works by setting a hardware bit in the
head-of-string unit for the DASD device concerned during the period of an update,
then resetting the bit at the end of the update to RELEASE the device. When the
RESERVE bit is set, the head-of-string will only allow I/O requests from the
RESERVing system to be processed, and requests from other systems will be
forced to wait. The RESERVE and RELEASE processes are, in effect, variations
on the ENQ and DEQ instructions respectively. Thus, when a process wishes to
protect the integrity of a DASD dataset across systems, it must issue the

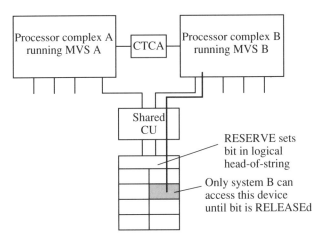

Figure 14.4. Use of RESERVE to obtain exclusive control of a device.

RESERVE instruction, perform its updates, then issue the RELEASE instruction. This is illustrated in Fig. 14.4.

In order for the RESERVE instruction to be effective, however, the device to be reserved must have been defined in your MVSCP deck with the FEATURE= SHARED parameter on its IODEVICE statement. Otherwise, MVS will assume there is no other system sharing the device and will not issue the subchannel request to set the RESERVE bit.

This process is thoroughly watertight, as long as the usual conventions on the use of ENQ and DEQ are followed to preserve integrity on the requestor's own system (see Sec. 3.6) — because the RESERVE/RELEASE mechanism will not prevent updates to the volume by other tasks running under the same system as the RESERVing task. However, it suffers from a major disadvantage — it locks out all tasks on all other systems from the whole of the device concerned for the whole duration of the updating process, which could be many minutes in the case of a typical batch job. While this may sometimes be acceptable for volumes containing only data used by batch jobs, it is obviously impractical for any volume containing system datasets or online datasets. In these cases, whole systems, or large numbers of online users, can be brought grinding to a halt for long periods of time waiting for the updating process to issue its RELEASE instruction.

It is because of this huge disadvantage that RESERVE/RELEASE is never used to control serious DASD sharing. The only situations where it is practical to use it as the main control over integrity are those where the production disks for each system are not shared but a few disks are shared simply for the purpose of transferring data between the systems. These disks must be dedicated to this purpose, at least during periods when data transfers are allowed, so that no other processes will be held up waiting for RELEASE instructions. In any other situation, you must use one of the alternatives discussed below if you wish to share DASD.

I should point out, however, that this does not mean that all RESERVE/ RELEASE instructions should be eliminated when we are using these alternatives. In some cases — notably where the length of time between the RESERVE and the RELEASE is exceptionally short — it can be more efficient to allow the RESERVE /RELEASE to occur than to suppress it and incur the overhead of either of the alternative methods of controlling serialization.

14.6   Multisystem GRS

IBM's answer to the unnecessary lockouts caused by the RESERVE process is to make the GRS components of MVS systems sharing DASD talk to each other about resources they wish to serialize, through channel-to-channel links. The complex of GRS systems and links is known as a ring, and information about ENQ requests is passed around the ring in the form of a ring system authority (RSA) message.

As each system receives the RSA message, it:

* Reads other systems' requests for ENQs from the RSA message and duplicates them in its own GRS control blocks.
* Adds its own new ENQ and DEQ requests to the RSA message.
* Removes its own requests from the previous round, which have now completed the journey round the ring and been added to the QCB/QEL chains of all the other systems (these chains were discussed in Chapter 3).

If a user attempts to ENQ a resource which is already owned by another requestor (i.e. there is a QCB for it in the GRS address space or a request for it in the RSA message already) the new requestor will have to wait. But even if it is not, the new requestor must wait until all the systems in the GRS complex have seen the request and built the relevant control blocks. Every ENQ and DEQ with cross-system implications therefore has to wait for the RSA message to arrive, be processed by GRS, then complete the circuit of the ring before GRS will allow the request to be completed. This process therefore extends the serialization of shared resources across multiple MVS systems, by ensuring that the control blocks in each system's GRS address space reflect ENQs and DEQs for shared resources issued in all of the sharing systems.

Each member of the complex is identified by a name or sysid, which is specified in the SYSNAME parameter of SYS1.PARMLIB(IEASYSxx). This should be kept the same as the system's SMFID to avoid the confusion caused by referring to the same system by different names in different contexts.

The multisystem component of GRS is activated by specifying GRS=START in member IEASYS00 of SYS1.PARMLIB for the first system in the ring to start, and GRS=JOIN in the subsequent systems. On MVS version 4 systems, you can specify GRS=TRYJOIN, which causes this system to join an existing multisystem ring or start a new one if there is not one already active. When multisystem GRS is not to be used, simply specify GRS=NONE — this does not prevent the single-system component of GRS from working.

In practice, it is unlikely always to be the same system which starts the ring, so GRS=TRYJOIN will usually be the logical choice when you are using multisystem GRS. On pre-version 4 systems, you can obtain a similar effect by coding GRS=JOIN for all members of the configuration. If a GRS ring has not already been started and a system attempts to JOIN, the system will issue the message

    `ISG006I GRS JOIN OPTION INVALID`

and your operators will have to be instructed to reply START to the subsequent WTOR.

Make sure they check first that there is no ring started already, because this message can be issued when there is one but this system cannot communicate with it because of a link failure, or because of improper closedown of the system now being IPLed. If they reply START in these circumstances you will end up with two GRS rings which are not talking to each other, but each believes they are controlling the integrity of the shared resources — a recipe for disaster! This is also a danger of the TRYJOIN option.

Likewise, the operator must not be allowed to reply NONE in these circumstances, or this system will go back to using RESERVE/RELEASE while the systems in the ring will eliminate RESERVE/RELEASE but fail to communicate the SYSTEMS scope ENQs to the newly-IPLed system — once again your integrity is exposed. The only option in these circumstances is to solve the link or closedown problem then reply JOIN.

The correct closedown actions are as follows:

1   After Z EOD on the system being closed down (say SYSA), enter V GRS(*),Q on the SYSA console. This informs the other system(s) in the ring (say SYSB and SYSC) that this system is being closed down and they will reform the ring without it. Without this command, you may find GRS on SYSB and SYSC grinding to a halt — if so, you can usually recover by entering the V GRS(ALL),RESTART command on a SYSB or SYSC console.

2   On a SYSB or SYSC console, enter V GRS(SYSA),PURGE. This removes the closed system from the list of currently connected systems, and allows it to JOIN again when it is re-IPLed. If this is not done, you will certainly get the ISG006I message described above when you IPL SYSA again. The correct solution if you do get into this situation is to issue the purge command on SYSB or SYSC as described above, then reply JOIN to the outstanding WTOR on SYSA.

It is vital that your operators are aware of these procedures, or you will be seriously endangering your data integrity. They should also be familiar with the D GRS command and its parameters so that they can check the status of GRS when required.

The configuration of the GRS ring is described in the GRSCNFxx member of SYS1.PARMLIB, where xx is an alphameric suffix. This is fairly straightforward, and is described well in [1]. Your GRSCNFxx member consists of one or more GRSDEF statements, each describing the GRS configuration for one of the systems in the ring, and if you duplicate the GRSDEF statement for one system in the other systems' GRSCNFxx members it must be identical on each of the systems in the ring. If a system being IPLed has a configuration which is inconsistent with those of the systems already in the ring, it will not be allowed to join the ring. This means that changes to the configuration could require all systems in the ring to be IPLed and the ring to be STARTed afresh.

The RESMIL value specified in GRSCNFxx is critical in determining the overhead your tasks will experience in waiting for GRS. The RSA message is held for this number of milliseconds by the system concerned, so the time taken for the message to go round the ring will be the sum of the RESMIL values for the systems in the ring and transmissions times. Because requestors of global resources must wait for their request to go round the whole ring before they can continue, the sum of your RESMIL values is the main factor determining this delay, and this is a good reason for making your RESMIL values as low as possible. On the other hand, if it is too low, you will experience very large numbers of I/O interrrupts from the CTCAs used by GRS, which will impact system performance. The impact of these I/O interrupts will depend on the cycle time of your processor, so the ideal RESMIL value has tended to fall as processor speeds have increased. The default (30) is appropriate to the cycle times of some rather old processors, so you should generally adopt a considerably smaller value — between, say, 5 for a recent model of 3090–180 upwards and 15 for a 3081. There is advice on setting and tuning RESMIL in [2].

14.7   GRS resource name lists

14.7.1   Use of RNLs

The most complex aspect of setting up multisystem GRS is the definition of how it should treat different types of serialization requests. By default, it will propagate around the ring those ENQs which are issued with the scope of SYSTEMS (as opposed to STEP or SYSTEM), but this default does not give adequate protection and can lead to numerous problems. It is therefore necessary for the systems programmer to provide GRS with a series of parameters known as resource name lists (RNLs), describing which ENQs are to be propagated around the ring and which ones are not. You can also use the RNLs to tell GRS to convert certain RESERVEs into simple ENQs, thus eliminating the problem of other systems being locked out of whole volumes when the requestor really only needs to serialize access to an individual dataset. The RNLs are held in member GRSRNLxx of SYS1.PARMLIB, where xx is an alphameric suffix specified in IEASYSxx or at IPL time.

There are three different lists in this member:

- *RESERVE conversion list* This specifies RESERVEs which GRS is to convert into ENQs (with a scope of SYSTEMS, unless this is altered elsewhere in the RNLs), thus eliminating the hardware RESERVE.
- *SYSTEMS exclusion list* This specifies resources for which ENQs with a scope of SYSTEMS are to be converted to ENQs with a scope of SYSTEM — in effect, making the ENQ a local rather than a global one (where local means 'confined to the current MVS system' and global means 'throughout the GRS ring').
- *SYSTEM inclusion list* This specifies resources for which ENQs with a scope of SYSTEM are to be converted to ENQs with a scope of SYSTEMS — in effect making the ENQ a global rather than a local one.

For each of these lists, you specify the ENQs or RESERVEs by their QNAME and, if required, their RNAME, i.e. the name of the resource to be ENQed.

The advice available from official IBM publications (see the bibliography) on the values to specify in these lists is unclear and inconsistent. I will set out some guidelines below, but if you are seriously considering implementing GRS for the first time, you should try to discuss your proposed lists with some existing GRS users (preferably with similar software portfolios to your own), and expect frequent problems with GRS for the first few weeks or months of use.

SYSTEMS exclusion list

The first class of resources to be considered is those which are currently RESERVEd and should continue to be so. The commonest reason for this is because the RESERVE is issued frequently for a very short period of time and the overhead of passing it round the ring is greater than the overhead of forcing other systems to wait for the RELEASE (remember to code FEATURE = SHARED on your IODEVICE macros, even if you do implement the multisystem component of GRS, to ensure these RESERVEs can still be issued). However, if you do not put them in your SYSTEMS exclusion list, GRS will pass the ENQ round the ring as well as issuing the hardware RESERVE, thus defeating the object of keeping the RESERVE. You should therefore consider including the following QNAMEs in your exclusion list:

- SYSIGGV2 and IEZIGGV3 Catalog RESERVEs — required for master catalogs (the ESA manual also states that SYSCTLG must be coded in this RNL), desirable for the rest.
- SYSVSAM VSAM RESERVEs — only required for some old versions of VSAM.

- SYSVTOC VTOC RESERVEs — required for SYSRES packs, desirable for the rest.
- SYSZVVDS VVDS RESERVEs — required by DFP.
- SYSZJES2 JES2 checkpoint reserves — required by JES2.
- SYSIAT (RNAME of CKPT) JES3 checkpoint reserves — required by JES3.

The other main category to be found in the exclusion list should be ENQs for datasets which are deliberately not shared for MVS reasons. Thus, for example, SYSRES datasets, page datasets, SMF datasets, SYS1.LOGREC, and temporary datasets will not be shared between the systems, and it is an unnecesary overhead to pass ENQs on them round the GRS ring. For some of these datasets, it could seriously impact the system to pass them round, as each system has its own copy of the dataset with the same name, and may need to serialize on its own copy for long periods of time. If GRS passes round the ENQs, system A's copy of SYS1.MAN1, for example, might be exclusively ENQed, and system B would be unable to access its own SYS1.MAN1, even though it is a completely separate dataset! Some examples of entries in the exclusion list for these reasons are:

- QNAME of SYSDSN and RNAMEs of PAGE, SYS1.DUMP, SYS1.MAN, SYS1.LOGREC, SYS1.PROCLIB, SYS1.NUCLEUS, SYS1.LINKLIB, SYS1.LPALIB, SYS1.PARMLIB, SYS1.STGINDEX, and any other key system datasets which are not shared, i.e. where each MVS system has its own copy. Note that the RNAMEs shown are 'patterns', so specifying an RNAME of PAGE in your RNL, for example, will be effective for all dataset names beginning PAGE.
- QNAME of SYSDSN and RNAME of SYS9 (unless you use SYS9 as a high-level qualifier in its own right, in which case you will have to go a little further, e.g. specifying SYS92, SYS93, SYS94, etc., in the RNL). This prevents allocation ENQs for temporary datasets being passed around the ring, as these always have a dataset name beginning with SYS followed by the last two digits of the current year. You should not need to make ENQs on these global as the other systems in the ring should never use them. This can, however, cause problems with DASD housekeeping — a housekeeping job running on one system could delete a temporary dataset belonging to a job running on another system. If you cannot prevent this happening through operational procedures, you may have to consider making temporary dataset ENQs global in scope.
- QNAME of SPFDSN and RNAME of SYS9 etc. — to prevent ISPF ENQs for temporary datasets being passed round the ring.
- QNAME of SPFEDIT and RNAME of SYS9 etc. — to prevent PDF EDIT ENQs for temporary datasets being passed round the ring.

In addition, there are some HSM QNAME/RNAME combinations which must be specified in the exclusion list if you use this product. See the chapter 'DFHSM multiple-processing-unit data set serialization' in [3] for details — but check with IBM too as some editions of this chapter are in error.

SYSTEM inclusion list

This should include the QNAMEs of the key resources to be shared between the systems, which are to be ENQed globally, i.e. on all systems in the GRS ring:

- SYSDSN — normal dataset allocation — note that many of the entries in the exclusion list were exceptions to this rule.
- SPFDSN and SPFEDIT-ISPF and PDF dataset allocation.
- SYSIKJBC and SYSIKJUA-use of SYS1.BRODCAST and SYS1.UADS — these should only be in the inclusion list if you are sharing these datasets, otherwise they should be in the exclusion list.

RESERVE conversion list

This lists the RESERVEs to be eliminated by GRS. Unless there is also an entry for them in the exclusion list, these will be converted to global ENQs. Common candidates are:

- SYSIEWLP — Linkage editor RESERVEs
- SPZAPLIB — Superzap RESERVEs (i.e. those issued by AMASPZAP)
- SPFDSN and SPFEDIT — ISPF and PDF RESERVEs
- SYSZRACF — RACF RESERVEs

In addition, RESERVEs issued by other products, such as DFHSM and CA-1, will commonly be converted. The chapter of [3] mentioned earlier gives details of the entries DFHSM requires; you should also consult the documentation of third-party products which may issue RESERVEs, and/or speak to the suppliers to determine how GRS should handle these.

14.7.2 Beyond the RNLs

Sometimes you may find that the RNLs do not give you enough control. A good example is DFDSS — this program has a nasty tendency to issue RESERVEs against the VTOC of the volume it is processing whether it really needs to or not. You will probably not want to convert other RESERVEs on SYSVTOC for performance reasons (see previous section), but you will have to prevent DFDSS from issuing these RESERVEs if you are going to allow its use alongside any work on other systems sharing the DASD involved.

There are GRS exits available for cases like this. However, in the case of DFDSS, there is also a user-replaceable module within the product (ADRUENQ) which allows you to eliminate the unnecessary RESERVEs quite nicely (all you need to do in ADRUENQ is to set a return code of 4 in register 15). I would recommend this to anyone using DFDSS in a GRS complex.

14.8   Multi-Image Integrity

By now you may be wondering how you can avoid the complexities of implementing the cross-system component of GRS. One answer, of course, is not to share DASD at all, or to keep DASD sharing to an absolute minimum. However, there is another option — the MII product from Legent. On the whole I am avoiding discussion of third-party products in this book, not because they are inferior in any way to IBM's, but because this book would probably run to half a dozen volumes if I did not. However, I have made an exception for MII, because I believe that in some circumstances it provides a vital function better than the available IBM software.

The most obvious difference between the two is that MII uses a control file on shared DASD to communicate between the sharing systems instead of a network of channel-to-channel links (though recent versions can also use CTCs). It intercepts ENQs and RESERVEs being processed by each MVS system's local GRS and decides (on the basis solely of your MII parameters) whether the ENQ should be propagated to the other systems in the complex, and whether RESERVEs should be converted to global ENQs. The default is always to treat the ENQ as local, but if your parameters override this, MII will propagate the ENQ by writing it to its control file. The full process for a global ENQ is as follows:

1   An ENQ on SYSA is intercepted and MII decides to make it global.
2   SYSA's MII reads the control file, which lists global ENQs and DEQs added by the copies of MII on other systems since the last time SYSA read it. It issues these ENQs and DEQs to the local GRS.
3   It now allows the new ENQ to proceed on SYSA's local GRS.
4   Finally, it writes back the control file, adding the new ENQ, marking those it has processed, and removing any now processed by all the active systems.

Thus, each local GRS system continues to function without the multisystem component, but by issuing any necessary ENQs and DEQs on all the required systems, MII ensures that the control block chains in each local GRS also reflect any outstanding ENQs for shared resources that have been issued on any other system. Because it always processes any outstanding requests from other systems before attempting to process the ENQ from the local system, it does not need to wait for other systems to see an ENQ before processing it on the system where it was issued.

In practice, this is just as quick as communicating through CTCs, and can be quicker, particularly for complexes containing more than two systems and particularly when the control file can be kept on a high-speed device (e.g. solid-state DASD or 3990 using the DASD Fast Write feature). Of course, it is subject to I/O contention, so you must take care to place the dataset favourably to minimize this.

The overhead of MII is therefore comparable to that of GRS, and its processing is equivalent. Why, then, do I say it is superior? There are several reasons:

- *Reliability* Although DASD are perhaps no more reliable than CTCs on average, a CTC failure will bring down your GRS ring and probably require an IPL of at least one of the systems in the ring; failure of the DASD on which the MII control file is placed should result in an automatic switch to an alternative control file on another device.
- *Flexibility* Prior to MVS version 4, GRS parameters could not be changed without IPLing every system in the ring (version 4 allows RNLs to be changed using the SET GRSRNL command), while MII parameters can be changed 'on the fly'.
- *Fewer IPLs* In addition to the previous two points, any failure of GRS requires an IPL; MII can be stopped and restarted at will.
- *Ease of use* As well as being easier to change if you get them wrong, MII's parameters are simpler and therefore easier to get right in the first place.
- *Better problem diagnosis facilities* MII provides more and better commands for finding out what it is doing, and will collect statistics on itself into the bargain.
- *Additional facilities* MII can be set up to issue messages on the console and to TSO users involved whenever a resource conflict occurs; it can stop and requeue jobs that are waiting for datasets to begin execution; it can provide additional integrity protection, e.g. stopping users from allocating a PDS as a sequential dataset then overwriting the directory; and it can automatically free unused datasets still allocated to a TSO user and required by another task.

On the other hand, of course, MII costs money and the multisystem component of GRS is free (although the CTCAs to support it are not), so more cost-conscious shops may find themselves forced to use GRS. The cost they may have to accept in return is regular loss of all the systems in the ring while you are getting GRS right, and occasional loss thereafter.

If you do implement MII, the key parameters you will have to define are the MIMQNAME member, defining ENQs to be propagated around the complex and RESERVEs to be converted, and the GDIEXMPT member, defining exceptions to the MIMQNAME rules.

MIMQNAME should include SYSDSN, SYSVSAM, SPFDSN, and SPFEDIT, i.e. dataset allocations of all kinds should be treated as global; and the same QNAMEs should be specified for RESERVE conversion as under GRS.

GDIEXMPT should exempt the same datasets from being global as we find in the exclusion list for GRS, but this can be achieved much more simply: in two lines you can tell MII to treat all SYS1.* dataset names as local and all PAGE.* dataset names as local, then in another three you can tell it to make all SYS1.A* (distribution libraries), SYS1.BRODCAST, and SYS1.UADS global. Any other SYS1 datasets you wish to share should, of course, be added to this second list.

Finally, although I have not used DFDSS with MII, it seems inevitable that if you do you will need to make the same modification I described in the GRS section. MII also has exits for finer control of ENQ propagation than is possible in the parameters.

14.9   Sharing system datasets

Once you have succeeded in sharing DASD between your multiple MVS systems, you can start sharing system datasets. Fortunately, this is usually a good deal simpler than setting up your shared DASD environment! Sharing system datasets allows you to maintain similar environments in each of your systems with the minimum of administrative overhead. A classic example is a shared security database. Whether it is an RACF, ACF2, or Top Secret database, this allows you to maintain a single set of userids and a single set of access rules with no danger of them being out of step in the different environments.

Some system datasets, however, cannot or should not be shared between multiple systems. We touched on these in Chapter 13, and they fall basically into three groups: datasets on the SYSRES pack, configuration datasets holding definitions unique to one system, and datasets used by the system for logging information or storing information on a temporary basis. The second group includes your master catalog, SYS1.PROCLIB, and SYS1.PARMLIB. The third includes the SMF datasets, system DUMP datasets, PAGE datasets, SYS1.LOGREC, and SYS1.STGINDEX, all of which must be dedicated to a single MVS system.

The remainder of this section considers the main system datasets which can be shared, some key things you need to know about how to share them, and why you might consider sharing them.

User catalogs

Indeed, you will find it very hard to use your shared DASD if you do not share the catalogs. If you are only sharing some of your DASD you need to enforce strict pooling rules. These must ensure: (a) that all datasets on shared DASD are cataloged in catalogs on shared DASD, or your users will not be able to locate these datasets from all the sharing systems; and (b) that datasets which are not on shared DASD are not cataloged in shared catalogs, or you will get REPLY DEVICE NAME OR CANCEL messages when users on systems which are not sharing the pack concerned find them in the catalog and try to access them.

To share user catalogs, first ensure they have been defined with SHAREOPTIONS (3,4) — use the IDCAMS ALTER command to change them if they have not. Next IMPORT CONNECT the catalogs to any master catalogs of sharing systems in which they are not already defined. Use the DEFINE ALIAS command to copy over any aliases at the same time (the master catalog conversion program provided with CBIPO can be used to generate a set of DEFINE ALIAS commands which will do the job), and ensure that your ALIAS maintenance procedures automatically update the alias entries in all catalogs simultaneously. Finally, if you are using the multisystem component of GRS, check your GRS parameters are set up as recommended earlier in this chapter.

SYS1.UADS

Sharing UADS will allow you to keep a single set of definitions of TSO users — and, incidentally, prevent a user from logging on to multiple systems in the complex at the same time using the same userid. Simply ensure your GRS parameters are set up as described in Chapter 13, copy your UADS dataset to a shared volume, and catalog it on this volume on all the sharing systems. Each system will use the shared version from its next IPL (as long as you have not changed the default master scheduler JCL by adding a volume serial number to the DD statement for SYS1.UADS).

SYS1.BRODCAST

Sharing BRODCAST will ensure that each TSO user will receive their notify messages from all systems regardless of which system they are logged on to. You should always share BRODCAST if UADS is shared, but never if UADS is not. The actions required to share BRODCAST are the same as those to share UADS.

HSM CDSs

The chapters 'Introduction' (to customization part) and 'DFHSM multiple-processing-unit dataset serialization' in [3] give details of how to do this. Sharing these control datasets is required if users on one system are to recall or recover datasets migrated or backed up under the control of DFHSM on the other system.

JES2 spool and checkpoint datasets

To share these, you must define a multi-access spool configuration to JES. This was discussed in Chapter 8.

Control files for other products

Security databases, tape catalogs, and many other control files used by IBM and third-party system software can be shared between multiple systems. Usually there will be a section in the product's manuals giving more information, but you should always check with the supplier as well — there may, for example, be fixes you need to apply to support a shared environment.

References and bibliography

IBM manuals

1. *MVS/ESA SPL: Initialization and Tuning Reference*, GC28–1635 (this title and order number is for the V4 version). Documents all the PARMLIB members and statements used at IPL time, including all those used by GRS.

2. *MVS/ESA Planning: Global Resource Serialization*, GC28–1621 (again the V4 version). The definitive manual on GRS.
3. *DFHSM Installation and Customization*, SH35–0084. Includes a chapter on sharing HSM resources across multiple systems, including GRS considerations.

Other

4. *Multi-Image Integrity System Manual*, Legent, Pittsburgh, 1990.

Part Five
Housekeeping and security

15
MVS security

15.1 Elements of MVS security

15.1.1 The role of systems programmers

Although different types of organization require very different levels of security, all MVS systems must be able to provide a guaranteed level of security for at least some of the data they control. For example:

- Any information used directly or indirectly in financial processes must be protected against fraudulent updates.
- Data describing living individuals is usually considered confidential, and there may be a legal requirement to restrict access to it.
- Some data may have commercial value to your competitors or even military value to your enemies.
- Almost any data which has enough value to be worth storing on an MVS system is likely to be worth protecting against malicious destruction.
- Availability of the system itself is a valuable resource worth securing against both accidental and malicious interference (e.g. from hackers and viruses).

In most installations the primary responsibility for data security will lie with a security administrator or a security team. However, these security staff are unlikely to have detailed knowledge of the MVS technical issues which are fundamental to an effective security policy. They will usually be dependent on systems programmers for assistance in this area, and for the installation and support of security software. Protecting the integrity and security of the operating system is therefore likely to be part of every systems programmer's job.

Since systems programmers are themselves (like all system users) dependent on the goodwill of the security team for the high levels of data access they need to do their job, there is an irrefutable case for close cooperation between systems programmers and data security staff. On the systems programmers' side, this may mean voluntarily relinquishing unnecessary levels of data access (such as unlimited access to production data) and helping the security staff identify potential exposures and remedies for them. In return, they should receive the levels of access on their user ids necessary to do all routine tasks, and controlled access to some sort of 'super id' which gives them the power to do anything at all in an emergency.

This chapter aims to introduce you to the knowledge required to ensure your MVS system is secure. The first part of it describes the components which are essential for effective security:

- Strict control of APF authorization
- A security package such as RACF or a third-party equivalent
- Product-specific security functions for products which do not support security administration via your main security package
- Network security
- Physical security

This part also describes password protection — this is now obsolete but is still referred to in the manuals, so you should understand enough about it to avoid confusion. The second part of the chapter lists some specific actions you should take to prevent loopholes in system security. The chapter will not cover the implementation of any particular security package, mainly because no single product dominates the market for MVS security software. In order to be a fully effective systems programmer, however, you will have to learn how to implement, use, and control your system security software, so you should aim to familiarize yourself with whichever package your installation uses.

15.1.2 APF authorization

For security to be truly enforceable under any operating system, that system must have a mechanism for ensuring that application programmers cannot modify or bypass the machine code and control blocks that make up the operating system at execution time (this is one of the US Department of Defense's requirements for secure systems — the de facto standard for computer security). APF authorization is the mechanism used by MVS. We have already discussed APF authorization in Sec. 3.3.3. Since this is critical to MVS security and integrity, however, we will recap briefly here:

- Each unit of work running under the control of MVS (including those which are part of MVS itself) has a storage protect key, which determines which areas of storage it can fetch and update. Work running with storage protect key zero can fetch almost any area of storage (the exceptions are minor, e.g. the PSA of other processors in the processor complex), and update any of these areas (except page-protected pages, such as pages in the PLPA). Application programs usually run with key eight.
- Each unit of work runs in either problem state or supervisor state. In problem state — the normal state for application programs—certain machine instructions may not be executed, such as those which change the PSW or the storage

protect key.

- The storage protect key and execution state of a unit of work are determined by certain bits in the PSW — which is why problem state programs are prevented from updating the PSW.

- The MODESET SVC is used to change the storage protect key or execution state. This SVC may only be issued by APF-authorized programs.

- A program is APF authorized if: (a) it was loaded from an APF-authorized library (unless that library was concatenated with one or more unauthorized libraries); *and* (b) it was link-edited with an authorization code of 1.

- APF-authorized libraries are those listed in the IEAAPFxx member of SYS1. PARMLIB which was invoked at IPL time (plus SYS1.SVCLIB, SYS1. LINKLIB, and other linklist libraries if LNKAUTH = LNKLST was specified in the IEASYSxx member of PARMLIB used at IPL time). SYS1.LPALIB is also considered to be APF authorized when it is opened at IPL time to load the LPA, and MVS 4.3 and some third-party software products allow you to add libraries to the APF list dynamically.

- Anyone can link-edit a module with an authorization code of 1 simply by specifying SETCODE AC(1) in their link-edit control statements.

In effect, this means that any piece of code which is APF authorized can do anything it likes. If it sets its storage protect key to zero, for example, it can update virtually any area of storage, including fundamental MVS control blocks and control blocks used by any security software you may be running on your system. This poses a major threat to both the integrity and the security of the system. Unauthorized code which accidentally attempts to overwrite an important system area, for example, is likely to experience a storage protection exception and abend 0C4 — but if a piece of code in key zero accidentally (or deliberately!) does this, it may bring down your system.

Similarly, an authorized program running in key zero could potentially overwrite the control blocks which define its own access rights to the security software, giving itself power to do almost anything — and bypassing audit processes built into the security software in the process. Or it could go still further and bypass security checks completely. For example, it could replace the system's dataset open routines (which call a security product to validate every open request) with its own routines. This last type of exposure would require such an advanced level of MVS expertise that it is not really a practical threat to most systems. Nevertheless, the simpler exposures are quite enough to make proper control of APF authorization an essential component of your MVS security strategy.

Since it is not practical to restrict the ability to assign an authorization code of 1 to a load module, this means you must restrict the ability of programmers to link-edit or copy modules into APF-authorized libraries. The only practical way to do this is to use a security package to restrict update access to all such libraries.

15.1.3 Password protection

Before we go on to discuss the use of security packages, we will look briefly at two
mechanisms which are now obsolete — and were never very effective. The first of
these, known as MVS password protection, used the PASSWORD dataset to
assign read and/or write passwords to non-VSAM datasets. The second, known as
access method services password protection, used the CONTROLPW,
MASTERPW, READPW, and UPDATEPW parameters of the IDCAMS
DEFINE statement to assign passwords to catalogs, VSAM clusters, and other
VSAM objects.

  MVS password protection is invoked when a user attempts to open a dataset, if
both: (a) the protection indicator for the attempted type of access (read or update)
is set in the dataset security byte of its DSCB (i.e. the dataset label or VTOC entry);
and (b) the system authorization facility (SAF) interface is inactive on the system.
The SAF interface is used by RACF (and some equivalent third-party products),
so if you have RACF or one of these products installed, password protection will
not be active.

  When password protection is invoked, the system searches the PASSWORD
dataset (which must have been allocated on the SYSRES pack) for a record
describing the dataset being opened. If it does not find one, access to the dataset
is denied. If it does, it checks the type of access required (read or write) against the
record. The record may specify one of three access combinations:

- PWREAD/PWWRITE A password is required for both read and write access.
- PWREAD/NOWRITE A password is required for read access, but write
  access is not allowed at all.
- NOPWREAD/PWWRITE A password is required for write access but not for
  read access.

If a password is required, the system will issue a WTOR to the operator console
requesting the password (or a message to the user's TSO session if the open request
came from a program running under TSO in the foreground). Only if the operator
(or TSO user) replies with the correct password will access be allowed to the
dataset. The password for each dataset is also kept in its record in the PASSWORD
dataset.

  The PASSWORD dataset can be maintained in a variety of ways. The simplest
of these are to use the IEHPROGM utility or the TSO PROTECT command. If
you were using password protection, the first dataset you should protect would be
the PASSWORD dataset itself! Clearly this is rather a clumsy way of protecting
datasets. Some of its disadvantages are:

- It requires operator intervention, and each time the operator must find a record
  of the correct password for the dataset concerned — this could easily become
  a full-time job.
- To do the job properly, the operator has to check each request against a manual

record of which users were allowed to access which datasets, making the process rather slow and prone to human error.

- In practice, many operators fall into the habit of always replying with the password to save them the trouble of checking whether the user is authorized for the requested access or not. This makes the system completely ineffective as a security mechanism.
- Anyone who knows the password for a particular dataset can pass it on to anyone else, so the system offers very little control over who can access which datasets through TSO.
- It offers no mechanism for controlling access to resources other than datasets, and it does not even give complete control of that — it does not control dataset creation, for example.

For all these reasons, password protection was found to be quite inadequate for securing MVS datasets, and it is now universally accepted that MVS system security requires a proper security package like RACF or one of its competitors instead.

There is still, however, a trace of the password protection mentality in the use of passwords to protect VSAM objects — known as access method services password protection. This uses the CONTROLPW, MASTERPW, READPW, and UPDATEPW parameters of the IDCAMS DEFINE statement to assign passwords to catalogs, VSAM clusters, and other VSAM objects. These four operands can be used to assign passwords at one or more of four different levels for any object:

- MASTER A user who supplies this password can do anything at all to the object.
- CONTROL A user who supplies this password can do control-interval pro-cessing on the object, in addition to reading and writing it in the normal way.
- UPDATE A user who supplies this password can perform read or write operations on the object.
- READ A user who supplies this password can read the object.

If no password is assigned to a level, you must supply the next lower level password, e.g. if there is no UPDATE password, you must supply the READ password to be allowed UPDATE access. If there is no lower level password, all users can perform operations at this level without supplying a password (subject to any restrictions enforced by your system security package).

If no passwords at all are assigned to an object, all users can perform all operations on it without supplying a password (subject to any restrictions enforced by your system security package).

Access to perform operations on catalog entries is slightly more complex, as both the password for the catalog and the password for the object whose entry is to be processed are relevant. Reference [5] documents which passwords are required for which operations.

AMS passwords can be supplied in a number of ways. They can be:

- Coded as parameters of IDCAMS commands.
- Supplied in control blocks which are referenced by the ACB macro if you wish to access a VSAM dataset (usually via OPEN) from a program.
- Supplied by the console operator (or TSO user for programs running in the foreground under TSO) in response to a message, if the correct password was not supplied by the program or IDCAMS command. The number of attempts allowed in response to this message is defined for each object by the ATTEMPTS operand of the IDCAMS DEFINE statement. The ability to supply a password in response to a message can be overridden by specifying ATTEMPTS(0).

AMS password protection, however, also suffers from the drawbacks of MVS password protection. If operator prompts are allowed, all the disadvantages listed earlier come into play. Even if they are not, there is still the fatal drawback that passwords can easily become ineffective by becoming widely known. Since the passwords must be hard-coded in any jobs which access the catalog, there are many potential opportunities for unauthorized users to find them out, e.g. by browsing an inadequately protected JCL library, or seeing the password over someone's shoulder on a terminal display. Furthermore, the need to hard-code them in regular jobs makes the process of changing them rather painful, as all of these jobs must also be changed.

Fortunately, security packages like RACF offer far more effective ways of controlling access to catalogs — simply by treating them as ordinary datasets and controlling read and update access in exactly the same way as for any other dataset. Although it is still possible to provide passwords for VSAM objects, they are therefore just as obsolete as the password protection mechanism.

The *coup de grâce* has finally been delivered to both types of password protection by DFSMS, which does not allow either type of password protection on DFSMS-managed datasets, catalogs, and VSAM objects.

15.1.4 System security packages

As you will have gathered from the last couple of sections, effective MVS security requires the use of a system security software package. The IBM offering is RACF, but there are several competitive products which are just as well established in the market-place, notably Top Secret and ACF2, both from Computer Associates. The basic ideas and processes used by all these products are similar, so most of the following discussion applies equally well to any of these, though RACF is generally used to provide examples.

The fundamental concepts used by security packages are users, resources, and access rights. Before any unit of work can obtain access to any resource, it must first identify to the security system the user on whose behalf it is performing work.

For a batch job, for example, this will be done at job initiation, and the user will be identified from the USER statement on the job card. It is not enough for a unit of work simply to claim to represent a user; it must prove it by supplying the current password of the user (in this case using the PASSWORD statement on the job card). This password has none of the drawbacks of the password protection type of password — because it is personal to the user, and only ever entered by the user directly, it is quite possible for each user's password to be kept thoroughly secure, and no operator intervention is required in the process.

Other types of work may identify themselves in other ways:

- TSO users identify themselves to the security package at logon time. The user id is taken to be the TSO logon id, and they must enter their password (into a non-display field, to prevent onlookers from reading it off the screen) during the logon process.
- Started tasks must be defined to the security package in advance of start time, usually using a table which associates each task with a specific user id (in RACF the ICHRIN03 table is used). There is no way to enter a password for a started task, so you must strictly control update access to all procedure libraries from which started tasks can be submitted.
- User ids can be propagated automatically to jobs which are submitted by users who have already identified themselves to the security package. This is commonly done to allow TSO users to submit jobs without having to enter their user ids and passwords each time (this also saves them from keeping passwords hard-coded in their JCL datasets). In effect, an additional JCL statement is automatically added to their jobstreams at submit time with the correct USER and PASSWORD statements on it. Note that PASSWORDs are held in a special undisplayable format on the spool, so it is not possible to find out a user's password by displaying one of their jobs on the input queue. Propagation of user ids is done by JES.

The items which the security system is going to protect are known as resources. Resources are divided into classes, such as DASD datasets, tape datasets, DASD volumes, CICS transactions, and VTAM applications. Certain resource classes are predefined to the security software, but you can usually add your own classes if required. RACF treats datasets a little differently from other resources, but the basic processing done by security software is essentially the same for all classes of resource.

Users can be granted access rights to resources using the security software. There are several possible levels of access to a resource, and each level has a name — typically these will be ALTER (or ALL), CONTROL, UPDATE, READ, and CREATE. The first four of these are a hierarchy similar to the equivalent levels of AMS password protection, while the last represents the right to create the resource (e.g. allocate a new dataset). Note, however, that the hierarchy works a little differently from the AMS password hierarchy. When a user attempts to perform an operation that requires a certain level of access to a resource, the request will be allowed if the user has been granted that level of access to the resource, or a higher level (or if the resource has been given universal access at this level or higher); otherwise it will be denied. Recent versions of security packages have introduced an additional access checking mechanism known as security classification checking, which is required by software aiming to meet the Defense Department's B1 security requirements. Most installations, however, do not use this mechanism.

Details of access rights are kept in a database (some security products keep a copy of part or all of this database in virtual storage). In RACF, the access rights relating to a particular resource are kept in a record known as the resource profile.

The structure of access rights is usually simplified (and should be wherever possible), by giving access at a general rather than at a particular level. There are two ways of doing this, and ideally both should be combined. On the user side, users can be associated with groups, and access to a resource can be allowed to a group rather than to an individual user. Each user acquires the access rights of the group(s) to which they are connected in addition to their personal access rights. Typically, the group will correspond to a set of responsibilities (e.g. 'production payroll users' or 'development staff working on the stock system'), so rather than granting each payroll user personal access rights to each payroll dataset, it is simpler to grant these rights to the payroll group, and simply connect each payroll user to the group. When individuals join, leave, or move between departments, all that is required is to connect them to or disconnect them from the relevant groups.

On the resource side, generality of access rights is accomplished using generic profiles. For example, rather than granting a user or a group separate access to each of a hundred datasets with the high-level qualifier PPAY, we grant access to a single generic profile PPAY.*, which has the effect of allowing access to all datasets whose names begin with this HLQ. Clearly the use of groups and generic profiles simplifies security administration enormously, and one factor which should always be considered when setting standards for resource names is the scope they give for using generic profiles.

Access rights, however, are not enforced by the security software itself. Instead, they are enforced by modules of the operating system known as resource managers (other software can also provide resource managers — including your own, if you make the necessary calls to the security software). Whenever a resource manager is asked to access a resource, it calls the security software to determine whether the current user has the necessary access rights. If, for example, a program attempts to OPEN a dataset for update, the OPEN routine asks the security system whether the current user has update access to the dataset. The security software will scan the accesses which have been granted to the resource concerned (and/or any appropriate generic resources), and determine whether or not the user, or any group it is currently using, is allowed the requested level of access. If not, the security software will issue a bad return code to the resource manager, which will in turn deny access to the resource — and, in our example, abend the program requesting access with a system 913 abend code.

In effect, then, the security software simply acts as a database of access rights. This is why we say that the security software processes all classes of resources in essentially the same way. Effective security depends on the relevant resource management routines: (a) calling the security software to check those rights before accessing a resource; and (b) taking the appropriate action when the security software indicates that the user does not have access to a given resource.

If you are writing your own code, you can use the same approach to control access to a resource. Say, for example, you are coding a security exit to control online access to a third-party product called XXX. In this case you could:

- Define a 'VTAM applications' resource class, containing an individual resource called XXX.
- Grant users who are to be allowed access to the application READ access to XXX.
- Whenever a user attempts to logon to XXX, use your exit to display a screen on which they must enter their user id and password, then invoke the security software using the SAF RACROUTE macro to: (a) identify the user to the security system (RACROUTE REQUEST=VERIFY); and (b) determine whether they have access to XXX (RACROUTE REQUEST=AUTH).

It is the fact that all MVS routines which access resources invoke SAF (or RACF directly) to check the user's access rights that makes security software an effective means of controlling MVS security. Furthermore, the essential simplicity of the process allows these products to be used to control access to any type of resource. It is highly recommended that all sites install such a package, activate it for all resource types in use at the installation, and define profiles which limit access to resources to only those who need such access to perform their jobs.

15.1.5 Product-specific security

Suppliers of software products often need to include security mechanisms within the product to control access to resources. A database management system, for example, will generally provide some mechanism for controlling access to database tables. As time goes by, more and more suppliers of software for MVS systems are recognizing that the simplicity and versatility of the SAF interface make it an ideal mechanism for controlling security processes within their products. It is very common, for example, for suppliers to provide exit points to control security and sample exits which use the SAF RACROUTE macros.

Use of your standard security product to control product-specific security has several advantages:

- Security administration for the new product is automatically placed in the hands of the same staff who control other aspects of system security.

- These security administration staff do not have to learn new skills and processes in order to administer security for the new product.
- Users do not have to be defined to lots of different products — they all share the same set of user definitions.
- Access rights can be granted and taken away by a process which is simple and quick — unlike many of the old-style product security mechanisms.
- Capabilities such as generic profiles and groups are readily available to simplify security administration for the product.

Unfortunately, IBM itself is still some way off universal usage of the SAF interface. DB2, for example, has an internal security system which makes the security database part of the relational structure of the DB2 system itself. CICS internal security is moving towards SAF compatibility, but historically has been quite separate.

Among the products which an MVS systems programmer is likely to control, SDSF prior to version 1 release 3 provided perhaps the worst example of a non-SAF internal security structure. Fortunately there is now a SAF-compatible alternative, but until you implement this, you must reassemble and relink your ISFPARMS module every time you need to change any user's SDSF access.

15.1.6 Network security

Although it may fall outside your area of responsibility, you should also be conscious of the importance of network security. If anyone who sits down at a terminal attached to your system can experiment until they find a way into an important application, you are at serious risk of a security incident. Most MVS sites have now installed 'front-end' software on their networks to prevent this sort of exposure. Typically, such software presents a sign-on screen on which users must enter a user id and password before they can do anything else at all. Once a correct combination has been entered, users are then presented with a menu showing applications they are allowed to log on to (and this menu will be different for different users, so no user sees options they are not allowed to access). They can then select the application they wish to use — but cannot enter any application other than those on their menu.

Software like this commonly provides lots of other features as well, such as the ability to log on to multiple applications concurrently and 'hot key' between them, but our interest here is restricted to the security aspects. The software should always use the SAF interface to validate user id/password combinations and to check access rights to applications, where this is appropriate, thus keeping the user's network user id and password the same as those used for TSO, batch jobs, etc.

It should also 'time out' user sessions when there is no input from the user after a certain period of time (typically between 10 minutes and half an hour), so that unattended terminals are not left logged on to sensitive applications, allowing unauthorized personnel to make use of other people's sessions.

Even if you have such a security product, you should also take precautions to prevent unauthorized users from dialling in to modems attached to your system and hacking into it. One method of doing this is to provide dial-in ports only on devices which hang up and call back to an authorized telephone number as soon as a dial-in user has identified himself or herself.

15.1.7 Physical security

The last essential element of your security strategy must be physical control over access to computer equipment. Obviously you must prevent unauthorized access to the machine room itself, given the immense potential for damage from deliberate or accidental interference with processors, DASD, etc. Equally important is the need to prevent unauthorized physical access to certain powerful terminals.

Consoles are the most obvious of these. Unless you have imposed strict control over the commands that can be issued from a console, a malignant or ignorant user could cause serious disruption with a few simple commands. It is probably even more important, though, to restrict physical access to the terminals of users with high levels of authority — such as security administrators and systems programmers. An interloper may be able to blow your security wide open if he or she has the opportunity to use a systems programmer's TSO session for a few minutes simply because it has been left logged on during a teabreak! So even in the most sophisticated software environments, locks on doors are still an essential security precaution.

15.2   Preventing MVS security loopholes

15.2.1 Controlling APF authorization

We have already seen that to prevent security and integrity exposures we must protect APF-authorized libraries against unauthorized updates; but there is more to controlling APF authorization than this. Broadly speaking, there are two main areas of potential exposure: people acquiring APF authorization for code when this has not been approved, and integrity problems in approved code.

The first should be prevented by careful control of all libraries and members which give potential access to APF authorization, i.e. prevent update access to them by all users other than systems programmers. The libraries and members you need to control include:

- The approved APF-authorized libraries themselves, i.e. those listed in any IEAAPFxx or LNKLSTxx member of PARMLIB which could be selected at IPL time, plus SYS1.LINKLIB, SYS1.SVCLIB, and SYS1.LPALIB. Remember that the current versions of these members and the current setting of the LNKAUTH parameter in IEASYSxx can be changed by operator intervention at IPL time, so do not keep redundant versions of these members around longer than necessary, and do restrict access to libraries listed in members other than the current ones.

- SYS1.PARMLIB Clearly you must prevent unauthorized users from modifying any of the members mentioned under the previous point, or they will be able to add their own libraries to the APF list. Other members of PARMLIB can also confer privileged status, such as the IEASVCxx member, and the PPT entries in SCHEDxx.
- SYS1.NUCLEUS A sophisticated hacker could attempt to replace an authorized SVC with one of his or her own. In fact it is sensible to prevent update access to all SYS1.* libraries, except a few which actually require generalized update access — notably SYS1.BRODCAST.
- Systems programmers' source and JCL libraries—so that casual snoopers cannot pick up any potentially dangerous code from them.

Furthermore, you should strictly control access to facilities (MVS from version 4.3 onwards and some third-party products) which allow users dynamically to update the linklist, APF list, and/or LPA.

Another potential exposure is the use of an 'authorization SVC', popularized by articles in some of the technical journals in recent years. These SVCs can be invoked by unauthorized programs to make them temporarily authorized. I cannot stress strongly enough that you should not allow such SVCs on your system. Even the versions which make some attempt to check the caller's right to call them represent a potential security exposure. Versions which do not perform such checks drive a coach and horses through system integrity. If code genuinely needs to be APF authorized, then it should be placed in an authorized library under strict control of the systems programmers.

More subtle exposures occur through lack of proper integrity checking in approved authorized code. Thus, for example, if a program running in key zero writes data into a user storage area whose address is passed to it by an unauthorized caller, it must validate that the address passed really is in the user's private storage; otherwise, the caller could use the authorized program to overwrite a system control block by passing that control block's address. Other potential exposures, and techniques for preventing them, are documented in [10] in the section called 'Protecting the system'.

IBM takes great care to prevent integrity exposures in its own authorized code, as do most third-party suppliers, but it is your responsibility as a systems programmer to ensure they are prevented in authorized code written in your installation. To enforce this properly, there is no alternative to reviewing every line of code before allowing it to be linked into an authorized library. When the code is your own, you should have someone else check it for you.

15.2.2 *Protecting your security package*

Just as proper system security requires measures to protect the APF authorization mechanism, it also requires measures to protect the security and integrity of the security software itself. Just like any other software, your security package depends for its functioning on data in MVS datasets, so these datasets must be protected. They include:

- Load libraries — these will usually be in the linklist and/or the LPA list, so your measures to protect APF authorization should already have covered these, but check that any other load libraries used by the security software are not updatable by anyone except the staff who install and maintain the software.
- The procedure library containing the startup procedure for your security product must be carefully protected, to prevent, for example, someone changing the name of the current security database, which is specified in the procedure when using some third-party products.
- Any datasets containing startup parameters must also be protected. One option with many packages, for example, is to start up in either FAIL mode, WARN mode, or even INACTIVE mode for different functions, so someone with access to these parameters could potentially inactivate a whole group of security functions from one startup to the next.
- The security database itself must be protected from all updates except those done through the security software.
- Backups of all secure datasets should also be thoroughly protected, including pack dumps which include them. Otherwise you open yourself to the risk of someone: (a) modifying the backup; then (b) corrupting the live version so that the backup is used to 'recover' the altered version.

You should also take great care to check any modifications to your security software thoroughly. It is all too easy to code up a RACF exit, ensure it allows access where required, and forget to check whether it still denies access when it is supposed to.

There may also be other precautions you need to take which depend on how the particular package you are using works. Some packages, for example, have an option to allow the operator to disable all or part of the function of the package at startup time. Clearly, such options should be suppressed on production systems. You should be wary, however, of assuming they can be allowed on non-production systems. Even a systems programmer test system should have full security enabled if it shares DASD with a production system.

15.2.3 *Protecting other MVS facilities*

Other facilities should also be protected using your security package to prevent system security exposures. For example:

- Recent versions of security packages allow you to control the use of console commands. You should take advantage of this facility, as uncontrolled console commands can cause serious disruption.

- You should restrict the ability to use certain programs. AMASPZAP, for example, can be used to read and amend DASD data without going through normal security procedures, and IEHINITT can be used to overwrite tape labels.
- The bypass label processing (BLP) facility can be used to read tape datasets without going through tape dataset security validation, so this should also be restricted to authorized staff.
- System dump datasets can also include passwords and other privileged information, so READ access to these should be restricted to systems programmers.
- JES2 offload datasets containing jobs from the input queue include the password field from the JOB cards in a viewable format, so READ access should be denied to all users.
- The master catalog—you must allow universal read access to your master catalog but you should restrict update access to systems programmers and staff responsible for creating alias entries for new high-level qualifiers. This prevents other staff from accidentally cataloging datasets in the master catalog with unauthorized high-level qualifiers. You can allow universal update access to development user catalogs, but you may wish to restrict access to production user catalogs, particularly if you have split them up in a way which allows you to restrict access simply and logically. For example, if you have a catalog for all production finance datasets, you can restrict update access to it to production finance work.
- SMF datasets and archived SYSLOG – these contain the records of attempted security violations and might therefore be amended or destroyed to remove incriminating evidence.

References and bibliography

IBM manuals

1. *MVS/ESA System — Data Administration*, SC26–4515. Includes a chapter on password protection.
2. *MVS/DFP V3R2: System Programming Reference*, SC26–4567. The DFP 3.2 version of SC26–4515.
3. *MVS/ESA VSAM Administration Guide*, SC26–4518. The security chapter includes a section on AMS password protection.
4. *MVS/DFP V3R2: Managing VSAM Datasets*, SC26–4568. The DFP 3.2 version of SC26–4518.
5. *MVS/DFP V3R2: AMS for ICF*, SC26–4562. Specifies what AMS passwords are required for each IDCAMS command.
6. *RACF General Information*, GC28–0722. Includes some useful high-level information on how RACF works.
7. *SPL: RACF*, SC28–1343. The systems programmer's guide to implementing RACF.

8. *MVS/ESA Planning: B1 Security*, GC28–1800. This is the place to look if you need to know how to implement more sophisticated security than that required by most commercial organizations.
9. *SDSF Guide and Reference*, SC23–0408. Includes documentation on how to define SDSF security (both the SAF and pre-SAF versions).
10. *MVS/ESA SPL: Application Development Guide*, GC28–1852. Includes a detailed discussion on protecting MVS system integrity, with particularly useful coverage of potential APF authorization exposures.
11. *MVS/XA SPL: System Macros and Facilities Volume 1*, GC28–1150. The XA version of *SPL: Application Development Guide*.
12. *MVS/ESA SPL: Application Development Macro Reference*, GC28–1857. Documents the SAF (RACROUTE) macros.

Other

13. Wachtel, H.: Dangers of User-written Security Mechanisms, *MVS Update*, September 1991, pp. 3–4.
14. Dattani, D.: Security Exposures and Controls for MVS, *Mainframe Journal*, August 1990, pp. 46–50.

16
DASD management

16.1   Systems programmers and DASD management

DASD management is one of those terms that means something different to everyone you speak to. A chief operator's definition will be different to that of a storage administrator, and a systems programmer's will be different again. Indeed, the systems programmer's view will be enormously different from site to site, depending mainly on how much of those other two roles they are expected to play. On larger sites, there is likely to be a dedicated storage administration team, and the systems programmer may only be called in to help with obscure problems and exit routines. On sites where the operations department is strong and stable, the systems programmer may never have to deal with the hardware side of DASD management, other than modifying the MVS I/O configuration and the IOCDS. On other sites, however, the systems programmer may take on far more of these roles.

The picture is further complicated by the appearance of system managed storage (SMS); indeed DASD management in the SMS era is quite a different subject from DASD management in the pre-SMS era. (Note that there is some confusion over the meaning of SMS. In this chapter I shall use the term SMS to mean system-managed storage, a concept which can be implemented in many different ways, including some which use third-party software products instead of IBM's. By contrast, I shall use the term DFSMS to mean IBM's implementation of SMS. In DFP version 3 this was a slightly woolly concept, embracing the DFSMS subsystem, which was a component of DFP itself, plus DFDSS and DFHSM. With MVS 4.3, IBM has merged DFP, DFDSS, and DFHSM into a new product called DFSMS/MVS, which only muddies the water further by detaching DFSMS from the concept of system-managed storage as such. No doubt new usages will develop to clarify this; until they do I shall stick to the old usage for DFSMS as well as continuing to call DFP, DFDSS, and DFHSM by their old names.)

Irrespective of the division of labour on your site, however, and of the status of

SMS, there are aspects of DASD management which every systems progammer should understand. These include:

- How to make DASD devices and volumes available to the system
- Why and how to implement DASD pooling
- Regular housekeeping required to make effective use of DASD space
- How to maintain an effective catalog structure
- How to deal with DASD I/O and VTOC problems

These are the subjects which this chapter aims to cover. It will not attempt to cover DASD performance issues, although it is certainly true that the performance of your DASD subsystem is usually one of the most critical factors contributing to overall system performance. DASD performance is therefore a crucial issue for any DASD manager, but it is beyond the scope of this book.

16.2 DASD initialization

16.2.1 Overview

Before a DASD volume can be used on an MVS system, it is necessary to:

- Physically connect the DASD device on which it is mounted to a control unit, which is in turn connected to a channel available to the system (see Chapter 2).
- Define the device to the processor complex using IOCP and define the device to MVS using MVSCP, or HCD for MVS version 4 (see Sec. 7.4).
- Format the volume with null records, a volume serial label, and a volume table of contents (VTOC), and optionally a VTOC index.
- Vary the device online (done automatically for devices available at IPL time), and on systems prior to MVS 2.2.3 issue a mount command to determine the mount and use attributes of the volume (see Sec. 7.5.12 for a discussion of mount and use attributes, and see the descriptions of the MOUNT and VARY console commands in Sec. 4.4).
- Optionally, define the device as belonging to one or more eligible device groups so that datasets can be allocated on it using the UNIT parameter with the associated esoteric device name (also covered in Sec. 7.4).

I have been quite careful to use the term 'volume' in some places here, and 'device' in others. In the days of removable DASD volumes, this was of obvious importance. Nowadays it is more a matter of semantics, as the volume mounted on a modern DASD device can never be changed (although its volume serial number can be). However, the old usage is still retained, so you should get used to it.

As you can see, most of these processes have been discussed already in this book. In this section we will therefore concentrate on the process of formatting DASD volumes for MVS. This is done using the IBM device support facility program (also known as ICKDSF).

16.2.2 Formatting MVS DASD volumes

In order to format a DASD volume for use under MVS, you must use the DSF
INIT command. For 3380 and 3390 devices, there are two alternative 'levels' of
initialization — minimal and medial. Minimal initialization creates a VTOC and
a volume label, and leaves the other data on the volume untouched. Medial
initialization creates the VTOC and volume label, but also rewrites the home
address and record zero on every track on the volume, and erases all other data on
the volume, and so may be preferable for security reasons. It does, however, run
for much longer (over an hour for a 3380 model E volume, for example).

DSF now also provides an INSTALL command, which does some physical
checking of the volume but also rewrites the home addresses and record zero on
each track and erases other data in the same way as medial initialization — and
takes about as long as a medial initialization. IBM recommends the use of
INSTALL on new devices, so INSTALL followed by minimal initialization is
probably preferable to a medial initialization.

The VTOC maintains a record of the datasets allocated on a volume, the
physical location of each extent assigned to each dataset, and the locations of the
free space remaining on the volume (i.e. available extents). By default, the VTOC
is allocated one track at cylinder 0, head 1. For most volumes this will be far too
small. Each track of the VTOC on a 3380 device, for example, can be expected to
hold around 50 dataset entries, so unless the volume is to be reserved for rather
large datasets, you should allow at least one cylinder for the VTOC, and preferably
two or three. Volumes which are to be used for particularly small datasets (e.g.
HSM migration level one volumes, and volumes reserved for TSO datasets) may
require even larger VTOCs. Unless you intend to squeeze a VTOC index onto the
same cylinder as the VTOC (see the discussion of VTOC indexes in Sec. 16.2.3), the
VTOC should end on a cylinder boundary.

On uncached devices, the default positioning is also far from ideal. The VTOC
is likely to be heavily accessed, and on uncached devices the default position will
lead to a head movement back to cylinder 0 for each access, causing performance
degradation by increasing the average seek distance for the disk. It is therefore
traditional to allocate the VTOC nearer the middle of the volume to reduce
unnecessary head movement. One popular location is one-third of the way across
the disk, to allow for the fact that disks are not always full and free space tends to
be at the end of the disk, so the centre of the occupied area of the disk will come
before the physical half-way point. VTOC positioning is less important with
cached devices, as heavily accessed areas of the disk will tend to be kept in cache
memory and can therefore be accessed without any head movement.

Example 16.1 gives an example of a DSF job to perform a minimal initialization,
allocating the VTOC in a central location on a 3380 model K volume. Note that:

- To initialize SMS-managed volumes, you must also specify the storage group
  (SG) parameter on the INIT statement—or convert the volume later using the

```
//*-----------------------------------------------------------------
//*          CLIP AND INITIALIZE A DASD VOLUME(MINIMAL)
//*          - SHOULD BE ONLINE TO THIS SYSTEM & OFFLINE TO ALL OTHERS
//*-----------------------------------------------------------------
//INIT       EXEC PGM=ICKDSF,REGION=4096K
//SYSPRINT   DD  SYSOUT=*
//INITVOL    DD   DISP=SHR,VOL=SER=XADLIB,UNIT=3390
//SYSIN      DD  *
    INIT       DNAME(INITVOL)                                      -
               VERIFY(XADLIB)                                      -
               VTOC(1325,0,45)                                     -
               INDEX(1328,0,15)                                    -
               NOCHECK                                             -
               NOVALIDATE                                          -
               VOLID(SYST04)
/*
```

Example 16.1. Volume initialization using ICKDSF.

DFDSS CONVERTV command.

• This example also changes the volume serial number of the volume from XADLIB to SYST04, and creates a VTOC index. VTOC indexes are discussed in the next section.

Optionally, the initialization process may also place bootstrap records on cylinder 0, track 0. These are required if you intend to IPL from the volume, i.e. if it is to be used as a SYSRES pack, or as the IPL pack for a stand-alone utility. You may, however, add the bootstrap records later using the REFORMAT command, which can also be used to change the volume serial number (generally known as 'clipping' the volume) without re-initializing it. Example 16.2 illustrates the use of the REFORMAT command. Note that if you relabel a volume with a different serial number, any cataloged datasets on it will be wrongly cataloged afterwards (unless it is a SYSRES pack with datasets cataloged using indirect volume references). Except in special cases such as SYSRES maintenance, it is therefore unwise to change the volume serial number of a volume unless you also clear it of all datasets first (including the VTOC index and VVDS, whose names usually include the volume serial number). In most cases, then, you may as well perform a minimal re-initialization and recreate the volume from scratch.

Whenever you do change a volume serial number, whether by relabelling it or re-initializing it, you should also:

• Update SYS1.PARMLIB(VATLST00) to reflect the change, if the volume appears in it.
• Modify your HSM parameters or SMS storage group definitions for the volume concerned.
• Change any backup jobs and housekeeping jobs which service this volume.
• Update your DASD configuration documentation.
• Change any hard-coded volume serial numbers in production JCL or IDCAMS statements which refer to this volume.

```
//*------------------------------------------------------------
//* DOC: CHANGE VOLSER ON ONLINE PACK
//*------------------------------------------------------------
//CLIP1    EXEC PGM=ICKDSF
//SYSPRINT DD  SYSOUT=*
//PACK     DD  UNIT=3380,VOL=DDSER=SP213B,DISP=OLD
//SYSIN    DD  *
  REFORMAT  DDNAME(PACK) VERIFY(SP213B) VOLID(SPOOL2)
/*
//*------------------------------------------------------------
//* DOC: CHANGE VOLSER ON OFFLINE PACK
//*------------------------------------------------------------
//CLIP2    EXEC PGM=ICKDSF
//SYSPRINT DD  SYSOUT=*
//SYSIN    DD  *
  REFORMAT  UNITADDRESS(21C) VERIFY(XA217R) VOLID(IBMRES)
/*
//*------------------------------------------------------------
//*        INSTALL IPL TEXT ON SYSRES PACK
//*------------------------------------------------------------
//INSTALL EXEC PGM=ICKDSF
//SYSPRINT DD  SYSOUT=*
//IPLVOL   DD  DISP=SHR,VOL=SER=IBMRES,UNIT=3380
//IPLTEXT  DD  DISP=SHR,VOL=SER=XA313R,UNIT=3380,
//             DSN=SYS1.SAMPLIB(IPLRECS)
//         DD  DISP=SHR,VOL=SER=XA313R,UNIT=3380,
//             DSN=SYS1.SAMPLIB(IEAIPL00)
//SYSIN    DD  *
   REFORMAT  DDDNAME(IPLVOL)                                   -
             IPLDD(IPLTEXT)                                    -
             NOVERIFY                                          -
             BOOTSTRAP   /* IPLRECS OF IPLTEXT DD WILL SUPPLY IT */
/*
```

Example 16.2. Use of the ICKDSF REFORMAT command.

16.2.3 VTOC indexes

Unless you coded the INDEX parameter on the DSF INIT statement (as shown in Example 16.1), there is usually a further step you will need to perform to complete DASD initialization. This is the creation of a VTOC index. While MVS can use a volume without a VTOC index, access to the VTOC is considerably faster when you use one, and if you intend to make a volume SMS-managed, a VTOC index is an absolute prerequisite.

If you do code the INDEX parameter of the DSF INIT statement, the VTOC index dataset will be created automatically as part of volume initialization, with the dataset name SYS1.VTOCIX.volser (unless the volume serial number begins with a numeric character, in which case it will be called SYS1.VTOCIX.Vxxxxx, where xxxxx is the last five characters of the volume serial number). The INIT statement also converts the VTOC into indexed format.

An unindexed (i.e. MVS format or OS format) VTOC can be converted to an indexed one using DSF's BUILDIX command with the IX operand — an indexed one can be unindexed using the OS operand of the same command. For the indexing operation, you must allocate the index dataset from your JCL, and its name must begin SYS1.VTOCIX. You can allocate an existing VTOC index dataset if there is one, or allocate the space for a new one in your DD statement.

Appendix E of [1] gives a formula for working out the exact size of a VTOC index, but on 3380 and 3390 devices you will find this can be simplified to provide an easy rule of thumb:

- If your VTOC is 12 tracks or less, allocate 3 tracks on the same cylinder as the VTOC for the VTOC index.
- If your VTOC is over 12 tracks but no more than 12 cylinders, round it up to a whole number of cylinders and allocate a single cylinder for the VTOC index.
- If your VTOC is any larger than this, allocate two cylinders for the index.

Since the VTOC index and the VTOC itself are always accessed in rapid succession, it is sensible on uncached devices to place them as close to each other as possible (ideally on the same cylinder, or adjacent cylinders if they are too large for this) to minimize the head movement involved. As with the VTOC itself, it is preferable to end the VTOC index on a cylinder boundary. The INDEX keyword of INIT allows you to specify where to place the VTOC index on the volume, but if you are using BUILDIX, you will have to use your DD statement to place it next to the VTOC yourself. If you ever have to unindex the VTOC, BUILDIX leaves the old index dataset in place, so once you have placed the dataset you should never have to recreate it, even if the index status of the volume changes backward and forward. Example 16.3 shows how to create a VTOC index using the BUILDIX

```
//*-------------------------------------------------------------
//*DOC: ALLOCATE VTOC INDEX DATASET & BUILD VTOC INDEX
//*-------------------------------------------------------------
//BUILD EXEC PGM=ICKDSF
//INDEX  DD DSN=SYS1.VTOCIX.volser,DISP=(,KEEP),UNIT=3380,
//          VOL=SER=volser,SPACE=(ABSTR,(15,19920))
//*
//*  NB:  (ABSTR,(PP,TT))—PP IS NO OF TRACKS
//*                TT IS TRACK NO OF FIRST TRACK
//*                  (= (CC X 15) + HH, ON A 3380 OR 3390)
//*
//SYSPRINT DD  SYSOUT=*
//SYSIN    DD  *
  BUILDIX  DNAME(INDEX) IX
/*
```

Example 16.3. Creating an indexed VTOC.

command, positioning it in the same place as the index created with the INIT command in Example 16.1 above. Note that the ABSTR parameter may not be used on SMS-managed volumes, so if you need to position a VTOC index on an SMS-managed volume you will have to use the technique discussed in the following section on VVDSs.

16.2.4 Allocating a VVDS

In addition to a VTOC and its index, volumes which contain components of VSAM datasets and/or DFSMS-managed non-VSAM datasets must contain a VSAM volume dataset (VVDS). The VVDS is a component of the ICF catalog structure, holding records describing VSAM components and SMS-managed datasets allocated on this volume. The VVDS is created automatically when the first VSAM component is allocated on the volume, but attempts to place DFSMS-managed datasets on a volume will fail if the VVDS does not already exist. In any case, the comments on sizing and positioning the VTOC index apply equally to the VVDS. For SMS-managed volumes containing large numbers of datasets, the default primary extent size will be too small and will lead to secondaries being allocated — and hence fragmentation of the VVDS. Also, because the VVDS is likely to be accessed immediately after the VTOC, it should be placed next to the VTOC (at least on uncached volumes). So rather than allowing the VVDS to be created automatically with the default space at the first available location on the volume, you should pre-allocate it yourself, preferably immediately after initializing the volume.

The default size for a VVDS (i.e. if it is allocated automatically when the first VSAM component is created on a volume) is a primary extent of 10 tracks, with secondary extents the same size. If you can predict the number of datasets on the volume, [8] gives a formula for calculating the size of VVDS you need. The default caters for a little over 500 VSAM datasets and 1000 SMS-managed non-VSAM datasets, so if you feel this may be inadequate, a larger primary allocation would be wise.

Positioning VSAM components is a little more difficult than positioning sequential datasets, as you may not specify an absolute track address when you are defining a component using IDCAMS. In order to place the VVDS (or any other VSAM dataset) where you want it, you must therefore:

- List the locations of all free extents on the volume (e.g. using IEHLIST with the LISTVTOC FORMAT statement).
- Prevent anyone else from allocating, extending, or deleting datasets on the volume.
- Fill up the empty extents up to the position you wish to use by allocating dummy datasets of a suitable size (making use of the fact that MVS always allocates a dataset in the first available extent on a volume which is large enough to hold the primary allocation).
- Allocate your VVDS, which will also be placed in the first available extent — this is now the place where you want it to go!

This can be a very tedious process, unless you do it when the volume is still 'clean' and so only needs one or two datasets to fill up the space prior to your desired VVDS location. Assuming you have a clean volume, Example 16.4 shows you how

```
//*----------------------------------------------------------------
//*DOC: PREALLOCATE VVDS
//*----------------------------------------------------------------
//ALLOC EXEC PGM=IDCAMS
//SYSPRINT DD   SYSOUT=*
//DUMMY1 DD   VOL=SER=volser,DISP=(,DELETE),UNIT=3380,
//            SPACE=(TRK,(14))
//DUMMY2 DD   VOL=SER=volser,DISP=(,DELETE),UNIT=3380,
//            SPACE=(CYL,(1324))
//*
//*   NB:   DUMMY1 FILLS UP CYLINDER ZERO
//*         DUMMY2 FILLS UP CYLINDERS 1 TO 1324
//*
//SYSIN     DD  *
  DEFINE CLUSTER( NAME(SYS1.VVDS.Vvolser) VOL(volser) -
         NONINDEXED TRACKS(15 15) )
/*
```

Example 16.4. Preallocating a VVDS.

to pre-allocate a VVDS next to the VTOC and VTOC index created in Example 16.1. For maximum simplicity, you should do this in a subsequent step of the same job.

The role of the VVDS in the ICF catalog structure is discussed in Chapter 3.

16.3   DASD pooling

16.3.1   Why pool DASD?

If we were to make all our DASD volumes available to our users then leave them to make use of them as they pleased, we would be foolish indeed. With no restrictions on which volumes they could use or how much space they could allocate, the most resource-hungry users would quickly fill up the space available, however much we provided. We would constantly have to supply more space for essential data, or waste time tracking down owners of datasets, establishing how important they were, and negotiating space reductions.

The traditional alternative was to allocate individual volumes to each application, type of use, or group of users. Each volume was mounted as 'private' and all allocations were done by volume serial number. This, however, was just as unsatisfactory as the first option. It was unlikely, for example, that each 'use' would always require exactly the amount of space available on a whole number of volumes, so the private volumes approach usually led to space being wasted through over-provision. Also, the requirement to specify volume serial numbers for allocations led to inflexibility, and an increased workload for storage administrators. For example, a space allocation on one volume might fail even though there was lots of space available on another volume available to this user. It is also difficult and time-consuming to change the volumes available to a user, when this could only be done by changing hard-coded volume serial numbers in JCL.

Much of DASD management is concerned with avoiding these problems, or, to put it in a more positive light, with making the most cost-effective use of the storage resource. At the heart of an effective storage management strategy is DASD pooling — grouping DASD volumes into 'pools', and reserving each pool for a different type of use or group of users. If it is done well, this means that each 'use' of DASD has space reserved for it (and cannot impinge on that reserved for other 'uses'), while users do not have to worry about which volume they are going to use, and can remove hard-coding of volume serial numbers with all the inflexibility that implies.

Of course, DASD pooling alone will not solve all your storage management problems, and there are several other components of effective DASD management, some of which we will touch on in the next section. Pooling, however, is the starting point for effective storage management — including SMS. Indeed, the implementation of SMS is far easier if your DASD is already pooled before you start.

16.3.2 The options

Technically, there are several different ways of implementing pooling, for example:

- Perform all allocation using the UNIT parameter, and enforce this via JCL vetting and cleaning up rogue datasets after the event.
- Control allocation using the DADSM allocation exits, failing all allocation requests to wrong pools.
- Implement SMS management of your data.
- Use a third-party storage management product.

This section will look briefly at the first three of these. Third-party software is beyond the scope of this book.

16.3.3 Defining your pooling policy

Irrespective of the technology to be used, the first step in any DASD pooling implementation is to set standards defining your pools and specifying which datasets belong in which pools.

A typical set of pools and pool names (pool names in parentheses) might be: system datasets (SYS), development data (DEV), work files (WRK), and production data for finance applications (FIN), stock applications (STK), and personnel applications (PER). Alternatively, production data might be subdivided by type of dataset rather than by application, e.g. into database files (DBA), VSAM files online to CICS (CIC), and sequential files (SEQ). The 'application' approach might be more suitable where production file allocation is devolved to users and developers and the main reason for pooling is to guarantee each application an

agreed amount of space. The 'file-type' approach is probably better where production file allocation is under the control of the storage administrators and the main
reason for pooling is to distinguish the type of service to be given to each pool; in
this case, for example, we would expect the DBA and CIC pools to be on relatively
fast devices, and the SEQ pool to be on relatively slow ones.

Having defined your pools, you must establish dataset-naming standards which
will enable you to determine which datasets belong to which group. In practice,
most installations should have such standards already in place — establishing them
from scratch in a mature installation is an enormous undertaking, though an
essential one if it has never been done. For example, the first character in the
high-level qualifier could be used to indicate if the dataset is test or production, the
next three could indicate to which application it belongs, and the fifth could
indicate the type of file. Thus, we might have high level qualifiers like:

PFINC   production finance CICS VSAM datasets

TSTKD   test stock database datasets

PPERS   production personnel permanent sequential

TPERW   test personnel temporary sequential (i.e. a work file)

In addition, most sites will have HLQs for system datasets which follow the CBIPO
conventions, and others which are the user id's of TSO users — your standards for
TSO user ids should ensure there is no danger of confusion between these and the
'batch' HLQs. For example, TSO user ids can be distinguished by containing a
numeric section (but remember IBM's SYS1 and IPO1 datasets, and temporary
datasets).

Finally, you must develop and agree the rules that define which high-level
qualifiers belong in which pools.

16.3.4 Pooling using the UNIT parameter

Having set out standards, we must find a way of implementing and enforcing them.
Our first option was to perform all allocation using the UNIT parameter, and to
enforce this via JCL vetting and cleaning up rogue datasets after the event.
Technically, this is relatively simple, but administratively it is relatively complex.
The technical steps required are:

1   Define UNIT names in your EDT which correspond to your pools (e.g.
    UNIT=SYS, UNIT=DEV, etc.), and assign devices to each UNIT name
    which will provide the storage for the corresponding pool.
2   Mount the volumes on these devices with the 'storage' use attribute, which
    allows them to be used for non-volume-specific allocations of permanent
    datasets.
3   Remove all volume serial numbers from all production JCL, using pool-specific

unit names instead, and ensure it allocates datasets to the correct pools. This
is reasonably feasible if production JCL is under centralized control, as it
should be.

4   Ban the use of volume serial numbers by all users except systems programmers
    and storage administrators. Note that IDCAMS requires you to allocate
    VSAM components to specific volume serial numbers, so in pre-SMS environ-
    ments this will be an unavoidable exception to the rule.

5   Implement a JESEXIT4 to vet all DD statements for the VOL=SER
    parameter and either cancel the job or remove the parameter (with the
    exceptions mentioned above). This exit can do further processing to enforce the
    standards (i.e. checking that the UNIT name used is the correct one for the
    given HLQ), but since it does not affect dynamic allocations, it makes more
    sense to use our second option (i.e. the DADSM exit) if you aim to do this. On
    the other hand, some simple checking is probably worthwhile, e.g. prevent
    non-production users from allocating on production unit names, and non-
    systems programmers from allocating on UNIT=SYS.

6   Set up a regular housekeeping job which deals with datasets in wrong pools.
    This housekeeping job could, for example:

    a   Use a table to tell the job which volumes belong in which pool (unless you
        are able to derive this from the volume name, e.g. by making all volume
        serial numbers begin with the UNIT name of the pool to which they
        belong).
    b   For each volume, invoke a utility such as IEHLIST to list the datasets on
        it.
    c   For each dataset on the volume, check the high-level qualifier against a table
        which lists valid HLQs for this pool.
    d   For datasets in the wrong pool, write out an IDCAMS DELETE statement
        (for test datasets) or an HSM MIGRATE statement (for production
        datasets) to an output dataset.

You must then check the output dataset after each run to be sure you are not
about to delete a crucial dataset, or to migrate a dataset which will simply come
back to the wrong place over and over again, and finally submit the commands
which are acceptable. Obviously, this manual validation and the research involved
are potentially quite time-consuming. Once such a system is in place, however,
relatively few datasets should go into the wrong pool, and the task of dealing with
those that do should be manageable if you have dedicated storage administrators.

16.3.5 Pooling using the DADSM exits

To go to the next level of control, you must implement something like our second
option. This option replaces the JES exit (or supplements it) with a DADSM
pre-allocation exit (IGGPRE00), which validates each allocation request (whether

done from JCL or via SVC 99) and rejects requests attempting to allocate a dataset to a volume in a pool for which it is not eligible.

This, of course, requires that your exit has some way of knowing which datasets are eligible for which pools. The obvious way of doing this, as in the housekeeping program, is to use a table. Maintenance of tables in exits, however, can be a problem, so a preferable approach, if possible, is to design your standards so that simpler 'rules' can be applied to determine in which pool a dataset belongs. This is only likely to be practical, however, if you are starting with a green-field site.

Examples of IGGPRE00 exits to control DASD pooling are fairly common in the technical journals (or were before the dawning of the SMS era). See Chapter 12 for references to some of these.

Once again, it is best to prevent the use of volume serial numbers and set up your UNIT names in the same way as in the first option, so that MVS is given the opportunity to allocate all new datasets on any volume in the esoteric device group. Once your exits are in place, you should find that no datasets are allocated in the wrong pools, but it is wise to run a regular checkup job just to be on the safe side.

16.3.6 Pooling using DFSMS

Our third option is to implement DFSMS 'storage groups'. The DFSMS concept of a storage group is identical to the pre-SMS concept of a DASD pool. Each DFSMS-managed volume is assigned to one (and only one) storage group, and DFSMS will only allow datasets to be allocated to that storage group if your automatic class selection (ACS) routines determine that they are eligible for it. ACS routines can determine a dataset's pool on the basis of any one of a large number of attributes, but the simplest to use, as in other pooling strategies, is the dataset name. If you have implemented dataset-naming standards which reflect your pooling criteria, then it is a relatively simple matter to assign datasets to the correct storage groups. The storage groups themselves are defined in the DFSMS control dataset, and these definitions are created and changed using the ISMF storage group dialog.

This option has many advantages over those discussed earlier:

- The software required is standard, vendor-supported, and rapidly evolving — unlike your own exits.
- DFSMS exercises watertight control over dataset placement on DFSMS-managed volumes — so no housekeeping jobs to do checking-up or cleaning-up are required.
- DFSMS does not fail attempts to allocate datasets to the wrong pool — it redirects them to the right pool, overriding JCL parameters and control statements which specify volume serial numbers or unit names. So there is no need for manual correction and resubmission of jobs which abend because an exit has refused a wrongly coded allocation.
- Changes can be made to storage group definitions and ACS routines at any

time, without bringing down your system or reloading exits.

• DFSMS also automates control of many other aspects of allocation and space management, e.g. DCB parameters for common dataset types, allocation of datasets to cached or uncached devices depending on their performance requirements, and how long each group of datasets should remain on 'primary' DASD before becoming candidates for migration to other devices.

Implementing SMS for the first time is a substantial undertaking, and describing how to do it is beyond the scope of this book. IBM has, however, provided a clear and practical set of manuals on the subject, in the form of their *Storage Management Library*. The XA version of this set of books [3] contains advice on DASD management without DFSMS, including work you can do to position yourself for DFSMS implementation. The ESA version [4] explains how to implement DFSMS.

16.4   DASD housekeeping

16.4.1 Objectives

To keep DASD space usage effective, it is necessary to do a certain amount of regular housekeeping on your DASD volumes. The objectives of housekeeping include:

• Identification and removal of unwanted datasets
• Clearing of space on WORK volumes, i.e. volumes reserved for temporary data
• Recovery of unused space from over-allocated datasets
• Defragmentation of unused space
• Migration of little-used data on to cheaper media
• Backing up data in case it needs to be recovered after a hardware error, a software error, or a user error

The precise method you use to perform this housekeeping will depend on the software used for storage management in your installation. The following sections describe some of the commonly used methods for sites using IBM storage management software. Whatever software you use, you will probably find it necessary to run daily, weekly, and monthly DASD housekeeping suites — usually during periods when little or no other work is running on any system with access to the DASD concerned.

16.4.2 Removal of unwanted datasets

One problem with DASD volumes is the tendency for unwanted datasets of various types to accumulate gradually as a result of failures and mistakes, for example:

• Datasets which were not cataloged at creation time due to a user error — and

worse still, uncataloged datasets with the same name as cataloged datasets on other volumes
- Temporary datasets left behind after system failures
- VSAM orphans (i.e. VSAM components which are unusable because their catalog entries have been destroyed)

What all these datasets have in common is that they are not found in the catalog, so to identify them you must generate a list of uncataloged datasets on each DASD volume. One way of doing this is to run a DFDSS job against each volume specifying the following command:

```
DUMP DS (BY ((CATLG EQ NO))) INDYNAM(volser)
OUTDD(OUT)
```

This will show uncataloged datasets as 'successfully processed' in the message listing. The OUT DD statement can be used to back up the datasets before deleting them, if you think this is necessary, but by putting OUT to DD DUMMY, you can suppress the backup. In either case, you should keep the message listing on disk by allocating SYSPRINT to a disk dataset. Now you can feed the listing into a program or REXX EXEC which generates IEHPROGM SCRATCH statements for the successfully processed datasets, and finally use these as input to an IEHPROGM step.

This process will remove most uncataloged datasets but will fail to delete VSAM orphans. You should therefore check return codes from the deletion steps of these jobs (or automatically generate a WTOR or an incident report when you get a bad return code) and follow up non-zero return codes. Normal VSAM orphans can be removed using the IDCAMS DELETE VVR command. See Sec. 16.6 for advice on what to do if any more intractable 'orphans' turn up. Unless you are in the habit of deleting catalogs without emptying them first, problems of this type are rare on mature, stable systems.

There are several points you should beware of if you intend to establish a process like this for your DASD:

1 There are some system datasets which are often not cataloged for a good reason, e.g. all datasets on an alternative SYSRES pack are likely to appear as uncataloged. Similarly, if a systems programmer is building a new CBIPO system (or has built a one-pack system), the datasets on the packs used will be cataloged in a separate catalog structure based on a separate master catalog, and will therefore appear uncataloged to the live system. You should therefore avoid automatic deletion of uncataloged datasets on system packs.
2 VTOC index datasets need not be cataloged, so exclude these from your deletion process.
3 If such a process has not been in place before, users may have become used to leaving uncataloged datasets lying around and expect them to be left there. In this case, you will need to do some 'expectations management' before starting

to delete these datasets, and it would be wise to back them up before deleting them.

Far better than removing uncataloged datasets, of course, is to prevent them ever appearing. DFSMS does this automatically in normal circumstances, but will not cover you against every error and system failure. In a DFSMS-managed environment you will therefore still need to run this process. I would recommend running this process weekly in a non-SMS environment and monthly if you have implemented SMS.

16.4.3 Removal of datasets in wrong pools

As we saw in our discussion of DASD pooling, some pre-SMS pooling technologies require you to run a regular housekeeping job to identify and remove datasets which have been allocated in the wrong pool. If you have DFSMS, this should not be required.

To identify datasets in the wrong pool, you must generate a VTOC listing for each volume (e.g. using IEHLIST), then run this through a program that checks which datasets are allowed on which volumes (e.g. using a table of HLQs allowed in each pool), and generate a list of wrongly placed datasets. In theory, you can turn this list into a deck of IDCAMS DELETE statements then submit these to IDCAMS. However, this may be risky, e.g. if your table is not up to date or someone puts a vital production dataset in the wrong pool. If you have already run a clearup job to ensure there are no uncataloged datasets on the volume, one nice alternative is to generate DFHSM HMIGRATE statements instead and migrate the datasets on to migration level one storage. Assuming your DFHSM control statements are set up to recall all datasets to the correct pool, this will automatically move the datasets where you want them if and when the user attempts to access them. On the other hand, this option does not penalize the user for wrong placement and so give them an incentive to obey the rules. A more time-consuming alternative is simply to follow up the list of wrongly placed datasets manually.

In a non-SMS environment, with DASD pooling implemented, cleaning up your pools should be a weekly process.

16.4.4 Clearing of WORK volumes

Many installations reserve a pool of volumes for use by temporary datasets (or short-lived datasets, such as those created by one job of a regular suite and deleted by a later job in the suite). The whole point of providing such a pool is that it always has space available because there is no accumulation of permanent datasets gradually filling it up. It is therefore essential if you have a WORK pool to clear down your WORK volumes on a regular basis.

The easiest way is to perform a minimal initialization of each work volume (see Sec. 16.2) and then create a new VTOC index and VVDS. This requires that all other work which might use the volume is stopped during the cleardown, and also that you run the cleardown at a point in the schedule where there are never any datasets in the process of being passed from one job to another. This approach is also inconsistent with a flexible policy on the use of such volumes, and will therefore be difficult to establish if users have grown accustomed to such a policy. It is, however, the ideal solution, since it effectively enforces the intended usage of work volumes.

If you want (or need) to be more flexible, an alternative approach is: generate a VTOC listing for each WORK volume; put it through a program which separates what is to be kept from what is to be deleted, and creates IDCAMS DELETE statements for the latter group; then run IDCAMS using these as input.

Work volumes should be cleared every day.

16.4.5 *Recovery of over-allocated space and defragmentation of unused space*

To prevent wastage of space, you should periodically recover space allocated to sequential datasets but not used, and space used to extend uncompressed PDSs. One method is to run a DFDSS RELEASE and COMPRESS against each volume (or equivalent functions of a competing product). For sites with DFP 3.2 or above, wastage of space by PDSs can be permanently stopped by converting them to PDSEs, which reuse space released by deleted members and so do not need regular compression.

Fragmentation of free space on volumes can also cause problems: an attempt to allocate a dataset on a volume will fail, for example, even though there is enough free space on the volume, if that space cannot be assembled in five or fewer extents. Fragmentation also leads datasets to be split over multiple extents and therefore impacts the performance of I/O operations to them. To control fragmentation, you can periodically run a DFDSS DEFRAG against each volume. Note that the DFHSM space management volume exit ARCMVEXT is passed a fragmentation index for each volume by DFHSM, so this is an ideal point at which to schedule DEFRAG jobs. DFHSM also provides a MAXEXTENTS parameter, which is used by its space management routines to determine whether it should consolidate extents belonging to individual datasets when it does volume space management. Any dataset which has gone to more extents than the MAXEXTENTS value will be migrated then immediately recalled and reallocated with a primary extent equal to the amount of space used.

Beware of running DEFRAGs against volumes containing linklist libraries, or LLA-managed libraries, since the system keeps information on the physical location of data in these datasets and bypasses the VTOC to access it, and will therefore suffer integrity problems if the data is moved.

In addition, DEFRAGS should be scheduled when the pack concerned is not being accessed by other work, as they enqueue on the VTOC and perform heavy

I/O to the volume, resulting in very poor response times for other work accessing the volume concurrently.

I would recommend running RELEASE and COMPRESS weekly against all volumes, and DEFRAGS against non-linklist volumes when the fragmentation index exceeds a given threshold. IBM recommends, for example, checking the fragmentation index of DFHSM migration level one volumes monthly, and running a DEFRAG if the fragmentation index exceeds 0.450. A threshhold of 0.300 to 0.350 may be more suitable for primary volumes.

16.4.6 Migration of little-used data

To prevent rarely used data from filling up your primary DASD volumes, you should regularly use DFHSM or an equivalent product to migrate data which has not been used for more than a given period of time. You need to understand the usage pattern of data on a volume before setting migration ages for it. For example:

- A daily backup GDG which will only be accessed in the rare event of an application failure could be migrated immediately.
- Development datasets can usually be migrated after a relatively short period of non-usage, say 10 days.
- Do not set a migration age of 30 days for datasets used by monthly batch jobs. These should either be given a short migration age (2 days, to allow for reruns if the suite fails), or a long one (32 days plus, which ensures they will never be migrated as long as the batch job continues to run).

While it is clear that the appropriate migration age depends on the dataset type, you need DFSMS management classes to be able to control migration age by dataset name. DFHSM only allows you to control migration ages at the volume level, so pre-SMS sites inevitably have to compromise in this area.

Migration should be done on a daily basis, as part of DFHSM's daily space management routines.

16.4.7 Backup

DASD data is usually extremely valuable — far more so than the hardware on which it sits. It is often claimed, for example, that many private companies would go out of business in a matter of days or weeks if they lost their information systems or data. It is therefore vital for every site to have backups of DASD data to prevent its loss in the event of hardware or software failure.

You should take full-pack dumps (e.g. using DFDSS) of all volumes at least once a week, and keep a copy of the most recent one offsite for disaster recovery purposes. For volumes where data changes frequently and changed data is difficult to reconstruct and important to your organization, back up the volume daily —

either full-pack dumps, or incremental ones — and once again, keep all tapes necessary to recover the most recent version of the data offsite. Incremental backups sound like a good idea in principle, but they are notoriously difficult to use for recovery, so conduct a few trials of what it would be like to recover with them in a worst-case scenario before deciding to depend on them. Indeed, whatever your backup strategy you should practice recovery so that you can be confident that it is possible and can be done smoothly should an emergency ever arise.

You should also take care to back up volumes containing related datasets simultaneously. If a VSAM dataset on one volume is used as an index to a VSAM dataset on another volume, for example, the integrity of your backups will be compromised if any updates occur between the backups of the two volumes. The simplest approach to preventing problems like this is to: (a) ensure that related datasets always reside in the same pool as each other; and (b) back up the whole pool at the same time, with no work running which can update any data on the pool.

The concurrent copy feature of the 3990 DASD controller provides a convenient way of backing up multiple packs or datasets at consistent points, with minimal interruption to other work. This feature allows backups to be taken virtually instantaneously and then copied to the output device asynchronously, allowing the data concerned to be updated by applications while the backup is completing. It is invoked by specifying the CONCURRENT operand on a DFSMSdss DUMP or COPY command. However, there is one potential problem to be aware of: if the backup fails due to problems on the output device (e.g. an I/O error on a tape drive), then you cannot recover it, and since further updates may have occurred to the data during the backup process, you will have lost the opportunity to take a backup at the original backup point. This alternative is therefore not suitable for data which must be backed up at a particular point in your schedule.

16.5   Catalog management

16.5.1 Overview

DASD datasets are usually located via catalogs. Indeed, VSAM and SMS-managed datasets are always located via catalogs, and it is good practice to ban uncataloged datasets on your DASD (except for system datasets of which you need multiple copies, e.g. SYSRES datasets). Ensuring that your catalogs are effectively managed is therefore a crucial aspect of DASD management. The elements of catalog management in which systems programmers are commonly involved are:

• Defining and maintaining the master catalog
• Defining and enforcing the alias/user catalog structure
• Establishing processes to remove redundant entries from catalogs

- Catalog backup and recovery
- Establishing processes to reorganize catalogs from time to time

The first of these is discussed in some detail in Chapter 7; the others are the subject of the remainder of this section.

16.5.2 The user catalog/alias structure

User datasets should be cataloged in user catalogs rather than the master catalog, and this requires that you create ALIAS entries in the master catalog for each valid user dataset name high-level qualifier. The ALIAS entry directs the catalog search process to a specific user catalog for a specific HLQ. It will be either part of the systems programmer's job or part of the storage administrator's to determine how many user catalogs to use, how large they should be, where they should be placed, and which HLQs will be associated with each user catalog.

My advice is to create one user catalog per DASD pool, and place it on a volume within the pool it is going to service. All HLQs which belong in a given pool should then be associated with the user catalog for that pool via suitable ALIAS definitions in the master catalog. This has two main advantages:

1 It prevents cross-contention between catalogs, which can occur when a catalog task using a catalog on volume A tries to access the VVDS on volume B while another is using a catalog on volume B and is trying to access a VVDS on volume A.

2 If you also follow my recommendation to perform backups a pool at a time, this ensures that each pool can be restored as a separate unit in a disaster recovery situation, and the catalog will automatically be in step with the datasets.

You should also have a separate catalog for tape datasets — obviously this cannot reside on a pack in the tape pool, but since the cross-contention problem cannot happen for tape datasets this is not too bad. If you use a tape management package, you should place your tape user catalog on the same pack as the tape management catalog, so that they will be in step if the volume ever has to be restored.

If you have an unsatisfactory catalog structure and wish to move to a more organized one, the best approach is to:

1 Create new, empty, user catalogs in the desired locations.

2 Back up your existing catalogs, and ensure recovery will be possible if you have a problem (see Sec. 16.5.4).

3 Use a series of IDCAMS jobs with the REPRO MERGECAT statement to move the catalog entries for each HLQ to the correct user catalog (and change the ALIAS pointer in the same job, using DELETE and DEFINE statements, if the REPRO MERGECAT completes satisfactorily).

4 Clean up any entries left over in the old catalogs and then delete them.

This is a lot simpler and quicker if you write a clist to generate the JCL to move a list of HLQs from one catalog to another (ISPF clists are very suitable for this because of the ease of using ISPF skeletons to generate JCL). Even with this assistance, however, it can be a major undertaking, as most well-established installations have literally thousands of HLQs in use. Each REPRO MERGECAT job also needs to allocate all VVDSs containing entries for VSAM clusters affected by the move, which adds a further complication to the JCL. Furthermore, HLQs used by online applications should only be moved when the online service is down.

Once you have your catalogs set up the way you want them, you must ensure that new HLQs are allocated ALIASes pointing to the right catalog. This is not too difficult if the process of setting up new HLQs is centralized in the storage management or security group, as it should be, and you use a clist or standard piece of JCL to set up new ALIASes. You can either include a prompt in the clist to ask for the pool to be used and rely on the administrator's knowledge of the pools, or use a program referencing a table to determine which user catalog to use for any given HLQ.

16.5.3 Removing redundant entries

Those of you with DFHSM can easily identify redundant entries in catalogs by running HSM AUDIT against each catalog. This will generate a list of catalog discrepancies. For datasets cataloged on DASD, it will list catalog entries which do not match VTOC entries on the device; for datasets cataloged on VOL = SER = MIGRAT, it will list entries which do not correspond to entries in the HSM control datasets. Different error codes are shown for different types of problem, and you must not simply delete every catalog entry shown on the listing. Datasets cataloged on tapes, for example, could be perfectly correctly cataloged, but they will appear on the listing because HSM will not attempt to mount the tape to verify the catalog entry against the label. Other datasets may appear in the listing when the catalog shows them on DASD volumes and the control dataset shows them as migrated — this could mean that two versions of the dataset exist, one on the primary volume and the other migrated, so deleting the catalog entry is clearly not the solution. Instead, you will have to familiarize yourself with the different types of error code and take the corresponding action for each. This process can be partially automated, e.g. by generating IDCAMS DELETE cards from the output of the AUDIT command for datasets cataloged on DASD volumes but showing error codes which unambiguously mean the dataset does not exist on that volume. Other errors will have to be resolved manually. Fortunately, bad catalog entries usually accumulate rather slowly, so once you have cleaned up your catalogs, it should be a relatively minor exercise to keep them clean, say once a month.

16.5.4 Catalog backup and recovery

Catalogs are critical system datasets, and the coming of SMS, with its rule that all datasets must be cataloged, is making them still more critical. It is therefore vital that they can be recovered in the event of a hardware or software failure (or systems programmer error!). If you take weekly pack backups, these will include your catalogs, but catalog backups can become seriously out of date in a matter of hours, so weekly dumps do not provide a suitable level of backup.

Even daily dumps are not really adequate for catalog recovery, though if you have a tape management package to cover the tapes you could probably reconstruct the lost catalog updates since the time of your backup by scanning all your DASD for new uncataloged datasets after restoring the catalog. This, however, would be a long and tedious process (though not quite so long and tedious if you are confident that the user catalog relates only to one DASD pool).

Fortunately, there is a way round this problem, which makes use of the fact that all catalog updates are recorded by SMF, using the following record types: type 61 —when an entry is defined; type 65—when an entry is deleted; and type 66—when an entry is altered.

If you ensure that SMF records these record types (via the current SMFPRMxx member of SYS1.PARMLIB), you can use these records to "roll forward" a restored user catalog from the time of the backup to the point of failure. This can be done manually, with the aid of a program to format the SMF records comprehensibly (see [13], for example), or it can be done automatically, with the aid of a more sophisticated program such as IBM's ICFRU (Integrated Catalog Facility Recovery Utility). ICFRU is used to merge updates recorded by SMF with an exported copy of the catalog before restoring the catalog from the exported copy. Anyone considering using ICFRU should read [14] for practical advice on how to do it.

One critical point made repeatedly by Martin Hoare [14] is that you must ensure that your catalog recovery process is completely independent of the catalogs themselves. In other words, any datasets you need to perform the process must be on a known volume.

Furthermore, these datasets should not be kept on the same volume as any catalog you may wish to recover, or on one volume of an HDA pair when the other volume of the pair contains such a catalog; otherwise, an HDA failure which takes out the catalog will also prevent you recovering it. This all requires careful thought in advance. In particular, you should:

1   Take a daily backup of all catalogs (using IDCAMS EXPORT if you are going to use ICFRU) to a GDG on a known DASD volume.
2   Write the SYSOUT data from the EXPORT to a dataset on the same DASD volume as the backup, so you know the date and time of the backup you are using when you try to perform recovery from it.
3   Ensure that the necessary SMF data will be available – I would suggest

extracting the relevant record types and storing them on a known DASD volume as part of your regular SMF housekeeping.

4 Keep your JCL and procedures in a special dataset on a known volume.

5 Ensure none of these datasets will be migrated by DFHSM.

You may also find it useful to take a 'snapshot' of all your DASD VTOCs on a regular basis and save this on a dataset on a known DASD volume, so that you can browse it to find a dataset when the catalogs are not available.

16.5.5 Catalog reorganization

Catalog reorganizations should be carried out regularly—say once every three to six months—to remove CI and CA splits (do it more frequently if you detect CA splits). This can be done by REPROing out the catalog entries into a temporary catalog, reallocating the original catalog, and REPROing the catalog entries back into it. Example 16.5 describes each job required and the IDCAMS control statements required for each of them. Note that it includes steps to disconnect the catalog from a second master catalog and reconnect it afterwards — you will only need to do this if you are sharing the catalog between two master catalogs.

```
//*-------------------------------------------------------------------*
//*   JOB 01 - LIST OFF THE CATALOG TO BE REORGANISED. PUT THE OUTPUT  *
//*            TO A DISK DATASET AS AN EXTRA LEVEL OF BACKUP. YOU       *
//*            SHOULD ALSO HAVE BACKED UP THE CATALOG, E.G. VIA DFDSS   *
//*-------------------------------------------------------------------*
  LISTCAT ENT(CATALOG.Vvolser) ALL
//*-------------------------------------------------------------------*
//*                                                                     *
//*   JOB 02  - DISCONNECT THE CATALOG FROM THE SECOND MASTER CATALOG   *
//*-------------------------------------------------------------------*
//* DOC: YOU MUST CHECK THE CATALOG ADDRESS SPACE IS NOT USING THE      *
//*      CATALOG. IF IT IS, ISSUE THE 'MODIFY CATALOG,UNALLOC' CMD      *
//*-------------------------------------------------------------------*
//STEPCAT  DD  DSN=CATALOG.MASTER.VSECOND,DISP=SHR
  EXPORT 'CATALOG.Vvolser' DISCONNECT
//*-------------------------------------------------------------------*
//*                                                                     *
//*   JOB 03  - ALLOCATE THE TEMPORARY CATALOG. IT IS EASIER TO REPRO   *
//*             THE DATASET IN AND OUT TO DISK THAN TO USE IDCAMS EXPORT *
//*-------------------------------------------------------------------*
     DEFINE   UCAT   (NAME (CATALOG.VBACKUP)   -
                      VOLUME (bkpvol)          -
                      ICFCATALOG               -
                      TRACKS (150 15) )        -
                      CATALOG(CATALOG.MASTER.VFIRST)
//*-------------------------------------------------------------------*
//*                                                                     *
//*   JOB 04 -   WILL COPY THE CURRENT CATALOG INTO THE NEWLY DEFINED   *
//*              BACKUP CATALOG. MUST COMPLETE WITH CC=0.               *
//*-------------------------------------------------------------------*
//STEPCAT   DD   DSN=CATALOG.Vvolser,DISP=SHR
//          DD   DSN=CATALOG.VBACKUP,DISP=SHR
  REPRO INDATASET(CATALOG.Vvolser)-
        OUTDATASET(CATALOG.VBACKUP)
```

Example 16.5. Reorganizing an ICF catalog.

```
//*-------------------------------------------------------------------*
//*                                                                   *
//*  JOB 05 —  WILL DELETE THE CURRENT CATALOG. THIS IS DELETED WITH  *
//*            THE RECOVERY OPTION SO THAT THE ALIAS POINTERS ARE NOT  *
//*            LOST IN THE MASTER CATALOG AND ALL RELEVANT VVDS'S.     *
//*-------------------------------------------------------------------*
//*  DOC: FIRST CHECK THE CATALOG IS NOT ALLOCATED TO THE CATALOG ADDR *
//*       SPACE. IF IT IS, ISSUE THE 'MODIFY CATALOG,UNALLOC' COMMAND  *
//*-------------------------------------------------------------------*
//SYSIN     DD  *
  DELETE CATALOG.Vvolser -
       RECOVERY               -
       USERCATALOG
//*-------------------------------------------------------------------*
//*                                                                   *
//*  JOB 06 —  ALLOC DEFINES THE NEW USER CATALOG. ENSURE THAT        *
//*            YOU SIZE AND POSITION THE DATASET CORRECTLY.           *
//*-------------------------------------------------------------------*
      DEFINE  UCAT  (NAME (CATALOG.Vvolser) -
                     VOLUME (volser)      -
                     ICFCATALOG           -
                     TRACKS (140 10) )    -

                    CATALOG(CATALOG.MASTER.VFIRST)
//*-------------------------------------------------------------------*
//*                                                                   *
//*  JOB 07  - THIS WILL REPRO THE CURRENT BACKUP COPY BACK INTO THE  *
//*            LIVE SYSTEM CATALOG. MUST COMPLETE WITH CC=O.          *
//*-------------------------------------------------------------------*
//STEPCAT   DD  DSN=CATALOG.VBACKUP,DISP=SHR
//          DD  DSN=CATALOG.Vvolser,DISP=SHR
  REPRO —
       INDATASET(CATALOG.VBACKUP) -
       OUTDATASET(CATALOG.Vvolser)
//*-------------------------------------------------------------------*
//*                                                                   *
//*  JOB 08  - WILL RECONNECT THE CATALOG BACK TO THE SECOND MASTER   *
//*            CATALOG. IT USES THE ALIAS STATEMENT TO ENSURE THAT    *
//*            THE ALIASES ARE RETAINED IN THE MASTER CATALOG.        *
//*-------------------------------------------------------------------*
  IMPORT CONNECT ALIAS OBJECTS((CATALOG.Vvolser -
                   DEVT(3380) VOLUMES(volser))) -
                   CATALOG(CATALOG.MASTER.VSECOND)
//*-------------------------------------------------------------------*
//*                                                                   *
//*  JOB 09  - DELETE THE BACKUP CATALOG SO YOU CAN RERUN THE PROCESS *
//*            FOR OTHER CATALOGS. DON'T RUN THIS JOB UNTIL THE REST   *
//*            OF THE PROCESS HAS COMPLETED SUCCESSFULLY!             *
//*-------------------------------------------------------------------*
  DELETE -
     CATALOG.VBACKUP -
     RECOVERY         -
     USERCATALOG
```

Example 16.5. (cont.)

16.6   DASD problems

There are two main types of DASD problem with which systems programmers may
need to get involved: I/O errors, and VTOC problems.

16.6.1 I/O errors

The I/O subsystem does a great deal of error recovery itself, including:

- Reconstruction of unreadable data using error checking and correcting (ECC) bytes which are recorded along with the original data.
- Offset recovery: when ECC recovery does not work, another read is attempted with the read/write heads slightly offset from the centre of the track to try to find a more readable area of the media; if this succeeds, it is recorded as a 'temporary error'

I/O errors detected by the I/O subsystem are recorded in the error-recording dataset (ERDS), which for MVS is SYS1.LOGREC, and every site should check the contents of this dataset on a daily basis using the Environmental Record Editing and Printing (EREP) Program. Usually this will be done by the operations department. The jobs required to save LOGREC data and print EREP reports from it are discussed in Chapter 17.

Errors which are shown on the EREP reports should be followed up, particularly as temporary errors tend to precede permanent errors, so by acting on temporary errors you can anticipate and prevent many permanent errors. Often, this will simply be a case of calling in your hardware engineer to look at the problem. However, when the problem is caused by defects on the magnetic surface of the disk, the systems programmer may be involved. Errors of this type can be analysed and prevented from recurring using facilities provided by DSF. The ANALYZE command can be used to determine if the data on a volume is readable and to report on errors. The INSPECT command can be used to do more rigorous checking of the surface of the disk and can take action to prevent future problems.

INSPECT can prevent future problems by invoking 'skip displacement' for bad areas of a track, if the SKIP parameter is coded on the INSPECT command. This means that bad areas of the track are marked as unreadable, and all data on the track after this point is shunted along. Seven skip displacement areas are available at the end of each track to accommodate data overflow due to skip displacement, and if these are all filled up, INSPECT will assign an alternate track to be used instead of the bad track. This will be assigned from one or more spare cylinders which are provided after the last cylinder on the volume for this purpose.

See [9] and [1] for further explanation and examples of the use of the ANALYZE and INSPECT commands.

16.6.2 VTOC problems

The other type of DASD problem which may fall into the lap of the systems programmer is the need to remove datasets from a volume which cannot be deleted using normal methods. The safest and most convenient thing to do with datasets like this is to accept the loss of space. Another alternative is to take a logical dump of the volume, re-initialize it, then perform a restore which excludes the datasets to be removed.

However, there are times when neither the loss of space implicit in the first solution nor the outage in service implicit in the second will be acceptable. On these occasions, it is possible to remove such datasets by the process of 'zapping the VTOC' to make the dataset deletable, then deleting as normal. This process can also be used to rename a dataset when there is another copy of the dataset allocated to the system or to a long-running task or job, so that it can then be deleted. This is a dangerous and unsupported process, but if you have to do it, here is how:

1   Take a physical backup of the volume, just in case.
2   Unindex the VTOC.
3   Run DFDSS PRINT to list the VTOC, as shown in Example 16.6.
4   From this print, find the CCHHR location of the VTOC entry you need to change. Example 16.7 shows the first four records of a VTOC print. Each record is preceded by its COUNT field, and the first 10 characters of this are the CCHHR address of the record (four hex characters each for the cylinder and head numbers, and two hex characters for the record number). The first record is always a 'format 4 DSCB', which is the VTOC's self-describing entry. The second is always a 'format 5 DSCB', which describes the first 26 available

```
//*---------------------------------------------------------------------
//*        DUMP VTOC
//*---------------------------------------------------------------------
//DUMP1    EXEC PGM=ADRDSSU,REGION=2M
//SYSPRINT DD   SYSOUT=*
//DASD1    DD   DISP=OLD,UNIT=3380,VOL=SER=TSOVOL,DSN=FORMAT4.DSCB
//SYSIN    DD   *
         PRINT INDDNAME(DASD1)
/*
```

Example 16.6. Printing out VTOC entries using DFDSS.

extents on the volume. These are then followed by 'format 1 DSCB' entries for each dataset on the volume — also known as the dataset labels.

5   Identify the bits you need to change (see the description of the DSCB in [11] for information on the function of bits in the VTOC record).
6   Run AMASPZAP (superzap) to change the bits concerned. Example 16.8 shows an example of what is required to make a VSAM orphan appear to be an ordinary non-VSAM dataset. Note that you should attempt to use the IDCAMS DELETE VVR command on VSAM orphans before trying the superzap option.

```
*** TRACK(CCHH)  012C0000           RO DATA  000000000000000
     COUNT  012C0000012C0060
0000  04040404 04040404 04040404 04040404 04040404 04040404 04040404  *................................*
0020  04040404 04040404 04040404 F4012E00 0E3505A3 03750000 000F8B01  *...............4....T.........IB*
0040  000FBB60 00000020 00000000 00000000 2E000E00 00000000 00000000  *...-............................*
0060  00000000 00010001 2C000001 2E000E00 00000000 00000000 00000000  *................................*
0080  00000000 00000000 00000000                                      *............*
     COUNT  012C0000022C0060
0000  05050505 00000000 00000000 00000000 00000000 00000000 00000000  *................................*
0020  00000000 00000000 00000000 F5000000 00000000 00000000 00000000  *..........5.....................*
0040  00000000 00000000 00000000 00000000 00000000 00000000 00000000  *................................*
0060  TO  007F  SAME AS ABOVE
0080  00000000 00000000 00000000                                      *............*
     COUNT  012C0000032C0060
0000  E2E8E2F1 4BE5E3D6 C3C9E74B E5E3E2D6 E5D6D340 40404040 40404040  *SYS1.VTOCIX.VTSOVOL........*
0020  40404040 40404040 40404058 F1D5E2D6 E5D6D300 015400A5 00000001  *..........1NSOVOL....V....IB*
0040  D4D6E2E5 E2F24040 40404058 00780000 00040000 80000800 08000000  *MOSVS2.........................*
0060  0000000E 12BB6000 00810001 2F000001 2F000E00 00000000 00000000  *.....-...A....................*
0080  00000000 00000000 00000000                                      *............*
     COUNT  012C0000042C0060
0000  E2E8E2F1 4BE2D6E4 D9C3C54B C3D5E3D3 40404040 40404040 40404040  *SYS1.SOURCE.CNTL.........*
0020  40404040 40404040 40404040 F1E3E2D6 E5D6D300 015A0074 00000001  *.........1TSOVOL....!.....IB*
0040  D4D6E2E5 E2F24040 4040405B 00BE0000 00000200 90000C30 00500000  *MOSVS2....$...&....{.*
0060  00000004 04A6E000 00810000 CA000000 CB000E00 00000000 00000000  *.....W...A....................*
0080  00000000 00000000 00000000                                      *............*
```

Example 16.7. Section of DFDSS VTOC print.

```
//*------------------------------------------------------------------
//* DOC:     MAKE UNCATALOGED VSAM DATASET DELETABLE
//*------------------------------------------------------------------
//*          SEE DATA AREAS VOL2 FOR DESCRIPTION OF DSCB1 FIELDS
//* REP     0038 000000      EXPIRY DATE
//* VER     0053 08          VSAM DATASET
//* REP     0053 00          TURN OFF VSAM DSN INDICATOR
//* REP     0052 40          CHANGE DSORG IND TO PHYSICAL SEQUENTIAL
//* VER     005D 10          PASSWORD REQUIRED FOR READ WRITE
//* REP     005D 00          TURN OFF PASSWORD PROTECTION BIT
//*------------------------------------------------------------------
//STEP1    EXEC PGM=AMASPZAP
//SYSLIB   DD DSN=FORMAT4.DSCB,DISP=OLD,UNIT=3380,VOL=SER=TSOVOL,
//         DCB=KEYLEN=44
//SYSPRINT DD  SYSOUT=*
//SYSIN    DD  *
 CCHHR 012C000005
    VER 0000 C3C1E3C1D3D6            CATALO
    REP 0038 000000                  EXPDT
    VER 0050 00000008                VSAM
    REP 0050 00000400                PS
    VER 005C 0010                    PASSWORD PROTECTED
    REP 005C 0000                    NOT!
/*
```

Example 16.8. Zapping VTOC to make VSAM orphan deletable.

7   Now delete the dataset as normal, e.g. using IEHPROGM.
8   Reindex the VTOC.

The requirement to unindex the VTOC means this process is not an option for DFSMS-managed volumes.

References and bibliography

IBM manuals

1. *DSF User Guide and Reference*, GC35–0033. Includes documentation of the INIT, REFORMAT, BUILDIX, ANALYZE, and INSPECT commands.
2. *MVS/ESA System Data Administration*, SC26–4515. Describes the VTOC and how it is used and managed (for DFP 3.2 onwards, this manual is called *DFP Systems Programmer's Reference*).
3. *MVS/XA Storage Management Library*. A useful and readable set of manuals on storage management policies and practices, designed for pre-DFSMS sites implementing policies to position them for DFSMS, e.g. the volume on *Managing Storage Pools*, GC26–4264, discusses DASD pooling in some detail. *Managing Data Sets*, GC26–4263, *Configuring Storage Subsystems*, GC26–4262, and *Leading an Effective Storage Administration Group*, GC26–4261 are also good value.
4. *MVS/ESA Storage Management Library*. The DFSMS version! Lots of good advice on implementing SMS — includes *Managing Storage Pools*, SC26–4656, *Managing Data Sets and Objects*, SC26–4657, *Leading an Effective Storage Administration Group*, SC26–4658, and *SMS Migration Planning Guide*, SC26–4659.
5. *MVS/DFP Storage Administration Reference*, SC26–4566. Covers the nuts and bolts of SMS.

6. *DFHSM System Programmer's Guide*, SH35–0083. Documents how to implement and control DFHSM.
7. *DFDSS User's Guide*, SC26–4388. Includes a chapter on using RELEASE, COMPRESS, and DEFRAG, and one on converting data and volumes to DFSMS management.
8. *MVS/DFP Managing Catalogs*, SC26–4555 (formerly *Catalog Administration Guide*). Discusses the creation and management of catalogs, including control of the catalog address space.
9. *DSF Primer for the User of IBM 3380 and 3390 DASD*, GC26–4498. Excellent short introduction to I/O errors and error correction on DASD.
10. *EREP User's Guide and Reference*, GC28–1378. Documents use of EREP to report on hardware errors.
11. *MVS/ESA Diagnosis: Data Areas, Volume 2*, LY28–1044. Documents formats of VTOC entries (listed as DSCB1 through DSCB5).

Also, see the reading list in Chapter 4 for documentation on IBM utilities referred to in this chapter, such as IEHLIST and AMASPZAP.

Other

12. Conner, C.: ICKDSF Initialize and Install Functions, *Enterprise Systems Journal*, April 1991, pp. 107–109.
13. Fairbrother, I.: Forward Recovery of an ICF Catalogue, *MVS Update*, February 1987, pp. 18–28.
14. Hoare, M.: User Experiences of Catalog Recovery using ICFRU, *GUIDE Europe conference proceedings*, Wiesbaden, Autumn 1990, pp. 299–305.

17
System data housekeeping

17.1 Housekeeping overview

In the course of normal operation, MVS generates useful management data of various types and records it in MVS datasets (or JES spool datasets, in the case of the SYSLOG). It will usually be part of the systems programmer's job to set up housekeeping processes for this data — processes which produce reports from the data, clear down the datasets used by MVS, and archive the data for future reference. There are four types of system data which you will need to deal with:

1. SMF data
2. LOGREC data
3. The SYSLOG
4. System DUMP datasets

This chapter describes the purpose of each of these and the normal housekeeping processes they require. Each of them is described in a separate section, but some parts of the housekeeping process are common to SMF, LOGREC, and SYSLOG data, and these are covered in this overview. Typically, housekeeping for these types of data consists of the following components (illustrated in Fig. 17.1):

- A 'cleardown' job which is triggered automatically, or submitted by the operators, when the dataset in which MVS collects the data becomes full. Typically, this job will MOD the data onto a DASD dataset which will accumulate all data for the current day or week, depending how much DASD space you have available. I shall refer to this DASD dataset as your temporary store. The job will then clear down the dataset used by MVS, making it available for reuse. As an alternative to adding the data to a single temporary store dataset, this job could place it in a new generation of a DASD GDG (one with no LIMIT to the number of generations).
- A regular first-level archiving job to copy the current temporary store dataset(s) into a new generation of an archive GDG, usually on tape, and re-initialize the temporary store. Each generation of your archived data should correspond to a standard time period, so that it is relatively easy to find the generation with

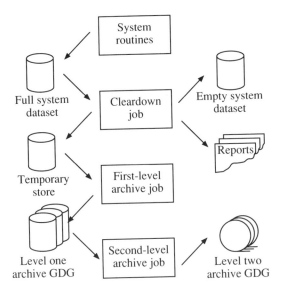

Figure 17.1. Typical system data housekeeping process.

the data for any given period. To achieve this you will normally need to run your cleardown job at midnight every day (or midnight on a given day of the week if your temporary store is big enough for a week's data), and wait for it to complete before submitting your archiving job, to ensure the temporary store contains the data for the right time period.

- If you want to keep data for a long time (SMF data may need to be kept for several years, for example), but only have enough DASD space for one day's data, you will probably want to consolidate your first-level GDG datasets into a longer term GDG to avoid keeping huge numbers of tapes. You would then have two archiving processes: a short-term one which builds a daily archive on tape, and a longer term one which consolidates all the data for a given week or month onto a single generation of the second-level GDG.

Many variations of these processes are of course possible. For example, if you have enough DASD space to keep a first-level archive GDG on disk, you could MOD onto the current generation of it in your cleardown job then simply roll the GDG forward in your daily job (by cataloging a new (+ 1) generation).

The MVS CBIPO supplies a number of sample jobs for system data house-keeping which illustrate some of these processes and provide a convenient starting point for creating your own jobs. These are documented in [1]. You should aim to handle various error conditions automatically, such as jobs being run twice or at the wrong time, and the examples given by CBIPO will give you some help on this.

17.2   SMF data

17.2.1   Uses of SMF data

SMF (system management facilities — though SMF is usually regarded as a singular) is used by MVS (and many other software products, including CICS and DB2) to record machine-readable management and performance data about many different kinds of events. SMF data has many uses, but the most widespread are:

- *Performance and capacity reporting* — Products like SAS, SLR, and MICS use SMF data as input to generate detailed reports on performance and capacity usage. RMF also records its data as SMF records and therefore requires SMF data as input to the RMF postprocessor which writes its reports.
- *Accounting and chargeback* — Accounting packages use SMF data to determine which jobs and users used how much of which resources.
- *Auditing* — If you ever need to know who deleted a dataset, for example, you can scan through the SMF records to find out.

17.2.2   Controlling SMF

SMF is started automatically at IPL time and should be kept running at all times. The IEASYSxx member of PARMLIB selected at IPL time should point to an SMFPRMxx member of PARMLIB which contains the startup parameters for SMF. You can change to a different set of parameters (or restart SMF after a failure) by issuing the T SMF=xx console command, and you can change individual SMF parameters using the SETSMF command.

Perhaps the most important of the SMF parameters are the TYPE and NOTYPE operands of the SYS and SUBSYS parameters. These determine which record types SMF will actually record. There is a large number of IBM-defined record types and subtypes, each identified by a number. Record type 4, for example, is the job step termination record, which is used to record the job, step, and program name, the start and end time of the step, the completion code, how many TCB, SRB, I/O, and storage occupancy service units the step used, etc. You must ensure that all record types required by your uses of SMF data are recorded — but it is also worth while excluding record types which are not going to be used in order to minimize both the overhead of running SMF and the amount of DASD space and tape cartridges required for current and archived SMF data. SMF record types are fully documented in [2].

17.2.3   SMF buffers and datasets

SMF records are written initially to buffers in the SMF address space, which are in turn written out to the active SMF dataset. The SMF datasets are specified in your SMFPRMxx member; they are VSAM ESDSs and must be named

SYS1.MANx, where x can take any value from 1 to 9 or from A to Z. The default CISIZE is 4096 but you can reduce SMF I/O activity substantially by increasing this to the optimal blocksize for the device type you are using. There must be at least two SMF datasets, so that when one fills up SMF can switch to an alternative dataset.

It is at this point that housekeeping requirements begin — the full dataset must be dumped and cleared using the IFASMFDP program so that when the other dataset(s) fill up, SMF can switch back to the first one without overwriting the data already recorded in it. The SMF datasets can also be switched manually, using the I SMF command, though it should not be done too frequently, as this can lead to SMF switching back to a dataset it has only recently finished writing to, and which has therefore not yet been dumped. The primary dataset should generally be made large enough to hold a full day's data, and it is worth having two others which can each take several hours' data, to minimize the danger of losing data due to problems with the dumping process.

17.2.4 SMF housekeeping

The first step in SMF housekeeping is to dump the SMF datasets after they are switched. It is wise to do this automatically to minimize the risk of loss of SMF data, either using a console automation product (such as an MPF exit) or using the SMF exit IEFU29.

If you choose the console automation route, you must trap the message

```
IEE362A  SMF ENTER DUMP FOR SYS1.MANx ON volser
```

and submit your cleardown job (or started task) in response to it. You should also trap

```
IEE366I  NO SMF DATA SETS AVAILABLE -- DATA BEING
BUFFERED TIME hh.mm.ss
```

and

```
IEE361I  SMF DATA LOST -- NO DATA SETS AVAILABLE, DATA
BEING BUFFERED TIME hh.mm.ss
```

in case you fail to catch one of the IEE362A messages.

Alternatively, you may code an IEFU29 exit to submit the job. The IEFU29 exit is invoked (if activated in SMFPRMxx) whenever an SMF dataset switch occurs, and also during SMF initialization if any of the inactive datasets is not empty. This will occur when MVS is re-IPLed after being closed down with the Z EOD command, which stops SMF and causes an SMF dataset switch, but does not give an opportunity to run a cleardown job. CBIPO provides a sample IEFU29 exit in IPO1.SAMPLIB, and a job to install it as an SMP/E USERMOD in IPO1.JCLLIB.

```
//*------------------------------------------------------------------*
//*      SMF DATASET DUMP/CLEARDOWN PROCEDURE                         *
//*------------------------------------------------------------------*
//SMFDUMP  PROC CLASS='*',MANXYZ=
//DUMP     EXEC PGM=IFASMFDP,REGION=4096K
//SYSPRINT DD   SYSOUT=&CLASS
//DUMPIN   DD   DISP=SHR,DSN=SYS1.&MANXYZ,AMP='BUFND=151'
//DUMPOUT  DD   DSN=SMF.TEMPSTOR,DISP=MOD
//SYSIN    DD   DISP=SHR,DSN=SYS1.CONTROL(SMFDUMP)
//*  INDD(DUMPIN,OPTIONS(DUMP))
//*------------------------------------------------------------------*
//CLEAR    EXEC PGM=IFASMFDP,COND=(0,NE,DUMP)
//SYSPRINT DD   SYSOUT=&CLASS
//DUMPIN   DD   DISP=SHR,DSN=SYS1.&MANXYZ
//SYSIN    DD   DISP=SHR,DSN=SYS1.CONTROL(SMFCLEAR)
//*  INDD(DUMPIN,OPTIONS(CLEAR))
```

Example 17.1. SMF dataset dump procedure.

Whichever method you use, your exit or automation routine must pass the name of the SMF dataset which is full, or at least the final suffix of the dataset name, to the cleardown job so it knows which dataset to dump. CBIPO also provides a sample cleardown job that uses a program called SMFDUMP to determine which dataset to dump and then invokes IFASMFDP dynamically.

Typically, your SMF dump job will MOD the SMF data onto a DASD temporary store dataset. Example 17.1 shows some suitable JCL. Note that:

- This procedure may be run as a started task.
- Because it is a procedure we have had to put the IFASMFDP SYSIN data into a control dataset rather than in stream — the comment statements following the SYSIN DD statements show what the SYSIN data actually contains.
- The temporary store dataset contains VBS records and IFASMFDP can reblock as it dumps, so the blocksize of this dataset should also be optimized to minimize I/O for the dump job (and the DASD space used).
- The BUFND parameter causes VSAM to read an entire control area into storage at a time, significantly reducing the I/O operations performed by IFASMFDP. See [10] for further discussion of how to optimize SMF dump processing.

In addition to running this procedure whenever an SMF dataset fills up, you should trigger it automatically at the end of the day (typically this will be done by automatically issuing the I SMF command at midnight) in order to ensure that your temporary store datasets contain all the data for the day just completed before starting your daily archiving process.

Daily/weekly/monthly archiving must then be done for your SMF data, as discussed in Sec. 17.1. You will probably need to keep your SMF data for a relatively long time — you are likely to need it for capacity planning purposes for well over a year, for example. If you use your SMF data as a basis for charging customers, you may find it necessary to keep it for several years — in at least one country there is a legal requirement to keep it for seven years.

Beyond this housekeeping process, of course, you may also be involved in setting up processes which actually make use of the SMF data, for example, to generate performance, capacity, or accounting reports. These jobs will vary enormously depending on both your installation's requirements and the software in use, so it is not possible to cover them here.

17.3 SYS1.LOGREC data

17.3.1 Uses of LOGREC data

We have already touched on LOGREC data in Chapter 16. SYS1.LOGREC is used by MVS to record information about system-detected errors of various kinds. All MVS-detected hardware errors are recorded in LOGREC, and the main usage of LOGREC data is to report on these hardware errors, using the EREP program. Certain software abends are also recorded in LOGREC, but more comprehensive and useful information about these is generally available elsewhere.

It is normally the responsibility of the operations department to check EREP reports on a daily basis, though sometimes it may fall into the systems programmer's court (or even that of a supplier's engineer, if you have one permanently assigned to you). The main objective is to detect any hardware problems which have not yet caused operational problems but could worsen to the point where they do so.

When errors are detected using EREP, the usual course of action will be to call in an engineer to look at the problem, and the engineers themselves will generally want to use EREP reports to show them the nature of the problem. Occasionally, however, the systems programmer or data administrators may be asked to deal with a problem, for example, using DSF to correct media errors on a DASD device.

17.3.2 LOGREC housekeeping

As with SMF data, LOGREC data must be regularly copied out of the dataset in which MVS records it, and this dataset cleared down so that it can be reused. The process is a little different because there is only one LOGREC dataset.

IBM provides two programs for offloading data from LOGREC, IFCEREP1 and IFCOFFLD, and each is suitable for different occasions. IFCEREP1 should be used when you are running your daily EREP housekeeping, and IFCOFFLD for emergency cleardowns which are required when LOGREC fills up.

IFCEREP1 is the program (usually just known as EREP) which is used to write the standard reports from LOGREC data, but it can also be used to perform the offload function. Example 17.2 shows EREP being used to offload SYS1.LOGREC. The ACC=Y parameter indicates LOGREC is to be copied to

```
//*------------------------------------------------------------------*
//*     LOGREC DUMP/CLEARDOWN PROCEDURE                              *
//*------------------------------------------------------------------*
//LOGREC1 EXEC PGM=IFCEREP1,REGION=1M,
//             PARM='LINECT=60,ACC=Y,HIST=N,ZERO=Y,SYSUM=Y'
//SERLOG   DD   DSN=SYS1.LOGREC,DISP=OLD
//ACCDEV   DD   DSN=LOGREC.TEMPSTOR,DISP=MOD
//TOURIST  DD   SYSOUT=*,DCB=BLKSIZE=133
//EREPPT   DD   SYSOUT=*,DCB=BLKSIZE=133
//SYSIN    DD   DSN=SYS1.CONTROL(EREP),DISP=SHR
//*
```

Example 17.2. Offloading SYS1.LOGREC using EREP.

the dataset with the **DDNAME ACCDEV**, **ZERO=Y** indicates LOGREC is to be cleared down afterwards, and **SYSUM** indicates that a system summary report is to be printed. When you run EREP with SYS1.LOGREC as input and select a system summary report, it also causes various statistical counters maintained by MVS to be dumped to LOGREC before creating the report, which ensures the report gives you full and up-to-date results. (See Sec. 17.3.3 for a description of the SYSIN dataset for EREP.)

The processing done by IFCOFFLD is very similar to this, except that it does not dump the statistical counters. This is what makes it more suitable in an emergency when LOGREC is already full. Example 17.3 shows the use of IFCOFFLD to offload SYS1.LOGREC. It automatically generates a system summary report as well.

You should therefore set up a procedure in one of your started task procedure libraries which uses IFCOFFLD to offload SYS1.LOGREC, and instruct the operators to run it when the following message is issued:

        IFB060E   SYS1.LOGREC NEAR FULL

This is issued when LOGREC becomes 90 per cent full; if action is not taken and LOGREC fills up completely, the following message is issued:

        IFB040I   SYS1.LOGREC AREA IS FULL, hh.mm.ss

This message should prompt urgent action!

Ideally, of course, LOGREC should be big enough for a whole day's data, but

```
//*------------------------------------------------------------------*
//*      OFFLOAD LOGREC TO TEMPSTOR                                  *
//*------------------------------------------------------------------*
//OFFLOAD EXEC PGM=IFCOFFLD
//SERLOG   DD   DSN=SYS1.LOGREC,DISP=SHR
//ACCDEV   DD   DSN=LOGREC.TEMPSTOR,DISP=MOD
//TOURIST  DD   SYSOUT=*,DCB=BLKSIZE=133
//EREPPT   DD   SYSOUT=*,DCB=BLKSIZE=133
//SYSIN    DD   DUMMY
```

Example 17.3. Offloading SYS1.LOGREC using IFCOFFLD.

occasionally it will fill up due to a recurrent error of some sort. When this happens, the operators should also initiate the process of finding out *why* LOGREC has filled up — or the recurrent error will simply fill it up again. This is also the reason for getting the operators to respond manually to this message, rather than automating it — unless, of course, you also automate a process for bringing the underlying problem to the attention of someone on duty.

Your daily housekeeping, though, can be completely automated. This should begin with an EREP step to offload the contents of SYS1.LOGREC, as in Example 17.2. It should then be followed by further EREP steps to produce whatever reports you require for daily fault monitoring. Note that EREP can only produce one type of report per run, so it is necessary to run it several times against the same data to produce several different types of report. These later steps should use the temporary store dataset as input. This has several advantages over using LOGREC itself as input in each step and offloading it in the last one:

- The input to EREP automatically includes any records offloaded earlier in the day using IFCOFFLD.
- Several of the EREP report types cause counters to be dumped to LOGREC if they are run using LOGREC as input. This could lead to counters being dumped several times by the same job, which is an unnecessary overhead.
- If you use LOGREC as input in successive steps it may be updated between (or during) these steps, with the result that inconsistent figures are produced by reports in the same job.

Finally, the daily job should archive the daily data using one of the processes discussed at the beginning of this chapter, and clear down the temporary store dataset. You will then require weekly and/or monthly jobs to complete the archiving process.

17.3.3   EREP control statements

Before you can run EREP, you may need to specify a set of control statements in the SYSIN dataset which describes your hardware configuration and certain thresholds you wish to be used in the preparation of EREP reports.

The control statements you can specify (and their use) are:

- CONTROLLER — To define control units to EREP. This statement is not required for 3880 control units used with 3380 DASD, 3990 control units, or control units with less than 16 devices attached to them. It is used by the system summary and threshold reports.
- DASDID and SHARE — To tell EREP what device id to assign to pre-3380 DASD devices which do not provide physical identifiers in their error data, and how to combine records from multiple CPUs that relate to shared devices with different device numbers on the different systems.
- LIMIT — Sets thresholds for EREP to use in subsystem exception reports.

```
LIMIT 3420,HR1600=013(2),HW1600=002(25),VR1600=013(2),VW1600=002(25)
LIMIT 3420,HR6250=026(1),HW6250=004(25),VR6250=026(1),VW6250=004(25)
LIMIT 3480,HR3480=026(1),HW3480=004(1),VR3480=026(1),VW3480=004(1)
```

Example 17.4. EREP control statements.

> With older devices (most notably reel tape drives), this is used to suppress
> reporting of devices with small numbers of temporary errors. LIMIT
> statements are required for tape devices to show up at all in this report, but are
> not required for modern DASD. They are invalid for 3390 DASD.
> • SYSIMG — Used to direct EREP to combine records from multiple processors
>   belonging to the same system, or to separate records from different systems
>   running on the same physical processors (e.g. under PR/SM).

If you are not running obsolete devices, you should be able to get by with just
a LIMIT statement for each type of tape device on your system, and a SYSIMG
statement for each MVS system you are running. Note that when you are running
multiple MVS systems and sharing devices between them, you should merge the
data from their LOGREC datasets before running EREP, so that all errors relating
to any given device are shown on the reports irrespective of which system they were
reported to.

Example 17.4 shows EREP control statements for a simple installation. Note
that:

• All DASD temporary errors will be reported on the subsystem exception and
  threshold reports because the LIMIT statements for these default to 1, i.e.
  report all errors.
• For tape devices, however, the default is to report only permanent errors, so
  you must code the LIMIT statements to ensure temporary errors are reported.
• The LIMIT statements for tape devices set separate reporting thresholds for
  different tape densities, reads and writes, and device/media errors. The HR1600
  parameter, for example, sets the threshold for hardware (i.e. device) read errors
  at 1600 bpi, while the VW6250 parameter sets the threshold for volume (i.e.
  media) write errors at 6250 bpi. The first operand of each parameter sets a
  megabytes per error threshold, while the second (the one in parentheses) sets an
  error count threshold. EREP only reports temporary errors for volumes/
  devices of the specified type when the number of errors recorded is greater than
  or equal to the error count threshold *and* the average quantity of data processed
  between errors is less than or equal to the megabytes per error threshold.
• The LIMIT statements in the example reflect the generally higher error rate on
  open-reel tape drives — it is not worth reporting occasional temporary errors
  on these devices. Errors, however, are much rarer on 3480 devices, so your
  limits should be more stringent for these. Note that recording density is not
  considered by EREP for 3480 devices, so it simply appears as 3480 in the
  LIMIT parameters.

17.3.4 *Using EREP to report on problems*

There are two occasions when you need EREP reports:

1 On a regular (daily) basis, to check whether any faults have occurred
2 On demand, when faults are known to have occurred, and further diagnostic
   information is needed

The first of these should be covered by your daily housekeeping job, as mentioned
earlier, and the second by a job or started task which the operators can submit as
required.

There is a large selection of reports which you can produce, and these are
documented in detail in [5]. The main report types are:

- *System summary* — A short statistical summary of all errors.
- *Trends* — Similar to the system summary, but showing the figures by Julian
  calendar day. Requires LOGREC data from at least a week for the results to
  be useful.
- *Event history* — A chronological listing of one-line abstracts of event records.
  Various parameters can be used to restrict the records printed, e.g. selecting
  those for a given device type or time of day.
- *System exception* — A set of exception reports covering processors, channels,
  DASD, and tape devices. The DASD and tape reports are quite detailed. They
  include reports on service information messages (SIMs), which are console
  messages issued by some recent device types, including 3990s and 3390s.
- *Threshold summary* — A summary report for your tape subsystem, showing
  errors which exceeded thresholds specified in your LIMIT statements.
- *Detail edit and detail summary* — These are both selected using the PRINT
  parameter. The detail edit report gives formatted and hexadecimal dumps of
  every selected record, and the detail summary shows important data from each
  selected record and/or the total number of records that meet your selection
  criteria. These reports are only likely to be run for small numbers of carefully
  selected records when detailed problem diagnosis is required.

In your daily housekeeping, you should produce the system summary and
system exception reports, and any others that the person doing the checking finds
useful. For ad hoc problem diagnosis, you will probably want more detailed
reports; here the best thing is to provide a procedure which will accept the type of
report and selection criteria as symbolic parameters, so that the engineer can select
the required report. Remember the engineer may be interested in records in your
temporary store as well as in LOGREC itself, or even in the archived data for
yesterday if your daily housekeeping happened to run between the hardware failure
and the request for more diagnosis. You should therefore either use symbolic
parameters to specify the input dataset, or provide several versions of the diagnosis
job using different input datasets.

17.4   The SYSLOG

17.4.1 Nature and uses of the SYSLOG

Strictly speaking, the SYSLOG on MVS systems consists of two separate logs: the hardcopy log and the system log. Once upon a time, it was normal to keep a hard copy record of console messages and operator commands for audit and diagnosis purposes. This was produced using the hardcopy log facility, by assigning the hardcopy log to a printer — you can still do this using the CONSOLxx member of SYS1.PARMLIB, at least on JES2 systems. Nowadays, however, it is normal practice to assign the hardcopy log to the system log instead of a physical device, which results in the hardcopy log being merged with the system log. Note that messages which are suppressed from appearing on consoles using MPF or other console management software are not suppressed from the hardcopy log, because of its function as an audit trail. The system log proper receives messages written using the write to log (WTL) macro or the LOG console command, which do not appear on consoles. For the rest of this chapter we shall refer to the merged log as the SYSLOG and ignore the distinction between the hardcopy log and the system log.

The SYSLOG is written to the JES spool as an output dataset until the number of lines in the dataset reaches the threshold specified at IPL time using the LOGLMT parameter in the IEASYSxx member of SYS1.PARMLIB (or until the WRITELOG operator command is issued). When this occurs, the current SYSLOG dataset is closed and released to the print queue, and a new spool dataset opened. The output class is determined by the LOGCLS parameter in the IEASYSxx member of PARMLIB, but can be overridden when the WRITELOG command is used.

The purpose of the SYSLOG is to provide a permanent, consolidated record of all console messages and commands, so that it is possible to review this for evidence of problems, errors, and other events at a later time — mainly in the course of problem diagnosis.

17.4.2 SYSLOG housekeeping

One reason why hardcopy logs are rarely assigned to printers these days is that they require a permanently assigned printer, which is far less cost-effective than assigning the same printer to JES and therefore sharing it with other print users. The other important reason, though, is that printed output is a lot harder to scan for a given message than a machine-readable dataset. Most installations therefore prefer to archive their SYSLOG in machine-readable format, rather than as printed output. There are several ways of achieving this, all of which require the SYSLOG datasets to be offloaded from the spool without printing:

1   Use an external writer to offload the SYSLOG to an MVS dataset.

```
//*---------------------------------------------------------------*
//*    EXTERNAL WRITER FOR CLASS L - USED FOR OFFLOADING SYSLOG    *
//*---------------------------------------------------------------*
//LOGDUMP PROC
//IEFPROC EXEC PGM=IASXWROO,PARM='PL'
//IEFRDER  DD  DSN=SYSLOG.TEMPSTOR,DISP=MOD,
//             DCB=(RECFM=VBA,LRECL=137,BLKSIZE=4088)
```

Example 17.5. Procedure to move SYSLOG to an archive dataset.

2   Use a JES OFFLOAD device to offload the SYSLOG to an MVS dataset.
3   Use a print management package (which may itself use external writers).

External writers offer much less flexibility than offload devices in the selection of datasets to move from the spool, but they create output in a more easily readable format, since the offload devices are designed to produce output which is easy to reload onto the spool, rather than output which is easy to browse. Since it is normal to assign a separate output class for SYSLOG datasets anyway, it is usually more convenient to use an external writer to move SYSLOG from the spool.

If you have a suitable print management package, it should be able to take the SYSLOG from the spool, archive it, and provide facilities to recall and browse it later. A good package will treat SYSLOG differently from other types of output, and allow you to specify which bits of log you wish to view by date and time, rather than requiring you to identify which SYSLOG dataset you wish to view (this is a useful evaluation criterion to include if you are evaluating such packages).

If you do not have such a package, however, you will have to set up your own archive/recall process. If you have enough space on disk to hold a full week's SYSLOG, you could perform your housekeeping as follows:

1   Set up a procedure which starts an external writer for the log class and MODs the output onto a DASD temporary store dataset, as shown in Example 17.5.
2   Start this procedure automatically via a console automation product whenever the current segment of system log fills up and the system issues the message

```
IEE043I  A SYSTEM LOG DATA SET HAS BEEN QUEUED TO
SYSOUT CLASS x
```

3   Use a console automation package to trap the message.

```
IEF176I  WTR ddd WAITING FOR WORK, ...
```

which is issued when the external writer has finished offloading eligible spool datasets. When this message occurs, submit the command P ddd to stop the external writer.

4   At midnight on the last day of the week, automatically submit a WRITELOG command. When this has completed it should issue message IEE043I as shown above, which will automatically kick off your external writer job. After the external writer has been stopped, copy the temporary store dataset onto the

(+1) generation of your SYSLOG archival tape GDG and clear down the temporary store dataset.

The general principles discussed in Sec. 17.1 apply here too, so you can vary this process to suit your circumstances as we discussed there.

Remember that you must also provide a mechanism for viewing old SYSLOG. The simplest mechanism is to copy the relevant generation of the tape GDG back onto DASD where it can be browsed from TSO. This is acceptable as long as:

- You have not accumulated so much data on each generation of the tape GDG to make the DASD space requirements for the dataset prohibitive.
- Generations which are copied back onto DASD are deleted from DASD again relatively quickly.
- You do not have to do it too often. In practice, it is rare to need SYSLOG datasets more than a week old, so if you keep a week's worth of SYSLOG on DASD you should not have a problem.

17.5   System DUMP datasets

17.5.1 Nature and use of system DUMP datasets

The system dump datasets are used by MVS to record dumps of virtual storage when it detects failures in a system task. These dumps can then be analysed to provide information required for problem determination. Each dataset can hold only one dump at any one time.

The dump datasets are sequential datasets and they must be named SYS1.DUMPnn, where nn is a numeric value from 00 to 99. While it is possible (on levels of MVS below 4.2) to define them as tape datasets, it is normal to use DASD datasets. These must be cataloged and allocated in single contiguous extents, and should be large enough to contain the largest system dump that is likely to occur: [3] includes a formula to help you calculate the necessary size.

You must also specify the DUMP parameter in the IEASYSxx member of SYS1.PARMLIB at IPL time to tell MVS where to find its dump datasets. The recommended option is simply to specify DUMP=DASD, which directs MVS to use all SYS1.DUMPnn datasets which are cataloged on DASD.

MVS maintains a record of the status of each dump dataset, which can be either empty or full. When it wishes to take a system dump, it will select the first available empty dataset. If none are empty, it issues the message

```
IEA994A  ALL DUMP DATA SETS ARE FULL AND NO SVC DUMPS
CAN BE TAKEN
```

and does not take the dump.

Clearly we must put a process in place which regularly empties out full dump datasets so that there are always empty ones available for new system dumps.

17.5.2 Dump dataset housekeeping

Emptying dumps can be done in one of two ways:

- Use the DUMPDS CLEAR console command, which clears the dump dataset without saving the data in it; or
- Copy the contents of the dump dataset to another dataset, then mark it as empty.

Prior to MVS/ESA, dump datasets could be copied, printed, formatted, and cleared using the AMDPRDMP program documented in [9], but from ESA onwards, they can only be processed using IPCS. The IPCS COPYDUMP command should therefore be used for copying dumps on ESA systems. From MVS 3.1.3 onwards, this has a CLEAR keyword which can be used to clear the dump dataset once it has been copied.

If all system dumps occurred in response to important system problems, it is clear we ought always to copy them out rather than simply clearing them down. However, a high proportion of them seem to relate to relatively trivial problems with no impact on the service to users (other than the significant overhead caused by writing out a system dump). In order to determine whether a dump dataset is to be cleared down or copied out, we must therefore determine the circumstances in which the dump was written and decide whether we need it for problem determination.

This is done by using the D D,T console command to display the titles of the full dumps, and the dates and times they were taken, and cross-referencing these with actual problems. If a dump relates to an unsolved problem, you should copy it out of the SYS1.DUMPnn dataset into a private DASD dataset and use IPCS to analyse it; if it does not, you should simply clear it down. If a problem is recurrently causing dumps to be taken without impacting the service in any other way, you should follow it up anyway, if only to eliminate the system overhead caused by the dumps and the job of constantly checking them.

Given that manual intervention is required to determine whether a dump is worth copying or not, it is clear that the dump housekeeping process cannot be fully automated. You can go part way, however, by using a console automation facility to inform you whenever a dump dataset is written, indicated by the message

```
IEA911E    COMPLETE/PARTIAL DUMP ON SYS1.DUMPnn FOR
ASID...
```

This should provide the necessary prompt for you to check the dump datasets before they all fill up. You may also trap the message

```
IEA994E    ALL ALLOCATED SYS1.DUMP DATASETS ARE FULL
```

which is issued when the last dump dataset is filled up, (you should also trap the IEA994A version of this message quoted earlier) to provide an extra level of warning.

Assistance with preventing dump datasets filling up is provided by the dump analysis and elimination (DAE) feature of MVS. This suppresses duplicate dumps when a problem recurs for which a dump has already been taken in the recent past. DAE is controlled by the current ADYSETxx member of PARMLIB. The default IEACMD00 member of PARMLIB causes the ADYSET00 member to be selected at IPL time by issuing the command SET DAE=00. The default values in ADYSET00 are very effective.

You may also find it useful to minimize the danger of losing a dump altogether by creating a few dump datasets that are large enough for a full dump plus a larger number of relatively small ones that will at least record the symptom and summary information if the large dump datasets are full. The smaller ones must have larger values of nn in their dataset names, or they will be used in preference to the larger datasets even when the large ones are empty.

MVS dump processing and the analysis of dump data are discussed in more detail in the next chapter.

References and bibliography

IBM manuals

1. *CBIPO MVS Customization* (provided in machine-readable format with the MVS CBIPO). Describes housekeeping processes for SMF, LOGREC, and SYSLOG data, including references to sample jobs provided in the CBIPO datasets.
2. *MVS/ESA SPL: System Management Facilities*, GC28–1819. Describes SMF, including the IFASMFDP program, and documents SMF record types in detail.
3. *MVS/ESA SPL: Initialization and Tuning*, GC28–1828. Includes descriptions of the SMFPRMxx and ADYSETxx members of PARMLIB, plus the LOGCLS and LOGLMT parameters in IEASYSxx.
4. *MVS/ESA SYS1.LOGREC Error Recording*, GC28–1854. Covers how to format and re-initialize SYS1.LOGREC and how MVS records data on it.
5. *EREP User's Guide and Reference*, GC28–1378. Comprehensive documentation on EREP, including control and parameter statements, samples of the different types of report it can produce, and formats of all the records it reports on.
6. *MVS/ESA Operations: System Commands*, GC28–1826. Describes the system log and hardcopy log, and commands for controlling these, the dump datasets, and external writers.
7. *MVS/ESA SPL: System Modifications*, GC28–1831. Includes a chapter on the external writer.
8. *MVS/ESA IPCS Command Reference*, GC28–1834. Explains IPCS commands, including COPYDUMP.
9. *MVS/XA SPL: Service Aids*, GC28–1159. Documents AMDPRDMP program.

Other

10. Heitlander, H.-J.: Optimizing the Processing of SMF data, *MVS Update*, January 1991, pp. 33–35.

Part Six
Dealing with problems

18
Problem diagnosis and resolution

18.1 How to approach problems

18.1.1 Overview

This chapter discusses one of the most interesting and difficult and sometimes one of the most frustrating parts of the systems programmer's job — dealing with problems. In most installations, the systems programmer is the problem solver of last resort — the expert to whom all others turn when a problem becomes too difficult or obscure for them to solve themselves. The mystique and reputation of systems programmers rests above all on their ability to deal with these situations — so cultivate this skill!

Effective problem resolution depends on a number of factors:

- Adopting a systematic and thorough approach to dealing with problems.
- Understanding where to look for diagnostic information and how to obtain it.
- Knowing where to look to find the correct interpretation of diagnostic information.
- Knowing when and how to turn to others for assistance.

This chapter cannot tell you how to solve every individual problem you might encounter — every problem is different (if only in the way it is presented by the person experiencing it) and even the well-defined problems occupy many volumes of messages and diagnosis manuals — but it will attempt to cover:

- An effective approach to problems.
- How to obtain and use dumps—perhaps the most mystifying of all the systems programmer's secret weapons!
- What other diagnostic information and tools are available to you and when to use them; and
- How to get help from IBM

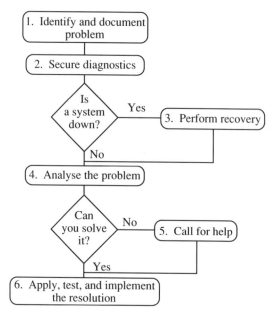

Figure 18.1. Problem determination flowchart.

18.1.2 An effective approach

To be consistently effective in handling problems, you must adopt a systematic approach. The fundamental steps of such an approach can be quite clearly defined. They are illustrated in Fig. 18.1, and examined in detail below.

Step 1 — Identify the problem

One of the easiest mistakes to make in problem diagnosis is to assume that you know what the problem is. The next easiest is to assume that the person reporting the problem knows what it is! In practice, the vast majority of problems reported to systems programmers are simple user errors, even where there is an intelligently staffed help desk filtering out the more obvious problems. Usually the person experiencing the problem has made a basic JCL or program coding error, but has assumed the problem is really something more obscure. On the other hand, you must avoid assuming that every problem reported to you is a user error — some of them will inevitably be something more serious.

Furthermore, the initial problem description you receive is likely to be highly partial, depending not only on the level of the user's familiarity with the system but also on what assumptions they have already made about the problem's cause, what their attitude is to you and the MIS department in general, what side of the bed they got out of this morning, etc.

The only way to start your diagnosis on a sure footing is to:

● Speak directly to the person experiencing the problem.

- Find out exactly what they were trying to do — ideally get a copy of any JCL, source code, etc., involved — including details of when the problem occurred, which terminal they were using if it is an online problem, and any other potentially relevant information.
- Find out whether they have done exactly the same thing before and what happened then.
- Find out what they have changed since the last time they attempted to do it. Do this (and pursue it mercilessly!) even if they do claim to have done 'exactly' the same thing before. Nine times out of ten they have changed something which to them seems trivial but is actually the cause of the problem (such as rearranging the statements in their JCL to make them look neater, changing the data fed into a process, renumbering their IEBUPDTE statements, or any one of a hundred things which might seem insignificant to someone who does not understand exactly what they are doing).
- Obtain hard evidence of the symptoms of the problem. If it includes a message or a return code, ensure you have a copy of the log or output dataset showing it. If it is an online problem or there is no hard evidence for any other reason, get the user to reproduce the problem, or show you how to reproduce it, so you can see the symptoms for yourself – and ideally take screen prints.
- If the user is unable to reproduce the problem: (a) be sceptical — perhaps they have just realized and corrected what they did wrong and are ashamed to admit it; but also (b) be conscious that some problems really are intermittent and may be very difficult to reproduce. You can generally cover both possibilities by telling them you cannot do anything unless they can reproduce the problem or produce some other hard evidence of it, and encourage them to take comprehensive notes and ring you straight away if the problem recurs.

Step 2 — Document the problem

There are several good reasons for documenting each problem as you deal with it. For example:

- If you need to call in external support, such as the IBM Support Centre, they are going to treat you in much the same way as you have treated the user who reported the problem to you — they are going to ask for a very precise definition of the problem, and if they cannot solve it at once they are going to ask for hard evidence.
- If anyone else is called in to deal with a related problem later, it may be possible for them to save a vast amount of time if they have full information as to what you have done already. Indeed, you may need this written record yourself if the problem recurs in a few months time or if it becomes so complex that it is hard to remember everything that has happened.
- You may need the full story carefully documented if there is a management

postmortem or if you need to argue the case for some contentious change in order to prevent recurrence of the problem.

In practice, the process of collecting and documenting the evidence should already have begun as part of step 1 and continues until the problem has been solved. The components of that process are:

- Collect and keep all relevant job output, dumps, copies of the system log at the time, screen prints, etc.
- Note down all the information obtained from the user.
- Log everything you learn about the problem as you learn it, along with supporting evidence, and dates, times, and names of contacts.
- Log all contact with software suppliers concerning the problem, including dates of phone calls, who you spoke to, and what their response was.
- Log any actions taken to solve the problem, including testing done to prove whether they worked or not.
- Log the eventual resolution.

If you use INFOMAN or a similar product for managing problem information, you will probably record this information on an online problem record or incident report. If you do not, you must substitute a manual alternative (e.g. a 'problem book' in which all problems handled by systems programmers are recorded and documented).

Step 3 — Take immediate recovery actions, if required

If the problem has interrupted a service, you will generally want to restore that service before analysing the problem further. When that service is your whole MVS system or a major subsystem, this will be an urgent requirement. Most problems which bring down major subsystems are not likely to recur immediately you restart the subsystem, so it is usually possible to restart the system and restore the service to the user before conducting detailed analysis of the reason for the failure. If it seems likely from the start that the problem is due to a recent change, you may choose to back out the change when restoring the service, to minimize the danger of the problem recurring.

Remember, though, that some diagnostic information might be destroyed as a result of restoring the service. The obvious example is the contents of processor storage when you re-IPL MVS. In cases like this you must ensure that any available diagnostic information is secured before you restore the service — in this case by taking a stand-alone dump. The delay in restoring the service may be irritating and even expensive for your business users, but without this step you may be unable to diagnose the problem which brought the system down, and so be unable to prevent further costly disruptions.

In some cases the original problem will prevent you from restoring the service — a hard I/O error on a critical system dataset, for example. If the situation is so bad that you do not have a usable system to work with, you will have to invoke emergency recovery procedures — these are discussed in Chapter 19. If it is not, you will still find management attention becoming heavily focused on your attempts to find an early resolution. Such attention can be helpful, as long as it does not lead to constant interruptions to your work on the problem, and you should encourage your managers to establish constructive (as opposed to interfering) ways to manage major problems. A five-minute meeting every hour, for example, can help to maintain your perspective on the issues as well as your management's, and could be used to provide you with any extra resources you need. A two-minute interruption every five minutes, however, is likely to prevent the problem ever being solved. It is best to make this universally understood before you experience this kind of problem.

Step 4 — Analyse the problem

This is the difficult bit! Be realistic about your capabilities. Always try to understand the problem and at least have a quick look at the relevant manuals, but if it becomes obvious then that you are out of your depth, do not hesitate to move on to the next step — call for help. You are a far more effective systems programmer when you pass a problem on to someone else who can fix it after 10 minutes than when you grapple uselessly with it for hours and still end up calling for help. If you do call for help, though, always try to learn how to deal with it better next time, by asking the person who does fix it to explain the problem and how they diagnosed it.

As you gain experience, you will deal with more and more of the problems yourself. Usually the evidence you have collected will point to several fairly obvious lines of enquiry: looking up messages in manuals; considering what has changed recently that could have affected the relevant area; reviewing reference manuals which tell you how to do what the user experiencing the problem was attempting; and following up any ideas as to possible causes which spring to mind. The exact action will depend very much on the type of problem and the tools available to you.

Later in this chapter we will discuss some different types of problem, what sort of diagnostic actions might be appropriate to each of them, and some of the diagnostic tools you might use. Familiarity with these tools is an enormous asset when it comes to problem diagnosis, so you should aim to develop your expertise with them before you need them in earnest.

Here we will confine ourselves to a few more general points. Perhaps the most important of these is to take a step back from the problem if it becomes clear that you are not going to solve it quickly. Be conscious that there are usually several different angles from which you can attack the problem — try listing them and spending a few seconds evaluating which is most likely to lead to a diagnosis of the problem. Consider whether you could involve someone else in following up one approach while you look at another. Once you have selected an approach, follow it for a reasonable period of time, but stop occasionally, take that step back, and re-evaluate whether this is the most useful angle of attack. Effective problem resolution is a loop between generating ideas as to possible causes, evaluating them to decide which ones are worth following up, and then investigating the most promising. (This loop is described brilliantly in [17].)

If you are sufficiently lucky and/or intelligent, and the problem is one which you have the tools to resolve, this process will produce a plausible explanation of the cause of the problem. If so, you will then move on to step 6 — resolving the problem. If not, however, you will soon need to take step 5 — call for help. Indeed, you may decide to call for help in parallel with your own problem analysis, and this is often an intelligent and effective course of action.

Step 5 — Call for help

As we have seen, it is often necessary or useful to call for help. This might be because you do not understand the problem, because your analysis leads you to suspect someone else is responsible for causing the problem so they are the right person to diagnose it, or simply because you are not making clear progress and you feel it would be useful to have someone else working on it in parallel. There is also the old theory that 'two minds are better than one', and one common experience is that when you start to explain a problem to someone else you realize what it was that you missed when you were looking at it on your own!

There are generally three groups of people you might turn to for help:

1 *Colleagues* — Not only more experienced systems programmers but also your peers and even your juniors can often generate new ideas to feed into the analysis process or follow up lines of enquiry for you.

2 *Software suppliers* — Whenever it seems possible that a problem is related to a malfunction in a software product, you should contact the supplier sooner rather than later and ask if there are any known problems with symptoms similar to those you are experiencing. When other lines of enquiry fail to produce progress, or when the problem is very obviously in one of their software products, most software suppliers are quite willing to analyse dumps and other diagnostic information for you. However, they can do nothing unless you are able to provide them with the relevant diagnostic information. IBM's facilities and procedures for dealing with customer problems are discussed in Sec. 18.4; other software suppliers tend to adopt a similar approach, though it is often simpler as they have fewer calls to deal with.

3 *Third-party sources of systems programming expertise* — Consultancy companies, training companies, and software suppliers (including IBM) will generally jump at the opportunity of sending in an expert (for a fee) to help you with the diagnosis. If it seems very obvious that the problem lies with a particular piece of software, you might even be able to persuade the software

supplier to do this for nothing. Frustrated managers are fond of suggesting this course if it seems to be taking a long time to solve a problem. It is only a good idea if the person to be brought in really is an expert in the problem area, and even then it is likely to lead to a minimum of several hours being wasted while they get on site, pick your brains as to what has happened, and retrace some of your steps. On the whole you should resist this option if you still have promising avenues to explore, but welcome it if you do not.

Step 6 — Implement the problem resolution

Once step 4 or step 5 has produced an explanation of why the problem occurred, the steps to be taken to resolve it are usually fairly obvious. If a user error was to blame, the user will simply have to correct it and carry on. If a software implementation error was the cause, you will have to determine the correct resolution yourself and apply it. If a software product was at fault, the supplier will usually provide a fix (though you may have to wait a while for them to develop the fix if it is a new problem) or a 'workaround' — a way of avoiding rather than solving the problem.

There is a temptation when fixing a problem to 'slap on' the fix or the resolution and get it into production straight away. Unless the service to your users is very badly affected, this should be resisted. Problem fixes and resolutions are no more likely to be error-free than any other change. They need to be tested before they are put into production (a dedicated test machine, or a virtual machine or logical partition for systems programmers comes in handy at this point). Not only is it possible that the fix will fail to solve the original problem, but it is also quite possible that it will introduce new problems which could be more serious than the original one. A small but significant proportion of even IBM's fixes turn out to be 'in error', so you should aim to test not only that the fix solves the problem but also that the system still works after you have applied it. Of course, it is usually impractical to test all system functions exhaustively after applying every fix to your test system, but you should at least prove that the system comes up and that the functions with a logical relationship to the component being fixed still work.

Step 7 — Close the problem

Having tested and implemented your problem resolution, you should check that the original problem has indeed been resolved to the user's satisfaction — and make sure they know you fixed it. It is astounding how often users are left to believe their problem 'just went away' — or worse still, carry on with a workaround for months or years after the original problem was fixed.

At this stage you should also check that the problem record has been fully written up. If you have an automated problem management system, you will probably have to 'close' the problem formally and obtain a management sign-off that the problem has been satisfactorily resolved.

Sadly, there will be a few problems which remain unresolved even in the best-run shops. One of the skills of problem management is to know when to give up. If you have been given insufficient information to diagnose the problem, if it is impossible to reproduce it, if you have somehow lost or forgotten to obtain full diagnostics, and if your relevant software suppliers have no record of anything similar, you will never resolve the problem. Close it off anyway, but make sure that procedures are put in place so that next time you will have the information you need.

18.1.3 Types of problem

This section lists some of the commoner types of problem which systems programmers must deal with, and the usual sources of diagnostic information for each of these. The types of problem it will cover are:

- Application program abends
- System program abends
- I/O errors
- System wait states
- Systems or applications 'hanging' for other reasons
- Program errors (bad return codes, error messages, and/or incorrect processing)

For further information, try [6], which includes a useful chapter on how to diagnose each major type of problem.

Application program abends

These are always accompanied by a message in the SYSLOG and job log indicating the abend code and usually a supplementary reason code. Many abends are also accompanied by a symptom dump in the SYSLOG and job log. Other abends are accompanied by system messages in the log which give more information on the cause of the problem, and it is not uncommon to find messages in either the job log or the job's output datasets which describe problems which led to the abend. By examining the SYSLOG, the job log, and the job's output datasets you should therefore obtain enough information to diagnose most problems.

If the problem is not immediately obvious you should find the appropriate messages manuals for further explanation of the messages. Abend codes are documented in [2], and IBM messages are documented in [1]. Third-party software messages are usually also documented in a message manual or a reference manual supplied with the software.

If this does not yield the answer you are looking for, your next source of information is likely to be a dump. If there was a SYSUDUMP, SYSABEND, or SYSMDUMP dataset allocated to the abending step, MVS will have written a dump. If there was not, you will need to add one and rerun the job to reproduce the problem and produce a dump. Dumps are discussed in Sec. 18.2.

System program abends

Like application program abends, these are generally accompanied by messages in the SYSLOG, but unlike them, there is usually no job log or output dataset in which to record other information. If there was a SYS1.DUMPnn dataset available at the time of the problem and the dump was not suppressed by the DAE facility of MVS, a system dump (or SVC dump) will also be written at the time of the abend. See Sec. 18.2 for more on these dumps too.

I/O errors

These are likely to come to your attention either because of a program abend or because of console messages noticed by operations staff. As with any other sort of program abend, abends caused by I/O errors will be accompanied by messages in the log, including reason codes which will give you a clue as to the type of error, and sense data which can be interpreted by an engineer. You must be conscious that I/O errors reported by programs fall into two very distinct groups — genuine hardware errors and 'soft' I/O errors. The latter group is merely logical errors and can be corrected by altering the program, the data, or run-time parameters such as the DCB. Typical examples would be: I/O errors which occur opening a PDS when a previous user has wrongly opened it as a sequential dataset and overwritten the directory; most examples of 'wrong length record' errors. Soft errors can always be eliminated by overwriting the data in error with valid data.

Genuine hardware errors, however, need more radical action. Diagnostic information for them is recorded in SYS1.LOGREC as well as in console messages, and reports on LOGREC data can be produced using EREP, as discussed in Chapter 17. DASD media problems can often be corrected using ICKDSF, while tape media problems can sometimes be resolved by reading the tape on a different drive, notably the one it was written on (you should then discard the tape, to prevent repetition of the problem). Other hardware problems, however, generally require an engineer to fix them.

There is an intermediate class of I/O errors — errors caused by a mismatch between the I/O configuration data used by MVS or the processor and the real I/O configuration. These generally surface immediately after a change in your IOCDS or your MVS I/O configuration, or immediately after the attentions of a hardware engineer. They can cause a wide range of effects including data corruption (usually MVS will detect an I/O error the first time this occurs and vary the affected channel offline, but if the first I/O corrupted your master catalog or JES checkpoint dataset this will be small consolation) and poor performance (e.g. due to channels failing to come online). The resolution is to correct either your actual I/O configuration or your configuration data, but recovery may be more difficult, and on pre-version 4 levels of MVS it is almost certain to require an IPL of your system.

System wait states

These are easily spotted — the machine is dead, the processor alarm is going off, and everyone in the machine room is in a state of panic. Fortunately they usually only happen while you are in the process of IPLing a newly built MVS system. When they occur there should be a message on the hardware console indicating that the system has entered a disabled wait and including a wait code (if you have lost this message, it should be possible to find it by viewing the hardware log, which is generally accessible from the hardware console). MVS wait codes are documented in [2]. Usually the reason is that you have tried to IPL a pack which does not contain everything required by the initial stages of IPL — IPL text or a copy of SYS1.NUCLEUS, for example.

System/subsystem/application hanging

'Hangs' are generally due to tasks waiting on an event which will either never happen or an event which is simply taking a long time. When one of the waiting tasks is a fundamental system task, or is holding control of a fundamental resource, then other tasks will start to queue up behind it and more and more of your system will gradually grind to a halt. If your whole system is dead, you must perform a stand-alone dump to provide diagnostic information, then re-IPL. Otherwise, various tools are available for investigating the cause of the delay, and sometimes for resolving it. Unfortunately, problems of this type do not automatically generate diagnostic information, and you may have to make and test a series of guesses on the possible cause of the problem. Typical examples include:

- Failure in a task which was holding exclusive control of a resource, where this exclusive control was not released by the MVS termination routines. This may be impossible to recover from without an IPL, but you should have some evidence of the problem in the form of termination messages for the failing task in the log at around the time your delays started, and possibly an SVC dump.
- A 'deadly embrace' between tasks enqueuing on the same group of resources. This can be detected for ENQ problems by issuing the

      D GRS,CONTENTION

  command at the console. The recovery action is usually to cancel the contending task whose failure will have least impact on the system and/or the users. Everything else is then likely to spring back to life. However, this is a classic example of the difference between problem recovery and problem resolution — the problem is not resolved until you have found out why it happened and prevented it recurring.

- A task waiting for operator action. If a task holding a critical resource is waiting for a tape mount, for example, and the operators have taken a tea break, the effect on the system can be disastrous. Use the D R,L command to display outstanding action messages.

- Shortage of a critical resource — console message buffers, for example — can have the same effect. In this case the recovery action is simply to put the offending consoles into roll mode; the resolution may be to put consoles into roll mode automatically at IPL time, or to rap the operators' knuckles. JES2 is particularly prone to grinding to a halt when a resource shortage occurs — for example, when it runs out of spool space. Fortunately such shortages are generally preceded by action messages for operators, so the D R,L command should show up this type of problem too. If not, scan the log for the period prior to the beginning of the reported delays.

- System in a loop. In a uniprocessor this will cause the entire system to hang; in a multiprocessor it will initially only tie up one processor, though sometimes the condition which caused the loop will occur on each processor in turn, eventually making them all unusable, or the looping task may hold control of a fundamental resource, in which case tasks on other processors will also be forced to wait. Even very tight loops (e.g. an instruction branching to itself) can be broken if the processor is enabled for interrupts and the looping unit of work can be shifted from the top of the dispatching queue. The usual action is to attempt to cancel the looping unit of work if you can identify it. If this cannot be done, and your system is not running under PR/SM, you can use the instruction address trace facility (see Sec. 18.3.2) to record the addresses of the looping instructions, then perform a stand-alone dump. Under PR/SM, you will have to do without this trace, but your best course of action will still be to perform a stand-alone dump then re-IPL MVS.

Program errors

When messages are produced, these will be the obvious starting point. Otherwise the errors should generally be referred to the developers of the program for them to debug. If it is the developer who has come to you, or you are the developer, then you will have to try and debug the program yourself. Usually this will involve obtaining and analysing dumps, the subject to which we will now turn.

18.2   Controlling and using dumps

18.2.1 Symptom dumps

Symptom dumps are written to the system log and job log when an application abend occurs. They are written to the log as a 10-line message, numbered IEA995I, and show the abend code, the time of failure, the PSW and registers at the time of the abend, a hex dump of 12 bytes of storage centred on the PSW address at the time of the abend, and some other information. Example 18.1 shows a symptom dump. Note that:

```
IEA995I SYMPTOM DUMP OUTPUT
SYSTEM COMPLETION CODE=0C4   REASON CODE=00000004
 TIME=16.37.46  SEQ=34505  CPU=0000  ASID=003D
 PSW AT TIME OF ERROR  078D2000    00006FCA  ILC 6    INTC 04
   ACTIVE LOAD MODULE=SAMPFAIL  ADDRESS=00006F58  OFFSET=00000072
   DATA AT PSW   00006FC4 - D207B048   70685840   40001244
   GPR  0-3   00000050   00005F60   00005FF8   00FD3858
   GPR  4-7   00F613B8   00000220   00F33200   00AA7CB0
   GPR  8-11  007FF008   807FF328   00F613C0   00005F60
   GPR 12-15  00006F5E   00005F60   80FD38A8   00005F60
 END OF SYMPTOM DUMP
IEF472I SYS001ST SAMP - COMPLETION CODE - SYSTEM=0C4 USER=0000
REASON=00000004
```

Example 18.1. MVS symptom dump.

- This job has abended with a system 0C4 abend code — a protection exception. The symptom dump provides enough information to identify both the failing instruction and the address of the control block it was trying to access.
- The abend message IEF472I is not part of the symptom dump but is included here for clarity. It may appear either before or after the symptom dump in the log.

Symptom dumps were introduced with MVS/XA and are regarded as part of the ABEND dump; they are therefore suppressed when the rest of the dump is suppressed (see the following subsection for more details). It is also possible to suppress all symptom dumps by specifying the NOSYM operand in any of the ABEND dump tailoring members of SYS1.PARMLIB. However, symptom dumps are extremely useful and often save you the trouble of reading a larger dump, so it is recommended that you do not suppress them.

18.2.2 ABEND dumps

ABEND dumps are written by the MVS recovery and termination manager when an application abend occurs. They are written to the dataset defined by the SYSABEND, SYSUDUMP or SYSMDUMP DD statement in the JCL for the job step in progress. If no such statements are present, no dump is produced, but a symptom dump is produced on the log. If more than one of these statements are present in the JCL of the current step, MVS produces only the dump corresponding to the last one coded.

The contents of each type of ABEND dump is determined by a corresponding member of SYS1.PARMLIB. Table 18.1 shows the relevant PARMLIB member for each type, along with the default contents as supplied by IBM. Note, however, that CBIPO installs a different set of options into these PARMLIB members if you allow it to. With either the defaults or the CBIPO values in effect, SYSUDUMP provides the next level of detail beyond a symptom dump, SYSABEND provides additional diagnostic data up to the maximum it would be reasonable to print, and SYSMDUMP provides a comprehensive dump of the address space (excluding

Table 18.1. Types of ABEND dump

DD statement	PARMLIB member	Dataset type for dump	Default contents
SYSUDUMP	IEADMP00	SYSOUT	Summary information only
SYSABEND	IEAABD00	SYSOUT	Summary information, LSQA, trace data, formatted control blocks, PSW and registers, the save area chain, modules used by the task, and user storage allocated to the task
SYSMDUMP	IEADMR00	DASD	The nucleus, SQA, LSQA, SWA, trace data, summary information, and the whole of the private area of the abending address space

CSA and LPA) suitable for analysis using IPCS. Whichever values you choose, the objective is to provide several useful levels of diagnostic information with the option to move on to a more detailed level by reproducing the problem with the next level of dump.

ABEND dumps can be suppressed using the SLIP command. The IBM-supplied version of SYS1.PARMLIB(IEACMD00) includes the SLIP commands shown in Example 18.2. The effect of these is to eliminate all dumps for 0F3, 13E, 222, 322,

```
COM='SLIP SET,C=013,ID=X013,A=NOSVCD,J=JES2,END'
COM='SLIP SET,C=028,ID=X028,A=NOSVCD,END'
COM='SLIP SET,C=0E7,ID=X0E7,A=NOSVCD,END'
COM='SLIP SET,C=0F3,ID=X0F3,A=NODUMP,END'
COM='SLIP SET,C=13E,ID=X13E,A=NODUMP,END'
COM='SLIP SET,C=222,ID=X222,A=NODUMP,END'
COM='SLIP SET,C=322,ID=X322,A=NODUMP,END'
COM='SLIP SET,C=33E,ID=X33E,A=NODUMP,END'
COM='SLIP SET,C=622,ID=X622,A=NODUMP,END'
COM='SLIP SET,C=804,ID=X804,A=(NOSVCD,NOSYSU),END'
COM='SLIP SET,C=806,ID=X806,A=(NOSVCD,NOSYSU),END'
COM='SLIP SET,C=80A,ID=X80A,A=(NOSVCD,NOSYSU),END'
COM='SLIP SET,C=9FB,ID=X9FB,A=NOSVCD,J=JES3,END'
COM='SLIP SET,C=B37,ID=XB37,A=(NOSVCD,NOSYSU),END'
COM='SLIP SET,C=D37,ID=XD37,A=(NOSVCD,NOSYSU),END'
COM='SLIP SET,C=E37,ID=XE37,A=(NOSVCD,NOSYSU),END'
```

Example 18.2. SLIP commands supplied in IEACMD00.

33E, and 622 abends, SVC dumps for 028 and 0E7 abends (plus 013 abends in JES2 and 9FB abends in JES3), and both SVC dumps and SYSUDUMPs (but not SYSABEND and SYSMDUMPs) for 804, 806, 80A, B37, D37, and E37 abends.

The dump analysis and elimination (DAE) feature of MVS also affects the production of SYSMDUMP dumps, so duplicate SYSMDUMP dumps for the same problem will generally be suppressed. This is discussed further under Sec. 18.2.4.

ABEND dump options can be further modified using the CHNGDUMP console

command, or by the macro invoking dump services (ABEND, CALLRTM, or
SETRP).

18.2.3 SNAP dumps

Address space dumps can also be taken when an application has not abended by
invoking the SNAP macro instruction from within the application code. SNAP
dumps are not taken directly by the MVS recovery and termination routines, and
they require a little more work from the programmer than ABEND dumps. The
output dataset to which the SNAP dump is to be taken, for example, must be
opened normally by the application before SNAP is issued, and the areas of storage
to be dumped must be coded explicitly on the SNAP macro.

SNAP dumps are useful for debugging assembler programs when you need to
know the contents of storage at a specific point in the program — particularly if
you have a good reason not to take the rather simpler course of creating a dump
by forcing an abend at that point. On the other hand, you can usually obtain
similar data more easily and flexibly using the TSO TEST command. SNAP dumps
do not have any other relevance for the systems programmer, so we will not cover
them in any more detail here. More detail on the use of the SNAP macro can be
found in [15].

18.2.4 SVC dumps

SVC or system dumps are produced when a system task abends, or when requested
using the SLIP or DUMP console commands. They are unformatted and are
written to the first available (i.e. empty) SYS1.DUMPnn dataset (management of
these datasets was discussed in Chapter 17). If you need to analyse an SVC dump
you will usually copy it out to a DASD dataset then format it using IPCS.

The exact contents of an SVC dump depend on the parameters specified on the
SDUMP macro which invokes the dump. Usually this will be deep within MVS
and hence beyond your control, but if you request a dump using SLIP or DUMP
you can specify the areas to be dumped as part of the command. In general, the
dump will contain virtual storage belonging to all address spaces associated with
the failing unit of work. The SDATA operands of the SLIP and DUMP commands
determine which parts of those address spaces will be dumped.

The DUMP command is an unconditional and immediate request for dumping
of an address space. Its only operand is the COMM parameter, which is used to
specify the comment to be included in the dump title. Once the command has been
accepted, however, message IEE094D will be issued, asking you to enter the dump
options required. In reply to this message you must specify the jobname(s), TSO
user name(s), or ASID(s) of the address space(s) to be dumped (data spaces can
also be selected), and the storage areas to be dumped. The full syntax of the reply
to IEE094D is documented under the DUMP command in [3]. Example 18.3 shows
an example of a DUMP command and the ensuing dialog. Note that:

```
DUMP COMM=(TSO USER HUNG)
99 IEEO94D SPECIFY OPERAND(S) FOR DUMP COMMAND
R 99,TSONAME=(DEVOO1),SDATA=(GRSQ,LPA,PSA,RGN,SUM,TRT),END
IEA911E COMPLETE DUMP ON SYS1.DUMPO3 FOR ASID (0090)
```

Example 18.3. DUMP command and subsequent console dialog.

- The END statement indicates there are no more dump operands. If you cannot fit all the operands on one reply, finish with the CONT statement instead, and message IEE094D will be reissued.
- The SDATA operand indicates which parts of the selected address space should be dumped; it is also possible to specify the STOR operand, which selects storage areas for dumping by specifying their virtual storage addresses.
- The address space being dumped is not terminated. If you want to do this, you can use the CANCEL command, with the DUMP operand, although this produces an ABEND dump rather than an SVC dump, and only does so if there is a SYSUDUMP, SYSABEND, or SYSMDUMP DD statement for the step being executed.

The SLIP command is used to make a conditional request for dumping of an address space (though it can also trigger off other actions, such as suppressing dumps or generating trace records). It works by defining a condition which is to trigger the required action, known as a 'slip trap'. The SLIP command is extremely complex and flexible — the description of it in [3] runs to almost 40 pages. Here we will simply illustrate the basic ideas.

There are three types of SLIP command:

1 SLIP SET, which defines a SLIP trap — this is the complicated one.
2 SLIP MOD, which enables or disables a SLIP trap that has already been defined using SLIP SET.
3 SLIP DEL, which deletes a SLIP trap.

Furthermore, you can place a series of SLIP commands in a member of PARMLIB called IEASLPyy and issue them all by entering the SET SLIP=yy command. This is the recommended way of using SLIP as it minimizes typing errors and allows you to build up a library of useful SLIP commands.

There are six types of keyword on the SLIP SET command:

1 Trap-type keywords, which indicate what type of program event the trap is to monitor. There are four alternatives: IF (instruction fetch); SB (successful branch); SA (storage alteration); and none, which indicates that an error condition is to be trapped.
2 Event filter keywords, which further qualify the type of event to be monitored. There are a large number of these, for example, ASID, which restricts the trap to events in the specified address space, or ADDRESS, which restricts the trap to events affecting a given range of virtual storage addresses.
3 Action-related keywords — there is one ACTION keyword but this can take

many operands indicating what is to be done when the trap is 'sprung'. Examples are SVCD, which causes an SVC dump to be taken, or TRACE, which causes a GTF trace record to be written (if a suitable GTF trace is active).

4 Trap control keywords, which control the enabling and disabling of the trap.
5 Dump and trace tailoring keywords, which allow you to specify the contents of the dump or trace records taken as a result of a trap.
6 Specialized keywords such as END, which indicates your command is complete.

Example 18.4 shows a sample SLIP command. Further useful examples can be

```
SLIP SET,SA,ENABLE,ACTION=SVCD,PVTMOD=(PRG1,3C0,3DF),END
```

Example 18.4. Sample SLIP command.

found under the description of SLIP SET in [3], and in the useful chapter on the use of SLIP traps in [6]. Note that:

• This command defines and enables a storage alteration trap.
• The trap will cause an SVC dump to be taken when the storage between offsets 3C0 and 3DF in the private module PRG1 is altered.

18.2.5 Stand-alone dumps

Stand-alone dumps are not produced by MVS at all, but by a stand-alone program called SADMP which is IPLed in place of MVS. This program dumps out real storage and parts of paged-out virtual storage to a tape dataset for later analysis using IPCS. It should only be used when your MVS system has failed and needs to be re-IPLed, and you need a dump for diagnosis of the failure.

Stand-alone dumps can be formatted or unformatted but you should always take an unformatted one. Not only is this much faster, but it also provides a dump which is suitable for online analysis using IPCS. Formatted dumps are intended for printing, which is an entirely unsuitable process for diagnosing operating system problems.

Before you can use stand-alone dumps, you must generate the dump program. Normally this is done as part of the process of installing a new version of MVS, as you will generally need to upgrade the stand-alone dump program when you upgrade MVS. You should select a DASD volume to use as the 'system residence' volume for stand-alone dump — this cannot be one of your MVS SYSRES packs, since the process of generating SADMP installs IPLTEXT on track 0, cylinder 0 which would overlay your MVS IPLTEXT. In theory, you can install SADMP on a tape volume instead, but most sites find it more convenient to keep it on DASD.

Generating your stand-alone dump program is usually a two-stage process. Example 18.5 shows an example of the stage 1 job. Note that:

```
//ASMBLR   EXEC  PGM=IEV90,REGION=1024K,
//               PARM='NOOBJECT,DECK'
//STEPLIB   DD   DSN=SYS1.LINKLIB,DISP=SHR,
//               UNIT=3380,VOL=SER=XA313R
//SYSLIB    DD   DSN=SYS1.MACLIB,DISP=SHR,
//               UNIT=3380,VOL=SER=XA313R
//SYSUT1    DD   UNIT=WORK,SPACE=(1700,(600,100))
//SYSUT2    DD   UNIT=WORK,SPACE=(1700,(300,50))
//SYSUT3    DD   UNIT=WORK,SPACE=(1700,(300,50))
//SYSPRINT  DD   SYSOUT=*
//SYSPUNCH  DD   DSN=IP01.SADUMP,DISP=OLD,
//               UNIT=3380,VOL=SER=SYST11
//SYSIN     DD   *
DMPBLD1    AMDSADMP   TYPE=HI,LOADPT=X'00001000',              +
               CONSOLE=((060,3278),(061,3278),(840,3278),(841,3278),(AA+
               0,3278),(AA1,3278),(B20,3278),(B21,3278)),        +
               MSG=ALL,IPL=D3380,VOLSER=SYST11,                +
               OUTPUT=T6A0
           END
/*
```

Example 18.5. Stage 1 of generating a stand-alone dump program.

- The assembly of this macro causes a jobstream to be written to the SYSPUNCH dataset. This includes the JCL necessary to assemble and build the stand-alone dump program, and invoke ICKDSF to install the SADMP IPL text on the selected DASD volume.

- The parameters on the AMDSADMP macro describe the type of dump program you want to have generated, the devices which are to be available to it as consoles at execution time, and the device on which to install the program and IPL text.

As well as IPLTEXT, the installation process creates a dataset called SYS1. PAGEDUMP on the selected volume, which contains the SADMP program itself. You must not delete this dataset or move it to another volume (but remember when you are generating your stand-alone dump to check there is not a SYS1. PAGEDUMP already on your selected volume — if there is you must delete it or your stage 2 job will fail).

Generation of the stand-alone dump program is documented in [11]. You will note that there is also a one-stage generation process available. If you are not using CBIPO and so have to build your own JCL from scratch, you may find it more convenient to use the one-stage version.

Having installed SADMP you should test it and ensure your operators have full instructions on how and when to use it, including the address of the device on which it resides.

The procedure for taking a stand-alone dump is also documented in [11]. Briefly, you must:

1 Perform a 'store status' operation on the processor, which causes processor status information such as the PSW and register contents to be written to a

predefined area of storage before they are corrupted by the stand-alone dump program itself.

2   IPL the device which contains the SADMP IPLTEXT and program (using the load option, not the load clear option, which would zero the storage you wish to dump).

3   Wait until the hardware console notifies you that the processor has entered an enabled wait (wait code × '140000'), then select a console which was defined to SADMP at generation time and press ENTER. This causes SADMP to use this as its master console and issue the message:

    AMD001A   ENTER ADDRESS OF OUTPUT TAPE.

4   Mount a tape (preferably unlabelled) on a tape drive, ready the drive, and reply with its unit address. If it is a labelled tape you will have to reply 'use' to message AMD045A to overwrite the label.

5   SADMP prompts you for a dump title, and once you have replied to this it dumps the contents of real storage.

6   If you specified PROMPT at SADMP generation time, you will then receive the message:

    AMD059D   ENTER DUMP OPTIONS, 'LIST', OR 'END'

which you may respond to by requesting extra storage to be dumped in addition to the defaults.

7   SADMP then dumps selected areas of virtual storage from the page datasets if these are available.

8   When the dump is complete, SADMP issues the message:

    AMD056I   DUMPING OF VIRTUAL STORAGE COMPLETED

Then unloads the output tape and places the processor in a wait state with reason code × '410000'.

Once produced, stand-alone dumps can be analysed using IPCS, though you will often have to send copies to IBM or other software vendors for diagnosis when the source of the problem is unidentifiable or is clearly in one of their software products.

18.2.6 What to look for

The information you need from a dump to diagnose a problem will vary enormously, depending on the nature of the problem and the type of dump you have available. There is not room here to go into all the various cases, but we will pick out some of the key 'symptoms' which you will often need to search for in a dump, and discuss what they are useful for and where to find them. [6] is worth consulting if you are unsure of what to look for in a particular dump — it includes a substantial chapter which sets out a step-by-step approach to diagnosing each main type of problem, and others which discuss some of the problem data available in various types of dump. [7] goes a step further, stepping you through sample dumps and explaining what is present in each section. It is well worth obtaining some real dumps and using this manual to work through them so that you are familiar with the significance of each section of each type of dump before you are faced with one in anger. Some of the main problem symptoms to look for include:

Abend code, job and step name

For most program failures, these define the problem, and you may well know them already before you start looking at the dump. If not, the job and step name will be shown in the dump title for SYSUDUMP and SYSABEND dumps, and the abend code at the top of the first page. You should also look in the RTM2WA (recovery and termination manager work area) for the abend code. Example 18.6 shows the first few lines of a SYSUDUMP dump and an extract of the RTM2WA summary. Note that there is sometimes more than one RTM2WA — for example, if there has been an abend in an ESTAE recovery routine after the initial abend — and in this case you will have to find the original RTM2WA in order to diagnose the original problem. For SVC dumps and SYSMDUMPs, this data can usually be found using one of several IPCS subcommands — STATUS FAILDATA, for example — and Example 18.7 shows an extract from the output of STATUS FAILDATA.

  Note that these two examples refer to different failures; the first comes from the SYSUDUMP for the same problem as the symptom dump in Example 18.1, while the second refers to the same problem as the output in Example 18.8 below.

Messages issued prior to failure

If your SVC dump, SYSMDUMP, or stand-alone dump includes the master trace table, you can scan this for console messages issued prior to the failure (even if these did not appear on the console itself due to a system problem) — this at least gives you an idea of the context of the problem, and may save you having to look any further. These messages can be displayed using the IPCS VERBEXIT MTRACE subcommand.

PSW at time of failure

The PSW includes a lot of useful information, including the address of the next sequential instruction, the PSW key at the time of the abend, whether the current unit of work was running in problem or supervisor state, whether the processor was running disabled for any kind of interrupt, the condition code returned by the last instruction, and the current addressing mode. It should appear in the symptom dump, in the RTM2WA (again, make sure you are looking at the right one), also near the top of the first page of a SYSUDUMP or SYSABEND dump, and in the output from an IPCS STATUS FAILDATA subcommand (as shown in Examples 18.1, 18.6, and 18.7).

```
JOB SYSOO1ST        STEP SAMP        TIME 163747    DATE 91336    ID = 000
COMPLETION CODE        SYSTEM = OC4    REASON CODE = 00000004
 PSW AT ENTRY TO ABEND  078D2000  00006FCA  ILC  06  INTC  0004
PSW LOAD MODULE = SAMPFAIL  ADDRESS = 00006FCA  OFFSET = 00000072

                        RTM2WA SUMMARY
                        --------------

+001C  COMPLETION CODE                    840C4000
+008C  ABENDING PROGRAM NAME/SVRB ADDRESS 00000000  00000000  00000000
+0094  ABENDING PROGRAM ADDR              00000000

       GPRS AT TIME OF ERROR
       0-3    00000050  00005F60  00005FF8  00FD3858
       4-7    00F613B8  00000220  00F33200  00AA7CB0
       8-11   007FF008  807FF328  00F613C0  00005F60
       12-15  00006F5E  00005F60  80FD38A8  00005F60
+007C  EC PSW AT TIME OF ERROR  078D2000  00006FCA  00060004  00011BA8

+016C  PREVIOUS RTM2WA FOR THE TASK       00000000
+0170  PREVIOUS RTM2WA FOR RECURSION      00000000

+00B8  ASID OF ERROR IF CROSS MEMORY ABTERM       0000
+036C  ERROR ASID                         003D
```

```
                    RTM2WA  BIT  FLAG  SUMMARY
                    - - - - - - - - - - - - - -

          PROGRAM CHECK
          ENABLED RB IN CONTROL AT TIME OF ERROR
          ERRORID INFORMATION AVAILABLE


REGISTERS AT ENTRY TO ABEND

FLOATING POINT REGISTER VALUES
  0-6  00000000 00000000   00000000   00000000   00000000 00000000   000000

GPR VALUES
  0-3   00000050   00005F60   00005FF8   00FD3858
  4-7   00F613B8   00000220   00F33200   00AA7CB0
  8-11  007FF008   807FF328   00F613C0   00005F60
  12-15 00006F5E   00005F60   80FD38A8   00005F60

ACCESS REGISTER VALUES
  0-3   00000000   00000000   00000000   00000000
  4-7   00000000   00000000   00000000   00000000
  8-11  00000000   00000000   00000000   00000000
  12-15 00000000   00000000   00000000   00000000
```

Example 18.6. SYSUDUMP dump headings and part of RTM2WA summary.

```
* * * DIAGNOSTIC DATA REPORT * * *

SEARCH ARGUMENT ABSTRACT

PIDS/566528418 RIDS/UNKNOWN&L RIDS/UNKNOWN AB/S00C4 PRCS/00000000 REGS/0E180
REGS/0C2CA RIDS/IGG0CLHC&R

Symptom               Description
-------               -----------
PIDS/566528418        Program id: 566528418
RIDS/UNKNOWN&L        Load module name: UNKNOWN
RIDS/UNKNOWN          Csect name: UNKNOWN
AB/S00C4              System abend code: 00C4
PRCS/00000000         Abend reason code: 00000000
REGS/0E180            Register/PSW difference for ROE: 180
REGS/0C2CA            Register/PSW difference for ROC: 2CA
RIDS/IGG0CLHC&R       Recovery routine csect name: IGG0CLHC


Time of Error Information

PSW: 075C1000 82948122   Instruction length: 04   Interrupt code: 0011
Failing instruction text: 00085E50 D14C9180 500A4770
Translation exception address: 00003098

Registers 0-7
GR: 7F631808 00000000 7F631AAC 00000000  00FD3858 00003090 82947E58 7F631808
AR: 00000000 00000000 00000000 00000000  00000000 00000000 00000000 00000000
Registers 8-15
GR: 000002A0 82947EAC 007C7938 007C7FB8  82947E58 7F63182C 82947FA2 00000000
AR: 00000000 00000000 00000000 00000000  00000000 00000000 00000000 00000000
```

```
Home ASID: 0056    Primary ASID: 0056    Secondary ASID: 0056
PKM: 8080          AX: 0000              EAX: 0000

RTM was entered because of a program check interrupt.
The error occurred while an enabled RB was in control.
No locks were held.
No super bits were set.

STATUS FROM THE RB WHICH ESTABLISHED THE ESTAE EXIT

  PSW: 070C2000 82938B74    Instruction length: 02    Interrupt code: 0001

Registers 0-7
GR: 00000001 007D537C 007D537C 007D3304 007D5380 829380A4 007D537C 7F6A3890
AR: 7FFFD5B0 00000000 00000000 00000000 00000000 00000000 00000000 00000000
Registers 8-15
GR: 829380A0 7F6A3AF5 02938E95 7F6A3B14 82937E96 7F6A3B14 80FD38A8 807FD4B8
AR: 00000000 00000000 00000000 00000000 00000000 00000000 011E4F60 811D799A
```

Example 18.7. Extract from output of IPCS STATUS FAILDATA subcommand.

Current module at time of failure

This is the module containing the storage at the PSW address. It will usually be a clear indication of whether you have a system or application problem — if it is an IBM or OEM module, you will probably need to call their support desk once you have obtained comprehensive symptom data; if it is an inhouse module you will usually have to start digging deeper in the dump yourself. The PSW module's name is shown in the first few lines of a SYSUDUMP or SYSABEND dump, and also in the symptom dump. If you are analysing a dump using IPCS you can find the failing module by issuing the SUMMARY TCBERROR subcommand, then looking through the output until you find a TCB with a non-zero value in the CMP (completion code) field. This is the failing TCB, and the lines between this and the next TCB entry describe control blocks belonging to this TCB. One of these will be for the contents directory entry (CDE) of the module in control at the time of the abend, and will show the name and entry point address of this module.

Note that occasionally the PSW address at the time of failure will be outside the failing program, since in some circumstances a program may succeed in branching outside itself when it was not supposed to. Example 18.8 shows an extract of the output from the SUMMARY TCBERROR subcommand.

Following the steps outlined above, you should find that the problem under analysis in this example was an 0C4 abend in a task executing the IDCAMS module.

Current instruction at time of failure

The PSW next-sequential-instruction field usually points at the instruction immediately after the failing instruction, although in some circumstances it points at the failing instruction itself (notably for page translation and segment translation errors). Usually it is fairly clear which instruction failed: if not, look in [16] (the sections on 'Interruption action' and 'Instruction-length code' in the chapter on interruptions) to determine which of these cases applies to the problem you are dealing with. If the failing instruction is the one before the PSW address, you can obtain its exact address by subtracting the instruction-length code from the PSW address. This code appears in the fourth line of a SYSUDUMP or SYSABEND dump, after the acronym ILC, and in the output from IPCS STATUS FAILDATA.

If you are collecting symptoms for a software supplier, the main use of this information is to inform them of the offset into the module at which the failing instruction was found, and you merely subtract the module address from the instruction address to obtain this offset. If you are analysing a failure in an inhouse module, you will usually use this offset to find the failing instruction in an assembly listing, and continue your analysis from there.

```
* * * * K E Y F I E L D S * * * *
BNAME TDPYN110
  SELECTED BY: TCBERROR

SCB: 00F71C00
  FWDP..... 00F53900  ASID..... 0056      TRQP..... 00FD2D68
  CSCB..... 00F74080  TSB...... 00000000  AFFN..... FFFF
  ASXB..... 007FDEF0  DSP1..... 80        FLG2..... 00
  SRBS..... 0000      LOCK..... 00000000  ASSB..... 0184E880
  Address space non-dispatchability flags from ASCBDSP1:
    System set non-dispatchable and this ASCB is not exempt

CB: 007FE168
  CMP...... 00000000  PKF...... 00        LMP...... FF        DSP...... FF
  TSFLG.... 00        STAB..... 007FD2F0  NDSP..... 00000000
  JSCB..... 007FDD74  BITS..... 00000000  DAR...... 00
  RTWA..... 00000000  FBYT1.... 00
  Task non-dispatchability flags from TCBFLGS4:
    Top RB is in a wait

RB: 007FDD50
  WLIC..... 00020001  FLCDE.... 00F3D058  OPSW..... 070C1000  81062B88
  LINK..... 017FE168

DE: 00F3D058
  NAME..... IEAVAR00  ENTPT.... 82FEC000

CB: 007D8D10
  CMP...... 940C4000  PKF...... 80        LMP...... FF        DSP...... FF
  TSFLG.... 20        STAB..... 007D7F98  NDSP..... 00002000
  JSCB..... 007FF214  BITS..... 00000000  DAR...... 00
  RTWA..... 7F62E090  FBYT1.... 88
  Task non-dispatchability flags from TCBFLGS5:
    Secondary non-dispatchability indicator
  Task non-dispatchability flags from TCBNDSP2:
    SVC Dump is executing for another task

RB: 007F3BC0
  WLIC..... 00020033  FLCDE.... 14000000  OPSW..... 070C1000  82AADAC2
  LINK..... 007FD348

RB: 007FF3B0
  WLIC..... 0002001A  FLCDE.... 007FE058  OPSW..... 078D0000  00014B78
  LINK..... 007D8D10

DE: 007FE058
  NAME..... IDCAMS    ENTPT.... 00012E90
```

Example 18.8. Extract from output of IPCS SUMMARY TCBERROR subcommand.

Register values at time of failure

These are important when analysing inhouse problems, since you can often make useful deductions about what the program was doing before the abend by comparing these register values with the instructions which should have loaded or manipulated those registers prior to the abend. Beware, though, of assuming values in registers 0, 1, 14, and 15 have been set by your program — these are often corrupted by SVC calls or programs called as subroutines. Also beware of instructions which modify registers other than the one specified in the assembler instruction, such as the divide instruction.

Register values at the time of the abend can be found in the RTM2WA (labelled as GPRS AT TIME OF ERROR, where GPR stands for general-purpose register), in the output from the IPCS STATUS FAILDATA subcommand (labelled as GR), or the IPCS STATUS CPU REGISTERS subcommand, and also in symptom dumps.

Symptom string

If you are going to report the problem, IBM will be interested in the symptom string generated for the problem by the dump routines. This includes some of the information we have discussed above in a standardized form suitable for input to searches of IBM's problem database. It can be found in SVC dumps, SYSMDUMP dumps, and stand-alone dumps using the IPCS STATUS FAILDATA or VERBEXIT SYMPTOM subcommands.

Contents of relevant areas of virtual storage

This includes program modules, working storage, and system control blocks. For inhouse problems, you may spend hours searching through these areas checking what effect your program has had on them in order to work out where it went wrong. If you are using a SYSUDUMP or SYSABEND dump you may find the dump index at the end useful for finding your way around, particularly as these dumps do not simply list storage in ascending address order. If the problem is a complex one, though, you might be best advised to reproduce the problem and obtain a SYSMDUMP instead so that you can use IPCS. The BROWSE facility in the IPCS ISPF dialog is very helpful for scanning through virtual storage, especially if you make use of the pointer stack facility to keep a list of useful addresses.

Events recorded in system trace table

Note that this will include events after the problem you are diagnosing, including the processing done by the dump task itself up to the time it dumped the trace table, so you will need to work back through it until you find the record corresponding to the failure you are analysing, and exclude later events. It also includes trace records for events which occurred while SVC routines called by your program were running — you may want to exclude these from the early stages of your analysis as well. Once you have done this, the trace table can give you quite a useful record of things your program did before it failed, including, for example, SVCs it invoked, parameters it supplied to them, and return codes it received from them. The trace table appears near the end of a SYSUDUMP or SYSABEND dump, and for other types of dump it can be formatted from IPCS by issuing the VERBEXIT TRACE subcommand.

18.2.7 Dump analysis tools

Essential tools for any systems programmer who is going to analyse dumps include:

- A copy of [10], which documents the machine instruction formats and op codes, the various interpretations of any given hex value of a byte, the PSW format, interruption codes, and hex-to-decimal conversion tables. This is invaluable in working out what any given area of storage in a program module really does.
- A hex calculator: hex-to-decimal and decimal-to-hex conversions, address calculations, and other hex calculations are an inevitable part of serious dump analysis, and you should either buy a calculator with hex function, or write a program to do it for you — REXX has some handy built-in functions for this sort of thing.
- IBM manuals [9] (pre-ESA versions of these were known as the *Debugging Handbook*) — these document the contents of every major MVS control block.

And one of the following:

- A 132-column terminal — if you are going to analyse non-IPCS dumps online, you will soon go crazy trying to use an 80-column screen.
- Highlighter pens and sticky bits of paper: if you are going to analyse dumps on paper, you need to be prepared to mark the interesting bits so you can find them again easily.
- A course on using IPCS — this is *the* tool for serious dump analysis. If you have a pre-ESA system you may find yourself using the Stone Age equivalent — AMDPRDMP. My advice is to forget about this and learn how to use IPCS instead. If you are determined to carry on bashing flints together, though, AMDPRDMP is documented in [11].

Plus, of course:

- Vast amounts of patience and determination!

18.2.8 Using IPCS

Although it used to be rather an unfriendly piece of software, IPCS has developed over the years to become a usable and powerful tool for online dump analysis. The ISPF interface in particular makes it easily accessible, although a certain amount of training is still required. The maturing of IPCS should make the production of huge piles of paper for debugging problems a thing of the past.

You use IPCS like any other ISPF application, but it is only available if you have issued the TSO IPCS command *before* entering ISPF in the first place. This is normally accomplished by setting up a special logon procedure for IPCS which issues this sequence of commands automatically. IPCS subcommands can then be issued from the command line in ISPF, or accessed through a menu system. Your IPCS logon procedure must also allocate a number of IPCS datasets (see [12] for

```
//LIST     EXEC PGM=IKJEFT01,DYNAMNBR=20,REGION=2M
//IPCSDDIR DD DSN=SYS001.DMPDIR,DISP=SHR
//SYSPROC  DD DSN=SYS1.SBLSCLI0,DISP=SHR
//SYSTSPRT DD DSN=SYS001.TEMP,DISP=(,CATLG,DELETE),UNIT=WORK,
//            SPACE=(CYL,(1,1))
//SYSTSIN  DD *
 PROFILE MSGID
 IPCS NOPARM
 SETDEF DSN('SYS001.SADUMP.D91137') LIST NOCONFIRM
 %BLSCSCAN
 END
/*
```

Example 18.9. JCL to run IPCS CLIST in batch.

information on these), including the IPCS dump directory you are going to use for the current session. The dump directory must be initialized using the IPCSDDIR command before it is used for the first time. This dataset contains information gathered by IPCS for its own use about dumps you process; notably pointers to different areas of the dump, known as a storage map. IPCS gathers much of this information during the first executions of the STATUS and SUMMARY subcommands against each dump, which therefore tend to take rather a long time to run.

You must select the dump you are going to work with using the IPCS SETDEF subcommand, or by specifying it on the initial screen of your ISPF session. If you plan to analyse an SVC dump or a dump dataset on tape, you should use the COPYDUMP subcommand to copy it to a private DASD dataset before starting your analysis. Note that you may also use IPCS to examine its own address space (including common storage areas) in real time by specifying the ACTIVE, MAIN, or STORAGE operand of the SETDEF command instead of naming a dump dataset.

You may also code IPCS CLISTs to perform standard analysis tasks and execute these from the command line, or even in batch. This is particularly useful for preliminary formatting activities for new dumps. IBM supplies some sample IPCS CLISTs for this purpose, which are documented in Chapter 1 of [13]. The BLSCSCAN CLIST supplied in SYS1.SBLSCLI0 is particularly useful for formatting stand-alone dumps and printing the symptom summary information (though personally I have found it useful to exclude the SRMDATA command from the supplied CLIST). The printout it produces is a good starting point for further diagnosis, and provides you with a hardcopy of lots of useful data for reference during your analysis.

Example 18.9 shows the JCL required to run BLSCSCAN in batch. Note that:

- The JCL executes TSO in batch; I have chosen to put the terminal output to a DASD file rather than SYSOUT.
- The SETDEF subcommand defines the dump to be analysed using the DSN operand, then the BLSCSCAN CLIST executes a series of IPCS subcommands against this dump.

- All the IPCS subcommands are documented in [13].

The IBM-supplied clists for initial analysis of SVC and SYSMDUMP dumps are also good — these are members BLSCBSVB and BLSCBSYB respectively of the same dataset. They both provide most of the symptom information discussed in the section on dump analysis earlier, which is useful both in itself and for reference while you are browsing through sections of the dump.

Once you have obtained this initial symptom information, you may find it useful, depending on the problem, to use some of the 'component analysis' options on the IPCS ISPF menu, to delve deeper. The TRACE option, for example, will show you the system trace table, which is often useful for SYSMDUMP dumps, and the MTRACE option will show you the master trace table, which can be very useful for stand-alone dumps. You should familiarize yourself with the output of all these options so that you know what is available if you should need it. There is a useful table in the IPCS chapter of [7] which tells you how to find and format many important storage areas using IPCS.

IPCS is also capable of doing things which are rather more sophisticated than formatting and displaying control blocks. One of the most powerful is the ability to scan through control block chains and verify their integrity. This is done using the RUNCHAIN, SCAN, and TCBEXIT subcommands. For example, to check the integrity of all control block chains in the shared system area, you can issue the subcommand

```
SCAN RANGE(COMMON)
```

This is another time-consuming command which is best issued in batch — and it is probably only worth doing if you have some reason to suspect control block integrity problems.

Finally, if you need to browse through program modules or working storage areas which are not occupied by control block chains, you will need to use the IPCS BROWSE subcommand, or the ISPF dialog which front-ends this. This allows you to define symbols to refer to addresses in the dump, and places these on a stack of symbols which you can easily jump to from the BROWSE front-end. A symbol can be defined simply by entering a single character against an area of storage you are browsing, or by using the IPCS EQUATE and STACK subcommands. IPCS EQUATE works in much the same way as the EQUATE subcommand of TSO TEST, and allows you to define symbols which represent complex strings of indirect addresses. The process of defining areas of storage to IPCS, including the use of symbols, is described in the section of [13] entitled 'Describing storage in a dump', and you should devote some time to understanding this process as it will vastly increase your effectiveness with IPCS. Once you have defined a symbol it can be used in place of an address (and other attributes) in many IPCS subcommands.

18.3   Other diagnostic information and tools

18.3.1 Messages and message manuals

The vast majority of problems generate one or more diagnostic messages from the failing software, and these are the natural starting point for problem diagnosis. Correct interpretation of the error message(s) is often all that is required to solve a problem. When the error message does not appear to be sufficient on its own, you should always look it up in the relevant message manual, which often offers further detail on the cause of the problem and even suggested solutions. IBM message manuals also document the procedures you should follow if you need to escalate the problem to IBM.

Messages from most components of MVS are documented in [1], and this manual also includes a message directory that shows which manual documents the messages from each component of MVS and each major program product. Each component/product issues messages beginning with a different three-character identifier, and the directory relates each identifier to the appropriate message manual. You should ensure that you have a full set of message manuals for the products you support, and remember if you are using Bookmanager to keep these manuals online that you must also have a version which you can access when your MVS system is down.

It is also useful to bear in mind that some products allow you to vary their message options, so that messages which are usually not produced can be written out on request in a debugging situation. For example, TSO CLISTs and REXX EXECs can have several different message options set, and problems which seem incomprehensible with the minimum message options can become as clear as day when you turn on more comprehensive message options and reproduce the problem. Other products, such as HSM, allow you to specify options to generate additional diagnostic messages when you have problems (in this case using the SETSYS MONITOR command). When you are writing your own programs you can make debugging easier by inserting WTO macros to write error messages with useful diagnostic data, and by temporarily inserting WTOs to show you which path you took through a program while you are diagnosing a problem.

18.3.2 Traces

Traces are processes which keep a record of system events for use in diagnosing problems. Unlike dumps, they are not kicked off in response to an actual problem — instead, you have to start them off explicitly in anticipation of the problem. They therefore divide in practice into two groups: traces which are run all the time so that the trace data is always available if a problem occurs, and traces which are started after you have experienced a problem so you can obtain more detailed information the next time the problem occurs.

Table 18.2 summarizes the five types of trace supplied by IBM, showing what

Table 18.2. Types of trace available

Trace type	Information recorded	When to use it	How to obtain data
Component trace	Events internal to an MVS component, e.g. real storage manager	When diagnosing problems within an MVS component — usually only at IBM's request	Start the trace using the TRACE CT operator command, then obtain a dump and format the trace data using the IPCS CTRACE subcommand
GTF trace	Can trace some or all of a wide range of system events, depending on the parameters supplied when GTF is started	Whenever any of the information GTF can supply is needed for diagnosis of a reproducible problem	Runs as a started task using the IBM-supplied GTF cataloged procedure or an inhouse version of this. Trace data can be written to a dataset or kept in storage then dumped; in either case format it using the IPCS GTFTRACE subcommand
Instruction address trace	Addresses of instructions executed by the processor	When the processor appears to be looping and cannot be stopped because it is disabled for interrupts	Start from the hardware console (not available on systems running under PR/SM), then obtain a dump (likely to be a stand-alone dump) and format the trace using the IPCS CPUTRACE subcommand
Master trace	Console messages, commands, and replies	In any problem, but especially when messages may have been produced but were not written to the console itself or the SYSLOG dataset	Switch on with the TRACE MT console command, obtain a dump, and format the trace using the IPCS VERBEXIT MTRACE subcommand
System trace	Various internal system events such as interrupts, dispatcher actions, I/O operations, and SVC calls and returns. Successful branches may also be traced	In any problem where the sequence of events prior to the failure is required for diagnosis	Started automatically at MVS initialization; if stopped may be restarted with the TRACE ST console command. Trace table may be dumped and then formatted using the IPCS VERBEXIT TRACE subcommand

information each records, when to use it, and how to obtain the information. The five types of trace are described in more detail in [5], and the format and contents of trace records are described in [7].

Usually system trace and master trace will be active at all times (the TRACE MT command to start master tracing should be issued automatically at IPL time by including it in the COMMND00 member of PARMLIB, while system trace is started automatically by MVS at IPL). The other traces will be started only for short periods of time when required for the analysis of a particular problem, as the overhead of running them at all times is unacceptable. You can check which traces are active at any one time using the DISPLAY TRACE console command.

By far the most complex and flexible of the trace services available is the generalized trace facility (GTF). GTF can trace a wide variety of events, including various types of I/O events, various types of interrupts, any events trapped by SLIP commands, invocations of SRM, recovery actions, VTAM events, and user-defined events, and tracing of events can be restricted to a given range of address spaces or job names. The events to be traced are defined in a member of SYS1. PARMLIB specified on the GTF start command, and the coding of this member is documented in [4].

The trace records created by GTF are kept in a trace table in the GTF address space, and unless you specify MODE=INT in your GTF EXEC parameter, they are also written to the dataset defined by your IEFRDER DD statement. It is usually easier to write the data direct to a dataset, as it saves the trouble of requesting and taking a dump; on the other hand, if you expect to take a stand-alone dump to analyse the problem anyway, you can reduce the GTF overhead by specifying MODE=INT. GTF operation is documented in [11] and trace record formats in [7].

Note that GTF can provide some very useful information which is not available from other IBM tools; for example, it can tell you the cylinders referenced in I/O operations to a DASD so that you can analyse the head movement on the device. In order to obtain useful results from this sort of data, however, you may have to develop postprocessing routines of your own.

18.3.3 Console commands

There is a large number of console commands that can provide useful diagnostic information in a wide variety of situations. If you have a system 'hang', for example, you can determine whether ENQ contention and catalog contention are factors simply by issuing the commands

```
D GRS
F CATALOG,LIST
```

(always assuming, of course, that the situation has not deteriorated to the point where the consoles are no longer responding). It is not possible to list here all the commands you might consider in different situations — you must simply familiarize yourself with the commands available and be ready to use them when the need arises. Some useful commands are listed in Chapter 4.

18.3.4 RMF and third-party monitoring software

RMF is a performance-oriented program product which records statistical information on the SMF datasets about SRM events, I/O activity, and transaction completions. This RMF data is often useful for analysing performance problems (which are beyond our scope here) after the event, but you should also be aware of the capabilities of the two online components of RMF. These are known as

RMF II, invoked from TSO using the RMFMON command, and RMF III, invoked from TSO using the RMFWDM command. RMF II provides online displays of system variables such as CPU activity, I/O rates and response times, paging and swapping activity, and breakdowns of these by performance group and domain. RMF III is a workload delay monitor which analyses the factors delaying each job and started task on the system. Both of them can be very useful for obtaining a little more detail on what is happening on your system, particularly for performance problems, but also where you appear to have a system or subsystem hanging. Detailed advice on how to use these facilities can be found in the RMF manuals.

If you have third-party MVS monitoring products installed, such as Candle's Omegamon or Landmark's The Monitor, these usually provide all the facilities of RMF II and III, and supplement them with others designed for more general problem diagnosis. On some occasions these monitors will do the entire job of diagnosing the problem for you, and all you have to do is log on and look at the currently highlighted messages. On others, they will provide tools which allow you to perform detailed diagnosis (and sometimes even problem resolution) easily and quickly. If you have such a tool, you should learn to use it, and make it one of your first ports of call whenever you are experiencing a system problem.

18.3.5 SMF and LOGREC data

Information to assist with problem diagnosis can also be obtained from other MVS facilities, for example SYS1.LOGREC and SMF.

The main use of SYS1.LOGREC is for recording hardware errors. If you have any reason to suspect that a problem you are diagnosing is related to a hardware error, you should use the EREP program to print the LOGREC records from the relevant period. In theory, software error records can also be recorded on SYS1.LOGREC, although in practice very few are. You can force error records to be written there using the ACTION=RECORD keyword of the SLIP SET command. Normally, though, there are better ways of getting diagnostics out of SLIP traps. Handling of SYS1.LOGREC data was covered in Chapter 17.

SMF data can also be useful in problem diagnosis. It is particularly useful for performance problems, as it contains large amounts of information on transaction completions and users of resources, but it can also be useful in other circumstances. For example, you may be able to determine from it that a certain critical dataset was deleted or amended by a certain user at a certain time. The usefulness of SMF data depends on which SMF records you are collecting. The use and control of SMF was also covered in Chapter 17.

18.3.6 TSO TEST

If you are attempting to diagnose a problem in an inhouse assembler program, you may find it useful to use the TSO TEST command. TEST provides an interactive debugging environment which allows you to set breakpoints in programs, step through them an instruction at a time, trap error conditions, and examine (and even amend) the contents of virtual storage and registers belonging to the program you are debugging while it is stopped at a breakpoint. It is a bit like stepping your way through a dynamic online dump, or 'playing computer' by changing the bits and bytes yourself as the program progresses.

TEST is another complex tool which requires a significant investment of time in learning how to use it, but is well worth while if you do frequent work on assembler debugging. If you want to learn it, there is a step-by-step tutorial in [14].

One handy feature of TEST is the ability to display areas of common storage which contain system control blocks. TEST is sometimes used in this way in diagnostic situations which do not involve detailed debugging of an assembler program. In these cases, you can specify any program as the program to be tested — IEFBR14 is usually used, so that nothing happens if you inadvertently start it — then examine storage without actually starting to execute the program 'under test'. A typical dialog using TEST in this fashion is shown in Example 4.1. Note that this usage of TEST duplicates the function provided by IPCS's ability to examine storage in real time.

18.4   Getting help from IBM

18.4.1 IBM staff roles and departments

IBM offers a range of services to assist you with software problems and issues (some chargeable, others free for licensed users). Although IBM's job titles and departmental organization seem to change as frequently as everyone else's, their software-related services generally remain divided into two broad areas, which we shall refer to as SE services and CE services.

SE stands for systems engineer, and all large IBM mainframe users are assigned a (full- or part-time) SE by IBM. Most systems programmers will be familiar with their IBM SE, who is in effect a liaison officer (the word 'engineer' in their job title is a complete misnomer). The SE actually reports to IBM's marketing department and his or her job is to keep in touch with what the customer is doing, ensure the customer is aware of relevant IBM products and services, and help the customer get good value from IBM. This is not quite as altruistic as it may sound — it is a highly effective part of IBM's famous marketing system, which encourages customer loyalty by maintaining a high level of customer confidence in IBM, and also maintains a high level of IBM awareness of potential sales opportunities.

Nevertheless, the SE is a useful resource for the systems programmer, and can assist with tasks such as determining appropriate levels of IBM software when upgrades are being considered, ordering software and preventative service, and escalating problems which are not being solved quickly enough through normal channels. SEs also have access to product specialists, who are experts on individual pieces of software; their services are often chargeable, but they ought to be able to provide the highest level of consultancy expertise available on IBM products.

SEs, however, do not deal with day-to-day problems. These are handled by CE services — customer engineering — which embraces both the hardware engineers who fix your CPUs and disk drives, and the support staff who deal with software problems. The latter includes the IBM support centres, which you will call when you have a problem, and staff who provide other fix-related services, such as tailored preventative service tapes.

18.4.2 The IBM support centre

Each IBM mainframe customer is assigned to an IBM support centre; there may be one for your country, one for a group of small countries, or one for each region of a larger country. The support centre's job is to help you resolve bug-type problems with IBM software (not to give you general advice or answer non-bug-related queries — these fall within the province of SE services). You should call them when you are suffering from a problem which might be due to a bug in an IBM product.

When you call the support centre, you will initially speak to a non-technical switchboard operator, who will take down details of your problem which you must have ready. These include your name, site, and customer number, the product with which you believe you have a problem, a one-line description of the problem, and an indication of its severity. Severity is indicated using a code as follows:

- *Severity 1* System or major product down, requiring immediate action
- *Severity 2* Severely restricted operation
- *Severity 3* Problem is non-critical and program is usable

Once the operator has taken details of your call, he or she will record it on a computer system and add it to a queue — there is a separate queue for each major group of products. You will be given a problem number, which you must note down and quote whenever you call in again to discuss the same problem. You will then be asked to hang up and wait for a call back.

Depending on the severity of the problem and the workload of the staff dealing with the relevant queue, you will be called back sometime between five minutes and a day later. The person who calls you back will still not be an expert on the product concerned, though they should at least understand the basics. Instead, the caller will be an expert at using IBM's computerized problem database, and will attempt to find problem records from previous customer calls which match the problem you are experiencing.

At this point, the process can take one of several paths, depending on what is found:

1 They may find records which match your problem, and for which a fix is already available. They will then send you the fix (unless you already have it on

an unapplied PUT), which you will have to apply to fix the problem.

2   They may find records which match your problem and indicate another course of action. For example, the problem may be due to a 'customer error' of some sort — sometimes a failure to observe a limitation documented in an obscure corner of the manual! Once again, you should be able to resolve the problem by following their advice.

3   They may find a match but a fix may not yet be available. If the problem is well defined and the match with the previous symptoms is 100 per cent, you will simply have to wait until a fix is produced — though sometimes the problem record may suggest a workaround to circumvent the problem until it is fixed. If the problem is less well defined or your experience is a little different from the previous one, you may be asked to provide diagnostic data.

4   There may be no match because no one else has yet experienced the problem. In this case you will generally be passed on to level 2 support — product specialists within the support centre who really do know the product better than you do. If these specialists also cannot identify the problem over the phone, you will be asked to provide diagnostic data — dumps, listings, etc. — for them to analyse. If the problem is urgent, you should ensure these are delivered as rapidly as possible. If you cannot provide requested diagnostics quickly, the support staff will naturally assume your problem is non-urgent, and if you cannot produce it at all, they will generally not pursue the problem further.

On the basis of your diagnostic data, level 2 support may come to the conclusion that there is no error in IBM software, in which case they will advise you to pursue the problem elsewhere, or they may conclude that there is an IBM bug. In the latter case they will open an authorized problem analysis report (APAR) and pass the problem to the change team for the product concerned, along with all the diagnostic information you have supplied. The change team is responsible for developing and testing fixes for all bugs in their product — most change teams are located in the USA, though a few are in other countries.

The change team may provide a temporary fix, known as an APAR fix, and will usually develop a permanent fix, known as a PTF, which will supersede the APAR fix if one was provided. Alternatively, they may come to the conclusion that it was not really a bug after all, and advise you to solve the problem in some other way, or they may occasionally be unable to develop a fix and advise you to circumvent the problem until it is fixed in a new version or release of the product. Occasionally a 'bug' might turn out to be an undocumented feature, so the manuals would be amended to reflect the 'bug' instead of the other way round! In any case, the complexity of most IBM software ensures that an effective and fully tested fix is unlikely to be available in a short period of time, so once a problem has gone to the change team, you are likely to have to find a workaround solution while you await a more permanent one.

Only a tiny fraction of the calls to IBM support centres result in APARs being raised (one IBM speaker quoted a figure of 1 per cent); a much higher proportion but still less than half (26 per cent, according to the same speaker) are 'rediscoveries' of such problems; and the majority are resolved without fixes being required.

If there is a delay in the resolution of a problem you have passed to the support centre which is causing genuine operational problems to your organization, you should normally ensure that your own management follows an escalation process, notifying your SE in the first instance, to ensure that IBM gives the problem the level of attention you require.

18.4.3 INFO/MVS and DIAL-IBM/IBMLink

Clearly the problem database used by IBM is of enormous assistance in diagnosing problems — indeed the other databases of technical information which are available internally in IBM are equally valuable. For example, IBM runs an internal 'question and answer' system, used by staff (typically SEs dealing with queries from customers) to get answers to technical questions from product specialists, including the authors of the product code. IBM makes this and other information available directly to customers via the INFO/MVS product. INFO/ MVS is an INFO/SYS application which allows users to install copies of a number of IBM's MVS-related databases on their own systems and search them for information themselves. To remain useful, of course, your INFO/MVS database has to be kept up to date, and IBM will supply you with regular updates (approximately monthly) which must be applied to the database.

If you have access to INFO/MVS, it is well worth while searching for information on problems (and more general queries) yourself, before calling the support centre, since you may be able to identify or exclude associated problems quickly and easily. On the other hand, you should still call the support centre, even if you believe you have found an obvious fix for your problem — you may have to call them to get the fix delivered anyway, but even more important, you must call them to ensure that the fix has not turned out to be in error since your copy of the database was generated.

Even better than keeping this information on your own system, though, is to access it directly on IBM's. This service is also available (at branch discretion) to mainframe customers, and is known by differing names in different countries. In the UK, for example, it is known as DIAL-IBM, while in the USA it is called IBMLink. To use it you must establish a comms link to IBM's network. Many users do this anyway in order to use other IBM communications services, in which case DIAL-IBM comes as an almost-free extra.

DIAL-IBM provides a whole range of services, including:

- Announcement details and product information and prices.
- The ability to raise orders online for courses, manuals, and other IBM products.
- The ability to send messages to IBM staff.
- A guide to IBM manuals, including extracts of certain key MVS manuals.

For systems programmers, though, the most useful service is access to INFO/ MVS. (Note: this is only available if you have a licence for the INFO/MVS product.) Accessing this through DIAL-IBM instead of building it on your own system has several advantages:

1 IBM's version is always more up to date.
2 You do not have to apply an upgrade to the database every month.
3 You save a large amount of disk space.

For further discussion of IBMLink — the US version — see [19].

References and bibliography

IBM manuals

1. *MVS/ESA Message Library: System Messages, Volumes 1 and 2*, GC28–1812 and 1813. These manuals document the vast majority of MVS messages, including possible problem causes and solutions and the meaning of reason codes included in the messages. Volume 1 also contains a table showing which manual contains the IBM messages with any given message prefix, for MVS components and major MVS program products.
2. *MVS/ESA Message Library: System Codes*, GC28–1815. Documents abend codes and wait codes, with possible problem causes and solutions and the meanings of reason codes.
3. *MVS/ESA Operations: System Commands*, GC28–1826. Includes documentation of commands such as DUMP and SLIP, and how to start a GTF trace.
4. *MVS/ESA SPL: Initialization and Tuning*, GC28–1828. Includes documentation of the PARMLIB members used to control dump options, GTF traces, and IPCS.
5. *MVS/ESA Planning: Dump and Trace Services*, GC28–1838. Describes the different types of dump and trace provided by MVS and how to customize each of them.
6. *MVS/ESA Basics of Problem Determination*, GC28–1839. Describes the different type of problem you may have to diagnose and defines the steps you should follow for each type; also explains how to develop search arguments for use with INFO/MVS and RETAIN, and what problem data you should have ready when reporting each type of problem to IBM.
7. *MVS/ESA Diagnosis: Using Dumps and Traces*, LY28–1843. Covers how to request and interpret dumps and traces, and provides documented examples of the contents of each major type of dump and trace, and samples of the output of the most useful IPCS dump analysis commands.
8. *MVS/ESA Diagnosis: System Reference*, LY28–1011. Various reference information such as sense bytes for I/O errors and a table of MVS SVCs.
9. *MVS/ESA Diagnosis: Data Areas, Volumes 1–5*, LY28–1043 to 1047. Gives full documentation of all major MVS control blocks, including the names, data formats, and contents of each field in each control block (on pre-ESA systems this was known as the *Debugging Handbook*).
10. *ESA/370 Reference Summary*, GX20–0406. A useful little handbook containing instruction and control-block formats and hex conversion tables for use in debugging.
11. *MVS/ESA Service Aids*, GC28–1844. Includes documentation of GTF trace and the stand-alone dump program. Pre-ESA versions also document AMDPRDMP, the dump formatting program which was replaced by IPCS.

12. *MVS/ESA IPCS User's Guide*, GC28–1833. Covers how to access IPCS, including how to use the ISPF dialog, IPCS CLISTs, and IPCS in batch.
13. *MVS/ESA IPCS Command Reference*, GC28–1834. Documents all the IPCS sub-commands and the IBM-supplied sample IPCS CLISTS.
14. *TSO/E V2 Programming Guide*, SC28–1874. Includes a tutorial on how to use TSO TEST.
15. *MVS/ESA Application Development Macro Reference*, GC28–1822. Includes documentation of the SNAP macro.
16. *IBM System/370 XA Principles of Operation*, SA22–7085. Includes documentation of all System/370 machine instructions and what happens when an interrupt occurs. Note there are different editions for different versions of the architecture (e.g. System/390 and System/370 ESA).

Other

17. Keller, T.: Improving your Debugging Skills through Problem Solving Techniques, *Technical Support*, August 1991, pp. 21–24. An excellent article which describes the different kinds of mental processes involved in effective problem determination, nicely illustrating the need for flexibility, versatility, and open-mindedness.
18. Tomiak, K.E.: Extending IPCS, *Technical Support*, August 1991, pp. 57–59 and September 1991, pp. 53–55. Describes how to code storage addresses and CLISTs for IPCS.
19. Goldberg, G.: IBMLink — An Information Cornucopia, *Enterprise Systems Journal*, December 1990, pp. 31–32 and 109–111. Describes some of the services available on IBMLink in the USA.
20. Westerling, K.: Getting the Most out of IBM's ASAP Information, *Technical Support*, September 1990, pp. 66–71. More on IBMLink and how to make use of the 'automated software alert process' it provides to keep you informed of new software problems.

19
Emergency recovery facilities

19.1   Why you need emergency recovery

There is a moment every systems programmer dreads. MVS is just coming up after
a change to a system parameter, and it stops. Perhaps it issues an explanatory
message; perhaps it goes into a disabled wait and starts ringing bells in the
computer room; or perhaps it just sits there and does nothing. So you try to go
back to the way things were before your change — and MVS still will not come
up. Suddenly you get that funny feeling in the pit of your stomach and start to
wonder if you will be able to handle Skid Row.

   If you want to wriggle your way out of those moments with the least risk to your
career prospects and peace of mind, let alone the service you provide to your
organization, you will make sure in advance that you have facilities available to get
you out of every conceivable MVS disaster. And not only that, but also every
conceivable JES, VTAM, TSO, DFP, and security software disaster, since any one
of these could make it impossible to bring up a system far enough to correct the
problem. It might not appear in your job description, but do not doubt for a
moment that it is part of your job to provide 'belt and braces' (suspenders for
American readers) recovery options for the systems you support. And of course
you need to allow for recovery in a multitude of situations — not just when you
have messed up a system change, but, for example:

- When an HDA crash has taken out any critical DASD volume.
- An I/O error during IPL has irretrievably mutilated SYS1.NUCLEUS, or
  perhaps the master catalog, or the JES2 checkpoint, or any one of the dozens
  of datasets you need for a successful IPL.
- Someone has deleted a vital dataset.
- A software bug has corrupted a critical dataset.

   Remember too, that you have got to be able to recover without any of the
facilities you usually rely on. Online documentation and search facilities are major
weak points here: how are you going to find any datasets you need if the catalog
is unavailable, for example?

The only safe solution to this potential nightmare is to provide as many levels of emergency recovery facilities as you can, document them, test them regularly, and keep them up to date. For the purpose of this chapter I have divided the facilities you need into four levels, each providing a safety net for the previous level. If these all fail, you will probably be sharing a piece of pavement (sidewalk to transatlantic colleagues) down on Skid Row with your former manager, while IBM picks up the pieces for your former employers! These four levels are:

1   Alternative system startup options
2   Alternative MVS systems
3   Non-MVS facilities
4   Standby sites

19.2   Level 1 recovery—Alternative start-up options

19.2.1   Overview

Nine times out of ten, when your system will not come up first time, you should be able to recover simply by selecting some different options at the console — assuming, of course, that you are properly prepared for the problem. There are a number of general techniques you should adopt to maximize your preparedness:

- Retaining usable backups of old versions of changed procedures and parameters
- Parametrizing startup procedures to increase flexibility
- Creating alternative versions of major subsystems

19.2.2   Making usable backups of changed procedures and parameters

This is an essential discipline. Problems caused by a small change you have made to a procedure or a set of parameters can almost always be solved by reverting to the previous version then correcting your mistake. To ensure this is possible, always follow a few simple rules when making system changes:

1   Save the member you are changing under an alternative name before starting to change it. It is best to follow a convention which makes it easy to remember the name of your backup version, such as always suffixing it 99, or always suffixing it with your initials.
2   Ensure there is a viable way of using the old version of the member before trying to use the new version.
3   Keep a written note of how to use the old version if it proves necessary.
4   Avoid making any related changes which make the old version unusable before proving that the new version works.

For example, let us assume you are about to move the page datasets on your

MVS system and you need to modify IEASYS00 to implement the change permanently. The procedure you should follow will go something like this:

1 Define the new page datasets.
2 Copy IEASYS00 to IEASYS99.
3 Modify IEASYS00, removing the old page dataset names and inserting the new ones.
4 IPL using the new version of IEASYS00.

Now, if your IPL fails — because, for example, you have made a mess of defining the new page datasets, or they are on volumes which are not accessible to the system, or you have missed out a comma in IEASYS00 — then you can simply re-IPL, specifying SYSP=99 in the reply to the SPECIFY SYSTEM PARAMETERS message, and go back to your old page datasets.

Once you have your page datasets and IEASYS00 right, and have proved it by IPLing a few times, you can then complete the task, by:

5 deleting the old page datasets.
6 Allowing IEASYS99 to be overwritten again when you start making your next change to PARMLIB (if there are several systems programmers who might consider changing IEASYS00 at the same time, avoid the danger of someone else prematurely overwriting your backup version by suffixing it with your initials instead).

Exactly the same logic can be applied to most changes to startup parameters, for both MVS and essential subsystems (where 'essential' means 'you need this subsystem up to fix your mistakes').

19.2.3 Parametrizing startup procedures

MVS and most MVS subsystems make heavy use of parameters which can be overridden from the console at startup time, precisely because this allows you to recover from difficult situations. You can further reduce the danger of disaster by parametrizing critical cataloged procedures to maximize your flexibility.

In Chapter 8, for example, we saw a version of the JES2 procedure (Example 8.1) in which the names of all procedure libraries were supplied as symbolic parameters. In the event that someone deleted one of these libraries, or the volume containing it was unavailable at IPL time, for example, JES2 would fail with a JCL error at startup time. With our parametrized procedure, however, you could name a different library (or even DSN=NULLFILE) in your start command for JES2 and bring up a working version of JES despite the absence of the procedure library. I strongly recommend the use of this technique to maximize the startability of your JES system.

VTAM is also a good candidate for this approach, as are security products which are started as cataloged procedures.

19.2.4 Providing alternative versions of subsystems

Another valuable insurance policy can be taken out by creating alternative versions of critical subsystems and procedures, which do not depend on the datasets that are critical to the usual production versions, notably:

- An alternative version of JES2 using different spool and checkpoint datasets
- An alternative version of your security system using a different security database
- An alternate master catalog which can be used at IPL time
- A minimal-dependency TSO logon procedure which can be used when any of the datasets in your usual logon procedures are unavailable

We will briefly discuss each of these in turn. You should consider each of them and decide whether to make it a component of your recovery strategy; certainly you must be prepared for failure of any one of these subsystems, but you may feel that having a stand-alone recovery system (discussed in Sec. 19.3) makes some of these alternative versions unnecessary (e.g. an alternative master catalog). On the other hand, alternative versions which are simple to set up and require little maintenance are well worth providing, just in case.

Providing an alternative JES2 subsystem

As long as you have parametrized your JES2 procedure as described earlier, it should be straightforward to provide an alternative version of JES2 to use when the normal version fails to come up due to spool or checkpoint problems. All that is necessary is to set up alternative spool and checkpoint datasets (the spool will usually be rather small), then copy the normal JES2 parameters into a separate member of PARMLIB and modify the spool and checkpoint parameters to point to your alternative datasets. Then, when you need to start your alternative JES2, you can simply override the name of the PARMLIB member containing the JES2 initialization statements on your start command. Using the procedure in Example 8.1, for example, and a set of alternative parameters in SYS1.PARMLIB(JESP-MALT), you could start JES using the command

```
S JES2, MEMBER=JESPMALT
```

If the JES2 procedure itself is inaccessible or contains a JCL error which cannot be corrected using symbolic parameters, you will need to IPL a system with a different master catalog pointing to a different SYS1.PROCLIB containing a different version of the procedure. This could be part of your 'alternative master catalog' recovery option, or a separate MVS system altogether (see Sec. 19.3).

Creating an alternative security system

The critical dataset on which most security subsystems depend is the security database (the profile dataset in RACF). If possible, you should set up your security software so that it keeps dual copies of your security database, on different HDAs. Now, when one copy is put out of action, you should be able to start up your security system using only the remaining copy until the first copy is available again. In this case, you need three versions of the startup process: a normal version which uses both copies of the database, and two alternative versions, each using only one of the dual copies. If you cannot keep dual copies, you should run a daily job to copy your live database to a backup version on disk, and keep an alternative version of the startup process which allows you to use the backup database.

If you are using RACF, you must name the current RACF profile datasets in the ICHRDSNT module in the LPA; to replace the normal profile configuration with an alternative configuration, you must therefore bring a different version of this module into the LPA at IPL time. To make this possible, you must set up suitable versions of ICHRDSNT in a linklist library or SYS1.SVCLIB and create IEALPAxx members of PARMLIB which can be used to bring whichever one of them is required into the MLPA at IPL time. (On MVS 4.2 systems and higher you may load into the MLPA from any authorized library which is cataloged in the master catalog.) Say, for example, you placed a version of ICHRDSNT pointing only to your normal secondary profile dataset in SYS1.LINKLIB and created a member of PARMLIB called IEALPAR2 which included the line

```
SYS1.LINKLIB    ICHRDSNT
```

or on MVS 4.2 or higher, the line

```
INCLUDE LIBRARY(SYS1.LINKLIB) MODULES(ICHRDSNT)
```

Now, you could IPL using your alternative version of RACF by replying SYSP = xx, MLPA = R2 (where xx is the suffix of your normal IEASYSxx member of PARMLIB) to the SPECIFY SYSTEM PARAMETERS message. (Note that you may have to change the load parameter on your hardware console to force this message to appear if you are using MVS 4.2 or higher with the LOADxx member to control the selection of IPL options — see Chapter 7 for discussion of this.)

It is also worth while if you are using RACF to code an ICHRCX01 exit to allow systems programmers unlimited access to RACF-protected resources when RACF cannot access its database and goes into failsoft mode; otherwise you will have to reply to hundreds of console messages in order to perform the simplest of tasks. [3] and [4] both provide samples of the necessary code.

Providing an alternative master catalog

If the master catalog becomes inaccessible, you will find it useful to have an alternative version available (located on a different HDA so it is not vulnerable to the same hardware failures as the normal master catalog), and an alternative SYSCATxx member of SYS1.NUCLEUS pointing to it (or on MVS 4.2 on higher, an alternative LOADxx member of PARMLIB or LOADPARM). You can then

```
//MINPROC  PROC
//TSO      EXEC PGM=IKJEFT01,DYNAMNBR=50,TIME=1440
//SYSPRINT DD   TERM=TS,SYSOUT=*
//SYSTERM  DD   TERM=TS,SYSOUT=*
//SYSIN    DD   TERM=TS
```

Example 19.1. Minimal-dependency TSO logon procedure.

IPL using the alternative master catalog by replying with the suffix of your alternative SYSCATxx member to the message SPECIFY MASTER CATALOG PARAMETER, or by selecting the alternative LOADxx member using the load parameter on the hardware console.

To prepare your alternative master catalog, you must first define it using IDCAMS (see Chapter 7), then build the essential catalog entries. You should be able to copy the essential entries from your live master catalog using the MCNVTCAT job from CBIPO. You must then put in place a process to keep it up to date. There are two main options: (a) ensure that your normal master catalog update process updates both the live and alternative catalogs; or (b) regularly rebuild the alternative master catalog from scratch. Fortunately, the system-critical master catalog entries are not usually changed except when you are making major system changes, such as upgrading MVS or moving major system datasets; when you do this you should ensure that the alternative master catalog is updated or rebuilt. At other times, the main update activity on the master catalog is the addition of new aliases, and if you have a standard process for adding these it is usually easy to add a step updating the alternative master catalog as well.

Minimal-dependency TSO logon procedures

Logon procedures, particularly those which allocate ISPF libraries using DD statements rather than dynamically allocating them, often specify large numbers of datasets on DD statements. If only one of these is deleted or unavailable, your TSO logon will fail with a JCL error. You should therefore ensure that all systems programmers have access to a logon procedure which does not depend on any dataset allocations, such as that shown in Example 19.1.

Once you have got into 'raw' TSO using a procedure like this, you should be able to allocate any other datasets you need dynamically. However, this can be a slow process, so you should also provide some clists which can be used to speed it up (see the discussion of logon clists in Sec. 10.3 for some ideas on how to do this).

Once you have set up alternative systems, you must test them to prove they are usable and continually retest them every few months to prove they are still usable. Otherwise they will get out of date, and you will not find out until that fateful day when you need them and they do not work.

It is also essential to document these facilities once you have set them up, in hardcopy so the documentation is accessible when you need it — when the system is down. You should ensure that all systems programmers are familiar with the facilities available and where to find the documentation, and that the documentation is kept up to date. If you do not have an inhouse standards/reference manual which covers this sort of thing, you should consider creating your own 'recovery manual', documenting the facilities discussed in both this and the other sections of this chapter.

19.3   Level 2 recovery — Alternative MVS systems

19.3.1   Overview

However careful you are to give yourself lots of options for starting up your primary MVS system in difficult circumstances, there are certain to be cases when you just cannot do it — times when you forget to cover one of the possible problems, when it is just not possible to cover all foreseeable problems, or when problems such as hardware errors make essential resources unavailable. In order to recover in these situations, you will need to bring up an alternative MVS system which you can use to fix the problem.

The first option, which everyone should have available as a by-product of the MVS maintenance process, is to use your test system. Ideally this should be up and running at all times, in parallel with the production system — on its own machine, a virtual machine, or a logical partition. If this is the case, and the problem with your primary system has not brought down the test system as well, then you should be able to recover very quickly. If not, you should usually be able to IPL the test system on your primary machine and recover from there. Both of these options require that your test system can access the system-critical disks used by your production system in order to fix problems on them. Test systems running in parallel with the production system should therefore be configured in such a way that they can share system-critical DASD volumes with the production system if necessary. Remember that you may want to use your production system for recovery of your test system too.

Similarly, if you are running multiple production systems on different machines or partitions, you will have multiple SYSRES packs, and you should be able to use any one of these as part of a recovery system for one of the other machines. In order to keep this option open, you should aim to keep all your SYSRES packs identical, particularly by including the I/O configurations for all your systems on each of your SYSRES packs. If you are running MVS 4.2 or higher and using an IODF off the SYSRES pack to define your I/O configuration, you must also ensure that you have multiple copies of the IODF on volumes on different HDAs.

However, your test system and your 'other machine' systems are unlikely to be 100 per cent reliable as fallback systems for system recovery for a number of reasons:

• You will often be part-way through installing maintenance on the test system, which may make it unusable from time to time.

- When all DASD are shared, test systems often share resources with production systems, and production systems on multiple machines often share resources with each other. If a system failure affects a shared critical resource, then all your systems may be equally unusable.
- When all DASD are not shared, a system which usually runs on one machine can be dependent on resources which are not available to other machines (even when your intention is to avoid this, it can occur without your realizing).

It is therefore important to have another alternative, and you should provide this by creating and maintaining a stand-alone system or one-pack system. This is a system which is completely independent of your production and test systems, sharing no resources with them whatsoever. The normal method of ensuring this is to dedicate a DASD volume to your stand-alone system and create all the datasets required to bring up a working system on that volume. You can (and should) prove this is truly stand-alone by varying all other volumes offline as early as possible in the IPL process.

The purpose of your stand-alone system is purely to provide a usable system for recovery purposes, and it need only provide facilities which are essential for this purpose. It can therefore be a minimal function system capable of supporting only a few TSO users, although like any system to be used in recovery, it must be able to access all DASD volumes which are critical to the systems it is to recover.

Building a stand-alone system is a fascinating exercise which is often assigned to relatively new systems programmers to teach them a few things about MVS. The rest of this section discusses how to go about building one, what facilities to provide, and what activities are necessary to ensure the system is usable and remains so.

19.3.2 Building a stand-alone system

The essential steps in building a one-pack stand-alone system are:

1   Initialize your DASD volume and install IPLTEXT.
2   Create a master catalog on the volume.
3   Copy SYSRES datasets onto the volume.
4   Copy any other PDSs required from other volumes.
5   Copy the IODF if you are using HCD to define your I/O configuration on MVS 4.2 or higher.
6   Build other required datasets, e.g. page, LOGREC, SMF, and JES2 spool and checkpoint datasets.
7   Modify the catalog pointer member of SYS1.NUCLEUS (or the catalog pointer record in the LOADxx member of PARMLIB/LOADPARM).
8   Customize SYS1.PARMLIB and SYS1.PROCLIB.
9   Customize VTAM and TSO.

```
//INSTAL1   EXEC PGM=ICKDSF
//SYSPRINT  DD   SYSOUT=*
//IPLTEXT   DD   DISP=SHR,VOL=SER=XA313R,UNIT=3380,
//               DSN=SYS1.SAMPLIB(IPLRECS)
//          DD   DISP=SHR,VOL=SER=XA313R,UNIT=3380,
//               DSN=SYS1.SAMPLIB(IEAIPL00)
//SYSIN     DD   *
INIT            UNIT(123)                                               -
                VERIFY(OLDVOL)                                         -
                VOLID(SASYSR)                                          -
                VTOC(0,1,11)                                           -
                NOVALIDATE                                             -
                NOCHECK                                                -
                INDEX(0,12,3)                                          -
                IPLDD(IPLTEXT)                                         -
                BOOTSTRAP   /* IPLRECS OF IPLTEXT DD WILL SUPPLY IT    */
/*
```

Example 19.2. Initializing DASD volume for stand-alone system.

10   Ensure your security software will not prevent use of the system.
11   Test and back up the system.

Each of these steps is discussed in a little more detail below. It is a good idea to save the JCL for each step in a PDS dedicated to the one-pack-system-build process. To avoid building a system with incompatible or unreliable components, you should select a single stable MVS system and use its system libraries for both the programs and the input for all the build and copy jobs discussed here. The safest and easiest version to use will usually be your live production system.

Initialize your DASD volume and install IPLTEXT
This is a straightforward ICKDSF job. Take care to load IPLTEXT at the same level as the rest of the system you are going to build. Example 19.2 shows the JCL required. Note that this DSF step will perform a minimal initialization of the offline volume at address 123, changing the volume serial number from OLDVOL to SASYSR, and install IPLTEXT from SYS1.SAMPLIB on volume XA313R.

Create a master catalog on the volume
The JCL for this will be the same as for any master catalog build — see, for example, that shown in Example 7.20. Give the catalog a name which makes its role clear, e.g. CATALOG.MASTER.STNDALON.

Copy SYSRES datasets onto the volume
Use DFDSS or an equivalent product to copy the SYSRES datasets you require. Avoid copying datasets which are not needed by the facilities you will be using on your system, as space will probably be at a premium on your single volume. Example 19.3 illustrates the JCL you need.

Copy PDSs required from other volumes
If you plan to use any third-party or inhouse software on your system you will need

```
//RESCOPY EXEC PGM=ADRDSSU,REGION=1948K
//SYSPRINT DD SYSOUT=*
//SYSUT3    DD UNIT=WORK,SPACE=(CYL,40)
//SYSUT4    DD UNIT=WORK,SPACE=(CYL,40)
//DDIN1     DD UNIT=3380,VOL=SER=XA313R,DISP=SHR
//SYSIN  DD *
 COPY DATASET(INCLUDE(GIM.**                    -
                      ISF.**                    -
                      ISP.**                    -
                      ISR.**                    -
                      SORT.**                   -
                      SYS1.CMDLIB               -
                      .
                      .
                      .
                      SYS1.VTAM*.**             -
                      )) INDD(DDIN1) CANCELERROR -
       OUTDYNAM((SASYSR,3380))                  -
       SHARE TOL(ENQF)
/*
```

Example 19.3. Copying SYSRES datasets onto stand-alone system.

to copy the load libraries and ISPF libraries for these; you might also find it useful to copy other PDSs, such as VTAM libraries with in-house configuration data, and your JCL library and CLIST/EXEC libraries. Again DFDSS should do the job.

Catalog the datasets you have copied in the one-pack system master catalog
You could, for example, use ISMF to generate a job to do this.

Build other required datasets
Here it is easiest to extract the required steps from the relevant CBIPO jobs (or whichever jobs you use to create these datasets on your live system) and amend them to point to your volume and allocate realistic amounts of space. Zeh's series of articles [5] provides a full set of sample JCL for building these datasets (and indeed the rest of your one-pack system).

Some of the datasets which you should create are as follows:

- JES2 spool and checkpoint — allocate these as shown in Chapter 8; initialization is done automatically by JES2 the first time you start it up. You will inevitably end up with rather a small spool, but do not make it too small or your system will constantly grind to a halt as it fills up.
- Page datasets — again, these will have to be much smaller than on your production system, but if they are too small you will not be able to run your system.
- SYS1.LOGREC — a required dataset.
- Dump datasets — not strictly essential, but one or two small ones might come in handy.
- SMF datasets — again, not essential, but might be useful. For example, your

security administrators and auditors might find it reassuring to have SMF data available so they can check up on what you have done while security systems were inactive.

- SYS1.BRODCAST and SYS1.UADS — and define your systems programmers in SYS1.UADS. You could copy your live SYS1.UADS, but you should avoid copying a UADS which defines lots of users outside systems programming. If other users log on to your stand-alone system then: (a) they will become confused because it is not like the system they are accustomed to; (b) they may have the power to do dangerous things if the security system is down; and (c) they will contribute to paging and spool space requirements which you may not be able to support. You should therefore aim to restrict UADS entries to systems programmers with a genuine potential need to use the stand-alone system.

Modify catalog pointer member of SYS1.NUCLEUS

You will need a SYSCATxx member of SYS1.NUCLEUS or a LOADxx member of PARMLIB/LOADPARM which points to your stand-alone system's master catalog. The ideal solution is not only to create a default member which points to your stand-alone system's master catalog, but also to create an alternative SYSCATxx member which points to the live master catalog so you can use this if it is available. See Chapter 7 for an explanation of how to create a suitable SYSCATxx member.

Customize SYS1.PARMLIB and SYS1.PROCLIB

This is really the only difficult part of the process. You need to review all your PARMLIB and PROCLIB members to determine what changes are required to make the subsystems you need work on your stand-alone system. You will almost certainly need to change the members listed below (but take care to review the others carefully as well):

- IEASYSxx The page dataset names will need to be changed. If you intend to share DASD with any other system and use GRS to control cross-system integrity, you may also need to change the GRS system name. Generally each physical machine or logical partition should always have the same GRS name, whichever version of the system is running on it, so if you are using GRS in this way you may need to provide several versions of IEASYSxx and select the appropriate one at IPL time, depending on which machine or partition you are IPLing.

- IEAAPFxx The volume serial numbers of APF-authorized libraries will have to be modified to point to the stand-alone versions, unless you include the stand-alone versions as well as the live ones in your live APF list.

- COMMNDxx and IEFSSNxx Remove commands and subsystem entries which start up facilities you do not want. It is worth creating a version of COMMNDxx which varies all DASD offline except the SYSRES pack itself, so you can use this when you are testing to prove your system really is stand-alone.

- LNKLSTxx and LPALSTxx Remove libraries which are not included on your system.
- JES parameters Modify volume serial numbers (and names if necessary) of spool and checkpoint datasets, and ensure the default PROCnn statements for JOBs, TSO users and started tasks relate to DD statements you are including in your JES2 procedure.
- SMFPRMxx If your SMF datasets have different names from the live ones (or you do not have as many), change the names in this PARMLIB member too.
- JES2 procedure Any volsers used in this procedure will need to be changed, and any PROCLIBs which were not copied onto your stand-alone pack should be removed, along with the corresponding PROCnn statements.

Customize VTAM and TSO

- SYS1.VTAMLST You may wish to customize your VTAM configuration, e.g. leaving out your NCP, in order to simplify startup, remove dependencies on components which change frequently (notably the NCP definitions), and deny access to your system to remote users. If you need the NCP to access the system yourself, then you must take care to keep the NCP definitions on your stand-alone system up to date.
- SYS1.VTAMLIB You may also find it useful to generate a modified version of the VTAMLIB member named in the USSTAB parameter of your VTAM terminal definitions, in order to show a special dormant-screen message while you are using the stand-alone system. A suitable message would be something like SYSTEM RECOVERY IN PROGRESS — PLEASE WAIT FOR NORMAL SERVICE TO BE RESTORED.
- TSO logon procedures You must ensure that the procedures you are going to depend on during system recovery reference only datasets on the stand-alone system pack in their DD statements. Personally, I prefer to set up an entirely separate TSO procedure library for the stand-alone system and include only stand-alone versions of essential logon procedures (including a minimal-dependency procedure).
- TSO logon CLISTs As with logon procedures, you will probably have to customize logon clists to ensure that they only attempt to allocate datasets which exist on the stand-alone system. Once again, I recommend creating a separate library for your stand-alone system CLISTs and EXECs.

Ensure your security software will not prevent use of the system
One of the dangers of a stand-alone system which is rarely used or tested is that of bringing it up one day when you desperately need it for system recovery, only to find that it is impossible to log on to it because every available userid has been expired by the security system and/or their passwords have all been forgotten.

One solution to this problem is to copy your live security database regularly onto the stand-alone system — you would need to do this weekly for it to be effective in most installations. Since the security database is always reasonably current, userids never expire and users should be able to remember their passwords, even if they have changed them since the last copy was taken. However, this option will fail if you ever have to restore your one-pack system, including the security database, from an old backup tape, for example because the one-pack system volume itself is on a device which has failed. It will also fail if the live security database becomes corrupt, gets copied onto your one-pack system, then makes your live system unusable. Since the whole point of your stand-alone system is to be thoroughly reliable in an emergency, this is not a satisfactory alternative.

The best solution is to disable your security software on your one-pack system, or at the very least to set up your system so that you have the option of disabling the security software at IPL time. While auditors and security administrators may not like this, you should be able to carry the day with the argument that this option could be vital to restoring a service to your business in a potential disaster. RACF provides a failsoft mode, which you can make usable in a practical situation by implementing an ICHRCX01 exit, as noted above, and its leading competitors provide a WARN mode, which logs security violations but does not prevent them. Either of these options can provide some peace of mind to your bureaucrats while still allowing you to get the job done.

19.3.3 Testing, backing up, documenting, and maintaining a stand-alone system

Once you have built the system, you must test all the facilities you plan to provide, and correct your mistakes. Ensure that all the people who might need to use the system can access the important facilities, and ensure that the system not only comes up successfully with all other packs offline but is also able to vary them back on again and access them.

When you have proved your system works, you should dump the pack and ensure copies of both the dump and a stand-alone restore tape are available at both your primary and backup sites. These dumps should be:

- On tapes which are clearly labelled as one-pack system backups, not to be reused without your agreement.
- Stored in a documented place
- Outside the control of any tape management system

This is essential in case your stand-alone system is itself corrupted or made inaccessible by hardware problems. In these circumstances, you must be able to restore the stand-alone system onto any available DASD pack and use it to perform your system recovery. You should be aware in advance which volumes are suitable for overwriting with your stand-alone system. Potential candidates include:

- Empty packs
- Packs used by test systems
- Any pack which has been backed up since it was last updated
- Dedicated paging packs
- Packs being used to build new systems

You must also document your system so that it is usable by anyone in your systems programming team who might need it in an emergency. The documentation must include the IPL address, the location and description of backup tapes, and a list of the facilities available and restrictions imposed (e.g. if only certain TSO userids are available, or only certain logon procedures, or if the system's VTAM definitions include only certain terminals). It must document how to bring up the system, including unusual replies to IPL messages, and how to log on to it as a TSO user. You should also describe how you have dealt with system security, and how to invoke any IPL options you may have created to bypass security when necessary. Having produced your documentation, you should ensure that each of your systems programmers reads it, and that a copy is available for reference (e.g. in the recovery manual mentioned earlier in the chapter).

Finally, having created a usable stand-alone system, you must take steps to ensure it remains usable. There are two components to this:

1 Applying changes to the system
2 Re-testing it periodically

Most changes to your live systems should *not* be copied onto your recovery system, since you should try to keep this system as stable as possible and thereby avoid the danger of copying changes which make both systems unusable. Preventative maintenance and PARMLIB changes, for example, should usually not be copied. On the other hand, changes in the I/O configuration usually should be copied, since your stand-alone system may not be able to do its job without them. New DASD devices, for example, must be defined to the stand-alone system or you will not be able to use it to deal with problems on them.

For each change to the live system, therefore, you need to evaluate whether it is necessary to copy the change across to the stand-alone system to keep that system usable; if it is not essential, then do not copy it. You should try to ensure this evaluation is done for each change by including a check on it in the change control process for system changes, e.g. a question on the change control form which asks: 'does this change need to be applied to the stand-alone system?'.

However, it is still possible that a critical change may not be applied to the stand-alone system, making it useless when you need it. To minimize the danger of this occurring and remaining undetected, test your stand-alone system regularly

— at least once every three months — using a documented test plan which proves each essential component is still functional.

19.3.4 Facilities required on a stand-alone system

You should aim to provide the following facilities:

MVS, JES, VTAM, TSO, ISPF, and PDF
The ability to use ISPF/PDF is the most fundamental requirement for most system recovery tasks, and you need each of these products to work in order to provide that ability.

SDSF
You should ensure that you will be in a position to use SDSF (or equivalent facilities for looking at the JES spool) against both the stand-alone system's own spool and the live system's spool. At levels of JES2 below 2.2.0, all that was required to look at another system's spool from SDSF was to allocate the relevant JES2 checkpoint dataset before going into SDSF for the first time in your session. Since then, however, it has become a little harder. You now need to define and start a secondary version of JES2 using the other system's spool, assemble a separate copy of ISFPARMS pointing to the secondary JES (via the JESNAME parameter), and create a separate logon procedure with a STEPLIB holding this copy of ISFPARMS.

The process of setting up a secondary version of JES2 is discussed in the JES2 migration guides for releases 2.2 and 3.1, and in [1]. The use of SDSF to access a secondary copy of JES2 is documented in an appendix to [2].

IBM utility programs
Utilities such as IEBCOPY, IEBGENER, IDCAMS, DFDSS, and ICKDSF are all included in the system libraries you will have copied across from the live system, so it should be straightforward to use these on your stand-alone system. You may also find it useful to provide the ISMF dialog libraries, as a front end to some of these utilities.

Third-party and inhouse utility programs
You will have to take special measures if you want any of these to be available, i.e. you will need to copy the relevant program libraries and perhaps include them in your linklist and/or lpalist.

Inhouse and third-party ISPF dialogs providing useful recovery facilities
These will require ISPF datasets to be copied (clist, panel, message, skeleton, and table libraries) and made available via your stand-alone system logon procedures or clists.

Monitoring products
Third-party performance monitors may well be useful in recovery situations, not for their performance features, but for the other diagnostic facilities they usually provide. Once again, you will need to copy the relevant product libraries, and ensure they are included in PARMLIB members where appropriate — the APF list, linklist, lpalist, subsystem names table, etc.

DFHSM or equivalent products
These are more difficult to provide on a truly stand-alone basis, since their control datasets are necessarily volatile, being updated every time a dataset is migrated, backed up, or recalled. It is, however, worth setting up procedures which start up DFHSM using the live control datasets, so that you can do this if you need to recall or recover a DFHSM-managed dataset during system recovery.

19.4   Level 3 recovery — Non-MVS facilities

19.4.1 Stand-alone utilities

We have already touched on circumstances where simply IPLing an available MVS system is not feasible despite all our efforts to maximize our options. In these circumstances, there are 'stand-alone' programs which can sometimes do enough to give us an IPLable system. The example we have already seen is the use of a stand-alone restore program to restore a usable SYSRES volume; however, there are other circumstances where stand-alone programs can help.
    The stand-alone programs available include:

- Stand-alone restore facility of DFDSS
- Third-party equivalents to stand-alone DFDSS
- Stand-alone ICKDSF
- Stand-alone dump
- Third-party stand-alone editors

Of these, stand-alone DSF and stand-alone dump are of little value for system recovery: stand-alone DSF is primarily used for initializing DASD volumes, while stand-alone dump simply dumps MVS storage to tape for diagnostic purposes (see Chapter 18 for a discussion on this). The others, however, are potentially very valuable, and indeed system recovery is one of their primary reasons for existence.

19.4.2 Stand-alone restore

The main usage of stand-alone DFDSS is to restore entire DASD volumes from tape. This can be invaluable for recovery. You may need to restore a volume back to the same device because a dataset on it has been lost or corrupted which is essential to the IPL process. Alternatively, you may have a hardware problem that has damaged an essential device or made it temporarily inaccessible, in which case you can restore the volume back to a different device. The affected volume could be any volume which is essential to your system — not just your SYSRES, but your master catalog volume, or a volume holding any dataset required for MVS, JES, VTAM, or TSO startup.

Stand-alone DFDSS, however, suffers from two key limitations:

1   It can only restore entire volumes. This means that you could end up losing updates to all the datasets on a volume when you really only need to restore one dataset to make your system usable.
2   It cannot back up volumes, so if you restore one volume over the top of a different one there is no way to secure the one which is going to be overwritten.

Some of its third-party competitors do provide the capability to perform stand-alone backup, which overcomes both of these problems. The partial restore problem is solved by backing up the volume stand-alone, restoring the entire volume to an earlier level, then using the 'normal' version of the utility to do a partial restore from the stand-alone backup once you have got your system up and running again.

Both DFDSS and its competitors depend on the availability of: (a) an IPLable stand-alone version of the utility; and (b) usable backups of the volumes to be restored. You must pregenerate the stand-alone utility (including suitable IPL text) and ensure it is kept on a known tape or DASD volume in a documented location so that the operators will be able to find it in an emergency.

The major obstacle to the usability of backups is usually the need to identify the tapes being used for each volume's latest backup without access to the catalog or tape management system, which are not available when the system is down. You should therefore ensure that your volume dump processes produce a hardcopy listing of the tapes used to backup each volume and that this is kept in a documented location.

However, even with the more flexible third-party stand-alone restore programs, there are volumes for which stand-alone restore may not be suitable. These are volumes containing highly volatile files, such as page datasets and the JES spool and checkpoint datasets. You can restore these datasets, but their contents will almost certainly be useless, and at best you can expect them to need re-initialization at the next system startup. This is usually bearable, since the contents of these datasets are not essential to the functioning of the system, although your users are likely to be miffed at the loss of their output if you have to cold-start JES.

More problematical are volatile datasets whose contents are more vital. These include not only application data files but also your user catalogs. To provide full recovery facilities for these you need to have the capability to roll forward after doing a volume restore. CICS and many database management systems provide roll forward functionality by journalling all updates in a journal dataset on a different volume, so they can be reapplied if the base dataset has to be restored to an old version. You can provide similar functionality for catalogs by getting SMF to record catalog updates and using the SMF records to roll forward catalogs which have to be restored to old levels. This, however, requires a certain amount of programming in advance, or the purchase of IBM's ICFRU. Catalog recovery is discussed in Chapter 16.

In summary, then, stand-alone restore programs sometimes give you an additional recovery option, and you should put in place the necessary facilities, procedures and documentation to make this possible. On the other hand, they are not suitable in all cases and can cause further recovery problems because the data they restore will sometimes be out of date.

19.4.3 Stand-alone editors

At least one independent software vendor (New Era Software) is now offering a stand-alone program which can provide a much greater variety of system recovery facilities, including the ability to edit ISPF datasets, search DASD volumes for datasets, update catalogs, change DASD volume serial numbers, and modify data and load modules. Clearly this means that in most circumstances you should be able to use it to fix whatever problem is preventing your MVS system from coming up. It can therefore be seen as a last resort option when other alternatives fail. Some sites also find it easier and quicker to go straight to this option than to use some of the recovery techniques I have discussed earlier in this chapter — but like any other recovery technique, you should avoid becoming too dependent on this option. And like any other stand-alone program, you must keep an up-to-date copy of it available on tape or DASD and ensure documentation is available.

New Era's product is discussed in [6].

19.5   Level 4 recovery–Standby sites

Every site which is running business-critical systems should have a disaster recovery plan which covers the transfer of those systems to an alternative site in the event of a disaster. This is usually conceived of in terms of physical disasters — fires, floods, bombs, or plane crashes rendering the computer room unusable — but it should also give you an extra level of security for systems disasters.

This means that you should be able to restore your system and your data at the standby site as they stood at the last full set of volume backups and get a working system up there. You may even be able to do a partial restore (e.g. just system volumes) from a backup that was taken before your problems started, then IPL a system, fix your problems, dump the volumes off again and restore them at your home site, thus avoiding the trauma of transferring your business systems to the backup site and back again later. These options, however, should be seen as a last resort — if your system recovery gets to this stage when you do not have a physical disaster on your hands, you are in deep trouble.

Providing a standby facility is a major task which is well beyond the scope of this book, and large data centres should have staff dedicated to this task. Systems programmers should, however, play a part in setting up and testing the disaster recovery plan, and should certainly be aware of the options it gives them.

References and bibliography

IBM manuals

1. *JES2 Multi-access Spool*, GG66–0289. Includes documentation on setting up and using a secondary JES2.
2. *SDSF User Guide and Reference*, SC23–0408. See appendix on use of SDSF with a secondary JES2.

Other

3. Miller, I.A.: I/O Errors and the RACF Data Base, *Technical Support*, August 1991, pp. 47–50.
4. Hawkins, N.: Disabling RACF in a stand-alone environment, *MVS Update*, March 1991, pp. 37–39.
5. Zeh, S.: Creation of an MVS Stand-alone System, *MVS Update*, February 1988, pp. 12–16, March 1988, pp. 12–19, and April 1988, pp. 22–28.
6. Pearkins, J.E.: New Era's Stand Alone Edit, *Enterprise Systems Journal*, September 1991, pp. 116–117.

Glossary of acronyms

AASF	advanced address space facility
ACB	access control block
ACS	automatic class selection
ACT	accounting control table
AFQ	available frame queue
AMS	access method services
AOR	application-owning region
APAR	authorized problem analysis report
APF	authorized program facility
ASCB	address space control block
ASID	address space identifier
ASM	auxiliary storage manager
ASVT	address space vector table
BASSM	branch and save and set mode
BCS	basic catalog structure
BDAM	basic direct access method
BLP	bypass label processing
BPAM	basic partitioned access method
BSAM	basic sequential access method
BSC	binary synchronous communication
BSM	branch and set mode
BTAM	basic telecommunications access method
CA	control area
CAS	catalog address space
CBIPO	Custom-Built Installation Process Offering
CBPDO	Custom-Built Product Delivery Offering
CCW	channel command word
CDE	contents directory entry
CE	customer engineer
CHPID	channel path identifier
CI	control interval
CICS	Customer Information Control System
CMS	Conversational Monitoring System
CPC	central processor complex
CSA	common service area
CSCB	command scheduling control block
CSI	consolidated software inventory
CTCA	channel-to-channel adapter
CVT	communications vector table

DADSM	direct access device storage management
DAE	dump analysis and elimination
DASD	direct access storage device(s)
DAT	dynamic address translation
DCB	data control block
DCI	direct-coupled interlock
DEB	data extent block
DFDSS	Data Facility Data Set Services
DFHSM	Data Facility Hierarchical Storage Manager
DFP	Data Facility Product
DFSMS	Data Facility Storage Management Subsystem
DS	data streaming
DSCB	dataset control block
DSF	Device Support Facility

EC	engineering change
ECB	event control block
ECC	error checking and correcting
ECSA	extended common storage area
EDT	eligible device table
EP	Emulation Program
ERDS	error-recording dataset
EREP	Environmental Record Editing and Printing
ESA	Enterprise Systems Architecture
ESCON	Enterprise System Connection
ESDS	entry sequenced dataset
ESQA	extended system queue area
ETR	external timer reference
EXCP	execute channel program

FCB	forms control buffer
FEP	front-end processor
FLIH	first-level interrupt handler
FLPA	fixed link pack area

GDG	generation data group
GPR	general-purpose register
GRS	Global Resource Serialization
GTF	generalized trace facility

HDA	head-disk assembly
HIPER	high impact or pervasive
HLQ	high-level qualifier
HSA	hardware save area
HSM	Hierarchical Storage Manager

ICF	Information Centre Facility/Integrated Catalog Facility
ICFRU	Integrated Catalog Facility Recovery Utility
IDRC	Improved Data Recording Capability
IDTF	interactive data transmission facility
IML	initial microcode load
IOB	input/output block
IOCDS	input/output configuration dataset
IOCP	input/output configuration program
IODF	input/output definition file
IOGEN	input/output generation

IOQ	input/output queue
IOS	input/output supervisor
IOSB	input/output supervisor block
IOSQ	input/output supervisor queue
IPCS	interactive problem control system
IPL	initial program load
IRB	interrupt response block
IRIM	IPL resource initialization module
ISMF	Interactive Storage Management Facility
ISPF	Interactive System Productivity Facility
ISPTCM	ISPF TSO command table
IVP	installation verification procedure
JCL	job control language
JCT	job control table
JES	job entry subsystem
JESCT	JES control table
JFCB	job file control block
JPA	job pack area
KSDS	key sequenced dataset
LAB	line attachment base
LIC	line interface coupler
LLA	library (linklist) lookaside
LLE	load list element
LPA	link pack area
LPAR	logical(ly) partition(ed)
LPDE	link pack directory entry
LU	logical unit
MAS	multi-access spool
MCT	master control table
MDF	Multiple Domain Facility
MII	Multi-Image Integrity
MIS	management information services
MLPA	modifiable link pack area
MLPF	Multiple Logical Partition Facility
MPF	message processing facility
MPG	multiple preferred guests
MPSD	multipath storage director
MRO	multi region operation
MVS	Multiple Virtual Storage
MVSCP	MVS configuration program
NCP	Network Control Program
NDF	NCP/EP definition facility
NIP	nucleus initialization program
NIT	node information table
NJE	network job entry
NVR	non-VSAM volume records
NVS	non-volatile storage
OEM	original equipment manufacturer
ORB	operation request block

PCM	plug-compatible manufacturer
PDF	Program Development Facility
PDS	partitioned dataset
PDSE	partitioned dataset extended
PEP	Partitioned Emulation Program
PF	program function
PFT	page frame table
PLPA	pageable link pack area
PPT	program properties table
PR/SM	Processor Resource/Systems Manager
PSA	prefixed save area
PSP	preventative service planning
PSW	program status word
PTF	program temporary fix
PU	physical unit
PUT	program update tape
QCB	queue control block
QEL	queue element
QSAM	queued sequential access method
RACF	Resource Access Control Facility
RIM	resource initialization module
RJE	remote job entry
RMF	Resource Monitoring Facility
RNL	resource name list
RSM	real storage manager
RTAM	remote terminal access method
SAA	systems applications architecture
SCT	step control table
SDLC	synchronous data link control
SDO	system delivery option
SDSF	Spool Display and Search Facility
SE	systems engineer
SID	system identifier
SIM	service information message
SMF	system management facility
SMP	System Modification Product
SMP/E	System Modification Product/Extended
SMS	system-managed storage
SNA	Systems Network Architecture
SPL	systems programming library
SQA	system queue area
SRB	service request block
SRM	system resources manager
SSCH	start subchannel
SSCP	system services control point
SSCVT	subsystem communications vector table
SVC	supervisor call
SVT	supervisor vector table
SWA	scheduler work area
SYSGEN	system generation
SYSMOD	system modification
TCAM	telecommunications access method

TCAS	terminal control address space
TCB	task control block
TCM	thermal conduction module
TLB	translation lookaside buffer
TLP	target logical partition
TOD	time of day
TOR	terminal-owning region
TSB	terminal status block
TSO	Time-Sharing Option
TSO/E	Time-Sharing Option Extended
UADS	user attributes dataset
UCB	unit control block
UCS	universal character set
UCW	unit control word
UIC	unreferenced interval count
UIM	unit information module
UPS	uninterrupted power supply
VBS	variable blocked spanned
VIO	virtual input/output
VLF	virtual lookaside facility
VSAM	virtual storage access method
VSE	Virtual Storage Extended
VTAM	virtual telecommunications access method
VVCR	VSAM volume control record
VVDS	VSAM volume dataset
VVR	VSAM volume records
WTOR	write to operator with reply
XA	Extended Architecture
XCF	cross-system coupling facility
XDF	extended distance facility

Index of IBM manuals

Manuals are referred to here with abbreviated titles; the full titles and order numbers can be found in the relevant chapter bibliographies.

31-bit Addressing, 144, 159
3725 Model 2 Introduction, 292
Access Method Services, 106, 231, 397, 406
Application Development Guide, 159
Application Development Macro Reference, 141, 159, 467
Assembler H Installation, 158, 159

B1 Security, 407
Basics of Problem Determination, 460, 469, 471, 491

Cache Device Administration, 96, 107
Catalog Administration Guide, 80, 414
CBIPO MVS Customization Guide, 132, 223, 231, 356, 450
CBIPO MVS Installation Guide, 231
CBIPO System Design Reference, 231

Data Administration Guide, 159
Data Administration Macro Reference, 141, 159
Data Areas, 37, 136–41, 152, 158, 432, 436, 480, 491
Debugging Handbook, 37, 137, 159, 432, 480
DFDSS Reference, 106, 355
DFDSS User's Guide, 106, 435
DFHSM Installation and Customization, 355, 384, 390
DFHSM System Programmer's Guide, 436
DFP Customization, 355
DFP Storage Administration Reference, 434
DFP Systems Programming Reference, 157, 159, 406

DSF Guide, 106, 231, 413, 432, 434
DSF Primer for 3380 and 3390 DASD, 106, 432, 435
Dump and Trace Services, 484, 491

EREP User's Guide and Reference, 436, 450
ESA/370 Reference Summary, 480, 491
Extended Addressability, 75, 80, 148, 157, 159
Extending JES2 Using Table Pairs, 355

Getting Started with DFSORT, 106

Initialization and Tuning, 77, 194, 201, 231, 321, 382, 450, 485, 491
Initialization and Tuning Guide, 201, 231
Initialization and Tuning Reference, 194, 231, 389
Installation Exits, 344, 355
Installation Guide for VM/ESA, 368, 372
Installing SMP/E, 134, 135
IOCP Guide, 231, 372
IPCS Command Reference, 450, 481, 482, 493
IPCS User's Guide, 480, 493
ISPF and PDF Planning and Customizing, 315, 321, 355
ISPF Dialog Management Examples, 316, 321
ISPF Dialog Management Guide and Reference, 313, 316, 321
ISPF/PDF Edit and Edit Macros, 319, 321
ISPF/PDF Services, 321

JCL Reference, 269

JES2 Command Syntax Booklet, 108
JES2 Commands, 108, 268
JES2 Customization, 159, 269, 345, 355
JES2 Initialization and Tuning, 238, 242, 245, 247, 248, 257, 262, 268
JES2 Messages, 247, 269
JES2 Multi-Access Spool, 510
JES2 User Modifications and Macros, 269, 355

Linkage Editor Guide, 78

Managing Catalogs, 414, 436
Managing VSAM Datasets, 406
MVS CBIPO Planning, 135
MVS Software Manufacturing Offerings Planning and Installation, 229, 231
MVS/ESA Planning: GRS, 390
MVS/XA Overview, 77, 231
MVSCP Guide, 231

NCP and SSP Resource Definition Guide, 292
NCP and SSP Resource Definition Reference, 286, 292
Network Program Products - Planning, 292

Operator Tasks for the System Console, 365, 372

PR/SM Planning Guide, 372
Principles of Operation, 15, 36, 78, 158, 477

RACF Command Language Reference, 302, 321
RACF General Information, 406
RACF Security Administrators Guide, 302, 321
REXX Reference, 106
REXX User Guide, 106

SDSF Guide and Reference, 345, 355, 407, 510
Service Aids, 106, 449, 470, 480, 485, 491
SMP/E Reference, 109, 113, 115, 117, 130, 134, 135, 342
SMP/E User's Guide, 131, 132, 135
SNA Network Concepts and Products, 292
SPL: Application Development Guide, 78, 141, 154, 157, 159, 202, 231, 404, 407

SPL: Application Development Macro Reference, 141, 159, 407
SPL: RACF, 406
SPL: SMF, 355, 450
Storage Management Library, 420, 434
Supervisor Services, 159
SYS1.LOGREC Error Recording, 450
Sysplex Management, 372
System Codes, 167, 460, 462, 491
System Commands, 98, 108, 231, 321, 450, 467, 491
System Commands Reference Summary, 108
System Data Administration, 219, 406, 434
System Generation, 231
System Initialization Logic, 231
System Macros and Facilities, 141, 159, 202, 231, 407
System Messages, 460, 483, 491
System Modifications, 152, 159, 231, 345, 355, 450
System Reference, 78, 139, 158, 491

TSO/E Administration, 302, 321
TSO/E CLISTS, 106
TSO/E Command Reference, 106
TSO/E Command Reference Summary, 106
TSO/E Customization, 299, 321, 355
TSO/E Program Directory, 321
TSO/E Programming Guide, 88, 106, 487, 493
TSO/E Programming Services, 159
TSO/E System Programming Command Reference, 106, 301, 321

User Exits, 344, 355
Using Dumps and Traces, 472, 482, 484, 485, 491
Utilities, 107, 219

VM/ESA Running Guest Operating Systems, 372
VM/XA Installation, Administration, and Service, 368, 372
VSAM Administration Guide, 406
VTAM Installation and Resource Definition, 278, 292
VTAM Operation, 108
VTAM Resource Definition Reference, 292

Index of subjects and authors

Italicized page numbers indicate references which define the index term concerned.

$EXIT macro, 346
$WAIT macro, 349

/*JOBPARM statement, 239, 250, 263
/*ROUTE statement, 268
/*XEQ statement, 268
/*XMIT statement, 268

2305 DASD, 192
24-bit addressing, 44, 64, 142
2914 switch, 375

3081 processor, 16
3084 processor, 16
3088 CTCA, 35
3090 processor, 16, 17, 36
31-bit addressing, 44, 64, 142–46
3174 terminal controller, 32
3203 printer, 34
3211 printer, 34
3274 terminal controller, 32, 36, 375
3380 DASD, 23–25, 36, 185, 186
3390 DASD, 25–26, 36, 186
3420 tape drive, 29, 30
3480 cartridge drive, 30, 36, 376
3490 cartridge drive, 30, 31, 376
3495 tape library, 31
3725 comms controller, 33, 36, 187, 376–77
3745 comms controller, 33, 376–77
3800 printer, 34, 92, 219
3803 control unit, 30
3814 switch, 375
3880 control unit, 23, 185
3990 control unit, 25–26, 180, 186, 425

4245 printer, 34

4248 printer, 92, 187
4381 processor, 16

5990 processor, 16

9021 processor, 16
9037 timer, 370
9121 processor, 16
9221 processor, 16

AASF, 76
abend, 460, 465
  S047, 153
  S0C2, 153
  S0C4, 145, 153, 395
  S222, 348
  S306, 153
  S322, 296
ACB macro (VSAM), 398
ACB macro (VTAM), 281
ACCEPT (SMP command), 107, 108–9,
    123–25
access method, 51, 146, 157, 159
access method services, see IDCAMS
access registers, 76, 148, 157
ACCOUNT (TSO command), 84, 85, 296,
    299
account code validation exit, 350
accounting, 438
ACF2, 388, 398
address space, 38, 72, 142
address space control block, see ASCB
addressing mode, see AMODE, 24-bit
    addressing; 31-bit addressing
ADRDSSU, see DFDSS
ADRUENQ exit, 352, 385

ADRUPSWD exit, 352
advanced address space facility, *see* AASF
Advanced Function Printing, *see* AFP
AFP, 34
AFQ, *42*
ALIAS entry, 69, 70, 210, 213
ALLOCAS address space, 171
ALLOCATE (TSO command), 84
allocated datasets, displaying, 99
alternate cylinders, 368
alternate track, *431*
alternative JES2, 495
alternative master catalog, 215, 496
alternative nucleus, 194
alternative security system, 495
ALTLIB (TSO command), 84, 303, 322
AMASPZAP, 68, 91, 92, 174, 178, 205,
    406, 432
AMBLIST, 92
Amdahl, 16
AMDPRDMP, 449, 480
AMODE, 64, 78, 143
ANALYZE (DSF command), 94
APAR, 106, 114, 125, 489
APF authorization, 50, 66, 141, 142,
    152–54, 157, 176, 200, 205, 275,
    314, 394–95, 403–4
APPLY (SMP command), 107, 108,
    119–23, 126
AR mode, 76
ARCBDEXT exit, 352
architecture, *15*
ARCMDEXT exit, 353
ARCMVEXT exit, 353, 423
Artis, P., 36
ASCB, 49, 138
ASM, 41, 52
assembler programming, 136–61
auditing, 438, 446
authorization SVC, 404
authorized commands, 297
Authorized Problem Analysis Report, *see*
    APAR
authorized program facility, *see* APF
automatic commands, 104, 242, 254
auxiliary storage manager, *see* ASM
available frame queue, *see* AFQ

B1 security, 400, 407
backspacing printers, 104
backups, 94, 332, 334, 424–25, 428, 493
BAL instruction, 146
BALR instruction, 146
Barnett, S., 357
BAS instruction, 146
basic catalog structure, *see* BCS

BASR instruction, 146
BASSM instruction, 144–45
batch LSR, 77
BCS, 70
BDAM, 52
bind request, 274
BLDL, 62–64, 67, 68
BLP, 248, 406
BLSCBSVB CLIST, 482
BLSCBSYB CLIST, 482
BLSCSCAN CLIST, 481
Bookmanager, xvii, 13
bootstrap, 165, 173, 411
Bordonaro, B., 78, 152, 161, 231, 269
Bowler, R., 137, 160
BPAM, 52
Brack, R., 357
Brunner, T. A., 78
BSAM, 51
BSC, 266, 271, 278–80, 290
BSM instruction, 144–45
BTAM, 270, 284
bypass label processing, *see* BLP

CA-1, 385
cache, 26, 28–29, 96, 99, 246
CANCEL (TSO command), 354
cancelling address spaces, 98, 101
Candle, 486
Candle Computer Report, xvii, 78, 160
card reader, 34
Carlson, P., 374
Carson, G., 357
CAS, 72, 98
catalog address space, *see* CAS
cataloged procedures, 238–39, 250
catalogs, 68–72, 425–31
    housekeeping, 427–31
    recovery, 428
    reorganization, 429
    structure, 210–13, 426
CBIPO, *4*, 111, 112, 126, 129, 131–32, 158,
    210, 216, 220–27, 325, 329–30
CBPDO, 126, 227–29, 325, 329–30
CCW, 27, 52
CDE, 63
central processor complex, *see* CPC
change management, 9–10
change team, 489
channel, 20–23
    block multiplexor, 21, 185, 187
    byte multiplexor, 21, 34, 185
    ESCON, 20–21, 22, 35
    parallel, 21
channel command word, *see* CCW
channel extender, *21*, 36

channel path, 363
channel paths, displaying, 99
channel program, 26, 52, 157
channel subsystem, 17, 20, 52, 181
channel switch, 375
channel-to-channel adapter, see CTCA
checkpoint/restart, 250
CHNGDUMP console command, 467
CHPID macro, 185
CICS, 372
Circle, 137
Clark, J. W., 80
clip (relabel DASD volume), 94, 411
cloning, 330–41
cluster controller, 32, 33, 271
CMG, see UKCMG and USCMG
CMS, 367, 368
CNTLUNIT macro, 180, 185
command identification character, 103
command procedure, 297
command processor, 297
COMMON page dataset, 170
common service area, see CSA
common storage, 44, 73, 74, 78, 167
communications controller, see FEP
Communications Vector Table, 38
compare and swap, see CS instruction
comparing datasets, 94
component trace, 484
COMPRESS (DFDSS command), 423
compressing PDSs, 94
Computer Associates, 398
concurrent copy, 425
configuration:
    3274, 32
    3380, 23–25
    3390, 25–26
    3480, 30
    3990, 25–26
    hardware, 5
    printers, 34
    processor complex, 164
    tape devices, 30
connect time, 28
Conner, C., 436
console:
    control of, 99, 198
    definitions, 177
    hardware, 19, 20, 163, 165, 180, 199,
        364
    master, 32, 171
    MVS, 32, 171, 271, 278
    NIP, 167, 188
    PF keys, 177, 198
    TSO, 199
CONSOLE address space, 171

console commands, 97–106, 142
consolidated software inventory, see CSI
contents directory entry, see CDE
control blocks, 37, 87, 136–41
control unit:
    DASD, 23–29
    terminal, 32
CONVERTV (DFDSS command), 94, 411
copying datasets, 94
Cornman, J., 357
corrective service, 125, 326
cover letters, 325
CPC, 15–20
CPU, see processor
cross-memory services, 74–76, 80, 142, 157
cross-domain sessions, 282
cross-system coupling facility, see XCF
CS instruction, 140
CSA, 45, 73, 150, 170
CSI, 105–35, 106, 220, 224
    entries, 112–14
    listing, 127
    structure, 110–12
CSVLLIX1 exit, 347
CSVLLIX2 exit, 347
CTCA, 35, 187, 266, 359, 360, 361, 371
cumulative service tapes, 326, 329
customization, 222, 223–25, 229
CVOL, 68, 92
CVT, 38, 45, 137, 139, 151

D NET console command, 284
DADSM, 72
DADSM exits, 352, 418
DAE, 450, 466
daisy-chaining, 21, 34
DASD, 23–29
    housekeeping, 418, 420–25
    initialization, 409–15
DASD pooling, 190, 208, 211, 352, 415–
    20, 422
DAT, 18, 39–41, 74
DAT-off nucleus, 166, 174
DAT-on nucleus, 166, 174
data control block, see DCB
data extent block, see DEB
dataset labels, 432
dataset security byte, 396
dataspace, 43, 68, 76–77, 80, 142, 157
Dattani, D., 407
DCB, 51, 149
DDDEF (SMP CSI entry), 108, 109, 130,
    333
deadly embrace, 59
DEB, 51, 66
DEFRAG (DFDSS command), 423

defragmenting DASD space, *see* frag-
    mentation
deleting datasets, 94
deleting JES2 output, 105
demand paging, *see* paging
DEQ macro, 57–60
device address, 185
device allocation, 55
device emulation, 181
device number, 185
DFDSS, xvi, *92*, 93, 334, 385
    exits, 352
DFHSM, xvi, 384, 385
    control datasets, 389
    exits, 352, 423
    SETSYS MONITOR command, 483
DFP, xvi, 92, 210, 408
DFSMS, 26, 71, 191, 398, 408, 419
DFSMS/MVS, xvi
DFSMSdfp, *see* DFP
DFSMSdss, *see* DFDSS
DFSMShsm, *see* DFHSM
DFSORT, 91, *93*
DIAL-IBM, *see* IBMLink
Dimond, S., 80
directed VIO, 192
disabled processor, 18, 49, 56–57
disabled wait, 167
disaster recovery, 509
disconnect time, 27
disk storage devices, *see*DASD
dispatcher, 47–49, 61–62, 201
DISPLAY console command, 99–101
displaying address spaces, 99
documentation, 11–12, 497
domain (SNA), 274
driver systems, 229
DSCB, 432
DSF, 92, 93, 173, 409–15, 431
DSI Times, 374
DUAL checkpointing, 244
dummy output class, 242, 255
dump analysis and elimination, *see* DAE
DUMP console command, 101, 467
dump datasets, 101, 216, 388, 406, 448–50
DUMPDS console command, 449
dumps, 463–82
DUMPSRV address space, 170
DUPLEX checkpointing, 243
DYNALLOC macro, 154–58
dynamic address translation, *see* DAT
dynamic allocation, 154–58, 191, 348
dynamic devices, *189*
dynamic path reconnect, 27
dynamic reconfiguration management,
    181, 189

dynamic storage reconfiguration, 362, 371

EC, 19
ECB, 52
ECC recovery, 429
EDIT (TSO command), 84, 85, 88–91
edit macros, 318–19
EDT, 188, 189–91, 204
EDTGEN, 189
eligible device table, *see* EDT
EMIF, 20
Emulation Program, *see* EP
ENQ macro, 57–60, 380–85
ENQs, displaying, 99
Enterprise Systems Journal, xvii, 28, 36,
    78, 135, 231, 269, 357, 372, 436,
    493, 510
EP, 284
ERDS, 429
EREP, 429, 441–45, 486
error recording dataset, *see* ERDS
ES/9000, 15, *16*, 32, 181, 189
ESCON, 22, 35, 189, 371
ESCON director, 22
Eshom, T., 135, 342
esoteric device name, 187, 189, 207
ETR, 197, *370*
evaluating software, 6
event control block, *see* ECB
EXCP macro, 51, 52, 157
EXEC (TSO command), 84
execute form of macros, 148–50
exits, 5, 13, 138, 343–57
expanded storage, 42–43, 78
Extended Distance Facility, *see* XDF
extents, 94
external time reference, *see* ETR
external writer, 258, 446

Fairbrother, I., 428, 436
Fairchild, W., 28, 36, 78
FCB, 34, 92, 219
Feinstein, A., 78
FEP, 32–33, 270, 273, 284–92, 376–77
fetch-protected storage, 44, *50*, 142, 153,
    154
file tailoring, 304
fixed LPA, *see* FLPA
fixed storage, *see* page fixing
FLPA, 63, 65
forms control buffer, *see* FCB
fragmentation, 94, 353, 423
FREE (TSO command), 84
FREEMAIN macro, 147–48, 150–52
Friedman, M., 78
front-end processor, *see* FEP

Fujitsu, 16
full pack minidisks, 366, 368

GENERATE (SMP command), 132, 223
generic device name, 190, 207
generic profiles, 400
GETMAIN macro, 147–48, 150–52
GIMMPDFT CSECT, 109, 134
GIMUTTBL CSECT, 134
global access checking, 312
global resource serialization, *see* GRS
GMT time, *171*, 197
Goldberg, G., 491, 493
Goldin, S., 78, 160
GRS, 57–60, 99, 370, 378, 380–85
   closedown, 381
   starting, 380
GRS address space, 170
GRS RNLs, 262, 349, 357, 370, 382–85
GTF trace, 484
guest operating systems, 365
GUIDE, xvi, 436
GVTCREQ field, 345

Hanson, P., 342
hardcopy log, 446
hardware configuration definition, *see*
   HCD
hardware errors, *see* I/O errors
hardware save area, *see* HSA
Haupt, M., 80
Hawkins, N., 510
HCD, 6, 21, 179, 188–89, 223, 232, 368
HCPRIO ASSEMBLE, 368
head movement, 485
Heitlander, H.-J., 440, 450
held output, 255
HELP (TSO command), 84
high-level qualifier, 70, 210, 302, 417
high-speed buffer, *17*
HIPER problems, 5, 225, 326, 327
Hiperbatch, 77
HIPERSORT, 77
hiperspace, 43, 76–77, 80, 142, 157
Hitachi, 16
HLQ, *see* high-level qualifier
Hoare, M., 428, 436
HOLDDATA, *108*, 110, 113, 114, 118,
   119, 121, 126, 228, 325, 327
Hollar, R. D., 80
hot I/O, 53
housekeeping, 6
   catalogs, 427–31
   DASD, 418, 420–25
   EREP, 441–43
   SMF, 439–41

   SYSLOG, 446–48
Houtekamer, G., 36
HSA, 179, 368
HSM, *see* DFHSM
hung system, 462

I/O configuration, 178–92
I/O definition file, *see* IODF
I/O errors, 94, 216, 243, 247, 430, 441, 461
I/O processing, 26–28, 36
I/O supervisor, *see* IOS
I/O supervisor block, *see* IOSB
IBM manuals, index of, 516
IBM support centre, 455, 488
IBMLink, xvii, 325, 490, 493
ICEMAN, *see* DFSORT
ICF, 68
ICFRU, 428, 436
ICHRCX01 exit, 496
ICHRDSNT module, 496
ICHRIN03 table, 399
ICKDSF, *see* DSF
IDCAMS, 69, 84, 92, 93, 96, 190, 210,
   211, 215, 398
IDRC, 31
IEA995I message, 463
IEALIMIT exit, 347
IEAVMXIT exit, 347
IEAVTRML module, 345
IEBCOMPR, *92*
IEBCOPY, *92*
IEBDG, *92*
IEBEDIT, *92*
IEBGENER, *92*
IEBIMAGE, *92*, 219
IEBISAM, *92*
IEBPTPCH, *92*
IEBUPDTE, *92*
IEE094D message, 467
IEECVXIT exit, 348
IEF472I message, 464
IEFACTRT exit, 348
IEFBR14, 87, *92*
IEFDB401 exit, 348
IEFQMREQ service, 141
IEFSD060 module, 205
IEFSDPPT CSECT, 205
IEFU29 exit, 439
IEFUJV exit, 351, 354
IEFUSI exit, 347
IEFUSO exit, 348
IEFUTL exit, 206, 348
IEHINITT, *92*, 406
IEHLIST, *92*, 418
IEHPROGM, *93*, 190, 396, 421
IEZIGGV3 RESERVEs, 383

IFASMFDP program, 439
IFCEREP1 program, 441
IFCOFFLD program, 441
IGGPOST0 exit, 352
IGGPRE00 exit, 352, 418
IGWSPZAP, *see* AMASPZAP
IKJEFF10 exit, 354
IKJEFF53 exit, 354
IKJEFLD exit, 354
IMASPZAP, *see* AMASPZAP
IML, 164
Improved Data Recording Capability, *see*
      IDRC
incorrect device type, 190
indirect volume references, 177, 332
INFO/MVS, 13, 326, 490
INFO/SYS, 490
Information Center Facility, 299, 302
initial microcode load, *see* IML
initial program load, *see* IPL
initializing DASD volumes, 94
initiator, 47, *54*, 55, 105, 233, 251, 254
input class, 247–51, 254
input output block, *see* IOB
INSPECT (DSF command), 431
installation exits, *343*
instream commands, 248
instruction address trace, 484
integrated catalog facility, *see* ICF
Integrated Catalog Facility Recovery
      Utility, *see* ICFRU
internal reader, *53*, 233, 257
internal text, 54, 233, 351
interrupt, 18, *48*, 52, 56
interrupt handler, 18, 56
interrupting printers, 105
intersect, 61–62, 157
IOB, 52
IOCDS, 19, 164, 179, 180, 189, 363–65,
    368, 376
  basic mode, 363
  LPAR mode, 363
IOCONFIG macro, 185
IOCP, 6, 21, 164, 178–92, 189, 377
IODEVICE macro, 185, 379
IODF, 179, 188–89, 194, 232, 498
IOGEN, 179, 201
IOQ, 52
IOS, 52, 53, 142
IOSB, 52
IOSQ time, 27
IOSVSUCB service, 141
IPCS, 142, 449, 465, 469, 480–82, 493
  BROWSE facility, 479, 482
  COPYDUMP subcommand, 481
  dump directory, 481

EQUATE subcommand, 482
IPCSDDIR command, 481
RUNCHAIN subcommand, 482
SCAN subcommand, 482
SETDEF subcommand, 481
STACK subcommand, 482
STATUS CPU REGISTERS subcom-
    mand, 479
STATUS FAILDATA subcommand,
    472
SUMMARY TCBERROR subcom-
    mand, 477
TCBEXIT subcommand, 482
VERBEXIT MTRACE subcommand,
    472
VERBEXIT SYMPTOM subcommand,
    479
VERBEXIT TRACE subcommand, 479
IPL, 163–73, 332, 334
IPL resource initialization modules, *see*
    IRIMs
IPL text, 165, 173, 411, 469, 500
IPO1.DOCLIB, 221, 223
IPO1.INSTLIB, 222
IPOUPDTE, 222
IRIMs, 166, 174
ISFPARMS module, 97, 402
ISGGREX0 exit, 349
ISGGRS00 module, 345
ISPF, 84, *293*, 302–21
  applications, 316
  command tables, 316–18
  dialogs, 315
  exits, 355
  menus, 312–15
  messages, 304
  panels, 304, 312–15
  profile dataset, 305, 306, 307, 316
  skeletons, 304
  tables, 305
ISPF/PDF, *see* PDF
ISPTCM, 315

Jackson, B., 357
Jackson, E., 78
JCL, 53
JCL validation exits, 350, 351
JCLIN, 115–17, 128, 131, 133
JCLIN (SMP command), 223
JES exits, 191, 239, 248, 251, 259–61, 418
JES2, 53–56, 232–69
  closedown, 237
  cold start, 235, 238, 258
  hot start, 235
  warm start, 235

JES2 checkpoint, 105, 243–47, 261, 269, 389
JES2 checkpoint lock, 246, 261, 262
JES2 command processing exit, 351
JES2 commands, 103–6
JES2 exits, 350–51, 354
JES2 initialization, 105, 172, 234–37
JES2 initialization parameters, 104, 215, 234, 237–38
  APPL, 266
  CKPTDEF, 243–47
  CONNECT, 267
  EXIT, 260
  INITDEF, 251
  INITnnn, 252
  INTRDR, 258
  JOBCLASS, 249
  JOBDEF, 247
  LINE, 264
  LINEnnn, 267
  LOAD, 260
  LOGONn, 264, 266
  MASDEF, 261
  NJEDEF, 266
  NODEn, 266
  OFFLOADn, 258–59
  OUTCLASS, 254–56
  OUTDEF, 254–56
  PRINTDEF, 256
  PRINTERn, 256
  RMTnnn, 265
  SPOOLDEF, 239–43
  STCCLASS, 249
  TPDEF, 264
  TSUCLASS, 249
JES2 macros, 349
JES2 procedure, 235, 238
JES2 system ID, 261
JES2 table pairs, 351–52
JES3, 53–56, 232, 265, 269
JES328X, 32, 256, 263–65
JFCB, 141
job class, see input class
Job Control Language, see JCL
job management, 53–56
job number, 53
job pack area, see JPA
JOB statement validation exit, 350
JOBLIB, 63
Johnson, R. H., 78
journals, xvi
JPA, 62

Keller, T. C., 493
key zero, see storage protection
Kidd, C. L., 233, 322

Klein, P., 78
Krause, B., 342

LA instruction, 146
LAB, 286
Lakein, A., 14
Landmark, 486
Legent, 376, 386
level 2 support, 489
library lookaside, see LLA
LIC, 286
line attachment base, see LAB
line interface coupler, see LIC
link pack area, see LPA
linkage conventions, 147–48
linkage editor, 143
linkage stack, 144, 148
linklist, 66–68, 170, 176–77
linklist lookaside, see LLA
list form of macros, 148–50
LISTALC (TSO command), 84
LISTBC (TSO command), 84
LISTDS (TSO command), 85
Little, D., 322
LLA, 62, 63, 66–68, 78, 101, 172, 347
Llana, A., 36
LLE, 62
LMOD (SMP CSI entry), 113, 127, 128
load address, *165*
load list element, see LLE
load parameter, 165
loader, 62
local printer, 256–57
local system queue area, see LSQA
LOCAL time, *171*, 197
lock, 52, 60–61, 78, 140, 157
logical swapping, 47
logmode, 279
logon procedure, 295–97, 299, 305–12, 497
loops, 463
LPA, *46*, 63, 94, 170
LPA list table, 87
LPDE, 63
LSQA, 45, 166
LU, 272–75, 280, 290

MAC (SMP CSI entry), 114
macros, 141–42, 148
Mainframe Journal, 36, 78, 80, 161, 233, 269, 292, 318, 322, 407, *also see Enterprise Systems Journal*
maintenance, 325–42
major node, *278*, 283, 285
manuals, 13–14
  see also index of IBM manuals, 516

master catalog, 68, 166, 170, 210–13, 221, 224, 226, 388, 406
master catalog pointer, 169, 174, 194
master JCL, 171, 178, 210
master scheduler, 166, 171, 178, 204
master trace, 484
MAXEXTENTS (DFHSM parameter), 423
McDonald, J., 374
McSweeney, A., 269
MDF, 357, 361–63, 372
message processing facility, *see* MPF
microcode, *19*
microfiche, 256
MII, 262, 385–87, 390
Miller, I. Z., 510
minidisk, 368
minor node, *278*, 283
missing interrupt, 53
MLPA, 63, 65, 175
MLPF, 357, 361–63, 372
MOD (SMP CSI entry), 114, 127, 128
modem, 272
MODESET macro, 50, 142, 152–54, 395
MODETAB, 279, 291
modified LPA, *see* MLPA
MODIFY console command, 101
Monitor, The, 485
mount attribute, 207
MOUNT console command, 102, 207
moving datasets, 95
MPF, 101, 446
MPF exits, 439
multi-access spool, 105, 243, 244, 246, 261–63
Multi-Image Allocation, 376
Multi-Image Console, 371
multi-image environments, 357–74, 390
Multi-Image Integrity, *see* MII
multi-level aliases, 210
multiple preferred guests, 365
multiprocessing, 140
multiprogramming, 140
MVS:
  initialization, 163–73, 231
  installation, 4–5, 220–30
  Version 1, xv
  Version 2, xv
  Version 3, xv
  Version 4, xv, 165, 233
MVS Update, xvii, 78, 80, 137, 138, 160, 161, 269, 322, 346, 357, 407, 436, 450, 510
MVS/370, xv
MVS/ESA, xv
MVS/Express, 230

MVS/SP, xv
MVS/XA, xv
MVSCP, 6, 21, 132, 178–92, 189, 194, 204, 223, 345, 376, 377, 379

naming conventions, 12, 278, 285, 286
NASPA, xvi, xvii
NCP, 33, *270*, 273, 274, 275, 284–92, 376–77
NCP/EP definition facility, *see* NDF
NDF, 285
Nearline, 31
Netview, 284
Netview Performance Monitor, *see* NPM
network control program, *see* NCP
network job entry, *see* NJE
next sequential instruction, 143
NIP, 167, 174
NJE, 264, 265–68
non-cancellable program, 66
non-reusable attribute, *64*
non-swappable program, 66
NPM, 284
nucleus, 46, 94
nucleus initialization program, *see* NIP
nucleus suffix, 166

object code only, 37, 141, 343
Odom, R., 357
offload datasets, 406
offload device, 258–59, 447
offset recovery, 429
Omegamon, 486
one pack system, 498–507
OPEN macro, 51, 149
OPER (TSO command), 85, 301
operation request block, *see* ORB
ORB, 52
OS/VS2, xv
OUTPUT (TSO command), 354
output class, 254–56

page datasets, 102, 195, 213–15, 223, 388
  moving, 493
page fault, 41, 43
page fixing, 42, 52, 61, 63, 142
page frame table, 42, 46, 167
page migration, 43
page protected storage, 49, 66, 147
page table, *39–41*, 44, 72
pageable LPA, *see* PLPA
paging, 39, 41–42, 46, 78, 142
Painter, D., xviii, 319
PARMLIB (TSO command), 85, 299
partition weights, 362, 364
Partitioned Emulation Program, *see* PEP

partitioning:
  logical, 361–63, 365
  physical, 360–61
PASSWORD (JOB card keyword), 399
PASSWORD dataset, 396
password protection, 395–98
PC instruction, 75
PCAUTH address space, 75, 170
PDF, 84, *293*, 302–21
  exits, 355
PDSE, 92, 423
Pearkins, J. E., 269, 510
pending time, 27
PEP, 284
performance, 7, 24, 26, 42, 43, 46, 67, 77, 99, 192, 201, 206, 211, 213, 215, 245, 252, 262, 306, 311, 438
performance group, 99
PLPA, 63, 65, 147, 213
PLPA page dataset, 170
POWER, 265
power-on-reset, *19*, 164, 181
PPT, 66, 204
PR/SM, 35, 164, 185, 226, 357, 361–63, 365, 371, 372
preferred guest, 365
prefix, 302
prefixed save area, *see* PSA
preventive service, *125*, 326
preventive service planning tape, *see* PSP tapes
primary subsystem, 204
print dataset, 55
print management packages, 447
printer, 32, 33–34, 256–57, 374
printing, 255
priority aging, 249
private storage, 44, 45
private volumes, 207
privileged instructions, 152
problem resolution, 5, 12, 453–93
problem state, *50*, 152, 394
procedure libraries, 238–39, 250
processor, 15–20
product tapes, 230, 326, 329
ProductPac, 230
professionalism, 3–4, 8–14
PROFILE PREFIX (TSO command), 302
program fetch, 52, 62–64, 68
program properties table, *see* PPT
program status word, *see* PSW
program temporary fix, *see* PTF
program update tape, *see* PUT tapes
project management, 8–9
propagating userids, 399
PROTECT (TSO command), 396

PSA, 38, *45*, 49, 57, 60, 138, 166
PSP tapes, *125*, 228, 326, 327, 329
PSW, 18, 44, 45, *48*, 49, 56, 85, 143, 148, 167, 395
PTF, 106, 113, 114, *125*, 127, 325, 326–29, 489
PTS, *see* SMPPTS
PU, 272–75, 280, 290
public volumes, 207
punch, 34
PUT tapes, *125*, 325, 326–29

QCB, 57, 58–59, 380
QEL, 57, 58–59
QNAME, 58, 78
QSAM, *51*
queue control block, *see* QCB
queue element, *see* QEL

RACF, 85, 98, 142, 171, 219, 302, 312, 388, 398–401, 496, 510
RACROUTE macro, 401
Ranade, J., 292
re-entrant program, 65, 79, 146–52
real storage, 166
real storage manager, *see* RSM
Reaugh, D., 357
RECEIVE (SMP command), 107–8, 117–19, 126
RECEIVE (TSO command), 85, 265, 299
reconfigurable channels, 362, 364
refreshable attribute, 65–66
refreshing LLA, 67, 101
region size, 249, 301, 347
register, 17
REJECT (SMP command), 119, 128
RELEASE (DFDSS command), 423
releasing held jobs, 105
releasing unused space, 96
remote job entry, *see* RJE
remote printer, 256
RENAME (TSO command), 85
RESERVE, 99, 186, 214, 246, 262, 369, 378–80, 383, 385
residency mode, *see* RMODE
resource capping, 362, 364
resource initialization modules, *see* RIMs
responsibilities of systems programmer, 4–8
RESTORE (SMP command), 109, 128–29
restricted SVCs, 153
reusable attribute, *65*
REXX, 311
REXX EXECs, 83–88, 296, 303
RIMs, 167, 174

ring system authority message, *see* RSA message
RJE, *263–65*
RMF, 485
RMODE, 64, 143
RNAME, 57
Rohwer, E., 357
role of systems programmer, 3–14
rotational position sensing, 27
RSA message, 380
RSCS, 265
RSM, 41–42
RTAM, 266
RTM2WA, 472

Sackett, G. C., 292
SADMP program, 469
SAF, 396, 401
Samson, S., xv, 14
scheduler work area, *see* SWA
SDLC, 271
SDSF, 85, *233*, 245, 302, 306, 354, 402
search operation, 27
secondary JES2, 506, 510
security, 153, 157, 259, 352, 393–407
security software, 398–401, 404–5
seek operation, 27
segment table, *39–41*, 44, 72, 74, 76, 166
SEND (console command), 102
SEND (TSO command), 85, 297
separator pages, 350
serialization, 56–62, 78
serially reusable program, *65*
service information message, *see* SIM
service request block, *see* SRB
session manager, 279
session parameters, 279
SGIEF0PT macro, 205
SHARE, xvi, 4
shared catalogs, 388
shared DASD, 180, 186, 211, 214, 226, 246, 261, 368–69, 377–87, 443, 499
Shein, D., 135, 318, 322
Sherkow, A., 372
Shourbaji, R., 342
SIE assist, 365, 369
SIM, 445
Sinclair, B. J., 78
skip displacement, *431*
SLIP console command, 465, 468–69
slip traps, 468–69
SMF, 102, 205, 218, 437–41, 486
SMF address space, 171
SMF datasets, 206, 218, 388, 406, 438
SMF exits, 206, 348, 351, 354, 439
SMF record types, 206, 438

SMF system ID, 262
SMP, *see* SMP/E
SMP/E, 13, 105–35, 326, 330–41
administration dialogs, 130
datasets, 109–10
distribution libraries, *106*, 131
distribution zone, *106*, 110–12, 131
DLIBs, *see* distribution libraries
FMID, *106*, 114, 127
FUNCTION, *see* FMID
global zone, *106*, 110–12
GROUP operand, 121
GROUPEXTEND operand, 121
HOLD problems, *see* HOLDDATA
implementation, 134–35
MCS, *106*, 114–15
modification control statements, *see* MCS
PTF temporary store, *see* SMPPTS
query dialogs, 127
re-runnable jobs, 133
recovery options, 129
RELFILEs, 114, 117
REPORT ERRSYSMODS command, 126
SELECT operand, 119
SMPTLIBs, 117
SOURCEID operand, 118, 119, 127
SYSMOD, *106*, 105–35, 114–15
target libraries, *106*
target zone, *106*, 110–12, 131
TLIBs, *see* target libraries
zones, *106*
SMPPTS, 108, 110, 127
SMS, 94, 99, 100, 103, *408*, 410
SNA, 265–68, *271*, 272–75, 280–81, 290, 292
SNAP dumps, 467
solid-state DASD, 181
SORT, *see* DFSORT
Soucy, J., 342
special stationery, 256
SPFDSN ENQs, 384, 385, 387
SPFEDIT ENQs, 384, 385, 387
spin lock, 61
spin loop, *61*
spool dataset, 54, 55, 105, 226, 233, 235, *239–43*, 261, 269, 389
SPZAPLIB RESERVEs, 385
SQA, 46, 166
SRB, 47–49, 73, 74, 78, 142
SRC (SMP CSI entry), 114
SRM, 46, 103, 142, 201, 213
SSCH instruction, 52
SSCP, 272–75
SSCVT, 204

stand-alone DFDSS, 507
stand-alone dumps, 469–71
stand-alone editors, 509
stand-alone restore, 96, 507
stand-alone system, 498–507, 510
stand-alone utilities, 224
stand-by sites, 509
standards, 12–13, 498
Stanislawski, L., 232
start sub channel, *see* SSCH instruction
STARTIO macro, 52
static devices, *189*
STATUS (TSO command), 85, 354
STCINRDR, 54, 233, 258
STEPLIB, 63
storage group, 211, *419*
STORAGE macro, 147
storage protect key, 394
storage protection, 44, 49, 78, 152
storage volumes, 207
Storagetek, 31
store status, 470
subareas (SNA), 274
SUBMIT (TSO command), 85, 301, 354
subsystem, 103, 152, 172, 204
SUPERC, 92, 96
supervisor call, *see* SVC
supervisor state, *50*, 142, *152*, 394
SUPERZAP, *see* AMASPZAP
suspend lock, 61
SVC, 48, 157, 201
SVC 34, 97, 98
SVC 99, 154–58, 348, 419
SVC dump, 216, 467–69
SWA, 45, 141
swap datasets, 213–15
swapping, *46*, 201
SWAREQ service, 141
symptom dumps, 463
SYNC (TSO command), 85
SYS1.AMODGEN, 140, 224
SYS1.BRODCAST, 85, 219, 299, 385, 389
SYS1.DCMLIB, 177, 199
SYS1.DUMPnn, *see* dump datasets
SYS1.HASPSRC, 224
SYS1.IMAGELIB, 34, 219
SYS1.LINKLIB, 175, 176–77, 201
MSTJCLxx member, 171, 178, 219
SYS1.LOGREC, 216, 388, 429, 441–45,
    486
SYS1.LPALIB, 175, 202
IKJTABLS member, 297, 299
SYS1.MACLIB, 140
SYS1.MANx, *see* SMF datasets
SYS1.MIGLIB, 176
SYS1.MODGEN, 140

SYS1.NUCLEUS, 166, 174, 404
IEANCTxx member, 179
IEANUC0x member, 165, 179, 189, 202
IEFEDTxx member, 179, 189
IOSIITxx member, 179
IOSUCBxx member, 179
SYSCATxx member, 69, 169, 195, 210,
    224, 496
SYS1.PAGEDUMP, 470
SYS1.PARMLIB, 53, 192–210, 226, 388,
    404, 502
ADYSETxx member, 450
CLOCKxx member, 170, 196, 371
COFVLFxx member, 208
COMMNDxx member, 172, 197
CONSOLxx member, 97, 171, 188, 198,
    446
COUPLExx member, 371
CSVLLAnn member, 101
DUMP parameter, 216
GIMOPCDE member, 134
GRSCNFxx member, 382
GRSRNLxx member, 383
IEAABD00 member, 465
IEAAPFxx member, 66, 176, 177, 200,
    395
IEACMD00 member, 172, 197, 465
IEADMP00 member, 465
IEADMR00 member, 465
IEAFIXxx member, 63
IEAICSxx member, 201
IEAIPSxx member, 201
IEALPAxx member, 63, 175, 496
IEAOPTxx member, 201
IEASLPyy member, 468
IEASVCxx member, 201
IEASYSxx member, 66, 166, 168, 171,
    192–210, 195, 380, 395, 446, 448
IEFSSNxx member, 151, 172, 204
IGDSMSxx member, 103
IKJTSOxx member, 85, 297
LNKAUTH parameter, 177, 200
LNKLSTxx member, 66, 170, 176
LOADxx member, 69, 165, 166, 168,
    188, 189, 192, 194, 210
LPALSTxx member, 63, 170, 175
MPFLSTxx member, 101, 347
MSTRJCL parameter, 178
PFKTABxx member, 171, 198
SCHEDxx member, 66, 189, 204
SMFPRMxx member, 102, 205, 428,
    438
TSOKEY00 member, 294
VATLSTxx member, 207
SYS1.PROCLIB, 215, 388
SYS1.SBLSCLI0, 481

SYS1.STGINDEX, 217, 388
SYS1.SVCLIB, 174, 175, 201
SYS1.UADS, 85, 219, 296, 299–302, 385, 389
SYS1.VTAMLIB, 276
SYS1.VTAMLST, 275
SYSABEND dump, 465
SYSDSN ENQs, 384, 385, 387
SYSGEN, 131–32, 177, 179, 189, 199, 205
SYSIAT RESERVEs, 384
SYSIEWLP RESERVEs, 385
SYSIGGV2 RESERVEs, 383
SYSIKJBC ENQs, 385
SYSIKJUA ENQs, 385
SYSLOG, 103, 171, 406, 445–48
SYSMDUMP dump, 465
SYSn.IPLPARM, 166, 194
SYSOUT dataset, 55, 233, 254–56
SYSOUT limit, 348
Sysplex, 23, 35, 199, 358, 359, 370–72
Sysplex timer, see ETR
SYSRES, 165, 173–78, 193, 201, 221, 330–41, 388
system authorization facility, see SAF
SYSTEM CONFIG, 368
system delivery option, 367
system generation, see SYSGEN
system log, 446
system managed storage, see SMS
system management facility, see SMF
system name, 206
system queue area, see SQA
system resources manager, see SRM
system trace, 204, 483
System/370, 15
System/390, 15
SystemPac, 230
systems engineer, 220, 487
SYSUDUMP dump, 465
SYSVSAM RESERVEs, 383, 387
SYSVTOC RESERVEs, 384
SYSZJES2 RESERVEs, 384
SYSZRACF RESERVEs, 385
SYSZVVDS RESERVEs, 384

T-bar, 375
tape devices, 29–31, 375–76
    cartridge, 30
    open reel, 29
tape libraries, automated, 31
task, see TCB
task control block, see TCB
tasklib, 62
TCAM, 270
TCAS, 282, 294–95
TCB, 38, 47–49, 138, 142

TCM, 19
Technical support, xvii, xviii, 80, 135, 137, 232, 327, 342, 357, 373, 493, 510
TEST (TSO command), 85–88, 486
testing, 10–11, 222, 224, 229, 330–41, 346, 358
The Monitor, 485
thermal conduction module, see TCM
TIME (TSO command), 85
time limit, 348
time-of-day clocks, see TOD clocks
TLB, 40
TOD clocks, 170, 261
Tomiak, K. E., 493
Top Secret, 388, 398
TRACE address space, 170
traces, 483–85
track groups, 240
Translation Lookaside Buffer, see TLB
TRANSMIT (TSO command), 85, 265, 299
TSO, 293, 294–302
    defining to VTAM, 282–83
    displaying users, 99
    user administration, 219, 299–302
TSO CLISTs, 83–88, 296, 303, 318, 320
TSO commands, 83–88, 297–99, 315
TSO exits, 353–55
TSO logon, 294, 295–97, 299, 305–12, 354
TSO session manager, 299
TSO USERMAX, 98, 283, 295, 354
TSOINRDR, 54, 233, 258

UCB, 52, 60, 141, 169, 179, 188
UCB scan routine, 141
UCLIN (SMP command), 113, 130
UCS, 34, 219
UCW, 179
UIC, 41
UIM, 345
UKCMG, xvi, 78, 357
uncataloged datasets, 421
unit control block, see UCB
unit control word, see UCW
unit information module, see UIM
UNITNAME macro, 190, 191
universal character set, see UCS
unreferenced interval count, see UIC
USCMG, xvi, 78
use attribute, 207
USER (JOB card keyword), 399
user catalogs, 69, 210–13, 388, 406, 426
USER DIRECT, 368
user exits, 343
USERMOD, 106, 114, 115, 127, 132–34, 202, 205, 220, 223, 229

USSTAB, 279
utility programs, 91–97

V NET console command, 283
varying devices online/offline, 99
VIO, 187, 190, 191–92, 217
virtual CTC, 365, 369
virtual lookaside facility, *see* VLF
virtual machines, *see* VM
virtual RESERVE/RELEASE, 369
virtual storage, *38*, 43–46, 78, 87, 166, 213
VLF, 63, 67, 80, 142, 208, 233, 311, 322, 357
VLFNOTE (TSO command), 85
VM, 164, 265, 365–70
volume table of contents, *see* VTOC
VSAM, *52*
VSAM catalogs, 68, 71
VSAM orphans, 421, 432
VSAM volume dataset, *see* VVDS
VSE, 265
VTAM, 52, 73, 101, 103, 200, 265–68, *270*, 272, 275, 284, 285
VTAM applications, 281–83
VTAM initialization parameters, 275–84
VTOC, 70, 71, 92, 94, 96, 211, *410*, 432

VTOC index, 94, 96, 211, 412–13
VVDS, 70–71, 413–15

Wachtel, H., 407
wait codes, 167, 462
wait state, 462, 471
Waterhouse, P., 232, 374
Weaver, B. J., 292
Westerling, K., 493
Wiedemann, W., 152, 161
work element, 233
work selection criteria, 257, 259
work volumes, 422
working set, *41*
Wright, F., 373
WRITELOG console command, 446
WTO exits, 347
WTO macro, 149
WTOR macro, 102

XCF, 35, 370
XDF, 20
XEDIT, 367
XRF, 372

Zeh, S., 510

Further Titles in the IBM McGraw-Hill Series

OS/2 Presentation Manager Programming
Hints and Tips
Bryan Goodyer

PC User's Guide
Simple Steps to Powerful Personal Computing
Peter Turner

The IBM RISC System/6000
Clive Harris

The IBM RISC System/6000 User Guide
Mike Leaver
Hardev Sanghera

MVS Systems Programming
Dave Elder-Vass

CICS Concepts and Uses
A Management Guide
Jim Geraghty

Dynamic Factory Automation
Alastair Ross

Writing OS/2 REXX Programs
Ronny Richardson